THE OXFORD HISTORY OF ENGLISH LEXICOGRAPHY

VOLUME I
GENERAL-PURPOSE DICTIONARIES

THE OXFORD HISTORY OF ENGLISH

LEXICOGRAPHY

Volume I
General-Purpose Dictionaries

Edited by
A. P. Cowie

CLARENDON PRESS · OXFORD

OXFORD
UNIVERSITY PRESS

Great Clarendon Street, Oxford OX2 6DP

Oxford University Press is a department of the University of Oxford.
It furthers the University's objective of excellence in research, scholarship,
and education by publishing worldwide in

Oxford New York

Auckland Cape Town Dar es Salaam Hong Kong Karachi
Kuala Lumpur Madrid Melbourne Mexico City Nairobi
New Delhi Shanghai Taipei Toronto

With offices in

Argentina Austria Brazil Chile Czech Republic France Greece
Guatemala Hungary Italy Japan Poland Portugal Singapore
South Korea Switzerland Thailand Turkey Ukraine Vietnam

Oxford is a registered trade mark of Oxford University Press
in the UK and in certain other countries

Published in the United States
by Oxford University Press Inc., New York

First published 2009

British Library Cataloguing in Publication Data
Data available
Library of Congress Cataloging-in-Publication Data
Data available

Typeset by SPI Publisher Services, Pondicherry, India
Printed and bound in Great Britain
by
MPG Books Ltd, Bodmin, Cornwall

ISBN 978-0-19-928562-4

Vol I 978-0-19-928560-0

Vol II 978-0-19-928561-7

1 3 5 7 9 10 8 6 4 2

CONTENTS

PREFACE

It is not uncommon for a book of the scale and complexity of *The Oxford History of English Lexicography* to undergo at the planning stage a number of major transformations. This was the case as the present project got under way, and certain major decisions can be recalled here whose implementation shaped the eventual content and structure of the *History*. The expert advice of readers played an essential part in this process and I express my appreciation to them all. I especially welcomed the involvement of Werner Hüllen. He gave freely of his expert advice and contributed a chapter which drew on his unequalled knowledge of thesauri. By the saddest of ironies, he did not live to see the book to which he had contributed so much.

Werner recommended that we should adopt a chronological approach throughout the work—then consisting of three volumes, of which the third was not historically oriented—otherwise we would fail to meet the expectations raised by the title 'The History of . . .'. Adopting this suggestion led to the breaking up of Volume III, with much of its content being incorporated in the other volumes.

This redistribution of material sometimes brought multiple benefits. In Volume II the emphasis was from the beginning topical. But it is sometimes forgotten that, in the *History*, there is constant interaction between the topical and the historical. The chief focus of interest throughout the second volume might be topic or use, but the dictionaries were often listed, analysed, and discussed in a historical dimension. Such interaction existed in the case of learners' dictionaries. They had a shared function in that all were concerned with the linguistic needs of foreign students, but they also represented a historical progression—Hornby coming to prominence in the mid-1930s, Sinclair in the early 1980s. But it so happened that each of the EFL dictionaries published in the intervening years was associated with a development in grammatical and/or lexical research and the application of each to dictionary design. Thus the various strands of historical progression, specialization according to users and uses, and involvement in relevant research and development were seen to interact—and in the design of the *History* could be brought to bear illuminatingly on each other.

At an early stage, I had considered the possibility of introducing English-speaking readers to some of the achievements of other national traditions in lexicography. However, experience of drawing up the detailed plan, and the views of referees, brought home the difficulty of doing full justice to a tradition such as the French in fewer than two additional volumes. Those ambitious but unrealizable aims were therefore abandoned. Yet the comparative perspective has not been neglected altogether. A quarter of the list of contributors consists of German, Italian, Russian, Belgian and French-Canadian scholars who, quite apart from having expertise in particular areas of English lexicography, are well able to view their chosen fields from within a broader European perspective.

Earlier, I expressed my indebtedness to the specialist readers for their help in arriving at a suitable framework for the *History*. But I have benefited also from advice and support given by contributors to the book itself. For his invaluable guidance on many matters and especially for his comments on an earlier draft of the Introduction I express my warmest thanks to Noel Osselton. Thierry Fontenelle has brought his expertise to bear on various technical problems and for this too I am very grateful. Sidney Landau, also, has given invaluable support to this project. Not only has he provided helpful advice but he also, at very short notice, agreed to provide a chapter on the American collegiate dictionary, to which his experience as lexicographer and editor lends unrivalled authority.

John Davey, Consultant Editor at Oxford University Press, has from the beginning been closely involved with the *History*. It was he who came to me with the idea of a book devoted to the history of English lexicography and kindly invited me to edit it. I have since then been the beneficiary of expert technical advice, a clear sense of direction, and unfailing encouragement, and I owe John a profound debt of gratitude. I am also indebted to his colleagues at Oxford University Press, especially Karen Morgan and Chloe Plummer, who have supported him in his central role.

Finally, no thanks would be complete without some reference to the practical and moral support provided by my wife, Cabu, throughout the progress of the *History*. A full measure of thanks goes to her.

A. P. Cowie

Leeds, December 2007

CONTENTS OF VOLUME II

NOTES ON CONTRIBUTORS

MICHAEL ADAMS teaches at Indiana University, in Bloomington, Indiana. He has written *Slayer Slang*: A Buffy the Vampire Slayer *Lexicon* (Oxford University Press 2003) and *Slang*: *The People's Poetry* (Oxford University Press 2008); with Anne Curzan, he is author of *How English Works: A Linguistic Introduction* (Longman 2006). He is currently writing *Dialect Dilemma: The* Middle English Dictionary *and Techniques of Historical Lexicography*. For several years, he was editor of *Dictionaries: Journal of the Dictionary Society of North America*; currently, he is editor of the quarterly journal, *American Speech*.

JEANNETTE ALLSOPP is Director of the Caribbean Lexicography Programme—Anglophone and Multilingual—and Senior Research Fellow in Caribbean Lexicography at the UWI Cave Hill Campus in Barbados. She holds a Ph.D. from London Metropolitan University and was the 1991 winner of the Euralex Verbatim Award for lexicography. She produced the *Multilingual Supplement* to the *Dictionary of Caribbean English Usage* (*DCEU*), and later authored the first *Caribbean Multilingual Dictionary* in the Anglophone Caribbean.

RICHARD W. BAILEY is a Fellow of the Dictionary Society of North America and its former President. *Dictionaries of English: Prospects for the Record of Our Language*, his 1987-edited book, and the conference upon which it was based set out an agenda for future work that has now begun to reach fulfilment as the dictionaries promised or described in it have begun to reach completion. He is Fred Newton Scott Collegiate Professor of English at the University of Michigan.

JANET BATELY is Professor Emeritus of English Language and Medieval Literature at King's College London. Her research interests are those of the two areas named in her title, concentrating on Old English and historical English lexicography. Her publications in Old English include editions of the Old English Orosius, the Anglo-Saxon Chronicle and the Tanner Bede and a number of word-studies, while her lexicographical articles and papers have covered aspects of both the monolingual and bilingual English dictionaries of the seventeenth century. She has a book on Guy Miège two-thirds completed.

CHARLOTTE BREWER is the author of a history of the *Oxford English Dictionary* after 1928, *Treasure-House of the Language: the Living* OED (Yale University Press 2007), and *Editing Piers Plowman: the Evolution of the Text* (Cambridge University Press 1996). Since 2005 she has directed the research project *Examining the OED* (http://oed.hertford.ox.ac.uk/main/), a study of the *OED*'s sources, its use of quotations, and its processes of compilation. She is a fellow of Hertford College, Oxford, and CUF Lecturer in English at Oxford University.

MONIQUE C. CORMIER holds a doctorate from the Université de la Sorbonne Nouvelle (Paris 3). She is a full professor in the Département de linguistique et de traduction at the Université de Montréal, where she has been teaching terminology since 1988. For several years, she has been researching French–English bilingual dictionaries from the sixteenth to the eighteenth centuries. Her research is funded by the Social Sciences and Humanities Research Council of Canada. Professor Cormier is a Fellow of the Royal Society of Canada.

ANTHONY COWIE is Honorary Reader in Lexicography at the University of Leeds. He was co-editor of the third edition of the *Oxford Advanced Learner's Dictionary* and chief editor of the fourth. He was a founder member of the European Association for Lexicography and, from 1998 to 2003, editor of the *International Journal of Lexicography.* His other publications include, as editor, *Phraseology: Theory, Analysis, and Applications* (Oxford University Press 1998) and, as author, *English Dictionaries for Foreign Learners. A History* (Oxford University Press 1999).

MARGARET GRACE (MARACE) DAREAU was Senior Editor, then Editorial Director, of the *Dictionary of the Older Scottish Tongue* (1987–2001). She was Editorial Director of Scottish Language Dictionaries (2002–05) and is now Principal Editor. She is Lexicographical Consultant of *Faclair na Gàidhlig.* She was an editor of the *Concise Scots Dictionary* (1979–84) and author of the Glossary of the *Encyclopedia of Language and Linguistics* (1994).

GEORGE DURMAN is an adjunct instructor of Russian at New Jersey City University (Jersey City). He received his master's degree in Russian literature and language from the Moscow Pedagogical Institute. Later he became a Senior Fellow at the Moscow Literary Museum in Russia. After emigrating to the United States, he received master's degrees in Slavic languages and literatures, and in library science, from the University of Illinois, Urbana. His research interests are Russian intellectual history, particularly of the eighteenth and nineteenth centuries; Russian language and literature; and Russian rare books.

DONNA FARINA is an associate professor in the Department of Multicultural Education at New Jersey City University (Jersey City). She received her Ph.D. in linguistics from the University of Illinois, Urbana, and a licence and maîtrise in linguistics from the Université des Sciences Humaines in Strasbourg. In St Petersburg and Moscow, she has conducted research under a fellowship from the International Research and Exchanges Board (IREX).

SIDNEY LANDAU has been the editor-in-chief of many different kinds of dictionaries over the course of a long career in lexicography. He is a Fellow and past President of the Dictionary Society of North America and the author of *Dictionaries: the Art and Craft of Lexicography* (Second edition 2001) as well as of numerous scholarly contributions to journals.

ISEABAIL MACLEOD was Editorial Director of the Scottish National Dictionary Association (1986–2002) and was joint editor of several of their dictionaries, also of *The Nuttis Schell: Essays on the Scots Language* (1987). She was an editor of the *Concise Scots Dictionary* (1979–85). She has a special interest in the language of food and drink, and in 1986 she edited *Mrs. McLintock's Receipts for Cookery and Pastry-Work* (1736). Her other publications include *The Pocket Guide to Scottish Words* (1986, 2006), and she was General Editor of *About Scotland: People, Places, Heritage* (2007).

CARLA MARELLO is Full Professor of Applied Linguistics in the Faculty of Foreign Languages at the University of Turin (Italy), and Co-Director of a Ph.D. School in Euro-Asiatic studies in the domain of Linguistics and Linguistic Engineering in the same university. She has published extensively on lexicography and lexicology, text linguistics, and applied linguistics. She is Associate Editor of the *International Journal of Lexicography* and Series Editor at Zanichelli and Guerra publishing houses.

LYNDA MUGGLESTONE is Professor of History of English at the University of Oxford. She has published widely on language in the late eighteenth and nineteenth centuries. Recent work includes *Lexicography and the OED. Pioneers in the Untrodden Forest* (Oxford University Press 2002), *Lost for Words. The Hidden History of the Oxford English Dictionary* (Yale University Press 2004), *The Oxford History of English* (Oxford University Press 2006), and *'Talking Proper'. The Rise of Accent as Social Symbol* (Second revised paperback edition, Oxford University Press 2007).

NOEL OSSELTON has divided his academic career equally between Holland and England, and has held chairs of English Language in both countries. His first book, on *Branded Words in English Dictionaries before Johnson*, appeared fifty years ago, and most of his publications since then, including *The Dumb Linguists. A Study of the First English and Dutch Dictionaries* (1973) and *Chosen Words. Past and Present Problems for Dictionary Makers* (1995), have been in the field of post-Renaissance vernacular lexicography. A founder member, and later President, of the European Association for Lexicography, he now lives in retirement in Durham.

ALLEN REDDICK is Professor of English Literature at the University of Zürich. Among his publications are *The Making of Johnson's Dictionary, 1746–1773* (Cambridge 1990; revised edition 1996) and *Johnson's Unpublished Revisions of his*

Dictionary: A Facsimile Edition with Commentary and Analysis (Cambridge 2005). The author of articles on subjects including eighteenth-century lexicography and Samuel Johnson, he is currently compiling a descriptive bibliography of books distributed by the eighteenth-century figure Thomas Hollis and writing an analysis of Hollis's exhaustive attempts to influence public opinion.

HANS SAUER is Professor of English at the University of Munich (LMU), Germany. He has also taught at Columbus/Ohio, Eichstaett, Dresden, Innsbruck, Lodz, Palermo, and Wuerzburg, among other universities. He has edited Old and Middle English texts, including the *Theodulfi Capitula* and *The Owl and the Nightingale*; he has published on word-formation and on plant-names in Old and Middle English, on Wulfstan's handbook, on translations of *Beowulf*, on the *Épinal-Erfurt Glossary*. He is an editor or co-editor of the *Lexikon des Mittelalters*, *Anglia*, Middle English Texts (MET), *Texte und Untersuchungen zur Englischen Philologie* (TUEPh), *Anglo-Saxon Heritage in Munich* (2005), *Poetica* 66 (2006)—on emotions—and *Beowulf and Beyond* (2007).

EDMUND WEINER is Deputy Chief Editor, *Oxford English Dictionary*. He has been a member of staff of the *OED* since 1977. He worked on the *Supplement to the Oxford English Dictionary* and was co-editor (with John Simpson) of the second edition of the *OED*. He has special responsibility for grammar and assists the chief editor in finalizing the text of the third edition for online publication. His publications include several works on English grammar and usage and (with Peter Gilliver and Jeremy Marshall) *The Ring of Words: J. R. R. Tolkien and the Oxford English Dictionary* (2006).

ILLUSTRATIONS

ABBREVIATIONS

adv phr	adverb phrase
Angu	Anguilla
Antg	Antigua
arch	archaic
attrib	attributive
Baha	Bahamas
BCET	The Birmingham Collection of English Text
Bdos	Barbados
Belz	Belize
Bhoj	Bhojpuri (a dialect of Hindi)
BM	*Basic Material* volumes of the SED
CarA	Caribbean Area
CayI	Cayman Islands
CD-ROM	compact disc read-only memory
CE	Caribbean English
CERN	Conseil Européen pour la Recherche Nucléaire
Clar	Parish of Clarendon
COBUILD	Collins Birmingham University International Language Database
COPAC	see http://www.copac.ac.uk
DTD	document type definition
EDS	English Dialect Society
EEBO	Early English Books Online
EEMF	Early English Manuscripts in Facsimile
EETS	Early English Text Society
EFL	English as a Foreign Language
ÉpErf	The *Épinal-Erfurt Glossary*
foll	following
FrCa	French Caribbean
Gen. Sc.	General Scots

Gren	Grenada
Guad	Guadeloupe
Guyn	Guyana
Hait	Haiti
Hin	Hindi
HTML	Hypertext Mark-up Language
IC	integrated circuit
id phr	idiomatic phrase
IPA	International Phonetic Alphabet; International Phonetic Association
IrE	Irish English
Jmca	Jamaica
LCD	liquid crystal display
LEME	Lexicons of Early Modern English
LSS	Linguistic Survey of Scotland
Mart	Martinique
ME	Middle English
MRD	Machine-Readable Dictionary
n (pl)	plural noun
NARP	North American Reading Programme
Nevs	Nevis
NEWS	New English Words Series
NLP	Natural Language Processing
OCR	optical character recognition
OE	Old English
OED	Oxford English Dictionary
OEDIPUS	OED Integration, Publishing, and Updating System
PC	personal computer
PDA	personal digital assistant
phr(s)	phrase(s)
POS	part of speech
PtRi	Puerto Rico
RP	Received Pronunciation
SAWD	Survey of Anglo-Welsh Dialects
Sc.	Scots

SDC	Scottish Dialects Committee
SED	Survey of English Dialects
SEU	Survey of English Usage
SGML	Standard Generalized Mark-up Language
SNDA	Scottish National Dictionary Association
SQL	Structured Query Language
StDo	Santo Domingo
StE	Parish of St Elizabeth
StKt	St Kitts
StLu	St Lucia
StVn	St Vincent
Tre	Parish of Trelawny
Trin	Trinidad
USVI	US Virgin Islands
XML	Extensible Mark-up Language

1

INTRODUCTION

A. P. Cowie

THE *Oxford History of English Lexicography* provides a broad-ranging and detailed survey of English-language lexicography, with contributions from leading authorities in Britain, Europe, and North America. General-purpose and specialized dictionaries are treated in two parallel volumes, within a common historical perspective. The present volume deals with English monolingual dictionaries and with bilingual works one of whose component languages is English. A second volume, with its own introduction and combined bibliography, explores in depth the extraordinarily rich diversity of specialized dictionaries. The term 'English lexicography' is interpreted broadly to embrace dictionaries of Scots, of American English, and of the varieties of English spoken in Australia, Canada, India, New Zealand, and South Africa. It is also taken to apply to dictionaries of the English-based Creoles of the Caribbean. The *History* provides detailed, fully documented, treatments of the various scholarly projects which have been central to the development of lexicography over the past 150 years, and takes full account of the impact, on English dictionaries of all kinds, of recent developments in corpus and computational linguistics.

The elaborate, large-scale dictionaries of today evolved by stages from simple beginnings. In the seventh and eighth centuries, as **Hans Sauer** explains, the practice arose of inserting in Latin manuscripts explanations (or 'glosses') of difficult words, in Latin or in Old English (sometimes in both). Later, the glosses were gathered together into 'glossaries'. Three types of glossaries are usually recognized. If glosses in texts are later collected, but without orderly arrangement, they are 'glossae collectae'. If they are then arranged alphabetically, they become 'alphabetical glossaries'. If, however, the glosses are arranged according to semantic fields (e.g. parts of the body, farm tools), they are 'class glossaries'.

Glosses and glossaries came to fulfil a vital function in teaching and the transmission of knowledge. Also to be noted are the important connections between glossing and the terms used to describe it, and the structure of modern dictionary entries. The gloss is a word or short phrase used to explain a difficult Latin word—the 'lemma'—a relationship which foreshadows the pattern of the modern dictionary explanation, with its 'definition' and 'headword'. But there is a further link with modern dictionaries. Latin words could be used to explain more difficult Latin ones, thus foreshadowing the monolingual dictionary, or the hard ones could be explained in Old English, in which case they pointed forward to bilingual (Latin–English) dictionaries.

It is a matter of convention that the early collections are called glossaries and the later ones dictionaries. Moreover, terminology in the Middle Ages was unstable. One picturesque name or another could be used in any given case. For instance, the first English–Latin dictionaries (fifteenth century) were called *Promptorium parvulorum* ('storeroom, or repository, for children') and *Catholicum Anglicum* ('the comprehensive English collection').

Later, in accounts of how bilingual dictionaries of the Renaissance were produced, we are given insights into the way compilers built up their alphabetical lists of headwords. Richard Huloet and John Baret, as **Janet Bately** shows, transformed the English equivalents given in their Latin–English sources into headwords in order to build up their own word-lists. So, for instance, *master* as the translation equivalent of *magister* would become a headword and, if not already independently treated, would be slotted into an English alphabetical word-list. There is a curious, but altogether predictable, result of such transfers. As many of the Latin headwords are translated not by one-word English equivalents but by a paraphrase, this reorganization has resulted in the introduction of multi-word entries. This then raises the further problem of which of the components of a multi-word unit should be regarded as determining order in the English word-list.

From the middle of the sixteenth century onwards, a number of bilingual dictionaries appeared featuring English and a modern European language. These were explanatory dictionaries for English learners of the language in question—Italian in the case of John Florio's *A worlde of wordes* (1598), French in the case of Randle Cotgrave's *Dictionarie of the French and English tongues* (1611). But people wishing to compose texts in these languages would not have been greatly helped by these dictionaries. Potential users had to wait for separate English–Italian and English–French volumes for their particular needs to be met.

By the end of the seventeenth century, with monolingual English dictionaries by that time well established, bilingual works which combined English and a modern foreign language profited from the general decline of Latin and played a major part in the promotion of the various national tongues. Bilingual lexicography, as **Monique Cormier** goes on to show, also benefited from the presence in England of two exceptional dictionary-makers, the Swiss Guy Miège and, a decade later, the Frenchman Abel Boyer. Miège's great achievement was to be the first to compile, as a single author engaged on a single project, a bi-directional French–English, English–French dictionary—the *Great French Dictionary* of 1688. The publication of a major rival, Boyer's *Royal Dictionary* of 1699, was soured by accusations of plagiarism—fully justified in the event, as Boyer had made extensive use of definitions and examples taken from Miège.

By the middle of the eighteenth century, monolingual dictionaries of English had so grown in scope and authority that several bilingual lexicographers, from various European countries, could contemplate using their word-lists as the basis of new dictionaries. The Spaniard Peter Pineda, for example, drew on Nathan Bailey's *Universal Etymological English Dictionary* to establish the word-list for the English–Spanish section of his *Nuevo dicionario*, published in London. The dictionary of Father Thomas Connelly and Father Thomas Higgens, also Spanish–English, and the first of the type to be published in Spain, greatly surpassed Pineda in originality. It drew on Johnson's *Dictionary* for its English headwords and definitions and on the dictionary of the Real Academia for its Spanish translation equivalents. It was thus a forerunner of the 'bilingualized' learners' dictionary of today, which in one of its forms has English headwords, definitions, and examples and also foreign-language translations of all three categories of information.

A hundred years on from those developments, English had gained much ground as the international language of commerce. But the language profited, too, as **Carla Marello** goes on to explain, from mass migration to the New World from all over Europe. At the simplest level there was a demand among English-speaking immigrants for everyday American vocabulary items; accordingly, American words and phrases were covered more extensively in dictionaries.

Generally speaking, and understandably, the linguistic needs of the time were often severely practical, so that bilingual dictionaries appearing in the nineteenth century, and featuring English, had increasingly to fulfil a demand for the *standard* language, but also satisfy a need for colloquial usage. By the end of the nineteenth century there was also—as far as English and French were concerned—a much greater emphasis on the explanatory needs of learners of English (i.e. 'decoding') with much less stress being laid on their productive needs (i.e. 'encoding').

Throughout the nineteenth century, German–English dictionaries were for the most part published in Germany. This tendency was fostered by the reputation that Germans had acquired in philological studies, including morphology and etymology.

This degree of understanding enabled lexicographers to make progress in the analysis of German and English, including the description of word-families.

An outstanding specialist in these studies, Elizabeth Weir, enjoyed the further distinction of being one of the few women to lead a dictionary team in the nineteenth century. She recognized that English–German dictionaries did not always help English students to select accurately from a dozen of so words the one corresponding to the meaning they wished to express. To help such students, Weir ensured that every meaning of a group of related German words was either preceded by an English synonym or followed by an explanatory word or phrase.

Despite early signs, in the reign of Ivan the Terrible, of Russians establishing trading contacts with England, it took a full century, taking 1600 as a starting point, to develop relations on a scale that would encourage serious language learning. Reports written at the time, as **Donna Farina** and **George Durman** indicate, suggest that Russians learning English did so through (limited) personal contact in the home country.

Learners of English had to wait till 1772 for the first English–Russian dictionary (and that an appendix to an English grammar) to appear. This was thematic in character, reflecting its function in language learning and teaching. And a further significant step forward was Zhdanov's *New Dictionary, English and Russian* (1784), in which the entries were listed alphabetically, parts of speech identified, and information about the register of words and meanings helpfully provided.

There were complaints in some quarters of 'the Want of ... any kind of Lexicon where the Russian words stand first'. But eventually, in 1840, the first Russian–English dictionary appeared, the work of James Banks. This was not for English users wishing to understand Russian, of course, but chiefly for Russians wishing to write in English—a target audience made more explicit in the case of Aleksandrov's *Russian–English Dictionary* (1883–85), which was prescribed for non-classical secondary schools.

Any account of Russian lexicography in the twentieth century must take account of the restrictions of the Soviet censorship. These fostered, for instance, a conservative approach to the inclusion of neologisms. However, official Soviet policy towards leading foreign languages carried certain benefits for lexicography. It led to the production of a wide range of dictionaries, bilingual as well as monolingual, aimed at learners of Russian and various other major languages, including of course English.

Change in lexicography may be seen not only in the introduction of new headwords but in the appearance and further development of new kinds of dictionaries. Such a progression can be traced from the appearance of the first monolingual dictionary—Cawdrey's *Table Alphabeticall* in 1604—to the stage where, a century and a half later, a recognizably modern work has emerged.

Noel Osselton suggests that the appearance of the first 'hard-word' dictionary can be seen as a development from the practice of appending short glossaries to various types of technical books. These helped the less proficient reader with the new words that were now needed, but included general learned vocabulary as well. Treating those learned words in a separate dictionary had the added attraction that users could find the items in one book instead of being obliged to search for them in several.

There were specific innovations within the development of the hard-word genre. Henry Cockeram, a successor to Cawdrey, took the unusual step of dividing his work—*The English Dictionarie*—into parts so as to meet both the 'decoding' (or 'explanatory') and the 'encoding' (or 'productive') needs of less proficient users. It was the second part which served as an encoding dictionary 'for writers aspiring to a loftier style'. The method by which this element was created was to take an English–Latin dictionary, copy the English headwords and then 'English' the Latin translation equivalents—a further instance of the imaginative use to which existing dictionaries could be put.

The second half of the seventeenth century saw the publication of a new type of monolingual dictionary, one which in scale and content was designed to appeal to an educated, leisured class of reader. Edward Phillips's *The New World of English Words* (1658) was the first of these folio dictionaries to appear. It was remarkable for presenting a broad range of encyclopedic information—from proper names and geographical descriptions on the one hand to an extensive listing of the arts and sciences on the other.

An altogether different feature introduced by Phillips was a dagger symbol, inserted in entries to warn readers that particular words were not acceptable in English. The introduction of this device marks the start of a prescriptive tradition in English dictionary-making, to be followed by other lexicographers in the next hundred years.

Johnson's *Dictionary* combined the best aspects of existing practice with features that were truly innovative, as **Allen Reddick** shows. As the essential basis of the work thousands of literary and other quotations were gathered, but Johnson also drew for ideas and material on the best dictionaries of his day. Nathan Bailey's folio *Dictionarium Britannicum* (1730) was exceptional in its treatment of etymology, and it was this dictionary, and especially the second edition of 1736, that served as a basis for Johnson and doubtless influenced his methods. Johnson also benefited from the publication of Ephraim Chamber's *Cyclopaedia* (1728), which provided entries for technical and scientific terms not previously covered. Of particular importance was Benjamin Martin's *Lingua Britannica Reformata* (1749), as this suggested a systematic plan for organizing multiple meanings in complex dictionary entries. Johnson started out by attempting to apply the *a priori* system of defining. He appears to have believed that any meaning would fit into his carefully constructed scheme. However, Martin's plan collapsed when put into practice, leaving Johnson to conclude that he must now turn to a method of establishing meanings by reference to their uses in texts.

This major change of direction is reflected in the *Dictionary* of 1755 and in the sombre realism of the 'Preface'. Instead of being merely the illustrations of the definitions, the examples became the groundwork of the semantic organization. One pioneering feature of the *Dictionary* for which Johnson is now justly applauded is his treatment of phrasal verbs, which in Bailey's dictionaries are almost entirely ignored. There were a number of possible sources. Major bilingual dictionaries would list them in the English ('encoding') part as entries, the assumption being that the writer would need ordinary words and phrases—such as phrasal verbs—as much as difficult, learned words. Johnson could also turn to the foreign language (say, French–English) part where phrasal verbs would be located as translation equivalents. But they would be scattered, and need reordering. However, Johnson would often have gathered as many examples from printed sources as he would have found in the dictionaries.

Charles Richardson, whose *New Dictionary of the English Language* appeared in 1837, is chiefly remembered for an approach to definition which laid great stress on etymology and for his criticism of the approach favoured by Johnson when compiling the latter part of his *Dictionary.* According to Richardson, Johnson mistakenly believed that a word had multiple meanings by virtue of its uses in context, when in fact it retained the one original and true meaning. Furthermore, Richardson quite accurately observed that Johnson had departed from his original procedure—the one which, as we saw earlier, he followed when first compiling the *Dictionary*—of determining meanings systematically.

The truth, according to one commentator, was that Richardson's determination to discover the 'literal roots' was founded upon superficial resemblances rather than a systematic examination of given words across different languages, or groups of languages. Richardson's etymologies were often absurd, but his dictionary nonetheless interested lexicographers because of the collection of quotations on which it was based and which foreshadowed the large-scale gathering of excerpts later seen as essential for the *Oxford English Dictionary.*

The first major dictionary compiled by an American chiefly for use in the United States was Noah Webster's *An American Dictionary of the English Language* (1828). In his earlier and much smaller work, *A Compendious Dictionary of the English Language* (1806), as **Sidney Landau** explains, he had revealed his intention to produce a much larger, more comprehensive dictionary, specifically to compete with and surpass Samuel Johnson's *Dictionary.* Johnson's *Dictionary,* especially its revision by Todd in 1818, was for many years the leading large-size dictionary in America, and a major source for Webster's great dictionary of 1828 as well as for Joseph Worcester's dictionaries.

The publication of Webster's *American Dictionary* is justly regarded as a landmark in American lexicography. According to Webster, the English language had developed a distinctive character in America and deserved its own dictionary. Webster's great rival in lexicography was Joseph Worcester. The two men engaged in a celebrated 'dictionary war', both producing larger dictionaries in quick response to each other's latest dictionary, until the matter was settled in 1864 by the publication of the first dictionary commonly referred to as 'the unabridged'. This was known as the Webster–Mahn and edited by Noah Porter after Webster's death in 1843. Worcester's dictionaries played an important part in raising the standards of American lexicography and his open acknowledgement of debt to his predecessors stands in marked contrast to that of most early dictionary-makers.

Then followed a period of development which brought great prestige to the unabridged dictionary. Publishers sought to persuade the educated public that their dictionary was the repository of all of the facts of the English language. It was entirely fitting that the *Century Dictionary,* a beautifully illustrated, printed, and bound work, edited by William Dwight Whitney, should have been published at this time (1889–91).

The two unabridged Funk & Wagnalls dictionaries of 1893–94 and 1913, and the first of the unabridged *New International* Merriam-Webster dictionaries, of 1909, set off a new dictionary war that was as fiercely competitive as the one between Noah Webster and Joseph Worcester half a century earlier, except that this was waged by corporations rather than individuals. The great strength of the Funk & Wagnalls position lay in its ability to recognize what kinds of information the user wanted, and to convey it as simply and accessibly as possible. Etymology was of little interest to the average user, whereas meaning, spelling and pronunciation were reckoned of great importance.

Despite such achievements, the end of the massive unabridged work could not be long delayed. Eventually, Webster's *New International* of 1934 settled the issue. It was widely recognized as being without equal for its coverage of the English language in America. Although Merriam-Webster produced a new edition in

1961, the *Third New International*, the era of the unabridged dictionary was already in a state of decline from which it would not recover.

The founding of the London Philological Society, in 1842, with its aims of extending 'study and knowledge of the structure, the affinities, and the history of languages', helped to create, for the 1850s, an intellectual climate in sympathy with a dictionary project along historical lines.

Initially, and as **Lynda Mugglestone** shows, the Society aimed at drawing up a supplementary list of words—not compiling a completely new dictionary—and a special committee was set up in 1857 with the task of gathering words and idioms. Already it was recognized that a wider public should be involved in the collecting, and titles of books to be read were listed in journals. A member of the special committee, Richard Chenevix Trench, spoke 'On some Deficiencies in our English Dictionaries', a seminal document in the history of the *OED*. He declared that they were to aim at a new dictionary, not a 'patch upon old garments'. The 'founding ideals' included objectivity, inclusivity, a respect for the historical record, and a commitment to original research.

Although much was done from that point to produce scholarly editions of early texts, the general activity of collection slackened by the early 1870s. It was at this stage that Henry Sweet pointed out in a letter to Oxford University Press the twin value of their taking on the dictionary project. He stressed the significance of lexicography in a national and international context, and argued that major dictionaries were now inconceivable without a basis in data and historical method. The Delegates, for their part, were only prepared to fund the project if James Murray would agree to take on the editorship. So it was that, early in 1879, Murray was appointed editor of the *New English Dictionary*, later to become the *OED*.

Murray straightaway recognized the need to reactivate the collecting programme, which he did by launching an *Appeal to the English-Speaking and English-Reading Public* (May 1879). By December 1880, two and a half million citations had been gathered, though only some were in alphabetical order and 'scarcely at all into chronological order under each word'.

In 1860, Trench had advocated the removal of scientific and technical terms from the Main Dictionary. However, in 1880, Murray asked readers to examine scientific works. Whatever the field of interest, however, not all items or senses could be included. Personal taste might be involved, and Murray was reminded that there is often a tension within the individual lexicographer between the objective appraisal of usage, and subjective evaluation.

The first *OED Supplement* was published in 1933, along with a re-issue of the parent dictionary; the second, consisting of four volumes, appeared between 1972 and 1986. What made the first *Supplement* so fascinating, as **Charlotte Brewer** indicates, was the reflection in its pages of a turbulent period of social and cultural history, and the increasing acceptability of informal language and slang in printed sources. It was the stated intention of the co-editors, Craigie and Onions, to devote space to colloquial idiom and slang, and to provide some indication of scientific and technical developments. And those were the very details that reviewers and commentators picked out for favourable comment.

In the 1930s and beyond, the publishers from time to time asked whether they should publish another *Supplement* or instead undertake a full reworking of the parent dictionary. It was important, among other priorities, to update the *OED* 'in order to breathe new life into the lesser dictionaries' (profitable off-shoots such as the *Concise Oxford*). As for the future of the *OED* itself, the production of further supplementary volumes would save OUP the enormous costs of complete revision and was the course eventually embarked on. Robert Burchfield, a distinguished medievalist, was appointed editor in 1957.

As Burchfield later remarked, it was impossible at the time to obtain expert guidance on the compilation of dictionaries. (In the 1950s, there were none of the conferences, journals and manuals which, fifty years on, are taken for granted.) He focused on three areas of vocabulary specified for treatment by his publisher—literary language, World English, scientific and technical terms—and to these he added 'coarse' expressions.

Assumptions concerning the superior status of literary language were at first unchallenged, but the absurdity was eventually recognized of guaranteeing inclusion of the name of a plant or shrub if it was used in a work of literature. The criterion was eventually dropped. Then, too, the growing importance that came to be attached to the treatment of scientific and technical terms led to the appointment of science consultants, and an extension of specialized coverage that was widely welcomed.

The study of English lexicography has a national and regional as well as a historical dimension: it encompasses the distinctive words and meanings used in the United States and in the independent countries of the Commonwealth, and the dictionaries in which they are recorded.

By the 1850s in America, lexicography had moved away from its earlier concern with lexical origins. As **Richard Bailey** puts it, 'American dictionaries were comprehensive, inclusive of Americanisms, and indifferent to opinions of Britain'. Such a general shift of attitude encouraged those wishing to compile large-scale dictionaries of Americanisms in a spirit of scholarly detachment.

The *Dictionary of American English* (*DAE*) was the first of these to be produced. In defining the scope of the work, William Craigie, its co-editor, narrowed the scope to material that would distinguish American English from usages employed in 'the rest of the English-speaking world.' But, even with this restriction, Craigie's scope was broad.

One of Craigie's assistant editors, Mitford M. Mathews, went on to edit *A Dictionary of Americanisms on Historical Principles* (*DA*) (1951). Of crucial importance was his limitation of 'Americanism' to 'a word or expression that originated in the United States'. The term embraced outright coinages (such as *appendicitis, hydrant*), and such words as *campus, gorilla*, which first became English in the US.

Dictionaries of national usages have appeared in several other countries, including India. But they are most comprehensive and scholarly in countries where there are long-established native-English-speaking populations, such as Australia, Canada, New Zealand, and South Africa. In all those territories, with minor differences, a particular pattern of dictionary development has come about. First, typically, a single scholar or individual enthusiast will appear and start noting down the vocabulary peculiar to the territory—often complaining as a result that the *OED* is deficient in covering those usages. A small scholarly dictionary might be the next step, as in South Africa at Rhodes University, where a modest 'dictionary unit' was established, resulting in the production of a *Dictionary of South African English* (1978).

Eventually, in response to the public and academic interest that had been stimulated, funding would be provided—often by the host university acting jointly with a leading publisher. This in turn would lead to the compilation of a full-scale dictionary aimed at satisfying the by now widespread desire to make an authoritative record of the words and senses that had arisen locally. The words 'on Historical Principles', appearing as part of the title of the major work, evoked the priorities of Murray and were a reminder of practical links to the parent *OED*, with which the South African dictionary had a uniform plan.

Scots was, by the late fifteenth century, 'the principal literary and record language of the Scottish nation', as **Margaret Dareau** and **Iseabail Macleod** indicate, but, throughout the sixteenth and seventeenth centuries, it became increasingly anglicized so that by 1707 English was the language of formal writing and the speech of the upper classes. What had been a formal, literary language in the past came to survive only as a dialect, though one with its individual history, its own internal dialect variation, its continuing use in a remarkable literature.

In the *OED* material there were many unused Scots slips and these were assigned to the *Dictionary of the Older Scottish Tongue* (*DOST*). The corpus eventually covered every available written source, and most manuscript sources, as well as a new, electronic source of data in the Older Scots Text Archive, from which listings of words could be made available to editors. The individual interests of editors—in syntax, pronunciation, etymology, and so on—were allowed to appear and, under the editorship of Jack Aitken, *DOST* became, according to one scholar, 'more fully than ever an encyclopedia of Older Scottish culture and a first-class reference book for Scottish historiography'.

The second major work to be produced by Scottish lexicographers was the *Scottish National Dictionary* (*SND*), which, despite its title, came about through a group of dialectologists forming a Scottish Dialects Committee (convenor William Grant) with a view to starting up 'a programme of investigation into the present condition of the Scottish dialects'.

Much of the collecting and preliminary editing was carried out by volunteers. To gather spoken evidence, the country was divided into dialect areas according to pronunciation. Written quotations, also excerpted by volunteers, came from a considerable number and variety of works. Regional dictionaries and glossaries were valuable, but many of these source books were descriptions of local dialects. Yet, alongside the highly specific words and senses, often from technical fields—*astragal* 'a glazing bar', *pirn* 'a spool'—that came to light, there were also formal terms from the language of the church and the law. Perhaps surprisingly, the proportion of words not restricted to one or a few regions—i.e. common-core items—were quite numerous.

William Craigie's annual lecture to the Philological Society in 1919 pointed to the need for a number of new dictionaries to supplement aspects of the coverage already provided by the *OED*, then nearing completion. One of the dictionaries envisaged would deal with the 'Older Scottish' element, mentioned above; the others would be devoted to periods of the English language—Early Modern English (EME), Middle English (ME) and Old English (OE).

Craigie would later go further, as **Michael Adams** explains, arguing that the 'period' dictionaries would, by collecting more material, 'carry back the date of words from one period into that preceding it' and serve to confirm 'the regional affiliations of certain words or forms of words' (1937). Craigie's call for more data was later strengthened by the German scholar Jürgen Schäfer, who challenged and questioned the accuracy and inclusiveness of the dating of words provided by the *OED*.

The EME project was the first to be launched, in 1927, and Craigie invited Charles C. Fries to take on the editorship. There were two million slips from Oxford at the outset, a number that was greatly increased by a reading programme. However, its abundance was not matched by the quality of Fries's leadership. The EME project was a failure, as was a later attempt to revive it, but it did succeed in establishing a culture of historical lexicography in America, extending into the twenty-first century.

The *Middle English Dictionary* project, which was set up at Michigan in 1930, made uneven progress. For some time, it was dogged by a succession of editors who, in one way or another, were unequal to the task. Hans Kurath, who succeeded to the editorship in 1945, and turned the tide for the *MED*, had an analytical approach much closer to that of a modern lexicographer, though he had no experience of dictionary-making, and was not a medieval scholar. Kurath introduced small but important innovations. His clear-mindedness is evident in the instructions he gave to editors, directing them to 'begin a paragraph with a quotation of earliest date', then to 'supply quotations at roughly twenty-five-year intervals'. But in doing so they were to make the quotations do double duty by exhibiting all attested spellings.

The Dictionary of Old English (*DOE*), the last of the period dictionaries to be launched (in 1968), was conceived and compiled at the University of Toronto's Centre for Medieval Studies. It was thoroughly planned and its editors benefited from close knowledge of the related historical projects and of their key editorial staff. They also profited from a series of conferences specially organized to chart the future of the project and gather international support and advice.

The *DOE* project was remarkable for the extent to which it exploited advances in computer technology. In fact it was recognized at an early stage 'that the DOE's innovative approach to automating lexical resources might guide us to new forms of dictionary and strategies of dictionary use'.

Four pioneering works—the first two focused on particular territories, the third and fourth encompassing the entire region—make of the Caribbean a major centre of English lexicography in the twentieth century.

The first serious undertaking, as **Jeannette Allsopp** explains, was *A Dictionary of Jamaican English* on historical principles (1967), by Frederic Cassidy and Robert Le Page. This was designed to be a complete inventory of Jamaican Creole as well as a record of more educated Jamaican speech. The bulk of its data was made up of recorded responses to a questionnaire, devised by Cassidy, which focused on the working lives of farmers, fishermen, and so on. The material was afterwards classified according to the language status and geographical distribution of the speakers. The next major title was *The Dictionary of Bahamian English* by J. Holm and A. W. Shilling (1982). It was intended to form 'a link between the Caribbean Creoles such as Jamaican English and the English spoken today by many black people in the United States'. Analysis was restricted to the language of the most accessible islands of the chain.

Richard Allsopp, eventually to assume the chief editorship of the *Dictionary of Caribbean English Usage* (1996), became aware while a student in Europe of differences between his own usage and British Standard English. This led to a personal collection based on his own Guyanese speech, to which he eventually cross-referenced his Caribbean items. These modest beginnings led on eventually to Allsopp's Caribbean Lexicography Project, housed at the University of the West Indies, Cave Hill Campus, and with himself as Director. Allsopp realized early on that he could not compile a dictionary on historical principles because of the scale of such an undertaking. But his synchronic project went forward, with data provided by informants in twenty-two territories.

Entries in the *DCEU* often have an exceptionally rich structure, indicating the written and spoken forms of headwords, including pitch-contour, which may play a crucial role in distinguishing between the senses of common words and phrases. There is also a remarkable cross-reference system, linking up the range of synonyms found for a given headword in different territories of the region. *The Caribbean Multilingual Dictionary* (2003), the work of Jeannette Allsopp, is a further major project introducing a fresh dimension into Caribbean lexicography—one that involves a thematic approach to description under such headings as flora, fauna, and foods.

In the early 1980s, as **Edmund Weiner** recalls, the publishers of the *OED* began to express concern about the future of the *Dictionary.* The fifty-year copyright of the 1933 first edition would soon come to an end. The best safeguard would be to integrate the contents of the *Supplement*—now nearing completion—with those of the 1933 *OED*, since an integrated dictionary would protect the copyright and keep the skilled staff at Oxford fully engaged. That was agreed to. However, the move that would have the most profound effects was to decide that, as computer technology was now making such rapid advances, the two texts should be computerized and then combined and edited.

Early on, it was realized that the entire process, from converting the texts into electronic form, merging them, revising and correcting, and then passing the text on for typesetting, was too much to manage in one stage. It was therefore decided to publish an integrated edition—first on paper and later in an electronic form—as a second edition. Revision and updating of the whole dictionary could be left to a later stage.

Important decisions had also to be made about converting the text to electronic form. Was it practicable, for instance, to convert the text by 'optical character recognition' (OCR)? The printed text of the first edition was of poor quality, necessitating much correction. But the company responsible for text conversion could keyboard and proof-read so as to make the output virtually error-free. Also, and most important, their skilled copy-editors could manage 'structural' mark-up (i.e. markers in the text that identified such aspects of entry structure as the headword, the part of speech, and so on). Keyboarding was therefore adopted.

In the period leading up to the publication of the second edition, the chief task was to integrate in their correct places in the main *OED* text *partial* entries from the *Supplement*—the *complete* entries being fitted in alphabetically. A component of the system was built that could, using the mark-up, match the corresponding pieces of text, first by headword, then by part of speech, then by other features of the entry structure, and could insert both definition text and quotations in the right place. Editors were partly helped by the fact that instructions were already present in the printed text of the *Supplement.* These might take the form 'Add to def.:', followed by supplementary definition text.

Moving on into the 1990s, the team began to prepare for the revision of the *OED.* Initially, it was thought that revision might be based on existing resources, such as the *Shorter Oxford Dictionary*, the *Middle English Dictionary*, and so on, and on the extremely large quotation files gathered since 1957 (i.e. since the beginning of the *Supplement* project). However, experiments had shown that these resources would not go far enough. Editors welcomed from Michigan, then, in 1997, the bodies of material gathered for the dictionary of Early Modern English, which had never been completed. These acquisitions, however, are overshadowed by the text collections published on the Internet which, with appropriate software, can be searched by lexicographers, whether at Oxford or elsewhere. Accessing such sites as the British National Corpus or JSTOR is now an everyday aspect of dictionary compilation.

Then, running in parallel with the expansion of text corpora, and of exceptional importance for the further development of the *OED*, have been the changes made possible by online editing and publication. One significant aspect has been the editorial revision of the dictionary, now ongoing, which has resulted in the online publication of large amounts of new and revised dictionary text.

PART I

EARLY GLOSSARIES; BILINGUAL AND MULTILINGUAL DICTIONARIES

2

GLOSSES, GLOSSARIES, AND DICTIONARIES IN THE MEDIEVAL PERIOD

Hans Sauer

2.1 THE PERIODS OF ENGLISH AND THEIR BACKGROUND

MEDIEVAL English is traditionally taken to comprise Old English and Middle English. Old English (OE, formerly also called Anglo-Saxon), the earliest form of English, spans the period from *c*.450 to *c*.1100; Middle English (ME) spans the period from *c*.1100 to *c*.1500. English has been attested in writing from *c*.700 onwards, that is, we are dealing with a period of roughly 800 years. Middle English was then followed by Modern English (*c*.1500 to the present, or spanning about 500 years so far). The period from *c*.1500 to *c*.1700 is often called Early Modern English. The periods are defined by their historical and cultural background as well as by changes in the structure of the language itself.

Historically, Old English corresponds to the Anglo-Saxon period, which according to Bede began in 449 with the conquest of Britain by Germanic tribes; it ended in 1066 with the Battle of Hastings and the Norman Conquest. The most far-reaching historical event during that period was probably the introduction of Christianity from the later sixth century onwards (597 was the date of arrival of the missionaries from Rome), which had a deep impact not only on religion but also on culture in general. Since language does not change radically from one year to another, the end of Old English and the beginning of Middle English is not clear-cut. It is often dated around 1100. Some Old English texts were copied until shortly after 1200; then the transmission of Old English came to an end.

Middle English historically comprises the reign of the Norman Kings and their successors till the early Tudors. The end of the Middle English period—unlike that of the Old English period—is not marked by one single historical event. There were a number of new departures around 1500 which signalled the end of the Middle Ages and the beginning of the Early Modern period, for example, the introduction of printing into England by William Caxton in 1476.

Anglo-Saxon society originally was an oral society. Literacy, that is, the ability to read and write, was introduced by the Christian missionaries from the late sixth century onwards, but probably reached only a fraction of the population, at first mainly the clergy. Even at the end of the Middle Ages, many people still could not read and write. Of course, teaching was also largely carried on orally, and pupils probably often took notes and wrote down what the teacher said. We have traces of the teaching of Theodore of Tarsus and Hadrian at Canterbury in the later seventh century in the form of biblical commentaries and also glossaries.

The main form of written transmission throughout the Middle Ages was the manuscript. Each text and each copy of a text had to be handwritten. The earliest written documents of English have been preserved from around 700, and by far the longest of the earliest documents is the *Épinal-Erfurt Glossary*. Originally texts were copied and manuscripts were produced mainly in the *scriptoria* of the monasteries and cathedrals. These remained important throughout the Middle Ages; later other centres such as the royal chancery also played a role. Right at the end of the Middle Ages, printing was introduced into England (1476).

The language of the Church and of learning was Latin, originally also introduced by the missionaries. Before the Norman Conquest, a large number of texts were also written in or translated into Old English. After the Norman Conquest, French (or rather 'Anglo-Norman', a variety of French) played an important role too, so that England was basically triglossic from 1066 to the fourteenth century: broadly speaking, French was the language of the ruling classes, English was spoken by the common people, and Latin was spoken and written by the clerics and the learned. Of course, some people were bilingual or even trilingual—for example, priests who celebrated the mass in Latin but preached in English.

Whereas Old English still had a relatively pure Germanic vocabulary, Middle English absorbed thousands of French loan-words. Thus English developed into a language with a mixed Germanic-Romance vocabulary. In glosses and glossaries, especially of the thirteenth century, we cannot always tell whether a French word was still regarded as a foreign word or whether it had been adopted as a loan-word into English. T. Hunt therefore does not distinguish between English and French words at all, but subsumes both under 'Vernacular Names', and he opposes Vernacular to Latin.[1] French died out as a native language in England in the course of the fourteenth century, and it had to be learned as a foreign language.[2]

2.2 THE FUNCTION OF GLOSSES AND GLOSSARIES

Glossing is still practised today as a study aid: schoolchildren and university students, for example, often write interlinear or marginal translations and explanations into their books, although they do not necessarily know that this activity is called glossing, and although teachers and professors often regard it as damaging school or public property. Glossing was not regarded so negatively in the Middle Ages; on the contrary, it was seen as a useful exercise, and it was essential for teaching, especially Latin. Although there seem to be few contemporary comments on this practice, the sheer number of glosses and the nature of the glossed texts show that glossing was important for an understanding of the Latin texts. It has even been said that 'glossing and the use of glosses was at the heart of the intellectual life' in the (early) Middle Ages.[3]

The main purpose of the glosses, as well as of the glossaries, thus must have been a didactic one: interlinear glosses facilitate the understanding and possibly also the learning of the glossed Latin text. Glossaries help with the acquisition of the Latin vocabulary (and probably also of the English vocabulary). Thus many of the glosses and glossaries must have been used for teaching purposes in schools, especially in monastic and cathedral schools. This seems particularly clear in cases such as Ælfric's *Glossary* as well as his Latin *Colloquy* and the Old English glosses added to it.

The didactic function of glosses and glossaries ranged from teaching and learning Latin at an elementary level to study at more advanced stages: whereas Ælfric's *Colloquy* was probably intended for beginners, some of the early glosses and glossaries explained the difficult (hermeneutic) Latin vocabulary which some early medieval authors such as Aldhelm (*c.* 640–709/710) or Abbo of Saint-Germain (later ninth century) employed in their poetry and prose. Specific glossaries (class glossaries) such as the plant name glossaries were perhaps intended for the use of physicians and healers, to help them to identify the plants

[1] In the indexes to his collections of plant names (Hunt 1989) and of teaching materials for Latin (Hunt 1991).

[2] For useful suggestions concerning my contribution, my thanks are due to Hedwig Gwosdek, Julia Hartmann, Ursula Lenker, Wolfgang Mager, Angelika Schröcker, and, of course, Anthony Cowie.

[3] Hüllen (1999: 56).

in Latin and English (and later also in Anglo-Norman) and to prepare the proper medicines.

It is also clear from the glossaries that learning and scholarship were international even in the early Middle Ages. In the Old English period, continental Latin–Latin glossaries were copied and augmented in England. Conversely, some of the early Latin–Latin and Latin–OE glossaries from England were also copied on the Continent, for example, the Erfurt manuscript of the *Épinal-Erfurt Glossary* in Cologne, or the *Leiden Glossary* in St Gall; see Ker (1957, esp. Appendix). How far the continental scribes and scholars understood the OE words is difficult to judge.[4] In the Middle English period, the great Latin dictionaries by, for example, Hugutio of Pisa, Johannes Balbus, and Papias were also used in England, whereas English scholars in their turn worked on the Continent.

Sometimes, especially in Old English, the glosses are possibly or probably loan-formations based on their Latin models, for example, *fræ-fætt* 'very fat' for L *prae-pinguis* 'very fat', or *frea-bodian* 'proclaim, announce' for L *pro-nuntiare* 'to make publicly known, announce, proclaim'. In such cases it is not always clear whether the glossators actually wanted to enrich the English vocabulary by providing new words or phrases, or whether they simply wanted to show the morphological structure or the meaning of the Latin words by imitating them with Old English material. Thus *fræ-*, *frea-* often had intensifying function (which it probably has in *fræ-fætt*), but in *freabodian* it seems just to mirror the *pro-* of *pronuntiare* and does not add to the meaning of *bodian*. The OE examples just given (*fræ-fætt*, *frea-bodian*) are *hapax legomena* (nonce formations); they were probably coined by the glossator(s), but never gained any currency and were not adopted by the speech community.

Sometimes, however, glossaries also record words that must have been of native origin and common in oral use, but are attested rarely or not at all in the literary texts of the period. This is, for example, the case with the plough and its parts, which obviously must have been very important to farmers.[5] The plough was, however, not part of the vocabulary of heroic poetry or of homilies, where farming does not play a role. Thus the word *share-beam* (OE *scearbeam*) for a part of the plough is only recorded in glossaries.[6]

[4] Thus the continental scribe of the *Leiden Glossary* remarks at the end 'Sicut inueni scripsi ne reputes scriptori' (Ker 1957, Appendix no. 18), 'I wrote it as I found it [sc. in my exemplar]; don't blame it [i.e. any mistakes] on the scribe'.

[5] See, for example, Roberts and Kay (2000, vol. I, no. 04.02.04.06.07).

[6] This also leads to the often difficult distinction between common (general) vocabulary and special purposes vocabulary (Fachwortschatz), that is, the vocabulary used by members of certain professions and occupations only. Thus OE *rap* (> ModE rope, for L *funiculus*) must have been a common word, whereas *wingeardes screadu-isen* 'vintner's knife' (lit. 'vineyard's pruning-knife') for L *surculus* must have been a fairly special term. On this question see, for example, Sauer (1999).

2.3 TERMINOLOGY AND TYPOLOGY

2.3.1 *Terminology: glosses, glossaries, dictionaries, etc.*

'Glosses' are words that explain other, normally more difficult, words. 'Interlinear' glosses are written between the lines of a text, usually above the words they explain; 'marginal' glosses are added in the margin. They can be synonyms or short paraphrases in the same language (e.g. Latin words explaining other Latin words), or translation equivalents in another language (e.g. OE words explaining Latin words). 'Glossators' are the people who provide glosses.[7] The word that is explained by a gloss is called its 'lemma'. The word which glosses a lemma is also called its 'interpretamentum'. A gloss (or *interpretamentum*) usually consists of a single word or a very short phrase, providing a synonym or a translation. Thus we have a lemma (or headword), which is explained by a gloss (or *interpretamentum*). A somewhat longer explanation is called a 'scholion'; the border between gloss and scholion is not always easy to draw.[8]

'Glossaries' are collections of glosses, that is, lists of words (*lemmata*), each with a brief explanation (gloss, *interpretamentum*). The explanation can be a synonym in the same language (e.g. in Latin–Latin glossaries) or a translation equivalent in another language (e.g. in Latin–Old English glossaries). The alphabetical OE glossaries in particular usually add partly Latin and partly OE glosses to their Latin lemmata and therefore are often mixtures of Latin–Latin and Latin–OE glossaries, less so the 'class' (synonym) glossaries, which are more consistently Latin–OE. The sequence and distribution of the Latin–Latin and the Latin–OE pairs seems often unpredictable. The Latin–OE glossaries can be regarded as the forerunners of bilingual dictionaries, and the Latin–Latin glossaries as the forerunners of monolingual dictionaries—but, as just stated, there was no strict division between those two forms in the Old English period. Some scholars employ the terms 'vocabulary' or 'wordbook' instead of or in addition to glossary. For types of glosses and glossaries, see 2.3.2. A collection of scholia (extended explanations) is a 'commentary'.

'Dictionaries' are systematic collections (with explanations) of the words of a language or a text. Dictionaries usually provide more information than glossaries do. Whereas glossaries normally just give the headword (*lemma*) and its meaning in the form of a synonym or a translation equivalent (gloss, *interpretamentum*), modern dictionaries—in addition to explaining the meaning—often also indicate

[7] Glosses and glossators also played a role in the medieval reception of Roman law and in Canon law, but we are not concerned with this here; see, for example, *LexMA*, ed. Auty, s.v. 'Apparatus glossarum', 'Glossa ordinaria', 'Glossatoren', 'Glossen', etc.

[8] On 'scholia' see, for example, *LexMA*, ed. Auty, s.v. 'Scholien', with further references.

the pronunciation, give grammatical information (e.g. word-class, inflexional patterns, possible constructions and collocations), and provide examples, either made-up or drawn from literature. They sometimes also supply information on the etymology (origin) and the development of the words they contain. But the difference between a glossary and a dictionary is one of degree and it is more by convention that the early collections are usually called glossaries and the later collections are usually called dictionaries.

Moreover, terminology was never fully fixed. The first author who named his (Latin) compilation *Dictionarius* was apparently John of Garland (*c*.1195–*c*.1272), but this title was slow to catch on. The large and popular Latin dictionaries from the Middle Ages have titles such as *Elementarium* (i.e. for beginners), *Derivationes* (i.e. assembling word-families), *Catholicon* (i.e. a comprehensive collection), *Medulla* (i.e. the quintessence), etc. The first English–Latin dictionaries, which appeared in the fifteenth century, were called *Promptorium Parvulorum* (i.e. a store-room [sc. of words] for young [sc. scholars]) and *Catholicon Anglicum* (i.e. the comprehensive English collection). The earliest monolingual English dictionaries had names such as *A Table Alphabeticall . . . of hard vsuall English wordes* (Cawdrey 1604), *An English Expositor* (Bullokar 1616), etc.

The term 'dictionary' came to be used more frequently in the course of the seventeenth century, and today it is the most usual English term for an alphabetical collection; for a collection that is arranged according to semantic groups (synonyms, topoi), the title 'thesaurus' is now preferred. 'Lexicon' is still used as a synonym for 'dictionary', especially for a dictionary of ancient languages, and the art of dictionary-making is called 'lexicography'. An 'encyclopedia' (encyclopaedia) usually gives more information than a dictionary; it explains not only the words but also the things and concepts referred to by the words.

The terminology just outlined (gloss, glossary, vocabulary, dictionary, thesaurus, lexicon, encyclopedia, etc.) is largely modern and originated mainly in the sixteenth century;[9] our knowledge about the OE and ME terminology (as far as this existed) seems rather limited.

2.3.2 *Types of glossaries and kinds of glosses*

Typologically, three kinds of glossaries are usually distinguished.[10] The starting point is (interlinear or marginal) glosses in texts. If these are subsequently collected,

[9] Most of these words go back to Greek or Latin, but they were taken over into English in the sixteenth century or later. The noun *gloze* was used in English from the thirteenth century onwards, but was re-latinized into *gloss* in the sixteenth century.

[10] Cf., e.g. Hüllen (1999: 56ff.).

but left in the same order as they appeared in the texts, they yield (1) 'glossae collectae'. These help to understand the vocabulary of specific texts. If they are then arranged alphabetically, (2) 'alphabetical glossaries' are the result; these can be regarded as the ancestors of alphabetical dictionaries. The process of alphabetization was a slow and gradual one, however. At first, glosses were arranged according to the first letter of the alphabet only, that is, in a-order. The next step was to arrange glosses according to the first two letters of the alphabet, that is, in ab-order, and so on. If, on the other hand, the glosses were arranged according to semantic fields, such as plants, animals, people, parts of the body, clothes, kinds of buildings, kinds of ships, etc., (3) 'class glossaries' (with various subtypes) were the result; the entries within the sections of the class glossaries could, of course, then be arranged alphabetically. Such collections were also called 'synonyma', for example, the plant name glossaries, because they provided synonyms, that is, words with the same or a similar meaning—or to put it differently—different names for the same thing (e.g. the same plant). The class glossaries can be regarded as forerunners of 'thesauri' or synonym dictionaries, such as *Roget's Thesaurus*. They are also called topical glossaries or onomasiological glossaries—on them, HÜLLEN, Vol. II.

A fourth kind of arrangement apparently became only prominent in the later Middle Ages, namely according to 'derivationes' (derivations); that is, words derived from the same base (or stem or root) were grouped together, yielding word-families. This is sometimes still done in modern alphabetical dictionaries (where it is called 'nesting'), e.g. when *swiftly* and *swiftness* are listed under *swift*, or *swindler* under *swindle*.

The chronology of the extant early collections does not necessarily coincide with the typology just mentioned. Glossaries of different types co-existed, and probably a number of manuscripts and compilations have been lost, too. Thus the *Épinal-Erfurt Glossary* is the earliest extant English glossary; typologically, however, it is an alphabetical glossary, a mixture of a Latin–Latin and a Latin–Old English glossary, that is, it reflects a later stage in the development than interlinear glosses and *glossae collectae*, although both of the latter categories are only transmitted in later copies than *ÉpErf*.

As far as languages are concerned, throughout the Middle Ages there were Latin–Latin glosses, glossaries, and dictionaries, as well as Latin–English ones (Latin–Old English, Latin–Middle English), and also mixtures of both. In the Middle English period there were also some trilingual glossaries (Latin–French–Middle English) as well as French–English glossaries. The first English–Latin dictionaries appeared in the fifteenth century (*Promptorium Parvulorum*; *Catholicon Anglicum*).

The density of glossing varies. Sometimes there were just a few occasional glosses in a Latin text; sometimes texts were glossed systematically and more or less continuously. Sometimes there are even multiple glosses to one lemma, for instance, one or several Latin glosses plus an Old English gloss (e.g. in the *Lambeth Psalter*). As far as the glossaries are concerned, none of the Latin–OE glossaries presents the entire vocabulary; they are selective.

In the majority of cases the glosses were added in a smaller script some time after—occasionally even centuries after—the original text had been written (as in the *Lindisfarne Gospels*); but sometimes the addition of the gloss was planned from the beginning and the gloss was entered by the same scribe as the original text.

Usually, glosses were, like the body of the text, written in ink; occasionally, however, 'scratched or dry-point glosses' were entered with a stylus. These are often very hard to detect or to distinguish from meaningless scratches.[11]

The majority of glosses are 'lexical glosses' (i.e. words glossing other words and explaining their meaning) and here we are mainly concerned with those, but, at least during the Old English period, a system of 'syntactic glosses' also existed, letters or other marks that indicated which elements of a sentence belong together.[12] These were obviously intended as a help to construct (parse) the Latin sentences correctly.

Glosses were sometimes also used in abbreviated form (as 'merographs'). If the beginning of the word is retained and its ending omitted, then the semantic information is usually preserved (e.g. *dælni* for *dælnimung* 'participation'); if the beginning of the word is omitted and only its ending is preserved, then the gloss approaches the status of a syntactic gloss, indicating, for example, the case of the lemma (e.g. *cere* perhaps for *werlicere–virili* 'manly').[13]

Sources: few if any of the glossaries, continuous interlinear glosses and dictionaries are independent; many are based on or incorporate earlier material. Since the glossators or the compilers of glossaries and dictionaries—in accordance with general medieval practice—mostly do not indicate their sources, much scholarly energy has been spent on investigating the sources of glosses and glossaries and the interrelation between them. There are, however, exceptions: thus the compiler of the *Leiden Glossary* has indicated his sources; the compiler or scribe of the *Cleopatra Glossaries* has also marked his sources (in the margins), albeit in abbreviated form.

[11] On scratched glosses see, for example, Page (1973 and 1979).

[12] On syntactic glosses in manuscripts from the Old English period, see, for example, Korhammer (1980).

[13] See *BEASE*, ed. Lapidge, s.v. 'glosses' (by M. Gretsch). A special case is the *Expositio Hymnorum*: in two manuscripts, Latin verse hymns were rearranged into prose and then provided with Old English interlinear glosses (ed. Gneuss 1968).

2.3.3 *The textual status of glossaries and interlinear glosses and the treatment of their evidence*

Should glosses and glossaries be regarded as texts? A positive answer to this question is implied in Henry Sweet's collection *The Oldest English Texts* (1885), which consists largely of editions of the earliest English glossaries and glossed texts. On the other hand, glosses and glossaries are excluded and thus not seen as texts (or at least not as literature) in the bibliography by Greenfield and Robinson (1980). Hüllen (1999: 22–27), however, argues that at least the onomasiological dictionaries (the descendants of the class glossaries) 'are texts in the full semiotic sense of this term' (1999: 22).

It is not always clear, either, where the borderline between variants of the same text and different texts lies. Thus the Épinal and Erfurt manuscripts are usually (and rightly) regarded as copies of the same text, the *Épinal-Erfurt Glossary*, but Cameron (1973: D 7 and D 36) lists them (less convincingly) as different glossaries.

Interlinear (and marginal) glosses to texts were intended as explanations of the words in the texts they gloss and not as independent texts in their own right. Nevertheless, continuous glosses, such as the OE glosses in a manuscript of Ælfric's Latin *Colloquy*, were occasionally printed without the Latin text by former editors. This, however, was probably not intended by the original glossators, and it distorts the evidence.[14]

As stated above, Old English alphabetical glossaries often contain a mixture of Latin–Latin and Latin–OE entries. Some editions intended for scholars of English print the Latin–OE pairs only and ignore the Latin–Latin entries, so, for example, Sweet (1885) or Pheifer (1974). From the point of view of scholars mainly interested in (Old) English this may be understandable, but nevertheless it is also a distortion of the evidence, as it plays down the importance of Latin.

Dictionaries and vocabularies from the later Middle English period often indicate the gender and declension of the Latin nouns (e.g. *hoc os, -ris, -i*) and the conjugation of verbs; in some editions this information is omitted.[15]

2.3.4 *Authorship*

Most of the Old and Middle English glosses, glossaries and dictionaries are anonymous, but there are exceptions. For example, in the *Lindisfarne Gospels* the original scribe as well as the later glossator are mentioned (see 2.6.1 below).

[14] Particular caution should for example be taken to regard continuous glosses as evidence of Old or Middle English syntax—generally they rather mirror the Latin syntax of the glossed text.

[15] See Ross and Brooks (1984: vii).

Ælfric (abbot of Eynsham; *c.*950–*c.*1010) is the most important Old English prose author and grammarian; his identity was, however, only established in the nineteenth century. Ælfric's teacher, Æthelwold (*c.*904/909–984; at first abbot of Abingdon and later bishop of Winchester), has only recently been identified as the probable author of the OE gloss in the *Royal Psalter* and of (some of) the glosses to Aldhelm's prose *De virginitate*.[16] The first known author of a Late Middle English (or Early Modern English) vocabulary is John Stanbridge (1463–*c.*1510). All of them, and probably also many of the anonymous glossators and compilers, were clerics who also acted as teachers.

2.3.5 *Relation of lemma and gloss*

Basically the gloss takes the form of a synonym or a translation equivalent or, more rarely, a short paraphrase of its lemma. In the case of English glosses to Latin words, the translation equivalent can be an existing English word or a loan-word or a newly created word, sometimes in the form of a loan-formation.

Usually lemma and gloss match, but occasionally the gloss does not quite fit its lemma, at least as far as we can judge. Such discrepancies can be due to many different reasons. Often they are just mistakes, but in some instances they were introduced on purpose. A few examples of possible causes for discrepancies are given in the following paragraph.[17]

The glossator (or a later scribe) may have made a simple spelling mistake; his eyes may have skipped from one word to another and thus he glossed a different word from the one he intended to; he may not really have known the Latin word or its referent and had to guess its meaning; the Latin word may not have had an Old English equivalent and the glossator may have used a more general term (e.g. *þæt seleste win* 'the best wine' for L *Falernum*); he may have glossed an explanation of the lemma and not really the lemma itself (the gloss thus approaching a scholion, an exegetical remark); he may have glossed a very rare meaning of the lemma and not its common meaning, and so on. Thus there is a cline from an accurate rendering, that is a fairly close correspondence of gloss and lemma (the normal case), over a loose correspondence, to what is (or at least seems to us to be) a mistake or something we cannot make any sense of.

A case of a rare Latin lemma (actually a *hapax legomenon*) is *bradigabo* (*badrigabo*) in *Épinal-Erfurt* 131, the meaning of which is unknown; it was glossed as *felduuop* (*Ép*) / *felduus* (*Erf*), the meaning of which is also unknown (the first

[16] See Gretsch (1999); *BEASE*, ed. Lapidge, s.v. 'Æthelwold' (by M. Lapidge).

[17] For more examples of difficult glosses and real or apparent discrepancies between lemma and interpretamentum (gloss) see, for example, Meritt (1954 and 1968); Sauer (1999).

element is 'field', but the second presents difficulties)—it may refer to an animal ('fieldhopper') or to a plant ('foxglove'), but this is speculation. Latin *digitalium munusculorum* (the latter probably a mistake for *musculorum*), *Erf* 346, seems to mean 'finger-muscles', but the Old English gloss *finger-doccuna* seems to refer to a plant, so the glossator either translated an otherwise unattested meaning of the Latin word or simply made a mistake. L *mulio* is a 'mule-keeper', but its OE gloss *hors-thegn* in *Ép* 658 changes the animal and imprecisely refers to a 'horse-servant'.

Some of the Latin lemmata in the Old English glossaries refer to the world of classical antiquity (its gods and goddesses, people, animals, plants, laws, etc.) and the glosses show us how the Anglo-Saxon monks and scholars interpreted and adapted this world. Specifically Roman terms were sometimes rendered by loan-formations, e.g. *centurio* by *hundredes ealdor* 'leader of a hundred [sc. men]' in Ælfric's *Glossary*; in other instances more general OE equivalents were used, as in *Épinal-Erfurt*, where for example *censores* 'Roman magistrates responsible for the citizens' morals' as well as *commentariensis* 'registrar of public documents' were rendered by OE *giroefa* (*gerefa* > ModE *reeve*) 'high official' (*ÉpErf* 197, 223). Occasionally there are cases of cultural substitution, as when *piraticum* 'pertaining to pirates' is glossed as *uuicingsceadan* 'damage done by Vikings' (or 'destructive Vikings') in *ÉpErf* 736, perhaps because the kind of pirates whom the Anglo-Saxons knew were the Vikings.[18] In rare cases a glossator even turned the meaning of the Latin word into its opposite, rendering the Latin lemma by its OE antonym, sometimes by mistake, but probably intentionally in the case of *res publica* 'republic', which is glossed by *cynidom* 'kingdom' in *ÉpErf* 859—the idea of a republic was probably unfamiliar to the Anglo-Saxons, whereas the idea of a kingdom was quite familiar, so here we have another case of cultural substitution.[19]

2.4 THE IMPORTANCE OF GLOSSES AND GLOSSARIES AND THE STATE OF SCHOLARSHIP

Glosses and glossaries are important records of Medieval English and its varieties: for example, the mid-tenth-century glosses to the *Lindisfarne Gospels* are the most comprehensive witness to the Northumbrian dialect of Old English, and the

[18] One of the problems with this entry in *Épinal-Erfurt* (*c.*700) is, however, that it predates the beginning of the Viking attacks on England (sack of Lindisfarne 793) by roughly a hundred years, so that it is questionable whether the Anglo-Saxons knew the Vikings as attackers and plunderers at that time.

[19] Cf., for example, Law (1997: 208–10).

mid-ninth-century glosses to the *Vespasian Psalter* are an important document of the Mercian dialect; the latter also represent the first extant partial English translation of the Bible. Glosses also show the interaction of English and Latin (and later French); they allow us glimpses of the culture of medieval England and record some aspects which are rare in or even absent from literary texts (poetry and prose). They indicate how Latin texts were read and interpreted and how Latin words were understood and rendered.

There are many editions and detailed studies of specific Medieval English glosses and glossaries, but few surveys covering the lexicography of the English Middle Ages. The only book-length overview from the beginnings to 1600 is Stein (1985). Brief sketches are included in recent encyclopedias such as the *LexMA* (ed. Auty *et al.*) and the *BEASE* (ed. Lapidge *et al.*).[20] On the whole, more research has been done on the Old English material than on the Middle English. Whereas most of the OE glosses and glossaries have been edited (although the editions vary in quality and accessibility), a number of the ME glosses and glossaries remain unpublished.

The OE material has also been catalogued. The standard description of all the manuscripts containing Old English (Anglo-Saxon) is Ker (1957), while Gneuss (2001) lists all the manuscripts from Anglo-Saxon England, including the purely Latin ones, until c.1100.[21] Cameron (1973) in his section C enumerates ninety-eight different Latin texts with continuous or occasional OE interlinear glosses. This number is an understatement, however, because many glossed texts exist in several manuscripts. Furthermore, there are fifty-nine Latin–OE glossaries listed in Cameron's section D.

The editions of the OE glosses and glossaries up to that time are also listed by Cameron (1973).[22] The two large collections of Latin glossaries (including some OE material) go back to the late nineteenth and the early twentieth centuries: the *Corpus Glossariorum Latinorum* (*CGL*) by G. Goetz (1888–1923), and the *Glossaria Latina* (*GL*) by W. M. Lindsay (1926–32). So does the big collection of Old High German glosses and glossaries by Steinmeyer and Sievers (1879–1922), which also contains some OE material, cf. Ker (1957: Appendix). The largest collection of Old and Middle English glossaries is still Wright and Wülcker (*WW*; 1884). Later collections of OE glosses include those by Napier 1900 and Meritt 1945.

[20] A survey covering OE and ME is given in *LexMA*, ed. Auty, s.v. 'Glossen, Glossare' esp. section IV (by H. Gneuss); a survey concentrating on OE is provided in *BEASE*, ed. Lapidge, s.v. 'Glossaries' (by P. Lendinara) and 'Glosses' (by M. Gretsch).

[21] Old English manuscripts written in the twelfth and early thirteenth century are thus covered by Ker (1957), but not by Gneuss (2001).

[22] For some of the more recent editions, see the references at the end of this volume.

Apart from providing editions, one of the main research activities has been the investigation of the sources and their interrelations; see, for example, Lindsay (1921) and Pheifer (1974); another has been to explain difficult glosses (*interpretamenta*) and to contribute to the study of the OE (and ME) vocabulary; see, for example, Meritt (1954, 1968). Of course, the glosses and glossaries have also been used in linguistic studies; for some recent work see, for example, Kittlick (1998); Sauer (2007). A relatively recent interest is to find out more about the intellectual background of the glossators and their audience; furthermore, whether they tried to imitate the stylistic level of the texts they glossed; see Gretsch (1999). There have been conferences devoted to medieval glossography—see Derolez (1992); Bergmann (2003)—as well as volumes of collected articles by leading scholars in the field; see Lindsay (1996); Lendinara (1999).

An overview of the Middle English material is now provided by Reiser (1998: esp. section 10, nos. 507–68). ME glosses and glossaries are also listed in the volumes of *The Index of Middle English Prose* (*IMEP*, ed. Edwards), which has been in progress since 1984. Many of the better-known editions of ME glossaries and dictionaries go back to the late nineteenth and early twentieth century, however, for example, Herrtage (1881; *Catholicon Anglicum*) or Mayhew (1908; *Promptorium Parvulorum*); a more recent edition is Ross and Brooks (1984). A number of glosses and dictionaries connected with teaching and learning Latin in thirteenth-century England have been discussed and partly also edited by Hunt (1991).

2.5 THE LATIN BACKGROUND

The Western tradition of explaining words and of compiling glossaries goes back to Classical Greece, and was then taken over by the Romans.[23] The first Latin lexicon was compiled by Verrius Flaccus in the first century BC, the *Libri de significatu verborum*; it only lives on in the abridged version (epitome) produced by Sextus Pompeius Festus in the second century AD. A further abridged version of Festus's epitome was then produced by Paulus Diaconus in the eighth century. An important source of Latin vocabulary were the *Etymologiae* by Isidore of Seville (*c.*570–636), one of the most popular encyclopedias throughout the Middle Ages. Among the glossaries and dictionaries that influenced the Old English glossators were also

[23] The first extended example of the discussion of words (in particular their etymology) is Plato's (427–348/347 BC) *Kratylos*. On the Latin tradition, see, for example, *LexMA*, ed. Auty, s.v. 'Glossen, Glossare I.' (by M. Lapidge).

the *Hermeneumata*, the *Abstrusa*, and the *Abolita* glossaries. The *Hermeneumata (pseudo-Dositheana)* had originally, i.e. in the second century AD, been compiled for Greeks wanting to learn Latin (as a Graeco-Latin class glossary); in the Middle Ages and especially in England they were used as a source of the Latin vocabulary. In England they were introduced early and used as one of the sources of *ÉpErf*. The *Abolita* and *Abstrusa glossaries* were probably compiled in the seventh century, perhaps in Spain; they were soon combined, and served as a source of numerous later glossaries, for example, also of *ÉpErf* and of the *Liber Glossarum*, the most important Carolingian glossary.

From around 1000 onwards, large Latin–Latin dictionaries became popular for learning Latin; some of them were imported to England from the continent, some were compiled by Englishmen. Among them are the dictionaries by (in rough chronological order): Papias (perhaps around 1000), an Italian about whom practically nothing is known; Hugutio (Uguccio, Huguccio, etc.) of Pisa (*c.*1140–1210); Osbern of Gloucester (first half of the twelfth century); Johannes Balbus de Janua (died 1298), who lived in Genua, and William Brito (the Breton, *c.*1159/69–*c.*1226).

Papias's alphabetical dictionary, which was probably written before 1045, is known under various titles; the original title seems to have been *Elementarium doctrinae rudimentum*. Among its sources is the *Liber Glossarum*. It was very popular throughout the Middle Ages and well into the Renaissance. It was used as a source by Hugutio of Pisa and Johannes Balbus, and even by Johannes Reuchlin in his *Lexicon Breviloquus* or *Vocabularius Breviloquus* (printed 1475/6).[24] Papias has been called the first modern lexicographer. He arranged his entries in abc-order. In addition to explaining the meaning he often gives quotations from literature (frequently, however, at second hand). For many lemmata he also provides 'derivations' (or derivatives, that is, words derived from the same stem or root), thus establishing a number of word-families.

Osbern's dictionary is known under at least two titles, *Derivationes* and *Panormia*. Each letter is subdivided into two sections: in the first section, as is implied in the title, Osbern provides many derivations; in the second, he repeats the words in the form of a glossary. Hugutio's *Liber derivationum* was also influenced by Osbern's *Derivationes*.

One of Johannes Balbus's most important works is the *Catholicon seu summa prosodiae* (also called *Summa quae vocatur Catholicon*, completed in 1286). It consists of five parts (the first four dealing with orthography, accent, etymology, syntax); the last is the lexicographical part. Apparently Balbus was the first lexicographer to achieve complete alphabetization (from the first to the last letter

[24] Reuchlin's dictionary thus shows that there was a certain amount of lexicographical continuity from late Antiquity until the Renaissance (Festus > *Abolita* > *Liber glossarum* > Papias > Reuchlin).

of each word). His *Catholicon* was among the first printed books (Mainz, 1460). William Brito in his *Summa* or *Expositiones difficiliorum verborum* used Isidore, Papias, and Hugutio of Pisa as some of his sources.

2.6 THE OLD ENGLISH PERIOD

2.6.1 *Old English interlinear glosses*

In the Old English period, religious texts mainly were provided with more or less continuous interlinear glosses, especially texts used for the liturgy or the monastic office, such as the Psalter (a collection of the Psalms), the Canticles of the Psalter, the Hymns, occasionally the Gospels, some prayers (such as the *Arundel Prayers*), and also texts of basic importance for the monks such as the *Benedictine Rule* and the *Regularis Concordia*; furthermore, texts by authors read in school such as the prose version of Aldhelm's *De virginitate* (= *De laudibus virginitatis* 'In praise of virginity') or Prudentius's *Psychomachia*. Among the less strictly religious texts which were glossed are also parts of Boethius's *De consolatione Philosophiae* and the third book of the *Bella Parisiacae Urbis* by Abbo of St Germain (second half of the ninth century), which was studied in English schools due to its unusual vocabulary. Abbo's work and the glosses to it then also served as the basis for *glossae collectae*; the same is true of the glosses to Aldhelm.[25]

Glossing (mainly in Latin) started in the later seventh century in Canterbury under archbishop Theodore of Tarsus (602–90) and his companion Hadrian (*c*.635–709/710), who arrived there in 669 and soon after founded a school. Some of their commentaries to passages of the Bible and to other texts have been preserved in the form of notes taken by their pupils, and mainly in continental manuscripts (ed. Bischoff and Lapidge 1994); some also survive in the form of later glossaries such as the *Leiden Glossary*. Hardly any OE glosses have been preserved from the eighth century. The main interlinear gloss from the ninth century is the gloss to the *Vespasian Psalter*. The bulk of the OE interlinear glosses dates from the second half of the tenth and from the eleventh century, and many of them are connected with the Benedictine Reform (Monastic Revival).

From Anglo-Saxon England about forty Latin psalters (including fragments) survive; about thirteen of them contain OE continuous interlinear glosses.[26] The

[25] See *BEASE*, ed. Lapidge, s.v. 'Glossaries' (by P. Lendinara).

[26] On the OE Psalter glosses see, for example, Schabram (1965: 21–34); Cameron (1973, section C no. 7.1–13); Pulsiano (2001).

earliest Latin Psalter with a continuous OE gloss is the *Vespasian Psalter.* Its Latin text was probably written at Canterbury around 720–30, its OE interlinear gloss was added there in the mid-ninth century. Psalters with interlinear OE glosses continued to be copied until the mid-twelfth century. The latest is Eadwine's *Canterbury Psalter,* written around 1150.The relations between the various Psalter glosses are quite complex. The *Vespasian Psalter* gloss and some later glosses are usually taken to represent the (Anglian) A-type, whereas the *Royal Psalter* gloss (written *c.*950 and perhaps composed by Æthelwold) and others are taken to represent the (West-Saxon) D-type (ultimately originating at Winchester). Relatively independent of the other types is the gloss of the *Lambeth Psalter,* which is regarded as the most scholarly of the psalter glosses and often contains multiple glosses to one lemma.

Whereas most glosses and glossaries are anonymous, the *Lindisfarne Gospels* are associated with names in the manuscript: they were probably written and illustrated at Lindisfarne around 700 by Eadfrith (bishop of Lindisfarne 698–721); the interlinear OE gloss was added around 970, that is, 270 years later, at Chester-le-Street by Aldred.

Another gospelbook with OE interlinear glosses from the later tenth century is the so-called *Rushworth Gospels* (Latin text: Macregol Gospels). These were glossed by two clerics, partly by Farmon in the Mercian dialect, and partly by Owun in the Northumbrian dialect, who may have copied his part from the *Lindisfarne Gospels.*[27]

A non-biblical and non-liturgical text that was glossed particularly often, and probably as part of the efforts of the Benedictine Reform, is Aldhelm's prose version of his *De virginitate,* a popular but difficult text.[28] At least fourteen manuscripts with OE glosses survive. Best known are the more than 5,000 *Brussels Aldhelm Glosses* from the first half of the eleventh century. Many of the Latin words have multiple glosses, in Latin and partly also in Old English. The different layers of glossing and their relation to glosses in other manuscripts are difficult to disentangle, but it was probably Æthelwold who originally composed many of those glosses.

One manuscript of Ælfric's *Colloquy* has a continuous interlinear gloss, but because the *Colloquy* was part of Ælfric's programme for teaching Latin and is thus connected to his *Grammar* and his *Glossary,* it is dealt with in the following section.

[27] These Northumbrian and Mercian glosses are probably not connected with the Benedictine Reform.

[28] Aldhelm composed his *De virginitate* in a poetic version as well as in a prose version.

2.6.2 *Old English glossaries*

The oldest English text of any length is the *Épinal-Erfurt Glossary* (*ÉpErf*). It exists in two manuscripts, which go back to a common exemplar. The archetype has been connected to Theodore's school at Canterbury (that is, to the period *c.*670–90) or to Aldhelm's school at Malmesbury (roughly at the same time). *ÉpErf* is an alphabetical glossary largely in a-order, with entries in ab-order added at the end of most alphabetical sections. It contains more than 3,280 Latin lemmata, most of which are glossed in Latin, but about 1,100, roughly a third, are glossed in English, so that *ÉpErf* is a mixture of a Latin–Latin and a Latin–Old English glossary. The Latin nouns, adjectives, and verbs are often given in inflected forms; this probably reflects the fact that the lemmata had originally been taken from texts and were arranged alphabetically later, but left in their inflected forms. This choice of forms was often imitated in the OE glosses, as far as this is possible in the OE inflectional system. Apparently the practice of giving the lemmata in a citation form (e.g. in the nominative singular with nouns) took some time to develop.

Many of the later OE glossaries are related to *ÉpErf*, that is, they incorporate material from this glossary, but also add new material, for example:[29]

(1) The *Corpus Glossary* was compiled around 800. The second of its two alphabetical glossaries includes most of the *ÉpErf* entries, thus providing virtually a third text of *ÉpErf*, but the compiler also added much new material.

(2) The *Cleopatra Glossaries* date from the middle of the tenth century. The manuscript consists of three OE glossaries: the first is an alphabetical glossary from A to P; the second basically a Latin–OE class glossary arranged by subjects; the third a Latin–OE glossary to Aldhelm, *De virginitate* (prose and poetry). The first two contain material from *ÉpErf*.

(3) The *Harley Glossary* dates from around 1000. It is preserved only as a fragment (letters A to F, arranged in abc-order). Nevertheless Pheifer (1974: xxxvi) calls it 'the fullest and most elaborate of the Old English glossaries, and the only one that treats its material at all intelligently'.

(4) Whereas the glossaries mentioned so far are mostly alphabetical glossaries (Latin–OE), the *Brussels Glossary* is a Latin–OE class glossary which was added in the margins of a collection of Latin glossaries that includes the *Hermeneumata*.

A representative of *glossae collectae* is the *Leiden Glossary*, which was copied at St Gall around 800, but goes back to an older exemplar ultimately connected with

[29] Extracts from *ÉpErf* are even found in some Continental glossaries.

the school of Theodore and Hadrian in Canterbury in the later seventh century. It consists of forty-eight sections containing glosses from sources which are usually indicated, for instance, the Bible, Cassian, Gildas, Gregory the Great, Isidore, Jerome, Orosius, Rufinus, Sulpicius Severus. The glosses are mainly in Latin, but they comprise also around 260 Old English (occasionally Old High German) interpretamenta.

The dominant author around 1000 was Ælfric. He was a dedicated preacher who wrote many OE homilies and saints' lives, but he was also a dedicated teacher. For teaching Latin to his pupils he wrote three related works: a *Grammar*, mainly for the morphology; a *Glossary*, usually appended to his *Grammar*, for the vocabulary; a Latin *Colloquy*, to practise oral skills.[30] The grammar is unique in that it is bilingual, that is, a grammar of Latin largely written in Old English. Judging from the number of extant manuscripts, it must have been quite popular in the eleventh century, and it was copied until the early thirteenth century. Incidentally, there is at least one manuscript which has Anglo-Norman glosses.[31]

Ælfric's *Glossary* is a Latin–OE class glossary, arranged onomasiologically according to word-fields (semantic fields), which include 'names of members [sc. of body parts], of birds, of fish, of animals, of plants, of trees, of houses'. Some of the groups contain more, however, than the headings imply.[32] The first and last groups, for example, include not only words for parts of the body and for buildings, but also a substantial number of words for people in various roles. Ælfric proceeds very systematically; for example, among the names of relationship, he starts with 'father' and continues as far as 'great-great-great-grandfather'; for terms referring to men he often adds the corresponding terms referring to women (e.g. 'male fiddler'–'female fiddler'), and he generally adopts a hierarchical sequence within the various groups, starting with the higher and proceeding to the lower, thus: 'God'–'angel'–'man'; or 'lord'–'servant, slave'. It has been said that Ælfric has 'a tendency to cover the whole world with words'.[33] A glossary which overlaps with Ælfric's is the *Antwerp and London Glossary*.

Ælfric's *Colloquy* is a kind of role-play designed to enable pupils to speak Latin: they pretend to be farmers, hunters, fishermen, bakers, and so on, and explain what their tasks and daily routines are. In one of the manuscripts, Ælfric's *Colloquy* was provided with a continuous interlinear gloss. This work stands in

[30] On Ælfric as a teacher and grammarian, see, for example, Law (1997: 200–23); especially on his *Glossary*, see Hüllen (1999: 62 ff.)

[31] See Hunt (1991: I: 99–118). It is an isolated forerunner of the English grammars which started to appear in the late sixteenth century. John Bullokar's *Pamphlet for Grammar* of 1586 is usually regarded as the first grammar of English.

[32] Cf. the list in Hüllen (1999: 64), and see Sauer (2007) for the words for people.

[33] Hüllen (1999: 65).

the tradition of the monastic colloquies; the tradition was continued by Ælfric's pupil, Ælfric Bata, who wrote a large number of Latin colloquies.[34]

From the twelfth century, that is, the post-Conquest era, date two alphabetical Latin–OE glossaries devoted specifically to plant names and perhaps intended for physicians: the *Laud Herbal Glossary* and the *Durham Plant Name Glossary*; the latter was written at Durham shortly after 1100.

2.7 THE MIDDLE ENGLISH PERIOD

2.7.1 *Middle English interlinear glosses*

In the Middle English period, that is, after about 1100 (with the twelfth century forming an overlap between late OE texts and early ME texts), glossing in English became rarer, whereas glossing in Latin continued, and there were now also glosses in French.

Of the 189 or so major Old English manuscripts, about forty-four, or almost a quarter, have, however, glosses that were entered in the Middle English period.[35] Most striking in this connection is the so-called 'Tremulous Hand of Worcester'.[36] In the first half of the thirteenth century, a monk at Worcester with shaky handwriting entered about 50,000 glosses in about twenty OE manuscripts, partly in early Middle English, but mainly in Latin. Apparently, even in the early thirteenth century, English had changed so much that Old English could no longer be readily understood and had to be explained. Why the Tremulous Hand took such pains to do this, is, however, not quite clear. Earlier scholars assumed that his hand was shaky because he was an old man who still remembered the language of his youth and wanted to pass it on to his younger brethren, but a more recent opinion (Franzen 1991) is that he could have been a younger man whose trembling was due to an illness and who also had to make an effort to learn Old English. Although he entered many glosses, they are usually not continuous and thus explain only fractions of the OE texts. Moreover, it is doubtful whether his fellow monks really wanted to learn Old English. 'There are always some people of an antiquarian turn of mind' (Ker 1957: xlix), and perhaps he was one of those.

[34] Ed. Stevenson (1929); Gwara and Porter (1997), who also provide information about the colloquy tradition.

[35] See Sauer (1997), with references to earlier literature.

[36] On the Tremulous Hand of Worcester see, among others, Franzen (1991); Sauer (1997); Reiser (1998, no. 546.)

Glossing continued to be important in texts intended for teaching Latin. There are glosses to some of the works by John of Garland (an Englishman, *c.*1195–*c.*1272), for example, to his *Dictionarius* and his *Distigium* (hexametrical distichs with particularly difficult words; Reiser 1998, no. 550), to *De nominibus utensilium* by Alexander Neckam (1157–1217, also an Englishman; Reiser 1998, no. 549), and to similar later works.[37]

One of the first documents which indicate that at least some members of the upper class had given up French (or rather Anglo-Norman) as their mother tongue and had started speaking English—and consequently had to learn French as a foreign language—is the *Traité* (or *Tretiz*) by Walter of Bibbesworth, written around 1250 (Reiser 1998, no. 507). This is a verse manual (in about 1,134 lines) of Anglo-Norman, presenting mainly its vocabulary (i.e. belonging to the class of the *nominalia*). It was originally written for a specific family, the children of Dionysia de Muchensy, but circulated widely subsequently.[38]

2.7.2 *Middle English glossaries and dictionaries*

In the Middle English period the tradition of producing Latin–English glossaries (vocabularies) was continued, but new types of dictionaries were also created. Examples of the older-type vocabularies are, for instance, *WW* no. XV, and the *Vocabula* (1496) and *Vulgaria* (1508) by John Stanbridge (1463–*c.*1510), written for teaching Latin to boys. The latter two are in the topical tradition of the class (or 'topical') glossaries and largely arranged according to semantic groups.[39]

It is said that four large dictionaries from the fifteenth century represent the culmination of Medieval English dictionary-making: two of them are Latin–English, the *Medulla Grammaticae* and the *Ortus Vocabulorum* (*ortus* for *hortus*); and two are English–Latin, the *Promptorium Parvulorum* and the *Catholicon Anglicum*. Whereas the former continue the tradition of the Latin–English glossaries, the latter are an innovation—both types of dictionaries complement each other.[40]

The *Medulla Grammaticae* has about 17,000 Latin entries. According to Reiser it was compiled in the later fifteenth century, but, according to others, before 1400 (Stonyhurst MS). Its main source was perhaps the *Catholicon* of Johannes Balbus.[41]

[37] See Hunt (1991: vol. I: especially chs. IV–V and VII; vol. II). Latin metrical vocabularies with partly Latin and partly English interlinear glosses are printed by *WW* nos. XVI–XVII.

[38] Some of its manuscripts also have English glosses, see Reiser (1998: nos. 507 and 509–11).

[39] On Stanbridge, see Starnes (1954: ch. V).

[40] On these four dictionaries (*Medulla Grammaticae, Ortus Vocabulorum, Promptorium Parvulorum, Catholicon Anglicum*), see, for example, Starnes (1954: Part I); Stein (1985); Reiser (1998: nos. 555–8).

[41] Apparently there is no easily accessible modern edition of the *Medulla Grammaticae.*

The Latin lemmata are partly explained in Latin and partly in English. The *Ortus Vocabulorum* has about 27,000 entries. The date of its compilation is also unclear: around 1500 according to Reiser (1998: no. 558), but around 1430 (Bristol fragment) according to others.

The *Promptorium Parvulorum* (ed. Mayhew 1908) lists about 12,000 English words, first nouns and other parts of speech, and afterwards verbs. It was compiled around 1440 by a Dominican friar in Lynn, Norfolk. The *Catholicon Anglicum* (ed. Herrtage 1881) presents about 8,000 English words in alphabetical order; it is partly based on John of Garland's *Synonyma*. It was compiled in the later fifteenth century (1483).

Both the *Promptorium Parvulorum* and the *Catholicon Anglicum* often give just one 'synonym' for the English lemma; however, sometimes they provide several Latin 'synonyms': for *foule* the *Catholicon* lists twenty-two Latin equivalents, for example, 'aceratus, deformis in corpore, turpis in anima, enormis, fedus, fedosus, fetidus, inmundus, inornatus', and so on. The *Promptorium* gives the Latin verbs in the first person singular and also provides information about their inflexion (e.g. 'ffowlyn, or defowlyn: Turpo, -as, -aui, -are'), whereas the *Catholicon* gives them in the infinitive. Thus the main purpose of those dictionaries seems to have been to help with Latin, and specifically with writing in, and translating into, Latin.

Building on the tradition of Alexander Neckam, John Garland, and others, wordbooks for teaching and learning purposes were developed. Often they concentrated on one word-class: those dealing with nouns (and adjectives) were apparently in the majority. They were called 'nominalia'; those dealing with verbs were called 'verbalia'. Some *nominalia* from the fifteenth century are printed by *WW* as nos. XVIII–XX, among them the so-called *Mayer Nominale* from the fifteenth century (no. XIX),[42] and a pictorial *nominale* with (rather crude) illustrations, a forerunner of illustrated dictionaries (no. XX). Many of them are arranged according to semantic fields; some cover several, others concentrate on one. Among them are also trilingual vocabularies, i.e. Latin–French–English; cf. Reiser (1998, no. 553). To indicate the gender, the nouns are usually preceded by *hic*, *hec*, or *hoc*. Collections of English sentences (often following or followed by the corresponding Latin sentences) for the purpose of learning Latin were called 'vulgaria'; see Reiser (1998: nos. 533–45).

A combination of a *nominale* with a *verbale* seems to be the vocabulary (glossary) in London, BL, Addit. 37075 from the late fifteenth century (*c.*1475; ed. Ross and Brooks 1984), where the nouns are largely arranged according to semantic groups.

[42] It is discussed, for example, in Hüllen (1999: 68–77).

There are a few French–English (or Latin–French–English) glossaries from the fourteenth and fifteenth centuries; like Walter of Bibbesworth's *Treatise*, they were intended as a help for teaching French to those who no longer used it as their mother tongue but spoke English. Some are arranged alphabetically, some according to word-classes, and some according to semantic fields; see Reiser (1998: no. 553). Even greater popularity was enjoyed by dialogues in French and English, where the vocabulary was embedded in a context. Caxton printed such a collection of dialogues in about 1483 (ed. Bradley 1900).[43]

A more specific type of glossary is represented by the numerous trilingual plant name glossaries which belong to the broader category of 'synonyma'. One of them, the *Trilingual Harley Glossary* from the thirteenth century, is printed in *WW* no. XVI, but not many apparently have been published so far; cf. Reiser (1998: no. 247).[44] In the *Trilingual Harley Glossary*, the sequence in an entry usually is Latin word–French word–English word, so: *abrotanum i. aueroine i. suþewurt*. The French word is often the etymological descendant of the Latin word, for instance, *saniculum i. sanicle (wudemerch)*. Some of the French words were later borrowed into English as loan-words, but at the time of the *Trilingual Harley Glossary* they probably were still French words (see 2.1, above, for Hunt's treatment of this question). These glossaries were perhaps intended for the use of medical practitioners.

Other specific vocabularies include a Latin–English glossary based on the names of the parts of the human body, which was apparently used as a school text. There was, furthermore, the so-called *Expositiones vocabulorum*, which exists in more than forty manuscripts from the twelfth to the fifteenth century, and explains Anglo-Saxon law terms.[45]

2.8 THE TRANSITION TO THE EARLY MODERN ENGLISH PERIOD

Period boundaries do not necessarily coincide with the end of all old traditions and the beginning of new ones. Whereas I have drawn the borderline between Middle English and Early Modern English around 1500, Stein (1985) finishes her

[43] See Hüllen (1999: ch. 4).

[44] On ME plant name glossaries (synonyma), see also Hunt (1989: xix–xxxvi).

[45] On the names of the parts of the human body see Reiser (1998: no. 553 e); on the *Expositiones vocabulorum* see Reiser (1998: no. 552 and cf. no. 553 k).

survey of early dictionaries just before 1600. Her main reason is that in 1604 Cawdrey's *Table Alphabeticall* was published. This was the first monolingual English dictionary, and thus began a new tradition of dictionary-making.

The late medieval bilingual dictionaries span both periods; moreover, they show the transition from manuscript to print. The English–Latin *Promptorium Parvulorum* exists in several manuscripts; it was first printed in 1499 (by Richard Pynson) and then frequently reprinted until 1528. No manuscript exists of the Latin–English *Ortus Vocabulorum*; it was first printed in 1500 (by Wynkyn de Worde) and then also frequently reprinted until 1532.[46] The manuscript tradition of the *Catholicon Anglicum* is comparatively weak and no early prints seem to exist. The *Medulla Grammaticae* is still preserved in more than twenty manuscripts, but apparently also not in early printed editions. Stanbridge's *Vulgaria* were reprinted until 1529,[47] but then their transmission also seems to have stopped.[48]

The first large Latin–English dictionary of the sixteenth century was Sir Thomas Elyot's *The Dictionary of Syr Thomas Elyot* of 1538, which apparently supplanted the *Ortus Vocabulorum*.[49] The first bilingual dictionaries of French, Italian, Spanish, Welsh, and so on were published in the sixteenth century; the first English–French dictionary was John Palsgrave's *Esclarcissement de la langue francoyse* of 1530. A new development was furthermore represented by polyglot dictionaries listing several languages.[50]

REFERENCES

Manuscripts of glossed texts and of glossaries[51]

Abbo of Saint-Germain: *Glossae collectae*: London, BL, Cotton Domitian I, fol. 37v–38v; London, BL, Royal 7.D.II; see Ker (1957, nos. 146, 258).[52]

Ælfric's *Colloquy*: London, BL, Cotton Tiberius A.III, fols. 60v–64v; see Ker (1957, no. 186).

[46] Of the *Ortus Vocabulorum* also no easily accessible modern edition seems to exist, but there is a facsimile of the first printed edition of 1500.

[47] See Stein (1985: 87, 101–2, 121); Starnes (1954: 41).

[48] An exception was apparently Stanbridge's *Vocabula*: between 1496 and 1631, seventeen editions were published.

[49] On Sir Thomas Elyot's dictionary, see Stein (1985).

[50] On continuations and new departures in the sixteenth century, see also Starnes and Noyes (1946: ch. 1).

[51] Mainly OE glosses and glossaries are listed here.

[52] See *BEASE*, ed. Lapidge, s.v. 'Glossaries', p. 207 (by P. Lendinara).

Aldhelm: (a) *Brussels Aldhelm Glosses*: Brussels, Bibliothèque Royale 1650; see Ker (1957, no.8); (b) Glossae collectae to Aldhelm: Oxford, Bodleian Library, Auct. F.2.14, fol. 11r–19r; see Ker (1957, no. 295).

Antwerp and London Glossary (*Junius Glossary*): Antwerp, Plantin Moretus Museum 47 + London, BL, Add. 32246; see Ker (1957, no. 2).

Arundel Prayers: London, BL, Arundel 155; see Ker (1957, no. 135).

Brussels Aldhelm Glosses: see Aldhelm.

Brussels Glossary: Brussels, Bibliothèque Royale 1828–30; see Ker (1957, no. 9).

Cleopatra Glossaries: London, BL, Cotton Cleopatra A.III; see Ker (1957, no. 143).

Corpus Glossary: CCCC 144; see Ker (1957, no. 36).

Durham Plant Name Glossary: Durham Cathedral, Hunter 100; see Ker (1957, no. 110).

Eadwine's *Canterbury Psalter*: Cambridge, Trinity College R.17.1; see Ker (1957, no. 91).

Épinal-Erfurt Glossary (*ÉpErf*): (a) Épinal, Bibliothèque Municipale 72(2), fol. 94–107, written in England by an English scribe around 700; (b) Erfurt, Wissenschaftliche Allgemeinbibliothek, Codex Amplonianus F.42, fols. 1a1-14va33, written in Cologne by a German scribe around 800. See Ker (1957: nos. 114 and App. 10); Sauer (2007); here quoted in the edition by Pheifer (1974).

Harley Glossary: London, BL, Harley 3376; see Ker (1957, no. 240).

Hermeneumatha (pseudo-Dositheana): see *Brussels Glossary*.

Junius Glossary: see *Antwerp and London Glossary*.

Lambeth Psalter: London, Lambeth Palace 427; see Ker (1957, no. 280).

Laud Herbal Glossary: Oxford, Bodleian Library, Laud Misc. 567; see Ker (1957, no. 345).

Leiden Glossary: Leiden, Bibliotheek der Rijksuniversiteit, Vossianus Lat. Q. 69, 7r–47r; see Ker (1957, Appendix no. 18).

Lindisfarne Gospels: London, BL, Cotton Nero D.IV; see Ker (1957, no. 165).

Royal Psalter: London, BL, Royal 2.B.V; see Ker (1957, no. 249).

Rushworth Gospels: Oxford, Bodleian Library, Auct. D.2.19; see Ker (1957, no. 292).

Trilingual Harley Glossary: London, BL, Harley 978, fol. 24v; ed. *WW* no. XIV.

Vespasian Psalter: London, BL, Cotton Vespasian A.I; see Ker (1957, no. 203).

3

BILINGUAL AND MULTILINGUAL DICTIONARIES OF THE RENAISSANCE AND EARLY SEVENTEENTH CENTURY[1]

Janet Bately

3.1 LATIN–ENGLISH AND ENGLISH–LATIN DICTIONARIES

3.1.1 *Latin–English dictionaries, from Elyot to Wase*

THE end of the fifteenth century saw the publication in print of two of the bilingual vocabularies and dictionaries that had previously been circulating in manuscript—the English–Latin *Promptorium Parvulorum* and Latin–English *Ortus vocabulorum*. Both were to be frequently reissued over the next thirty-two years. Yet there is little evidence of their influence on subsequent lexicography, a circumstance which in the words of DeWitt Starnes (1954: 37) 'might be explained by the desire of the Humanists to start afresh and to avoid the use of medieval sources'.

Instead, it was to the Continent that English lexicographers of the sixteenth century turned for models and materials.[2] So, when, in 1538, Thomas Elyot, scholar

[1] Length restrictions permit only short titles to be given here and in the References, with editions other than the first not normally listed. For fuller details, see Alston (1965–), COPAC and EEBO.

[2] For an invaluable exploration of sources in this section, see Starnes (1954).

and diplomat, produced his unidirectional Latin–English *Dictionary*,[3] the authorities he cited included French, Dutch, and Italian contemporaries, who, like him, were seeking to provide the linguistic tools demanded by the 'New Learning'. It was the monolingual Latin *Dictionarium* of 'Calepinus'—Augustinian friar Ambrogio Calepino of Bergamo—, first published in 1502, that was his chief source. And when Elyot's dictionary was reissued in 1542 as the *Bibliotheca Eliotae. Eliotis librarie*, it was from the *Dictionarium Latino–Gallicum* (1538) of French printer Robert Estienne (or 'Stephanus') that much of its new material was derived. Elyot died in 1546, but publication of his dictionary continued, with revisions by Thomas Cooper appearing in 1548, 1552, and 1559. Cooper, who was to become successively headmaster of Magdalen College School, dean of Christ Church, vice-chancellor of Oxford University, and bishop, first of Lincoln, then of Winchester, also drew directly on Robert Estienne. And when he abandoned his work as reviser to produce a Latin–English dictionary of his own, he continued to turn to the Continent for his materials, the sources of his *Thesaurus linguae Romanae & Britannicae* (1565) including not only the revised *Bibliotheca Eliotae* but also Johannes Frisius's *Dictionarium Latino–Germanicum* (1556) and an edition of Estienne's *Dictionarium Latino–Gallicum.*

A revised edition of another dictionary by Estienne/Stephanus—the Latin–French *Dictionariolum puerorum* (first edition 1542)—had already been published in London in 1552, with its French element removed, and with the addition of an English translation of its definitions by French émigré John Veron, rector of St Alphage within Cripplegate. Renamed *Dictionary in Latine and English*, 'for the vtilitie and profit of all young students', this publication was subsequently twice revised: firstly by Rudolph Waddington, *Ludimagister* at Christ's Hospital School (1575), and secondly by the clergyman, poet, and translator, Abraham Fleming (1584). Added material included English definitions from Elyot–Cooper 1548 and both definitions and illustrative phrases from Cooper's *Thesaurus.*

The *Thesaurus* remained in print until 1587, the year of publication of Thomas Thomas's *Dictionarium lingvae Latinae et Anglicanae.* Thomas, first printer to Cambridge University, died in the following year. However, his dictionary continued to appear in up to fourteen editions over the next half-century. One of Thomas's sources was Cooper's *Thesaurus.* Another was the *Verborum Latinorum cum Graecis Anglicisque coniunctorum commentarij* (1583), in which someone, arguably Abraham Fleming[4]—himself drawing heavily on Cooper's *Thesaurus*—

[3] The earliest instance of the word 'dictionary' recorded by the *Oxford English Dictionary* dates from 1526.

[4] I accept with some hesitation LEME's attribution to Fleming rather than that of Starnes (1954: 112) to publisher Richard Hutton.

had substituted English for the original French of the *Verborum Latinorum cum Graecis Gallicisque conjunctorum commentarij* (1558) of French Humanist Morelius (Guillaume Morel). The revised editions of Thomas drew still further on Cooper and Morelius–?Fleming, adding illustrative quotations from Latin texts from the former and (in some editions) Greek equivalents from the latter, as well as a dictionary of proper names, based on the *Dictionarium historicum, geographicum, poeticum* (1553), attributed to Carolus Stephanus (Charles Estienne),[5] and Cooper's *Thesaurus.* Other sources include recent editions of dictionaries by Calepinus and Robert Estienne, and Dutchman Hadrianus (or Adrianus) Junius's *Nomenclator omnium rerum propria nomina* (probably in John Higgins's translation, 1585). A major development is the addition (edition of 1615) of a *Supplementum*, or *Paralipomena* by schoolmaster-physician Philemon Holland and a *Vocabularium Anglo–Latino ex Dictionario.* This edition contains numerous new quotations from, and references to, classical authors, and some entries ascribed to a 'Medull.Gram.', probably the English–Latin *Promptorium parvulorum.*[6]

The final edition of Thomas's dictionary was published in 1644. However, already in 1606 there had appeared the first fully bi-directional (though co-authored) English–Latin—Latin–English dictionary, under the title *Rider's Dictionarie*, created by the 'transform[ation] into a Dictionarie Etymologicall'[7] of a Latin–English Index in John Rider's English–Latin *Bibliotheca scholastica*,[8] and providing for the first time under a single cover material for both the English reader of Latin and the would-be writer in it. The new Latin–English component, which included also a dictionary of 'Barbarous words', and a brief Index of proper names, the work of clergyman Francis Holyoke, drew heavily on Thomas's *Dictionarium. Rider's Dictionarie* subsequently appeared in eight revised editions between 1612 and 1659 (one by Nicholas Gray, headmaster of Merchant Taylors' School, 1626), with an edition of Thomas Thomas's dictionary once again a major source,[9] but incorporating also material from the publications of continental authors, including Johannes Fungerus (1605), Christianus Becmanus (1619), and Calepinus. And 124 years after the publication of Elyot's dictionary, with wheels turning full circle, we have 'an Abridgement [by Schrevelius] of the last Calepine, augmented by Passeratius',[10] entitled *Compendium Calepini*, and part of

[5] *Recte* Robert? See Starnes (1963).

[6] Starnes (1954: 136–7). Less convincing are Starnes's arguments for use of the *Catholicon Anglicum, ibid.*

[7] *Riders Dictionarie*: Title page.

[8] See below, p. 50.

[9] For contemporary accusations of plagiarism see Starnes (1954: 240 ff.).

[10] Wase 1662: Title page of Latin–English dictionary (dated 1661) and *Advertisements.*

another bidirectional compilation, the single-authored *Dictionarium minus* (1662) by Christopher Wase, then headmaster of the Free School, Tonbridge.[11]

3.1.1 (i) *The Latin headwords*

The continental dictionaries in their various editions provided not only materials for the Latin–English lexicographers but also a choice of models. Arrangement of headwords is roughly alphabetical, but in some cases disrupted by the practice of grouping 'derivatives' after their 'primitives' (i.e. root-words). Latin authorities are often named and illustrative quotations provided, some of considerable length, but proper names and encyclopedic detail, at first incorporated, are in later publications removed to a separate section or omitted altogether. The cover of pronunciation and grammar also varies.

Similar variation is found in the Latin–English dictionaries. Elyot, for instance, following a monolingual edition of Calepinus, frequently groups derivatives with their primitives in his otherwise alphabetically ordered word-list,[12] which is also occasionally disrupted by the inclusion of quotations. Subsequent editions are progressively more completely alphabetical, with straight alphabetical order becoming the norm in Elyot–Cooper and Morelius–?Fleming. Cooper, *Thesaurus*, however, regularly places 'Deriuatiues' after their 'Primitiues'—an arrangement already found in Estienne–Veron and its subsequent revisions and later (under the influence of a contemporary revision of Calepinus) followed by Wase.

The criteria adopted for the selection of headwords also vary. Elyot, for instance, enters personal names and place-name in the body of the work. However, Cooper, after making an initial incomplete attempt at reorganization in Elyot–Cooper 1559, follows the Estienne brothers in removing them to a separate *Dictionarium historicum & poeticum* in his *Thesaurus*. A similar two-part arrangement is found in Thomas 1589 and in Rider–Holyoke 1606. Other dictionaries, including the first edition of Thomas's dictionary, omit proper names altogether.

At the same time, from Elyot–Cooper 1548 onwards, we find an increasing reaction to the inclusion of Latin words not used by 'probatis autoribus'.[13] So, for instance, Holyoke initially 'ranged' a collection of 'barbarous words' into 'a Dictionarie by themselues' (*Rider's Dictionary* 1606: title page), and later 'expunged' them 'to the helpe of young Scholars' (*idem*, edition of 1640, title page). Wase's dictionary, also intended for young scholars, contains only 'the Classical words of the *Latine* Tongue' (title page, Latin–English section). In contrast,

[11] See *Oxford Dictionary of National Biography* (ODNB): Wase.

[12] I/J and U/V are treated as single letters.

[13] Rider–Holyoke 1606: *Ad Lectorem*.

specialist terms relating to a range of disciplines abound. So Elyot includes words belonging to 'lawe and phisike' and the names of 'herbes' and fishes, as well as quoting many proverbs. Cooper prides himself on having collected a number of technical terms relating to trades and crafts; Holyoke makes special mention of civil and canon law and glossaries.

One-word headwords are the norm. However, prefixes are occasionally given individual cover, as in:

(1) AD, **by hym selfe, or ioyned to an other word, signifieth to, or at, as** Vado ad oppidum, **I go to the towne** (Elyot 1538).

(2) **Syn**, Præpositio Græca, quæ in compositione significat Simul: quemadmodum apud nos CON (Cooper, *Thesaurus*),

while homographs are sometimes entered in a single entry, sometimes separately. And in some dictionaries headword entries[14] include combinations of words or phrases (syntagmas) as, for instance, Estienne–Veron's *Cantheriàta vinea*, Cooper's *Ephemera febris*, and Thomas Thomas's *Enula campana*. And in Elyot, Cooper's *Thesaurus*, Morelius–?Fleming, and revisions of Thomas from 1592, numerous phrases and illustrative sentences are provided from named Latin authors, usually as sub-entries, as in Elyot 1538, under headword *Species*:

(3) a Per speciem legationis in Asiam ablegatus est, **Under the coloure of ambassade, he was banyshed into Asia.** [*margin*] Plin. de uiris illustr.
b In Speciem esse, **to be to the honour.** [*margin*] Plautus

Usage in other dictionaries varies considerably, with, for instance, unattributed quotations in Cooper's revisions of Elyot, attributions without supporting quotations in Thomas 1587 and in Holyoke, and quotations, but only a few references to authors, in Wase.

Comment on register usually takes the form of descriptions, in Latin or in English, such as 'a barbarous word', 'in holie Scripture', 'as Poets say', 'anciently', and 'old writers vsed for . . .' beside 'veteres dixerunt', 'olim pro', and 'antiqu in script'. A usage is sometimes explained as 'metaphor' or as 'metonymie', while in Wase's dictionary 'the Tropical or Figurative Sense is set after the Proper and Natural' [1662, title page]. And references to technical-field membership serve to distinguish between homographs in Wase, as in the case of the following:

(4) Abdico, are. (*An augural word*) *To forbid, or forbode.* (*A Law word*) *To cast one, or overthrow* . . . *Addico'.

[14] For this term see Stein's comment in her important study (1985: 185–6).

Word-origins are occasionally commented on, as here:

(5) Symptoma, **a greke woorde vsed among phisicions, for lacke of a latine woorde fyt forthe thyng which it signifieth, it is a certaine effecte folowyng sicknesse, like as cause doeth procede, or is before sicknesse, it is a sensible griefe ioyned with sicknesse** (Elyot–Cooper 1548).

In the provision of details of pronunciation and grammar there is considerable variation, with consistency apparently never a prime consideration. Pronunciation is covered by either verbal comment, or the use of diacritics, or both. Verbal comment mainly takes the form of a range of tags indicating stress and quantity, often in abbreviated form. So, as in Calepinus and Robert Estienne, we find '*priore producta*', '*penultima correpta*', '*pen.prod.*' etc. in Cooper's *Thesaurus*, and—occasionally—Waddington's revision of Veron. Fleming[?]'s version of Morelius, and Thomas Thomas 1587, in contrast, make specific references to vowel length in the form *prima longa*, *prima breui*, *p.l*, *p.b*, etc., though in Thomas's case there are a handful of exceptions, as, for instance:

(6) a Ador, oris, penult. gen. modò producit, modò corripit Scalig. *A kinde of pure wheat, called also* Far, *in olde time vsed in sacrifice.*
b Alĭus, a, ud. genit. aliūs, dat. alij, p.b. penult. prod. quamuis in carmine sit indifferens. *Another, diuerse, contrarie* … & gemin. signif. *One, another*…

And from time to time we find comment in English, as in Elyot 1542's entry *Plâga*:

(7) Plâga, **the fyrste syllable beynge longe, sygnyfieth a wounde, the fyrste syllable beinge short, it sygnifieth the armynge corde of a nette, also a great space of heauen and earthe callyd also** Clima.

Use of diacritics is similarly varied, with acute and grave accents and the circumflex over vowels found in increasing numbers from Elyot 1538 through to Morelius–?Fleming. In Thomas Thomas's dictionaries and Holyoke, they are replaced by macron and breve (diacritics previously used only very sporadically, as in Elyot–Cooper 1559, *Angŭlātim*); Wase has very occasional instances of both kinds.

Cover of grammar in the Latin–English dictionaries is both highly variable and internally inconsistent, with inflections frequently provided only 'as far as it is needful'[15] to indicate conjugation and declension. Explicit reference to gender is at first normally confined to exceptional circumstances, as for instance where it serves to distinguish between homographs, as in the following pairs:

[15] Rider 1589: Directions for the Reader. Readers are presumably assumed to have access to a Latin grammar.

(8) a Calx, hic, calcis, **the heele. it sometyme signifieth the ende of a matter. sommetyme a stroke with the heele.**

b Calx, hæc, **lyme made of burned stones,**[16]

replaced in the *Additions* to the dictionary by:

c Calx, calcis, **masculyne gender, the hele.**

d Calx, **the feminyne gender, lyme made of stones burned, it is taken somtyme for the ende of a thynge** (Elyot 1538).

And although subsequently gender-marking is found in most dictionaries, with a variety of abbreviations, its distribution is uneven. Wase indeed expects his young readers to 'find out the Gender' for themselves, 'from the Nominative and Genitive accented given' (1662: *Advertisements*).

Greatest variation is found with respect to the verb. Here the Latin–English dictionaries all follow Calepinus and Robert Estienne in normally giving the first person singular present indicative as the headword, while using the infinitive in the English equivalents. However, the number of the principal parts cited varies from one to five, both between and within dictionaries, and, as the following entries show, there is disagreement even over basic patterns:

(9) a Conflare; Flo, aui, are (Elyot 1538)

b Conflo, aui, are; Flo, aui, are (Elyot–Cooper 1548)

c Conflo, conflas, conflàui, conflátum, conflàre; Flo, flas, flaui, flàtum, flàre (Estienne–Veron, similarly[17] Morelius–?Fleming)

d Conflo, conflas, conflare; Flo, flas, flare (Cooper *Thesaurus*)

e Conflo, as; Flo, flas, flāui, flātum, flāre (Thomas Thomas; similarly Rider–Holyoke)

f Conflo, are; Flo, are (Wase)

Variation is also to be found in the handling of the formal identification of grammatical categories (metalanguage Latin). Even those dictionaries which name parts of speech with any frequency do not routinely tag nouns and verbs, for, as Cooper explains (*Thesaurus*: Annotationes): 'Nownes[18] and Uerbes may be knowen by their declining'. However, we find references to the case governed by some prepositions and verbs from Elyot onwards.

Finally, a wide range of typesizes and faces, including black letter (here represented by bold type), special punctuation marks, and symbols, such as the asterisk and obelisk, is employed for a variety of 'linguistic' purposes, culminating in Wase's occasional and innovative use of '—' to indicate omission of what would otherwise be a repeated lemma, as in the following:

[16] Following entry *Calathus*.

[17] With different diacritics.

[18] Subdivided into 'Nouns Adiectiue' and 'Nouns Substantiue'.

(10) *Ago*, ere. *To do.* Agere mulas, *to drive.*— vitam, *to pass.*—caussas, *to plead* ...

3.1.1 (ii) The English equivalents

In the Latin–English dictionaries, as in their continental counterparts, the norm is for headword and equivalent or equivalents to be juxtaposed. However, linking words are also found, as '(It) is a ... .', '(It) signifyeth', or comments such as Cooper's 'Of some is taken for Brionia' (*Thesaurus*: *Ampelomelæna*), while sometimes we find an explanatory phrase, with no functional correspondence, as in:

(11) a Aequilíbrium, æquilíbrij, n.g. **when the balaunce doeth hange neyther on the one syde nor on the other, when the weyghtes be ryght**: *Quand la balance ne pend d'ung costé ne d'autre, & ne trebuche point* (Estienne–Veron 1552).

b Aequidiālis, le, adj. & æquidiale, lis, n. *of* ęquus & dies, *when dayes and nights are both of a length*, Fest. (Holyoke in *Rider's Dictionary* 1606).

And sometimes no translation equivalent is provided at all.

Although for their English materials the lexicographers of this period are frequently heavily dependent on Latin or French sources, the language they use is generally idiomatic. Cooper indeed tells his readers that he is aiming at providing renderings that are '*iuxta mentem & sententiam authoris, quem citaui[t]*' (*Thesaurus: Annotationes*). A notable feature is the striving after 'copie', the copiousness so much admired at the time,[19] with long strings of equivalents, 'quasi uno aceruo congesta' (Elyot–Cooper 1548, *Candido Lectori*), only occasionally broken up by what Stein (1985: 147) calls 'verbal discriminators', such as 'also', 'sometime(s)', 'properly'. Language varies from formal to informal, as in this entry:

(12) Homo aridus, **a veraie nygarde, a myser, a chinche, a pinche peny, a pelter, one that will scantly bestowe a peny vpon hym selfe** (Elyot-Cooper 1548: *Aridus*).

However, 'hard' or 'inkhorn' English terms are conspicuously absent. Paraphrase and explanatory detail are often provided, and sometimes personal opinions are expressed. So, for instance:

(13) a Acŏnītum, i, n.g.p.b. Plin. *A venimous hearb,whereof there be 2. kindes, as Turner saith: the one may be called Libarbdine, the other woolfebaine. In Dutch it is called woolfewoorte* (Thomas Thomas 1587),

[19] See, e.g., Starnes (1954: 66 and 134).

b Lagopus, **an herbe, whyche I suppose to be Auyns** (Elyot 1538: *Additions*).

Attention is drawn to old or new terminology by comments such as 'was . . .' or 'now called', while equivalents are occasionally identified as dialectal, as, for instance, the 'northern' words *banwort*, *myrke*, and *slanke* in entries for *Bellis*, *Scotos* (**in Greke, darknes: It is more aptly callyd in the northerne tunge, myrke**'), and *Bryon thalassion* (Elyot), and the 'Cambridgeshire' words *modder* and *whine* in entries for *Puella* (Elyot), and *Onōnis* (Thomas Thomas).[20] And although English pronunciation is not normally covered, Cooper, in discussing the supposed etymology of headword *Albion*, compares northern and southern pronunciation of words such as 'bone' and 'stone' (Elyot–Cooper 1548).

3.1.2 *English–Latin dictionaries, from Huloet to Wase*

Elyot's Latin–English dictionary was first published only six years after the final edition of the *Ortus vocabulorum* (1532). In contrast, almost a quarter of a century elapsed between the last appearance of the *Promptorium parvulorum* (1528) and the publication of another English–Latin dictionary (with a scattering of French equivalents), Richard Huloet's *Abcedarium Anglico–Latinum, pro tyrunculis*, 1552. There is some slight evidence that one of Huloet's sources—direct or indirect—may have been that medieval text.[21] However, his greatest debt was to Elyot, with much material taken from Elyot–Cooper 1548, though he borrowed also from Calepinus and other continental authors.

Huloet's dictionary was followed by two small specialist English–Latin compilations, a topical dictionary by schoolmaster(?) John Withals (1553), and a rhyming dictionary by Yorkshire physician, Peter Levens (1570). Levens (or Levins) is the only English–Latin lexicographer who can convincingly be claimed occasionally to have used the *Promptorium*.

The 1570s also produced two trilingual dictionaries: a revision of Huloet by poet and compiler John Higgins (1572), with French equivalents added throughout, and John Baret's *Aluearie or triple dictionarie, in Englishe, Latin, and French* (1574), with Tables containing numbered lists of the Latin and French equivalents used in the body of the work. For his revision of Huloet, Higgins turned once more to the Continent, drawing primarily on revised editions of Robert Estienne's *Dictionarium Latino–Gallicum* and *Dictionnaire francois–latin*, but also using among other works a recent version of Calepinus, and Junius's *Nomenclator* (first published 1555), a work which he was later to translate. He

[20] For French dialect see Stein (1985: 175).

[21] Starnes (1954: 154).

also returned to Elyot–Cooper for additional material, while classical sources included Latin poets, Pliny, Vegetius, and Vitruvius.

Baret, Cambridge graduate and 'doctor in physick', admits to having begun work by requiring his students to 'write the English [of 'Elyots Librarie'] before ye Latin' [*Address to the Reader*]. However, his main source was Cooper's *Thesaurus*, and he also drew on a number of other dictionaries, including Levens, Withals, Estienne–Veron, Huloet–Higgins, an edition of Calepinus, and Robert Estienne's *Dictionarium Latino–Gallicum* and *Dictionaire francois–latin*. Baret's trilingual dictionary was retitled *An Alvearie or quadruple dictionarie* in 1580, in acknowledgement of the expansion of its previously insignificant Greek component, in a new edition, with added material by Abraham Fleming. Fleming, reviser in 1584 of Withals and of Veron, borrowed further from Huloet–Higgins. 1580 also saw the publication of an English–Latin version of Simon Pelegromius's Flemish–Latin *Synonymorum sylva*, by one H.F.[22] This was followed in 1589 by the first edition of John Rider's *Bibliotheca scholastica*, a publication containing not merely a comprehensive English–Latin dictionary but also topical lists and a Latin index with numbering for cross-reference. Rider, subsequently dean of St Patrick's Cathedral, Dublin, and then bishop of Killaloe, 'Master of Artes, and preacher of Gods word', described his work as 'Uerie profitable and necessarie for Scholers, Courtiers, Lawyers and their Clarkes, Apprentices of London, Travellers, Factors for Marchants, and briefly for all Discontinuers within her Majesties Realmes of England and Ireland',[23] a claim which was to be echoed in the bilingual dictionaries of the seventeenth century. And it was Rider's dictionary which was taken over by Francis Holyoke in that century and transformed, as we have seen, into the first bidirectional English–Latin, Latin–English dictionary. Rider's major source was Thomas Thomas's Latin–English *Dictionarium*, supplemented by material from Pelegromius, Gualtherus's Latin edition of Julius Pollux's *Onomasticon*, Huloet–Higgins, Baret, and Junius. Despite Holyoke's claims, the revisions of Rider's dictionary (from 1606) seem to have involved very little alteration to the English–Latin section. Finally, in 1662, we have a short English–Latin dictionary, aimed at young scholars and forming the first part of Wase's bidirectional *Dictionarium minus*.[24] Although much material goes back ultimately to Rider, and he may have used James Howell's *Lexicon Tetraglotton* (1660)[25], a work in which Howell in his turn had drawn heavily on his own revision of Randle Cotgrave's French–English dictionary (1650), all the evidence

[22] See further Starnes (1954: 355–6) and Stein (1985: 296–311). [23] Title page.
[24] See also above, p. 43. [25] See Bately (2001: 28).

points to Wase's primary source as the English–Italian dictionary inserted in Torriano's revised edition of Florio's *Worlde of Words* 1659.[26]

3.1.2 (i) The English headwords

The English–Latin dictionaries of this period all reflect directly or indirectly the practices and concerns of the Latin–English dictionaries that preceded them, with, for instance, their basic word-lists arranged in roughly alphabetical order, but with some etymological grouping,[27] and a variety of fonts, font sizes, and symbols. However, there are major differences of presentation between the English and the equivalent Latin lists. One is the result of the lexicographers' practice of transforming the English equivalents of their Latin–English sources into headwords in order to build up their word-lists. Since many of the Latin lemmas are rendered not by one-word English equivalents but by a paraphrase or explanation, this relemmatization has resulted in the introduction of multi-word headword entries and sub-entries, of varying degrees of helpfulness to a would-be writer of Latin. So, for instance, an entry in Elyot—'Venustas, tatis, **beautie, proprely of women, somtime a delectable pronunciation or**[28] **speche**'—is the source of four entries in Huloet, all with the Latin equivalent *Venustas, tis*:

(14) a **Beautye properlye in women** (running head *B ante E*)
b **Delectable pronunciation of speache** (running head *D ante E*)
c **Pronunciation of speache pleasauntly made** (running head *P ante R*)
d **Speache aimablye, aptlye, delectablye, pleasauntly or properly pronounced** (running head *S ante P*)

Baret's long headword entry '¶To **Serue: to giue all ones endeuour and diligence to a thing: to labour or doo the best he can to helpe**', is taken almost word for word from Cooper's *Thesaurus* entry *Seruio*. In its turn, Rider's entry, under running head *CH*, '*To make* Chamfering *chanels, or rebates, in stones or tombes*. 1. Strio', is derived via Baret ultimately from Elyot. Note, though, that these texts, like Rider's immediate source, Thomas Thomas, read 'timber' not 'tombs'.

Where relemmatization results in the creation of strings of English entries with the same or an etymologically related lemma, Huloet presents them as individual entries. However, Baret, followed by Rider, arranges them in a single list, under a selected, distinctively marked, headword, while Wase has compound entries, such as:

[26] See Bately (2001: 24–8).

[27] With 'to' before verbs and, where appropriate, an article before nouns, except in Huloet's dictionary.

[28] Subsequent editions 'of'.

(15) *To abide (or dwell,)* Commoror ari (*or* tarry,) Praestolor ari ... (*or suffer,*) Tolero are, perpetior i.

And a large number of the phrases and sentences used as headword entries begin with some word other than the lemma that determines their position in the word-list. So Baret, in reversing entries from Cooper, leaves groups of English synonyms unrearranged, as, for instance, '***A littell sacke, bagge or purse.** Sacculus, li, pen.corr.m.g. Cic. *Sachet, pochette, bourse*', as part of a sequence which begins '¶ **a Bagge of leather, purse, or pouche**', and with 'Bagge' set in larger type to indicate a new headword entry. Huloet, in contrast, achieves regular alphabetical order for his entries by employing inversion where necessary to bring the lemma to head position, as, for instance, in 'Gyltye to be of felonye. *Teneri furti*'.[29] However, he sometimes incorporates an etymologically related syntagma in a single-lemma main entry, thus avoiding the need to change the order of his Latin–English source, as here:

(16) **Garden,** *Custos, Tutor, ris, Et Tutorius, a, u[m], ang:* **perteyninge to a gardaine.**

Since in the Latin–English dictionaries 'hard' Latin words are regularly given 'ordinary' English equivalents or explanations, it is 'easy' words that form the bulk of the relemmatized English word-lists. Not until 1662, and apparently mainly under the influence of Florio–Torriano, do we find Wase entering 'hard' English words in any numbers—and these are frequently rendered in the equivalents by the Latin word from which they immediately or ultimately derive. With the Latin–English entry 'Celsitudo, ĭnis. *Highness*' we may compare his English–Latin '*Celsitude,* Celsitudo inis', and Florio–Torriano '*Celsitude,* celsitudine, altezza'. Proper names are not normally included, except in Huloet and (in particular) Huloet–Higgins, where they are often accompanied by some encyclopedic detail.

Register is normally formal, though idiomatic expressions, such as Baret's '**to buy a pigge in the poke.** Emere aleam' (under '¶ **a Poke and poket**'), are occasionally found, and some instances of 'vulgar', that is, 'colloquial', usage are labelled as such. So, for instance, Huloet's split entry:

(17) **Borowe of Peter to paye Paule, whyche is a vulgare speach, properly wher as a man doth**
Borow of one to paye an other.

[29] In section *G ante I.* Based ultimately on Elyot 1538 Teneri furti, to be giltie of felonye.

Huloet's own usage is in its turn sometimes modified by his reviser, Higgins.[30] So the (by now mainly dialectal) verb *warye* is dropped from the entry '**Bande** [Huloet–Higgins *recte* 'ban'], **curse, or warye**', while new entries have 'normal' word-order.

Single-lemma entries are frequently provided with a plentiful supply of English synonyms—again an offshoot of the lexicographers' dependence for headwords on English equivalents in Latin–English dictionaries. So, for instance, as a sub-entry to the (enlarged) headword '¶to Bribe', Baret's '***Uncleanly: filthily: sluttishly: dishonestly: couetously: with taking bribes in dishonest matters.** Sordidè, pen.cor. Aduerb. vt Proconsulatum, sed sordidè gesserat. Plin.' is a very close inversion of Cooper, *Thesaurus*'s entry *Sórdide.*

The inclusion of illustrative examples—in English, but rendering quotations from named Latin authors (and sometimes an abridgement of the accompanying Latin)—is mainly restricted to Baret, again mirroring Cooper's *Thesaurus*, though Higgins introduces a number of his own verse translations of Latin poets into his revision of Huloet (1572). Rider deliberately excludes such examples. A feature of the revised Baret 1580 is the inclusion of some 260 proverbs.

The layout of sub-entries varies, the most striking being that of Rider's 'very thoroughly planned and structured dictionary' (Stein 1985: 336–42), with a range of fonts, antonyms as well as synonyms, and arrangement according to word-class, with verbs followed by participles, then 'Nownes substantiues, and adiectiues, and lastly the Adverbs'—an arrangement which has some rather strange results, with, for instance, '*A haft, hilt, or handle* 1 Manubrium n. capulus, m.' and '*A little haft* 1 Manubriolum' appearing as sub-entries under 'To Haft, *vi.* dodge'. Wase, as we have seen, follows the English–contemporary-foreign-language dictionary tradition.[31]

Discussion of English spelling and pronunciation is only very exceptionally found, and parts of speech are not labelled. Some comment on etymology is provided by Baret, as '¶**Abbay is a french woorde, & signifieth barking against somme thing** . . .', while in the entry '¶**an Acorne**' he muses '(**or rather Oke corne as it were the maste or corne of an Oke**)'.

Finally, the metalanguage is sometimes Latin, sometimes English, with, for instance, both *vide* and *look in* used by Huloet.

3.1.2 (ii) The Latin equivalents

Latin equivalents range from mainly one- or two-word entries (as in Wase) to strings of synonyms up to nearly thirty items long (as in Huloet). A very large proportion of these equivalents have been assembled from the Latin word-lists of

[30] See, e.g., Knappe (2004: 255–62).

[31] Bately (2001) and section 3.1.1.

the Latin–English dictionaries. So, for instance, Baret's 'To staye or stoppe the **flixe or laske, to binde**' (one of numerous sub-entries under '¶**to Binde**') includes not only English synonyms from Cooper's *Thesaurus* but also all eleven Latin alternatives from its entry *Aluum astringere* (main headword *Aluus*). These strings are frequently presented without any connecting material or attempt at differentiation between them. Huloet indeed expressly states that he intends such differentiation to be the task of the users of his dictionary. However, Baret occasionally identifies alternatives among the Latin terms (introduced by 'is also taken for'), as well as instances of proper, occasional, and metaphoric usage, and Rider distinguishes (by number) three levels, 'proper', 'figuratiue or translate', and 'obsolete, or words out of vse'. Obsolete words, he explains, are included and identified so that the reader may understand them but know not to use them. However, Baret tells us he has omitted '**olde obsolet words, which no good writer now a dayes will vze**', and the revised *Alvearie* (1580) also eliminates uncommon words and usages, and 'vulgar' forms. Comment on the etymology and derivation of Latin words is a feature of Rider's dictionary.

Variant Latin forms are occasionally cited, while Huloet and Baret include comment on individual letters of the alphabet. However, apart from Baret's adoption of abbreviations such as *penult. prod, pen. corr.*, in selected entries, pronunciation of Latin is not normally indicated. Very occasionally we find a diacritic, such as the circumflex or accent grave. In Rider's *Bibliotheca* macron, breve, and circumflex are used in the Latin Index to show quantity.

The amount of grammatical detail provided varies both within and between dictionaries and generally reflects the variety and lack of consistency of the Latin–English dictionaries.

3.2 BILINGUAL DICTIONARIES COUPLING ENGLISH WITH A CONTEMPORARY FOREIGN LANGUAGE[32]

3.2.1 *Foreign-language–English dictionaries from William Thomas to Hexham*

The first foreign-language–English dictionary to appear in print was A *Dictionary in Englyshe and Welshe* (1547) by humanist scholar William Salesbury, a Welshman. Alphabetically ordered Welsh headwords, consisting mainly of single lemmas or

[32] See Alston (1965–, vols. XII and XIII); Stein (1985).

short phrases, with some proper names, and accompanied by occasional synonyms and spelling variants, are entered with their English equivalents, while introductory material in Welsh gives advice on the pronunciation of English.

Salesbury's dictionary was thus aimed at native speakers of the headword language, Welsh, with English the 'foreign' language. It is not until 1550 that we find the first foreign-language-into-English dictionary directed at an English audience: a brief Italian–English dictionary by William Thomas, attached to his *Principal rules of the Italian grammar.* Thomas—a Protestant and at one time Clerk of the Council to Edward VI—was later hanged, drawn, and quartered for alleged complicity in Wyatt's rebellion against Catholic Queen Mary. His compilation was followed by two French–English dictionaries: *A dictionarie French and English* (1571), with English equivalents provided by 'L.H.' (London bookseller, Lucas Harrison), and *The treasurie of the French tong* (1580) by 'Claudius Hollyband' (or Holyband), the English equivalent of the surname of Claude deSainliens, who also used its Latin translation, *a Sancto Vinculo.* DeSainliens, a Huguenot émigré and teacher of French and Italian in London, was author of several books on these languages. A second edition of his *Treasurie,* renamed *A Dictionarie French and English,* appeared in 1593.[33]

The beginning of the 1590s also saw the publication of two Spanish–English works: *The Spanish Dictionarie* by John Thorie, 'graduate in Oxenford', accompanying his *Spanish Grammer* [sic] (1590), a translation of Antonio de Corro's *Reglas gramaticales para aprender la lengua Española y Francesa* (1586), and Richard Percyvall's *Bibliotheca Hispanica* (1591), containing a Spanish–English–Latin dictionary and offering readers 'the toonge with which by reason of the troublesome times [they are] like to haue most acquaintance'. Percyvall, who was helped in his work by prisoners from the Spanish Armada, was at that time teaching at Merchant Taylors' School, but later entered Robert Cecil's secretariat and became MP for Richmond, Yorkshire. A significantly enlarged revised edition by John Minsheu (1599) omitted the Latin component, but added an English–Spanish index. The final decade of the century also saw the publication of *A worlde of wordes, or most copious, and exact dictionarie in Italian and English,* by John Florio (1598). Minsheu, a London schoolmaster called rogue by Ben Jonson, was 'educated by extensive travels rather than in a university'.[34] Florio, author, translator, and like Minsheu teacher of languages, born in London to an Italian refugee father and an English mother, was a highly distinguished humanist scholar. He issued a second 'much augmented' edition of his dictionary, retitled *Queen Anna's new world of words,* in 1611. Further editions appeared

[33] Cormier and Francoeur (2004: 160–75).

[34] Vivian Salmon, ODNB.

after his death, the first 'most diligently revised, corrected, and compared with La Crusca and other approved dictionaries' by Italian Giovanni Torriano, who also added an English–Italian dictionary.[35]

Finally, the first half of the seventeenth century saw the publication of a *Dictionarie of the French and English tongues* (1611) by Randle Cotgrave, secretary to William Cecil, Lord Burleigh, and *Het groot woorden boeck: gestelt in't Nederduytsch, ende in't Engelsch* by Henry Hexham. Hexham was a soldier turned scholar and translator, an Englishman resident for most of his adult life in the Low Countries. His *Groot Woorden-boeck* was first published in Rotterdam in 1648 as companion volume to his *Copious English and Netherduytch dictionarie* (1647), and has the distinction of being part of the first-ever-published single-authored fully bi-directional dictionary with English as one of its components. A second edition of Cotgrave's dictionary, 1632, with an English–French dictionary by Robert Sherwood[36] attached, was subsequently augmented by James Howell, a prolific writer on political, literary, and linguistic subjects, who ended his life as historiographer royal.

These dictionary-makers, like their Latin–English counterparts, were heavily dependent on continental models and sources. William Thomas tells us that material in his Italian–English *Dictionarie* 'for the better vnderstandyng of *Boccace, Petrarcha*, and *Dante*', is taken from Alberto Accarigi's *Vocabolario, grammatica, et orthographia de la lingua volgare* (1542), and Francesco Alunno's *Ricchezze della lingua volgare* (1543). L.H.'s French–English dictionary had as its primary source an edition of Estienne's *Les mots francois selon lordre des lettres tournez en latin pour les enfants* (1544), while Hol(l)yband in his publications, though taking as their basis L.H.'s *Dictionarie*, also drew on a number of other sources, including revised editions of Estienne's *Dictionaire francois–latin*.[37] Cotgrave's French word-list in its turn was derived from Nicot's *Thresor de la Langue Françoyse* (1606)—itself based on a revision of Estienne—but he also used numerous other sources, both French and English. A large proportion of his English equivalents are taken directly or ultimately from the Latin–English dictionaries. Other material is from Palsgrave and Hol(l)yband.[38]

Thorie's 1100-word dictionary claims to be composed 'of all the Spanish wordes cited in [Corro's Spanish Grammar] and other more wordes most necessarie for all such as desire the knowledge of the same tongue', while Percyvall names his own main sources as the *Diccionario Latino–espanol* of Elio Antonio de Nebrija (first published 1495) and Cristobal de las Casas, *Vocabulario de las*

[35] See section 3.2.2.

[36] Below, p. 61.

[37] Recent discussions of these dictionaries include Stein (1985: 245–72) and Cormier and Francoeur (2004).

[38] Smalley (1948: 245–72) and Cormier and Francoeur (2004).

lenguas toscana y castellana (1570). Percyvall's reviser, Minsheu, in his turn was to use Thomas Thomas's Latin–English *Dictionarium*, Florio, and possibly also Junius.[39] Florio himself drew not only (as he claims) on his own wider reading but also on earlier dictionaries, in particular that of Thomas Thomas (edition of 1592),[40] turning many of Thomas's Latin entries into their Italian equivalents and borrowing many of his English definitions. Finally Hexham's Dutch–English dictionary is based almost totally on the Dutch word-list in *Le Grand dictionaire françois—flamen* (first published 1618), with French definitions converted into English. This text was in its turn heavily dependent on dictionaries in the Latin lexicographical tradition.[41]

3.2.1 (i) The foreign headwords

Like their Latin–English counterparts, these dictionaries exhibit considerable variation in layout and presentation. Headwords are arranged in a roughly alphabetical order, though Percyvall (but not Minsheu) follows contemporary Spanish practice, locating initial CL after CA, ÇA after CV, etc., and the practice of grouping of 'derivatives' with their 'primitives' is not infrequently observed. Furthermore, some dictionaries include entries with headword embedded in a phrase or sentence, as, for instance, Hexham's sub-entry '*Gaerne by den back zijn*, To Have his nose alwayes in the pot, or, to make good cheere' (located under headword *Back*, with Dutch syntagma from *Le Grand dictionaire*)[42] and L.H and Hol(l)yband's '**Femme qui accouche de son premier**, *shee that lyeth in of hir first childe*' (based on Estienne, and under running head *A ante C*), while Cotgrave too has sub-entries with embedding, as, for instance, some of the many thesaurus-type syntagmas accompanying headword *Chien*.

In all the dictionaries, the basis of the word-lists is a selection of the more common words of the foreign language. Some have a scattering of proper names, while William Thomas, Hol(l)yband, Florio, and Cotgrave include also a number of dialect terms. Cotgrave and Florio's dictionaries stand out for the extent of their coverage of specialized vocabulary.[43]

Homographs are sometimes dealt with in a single entry, sometimes separately, as in the following:

(18) a *Se*, **beying a pronoune betokeneth him selfe. And beeyinge a verbe, signifieth, art thou.**

b *Secondo, seconda, secondi, seconde*, **adiectiuelie, somtimes dooe signifie, the seconde in nomber, and somtimes, happie or prosperouse.**

[39] Steiner (1970: 360).
[40] Starnes (1965: 407–22).
[41] Osselton (1969: 355–62).
[42] Cited Osselton (1973: 47).
[43] See further Smalley (1948); Stein (1985: 401).

Secondo, beying a preposicion signifieth accordyng (William Thomas 1550).

Synonyms and variant forms in the headword language, located alongside the headword, are a common feature of the French–English dictionaries and Percyvall–Minsheu, with the occasional antonym in Hol(l)yband, Percyvall–Minsheu, Florio, and Cotgrave. Cross-reference is of general occurrence, introduced variously by words such as 'looke (under/in)', 'seeke', 'idem', 'id est', 'vide'.

Regular indication of derivation and etymology is a feature of Percyvall–Minsheu, with an internal capital to indicate an underlying primitive, as in '*aCiégas, *blindfold*', and with 'sundrie Arabian and Moorish words vsuall in the Spanish tongue' marked by an obelisk and also listed in a Table. Occasional instances in other texts, located along with the 'English equivalents', include Thomas's '*Meschite*, **a Turckishe woorde that signifieth with them as muche, as Churche with us**'; Hol(l)yband 1580, 'Traimontaine, *an Italian word, the Northern winde*'; and Cotgrave: 'Empacqué: m. ée: f. Il s'est empacqué ... *from the sheepe* Pacos *(whereon th'Indians, in stead, or for want, of horses, carrie their marchandise)* ...'. 'Old' words are noted by Florio, Minsheu, and Cotgrave, and words 'rarely used', by William Thomas and by L.H., whose description (following Estienne) of '*Accoinctement*' as 'mot peu vsité *an attonement*' is adapted by Hol(l)yband as 'mot peu vsité, *a word little in vse*'. The status of a word or usage is frequently noted in the French and Italian dictionaries, as in these cases:

(19) a *Abbarbagleare*, **to darken or bleamishe the sight, vsed most in verse** (William Thomas 1550).
b Loo, *or* lof, *a terme that is vsed among Mariners* ... (Hol(l)yband 1580).
c Calcimia, *a word vsed of alchimists for calcination* ... (Florio 1598).

Identificatory, explanatory, or illustrative phrases and quotations, in the headword language, are found mainly in the French dictionaries, either as sub-entries or incorporated within a main entry by words such as 'whence'. Proverbs are a feature of Hol(l)yband, Minsheu, Florio, and Cotgrave. Authorities are occasionally named in the dictionaries of William Thomas, Florio, and Cotgrave; encyclopedic comment is fairly common.

Unlike Salesbury's Welsh–English dictionary, all these dictionaries were designed for the native speaker wishing to learn the foreign language of the headwords—for 'comprehension and not composition'.[44] However, in some cases, these headwords were drawn from dictionaries whose word-lists (unlike those of the Latin–English dictionaries) were themselves in the language of the intended user. (One notable instance is L.H.'s French–English dictionary, which

[44] Cormier and Francoeur (2004: 84).

contains a headword list most of whose members had previously performed the same role in a French–Latin dictionary, whose own headword list was in its turn a relemmatization of the French equivalents in a Latin–French dictionary.) In these sources, geared to the needs of native speakers of the headword language, it was of course not necessary to provide information about the pronunciation or grammar of that language. Moreover, there are separate sections on the pronunciation and grammar of the headword language in the dictionaries of Thorie, Percyvall, Hexham, Florio (edition of 1611) and Cotgrave–Sherwood, while Hol(l)yband's publications included books on this subject. So it is unsurprising that in the foreign-language–English dictionaries the use of diacritics, occasional in Percyvall and Florio 1598, is regular only in Minsheu and later editions of Florio, while William Thomas's comment on the length of the *i* that distinguishes homographs in entry *Balio* and Hol(l)yband's 'three syllables' for *Mercier* are exceptional. Explicit and regular gender-marking occurs only in Hol(l)yband 1593 and Cotgrave, and in Minsheu's revision of Percyvall, though L.H and Hol(l)yband sometimes prefix their nouns with an appropriate form of the article, and we occasionally find comments, such as these in William Thomas: '*Citella*, **or** *Zitella* ... **as in** *Apuglia*, **they call a maide** *zitella* **or** *zitello*, **masculine and feminine** ...' and L.H./Hol(l)yband: 'LA, *this article* La, *is signe of the feminine gender.* La femme, *the woman*'. (Except in L.H./Hol(l)yband, where usage is mixed, metalanguage is generally English.) Verbs are normally given in the infinitive form. Citation of irregular verb forms (and sometimes other parts of speech) is a feature of the dictionaries of William Thomas, Hollyband, Percyvall, Percyvall–Minsheu, and Florio. Occasional explicit naming of parts of speech is provided by William Thomas, Florio, Minsheu and Cotgrave.

3.2.1 (ii) The English equivalents and other materials

Florio describes his dictionary as 'copious', and copiousness in respect of the number of English equivalents provided is a feature of several of the dictionaries. So, for instance, in Cotgrave, we find:

(20) a Babouïnnerie: f. *Apishnesse, fopperie, foolerie, childish trifling, baboonizing; also, an vnhappie tricke, waggish part, knauish, wilie, or busie pranke; also, a deceit, cosenage, gullerie.*
b Barbiere: f. *A Barbers wife, a barbaresse; a woman, or she, Barber.*

And, most strikingly, in Florio himself, and revisions of Florio, as in:

(21) a Nocchio, *a knot, a knob, or ruggednes of any wood. Also as* Nocciolo.– Nocciolo, Nocciuolo, *the stone of any fruite, as peach or oliue. Also a hazell*

nut tree. Also a kinde of play that children vse, or else the nut to throw at Castelletto. (Florio 1598).

b Nócchio, *any bosse, bladder, puffe, bunch, knob, knur, wen, nodositie, node, snag, knap, measill, snar, or ruggednesse in any tree or wood. Also the stone of any fruite, as Peach, or Oliue, or Date. Also the knuckle of ones fingers. Also the nocke of a bow. Also a notch in any thing.* [Florio 1611; 1659 Nócchio, Nócco, adds: *also a bunch, a knob, or swelling of any stripe, blow, or thump.*] *Also an hazell nut-tree. Also the play* [*that children use* 1659] *called kob-nut. Also a gull, a ninnie, a foole, a sot.* [1659 reads here '*cob nut, or castle-nut, by Met. used for a dull-pate, a shallow-brain, a ninnie-hammer*'.][45]

In these strings of equivalents, the items are separated by punctuation alone, or linked by words such as 'sometimes', 'also', 'as', 'in some places it standeth for . . . ', 'sometimes it signifieth . . . ', 'is taken for'. On occasion, however, we find the verbal discriminators 'properly', 'more/most properly', 'but properly', 'or rather', or 'by metaphor', as in:

(22) a Azogado, **one that is ouercome with the aire of quicke siluer, by metaphor a fearefull wretche, a poore quaking wretch.** *Timidus, pauidus* (Percyvall 1591).

b †Azogádo, **one that is ouercome by the sauor of quickesiluer: by metaphor it signifieth a fearfull silly wretch** (Percyvall–Minsheu 1599).

Where a headword is informal, then the English equivalents usually include colloquial and even slang expressions. So:

(23) a Babillard, *a bablar, a prattler, a clatterer, a tittle tattle* (L.H and Ho(l)lyband 1580; [Hol(l)yband 1593 adds gender-marker 'm.'].

b Babillard: m. *A babler, tatler, prater, pratler, chatterer, iangler, word-monger; talkatiue companion; one whose tongue neuer lyes (and yet he often lyes.)* (Cotgrave 1611).

(24) Nigauld, *as* c'est le plus grand nigauld que je vi jamais, *he is the greatest loubie, lumpish, or doltish, that euer I saw* (Hol(l)yband 1580).

(25) Truhan, **a parasite, a belly feast** (Corro-Thorie).

A common practice is to illustrate the meaning of a word by means of comparison—as in William Thomas's entry: '*Accostiare*, **to sitte as the taylours dooe, with the legges a crosse**'; Florio's 'Acquattare, *to hide or squat as a hare doth*'; and Cotgrave's 'Accroüé: m. ée: f. *Drooping, as a bird that sits with hir feathers loose, or*

[45] For Florio's tendency to progress from formal to colloquial and slang, see Rosier (1963: 417–18).

staring, about hir'. Another practice is to produce what Stein has called a 'cultural equivalent', sometimes with encyclopedic detail, with introductions such as, 'we call it', 'as we say', or, as in Florio, 'Monina, *a womans geere or conie, a quaint as Chaucer calles it*.' Hol(l)yband also provides the occasional Latin, Italian, or Spanish equivalent.

Grammatical imbalance between headword and its equivalent is found in several dictionaries, as well as straight run-ons from headword to explanation. So, for instance, 'Beuer la briglia, *when a horse drawes vp the bit with his toong*', and 'Affalcarare, *is properly taken when a horse doth stop and stay vpon his hinder partes*' (Florio 1598); '*Bizzarro*, **is such a person, as we commonlie call an harebraine**' (William Thomas 1550). Imbalance of a different kind is found in Cotgrave's entry, 'Davier de barbier. *The Pinser wherewith he drawes, or puls out, teeth*'.

3.2.2 *English and foreign-language dictionaries, from Hexham to Torriano*

Already in 1530, schoolmaster John Palsgrave, one-time tutor to Henry VIII's sister, Mary Tudor, had published his *Lesclarcissement de la langue francoyse*, a three-part work containing a 'frenche vocabulist' as a complement to studies of French pronunciation and grammar. In this section, or 'Book', ordinary English words, followed by their French equivalents and a number of illustrative examples, are arranged in 'Tables' according to word-class.[46] However, in the sixteenth century, the only dictionaries to have an alphabetically arranged English word-list with equivalents from a contemporary foreign language were revisions of Huloet and Baret (1572 and 1580 respectively), with French joining Latin in the equivalents, and Percyvall–Minsheu with its English–Spanish index. It was not until 1647 that *A Copious English and Netherduytch dictionarie* was published as the first part of Henry Hexham's pioneering bidirectional work,[47] while in 1632 and 1659 Robert Sherwood and Giovanni Torriano added English–French and English–Italian dictionaries for English speakers to the monodirectional publications of Cotgrave and Florio. The main source of Hexham's English word-list has been identified as Rider's English–Latin dictionary, in a Holyoke revision.[48] Sherwood, master of a school in St. Sepulchre's churchyard in the City of London, had Cotgrave as a major source for his numerous sub-entries in his *Dictionarie English and French*, but for his English word-list the arrangement of items seems to have used a combination of an edition of Rider–Holyoke's English–Latin dictionary (1627) and the English–Spanish components of John Minsheu's *Ductor in Linguas* (edition of 1625).[49] Sherwood

[46] See the definitive study by Stein (1997).

[47] For the second part see above, section 3.2.1.

[48] Osselton (1973: 44–5).

[49] Starnes (1937: 1018); O'Connor (1977: 95); and Bately (2001: 15–24).

also acknowledges words from a range of foreign lexicographers, including Calepinus, Robert Estienne, Nicot, Passerat, while for his *Dictionary English and Italian*, Torriano, Professor of Italian in London, has Sherwood as his main source.[50]

3.2.2 (i) The English headwords.

Rather surprisingly there seems to have been little or no attempt by Sherwood or Torriano to copy the layout and manner of presentation of the foreign-language–English dictionaries that they are supplementing. (Similarly, Hexham's Dutch–English dictionary differs in its appearance from his English–Dutch compilation.) The normal pattern is for a single alphabetically ordered headword, with an occasional synonym, or string of synonyms, followed by a sequence of entries containing that word or an etymologically related form. The use of an article with nouns and 'to' with verbs, and the inclusion of many syntagmas among the sub-entries, means that these lemmas are frequently not in initial position. Homographs from more than one word-class are sometimes separately entered, as *Gastly*, identified as adjective and adverb respectively in Sherwood and Torriano, and sometimes placed under a single headword.

Dependence on Cotgrave has resulted in both Sherwood and Torriano including some 'old words' (as for instance 'High(t)', Cotgrave 'Nommé') and occasionally also English dialect words, as 'northern' *Weebit*. (Proper names are confined to the occasional personal name in Torriano.) Colloquial or slang expressions shared by the two dictionaries include 'To flie off the **hinges**. (or be impatient, &c.)' and 'a smell-feast'.

Many of the English syntagmas are relexicalizations with a venerable ancestry. So, for instance, Torriano, '*A dog with wide nostrils*, cane colle nari larghe' (in a list headed The nostrills), is based on Sherwood 'A dog with wide **nosethrills**, or narrells. *Chien de haut nez*' (under The **nose-thrills**), which in its turn is a relexicalization of Cotgrave's sub-entry (under Nez: m.), 'Haut nez. Chien de haut nez. *A dog of a deepe nose, or good sent; also, a dog that hath wide narrells*', which itself goes back to a French dictionary source, such as Nicot. Similarly, Torriano's entry (headword A Rogue): '*A nastie place where rogues haunt and lowse*', goes back through Sherwood to Cotgrave, 'Caignart: m. ... *a nastie, and filthie place, or corner, wherein beggars lye in the Sunne, or lowse themselues* ... '. Both parts of Hexham's entry under 'Heaven', 'halfe the compasse of the visible Heavens, *De halve circkel van de sienelicke hemelen*' clearly go back to a dictionary gloss on Latin *Hemispherium*, such as is found in Elyot 1538.

English grammar and punctuation are not normally covered within the dictionaries, exceptions being Sherwood, '**Fled.** *Fui, enfui. Participe du verbe* to Flee, to Flie'

[50] O'Connor (1977: 95); Bately (2001: 24–6).

and Torriano (under *The even, or evening, or eventide*): '*Good even (corruptly pronunced good een)*'. However, Hexham has an English grammar for Dutch speakers, and Sherwood includes a section on pronunciation and inflections for non-English speakers. Sherwood's metalanguage is sometimes English, sometimes French, Torriano's English and Hexham's Dutch.

3.2.2 (ii) Foreign-language equivalents

Strings of up to half-a-dozen one-word equivalents are common in Sherwood and Torriano. In Sherwood's dictionary these strings (which include French dialect terms) are normally linked only by punctuation. However, he comments that he has 'for the most part, obserued to set downe first the Proper; then, the Translated and Metaphoricall'. Torriano uses the occasional connective, as 'also', 'or'; Hexham in contrast often paraphrases. French authorities are acknowledged by Sherwood. However, he omits much of Cotgrave's encyclopedic detail, while occasionally inserting details relevant to England, as in the following entry:

(26) a A **kitchin-stuffe** wench. *Marmitonne, celle (à Londres) qui vend du suif & de la graisse aux chandeliers, pour en faire chandelles* (Sherwood 1632), beside

b Marmitonne: f. *A Kitchin-stuffe wench, or Kitchin wench; a filthie, greasie queane* (Cotgrave 1611).

Italian and Dutch syntagmas are frequently straight translations of English ones—which in their turn are usually the result of relemmatization.

Grammatical detail is rare in all three dictionaries. As Sherwood observes, 'It could not be expected in so small a volume, as I was inforced to contract my selfe into, that (in this English Dictionarie) I should shew the Genders of all French Nounes, and the coniugation of all French Verbes, which are most sufficiently … alreadie done by M.COTGRAVE' [To the English Reader]. However, Sherwood does identify some irregular English verb forms.

3.3 POLYGLOT DICTIONARIES

The first Latin–English dictionary to include equivalents from a contemporary foreign language on a regular basis was Stephanus (Estienne)–Veron's trilingual Latin–English–French *Dictionariolum* (1552). Other Latin–English dictionaries also included some Greek equivalents, while Holyoke 1633 introduces Hebrew words. However, during this period a large number of dictionaries whose purpose was from the first to give brief cover to five or more languages were in circulation. These originated on the Continent, with Latin as their headword language and at first did not contain English. However, this was remedied in the 1530s and 1540s, when three dictionaries covering six, seven, and eight languages respectively were published. The first polyglot dictionary with English headwords, John Minsheu's *Ductor in Linguas: the Guide into Tongues*, appeared in 1617, covering eleven languages and including cognates, citations, and etymological explanations. The English headwords are frequently accompanied by synonyms and brief explanations. This was followed by the first Anglo-Saxon–Latin–English dictionary to appear in print—antiquary William Somner's *Dictionarium Saxonico–Latino–Anglicum* (1659), with Old English words set in special Anglo-Saxon type[51]—and by James Howell's *Lexicon Tetraglotton* (1660),[52] providing English headwords with lists of French, Italian, and Spanish equivalents.

[51] See further Gneuss (1996: 41).

[52] See most recently Hüllen (1999: 202–43).

4

BILINGUAL DICTIONARIES OF THE LATE SEVENTEENTH AND EIGHTEENTH CENTURIES[1]

Monique C. Cormier

4.1 INTRODUCTION

UNTIL the middle of the seventeenth century, relations between European countries were facilitated by the common use of Latin in many areas of human endeavour. Latin remained the customary language not only of scholars and theologians but also of philosophers and scientists. At the end of the seventeenth century, however, this situation changed drastically: national languages gained influence everywhere, almost entirely replacing Latin in all areas of intellectual activity. Although Latin continued to maintain a strong bulwark in education—the demand for dictionaries for Latin translation and writing remained high—it no longer met society's needs outside the classroom. Bilingual dictionaries responded to the trend and numerous bilingual dictionaries were published for modern European languages, with a plethora of reprints and augmented editions.

Bilingual dictionaries thus played a major role in the promulgation of the various national languages. Owing to the increasing influence of France under

[1] The author would like to thank David Vancil, Head of Special Collections, and Dennis Vetrovec, Library Associate, of the Cunningham Memorial Library at Indiana State University for their invaluable assistance, as well as Anthony Cowie, Franz Josef Hausmann, Noel E. Osselton, and Paul St-Pierre for their perceptive comments.

Louis XIV, French held a privileged position among European languages in England until the middle of the eighteenth century. However, the play of alliances, life at the royal courts, and English trade in the ports of Europe resulted in a substantial increase in contacts between speakers of English and of other languages, such as Italian, Spanish, German, and Dutch. These contacts brought about change and created a legacy that has persisted to the present day: that of the ideas and power of England and the English language. Throughout Europe, the prestige attached to bilingual dictionaries soared and their numbers multiplied. These dictionaries were often the work of language teachers: as frequent dictionary users, they were well aware of the shortcomings of existing references and endeavoured to improve upon them, while borrowing—sometimes extensively—from the works of their predecessors.

4.2 ENGLISH AND LATIN

4.2.1 *Elisha Coles*

Elisha Coles, born in Northamptonshire around 1640, was the son of John Coles, a schoolmaster at Wolverhampton Grammar School. He attended Magdalen College, Oxford, for a few years, but left without obtaining a degree. He then became a schoolmaster in London, where he taught Latin to English pupils and English to foreigners. In 1674, he published *The Compleat English Schoolmaster* and, in 1675, two Latin textbooks (Life 2004). In August 1677, he became second undermaster at Merchant Taylors' School, but resigned in December 1678 to become master of the free school of Galway, Ireland. He died in Galway on 20 December 1680 (Life 2004).

In 1677, Coles published *A Dictionary, English–Latin, and Latin–English* in London. The second edition mentioned that on 27 February 1677 Coles obtained a Royal licence and the privilege to print and publish the dictionary for fourteen years. According to the address 'To the Reader', the first part of the dictionary contained all the words used in Latin, followed by their English equivalents, and the second part provided all sorts of words, terms of art, and phrases used in English, with their Latin equivalents. In both cases, entries were listed in alphabetical order. In the Latin–English section, insofar as possible, words were rendered by other (single) words, rather than by long and tiresome periphrasis. Care was also taken to avoid providing too many synonyms in the target language; explanations, directions, and references, usually provided in Latin, were instead given in simple, intelligible

English. Etymologies were also omitted, since for the most part they were hypothetical and of little use, and of no use at all to children. As sources, Coles mentioned using Calepine, Ferrarius, and others. He followed Calepine's method of putting common and proper nouns in one alphabetical list but did not follow that author in placing derivatives under their primitives (or roots), since that would make consultation of the dictionary difficult. As for the English–Latin section, Coles claimed he had added thousands of words, particles, idioms, phrases, and proverbs, in addition to proper nouns.

As Starnes notes (1954: 301), this address to the reader clarified certain aspects of the dictionary's title page. Coles's predecessors, with the exception of Christopher Wase (1662), who did not include proper nouns in his dictionary, generally separated common from proper nouns. The same is true of the list of birds, animals, and so on, which was placed at the end of the Rider–Holyoke dictionaries. As for the explanations in English, Coles was referring to the practice of Francis Holyoke who often included explanations in Latin. Finally, the reference to long periphrasis and obscure etymologies specifically concerned the dictionaries by Rider–Holyoke and Francis Gouldman (1664), which provided explanations in Latin and etymological information. For the compilation of his dictionary, Coles's main source was the second edition (1675) of the *Dictionarium minus* by Christopher Wase; he also made use of the third edition (1674) of Gouldman's dictionary (Starnes 1954: 302–5). Coles's dictionary went through eighteen editions, not counting new reprints (Alston 2002), and was published regularly until 1772 without substantial enlargement.

4.2.2 *Adam Littleton*

Adam Littleton was born on 2 November 1627, in Halesowen, near Birmingham. He attended Westminster School and was later admitted to Christ Church, Oxford. He then became an usher at Westminster School, where he was appointed second master in 1658. During the 1660s, Littleton obtained the position of chaplain in ordinary to King Charles II. In addition to his preaching, Littleton continued his philological activities throughout his lifetime. He died in Chelsea on 30 June 1694, and was buried at St Luke's (Key 2004).

In 1678, in London, Adam Littleton published *A Latine Dictionary, In Four Parts.* In his address to the reader, Littleton described the four parts of the work in detail and stated what could be expected from them. His principal aim was to 'carry the purity of the Latine Tongue throughout'. In the English–Latin part of the dictionary, Littleton declared that he wished to present English 'as now spoken'; he therefore added several thousand words that had not appeared in previous publications. To make room for the additions, he rejected 'old-fashioned' words, as well as uncouth expressions and insignificant circumlocutions. In the 'Latine–Classick' section, not only were the etymology, meaning, and use of each word indicated but also parts of speech, primitives—written in capital letters—and obsolete words. Scientific terms were labelled with an obelisk; synonyms and antonyms were also labelled. The third part of the dictionary—'Latine–Proper'—included proper names from history, poetic fiction, and geography. As for the fourth part, the glossary of 'Latine–Barbarous', Littleton hoped that the 'right-bred Latinist' would not be offended by the inclusion of such words, since he believed it necessary for the young to be able to distinguish between these and classical words.

In compiling his dictionary, Littleton followed his predecessors, reproducing even their errors (Starnes 1954: 312). For both the English–Latin and Latin–English sections, Littleton made extensive use of the third edition (1674) of Francis Gouldman's dictionary, which had been augmented by William Robertson, and, on occasion, of the first edition (1677) of Elisha Coles's dictionary. For the section containing proper nouns, Littleton also had recourse to Gouldman, as well as to Thomas Cooper's dictionary. As for the 'Latine–Barbarous' part, likely sources were the dictionaries by Rider–Holyoke, Gouldman, and Thomas Thomas (Starnes 1954: 313–16).

A second edition of Littleton's dictionary appeared in 1684 and apparently was identical to the first. An anonymous edition, reproducing most of Littleton's dictionary but with a different title and title page, was published in 1693 in Cambridge (Starnes 1954: 317). Although not printed as an edition of Littleton, it was later considered the third edition of Littleton's dictionary and known as the 'Cambridge Dictionary'. It is a revised and augmented edition of the 1678 and 1684 versions. Also in 1693, two other reprints of the work appeared, one in London and one in Cambridge. In all, there were six editions of Littleton's dictionary, the last appearing in London in 1735, one year before the publication of Robert Ainsworth's dictionary.

4.2.3 *Robert Ainsworth*

Robert Ainsworth was born in September 1660, probably in Wordsall, in Eccles Parish, Lancashire (Smith 2004). It was in or around 1714 that he was asked to compile a new English–Latin dictionary. According to Samuel Patrick (1746: xxvi), the task was so arduous that it went slowly and was even suspended for some years. Given Ainsworth's advanced age and a disorder affecting his eyesight,

Samuel Patrick helped him complete the dictionary. Although obviously finished in 1728, the *Thesaurus Linguae Latinae compendiarius* was only published in 1736.

In the preface, which is nearly thirty pages long, Ainsworth gave a brief history of English–Latin dictionaries published between 1499 and 1678, then explained why he had undertaken such a tedious task, going on to outline his dictionary's content. The principal reason invoked was 'an earnest desire of contributing all that lay in my power to the preservation of the purity of the *Latin* tongue in our grammar schools' (Ainsworth 1736: iv). His dictionary was thus compiled for English students.

The dictionary is in three parts. According to Ainsworth, the English–Latin section contained all the words and forms of speech commonly used in English, followed by their Latin equivalents 'as may fairly be supported by the authority of the *Roman* writers, commonly called *classics*' (Ainsworth 1736: v). It also comprised, still according to the lexicographer, many terms from the arts and sciences—included for the first time in an English–Latin dictionary. Ainsworth pointed out (1736: xiii) that his primary aim was to ensure that only classical words, when they existed, were used as equivalents in this part. He added that the Latin–English section of the dictionary contained not only all the words found in good editions of Latin classics, with appropriate labels and notes when such was not the case, but also their etymologies, when these could be determined with sufficient certainty, and an accurate, clear interpretation of their different meanings, numbered and arranged in a natural order, all supported by pertinent examples from the best Roman authors, with references given for the quotations. As for the historical and poetical part, the third section, this contained the Latin names of the more noteworthy people and places mentioned by classical authors, as well as their modern names.

As Starnes remarks (1954: 328), Ainsworth modelled his dictionary, in terms of both structure and content, on that by Littleton. Like the latter, Ainsworth emphasized the classical nature of the Latin in his dictionary. A difference, however, was that Ainsworth closely followed a well-defined plan, which was thoroughly explained in the preface. For the English–Latin part, Ainsworth based his work especially on Coles, both for the numerous definitions and for the methodology, whereas for the Latin–English part, Ainsworth used Littleton for the word-list and the definitions. As for the illustrative phrases and specific references to their classical sources, these were taken from one of the editions of Robert Stephanus's *Thesaurus*. For the proper nouns, once again Littleton was the main source.

In truth, Ainsworth's objective was not to collect new words and new definitions but rather, from what he had already amassed, to 'systematize, correct, verify, and supply for the Latin words grammatical information' (Starnes 1954:

331). As far as these aims were concerned, his dictionary was a success, but there was nothing totally new or original in it. Building on the experience of his predecessors, he was however the first to create a classical dictionary in which the different meanings of words were ordered, numbered, and illustrated by examples from classical authors, with references systematically identified.

4.3 ENGLISH AND FRENCH

4.3.1 *Guy Miège*

Guy Miège, a Calvinist, was born in 1644 in Lausanne, Switzerland, where his education focused on philosophy. At the age of sixteen, keen to travel, he left Lausanne for England by way of France, arriving in London in March 1661, a few weeks before the coronation of King Charles II. Shortly afterwards, he joined the household of the Earl of Elgin, the grandfather of the Earl of Aylesbury.

In 1668, he decided to settle permanently in England and seems to have lived there until 1718, his presumed year of death. During this fifty-year period, Miège devoted himself to teaching, translating, and writing works on a variety of topics. He first taught French and geography, and then English, to the ever-increasing number of Huguenot refugees after the Revocation of the Edict of Nantes.

As a language teacher, Miège must certainly have made use of such teaching aids as dictionaries and grammars. At the time he began teaching—around 1669—there were no monolingual dictionaries covering everyday vocabulary in either French or English. He was thus obliged to base his teaching solely on bilingual works. For anyone teaching in the last quarter of the seventeenth century, the most recently published bilingual French–English dictionary would have dated from 1611—the *Dictionarie of the French and English Tongues*, by Randle Cotgrave, which appeared, relatively unchanged, in a new reprint in 1673. Cotgrave favoured the language of sixteenth-century France. As a result, his dictionary presented an antiquated view of the French language at the time Miège was producing his first dictionary, *A New Dictionary*, published in 1677 in London. Miège's preface clearly set out his purpose, which was in marked contrast to that of Cotgrave: to describe a French that was current, rich, and had been 'purified' by the Académie française. Miège's aim was to describe the language of the French court, and he thus deliberately excluded obsolete words. For the presentation of the entries, he adopted a derivational system of classification, grouping in the same article words belonging to the same family.

Miège claimed to have based the French–English part of his dictionary on the most recent edition of the French–Latin *Dictionnaire Royal des langues françoise et latine* by Father François Pomey. The 1671 edition of Father Pomey's dictionary—the second edition—included a number of words that had not appeared in any previous dictionary. Miège said nothing about his sources for the English–French part.

In *A New Dictionary*, Miège adopted a synchronic perspective, focusing on current usage and more in keeping with the literary tastes of the day (Hausmann 1991: 2957). Following the example of his predecessors, Miège targeted an English-speaking public who wished to gain access to French in order to extend their 'passive' reading knowledge of French. However, the dictionary did not meet the expectations of this readership, which was attached to French literature of the sixteenth century and wedded to the tradition of hard-word dictionaries. *A New Dictionary* thus received a lukewarm reception from the English (Hausmann 1991: 2957).

In response to this unexpectedly disappointing reception, Miège felt obliged to publish a second bilingual work in 1679. Entitled *A Dictionary of Barbarous French*, it was devoted to obsolete and provincial words, taken for the most part from Cotgrave's dictionary. That same year, the *New Dictionary* was reprinted in a single volume with the *Dictionary of Barbarous French*.

Despite the lack of interest shown in his first dictionary, Miège undertook two new works based on it. First, an abridged version, *A Short Dictionary English and French, with another French and English*, which he published in 1684 and which went through six editions (Alston 1985). This time derivatives were presented strictly in alphabetical order, as main entries, not grouped in word families. The intended readership for the dictionary consisted of French speakers who wished to read English works of literature. In the preface, Miège clearly pointed out that the English, too accustomed to hearing and speaking French, would not be satisfied with an abridged dictionary, and that he was in the process of compiling his great dictionary from which nothing would be missing. In 1688, *The Great French Dictionary* was duly published. This time, Miège included ordinary words as well as obsolete words and 'the most remarkable' barbarous words, which he declared he disliked. Miège made no mention of his sources in his preface. For the French–English part, however, it seems likely that, in addition to his own dictionaries, he used the first dictionary of classical French, the *Dictionnaire français* by César-Pierre Richelet, published in 1680 (Cormier 2006). As for the English–French section, numerous possible sources exist (Bately 1983: 5–6).

Although Miège would be overshadowed by Abel Boyer a decade later, he is remembered as a single author engaged in a single project, as the first lexicographer to compile a bidirectional French–English/English–French dictionary, a work which was to become the dominant model by the end of the seventeenth century. His predecessors, from John Palsgrave—who added an English–French dictionary to his French grammar—to Claudius Holyband and Randle Cotgrave, had produced monodirectional dictionaries. Although the first two-part dictionary (French–English and English–French) was published in 1632 (Cotgrave 1632), it was not originally intended to be bidirectional: it was actually a reprint of Cotgrave's French–English dictionary published twenty years earlier, with an English–French part compiled and added by Robert Sherwood. Miège was also the first person to produce an abridged dictionary, and the first to inventory the French of seventeenth-century France in a bilingual French–English dictionary, combining both ordinary and hard words in one volume (Cormier and Francœur 2004: 90).

4.3.2 *Abel Boyer*

Abel Boyer was born on 13 June 1667 in Castres, in the Haut Languedoc, a well-known centre of French Protestantism. He was baptized on 24 June of the same year. His parents were Huguenots: his father, Pierre Boyer, was a magistrate and his mother, Catherine de Campdomerc, was the daughter of Éléazar de Campdomerc, a well-known doctor in Puylaurens and later in Castres.

Abel Boyer received his early education from his uncle, Pierre de Campdomerc, before attending the Protestant Academy in Puylaurens. His studies were interrupted by the Revocation of the Edict of Nantes, and, in 1685, he left France for Amsterdam. In 1689, he reached England, where he remained until his death on 16 November 1729.

With the encouragement of Princess Anne of Denmark, Boyer undertook, in 1694, to compile his *Royal Dictionary.* He consulted Thomas Henshaw, who, in 1671, had edited the philological works of Stephen Skinner and sent him a sample of his dictionary for his comments. In compiling the English section, Boyer was not able to consult dictionaries with complete descriptions of the contemporary language; he decided, therefore, to work in collaboration with John Savage, who, in 1696, sent him a list of words that, Savage said, completed the words already inventoried. In fact, Savage added more than one thousand English words to Boyer's dictionary (Boyer 1699: Preface). By 29 April 1699, Abel Boyer had finished his dictionary and had sent it to the printers. *The Royal Dictionary* was published in May 1699. With its numerous editions, it remained in print throughout the eighteenth century.

In the preface to his dictionary, Abel Boyer listed the French and English sources used in the compilation of his dictionary. For the French–English part, in addition to material from Vaugelas, Ménage, and Bouhours, and the dictionaries of Richelet (1680) and Furetière (1690), there were the dictionaries of Father Tachard (1689) and of the French Academy (1694). Although traces of the influence of Richelet and Furetière on Boyer's dictionary are evident, his indebtedness to the Academy is most obvious (Cormier 2006).

For the English–French part, Boyer stated that he had consulted the best dictionaries and taken a number of words from the best authors, such as Archbishop Tillotson, Bishop Sprat, Sir Roger L'Estrange, John Dryden, and Sir William Temple. Yet the front matter of the *Royal Dictionary* does not mention that one of his sources was the *Great French Dictionary* by his predecessor and rival Guy Miège. When Boyer alluded to that dictionary in his preface, it was only to note its faults. Although he certainly had recourse to Littleton (1684) and, to a lesser extent, Gouldman (1678) and Holyoke (1677) for certain definitions and subentries, Boyer made extensive use of the definitions and examples of the *Great French Dictionary* (Cormier and Fernandez 2005).

In May 1700, Boyer published his *Royal Dictionary Abridged*, which was also very successful, with more than forty editions. In his preface, Boyer insisted on the originality of his work; for instance, accents were indicated on all the English headwords with a view to facilitating pronunciation of the language by foreigners. *Decémber*, *Décency*, *Decénnial* and *Décent* are examples.

Abel Boyer's contribution to the English–French lexicography of his time was very important, particularly because of the methodological innovations he introduced. First, Boyer systematically indicated the gender of words and their part of speech. Second, he was the first to recognize the necessity of clearly and systematically separating the different meanings of words, using for this purpose the ☞ symbol—which Miège had already occasionally used—to distinguish between them and inform readers that what followed was a new sense of the word. Boyer was also the first to provide and incorporate into his dictionary a series of precise usage labels to guide readers as to how words were used. For example, the English entry *Palpation* was preceded by the label D†, which meant that it was doubtful, its usage was not well established, and authors did not agree on its currency. Finally, Abel Boyer went further than previous lexicographers in indicating pronunciation in the body of the dictionary. The *Royal Dictionary Abridged* contained primary stress marks on English words, a practice which would become generalized only somewhat later in monolingual English dictionaries and only in the second half of the eighteenth century for bilingual English–Italian, English–Dutch, and English–Spanish dictionaries (Hausmann and Cop 1985: 185–6).

4.4 ENGLISH AND ITALIAN

4.4.1 Ferdinando Altieri

Little is known about Ferdinando Altieri, other than that he was a 'Professor of the Italian tongue' in London, where in 1726–27 he published his *Dizionario Italiano ed Inglese.* The dictionary, Italian–English and English–Italian, was produced for members of the nobility and gentry, as Italian was spoken in most of the courts of Europe and English was used widely outside England. Merchants were also targeted as potential users of the dictionary, since there was extensive trade by English merchants through Italian seaports. Altieri's dictionary broke with the tradition established by John Florio and Giovanni Torriano of simply compiling lists of words and including the largest number possible (O'Connor 1990: 63). For the Italian section, Altieri reproduced the entire *Vocabolario* of the Accademia della Crusca (1691), to which he added several hundred words from the texts of well-known authors. His method consisted in transcribing the entry and definition provided by the Crusca dictionary, enclosed in brackets, and adding an English gloss. As for the English part of the dictionary, Altieri based it for the most part on the *Royal Dictionary* of Abel Boyer (1699), while also making use of the dictionaries of Giovanni Torriano (1659) and Nathan Bailey (1721). From Boyer's dictionary he borrowed part of the word-list and most of the illustrative, idiomatic, and proverbial phrases (O'Connor 1990: 74).

Several characteristics of Altieri's dictionary, summarily presented in the preface, are worth noting, and some are innovations: for Italian words, the accentuated syllables were marked; the grammatical category of words other than verbs was indicated, as well as the gender, where appropriate, for both headwords and equivalents; the meanings of words were carefully differentiated and listed in the order of proper (i.e. literal) meanings, metaphorical meanings, and figurative meanings. In addition, numerous set phrases and proverbs were provided.

A second edition of Altieri's dictionary, corrected and improved by Evangelist Palermo, who also taught Italian in London, appeared there in 1749 and again in 1750, and in Venice in 1751. No additions were made to Altieri's dictionary; as Palermo stated in the preface to the 1749 edition, only the numerous 'inaccuracies of press' had been corrected. No further editions of this dictionary, identified as being by Altieri, were published.

4.4.2 Giuseppi Baretti

Giuseppe (Joseph) Baretti was born in Turin, Italy, on 24 April 1719. From his mother's death in 1735 to his father's death in 1744, he is known to have lived in

Guastalla, Venice, Milan, and of course Turin. He arrived in England in 1751 and remained there until 1760. It was probably through Charlotte Lennox that he met Samuel Johnson, who would become his friend. In 1757, a group of eight booksellers engaged him to correct and augment Ferdinando Altieri's dictionary.

A Dictionary of the English and Italian Languages was published in London early in 1760, with a dedication by Samuel Johnson. The work was immediately successful and remained in print until the beginning of the twentieth century. While admitting in the preface to the dictionary that Altieri had gone further than his predecessors Florio and Torriano, Baretti noted that many of his definitions 'awakened my risibility'. He criticized the obscene words and phrases included by Altieri, as well as the coarse language and absurd proverbs used to refer to women. Baretti claimed to have added about ten thousand new words or senses. He also retranslated numerous phrases, corrected the accents on the Italian words, and indicated stress for English words. The various changes Baretti introduced, and which he maintained were important, in his opinion justified putting his name on the title page of the dictionary. In actual fact, however, the additions and modifications were relatively minor (O'Connor 1990: 84). The additions came from two sources. As O'Connor explains (1990: 84–5), in the Italian–English section the lexicographer added a limited number of words from the fourth edition of the *Vocabolario* of the Accademia della Crusca (1729–38). These were either derivatives or variants of words already in Altieri's dictionary. In the English–Italian section, he added some words from Dr Samuel Johnson's dictionary, such as *Came'lopard* and *To Dap*. As for omissions, those affected in the Italian–English part of the dictionary were taboo words and words relating to the natural sciences. Few words were dropped from the English–Italian section.

The dictionary was reprinted in 1771 and, in 1778, a new edition was brought out, though without any obvious changes. In 1787, an edition was published in Venice. According to O'Connor (1990: 88), Baretti spent the last years of his life revising his dictionary. It is not clear, however, whether he played a role in the edition—corrected and improved by Pietro Ricci Rota—which appeared in 1790, one year after his death.

4.5 ENGLISH AND SPANISH

4.5.1 *Captain John Stevens*

Captain John Stevens (*c.*1662–1726) was born in London. His mother was probably Spanish and his father was in service to the Earl of Clarendon in Madrid, then to Catherine de Braganza, a Portuguese princess who later married King Charles II of England. After a military career lasting into his thirties, Stevens became a productive and distinguished scholar and translator. In 1705–06, he published *A New Spanish and English Dictionary*, the first bilingual dictionary for this combination of languages to appear in almost a century. A Spanish grammar and dialogues completed the dictionary, the first section of which, Spanish–English, is dated 1706, whereas the English–Spanish section, *Part II*, has a separate title page and is dated 1705. A second edition of the dictionary appeared in 1726, without the grammar and the dialogues.

The front matter preceding *Part I* contains a 'Preface', an 'Advertisement', and a 'Catalogue of Authors from whom this Dictionary is collected'. There is no separate introductory material to *Part II*, and the front matter refers only to the Spanish–English section of the dictionary. The sources mentioned in the 'Catalogue' refer only to this part and include six dictionaries, as well as a large number of works in Spanish on a variety of subjects, including literature, history, and politics. Of the former, only John Minsheu's dictionary of 1599 contained an English word-list. There is no indication of what sources were used for the English–Spanish section of the dictionary.

Steiner (1970: 58–67, 105) has demonstrated that much of the material included in the Spanish–English section was taken from two sources: Minsheu's dictionary (1599) and César Oudin's *Tesoro de las dos Lenguas Francesa y Española*, published in 1607. Cormier and Fernandez (2004) have also shown that for the English–Spanish part, Stevens made extensive use of Minsheu's dictionary (1623), as well as Torriano's dictionary (1659), and the *Royal Dictionary* by Abel Boyer (1699). Among the additions were a number of proverbs, the etymology of certain entries in the Spanish–English section of the dictionary, and information of an encyclopedic nature (Steiner 1991: 2950).

As Steiner explains, Stevens's dictionary did not contribute significantly to bilingual Spanish–English lexicography and even represented a backward step, because of 'the elimination of all gender labels so faithfully provided by Minsheu, because of the less-than-rigorous application of alphabetical ordering of entries, and because of the technique of glossing which includes the use of the leisurely exposition of learned and obscure meanings, the redundant explanation, and the discursive definition' (Steiner 1970: 105).

4.5.2 *Peter Pineda*

Peter Pineda left his native Andalusia for religious reasons, later earning his living in London as a teacher of Spanish (Steiner 2003: 89). He was the first Spaniard to develop a Spanish–English dictionary. This was the *Nuevo Dicionario, Español e Inglés e Inglés y Español*, published in 1740 in London.

The title page of the dictionary stated that Pineda's work contained six thousand Spanish words and twelve thousand English words more than previous dictionaries. In his preface, Pineda noted that, in the Spanish–English part, he had marked with an asterisk the words not found in any other dictionary, adding that readers would easily see that words had also been added to the English–Spanish section.

Steiner (1970: 68–75) has shown that Pineda's dictionary was not merely a copy of Stevens's dictionary and that Pineda did indeed make additions, even though, in the Spanish–English part, a number of these were merely derivatives of roots already present in Stevens's dictionary. Others were illustrative expressions, and a large number were idiomatic expressions. Furthermore, Pineda was the first lexicographer in the history of bilingual Spanish–English lexicography to use a monolingual English dictionary—the fourth edition of Nathan Bailey's *An Universal Etymological English Dictionary* (1728)—to establish the word-list for the English–Spanish section, making it much richer than the work of his predecessors.

For Steiner (1970: 74), Pineda's contribution to lexicography consisted principally in 'the introduction of much living speech into the dictionary proper; the sound doctrine of short, concise glossing; the designation in a systematic manner of all the parts of speech of vocabulary entries; the indication of the pronunciation of Spanish letters'. One aspect of Pineda's work, however, served to discredit him: in some of his definitions, he insulted the Spanish Academy and the Pope.

4.5.3 *Joseph Giral Delpino*

Like Pineda, Joseph Giral Delpino also taught Spanish in London. In 1763, he published *A Dictionary Spanish and English, and English and Spanish*, which, according to the lexicographer, contained several thousand words more than any other dictionary, with accents on the Spanish words and spelling based on the observations of the Real Academia Española.

Giral Delpino was not particularly kind to Pineda. In his preface he called him ignorant and selfish, and 'an obstinate writer'. Furthermore, he reproached Pineda for having filled his dictionary with 'silly tales and stories', and having included unjustified 'pedantical declamations against the Pope, the King of Spain and the Spanish nation'.

Steiner has shown that the entries added by Giral Delpino were taken from the works of his predecessors, as well as from two additional sources: Samuel Johnson's dictionary (1755) and, especially, the *Diccionario de Autoridades* (1726–39) of the

Spanish Academy. Although Giral Delpino omitted the objectionable elements in Pineda's work, as well as the proper nouns, his dictionary was, for the most part, simply a reproduction of Pineda's, retaining even its 'inconsistencies and lexicographical idiosyncrasies' (Steiner 1970: 76–84).

While not an innovator, Giral Delpino nevertheless had the merit of acknowledging the authority of the Royal Spanish Academy of Madrid. He was also the first Spanish–English lexicographer to introduce a symbol—the dagger—to indicate the level of speech of an entry, thereby recognizing the importance of such information for the reader. Finally, in the English–Spanish section of the dictionary, and at the beginning of certain letters, Giral Delpino provided information regarding the pronunciation of English words.

In 1778, a second edition of Giral Delpino's dictionary, the *Dictionary, Spanish and English, and English and Spanish*, was published in London. It had been corrected and improved by Giuseppe (Joseph) Baretti, who himself—as we have seen—had published an English–Italian dictionary in 1760. The 'Advertisement' claimed that many corrections and additions (nearly ten thousand words) had been made, mostly based on Johnson's dictionary for the English part, and gleaned from Spanish scholars for the Spanish part.

According to Steiner (1970: 85–91), the samples studied reveal that Baretti added less than half of what he had claimed. He deleted almost twice as many words as he added. He did extensive editing, and this was undoubtedly his main contribution to English–Spanish bilingual lexicography, as his dictionary did not comprise any innovations. Editions of this dictionary were published in 1786, 1794, and in the nineteenth century.

4.5.4 *Thomas Connelly and Thomas Higgins*

In 1797 and 1798, the four-volume *A New Dictionary of the Spanish and English Languages* was published. It was the work of Father Thomas Connelly, a Dominican who was the 'family confessor to his Catholick Majesty', and his collaborator Father Thomas Higgins, a Carmelite and 'family confessor at the Royal Seat of St. Ildephonsus'. This dictionary, which was the first bilingual Spanish–English dictionary published in Spain, broke with the well-established tradition of compiling dictionaries that were based on those of predecessors.

The preface to the Spanish–English part noted that Connelly had devoted his spare time for fourteen years to compiling this dictionary. Because of the scale of the task, he asked Father Thomas Higgins, his 'companion and relation' to come from Naples. According to Connelly, this dictionary included more words than the three best English dictionaries published in England and eight thousand more than that of the Real Academia Española. The preface also stated that the authors had added numerous 'technical terms of arts and sciences, trades and offices'.

The originality of Connelly's and Higgins's dictionary lies in the fact that the authors mainly relied on two monolingual dictionaries in compiling their own. Steiner (1970: 92–102) has demonstrated that they used the dictionaries by Samuel Johnson and the Real Academia to produce a work that provided not only target-language equivalents but also definitions following the source-language headwords. The result can therefore be considered three dictionaries in one: a monolingual English dictionary, a monolingual Spanish dictionary, and a bilingual English–Spanish dictionary.

4.6 ENGLISH AND GERMAN

4.6.1 Christian Ludwig

Christian Ludwig was born in 1660 in Eilenburg, Saxony. A master of philosophy, he was, as a young man, a ship's doctor in New England, where he lived for some time. He arrived in England in 1696 and remained there several years before moving to Leipzig, where he taught English until his death on 21 May 1728.

A Dictionary English, German and French, by Christian Ludwig, was published by Thomas Fritsch in Leipzig in 1706, five years after the British Parliament passed the Act of Settlement, thus creating a dynastic link between England and Germany (Hausmann and Cop 1985: 183). The Act provided for the transfer of succession to the House of Hanover after the death of Queen Anne, making Sophie of Hanover a potential heir to the English throne. At the time, no bilingual English–German or German–English dictionary had yet been published. Although three languages were included in the dictionary, it is considered in practice to be the first English–German bilingual dictionary, since it was possible to use the dictionary without reference to the French equivalents provided (Stein 1985: 148).

Ludwig's dictionary of 786 pages was dedicated to the Electress Sophie, Dowager Duchess of Hanover. On the title page Ludwig declared that his dictionary contained not only English words in alphabetical order but also their several significations (i.e. senses), their proper accent, phrases, figurative expressions, idioms and proverbs, and that it was compiled from the best newly published dictionaries. Hausmann and Cop (1985: 185–7) have shown that Ludwig based his dictionary on Abel Boyer's already famous *Royal Dictionary* (1699) and on the abridged version of the same dictionary. The fact that Ludwig indicated the accentuation of English headwords—a practice Boyer used in the abridged version but not in the complete edition—proves that he consulted the modified version of the dictionary. However, in the abridged version, Boyer essentially reproduced the word-list of the 1699 edition, limiting his omissions to a few rare entries (Cormier and Francœur 2006). It is therefore also certain that Ludwig borrowed from the articles of the complete edition of 1699, as is clearly demonstrated by scrutiny of the articles for *mouth* and *to get*, for example. Ludwig's actual contribution to the dictionary was rather limited, consisting in the insertion of equivalents and definitions in German between the English and French. Despite this, his importance for the English–German lexicography of the time should not be underestimated. Ludwig introduced the accentuation of English words with a view to facilitating their pronunciation by non-English speakers; he was one of the first lexicographers to do so and the first among English–German dictionary-makers. He also used grammatical labels to distinguish between homographic headwords, and semicolons to mark the different meanings of words. In addition, a system of usage symbols was used to guide the reader. A second edition of the dictionary was published in 1736, a third in 1763, and a fourth in 1791.

In 1716, the *Teutsch–Englisches Lexicon*, a German–English dictionary of 2,672 pages dedicated to King George I, was published in Leipzig by Thomas Fritsch. The dictionary contained only two languages—French was not included—and was designed for Germans who wished to express themselves in English. No author's name appeared on the cover page. Stein (1985) believes the author was clearly Ludwig, whereas Alston (1999) merely attributes the dictionary to him. For Hausmann and Cop (1985), authorship is even less certain, and they note that a passage in the publisher's preface would seem to indicate that Ludwig was not in fact the author. Because of the large amount of material it contains and because it presents the German words in alphabetical order, the dictionary is considered to be one of the most important with German as the source language. New editions were published in 1745, in 1765, and in 1789.

4.6.2 *Theodore Arnold*

In 1736, *Mr. Nathan Bailey's English Dictionary*, translated into German and improved by Theodore Arnold, was published in Leipzig. This volume was the translation of the second part—the orthographical dictionary—of what is known as the second volume of *The Universal Etymological English Dictionary*, published in London by T. Cox, in 1727.[2] Bailey compiled his orthographical dictionary for

[2] The first volume appeared in 1721 under the title *An Universal Etymological English Dictionary*.

both English and foreign readers. This dictionary provided accentuation for English words as an aid to pronunciation; asterisks distinguished those words of approved authority from those that were not approved; and the different meanings were given in English, French, and Latin to help foreigners who were interested in learning English. Idioms, set phrases, and proverbial sentences are also included. Arnold's dictionary is substantially the same as Bailey's, with the difference that Arnold provided German translations for the existing meanings in English, French, and Latin. Arnold's dictionary was also a collection of common and familiar words intended to help users with spelling and pronunciation. The resulting publication was therefore an English–French–German dictionary. To this first volume, Arnold added *A New German–English Dictionary* (Neues Deutsch–Englisches Wörterbuch) in 1739 (Hausmann and Cop 1985: 188).

In 1783, the German lexicographer Johann Christoph Adelung published the first volume of his *Neues grammatisch-kritisches Wörterbuch der englischen Sprache für die Deutschen* in Leipzig. This was a translation of the fourth edition of Samuel Johnson's famous dictionary, and contained entries for the letters A to J. The second volume of this English–German dictionary, for the letters K to Z, appeared in 1796. The German–English part of the dictionary was compiled by Johann Ebers and published in three volumes between 1796 and 1799 (Hausmann and Cop 1985: 188).

4.7 ENGLISH AND DUTCH

4.7.1 Willem Sewel

Willem Sewel was born in Amsterdam on 19 April 1653 and died on 13 March 1720, most probably in Amsterdam (Hall 2004). Known as 'the first Quaker historian of Quakerism' (Hull 1933), some thirty translations are also attributed to him, including those of important authors such as Gilbert Burnet, William Congreve, and Sir William Temple.

In 1691, Sewel published in Amsterdam his *New Dictionary English and Dutch*, in two parts, English–Dutch and Dutch–English, and included a short treatise on Dutch pronunciation as well as a guide to the Dutch particles *de*, *die*, *deeze* and *het*, *dat*, *dit*. In his preface, Sewel declared his certainty that readers would find his dictionary more satisfactory than Hexham's, from which he claimed to have borrowed nothing. Indeed, he asserted that while producing his own dictionary he had neither consulted Hexham's nor even had it in his house. Sewel addressed his dictionary to translators and readers of foreign works, rather than to language learners (Osselton 1991: 3036).

In his study of the first English–Dutch dictionaries, Osselton (1973: 58–75) demonstrates that for the English–Dutch section of his dictionary Sewel made particular use of the second edition of Elisha Coles's English–Latin dictionary, translating the Latin definitions into Dutch. Sewel reproduced approximately two-thirds of this dictionary, omitting the proper nouns and the more technical or specialized words. To a lesser extent, he also used William Robertson's Latin–English dictionary, *Phraseologia Generalis* (1681). Although Sewel's dictionary owed a great deal to English–Latin dictionaries, Osselton (1973: 67) considers it 'more varied, informative and up-to-date than that of Hexham'. It is also clear that Sewel's translations provided material for his dictionary: several English terms, specifically legal and ecclesiastical terms for which no equivalent Dutch terms existed at the time, such as *canon law* and *simony*, were included in his English word-list. The definitions in Sewel's dictionary are more precise than those in Hexham's, and meanings are more clearly differentiated.

As for the Dutch–English section of the dictionary, Osselton (1973: 72–5) has shown that Sewel based it on the third edition of Casparus van den Ende's Dutch–French dictionary, published in 1681, and on a nautical dictionary, *Wigardus à Winschootens Seeman*, which also appeared in 1681. This second part of the dictionary was not as rich as the first and was extensively reworked for the second edition.

The second edition was published in Amsterdam in 1708. According to Osselton (1973: 77), Sewel's revisions in this edition were significant and included a large number of minor modifications and improvements. In the English–Dutch section of the dictionary, more than twenty per cent of the English word-list was replaced; for every two new entries an existing one was deleted. Sewel made use of the sixth edition of Edward Phillips's dictionary, *The New World of Words* (1706), which had been revised by John Kersey. His debt to this work is substantial; about one entry in twenty clearly comes from this source, most notably political, ecclesiastical, literary, and technical vocabulary. In the Dutch–English section the number of entries is almost double what it was in the first edition. More than half of the new entries are common and familiar words taken—along with many of the accompanying definitions—from the Dutch–French dictionary of Pieter Marin, published in 1701.

No other edition of the dictionary appeared during Sewel's lifetime. The third edition was published in 1727 and reprinted in 1735. There were few changes from the previous edition. The English–Dutch part contained more quotations from the Bible and a number of terms related to publishing. In the Dutch–English section, certain geographical names were added (Osselton 1973: 87).

The fourth edition was published in 1749, also with minimal alteration; the English–Dutch part contained some new entries gleaned from the second edition of Nathan Bailey's *Dictionarium Britannicum* (1736) (Osselton 1973: 88). These were mainly technical terms, hard words, and bookish Latinisms. A fifth edition appeared in 1754, again essentially unchanged from the previous edition.

The sixth edition, revised by Egbert Buys, 'counsellor of their Polish and Prussian Majesties', as noted on the title page, was published in Amsterdam in 1766. Buys stated in the preface that he included a certain number of words not found in Sewel's dictionary along with others from his reading in English and a certain number from dictionaries by Littleton, Boyer, Marin, and Halma. As Osselton has noted (1973: 90), the 1764 edition of Abel Boyer's *Dictionnaire royal* was the principal source for the additions. The Dutch–English section of the dictionary was also considerably enriched. With all of this new material, the sixth edition of Sewel's dictionary presents a relatively faithful image of the vocabulary of the seventeenth and eighteenth centuries.

4.7.2 Samuel Hull Wilcocke

In 1798, in London, Samuel Hull Wilcocke published *A New and Complete Dictionary of the English and Dutch Languages* based on Willem Sewel's dictionary. The book targeted travellers, sailors, merchants, and colonists, with a convenient format and at a reasonable price. In fact, it was the first English–Dutch dictionary in small format. The lexicographer stated he had retained all the primary words in Sewel's dictionary, except for a few, and had enriched it with a number of words not found in the work of his predecessor. At the same time he had avoided the phrases and explanations that made the former dictionary voluminous and expensive. Working on the principle that dictionaries were usually used for translation from rather than into a foreign language, only equivalents for each word or each meaning had been provided.

An examination of the English–Dutch section of Wilcocke's dictionary shows that it contains far fewer entries than did Sewel's original 1691 edition (Osselton 1973: 96). It does, however, include some new entries, which the lexicographer said he had taken from the dictionaries by Johnson (1755)[3] and Sheridan (1797), as well as from Barclay (1792) and the pocket dictionary by Entick (1796). As for the Dutch–English part of the dictionary, Wilcocke stated he used the eighth edition (1773) of Marin's Dutch–French dictionary, Johannis De Wilde's Dutch–Latin

[3] According to Osselton (1973: 96, note 12), Wilcocke could have used any edition published before 1796.

dictionary (Binnart 1744), and a glossary of technical terms and obsolete words by Lodewyk Meijer (1745). There are more additions in this section, mostly Latinisms (Osselton 1973: 96–7).

4.7.3 *John Holtrop*

Most likely foreign born, John Holtrop moved to Dordrecht shortly before his first marriage and obtained Dutch citizenship after he remarried in 1759. He died in 1792 (Scheurweghs 1960: 141–2).

In 1789, the *New English and Dutch Dictionary* by John Holtrop was published in Dordrecht. It was an English–Dutch dictionary for settlers and merchants. The Dutch–English part of the dictionary was published only in 1801, but Holtrop was able to begin work on it before his death. According to Scheurweghs (1960: 142), Holtrop most likely produced his dictionary at the request of his son, the printer William Holtrop.

Approximately eight out of every ten entries in the English–Dutch section of the dictionary are included in the 1766 edition of Sewel's dictionary. As for the new entries, approximately two-thirds were taken from Johnson's dictionary (1786) and others possibly come from Bailey's dictionaries (1736) (Osselton 1973: 102–4). Holtrop reworked the internal organization of the articles, indicating parts of speech, rewriting definitions and providing accentuation for the pronunciation of vowels in English (Osselton 1973: 101). As for the Dutch–English section, the 1766 edition of Sewel's dictionary also formed the basis for the Dutch word-list. One seventh of the entries were omitted, mostly variant spellings or self-explanatory derivatives but also certain less common—regional, obsolescent, or foreign—words. Most of the additions were taken from Pieter Marin's Dutch–French dictionary (1787). On the whole, the Dutch vocabulary was treated more fully than in previous dictionaries and, as in the English–Dutch part, meanings were more clearly distinguished and the articles better structured (Osselton 1973: 106).

4.8 CONCLUSION

The end of the seventeenth century and the beginning of the eighteenth saw the compilation of the first large-scale fully bilingual dictionaries in which English was one of the languages. Bilingual dictionaries were aimed at a wide and diverse readership, and compilation often took place within an intensively competitive climate. Fresh challenges, including the treatment of current usage, led to the development of new and more effective lexicographic methods. By trial and error—with attention mercilessly drawn to error by competitors and successors—lexicographers during this period succeeded in producing bilingual dictionaries whose form and presentation of entries correspond to a large extent to those of today. Ainsworth, Boyer, and Sewel—to mention only three leading figures—greatly contributed to improving a model that would prove its worth in the centuries to come. Whereas the readership for English–Latin dictionaries would henceforth be limited mainly to students of Latin, bilingual dictionaries in which English was combined with another national language would see their markets expand indefinitely, a growth which, in its turn, would promote further innovation and creativity.

5

BILINGUAL DICTIONARIES OF THE NINETEENTH AND TWENTIETH CENTURIES[1]

Carla Marello

5.1 INTRODUCTION: ENGLISH BECOMES A WORLD LANGUAGE

BY the end of the nineteenth century English had gained considerable ground as the international language of commerce and travel, and the number of general- and special-purpose bilingual dictionaries compiled for non-English speakers had correspondingly increased. The language began gradually to take on the role of *the* language in which to write in order to reach an international audience of scholars and businessmen. French still played a similar role as the international language of culture and diplomacy and, as a matter of fact, during the nineteenth and twentieth centuries bilingual dictionaries of English and French published in Great Britain (and meant to serve an English-speaking audience) exceeded by far those pairing English with other European languages also spoken outside Europe, such as Spanish and Portuguese.

A complex of well-known factors determined in the twentieth century the worldwide expansion of English: bilingual dictionaries with English mirror such a development, and American production of bilingual dictionaries featuring European languages also increased. Already noticeable in the nineteenth century was the larger coverage of American English words in such dictionaries, meeting

[1] The author would like to thank Anthony Cowie for his comments.

the needs both of new American citizens migrating from Europe, and of the French- and Spanish-speaking communities inside the borders of the USA or in neighbouring countries.

The 1960 Bloomington (Indiana) Conference on Lexicography (Householder and Saporta 1962) and European metalexicographical debate originating with Ščerba (1940) and Quemada (1967) brought about changes in European bilingual dictionary design and production. We are still experiencing the benefits of these influences, also of their long-term effects on experimental research into dictionary use and users, and we are as a result provided with effective analytical tools for evaluating bilingual dictionaries (Steiner 1984; Hausmann and Werner 1991; Béjoint and Thoiron 1996; Atkins 2002).

5.2 ENGLISH AND LATIN

By the beginning of the nineteenth century, Latin had lost a great part of its function as a language of culture in favour of national languages. In the first half of the nineteenth century, we still find scientific reports written in Latin, above all in the fields of the natural sciences, anatomy, and medicine, with the aim of reaching an international audience. Gradually, however, the study of Latin lost this communicative use, without altogether losing its cultural function. Dictionaries combining Latin and a national modern language testified to the improvements that had taken place in historical and comparative linguistics and remained the keys to accessing classical literature.

Ethan Allen Andrews (1787–1858) published in 1852 a Latin–English dictionary which was a condensed version of the *Wörterbuch der lateinischen Sprache* compiled by the German philologist Wilhelm Freund. Andrews's dictionary met with great success in the USA, and in British colleges, often in abridged editions. *A Latin Dictionary* (1879) by Charlton Thomas Lewis (1834–1904) and Charles Lancaster Short (1821–86), of 2,019 pages, was based on Andrews's dictionary 'revised, enlarged, and in great part rewritten' by Lewis and Short, as stated in the Advertisement.[2] *An Elementary Latin Dictionary* (also called *Elementary Lewis*) was an abridged version, published in 1891, for the use of students.

The Oxford Latin Dictionary, planned in 1931, appeared in its first fascicle in 1968 and its eighth and final one in 1982, when it was also made available in a single bound volume. It is based on a reading of the Latin sources (it boasts over

[2] The dictionary's full text is available online from the Perseus Project. http://www.perseus.tufts.edu.

1,000,000 quotations), whereas Lewis and Short had brought together material from older dictionaries. *The Oxford Latin Dictionary* covers classical Latin with entries for approximately 40,000 words. It does not include pagan and Christian writers after AD 200, these being covered by Lewis and Short. There was a corrected reprint in 1996, edited by P. G. W. Glare.

J. F. Niermeyer's *Mediae Latinitatis Lexicon Minus*, completed in 1976 by C. van de Kieft after Niermeyer's death, has become a standard reference work for medieval usage. In recent editions on CD-ROM (2004), all headwords are defined in English, French, and German. Beside these works for scholars, we should mention the *Pocket Oxford Latin Dictionary* (1994), designed for students, with Latin words added from the writings of Plautus and Terence, and from the study of writings belonging to the so-called Silver Latin period. This work was edited by James Morwood, as was the *Oxford Latin Minidictionary* (1995). The *Follett World-Wide Latin Dictionary, Latin–English/English–Latin* (1967) was an attempt to coin Latin words for modern objects. Similar attempts are also periodically made by other bodies which foster a return to Latin as an international auxiliary language. Recent English–Latin dictionaries of modern terms can be found on the Internet.

5.3 ENGLISH AND GREEK

German philological work played an important role, also, in ensuring a surviving market for Greek–English dictionaries. Henry George Liddell (1811–98) and Robert Scott (1811–87) based their great *Greek–English lexicon*, first published in 1843, on the fourth edition (1831) of Franz Passow's *Handwörterbuch der griechischen Sprache*. As Collison (1982: 132) remarks of the former, 'words beginning with the same element were usually grouped together, an arrangement that impeded or delayed reference from time to time.' A *Supplement* edited by E. A. Barber was published in 1968 and a revised edition appeared in 1996. Liddell and Scott included Latin and Semitic words in Greek form but did not cover Byzantine and Patristic literature. G. W. H. Lampe began compiling in 1961 a *Patristic Greek Lexicon* (completed in 1968), including all words of Greek Christian writers to AD 800 not treated or poorly treated in Liddell and Scott's ninth edition (1925–40). W. F. Arndt and F. W. Gingrich prepared an adaptation of W. Bauer's Greek–German Dictionary (1949–52, 1958), which was published in Cambridge and Chicago with the title *A Greek–English Lexicon of the New Testament and Other Early Christian Literature* (1957; 1979). J. P. Louw and

E. A. Nida edited for the United Bible Societies a *Greek–English Lexicon Based on Semantic Domains* (1988).

For beginners there is the *Pocket Oxford Classical Greek Dictionary* (2002) edited by James Morwood and John Taylor. It has 20,000 Greek words and phrases, and of course narrower coverage (4,000 words) in the English–Greek part; for intermediate students there is the *Intermediate Greek Lexicon Founded upon the Seventh Edition of Liddell and Scott's Greek–English Lexicon* (1963).

5.4 ENGLISH AND FRENCH

The number of new bilingual dictionaries appearing in the early nineteenth century and featuring English—and of updated editions of eighteenth-century dictionaries—certainly bore witness to an enlarged market and an increased demand for treatment of the up-to-date *standard* language and for colloquial usage, since dictionaries are used in everyday situations and not only for reading literature or philosophical works.

For instance, in the Preface (signed 'the editors') of L. Ph. R. Fenwick De Porquet's dictionary (1832—by 1856 it had reached its tenth edition), we read: 'We have unsparingly omitted the provincialism both in French and English; ... we have simply given the UNIVERSAL LANGUAGE, – a term by which liberal and generous minds throughout Europe have been pleased to do honour to our nation; and upon this we have imprinted the genius and true nature, the taste and spirit, of the French language of the Nineteenth Century' which 'has benefited by the invigorating impulse of political convulsions and national agitation.'

Though most bilingual dictionaries have two parts, we find Gasc's dictionary (1873; printed in London and reprinted in Great Britain till the end of the century) composed of just the French–English part, and the author declares that he 'does not bind himself to issue an English–French Dictionary'. It is a clear sign that in Great Britain at that point there was a larger market for reading French texts than for writing in, or translating into, that language (1873: 595).

5.4.1 'A just and agreeable pronunciation of the English tongue: a Herculean labour' (Smith 1814).

Correct pronunciation of English and French was a problem for teachers of both as foreign languages. Boyer's *Royal Dictionary Abridged* (1700) broke new ground in that it included primary stress marks on English words, a practice which would become generalized later in monolingual English dictionaries and in bilingual dictionaries combining English with Italian, Dutch, and Spanish. The most influential pronouncing norms and systems of respelling in late eighteenth- and early nineteenth-century bilingual dictionaries were those of Walker (1791) for English and those of the French Academy and Abbé D'Olivet for French.

Chambaud (1805) followed Walker and gave for **fence** the pronunciation (fĕn'ce); Tarver (1847), modelling himself on Tardy (1811), and Spiers (1846) also imitated the Walker system. It is worth noting that in Tardy the pronunciation transcriptions for headwords such as **alonger**, **éloigner** are as for the pronominal **s'alonger**, **s'éloigner**. An interesting case of usage pronunciation winning out against the artificial reduction of the **se** in the headword.

Smith (1814) grouped French words, flanked by an English equivalent, according to their initial and final sounds and number of syllables. We find **bonbance**, **constance**, **contenance**; **auvent**, **content**, **onguent**; **couche**, **bouche**, **mouche**, **souche**, **rouche**; **doute**, **route**. Of course, he also provided an alphabetical index so that users could retrieve words from where they were located. Spiers (1846) has at the bottom of each page a reminder of the use of diacritic systems for representing vowel qualities: a device shared also by other dictionaries of all dimensions and of different language pairs.[3] We find printed in quite a small font size:

1 2 3 4 1 2 3 1 2 3 4 1 2 3 4 5 1 2 3 4 5
Fate, fat, far, fall. Me, met, her. Fine, fin, sir, vanity. No, not, nor, oil, cloud. Tube, tub, bum, rule, bull.

English pronunciation is so difficult for non-English speakers that even modest pocket dictionaries need to provide some indications. But it is not easy either to teach French nasal sounds to English speakers. J. Ch. Tarver, 'French Master at Eaton [sic] and French Master of Prince George of Cambridge', as we read in the frontispiece of his dictionary (1858), mentions 'the thousand obstacles the teacher has to face to fight the consonant sounds produced by English students of French' (1858: xi).

In the second half of the century, numbers above vowels were abandoned in favour of other systems, slightly less complex to print, using non-numerical diacritics and more easily readable. Weller (1863), Professor of English at the

[3] Boyer's edition published in Boston (1822, 1825, and with the addition of Abbé Tardy's transcriptions, Spiers and Surenne's *The Standard Pronouncing Dictionary of the French and English Languages* (New York 1873), have the pronunciation keys strung at the top of the page. Fleming and Tibbins (edition of 1844), Triebel (1923), and William (1929) present pronunciation keys running at the bottom of the page; William (1929) adopts the Stormonth system.

Athenaeum and Episcopal College of Bruges, offers an 'English Pronouncing Dictionary' in the front matter of his dictionary, where he uses a representation somewhat simpler than Walker's. Consider some of the respellings clearly directed at French-speaking people:

(1) **Aborigenes** éb'-o-ridj-i-n'z **Acclaime** ak-kléme'

(2) **Thank** tshan'gk **That** tzhate **Tradition** tra-dich'-eune

It is not by chance that a group of English and French language teachers developed, in 1888, the International Phonetic Alphabet (IPA), a standardized method of phonetic transcription (→ Collins and Mees, Vol. II). Surveys of phonetic indications in English dictionaries are devoted to monolingual dictionaries (Wells 1985, Bronstein 1986). The first multi-purpose monolingual dictionary to adopt IPA, the *Idiomatic and Syntactic English Dictionary* (1942), was aimed at learners of English as a foreign language. Bilingual lexicographers outside Great Britain, pressed by teaching necessity, adopted the IPA earlier, as the 1938 German and English dictionary, revised by K. Wildhagen, shows.

By the beginning of the 1960s, almost every bilingual dictionary featuring English had English headwords flanked by IPA phonetic transcriptions. The few not having it were children's bilingual dictionaries and those produced in the USA and Great Britain, which not only adopted respelling for English and American headwords but also for headwords in foreign languages. CD-ROM versions of bilingual dictionaries—containing recorded pronunciation which you can easily activate by clicking on the loudspeaker symbol—caused IPA transcriptions to disappear from paper dictionaries. Since their CD-ROM editions speak, bilingual paper dictionaries remain dumb.

When a phonetic transcription is present (in the IPA or some other system) it is generally positioned after the headword. If it is not present, the headword may carry primary stress and some other features (division into syllables, vowel length) which do not prevent the user from reading the spelling of the headword.

Phonetic indications in an encoding dictionary are more conveniently placed after the translation equivalent, but when the microstructure gives many equivalents it becomes impossible to give the phonetic transcriptions of each equivalent. Therefore, they are given in the L2–L1 part of the dictionary, where the equivalent is in headword position.

5.4.2 *Recent French and English dictionaries*

Truly bilingual dictionaries are Ledésert's *Harrap's New Standard* (1972) and *Robert Collins* (1978), edited by B. T. S. Atkins, A. Duval, and R. C. Milne. The latter was remarkably successful in balancing readability and in-depth description of equivalents. American idioms and spelling on one side, and French-Canadian idioms and 'the notoriously slippery area of French slang' on the other, have been given special attention. The user has to follow style labels to find out whether a word is formal, informal, literary, vulgar, dated, or euphemistic. The editorial decision to omit uncommon words and specialized terms and meanings in favour of 'more colloquial usage than any other French–English dictionary' has enabled the publishers to claim coverage of '222,000 references and 460,000 translations' in the edition of 1987 and '820,000 entries and translations' in the last updated edition of 2006, known as the *HarperCollins Robert.* A seventy-six-page 'Language in Use' section, which deals with ways of expressing ideas in both languages, recalls the goals and methods of the sixteenth-century 'conversation books' by Noël de Berlaimont and Claude de Sainliens (Quemada 1967). The *Hachette-Oxford*, edited by Corréard and Grundy, is also a large dictionary, first published in 1994 and revised in 2001. It includes collocates in both parts (for discussion of exemplification of these, see 5.5).

5.5 ENGLISH AND ITALIAN

Baretti's celebrated *Dictionary of the English and Italian Languages* was published in London in 1760 (→ CORMIER). There were numerous updatings and reprints up until 1928. The dictionary had received a major revision in 1854 by J. Davenport and G. Comelati, Davenport having previously collaborated with S. E. Petronj to compile a new dictionary. In that work (Petronj and Davenport 1824), both Italian and English headwords and translation equivalents were marked with a primary accent. French equivalents were rather casually added, though with no pronunciation indicated, nor change of gender signalled.

(3) **fiúme**, s.m. a riv'er: fleuve, rivière.

A succession of works then appeared, such as Meadows (1834), Millhouse (1849, 1853), and James and Grassi (1854), all stigmatized by O'Connor (1991) as popular, comprehensive but relying too much on Baretti's limited and dated English list of words and on D'Alberti's (1797, 1805) for the Italian side. Melzi (1892) used for the Italian word-list his Italian–French dictionary, and for the English list a bilingual dictionary with French, possibly that of Spiers (1846). His work is marred by many false friends and near translations: 'inaccurate translation into the target language was to become one of the most noticeable shortcomings of the lexicographers who followed immediately after him' (O'Connor 1991: 2972).

Edgren (1902) added the etymology of Italian headwords and included Americanisms. Lysle (1913, 1915) and Spinelli (1929, 1930) were designed for Italians, therefore their meaning discriminations were in Italian on both sides. Hoare (1915) was intended for the English speaker, and therefore his Italian–English side is much bigger than the English–Italian.

After the Second World War the Italian lexicographical scene was overflowing with bilingual dictionaries featuring English. Hazon (1961, updated 2006) was the best seller among medium-sized dictionaries till Ragazzini (1967, constantly updated) appeared and gradually established itself. Barbara Reynolds's *Cambridge Italian Dictionary* (1962) is, on the contrary, mainly intended for English readers of Italian literature; its English–Italian part was compiled much later, in 1981.[4]

While other dictionaries group phraseology according to meaning and in a section which follows immediately after the suggested translation equivalent, Sansoni–Harrap (1970) and Sani (1974) do not. They give all the equivalents divided and numbered corresponding to their different meanings (possibly explained through meaning discriminators) at the top of the microstructure. Then, examples and idioms are arranged below according to some formal arrangement, such as, for instance, alphabetical order of the head of the characterizing phrase in the example or idiom or of the most semantically significant word when it is not the head of the phrase (see Marello 1989: 77–98 and 5.7.2, 5.7, in this chapter).

Skey (1978) has the English–Italian part based on the second edition of the *Oxford Advanced Learner's Dictionary* (1963) with adaptations to suit the Italian learner. For example, it deals prominently with phrasal verbs, listing them as separate subentries.

The publishing house of Paravia first launched the Passerini Tosi dictionary in 1989. This later became the *Oxford-Paravia* (2001; second edition 2006). The English–Italian section was based on the *Oxford-Hachette French Dictionary* (third edition), and the examples given 'come from OUP's vast electronic corpus'. The word-list and examples in the Italian–English part come from the research involved in preparing the innovative Italian monolingual dictionary by T. De Mauro (2000). The *Oxford Paravia* introduces collocates, 'words that frequently appear together with the headword, thereby forming typical combinations that a native speaker would consider "natural"'. We can then see how the Italian team at Paravia mirrors the microstructure design of the *Oxford Hachette English-French Dictionary* and renders the interplay between meaning discriminators (within

[4] And, in 1985, the publishing house of Signorelli prepared an edition updated and revised for Italian users.

parentheses) and collocates (within square brackets). See the microstructure of the Italian adj. **forte** and, on the English side, the entry for **hard.**

(4) **forte** agg. 1. *(potente)* [*persona, paese, cannocchiale*] powerful; [*economia*] strong; [*moneta*] strong, hard; ... 3. *(moralmente)* [*persona, carattere, personalità*] forceful, strong, rugged; ... 4. *(accanito)* [*mangiatore*] hearty ... ***essere un~ bevitore*** to be a hard *o* heavy drinker ... 6. *(intenso)* [*rumore, musica, urlo, suono*] loud; [*colore*] deep, bright; ...

(5) **hard** adj ... 2. *(difficult, complex)* [*problem, question, puzzle, bargaining, negotiations*] difficile, complesso ... 3. *(harsh, unpleasant)* [*life, childhood, year*] difficile; [*blow, knock*] FIG. duro, brutto; [*climate, winter*] rigido ... ***this is a~ world*** viviamo in un mondo difficile.

Examples may or may not include the equivalent suggested; therefore there is interplay also with examples. In the *Oxford-Paravia*, grammatical, semantic, and usage notes appear at the beginning of the entries on a grey background. Cultural notes such as those devoted to *Academy Awards, Independence Day, Quango*, are located at the appropriate alphabetical positions in the word-list and are in Italian in the English–Italian section, in English in the Italian–English section. (See also *CartaSì, Palio di Siena, Stellone.*)

Picchi (1999) is innovative in his treatment of syntactic information; it will be noted how first the verb patterns are inserted—in the Italian–English section—according to the traditional Italian scheme transitive (A), intransitive (B), reflexive (C). But then the B pattern is subdivided according to whether the verb is followed by a prepositional phrase (V(+*su*)+IN) or some other construction.

(6) **pesare** A *vt* V+D(+IN) *1* (= *misurare il peso di*) to weigh,... **2** (= *valutare/soppesare, fig*) to judge... *B aus* avere o essere *vi 1* V(+IN) to weigh;... **2** V+IN (+INF) (= *essere gravoso, fig*) to *be heavy (...) *3* V(+*su*) + IN (= *ripercuotersi/essere importante*) to weigh, to impinge... *4* V+ *su*+ IN (= *incombere*) to *hang (over), to loom,... *C* **pesarsi** *vr* V+RIF(+IN) to weigh oneself.
(After Picchi 1999.)

5.6 ENGLISH AND SPANISH

5.6.1 *Nineteenth-century dictionaries*

In 1802, Henry Neumann's *A New Dictionary of the Spanish and English Languages* was published in London. In his preface Neumann admitted having 'particular recourse' to Connelly and Higgins (→ Cormier). The 1817 edition kept the two sections more in balance than the previous one, which had about 40,000 Spanish headwords compared with 25,000 English headwords. In 1823, the same 1817 edition was issued by a different firm of publishers, who added the name of Baretti to the title page.[5] A true revision was later made by Mateo Seoane y Sobral—a physician from Salamanca and political refugee in England (1831)—and printed by Longman, Rees, and Co.

Seoane, Neumann, and Baretti's work was revised by Mariano Velázquez de la Cadena, a professor of the Spanish language at Columbia University, who published it in 1852. Velásquez's *Pronouncing Dictionary*, incidentally, was reprinted till 1900 with the collaboration of Juan S. Iribas and E. Gray.

A compilation by Lopes and Bensley was published in 1878 by Garnier Frères in Paris. The dictionary ought to have been completed by F. Corona Bustamante, who had produced for Garnier, in the same year, a *Diccionario abreviado*. Corona Bustamante, however, did not get beyond page 240 and so Lopes edited the English–Spanish part, while Bensley produced the Spanish–English. The Spanish Preface expresses warm approval of what today's applied linguists call 'inter-comprehension', a mainly receptive knowledge of foreign languages, whereby everyone can 'write in his/her own mother tongue and understand the answer in another language'.

5.6.2 *Twentieth-century dictionaries*

5.6.2 (i) Arturo Cuyás

In 1903, a new Spanish–English and English–Spanish dictionary appeared from the New York publishers Appleton. Edited by Arturo Cuyás, it contained 'more than four thousand modern words and twenty thousand senses (*acepciónes*), idioms, and technical terms not in the latest edition of any similar work'. Cuyás adopted as a ground-work the Funk and Wagnalls *Standard Dictionary* (1893–1985) for English and the thirteenth edition (1899) of the Dictionary of the Royal Spanish Academy, but he included also words used in the Philippine Islands and, above all, in the Latin-American countries. Consider, for example:

(7) **Tiquin** [te-keen'], m. (Philip.) bamboo pole used in place of oars.

(8) **tortilla** f. dim. omelet; (Mex.) pan-cake.

And, as a further indication of the interest in Spanish after the war of 1898 between the United States and Spain, the author declares: 'The ties that now bind

[5] The so-called Neumann and Baretti was reprinted by a Boston firm and sold till the middle of the century.

to the United States several million people whose vernacular is the Spanish language have been kept steadily in view during the preparation of the work, which is intended to be as helpful to the American or English student of Spanish as to the great number of Spaniards who are now studying English.'

As illustrative examples of the exhaustiveness of Cuyás's work, the reader is referred to such words as the following—many being 'core' vocabulary items: *á, de, con, por, que, le, se, nos, ese, uno; dar, hacer, coger, estar, correr, echar, ser, salir, seguir, poner, tirar, ver, venir; llave, medio, fuerza, ropa, tiro, título, viga, vida.* On the English side the reader is referred to the entries for the combining forms *electr-* (30), *hydr-*, *micro-* (24), *photo-*.

Steiner (1991: 2952) mentions other American and South-American bilingual dictionaries with Spanish but none deserves the attention which has to be paid to the dictionaries of Edwin B. Williams.

5.6.2 (ii) Edwin B. Williams

One of the outstanding features of the English–Spanish dictionary edited by Edwin B. Williams (1955) is the close attention given to 'meaning discriminators'. The Explanatory Notes (p. vi) clearly state which meaning discriminator has to be chosen to particularize a given part of speech: 'The particularizing word or phrase may be (a) a noun (to particularize the meaning of an adjective), (b) a noun in apposition (to particularize the meaning of another noun), (c) a direct object (to particularize the meaning of a verb), (d) a subject (to particularize the meaning of a verb), (e) an adjectival expression (to particularize the meaning of a noun), or (f) an adverbial expression (to particularize the meaning of a verb).' Meaning discriminators were also used in the nineteenth century—Spiers in his Préface (p. x) dealt with such 'moyens de distinction', or 'means of discrimination'—but Williams focuses attention on their grammatical nature and on the language in which they should be indicated: he placed them before the target word and in the source language, i.e. the language of the headword, to serve both communities while encoding in L2 (see also 5.5 and 5.7.2). Meaning discriminators have generally been adopted in bilingual dictionaries since the second part of the twentieth century, but when they are not in a substitutive relation (such as synonyms or hyperonyms) with the headword and 'particularize' the headword via a combinatorial relation, as in 5.5 **forte** *(moralmente)*, lit. **strong** *(morally)*, they are not always easily distinguishable from collocates, especially in the case of headwords which are verbs or adjectives.[6]

[6] Bilingual discriminators, on the contrary, did not spread. Iannucci (1962) gives two examples of microstructures using French and English. In the first, bilingual discriminators precede the target word: '**nice** adj. (delightful – *charmant*) joli; (delicate – *délicat*) délicat, fin; (exact – *correct*) exact, juste'. In the second, they are in front in the source language and they follow the target word in the target language: '**ouverture** (d'un objectif) (*n.f.*), aperture (of a lens); (d'une caverne) (*n.f.*), mouth (of a cave)'.

The pronunciation of all English words listed in the dictionary is shown by means of a simplified adaptation of the IPA. All English compound words are listed as separated entries. Multiword Spanish expressions (i.e. idioms and the like) are listed as subentries. E. B. Williams took account of 'considerations of frequency and range' when deciding the words to be listed. He expanded the dictionary in 1962–63, but in 1968 he prepared a shorter, completely new dictionary, the *Bantam New College Spanish & English Dictionary*, considered one of the best bilingual dictionaries, with regard to the handling of sense discriminations, that had ever appeared till that date.

5.6.3 *Recent large dictionaries*

During the last quarter of the twentieth century a number of very large dictionaries have appeared, including those of Gámez *et al.* (1973) for Simon and Schuster and of Colin Smith (1971) for Collins. There is also the *Oxford Spanish Dictionary*, which in its third edition has acquired collocates. The Colin Smith dictionary (first edition 1971), appeared in an eighth edition in 2005. It featured long, completely translated examples and cultural notes. It was the first large bilingual dictionary on which Collins publishers embarked and it set high standards which were maintained and indeed surpassed by the later French and English dictionary edited by Atkins *et al.* (1978). Then, in 2003, there was Chambers Harrap, which boasted 'over 400,000 translations', and had a section devoted to false friends, but also signalled false friends in the main text after the article(s) concerned.

5.7 ENGLISH AND GERMAN

German and English bilingual dictionaries continued, in the nineteenth century, to be published mainly by German publishers. Fick (1802), Hilpert (1828–45), Burckhardt (1839), Grieb (1842–47), James (1846), and Wessely (1883) were all published in Germany. Nineteenth-century German philological studies made great strides in etymology, comparative grammar and morphology, and German lexicographers often used such studies as a springboard to discuss the grouping of English and German word families, or to decide at which point to start an incomplete subentry, i.e. whether to replace by a tilde mechanically the part of the subentry that was common to the entry or to identify a root. They did the same with words prefixed by *after-*, *all-*, *demi-*, *non-*, *out-*, *self-*, *semi-*, *under-*, etc.

For German headwords, equivalents, and translations of examples, or any other German part of the microstructure, including abbreviations in both sections of the dictionary, German–English dictionaries of all sizes maintained Gothic fonts till midway through the twentieth century and even beyond. It is a feature that, added to other indications, e.g. plurals of nouns, cases in verb constructions, has made German and English dictionaries difficult to read for non-German users. German and English dictionaries printed in the US were Kunst (1840), Elwell (1850), Grab (1897), and Adler (1848, 1857, 1902). Adler's dictionary, which first appeared in 1848, was based on Flügel, and also made 'free use' of the most recent works of its day, including those of Hilpert, Grieb, and others. In their revised edition, Foster and Althaus expunged obsolete words, introduced new words and new meanings brought to lexicographers by 'the wonderful progress of the arts and sciences', and dropped the *to* in English verb headwords and the second *s* in German words ending in *-nis(s)*.

In Adler (1902), the explanatory section of entries for nouns, adjectives, and verbs contained a separate part introduced by the abbreviation *Syn.*(onyms). **Schärfen**, for instance, had a *Syn.* part in which one might read: 'We *schärfen* that which is still blunt and not able to cut; we *wetzen* that which already cuts, but which we wish to cut better; and that which we *schleifen* not only is *schärfer*, but it becomes also smoother and more polished, or acquires the particular form we wish to give it.' In the English–German section of Adler's dictionary the *Syn.* part is not present and this indicates that Adler's dictionary was meant for American users.

Grab's 164-page pocket dictionary of 1897 boasts of its 'Thoroughness and Accuracy, by using the best results obtained from the lifelong works of the greatest philologists in German–English, the Grimm Brothers and Noah Webster'. But behind its impressive frontispiece there is a one word–one equivalent dictionary. It contains a few tables with sketches of Buildings, Animals, a Telegraph machine and a Telephone, and so on. Its Chicago publishers, Laird & Lee, claim that their 'long experience in preparing reference books for the masses has taught [them] the best methods to follow in the construction of standard works for everyday use'. Illustrated dictionaries are popular in German lexicographic production, which has always, in addition, cherished an encyclopedic approach to compiling language dictionaries. Muret and Sanders (1891–1901) is the best-known encyclopedic English and German dictionary, similar in its design to a classical language–modern language dictionary.

Baedeker's *Conversation Dictionaries* contain bilingual or multilingual lists of words. The German tradition for Reiseführer and Reisewörterbuch ('travelling companion book', 'globetrotter dictionary'), in bilingual and multilingual editions with English, is renowned: in 1889, a four-language edition, English, French, German, Italian, was published. Also other publishers offered similar works, but the Baedeker trademark was so famous that in some languages it became a common name for 'travelling companion book'.

5.7.1 *J. G. Flügel* A Complete Dictionary of the English and German Languages *(1830)*

The most impressive English–German dictionary of the first half of the nineteenth century was that of J. G. Flügel (1830, 1847–56). His prefaces to the first, second, and third editions, plus introduction, are written both in English and in German and displayed in two columns: these are true essays, each of more than fifty pages.

Flügel starts with a criticism of previous dictionaries. In a note (p. vi), he makes a comparison between the number of entries, at letter A, in his dictionary and in other large dictionaries, both monolingual and bilingual, such as Hilpert, and shows that his own section contains 5,097 entries, or at least 1,000 more than the others. In total, the dictionary contains 30,000 words more than the (monolingual) Johnson-Todd, including the compounds. He has inserted obsolete terms as far back as Chaucer, and American words and phrases, because 'the works of the ingenious authors of the new world in our days are read with so much delight but are new and foreign to the German translators' (p. vii). Flügel, a United States consul, had had close contact over 'twenty years with English, Scotch and Irish of all classes, a residence of ten years in America'. He had studied the English classics and he made use of nearly one hundred dictionaries.

In the second edition (p. xii), Flügel remarks that he has increased the size of the dictionary by about 5,000 words and 7,000 compound words. A great part of the Preface is devoted to defending his pronunciation guide from the criticism received. We gather from his defence that he was concerned to recommend the 'right' model of English pronunciation and about the best way of presenting it. In the preface to the third edition much space is devoted to denouncing the plagiarism of C. A. Feiling and A. Heimann (1841) in 'adapt[ing for] the English Student' Flügel's second edition. Together with his son Felix, Flügel also prepared a shorter *Praktisches Wörterbuch der englischen und deutschen Sprache* (1839) and in 1891 Felix prepared the completely revised fourth edition, which was to remain in print till 1912.

5.7.2 *Elizabeth Weir (1889) pioneer in meaning discriminations*

Elizabeth Weir is one of the few women to lead a lexicographic team in the nineteenth century. She worked in Stuttgart and prepared her 'handy volume' for the publisher Cassell, aiming specifically at English students. She was aware that 'English–German dictionaries, being for the most part compiled by Germans, had not provided for the difficulty which the English student feels when called on to select from some dozen German words the special one which answers to the sense in which the English word is to be used' (p. v). In her remarkably clear *Explanation of method*, she explained that words etymologically related, and having an initial syllable or syllables in common, are grouped under this initial syllable or syllables. In the English–German section of the work 'every new sense in which a word is taken is either preceded by an English synonym bracketed in italics, as *to doom* (*sentence*) **verurtheilen**, (*destine*) **bestimmen**. Or it is followed by some explanatory word or phrase which, when a completion of the idea of the preceding word, is bracketed in roman type, as to do, **erweisen** (kindness); when not a completion, in italics, as to drivel, **geifern** (*as infants*); in place of a synonym, a word is occasionally preceded by an explanatory clause in italics, as to drink (*of beasts*) **saufen**' (p.viii). Meaning discrimination through substitution relation, as in *doom/sentence*, or through explanation, e.g. *as infants [do]*, or collocates as in *erweisen–kindness* ('to show kindness') are there and given in English, the mother tongue of the students who are expected to use the dictionary to translate into German.

5.7.3 Modern German and English dictionaries

In the second half of the twentieth century, the production of large bilingual dictionaries for English and German consisted of an updated reprinting of Weir's dictionary, completely revised by H. T. Betteridge (1978) in England for Cassell, and of the already mentioned Muret and Sanders (1962–75) by Langenscheidt in Germany. There are also new dictionaries, such as the *Pons-Globalwörterbuch* (1983), the Collins German and English dictionary (1980), Langenscheidt's *Großwörterbuch* (1985), and the Duden-Oxford *Großwörterbuch* (1990).

Publishing houses also offer shorter, concise, and pocket editions. Note, for example, the Bantam *New College German and English Dictionary* (1981), Harrap's *Concise German and English Dictionary* (1982), and the East-German VEB dictionary (1986). As a whole, modern English–German bilingual lexicography has capitalized well on German metalexicographic research, the most developed in the world, but as Pätzold (1991: 2967) has observed: 'Lexicographers ... will have to make a more thorough analysis of structural differences between German and English.' This requirement still applies in the early twenty-first century.

5.8 ENGLISH AND DUTCH

Bilingual dictionaries combining English and Dutch have been, and still are, mainly compiled in the Netherlands for Dutch speakers. In the early nineteenth century, a prominent name was Bomhoff, whose bilingual dictionary (1822) went through five editions. Bomhoff also inaugurated the tradition of Dutch publishers having a series of four dictionaries in their catalogue: a monolingual Dutch title and three bilingual dictionaries for the languages of the neighbouring countries with the greatest number of speakers—English, French, and German. As Claes's bibliography (1980) clearly shows, in the eighteenth century, bilingual dictionaries combining French and Dutch were two times more than those with Dutch and English. In the twentieth century, English–Dutch bilingual dictionaries equal in number those combining French and Dutch.

A number of pocket English–Dutch dictionaries appeared towards the end of the nineteenth century. The well-known dictionary publisher Tauchnitz of Leipzig had printed in 1857 a new pocket dictionary which by the end of the century (1893) was also being sold in London by Hirschfeld Brothers. Of a similar format were Hill's *Vest-Pocket Dictionaries*, and in that series appeared *Hill's Miniature English–Dutch and Dutch–English Dictionary* (1908–09). The *Patriot woordeboek Patriot Dictionary* (1902–04) was the first bilingual dictionary with Afrikaans and English as language pair. Although published anonymously, we know that the editor was S. J. du Toit; it contained only 16,500 headwords but it was significant in its role of promoting 'co-operation between the leading races, English and Dutch, in South Africa', as stated in its preface. In 1908, Elffers and Viljoen had prepared a bilingual dictionary in Capetown, which in 1912 appeared as the anonymous *South African Pocket Dictionary, Dutch–English English–Dutch*, 'in simplified spelling and containing many Cape Dutch words'.[7] Kritzinger's *Woordeboek Afrikaans–Engels Engels–Afrikaans Dictionary*, first published in 1926, reached its fourteenth edition in 1997 with the title of *Groot Woordeboek Major Dictionary* and Bosman *et al.*'s *Bilingual Dictionary* English–Afrikaans (1931) and Afrikaans–Engels (1936) had its eighth edition in 1984. As a successor to Bosnam's dictionary, the publishing house Pharos published the new *Pharos Woordeboek Afrikaans–Engels English–Afrikaans* in 2005 (see Gouws 2007).

In the early twentieth century, A. Swaen edited for Harrap a large bilingual work (printed in Holland in 1933). F. Renier prepared in 1949 a compact dictionary for

[7] As Gouws (2007: 316–20) points out, such dictionaries are also an authoritative source of information about Afrikaans.

Routledge, reprinted till 1989. On the back cover it was claimed that the dictionary gave clear indications of the stylistic level of Dutch words and phrases. In the Preface the author emphasized the claim that, 'where possible, formal words and expressions in the one language have been translated by words and expressions used formally in the other. Idioms and colloquialisms have, wherever possible, been translated by idioms and colloquialisms'. Then, in 1952, F. P. H. Prick van Wely edited for Cassell an English–Dutch Dutch–English dictionary of almost 1,400 pages. A compact edition was printed in 1955.

In the second half of the twentieth century, the publisher Van Dale undertook the publication of a number of large monolingual and bilingual dictionaries with an innovative microstructure. The *Van Dale Groot woordenboek Engels–Nederlands*, a volume of almost 1,600 pages edited by W. Martin and G. A. J. Tops, appeared in 1984 and was a 'decoding' (i.e. explanatory) work for Dutch users. The Dutch–English, which appeared later, was an 'encoding' dictionary, also for Dutch users.

The microstructure is so arranged that the translations are at the top of the article, while phraseology comes after a diamond sign, and is then ordered by part of speech. Parts of speech are always assigned the same number: 1 is noun, 2 adjective, 3 verb, 4 pronoun, and so on. Therefore 1.1 is the code which signals a combination of the headword, taken in the first meaning, with a noun (interposed preposition *of* can be ignored); 3.3 means combination of the headword, taken in the third meaning, with a verb; 6.1 is a combination of the headword, taken in the first meaning, with a preposition. Since combinations with a noun are the most frequent for a headword of any part of speech, they come first. Since most headwords are nouns, combination with adjective is the second most frequent, and so on. The symbol ¶ is used in the first position when the relation of the headword is not with a particular part of speech; it is in the second position when the meaning of a combination cannot clearly be attributed to the first, second, etc., meaning. This new organization of the examples and phraseology was considered favourably by metalexicographers, because it offered a balanced mixture between formal and semantic criteria. In the electronic version linguists can appraise even more the advantages offered by the Van Dale microstructure. This, however, is confined to Van Dale dictionaries of this size: the mainstream of bilingual lexicography favours ordering by meaning and tries to convey possible combinations of the headword by means of a section of collocates kept separate from examples.

Van Dale itself publishes smaller dictionaries with usual microstructures such as M. Hannay's *Van Dale Handwoordenboek Engels–Nederlands*, a work of 988 pages which reached its third edition in 1996. In 2001, Van Dale published also the fourth edition of the *Ster Woordenboek* by N. Osselton and R. Hempelman, a bilingual dictionary with a traditional meaning-oriented microstructure. Two years later Routledge published it with the title *The New Routledge Dutch Dictionary.*

5.9 BILINGUALIZED LEARNERS' DICTIONARIES

Bilingualized learners' dictionaries are learners' dictionaries with English headwords followed by a definition in English (possibly using a restricted defining vocabulary), followed by translation equivalents in another language, usually the mother tongue of the user.[8]

In the tradition of West and Hornby (see Marello (1998) for a survey of bilingualized versions of Hornby's monolingual dictionaries) users are assumed to understand a definition in English, because it is written in a restricted defining (or at least simplified) vocabulary; therefore they should use the translation provided by bilingualized learners' dictionaries as a confirmation that the definition has been understood. Actually, observational user studies have produced evidence that beginners and intermediate students often do not understand definitions in English and jump straight away to the translation equivalent in order to understand the headword and the definition. This is all the more true when the users' mother tongue does not use the Latin alphabet.

Cowie (1999: 192–7) sums up very clearly the discussion concerning the notion of a progression within a given language-teaching programme from standard bilingual to bilingualized learners' dictionaries to fully-fledged monolingual works. Zöfgen (1991) explains the difference between a bilingualized learners' dictionary and a truly bilingual learners' dictionary and finds in the Russian tradition and in Dubois-Charlier (1980) the best instances of the second type.

The fact that bilingual dictionaries with English in the seventeenth and eighteenth centuries sporadically—or systematically, as Connelly and Higgins did in their four-volume *A New Dictionary of the Spanish and English Languages*

[8] Kernerman (2006) who, as a publisher, has in his catalogue a series of bilingualized learners' dictionaries, calls them semi-bilingual dictionaries because he is comparing the *Oxford Student's Dictionary for Hebrew Speakers* (1986), which provides a separate Hebrew translation of the English headword for each meaning of every entry, sub-entry, derivative, and idiom to the Korean bilingualization (1981) of the *Oxford Advanced Learner's Dictionary of Current English,* in which all those categories and also examples were translated into Korean. Quemada (1967: 52) was the first to use the term semi-bilingual dictionary, but he referred to vernacular–Latin dictionaries of the sixteenth century in which the headwords in the vernacular–Latin part were not true entries but phrases that interpret Latin words in specific contexts.

(1797–98) (→ Cormier)—provided definitions in the language of the headwords does not make them bilingualized dictionaries; they provided translations of part of the relevant monolingual dictionaries. Detractors asserted that definitions were provided because their authors could not find the appropriate translation equivalents; admirers praised the fact that the word was explained, giving users the chance to find themselves a good contextual translation in case the suggested equivalents were not suitable. The users who had a poor knowledge of a foreign language could not take advantage of those definitions, since it was not until the twentieth century that restricted defining vocabularies were available.

5.10 CONCLUSION

Bilingual dictionaries compiled by English lexicographers in the nineteenth century were not of exceptional quality. Dictionaries combining English and a foreign language were often commissioned by foreign publishers specializing in lexicography, notably Teubner, Brockhaus, and Langenscheidt in Berlin, and Garnier in Paris. More often still, British publishers bought dictionaries produced abroad by local publishers for their respective French, German, or Italian markets—products which were afterwards sold by those same English publishers in their hard covers, though they were not originally intended for English-speaking users.

The situation for dictionaries of the major European languages was rather stagnant in the first part of the twentieth century. The radical shift for bilingual lexicography featuring English with a European language came about as a result of the great success of monolingual learners' dictionaries and, with it, the possibility of access to electronic versions of those dictionaries (→ Nesi, Vol. II). Their databases became the starting point of a new generation of bilingual dictionaries. In the beginning, British publishing houses sold the rights to process the lists of headwords and entries of their learners' dictionaries, but then they decided to exploit the expertise accumulated when preparing large bilingual dictionaries—and began to work in co-edition with French, Spanish, and German publishers.

Bilingual dictionaries in the electronic era serve both as a starting point and as a by-product of bi- and multilingual electronic databases, as well as products which with multimedia (audio and video) aspects of an entry will reach larger and younger audiences.

6

BILINGUAL DICTIONARIES OF ENGLISH AND RUSSIAN IN THE EIGHTEENTH TO THE TWENTIETH CENTURIES

Donna M. T. Cr. Farina and George Durman

6.1 EARLY ENGLISH–RUSSIAN LEXICOGRAPHY

ENGLISH–Russian lexicography developed over more than four centuries, in conjunction with the gradual increase of commercial and cultural contacts, first between Russia and England, and much later between Russia and the United States. England's first direct contact was the landing of Richard Chancellor's ship, the *Bona Fortuna*, on the northern coast of Russia in 1553; Chancellor was immediately invited to appear at the court of Ivan the Terrible (Simmons 1964: 6). The first English translations from Russian began to appear in the sixteenth century. By contrast, the first Russian translation from English, a geometry textbook, did not appear until 1625 (Alekseev 1944: 86).

During the reign of Boris Godunov in the early seventeenth century, young Russians were sent abroad to France, Germany, and England (Ispolatov 1971: 131), but most of them never returned to Russia. Most Russians who learned English or other languages did so through limited contacts with native speakers (often merchants) living in Russia. There still exist so-called *azbukovniki* in manuscript form, compendia written by Russians studying languages, dating from mid-century.

Alekseev (1968: 4) discusses one *azbukovnik* that provides 'the content of conversations with foreigners, the nature of their interests, and preserves the originality of actual conversation'. In England, similar works are preserved in manuscript form, usually created by English people studying Russian or other languages. They include Mark Ridley's *A Dictionarie of the vulgar Russe tongue* (1996), considered 'a valuable source for the spoken language of the sixteenth century' (Cleminson 1995: 1), and Richard James's *Dictionariolum Russico–Anglicum* [Russian–English lexicon][1] of 1618–19 (Larin 1959).

Contacts with England increased during the reign of Peter the Great (1682–1725). Peter visited England in 1698 and returned with around sixty Englishmen from various fields of specialization (Simmons 1964: 57). Words of English origin began to appear in Russian books (Alekseev 1944: 86). Around the same time, the first grammar of Russian for foreigners was published in England. Heinrich Wilhelm Ludolf's *Grammatica Russica* (1696) contains a thematically organized Russian glossary as well as conversational phrases and dialogues, with Latin translations (Alekseev 1982: 45; Cleminson 1995: 2).

Russian–English contacts broadened further in the eighteenth century and the need for reference works grew. Catherine the Great and others wrote of their interest in English culture. In the 1760s, Russian students were sent to study in foreign universities, and they later became 'professors and scholars, translators, lexicographers and authors of textbooks for the study of English' (Alekseev 1944: 87–8).

The first English grammar to appear in Russian (1766) was published seventy years after the first Russian grammar was printed in England (Ispolatov 1971: 132 and ff.). The first dictionary in Russia to include English words (1763) was multilingual: *Slovar' na shesti iazykakh: Rossiiskom, Grecheskom, Latinskom, Frantsuzkom, Nemetskom i Angliskom* [A dictionary in six languages: Russian, Greek, Latin, French, German, and English]. While the title page does not name an author, some attribute it to Grigorii Poletika (Ispolatov 1971: 133). This dictionary was preceded by a variety of works that treated Latin, German, and French with Russian. Its preface identifies the 1696 trilingual dictionary of 'the famous Mr. Rei' as its predecessor; this is most likely an English–Latin–Greek dictionary by the distinguished English naturalist John Ray (1627–1705).[2] The

[1] In this chapter, square brackets are used for: English translations of foreign-language titles, translations of quotations, and parenthetical remarks. In addition, we use square brackets within examples provided from dictionaries to add clarifying information. Most frequently, this additional information is a more precise rendering of a dictionary's translational equivalents.

[2] Ray's dictionary, originally *Dictionariolum trilingue: secundum locos communes, nominibus usitatioribus Anglicis, Latinis, Graecis...*, was re-issued under the name *Nomenclator Classicus* in 1696 due to the existence of competing pirate editions from 1692 and 1694 (Cram 1991).

dictionary contains four thousand words and thirty-two themes (Ispolatov 1971: 133–4). Six columns make up a two-page spread, each column containing a different language. Within a single theme, it is not clear how (or whether) the words are organized: while Russian is the first language appearing on each two-page spread, words are not in alphabetical order in Russian or in any of the other languages.

6.2 ZHDANOV'S ENGLISH–RUSSIAN DICTIONARIES OF THE LATE EIGHTEENTH CENTURY

Nine years after the publication of the multilingual dictionary, the first bilingual English–Russian dictionary appeared (1772) as the appendix to an English grammar translated into Russian by Prokhor Zhdanov. This *Angliskaia grammatika* [English grammar] was republished in 1801. In his preface, Zhdanov notes that he has had 'the honour of having taught English for thirty years to the noble pupils of the Naval Military Academy' (1801: vi); this institution had fostered the study of English speech in Russia for more than one hundred years (Alekseev 1944: 91). As in the earlier multilingual dictionary, this bilingual work is thematic in structure. Ispolatov (1971: 135) estimates three thousand words and seventy-nine themes, including: 'Of the World in general/*O svete voobshche*' (p. 189), 'Of time/*O vremeni*' (p. 191), 'Things made use of for Clothing/*Veshchi upotrebliaemyie na plat'e*' (p. 208), 'Of Eating/*O pishche*' (p. 209), 'Of Drinking/*O pit'e*' (p. 213). Each page of the dictionary section has two columns, with the English words on the left and Russian equivalents on the right. Usually only one equivalent is provided in each language.

In 1784, Zhdanov published a new bilingual work of 30,000 words, entitled: *A New Dictionary English and Russian/Novoi slovar' angliskoi i rossiiskoi*, without numbered pages. In his preface, Zhdanov urges Russians to make an effort to learn English through his dictionary, so that they can translate 'all the best writing', which England has in greater abundance than other countries. This dictionary improves upon its predecessors in numerous respects. It is organized in alphabetical order rather than by themes. In addition, it includes grammatical information about English words, such as information about the parts of speech. Nouns are designated as 's' for substantive or *substantivum*, as in 's. Affinity (likeness). *skhodstvo, podobie*'. Verbs as well as idioms or expressions containing a verb are labeled 'v': 'v. to quack (as a duck) *Krichat' po utinomu, kriakat*'' [to cry as a duck, to clack]. The abbreviation 'p' is used for prepositions, adverbs, and phrases. This information would not be necessary for a Russian reading English texts, because the form of the Russian equivalent(s) usually makes the part of speech clear.

Zhdanov's dictionary of 1784 does more than simply list equivalents. For instance, it gives information about register: 'Gerund (in grammar) *Gerundiia (v gram.)*', 'Affirm (in law). *Podtverdit'*'. Each sense of a polysemous word is treated in a separate entry, and English synonyms or other types of explanation in parentheses help to differentiate between senses:

(1) s. chance (accid.) *Sluchai.*
  s. chance (fortune) *Shchastie, shchast'e* [happiness].
  s. chance (event) *Sluchai.*
  s. chance (hazard) *Shchast'e, udacha* [happiness, luck].

Despite the indication in his preface, Zhdanov's dictionary goes beyond the decoding function and would help Russian learners to produce English sentences.

6.3 ENGLISH–RUSSIAN DICTIONARIES OF THE NINETEENTH CENTURY

In the late eighteenth and early nineteenth century, English/Russian contact grew significantly. Some was indirect: during the reign of Catherine the Great (1762–96), knowledge of English culture was transmitted through French and German translations of English books (Simmons 1964: 82). For example, Defoe's *Robinson Crusoe* was first translated into Russian from French in 1762–64 (Simmons 1964: 140; Terras 1991: 119). The number of English teachers, governesses, and nannies in Russia increased; this is recorded in memoirs and travelogues published in Russia and in England, as well as in Russian literature. English merchants in Russia were numerous as well. Nikolai Karamzin (1792) tells how in London he encountered a group of English merchants who had gathered to speak Russian in the coffee house of the stock market; it turned out that they had lived and done business in Saint Petersburg (Alekseev 1982: 182).

Cross (1993: 27; 1997: 394) mentions *A Commercial Dictionary, in the English and Russian Languages with a Full Explanation of the Russia Trade* (1800) as the first publication in England of an English–Russian dictionary. The author, Adam Kroll, a naturalist and a British subject, was originally from Riga,

Latvia. Cross notes (1997: 394) 'The work promised more than it delivered, offering merely a sixty-page list of English words with their Russian equivalents in would-be phonetic transcriptions.' Alekseev (1944: 127) says that, until the mid-nineteenth century, there were no dictionaries, grammars, or other reference works published in England for the study of Russian; Americans and the English had to use French and German books instead.

6.3.1 Grammatin and Parenogo's dictionary

The publication of the first multi-volume English–Russian dictionary (1808–17) was a significant development in lexicography in Russia. The title page of Volume I is in both Russian and English; the English reads: '*A New Dictionary English and Russian, Composed upon the Great Dictionary English and French of M. Robinet*, by Nicholas of Grammatin, Candidate of Belles-Lettres at the Imperial University of Moscow.' Volumes II–IV add the dictionaries of Johnson and Ebers to that of Robinet as sources for the work. As author, Volumes II–IV credit 'Michel Parenogo, Counsellor of the Court'. In the preface to Volume I, Grammatin notes:

> Precise and complete dictionaries provide one of the first and most essential ways to ease the study of foreign languages.... [U]ntil now there has been no other available English dictionary except Zhdanov's, which in addition to being almost sold out in the stores, is too short and incomplete, and is useful... only for those... beginning language study.

Grammatin and Parenogo's dictionary of about 1,400 pages contains around 45,000 entries—by Ispolatov's count (1971: 138). A comparison with the preceding dictionaries shows that it is a vast improvement. While for the most part Zhdanov gives simple equivalence, in Grammatin–Parenogo many entries contain explanations of

Table 6.3.1 **(i) Nouns from Zhdanov and Grammatin–Parenogo**

Zhdanov (1784)	Grammatin (1807, Vol. I)
s. Abhorrer. *Nenavistnik* [hater].	Abhorrer, s. *kto chuvstvuet uzhas, otvrashchenie k komu nibut'* [someone who feels horror, repulsion towards someone else].
Zhdanov (1784)	**Parenogo (1811, Vol. II)**
s. Puritan. *Sviatosha, strogo nabozhnyi chelovek* [sanctimonious person, strictly religious person].	Puritan, s. *v Anglinskoi tserkve tak nazyvaetsia sekta, kotoraia khvalitsia chisteishim zakonom, chistozakonniki, puritane; v in. sm. litsemer, sviatosha, pustosviat, tartiuf* [A so-called sect in the English church, which prides itself on its pure rule, people who follow strictly the letter of the law, puritans; in other words, a hypocrite, a sanctimonious person, a vacantly pious person, a Tartuffe].

Table 6.3.1 (ii) Verbs from Zhdanov and Grammatin–Parenogo

Zhdanov (1784)	Grammatin (1807, Vol. I)
v. Abet (to encourage) ing, ed. *Pobuzhdat'*, *obodriat'* [to induce (to), to encourage].	Abet, v. a. *pooshchrit'*, *vozbudit'* [to encourage, to excite].
v. abet (to back or assist) ing, ed. *Pomogat'* [to help]	Abet, v. a. (*v Iurisprud.*) *pomogat'*, *podkrepliat'*, *vziat' ch'iu-nibud' storonu* [(in Jurisprudence) to help, to back, to take someone's side].
v. to Consider, ing, ed. *Rassuzhdat'*, *imet' pochtenie* [to reason, to have respect].	Consider, v. a. *rassmatrivat'*, *issledovat'*, *razmyshliat'*, *uvazhat'*, *pochitat'*, *voznagradit'*, *udovol'stvovat'* [to examine, to investigate, to reflect on, to respect, to honour, to reward, to satisfy].
v. to consider (requite) ing, ed. *Nagradit'* [to reward].	Consider of, v. n. *dumat'*, *sovetovat'sia*, *rassuzhdat'* [to think, to ask advice of, to reason].

meaning, either alone or in addition to an equivalent (for example, *abhorrer* and *puritan* in Table 6.3.1. (i)). Moreover, Grammatin–Parenogo regularly include multi-word units as part of the entry for one of the words within the unit.

For *abhorrer*, Zhdanov's single-word Russian equivalent does not promote full understanding of the English word: someone who hates is not the same as someone who abhors. The Grammatin–Parenogo entry for *puritan* contains many elements of interest. The explanation of meaning indicates full familiarity with English culture. The use of the abbreviation *v. in. sm.* 'in other words' shows that Grammatin–Parenogo recognized the transferred meaning of *puritan*. Volume II of the dictionary appeared in 1811. The first dictionary citation of Russian *tartiuf* 'Tartuffe' appeared in 1806;[3] so Parenogo uses it in a bilingual dictionary definition only five years later.

While Grammatin–Parenogo's dictionary made improvements in the definition of nouns, both Zhdanov and Grammatin–Parenogo achieve mixed results with English verbs. Zhdanov's system of allocating senses to separate entries seems to be applied less systematically with verbs. For example, as shown in Table 6.3.1 (ii), he assigns two meanings of *abet*—'encourage, induce' and 'assist, help'—to two entries. In the case of *consider*, he includes two distinct meanings—'reason' and 'respect'—under one entry. Then he separates the meaning 'reward'—which is closer to 'respect'—into its own entry.

Grammatin–Parenogo tended to avoid multiple entries for nouns, so that polysemy is not usually distinguished from homography. In the case of verbs, this principle does not seem to apply consistently; for example, *abet* has two

[3] See *Slovar' sovremennogo russkogo literaturnogo iazyka* [dictionary of modern standard Russian], Vol. XV, 1963, s.v. *tartiuf.*

separate entries in Grammatin. Like Zhdanov, Grammatin separates the meaning 'encourage' from 'help', but Grammatin restricts the sphere of usage for 'help' to jurisprudence. The first Grammatin entry for *consider* is more in line with that dictionary's treatment of nouns: a full series of equivalents are provided, each separated from the preceding by a comma. While the different meanings within the series are not distinguished, the ordering and progression of equivalents conveys the polysemy; the four main meanings—'examine', 'reflect', 'respect', and 'reward'—are among the meanings distinguished in the *Oxford English Dictionary* (1933). Grammatin's second entry for *consider* distinguishes the intransitive (label: *v.n.*) from the transitive meaning (label: *v.a.*).

6.3.2 *Banks's dictionary*

The next English–Russian dictionary to appear was the two-volume work of the Englishman James Banks: *A Dictionary of the English and Russian Languages/ Angliisko–russkii slovar'* (1838). Banks was well known as an active member of Moscow's English community.[4] Banks claims that he 'received but little assistance from preceding English and Russian dictionaries', but acknowledges acquaintance with the dictionaries of Zhdanov ('wholly useless to me') and Grammatin–Parenogo ('did not contain all the information required') (p. ii). More useful to Banks were two French and Russian dictionaries.[5] Press reviews of Banks's work were extremely favourable; they rated it as far superior to its predecessors and called for swift publication of the Russian–English dictionary which Banks was then preparing (Ispolatov 1971: 139; Alekseev 1944: 117–18).

Three main improvements stand out in Banks. First is the inclusion within the entry of numerous phrases containing the entryword (indicated by a dash) with their translations; for example (Vol. I):

(2) Giddy, a. *vertlianyi, vertoprashnyi* [fidgety, unstable];– brained,– headed, *legkomyslennyi* [frivolous];– head, *verchenaia golova* [flighty head];– paced, *vertkii, shatkii* [restless, unreliable];– fellow,– girl, *vertushka* [capricious boy/girl]; she is –, *u neia golova kruzhitsia* [her head is spinning] . . . .

[4] *Chronik der Evangelischen Gemeinden in Moskau* (1876, Bd. II: 136–7, 526), Moscow, as cited by Ispolatov (1971: 139, f. 33) and Alekseev (1944: 117, f. 2).

[5] While Banks does not give full information about the dictionaries he used, he most likely has in mind C. P. Reiff (1835–36). Banks probably used an earlier edition of Oldecop (1841) published in the late 1820s or early 1830s.

Another improvement is the inclusion of as many inflected forms and derivatives as possible; and finally, the very occasional indication of pronunciation; both features are exemplified in the entry for *gill* (Vol. I):

(3) Gill, (*gil'*) (in fish) *zhabra*; pl. *zhabry*, (brook) *ruchei*; a. *zhabernyi*.

Banks provides *zhabr-y*, the plural of the feminine *zhabr-a* '(fish) gill'. The adjective at the end of the entry only refers to the first equivalent, *zhabra*, and not to the second, *ruchei*. The pronunciation immediately following the entry-word was included to distinguish this word from that of the following entry with the same spelling (i.e. homograph) (Vol. I):

(4) Gill (*dzhil'*) (1/4 pint) .078 *shtofa vina* [.078 of a *shtof* or glass of wine], .095 *shtofa piva* [.095 of a *shtof* of beer]; (ground ivy) *budra*; (Juliana) *Iuliana*.

Banks divides the meanings of (3) and (4) solely according to the difference in pronunciation: two meanings ('organ of a fish' and 'brook') appear under the first entry, and three ('unit of measurement', 'ivy', and 'woman's name') under the second. All five meanings are apparently unrelated (*OED1*); there is no polysemy. Banks's use of English phrases in parentheses to distinguish meanings recalls the technique used earlier by Zhdanov. Neither Banks nor Zhdanov structured their entries to bring out semantic relationships between equivalents: while Zhdanov divided meanings into separate entries and Banks put everything together, both authors put form (both written and oral) before meaning as an organizing principle.

By including information on inflection and pronunciation, Banks goes beyond what would be necessary for reading English texts, and provides the Russian learner with encoding information for the more active use of English. This tendency in English–Russian lexicography (practised in Russia) began with Zhdanov, as indicated above.

6.3.3 *The Aleksandrov Collective's dictionary*

Drawing on the experience of its predecessors, the *Polnyi anglo–russkii slovar'/ Complete English–Russian Dictionary* was published in 1879, in two parts, under the name of A. Aleksandrov, a pseudonym for a group of Russian and English compilers ('Entsiklopedicheskii slovar' 1890: Vol. I, 384). According to the authors, an important development in their work was the treatment of pronunciation, influenced by Webster's dictionary (Aleksandrov 1879: v); the 1864 Webster's is probably meant.[6] Pronunciation is conveyed through phonetic

[6] In his preface to *Webster's New International Dictionary of the English Language* (1930), W. T. Harris mentions (p. v) that the 1847 edition had Chauncey A. Goodrich as editor. In the 1864 revision, Noah Porter was editor-in-chief. The Aleksandrov preface states (p. vi): '... we took as a model ... the most recent edition, revised by three famous philologists, Chonse, Gudrich, and Porter'.

Table 6.3.3 Derivatives of *abandon* in Grammatin, Banks, and Aleksandrov

Grammatin (1811, Vol. I)	Banks (1838, Vol. I)	Aleksandrov (1879, Part I)
Abandoned [not in the dictionary]	Abandoned, a, *ostavlennyi, pokinutyi, predannyi* [left, forsaken, betrayed]; (dissolute) *rasputnyi* [depraved].	**Abandoned** (ä-bän′-don-d), adj. *ostavlennyi, pokinutyi* [left, forsaken]; – to sottish credulity, *rab nelepogo sueveriia* [a slave to absurd superstition]; – to the wrath of the gods, *predmet gneva bogov* [an object of the gods' anger]; – wretch *ot'iavlennyi negodiai* [a complete scoundrel].
Abandoner, s. *tot, kotoryi ostavliaet* [the person who leaves (someone)].	Abandoner, s. *ostavliaiushchii, pokidaiushchii* [a person who leaves, forsakes].	**Abandoner** (ä-bän′-don-er), s. *ostavliaiushchii, pokidaiushchii* [a person who leaves, forsakes]; – of trust, *narushitel' doveriia* [a violator of trust].
Abandoning, Abandonment, s. *ostavlenie* [leaving].	Abandoning, Abandonment, *ostavlenie, pokidanie, predannost', rasputstvo* [leaving, forsakening, surrendering, depravity].	**Abandoning** (ä-bän′-don-ing), s. *ostavlenie, zapushchenie* [leaving, neglecting]. **Abandonment** (ä-bän′-don-ment), s. *ostavlenie, ustupka* [leaving, concession]; *odinochestvo* [solitude].

transliterations (in the Cyrillic alphabet) of English headwords. In the introduction (p. iv), the authors explain their organization of senses:

> To make possible a more complete explanation of meaning of each English word, we tried to establish first the main and most frequently encountered meaning. Next, we moved gradually toward the more remote senses of the word; we indicated those phrases which demonstrate this movement [i.e. from the core meaning to the extended ones]. Likewise, we indicated the shades of meaning which a word gradually acquires. When necessary for increased clarity we brought in examples … which demonstrate appropriately these various shades of meaning within a single word.

A comparison of related entries in Grammatin, Banks, and Aleksandrov (Table 6.3.3) demonstrates how the Alexandrov dictionary indicates a word's 'shades of meaning'.

Aleksandrov's entries for *abandoned* and *abandoner* provide more information than Banks's or Grammatin's. Aleksandrov's Russian translations of *abandoned to the wrath of the gods* and *abandoner of trust* are fixed phrases that do capture the meanings of the English expressions; their translation of *abandoned to sottish credulity*, another fixed phrase, comes fairly close to the meaning of the English. The Aleksandrov translation of *abandoned wretch* is accurate but limited, because it displays only one of two possible meanings. In English, *abandoned wretch* can mean an immoral or dissolute person, as is captured by Aleksandrov's equivalent *ot'iavlennyi negodiai* [complete scoundrel]. But it could also mean a forsaken and miserable person; the *Oxford English Dictionary* (1933, s.v. abandoned) has *abandoned woman* as part of phrases under its senses 'forsaken' and 'immoral'. By providing a Russian equivalent with the meaning 'complete scoundrel', the Aleksandrov dictionary illustrates the extended meaning 'immoral' and not the core 'forsaken'. However, this extended meaning is not among the senses listed, so a reader might be left confused.

A unique English–Russian dictionary for its time, the work of V. Butuzov deserves brief mention. Published in 1867, this had the (translated) title: *A dictionary of special words, phrases and locutions in colloquial English and the most frequently used Americanisms, not included in regular dictionaries. A manual for those studying English, for translators and readers of English literary works.* Alekseev (1944: 123) notes both the uniqueness and the timeliness of this work: good English slang dictionaries appeared in England after Butuzov and scholarly work on slang and cant began only in the 1870s and 1880s; after the American Civil War (1861–65), American literature had begun to interest the Russian reading public, and Butuzov's lexicon of Americanisms was available.

6.4 THE DEVELOPMENT OF RUSSIAN–ENGLISH DICTIONARIES IN THE NINETEENTH CENTURY

Except for the seventeenth-century *azbukovniki* and manuscripts such as that of Richard James from the same era, all of the bilingual works discussed so far have been English–Russian dictionaries. In 1751, a British chaplain, Daniel Dumaresq, complained of a 'Want of . . . any kind of Lexicon where the Russian words stand first' (Cross 1997: 393). The first Russian–English dictionary appeared in Russia in the early nineteenth century. Alekseev (1944: 93, f. 4) cites the two-volume work of Ivan Shishukov, a teacher at the Naval Military Academy (Zhdanov was also a teacher at this academy). This work, published in Saint-Petersburg between 1808 and 1811 under the title *Slovar' rossiisko–angliiski* [Russian–English dictionary], was only completed up to the letter 'R'.

6.4.1 *Banks's Russian–English dictionary*

James Banks's two-volume *Russko–angliiskii slovar'* [Russian–English dictionary], published in 1840, was the companion to his English–Russian dictionary

(1838) discussed above. Banks mentions Shishukov in the preface to his English–Russian work: as with other dictionaries available to him, he notes that it was of 'little assistance'. It was 'of less use than it might have been, from the circumstance that only two of the three volumes have ever been published' (p. ii).

Banks begins his Russian–English dictionary with information on letter sounds, spelling changes in Russian words in various contexts, tables providing information about grammar (singulars and plurals of nouns, adjective endings, declensions, etc.); below, we will see how the tables are used in the entries of the dictionary.

A comparison of entries in Banks's English–Russian work with those in his Russian–English dictionary reveals some similarities in style of presentation and treatment. In many cases, the treatment of a given word goes no farther than a one-word equivalent. However, this is much more likely to be the case in the Russian–English dictionary than in the better developed English–Russian. It is unusual for more than one English equivalent to be given for a Russian noun entryword, though note: '*Izbá*, *f.* hut, cottage, peasant's house' (Vol. I). Verbs in the Russian–English dictionary usually show slightly more development than nouns; for example, *Idtí* 'to go' (Vol. I) is treated in an entry that covers almost a full column of a two-column page. More typical verb entries are given below (Vol. I):

(5) a *Adressovát'*, 58, *v.* to address, to direct; —*sia*, to address one's self, to make application, to apply; *p.v.* [passive verb] to be addressed (p. 3).
   b *Izbavliát'*, 60, *izbávit'*, 65, *v.* to deliver, free, set free, exempt; rescue, save; —*sia*, *r.* to free one's self, to escape; *p.v.* to be delivered, etc. *s. Izbávlennyi* (p. 389).

The numbers appearing in the entries above refer to columns in a table in the front matter; thus each verb is cross-referenced to its full conjugation. One aspect of the treatments shown above can be seen in the 'reflexive' forms in —*sia*, such as *adressovát'sia* and *izbavliát'sia* or *izbávit'sia*.

6.4.2 *Aleksandrov's Russian–English dictionary*

As already noted, a group of lexicographers published an English–Russian dictionary under the pseudonym A. Aleksandrov in 1879. Under the same pseudonym, *Polnyi russko–angliiskii slovar'/Complete Russian–English Dictionary* was published in two parts (1883 and 1885), with a revised and expanded one-volume edition appearing in 1897. The title page of 1897 states that it 'is recommended by the Academic Committee of the Ministry of Public Education as a textbook for non-classical secondary schools [i.e. schools that do not teach classical languages, unlike gymnasiums] and for those educational institutions in which English is taught....'. Clearly the authors envisaged a Russian-speaking/English-learning audience.

While Banks capitalized his (Cyrillic alphabet) headwords and used italics for grammatical labels, other labels, and Latin phrases, the Aleksandrov dictionary exploits more fully the possibilities of print to make a variety of lexicographic distinctions. First, headwords appear in bold face and are capitalized, following the same format as Aleksandrov's English–Russian dictionary. As in Banks, grammatical labels are italicized; in addition, Aleksandrov italicizes and puts in parentheses a variety of English-language phrases designed to specify the contexts of a word's use; for example: Russian *poliàrnost'* is defined as 'polarity (*of the magnet*)'; *pomìgivat', pomigàt'* is defined as 'to wink (*the eyes*) a little' (Part II). Finally, Aleksandrov puts illustrative examples in italics, with the headword indicated by a dash. For example, in the entry for Russian *pol* 'sex', the English equivalent 'the fair sex' is given for *prekrasnyi* —.

Just as Banks's English–Russian dictionary had, generally speaking, better developed entries than his Russian–English, so the Aleksandrov Russian–English work is less fully developed than their English–Russian counterpart. Aleksandrov's Russian–English dictionary shows fuller development of entries than Banks's Russian–English, as is seen in Table 6.4.2.

Banks's entry for *izbá* provides equivalents that could be useful to a Russian speaker who is writing in English (encoding). While Russian students are the targeted audience of Aleksandrov's dictionary, it nevertheless contains information for English speakers, such as the diminutive form of *izbá* (*izbùshka*) and the proverb. An English speaker would find Banks's equivalents useful for understanding a Russian text (decoding), but would not be able to perceive the cultural importance of *izbá*. The English saying, in Aleksandrov, *a fine cage does not fill a bird's belly*, is not satisfactory as a translation for the Russian proverb, as it misses entirely the emphasis on hospitality in the Russian original.

For the Russian verb *izbavliat'/izbavit'* and the reflexive verb *izbavliat'sia/izbavit'sia*, both Banks and Aleksandrov contain similar information and have several equivalents in common. However, each dictionary makes different decisions about sense discrimination. In Banks, 'deliver/free/set free' is distinguished from 'rescue/save' but this distinction is not noted in Aleksandrov; meanwhile, the information provided in Banks does not support his division of meaning. In Aleksandrov, there is a sense 'rid of/disencumber' which is missing in Banks; in addition, Aleksandrov distinguishes a third sense 'to set clear'; these senses likewise are not supported by the contexts provided.

A look at several Russian monolingual dictionaries seems to indicate that neither Banks's nor Aleksandrov's sense distinctions are sound; this is not surprising given

Table 6.4.2 Noun and verb entries from Banks and Aleksandrov[7]

Banks (1840)	Aleksandrov (1883–85)
Izbá, f. hut, cottage, peasant's house.	**Izbà**, *s.f. dim.* **izbùshka**, peasant's house, cottage, cot, hut;||*prov. Ne krasna – uglami, a krasna pirogami* [literally, a cottage is not beautiful in its corners but in its pies; i.e. the hospitality of its inhabitants, and not a house's appearance, makes it attractive], a fine cage does not fill a bird's belly;||servant's lodging. ||**–bianòi**, *adj.* (1883, Part I).
Izbavliát', 60, *izbávit'*, 65, *v.* to deliver, free, set free, exempt; rescue, save;–sia, *r.* to free one's self, to escape; *p.v.* to be delivered, etc. *s. Izbávlennyi.*	**Izbavlìàt', izbàvit'**, *v.a.* to deliver, release, free, set free from; to rid of, disencumber; to set clear; **–vi** *nas ot lukavogo*, deliver us from evil; *on* **–vil** *menia ot bol'shogo bezpokoistva*, he has relieved me from great uneasiness; **–v'te** *ego ot etoi pechali*, spare him that grief; **–vi** *Bozhe*, God forbid; || **–sia**,*v.r.* (*ot chego*) [(from something)] to free one's self, deliver one's self, from, of; to get rid of; to escape from; || *part. p.* **izbàvlennyi**; *nikto ne* **–vlen** *ot smerti*, nobody is exempted from death (1883, Part I).

the probably limited information that these lexicographers had available to them. Ozhegov (1960) and Ozhegov–Shvedova (1993) have a single (paraphrased) sense: 'save, allow to escape from,' and Ushakov (1935, Vol. I) is close to this: 'save, bring about freeing from'. The *Slovar' sovremennogo russkogo literaturnogo iazyka* [dictionary of modern standard Russian] (1956, Vol. 5) divides the meaning into two senses, similar to Banks: 'help to escape from; save'; however, this distinction is not supported by the numerous contexts, which show the more metaphorical meaning of 'save' rather than a physical escape. Ushakov and the seventeen-volume *Slovar' sovremennogo ...* have an additional meaning that they label as colloquial: 'free; leave alone'. This colloquial meaning appears to be similar to Aleksandrov's 'rid of, disencumber'. No evidence in any of the dictionaries consulted could be found for Aleksandrov's 'to set clear'. In distinguishing (or not distinguishing) the different meanings of the verb *izbavliat'/izbavit'*, Aleksandrov's treatment is superior to Banks, but neither dictionary demonstrates a high level of sophistication.

6.4.3 *Riola's lexicon*

Most of the dictionaries examined so far originated in Russia. While nineteenth-century England saw the publication of a few textbooks or other reference books for learners of Russian (this activity increased in the 1890s), there were no

[7] In Russian, word stress is usually not indicated graphically. Banks and Aleksandrov use grave or acute marks (*izbà/izbá*) to indicate stress for non-native speakers.

dictionaries to speak of. Noteworthy among the reference books were those by Henry Riola, a teacher of Russian in England who was educated in a gymnasium in Taganrog, Russia (Alekseev and Levin 1994: 66). Riola's 1878 *How to Learn Russian: A Manual for Students of Russian*, and its companion volume *Key to the Exercises of the Manual for Students of Russian* (1878) received favourable critical notice.[8] Riola's *Manual* and *Key* did not contain a lexicon, but there is one in his *Graduated Russian Reader, with a Vocabulary of all the Russian Words Contained in It* (1880). In this 113-page, two-column Russian–English lexicon, several single-word equivalents are listed for each entryword. A few interesting verb entries are worth examination:

(6) a *Motat', va.* to wind, reel, shake, squander, spend.
b *Podtibrivat', -tibrit', va. fam.* to swindle, juggle away.
c *Podkhodit', podoiti, vn.* to come, approach, resemble.

In his Preface (p. iv), Riola emphasizes that his lexicon only includes word meanings that are relevant to the *Reader*'s texts; it is not meant to be a complete dictionary. Riola does not distinguish between different meanings represented by his equivalents, so that the basic meaning of the verb *motat'* 'to wind, reel' is not separated from the extended meaning 'squander, spend'. The same is true of the two meanings of *podkhodit'*: 'to come, approach' and 'resemble'. To facilitate an understanding of the *Reader*'s texts, Riola includes very few colloquial words with the label *fam.* 'familiar', such as *podtibrivat'*. It could be that Riola consulted the earlier, 1879 edition of Aleksandrov for *podtibrivat'*; Aleksandrov (1897) has 'to cheat, dupe, rob; to swindle, juggle away'.

6.5 DICTIONARIES OF THE TWENTIETH CENTURY—A BRIEF SURVEY

6.5.1 *The dictionaries of Müller and Miller*

The twentieth century saw the publication of numerous important general English–Russian and Russian–English dictionaries in the then Soviet Union, England, and the United States. In addition, many specialized dictionaries were published,

[8] The journal *Vestnik Evropy* [European herald] (1878: 398–9) quotes William Ralston (from the preface to the *Manual*) on the growing interest in the Russian language in England. Ralston (1828–89) was a librarian at the British Museum who became a well-known promoter of Russian literature and language in England (Alekseev and Levin 1994: 8).

covering fields such as engineering and computer science. Another well-represented type of specialized dictionary is the phraseological dictionary, some of which are intended as learners' dictionaries (see Kunin 1967). Russian–English dictionaries became increasingly necessary as relations between Russia and English-speaking countries developed, while at the same time greater sophistication in lexicographic theory moved dictionaries towards comprehensive descriptive records of the Russian and English linguistic systems. While twentieth-century dictionaries are too numerous to discuss in the present context, some important general works will be mentioned, including some that have theoretical significance.[9]

In the early twentieth century, political alliances and hostilities provided the impetus for the further development of English–Russian lexicography. The years of the First World War (1914–18) saw an increase in the number of Russian reference books published in England, although British and American collective knowledge of the Russian language remained far behind if compared—in the number of books alone—to Russian knowledge of, and interest in, English (Alekseev 1944: 135–7). As might be expected, many of the English–Russian bilingual dictionaries of the twentieth century became 'standards' that, with changed titles and/or authors, spanned many editions. As we turn first to discuss English–Russian dictionaries, we must mention the name of V. K. Müller, whose dictionary was attributed initially to Müller and Boyanus (1928). Another well-known name is that of A. D. Miller. While his dictionary was originally attributed to Miller and Mirskii (1936), for political reasons it later became Miller and Ozerskaia (1937).[10] Miller–Mirskii provide interesting information about Müller–Boyanus in their preface. They declare that, although their own work was based on the earlier publication, they observe strict alphabetical order and avoid many of the errors of the preceding dictionary, errors which were often due to an over-reliance on a single source, the *Pocket Oxford Dictionary*. In addition, Miller–Mirskii (1936) claim fuller coverage of the American–English lexicon, something that was clearly becoming a desirable feature.

In his turn, Müller credits Miller in the preface of his second edition (1946: 4) with having reviewed the entire manuscript prior to publication. This edition of Müller includes many items not in the first (1943)—terminology that appeared

[9] There are numerous twentieth-century dictionaries that are not included in our discussion. Among these are: Apresian *et al.* (1979), Kunin (1967), and Wilson (1982). Many of these depart from the usual expectations of bilingual dictionaries; their insights most likely have informed the more standard works.

[10] Dmitrii Petrovich Sviatopolk-Mirskii (1890–1939) was a famous Russian literary scholar. In 1920, he emigrated to London but repatriated to the USSR in 1932. He was arrested in 1937 and died a prisoner in the Far East. His name was deleted as joint editor of the dictionary after the edition of 1936 (Smith, 1989: 13, 29); the 1937 edition lists as authors Miller and Ozerskaia.

during the Second World War, and American expressions that 'are more and more solidly rooted in the English language'. By the seventh edition (1960), although Müller's name remained on the title page, the dictionary's preface tells us that it was revised by an editorial board of three; we are also informed of the switch from a historical ordering of senses to one that lists general meanings before more specialized ones (1960: 5). The seventh edition includes many new entries (an increase from approximately 60,000 to 70,000 words) as well as 'revisions of old ones, by means of greater differentiation in the meaning of individual words, along with an increase in illustrative material and phraseology'. In Table 6.5.1, some examples of Americanisms will enable us to make a comparison of the 1946 and 1960 editions of Müller.

By the seventh edition, the dictionary has certainly developed a more uniform structure. In the entry for *date*, the label **razg.** (*razgovornyi* 'colloquial') is used once at the beginning of meaning 3 and is meant to apply to the entire meaning; the same label appears twice in the earlier work. In the later work, the microstructure leads us to understand that the expression *to make a date* has two labels, 'colloquial' and 'American'. The expression *blind date*, labelled 'American slang' in both dictionaries, is moved in the later edition to the headword *blind*, where it retains the same label. For the entry *rattle*, the seventh edition changes the label

Table 6.5.1 American items from two editions of Müller

Müller (1946, 2nd ed.)	Müller (1960, 7th ed.)
	blind . . . 1. . . . , ~ date ***amer. sl.*** *svidánie s neznakómym chelovékom* [a meeting with an unfamiliar person]
date . . . I *n* . . . 3. ***amer. razg.*** [American colloquial] *svidánie*; blind d. ***amer.*** *sl.* [American slang] *svidánie s neznakómym chelovékom* [a meeting with an unfamiliar person]; to have (got), to make a d. ***amer. razg.*** *poluchít' priglashénie* [to receive an invitation]	**date** I . . . 1. *n* . . . 3). ***razg.*** [colloquial] *svidánie*; I have got a ~ *u meniá svidánie*; to make a ~ ***amer.*** *naznáchit'* svidánie [to set up a meeting]
rattle . . . I *v* . . . 4. ***amer. razg.*** *smushchát'* [to embarrass], *volnovát'* [to agitate], *pugát'* [to scare]	**rattle** . . . 2. *v* . . . 6) ***razg.*** *smushchát'* [to embarrass], *volnovát'* [to agitate], *pugát'* [to scare]; to get ~ d *teriát' spokóistvie* [to lose composure], *nérvnichat'* [to be nervous]
windshield . . . ***amer.*** = windscreen	**windshield** . . . ***amer.*** 1) = windscreen 1); 2) *attr.*: ~ *wiper* **avt.** [auto] *stekloochistítel' vetróvogo steklá* [glass cleaner of the front glass], «*dvórnik*» ['street sweeper']

from 'American colloquial' to just 'colloquial'. Müller's later entry for *windshield* is more fully developed than in the earlier work; especially welcome is the inclusion of the Russian colloquial term *dvórnik* [literally, caretaker or street sweeper] in the meaning 'windshield wiper'. The principles governing the seventh edition of Müller were used in subsequent editions into at least the late 1970s. The seventeenth edition (1978) has some interesting remarks about its decisions to delete or add material. Since Gal'perin's two-volume English–Russian dictionary had appeared in 1972 (see below) and included special terminology, archaic words, and archaic senses of words, these could now be omitted from Müller in favour of new socio-political words, new words from everyday life, and new words from English, American, Australian, and Canadian literature of the previous fifteen years (Müller 1978: 5). 'New' editions of Müller continue to appear to the present day.[11]

6.5.2 *The dictionaries of Gal'perin and Apresian–Mednikova*

Another landmark in English–Russian lexicography is the dictionary of I. R. Gal'perin, which first appeared in 1972. The publisher's note underscores the claim that 'This is the first time . . . a two-volume English–Russian dictionary has been published in the USSR' (1977: 7); however, Banks and Aleksandrov had published two-volume dictionaries in Russia. Gal'perin's long introduction is less significant for any of the specific decisions about what (or what not) to include in the dictionary, and very significant for the character of the discussion overall. In a tone completely different from that of Müller, Gal'perin discusses the dictionary as a *linguistic* work. Words are classified using style or usage labels (such as archaic, nonce, neologism, etc.) and decisions about how to treat them were made on that basis. For example, concerning neologisms he writes: 'A bilingual dictionary should be more up-to-date than a defining [i.e. monolingual] dictionary since it is destined to serve in direct communication and hence cannot aspire to set down standards [norms] accepted in the language' (pp. 11, 21). In his use of the term *linguistic*, Gal'perin is most likely indicating efforts to address the lexicon in a more scientific manner than was done in previous dictionaries. Certainly, his entries are more tightly structured and dense in information. In his comments about the inclusion of more neologisms, Gal'perin is addressing, and to some extent departing from, the lexicographic traditions of his country.

[11] The title of Müller's dictionary remained the same through at least the twentieth edition (1990). Then, the word *modern* [*novyi* 'new'] was added (e.g. Müller 1994). The twenty-first century has seen another name change, to *complete* [*bol'shoi* 'large'] (e.g. Müller 2004).

Soviet monolingual lexicography adopted a conservative approach to the inclusion of neologisms. Until a new word or new sense of an existing word was considered to have become part of the standard language, it was unlikely to be included in monolingual dictionaries. Gal'perin is justifying including more neologisms by saying that communication in the foreign language would be hindered if they were left out. Gal'perin's dictionary is noteworthy for the copiousness of its equivalents, whether translational or explanatory.[12] It certainly provided translators with a tool that was superior to any previously available in an English—Russian dictionary. Gal'perin states:

> In a number of cases several possible variants have been given .... As a result, some of the entries have been considerably lengthened, but we firmly believe that variants will be very useful ... .Translation variants sometimes disclose the potentialities of a word more profoundly than a mere listing of customary combinations might (pp. 19, 28).

The entries below from Gal'perin (1977) give some understanding of the richness of his work, as well as affording a comparison with Müller (above):

(7) **blind II** ..., ~ date ***amer.*** a) *svidánie s neznakómym chelovékom* [a meeting with an unfamiliar person] b) *neznakómyi chelovék, s kotórym predstoít vstrécha* [an unfamiliar person with whom a meeting is set]

(8) **date**[2] I... *n* ***amer. razg.*** [American colloquial] 1) *svidánie, vstrécha* [appointment, meeting]; to make a ~ with smb. *naznáchit' svidánie s kem-l.* [to set a meeting with someone]; I have (got) a ~ with him *u meniá s nim svidánie*; 2) *chelovék, s kotórym naznácheno svidánie* [a person with whom a meeting is arranged]

(9) **rattle II** ... 4. ***razg.*** *vzvolnovát'* [to disturb], *smutít'* [to embarrass]; *vývesti iz sebiá* [to drive out of one's mind]; *ispugát'* [to scare], *pripugnút'* [to intimidate]; *oshelomít'* [to stun]; to get ~d *perepugát'sia* [to become frightened]; *smutít'sia* [to get embarrassed]; *výiti iz sebiá* [to lose one's temper], *poteriát' samoobladánie* [to lose self-control]; don't get ~d! *spokóinee!* [be calm!]; *ne volnúites'!* [don't worry!]; the interruptions rather ~d the speaker *vózglasy s mest néskol'ko smutíli orátora* [the cries from the audience slightly disturbed the speaker]; the team were ~d by their opponents' tactics *kománda bylá sbíta s tólku táktikoi svoíkh protívnikov* [the team was confused by the tactics of their opponents]

Blind date is given two meanings in Gal'perin (the meeting itself, or the person whom one meets) compared to one in Müller. The entry for *rattle* provides

[12] For discussions of translational equivalents versus explanations of meaning, cf. Zgusta (1987) and Farina (1996).

numerous translation equivalents as well as equivalents for expressions such as *don't get rattled.*

Apresian and Mednikova (1993) is the revision and expansion into three volumes of the two-volume Gal'perin dictionary. In the introductory article (1993: 8)—and in words that echo James Murray's—Apresian defines what he means by the central lexicon (the standard language) and the peripheral lexicon (e.g. technical vocabulary, neologisms, archaic words, slang, etc.) of a language. He considers a dictionary as a momentary snapshot of a constantly changing language; to obtain a true likeness of the language in the static snapshot, the lexicographer must focus on the core of the language and the interrelationships of the core and the various layers of the periphery. Apresian mentions (p. 12) that, by some estimates, *Webster's Third* (Gove 1961) contains up to forty per cent technical terminology (peripheral language); among bilingual dictionaries, he considers Harrap's as having the same flaw, with more illustrative examples given for peripheral vocabulary than for core meanings. In contrast, Apresian places his dictionary in the indigenous Russian tradition of 'explanatory' (*tolkovaia*) lexicography; the goal is to present 'a more balanced picture of the interrelations between the central and peripheral lexicon'.

Apresian and Mednikova (1993) deserves an article (or book) of its own. In the present context, one example (compared with corresponding entries from Gal'perin and Müller) will suffice to give a taste of how Apresian's principles are reflected within an entry.

It is clear that each dictionary builds on the work of its predecessor. All three works distinguish the two main meanings of *putrid* that were also documented in Grammatin–Parenogo and Banks in the nineteenth century: 'rotten' and 'smelly'. In addition, they cover the metaphorical meaning 'depraved' that was not treated

Table 6.5.2 Putrid in three dictionaries

Müller (1960, 7th ed.)	Gal'perin (1977)	Apresian–Mednikova (1993)
putrid ... 1) *gnilói* [rotten]; 2) *voníúchii* [stinking]; 3) *ispórchennyi* [depraved]; 4) *sl.* [slang] *otvratítel'nyi* [disgusting]; , ~ fever *ust.* [archaic] *sypnói tif* [typhus]	putrid ... 1. 1) *gnílostnyi*; 2) *gnilói* [rotten]; 2. *voníúchii* [stinking]; 3. *ispórchennyi, izvrashchënnyi* [depraved, perverted]; 4. *razg.* [colloquial] *otvratítel'nyi* [disgusting]; ~ weather *otvratítel'naia pogóda* [terrible weather]; , ~ fever *sypnói tif* [typhus]	putrid ... 1. 1) *gnílostnyi* 2) *gnilói* [rotten] 2. *voníúchii* [*stinking*] 3. 1) *ispórchennyi, izvrashchënnyi* [depraved, perverted] 2) *naskvóz' prodázhnyi* [completely mercenary] 4. *razg.* [colloquial] *otvratítel'nyi* [disgusting]; ~ weather *otvratítel'naia pogóda* 5. *med.* [medical] *putrídnyi, gnílostnyi*; *gniíúshchii* [rotting]; *raspadáiushchiisia [decomposing]*

in the eighteenth-century Zhdanov or in Grammatin–Parenogo. In Banks, it is not clear whether he meant to include the meaning 'depraved' or a fourth meaning, 'disgusting, unpleasant'. But in the three twentieth-century dictionaries, all four meanings are included and clearly distinguished. Gal'perin's work introduces more equivalents and phrases that could be helpful to the professional translator of English texts. And Apresian–Mednikova do capture the interplay between the core and the periphery in the organization of their entry, with the expressions requiring labels such as *medical* (the peripheral lexicon) appearing at the end of the entry. Apresian–Mednikova's inclusion of the equivalents from medical terminology are particularly interesting: the equivalent *putrídnyi* shows how the Russian language has used borrowing to develop its terminological vocabulary. As was previously mentioned, borrowing from the English language began in the late 1600s when specialists from England arrived in Russia.

6.5.3 *Falla's dictionary*

Falla (1984), published in Britain, is an English–Russian dictionary based on the work of Russian native speakers as well as on Gal'perin's dictionary and *Supplement* (Gal'perin 1980). The introduction (1984: vii) states that the dictionary 'is intended to reflect the general and colloquial vocabulary of present-day English (including the better-known Americanisms)'. While 'copious examples' are included, some scientific and technical terminology has been excluded. The size of Falla's one-volume dictionary (90,000 words) means that it is of necessity very different in character from Gal'perin (150,000 words) or Apresian–Mednikova (250,000 words). Apart from differences in entry size, there are differences in the type of information included, since Falla is intended for use mostly by English native speakers. Below are some examples from Falla:

(10) **blind**... *adj.* ...2. ...a ~ date (*Am. coll.*) *svidánie s neznakómym/neznakómoi* [a social meeting with an unfamiliar (male/female) person].

(11) **date**[2] *n.* ... 3. (*coll., appointment*) *svidánie*... *v.t.* ...3. (*coll., make appointment with*) *nazn|achát', -áchit' svidánie + d. or s + i.*

(12) **putrid** *adj.* (*decomposed*) *gnilói*; (*coll., unpleasant*) *otvratítel'nyi.*

(13) **rattle**... *v.t.* ...2. (*coll., agitate*): he is not easily ~d *egó nelegkó vývesti iz ravnovésiia.*

The entries for *blind* (containing *blind date*) and *date* have information that would be unnecessary for a Russian speaker but is extremely useful for an English speaker. The inclusion of the equivalent *svidánie s neznakómym/neznakómoi* [social meeting with an unfamiliar male/female] for *blind date* assists the learner of Russian in using the instrumental case correctly—in both masculine and feminine. Likewise, the equivalent of the transitive verb *date* indicates that it can be used with no preposition and a dative object following, or else with the Russian preposition *s* followed by an instrumental object. The most useful feature of the dictionary is the inclusion of English synonyms for each possible meaning of the entryword, synonyms which provide the key to the exact meaning of a given Russian equivalent. So, while an English speaker might know that English *putrid* can mean 'rotten, smelly, depraved', or 'disgusting', he or she may not know which of the four meanings is closest to *gnilói*. The inclusion of the synonym *decomposed* provides the necessary key.[13]

6.5.4 *Katzner's dictionary*

In the same year that Falla's dictionary was published, the first American effort, a combined Russian–English and English–Russian dictionary, appeared in one volume (Katzner 1984). Piotrowski (1988: 127) gives a rough estimate of 65,000 words for both halves together, putting Katzner's work closer in size to Müller or Falla than to Gal'perin or Apresian–Mednikova. In his preface, Katzner discussed what was most important to him: the fact that the 'two halves of the dictionary mirror each other exactly' (p. v). All of the Russian words used as equivalents in the English–Russian part of the dictionary have their own entry on the Russian–English side, and vice versa. Katzner looked at his work as a unified whole (L. 2003) and compared it with later editions of Oxford Russian dictionaries (e.g. 1995) that combined the English–Russian component of Falla with a Russian–English component that had appeared earlier as a separate edition (Wheeler and Unbegaun 1972; see below). The entries below, if compared to those above from other dictionaries, demonstrate the originality of Katzner's work:

(14) **blind** [no information on *blind date*]

(15) **date** *n.* ... 4. (social engagement) *svidánie*: *go out on dates. khodít' na svidániia.* ...—*v.t.* ... 2. (see socially) *vstrechát'siia s.*

(16) **putrid** *adj.* 1. (rotten) *gnilói.* 2. (stinking) *voníúchii.*

(17) **rattle** ... —*v.t.* ... 2. *colloq.* (fluster) *sbivát' s tólku* [to knock (one's) sense away]. *Get rattled, (ras)teriát'sia* [to get lost; lose one's head].

[13] See Piotrowski (1988: 136–7).

Since Katzner is describing American English, he can do without the 'American' label; he also finds it unnecessary to include *blind date*. His entry for *putrid* includes only the two core meanings of the word; notably absent is the meaning 'disgusting' (*otvratítel'nyi*), which is more British than American. The most unique treatment is under *rattle*; the expressions Katzner chose are apt and missing from the copious material of Gal'perin.

Our discussion of Katzner's combined English–Russian and Russian–English dictionary provides a bridge to a broader discussion of the twentieth-century beginnings of Russian–English lexicography. As could be guessed from the pattern of English–Russian dictionaries, the activity begins within Russia/the Soviet Union and only moves to Britain and the United States later in the twentieth century. Müller–Boyanus, whose English–Russian dictionary appeared in 1928, published a Russian–English dictionary in 1930. While, according to the authors (1935), the dictionary was primarily intended for a Russian audience, nevertheless they believed it could serve an English-speaking public as well, because of its inclusion of Soviet expressions. The authors discuss their use of descriptions (i.e. explanatory equivalents or explanations of meaning) in place of or in addition to (English) translational equivalents, in cases where a good equivalent for a Russian word does not exist. This, they say, is particularly problematic in the case of political words such as:

(18) ***edinonachálie*** one-man management, management on unitary responsibility (in the USSR). (c. 344)

(19) ***militsionér*** militiaman; '~ *tsia* militia (civil force in the USSR responsible for maintaining public order). (c. 616)

Inclusion in the entries above of explanations can be understood as a solely linguistic concern by Müller–Boyanus to translate 'culture-bound words' (Zgusta 1971: 324). It is nevertheless true that Soviet lexicographers had other, non-linguistic concerns about transmitting the reality of Soviet life to the West through dictionaries. It is fair to say that lexicographers of the Soviet period were painfully aware of the consequences of erring politically in dictionaries. While perhaps Russian monolingual lexicography suffered the most from this Soviet sword of Damocles (cf. Farina 1992, 2001a, 2001b), it is evident in bilingual lexicography as well. Our discussion of the dictionaries below will make this clear.

6.5.5 *The dictionaries of Smirnitskii–Akhmanova and Wheeler–Unbegaun*

First appearing in 1948 and going through numerous editions, the dictionary of Smirnitskii and Akhmanova is significant because of the authors' adherence to the lexicographic theories of L. V. Shcherba, 'who so strongly advocated the principle of the absolute predominance of the translational equivalent ... that he was originally disinclined to admit any explanation whatsoever in his dictionaries' (Zgusta 1987: 13). Two examples from Smirnitskii–Akhmanova (1975) demonstrate this principle at work; all of the explanatory information that was contained in Müller–Boyanus (see above) has been removed, despite the fact that translational equivalents alone do not permit an understanding of the meanings of the headwords:

(20) ***edinonachálie*** óne-mán manage|ment.

(21) ***militsionér*** militia|man*.

In 1972, the first edition of the Russian–English dictionary of Wheeler and Unbegaun was published in England. In physical size, it is comparable to Smirnitskii–Akhmanova, whose 1958 (third) edition is among the dictionaries acknowledged as its sources. The preface to Wheeler–Unbegaun indicates that, while its purpose is to present 'translations, not definitions', it admits to the need for explanation, particularly in cases 'of words denoting specifically Russian or Soviet concepts' (p. x). The Russian–English half of Katzner (1984), while smaller in size than the other two dictionaries, can stand in comparison with them due to its innovative character. Below, the treatment of 'culture-bound' words is compared in Smirnitskii–Akhmanova, Wheeler–Unbegaun, and Katzner:

Table 6.5.5 Treatment of 'culture-bound' words in three dictionaries

Smirnitskii–Akhmanova (1975)	Wheeler–Unbegaun (1972)	Katzner (1984)
bespartíin||yi 1. *pril.* nón-Párty (*attr.*); ~ *bol'shevík* nón-Párty Bólshevik; 2. *Kak sushch. m.* nón-Párty man*; *zh.* nón-Párty wóman*... ; *mn.* nón-Párty people....	**bespartíin|yi**, *adj.* non-party; *as noun* **b.**, ~ **ogo**, *m.*, *and* ~ **aia**, ~ **oi**, *f.* non-party man, woman.	**bespartíinyi**, *adj.* non-party. –*n.* person not a member of the party.
dách||a II *zh.* 1. (*zagorodnyi dom* [house outside the city]) cóttage (in the cóuntry)..., cóuntry-cóttage... ; (*letniaia tzh.* [summer also]) súmmer cottage; *snimát'* ~ y rent a súmmer cóttage; *zhit' na* ~ e [live in a *dacha*] live in the cóuntry... ; *ékhat' na* ~ *y* [go to one's *dacha*] go to the cóuntry.	**dách|a**^{2}, **i**, *f.* 1. dacha (*holiday cottage in the country in environs of city or large town*). 2. *byt' na* ~ e [to be at one's *dacha*] to be in the country; *poékhat' na* ~ *y* [to go to one's *dacha*] to go to the country.	**dácha** *n.* 1. country house; summer cottage; dacha 2. the country: *zhit' na dáche*, to live in the country....
stukách [not in the dictionary]	**stukách**, **á**, *m.* (*sl.*) knocker (= informer).	**stukách** [*gen.* **–kachá**] *n. colloq.* informer; stool pigeon.

The adjective and noun *bespartiinyi* [literally, without party] describes a reality of the Soviet era that was foreign to the West. Someone who was *bespartiinyi* had not joined the only available political party, the Communist Party. This could either be by choice or because the person anticipated rejection or had been rejected. Wheeler–Unbegaun do not capture this with their equivalents. Smirnitskii–Akhmanova do better in a subtle manner. Their strict reliance on the translational principle allows them to avoid explaining what the word means, while their use of capitalization gives a hint that the Party being spoken of is not just any party. Katzner's explanation is somewhat more useful than the strict equivalence in the other dictionaries; however, his inclusion of the definite article *the* ('not a member of *the* party') seems an unnecessarily vague approach to the politics of this culture-bound word.

In the case of Russian *dacha*, Smirnitskii–Akhmanova and Wheeler–Unbegaun include explanations in addition to equivalents, and both manage more or less to capture the meaning: a *dacha* is located on the outskirts of cities, and people usually visit it in the summer to escape city life. Wheeler–Unbegaun omit the summer association; in addition, their inclusion of the word *holiday* (with its connotation of infrequent, special occasions) in the explanation seems overly restrictive. Katzner's treatment is the most succinct and the most satisfying of the three: he manages in fewer words to say almost everything that the other two dictionaries do. He does, however, miss specifying the location of the *dacha* near a city.

Our final word, *stukach*, is one that could not have appeared in a Russian-made dictionary of the Soviet era, such as Smirnitskii–Akhmanova. A post-Soviet edition of the one-volume monolingual Ozhegov dictionary (Ozhegov and Shvedova 1993) gives the following definition: '(prost prezr.) *To zhe, chto donoschik*' [(popular speech, contemptuous) the same thing as an informer]. Wheeler–Unbegaun give the literal meaning, 'knocker', which is not useful at all as an insertable translational equivalent. Katzner gives the standard-language meaning 'informer' (Ozhegov–Shvedova's *donoschik*) and then hits on an insertable expression, 'stool pigeon', which is at a similar stylistic level to *stukach*.

Taken as a whole, Russian–English lexicography of the twentieth century produced dictionaries based on well developed linguistic and lexicographic theories, with more uniform organization and presentation, and with more information for the user. It is not clear what to expect for this new century. The changes in world politics mean a decreased importance for the Russian language, just at the moment when Russian lexicographers are able to practise their craft with a lessening of the censorship that interferes with lexicographic technique. It is to be hoped that real revision (rather than stereotyped republications) of Russian–English dictionaries will continue in both the Russian- and the English-speaking world.

PART II

THE HISTORY OF ENGLISH MONOLINGUAL DICTIONARIES

7

THE EARLY DEVELOPMENT OF THE ENGLISH MONOLINGUAL DICTIONARY (SEVENTEENTH AND EARLY EIGHTEENTH CENTURIES)

N. E. Osselton

7.1 INTRODUCTION

FROM the first beginnings in 1604 it took one and a half centuries for the monolingual dictionary of English to evolve as a new, distinctive type of reference work, stable in contents, more or less settled in methodology, and such that the modern reader might have felt quite at home in using it.

Three stages in this development may be discerned: in the *hard-word dictionaries* of the first half of the seventeenth century the focus was almost entirely on the learned vocabulary of English; the *encyclopedic dictionaries* of the later seventeenth century were agreeably readable reference books with names treated equally alongside words; finally, the so-called *universal dictionary* in the early years of the eighteenth century was more narrowly linguistic, generally cutting out extraneous matter and with the aim of including all the words of the language, even the simplest ones.

7.2 THE HARD-WORD DICTIONARY

Alphabetical (or partially alphabetical) lists of English words had been drawn up for various purposes before Cawdrey compiled the first monolingual dictionary of difficult words in general use. As early as the fifteenth century, manuscripts of the *Promptorium parvulorum* had circulated with some 12,000 English words and their Latin equivalents (Stein 1985: 91–106). Learners of French in the sixteenth century could find extensive 'tables' of English words and their meanings in Palsgrave's *Lesclarcissement de la langue francoyse*—tables which the author rather grandly claimed would contain 'all the wordes in our tong' (Stein 1997: 125). Schoolboy English–Latin dictionaries were popular from the mid-sixteenth century, and Huloet's *Abcedarium anglico-latinum pro tyrunculis* (1552) was the first to range the words for each letter in one continuous alphabetical list, rather than in separate clusters for nouns, adjectives, etc. (Starnes 1954: 147–66). For the schoolroom there were also alphabetical lists of English words intended solely for the purpose of helping with the spelling—later always to be one of the commonest look-up purposes of the monolingual dictionary; Richard Mulcaster in his *Elementarie* (1582) has for instance a fine 56-page four-column list of undefined English words from *abaie* to *zealousnesse* 'for the right writing of our English tung'.

The emergence of the first English dictionary proper—a separate book solely for English words with English explanations—is however perhaps most usefully to be seen as a logical development from yet another type of alphabetical listing. With the more widespread habit of printing scholarly works in the vernacular (rather than in Latin) a need had arisen to add a short glossary to your book to help less able readers with the new (or newish) words that were now needed. For the sixteenth century alone Schäfer (1989) has listed more than seventy such glossaries from English books on architecture, heraldry, mathematics, medicine, theology, etc. Alongside purely technical terms (*chirurgeon*, *quarantine*, *tabernacle*, etc.) they include many words such as *augment*, *compatible*, *hypothesis*, *participate* and *transition* which belong rather to the general vocabulary of scholarly discourse.

These were the 'hard usual words', and the invention of the hard-word dictionary with a unified alphabetical list between one set of covers was to do away with the need for further reduplication of such glossaries of English words appended to the texts in which they were used: better one book on your shelf with explanations of the learned vocabulary of the day than twenty books each with its specialized (but often overlapping) glossary.

7.2.1 *Robert Cawdrey:* A Table Alphabeticall, *1604*

The monolingual English dictionary had a very modest though surprisingly successful start in Robert Cawdrey's slim little volume of 1604. With large lettering and a print area of only 2½ by 4½ inches on each page, it gives the reader the meanings of little more than 2,500 English words. Even so, Cawdrey may be seen to have set the pattern of selection (difficult words, but ones in general use) for his immediate successors, and to have tried out (at times successfully) various well-known devices of the lexicographer's trade.

7.2.1 (i) Users

Robert Cawdrey was a schoolmaster and his dictionary is aimed primarily at learners. The very choice of title—*Table Alphabeticall*—suggests a concern for those who are not (or not yet) literate, and the compiler even patiently repeats (from his source-book Coote) an instruction on how to set about finding a word in a fully alphabetized list: 'if thy word . . . beginne with (ca) looke in the beginning of the letter (c) but if with (cu) then looke toward the end of that letter' (*To the Reader*, sig. A4v). For use outside the schoolroom, he advertises his book as being also of benefit to Ladies and Gentlewomen (it is dedicated to five noblewomen), and to 'strangers'—that is, foreigners: a target user-group frequently invoked in the early monolingual works.

7.2.1 (ii) Character of the word-list

The general run of entries in Cawdrey may be said to answer to his stated intention of helping the less literate readers with the more learned words: *descend* 'goe downe', *evident* 'easie to be seene, plaine', *lassitude* 'wearines', *responses* 'answers'—these were all perfectly well-established English words in 1604, but the untutored reader will have felt less at home with them (whether in spelling or in meaning) than with the native equivalents the dictionary provides. Purely technical terms ('Terms of Art') such as *axiome*, *calcinate* ('to make salt'), *catharre*, *hemisphere*, *simonie*, or *transome* are relatively rare, and there are a few words (only a few) such as *frigifie* 'coole, make cold,' and *illiquinated* 'unmelted' which appear never to have had any real currency in English. Everyday homely words (e.g. *boate*, *gnible* 'bite', *shackle*) crop up only very occasionally.

7.2.1 (iii) Sources

Cawdrey justly deserves his fame as the originator of the English dictionary: none had been produced before 1604—though at least one abortive attempt appears to have been made (Osselton 1995: 104–16)—and his collection of words may be regarded as the foundation list of English monolingual lexicography. It was, however, based primarily on an alphabetical list of 1,368 English words printed eight years earlier in Edmund Coote's *English Schoole-maister* (Starnes and Noyes 1946: 13–19). In this little educational manual Coote was in turn indebted to a list of words given in Mulcaster's *Elementarie* (1582) to illustrate the 'right writing' of the English tongue. But whereas Mulcaster's collection was intended merely as a spelling-list, Coote gave his pupils brief explanations of the words, thus providing Cawdrey with a convenient body of ready-made entries:

(1) **Coote 1596**	**Cawdrey 1604**
Lapidarie **skillful in stones.**	lapidarie, **one skilfull in pretious stones or** jewells
largesse **or** *largis* **liberalitie.**	§ largesse, **or** largis: **liberalitie**
Lascivious **wanton.**	lascivious, **wanton, lecherous**

Such items from Coote make up roughly two-thirds of Cawdrey's entire word-list.

Another important source (for Cawdrey as also for his successors) was the Latin–English dictionaries of the day. Typically, the Latin headword will be Englished, and the English definition retained so as to construct a monolingual entry, as in the following examples from the *Dictionarium linguae Latinae et Anglicanae* (1587) of Thomas Thomas:

(2) **Thomas 1587**	**Cawdrey 1604**
Fraudulentus, a. um. *Deceitfull, craftie, full of guile.*	fraudulent, **deceitfull, craftie, or ful of** guile.
Glossa, ae, f.g. Plaut. *A tongue:* also *a glose or exposition of a darke speach,* Quint.	glosse, **a tongue, or exposition of a darke speech.**

The orderly and comprehensive sequence of Latin words in the Thomas dictionary has served as a highly convenient compiler's prompt for items such as *fraudulent*, which had been borrowed into English, while others such as *fraudatio* ('*fraudation'), which had not been adopted, are passed over silently. It was a compiling technique well suited to an age which had seen an enormous expansion of the vernacular, and it was to be widely adopted by later dictionary makers bent on embellishing their collections of English (or near-English) words.

7.2.1 (iv) Definitions

Entries in Cawdrey are mainly one-liners, often with only a single-word definition (*predominante*, 'ruling'), or else an undifferentiated string of synonyms (*proroge*, 'put off, prolong, deferre'); the longest entries in the book (*cypher*, *hipocrite*) run to no more than twenty-five words. Homographs tend to get short shrift in a single entry, sometimes with 'or' (§ *legacie*,'a gift by will, or an ambassage'), and sometimes with 'also' (*divine*, 'Heavenly [,] godly, also to gesse, conjecture, or prophesie'). Though some words are given refreshingly clear and informative explanations (*laborinth* 'a place so full of windings and turnings, that a man cannot finde a way out of it') in general it may be said that the definitions in the *Table Alphabeticall* remain scrappy and imprecise.

7.2.1 (v) Lemma structure

Cawdrey does little to give his users additional information about the words he defines. One lexicographical refinement is the use of the symbol § to mark recent and unassimilated borrowings from the French, as seen above in the entries for *largesse* and *legacie*. Another convention in Cawdrey is the insertion of (**g**) for words 'drawne from the Greek' such as *catholicke*, *decalogue*, *gnomen* and *poligamie*—hardly to be called the beginning of etymology in English dictionaries, but it would doubtless have had its value for beginners with little Latin and no Greek. Finally, he adopts (probably from Coote) the use of (**k**) for 'kind of'—a useful abbreviation for a very small dictionary in entries such as *barnacle* '(k) bird' and *cowslip* '(k) hearb', though it was never to be favoured by later compilers.

7.2.1 (vi) 'This simple worke'

The *Table Alphabeticall* is not a well-balanced piece of work. Like most of the other English dictionaries of the seventeenth and early eighteenth centuries it is badly skewed towards the beginning of the alphabet, and there is little consistency in the defining of words: for instance, we are told that *tragedie* is 'a solemne play, describing cruell murders and sorrowes' (a fair enough description for 1604, the year when *Othello* was first performed), but *comedie* comes out merely as '(k) stage play'. Even so, there can be no doubt of its practical value in giving simple explanations to a limited range of recently introduced or otherwise troublesome words; and the number of entries is nearly doubled in the three subsequent editions down to the year 1617.

7.2.2 *John Bullokar:* An English Expositor, *1616*

The second dictionary of English, John Bullokar's *English Expositor*, has nearly twice the number of entries contained in the original volume of Cawdrey, while sharing the same general aim of helping the linguistically insecure with learned terms—'the great store of strange words, our speech doth borrow' (*To the Courteous Reader*, sig. A3v). Bullokar was a physician in the city of Chichester, and tells us that his collection of English words had originally been put together for private use—for nearly seven years before publication, he says, he had not even had 'any leasure as much as to looke on it'. This suggests a measure of detached scholarly interest, and his dictionary will certainly have had a wider appeal than the narrowly informative little book of the schoolmaster Cawdrey, with its bare succession of jerky definitions.

7.2.2 (i) Word-list and sources

Bullokar takes over about one third of the entries he found in Cawdrey. Some of these he left quite unchanged ('O*bstacle.* A hinderance or lette', '*Reduction.* A bringing backe'), thus establishing from the start what was to be a long-lasting tradition in the early English dictionary of near-plagiaristic copying from predecessors. In many other Cawdrey items the wording of the definition has been improved and new senses are added.

The matter derived from Cawdrey is supplemented by a much larger number of entries adapted from the Latin–English dictionary of Thomas Thomas (Starnes and Noyes 1946: 21–3). The resulting assemblage of Latinate 'hard words' in Bullokar may seem daunting today, but in his favour it must be said that very few of them were mere 'dictionary' items which had never been recorded elsewhere, and there is a high percentage of recent borrowings: under *ex-*, for instance, *exhortatorie*, *exiccate* 'to dry', *exprobrate* 'to upbraid, to cast in ones teeth' and *extrinsecall* had all entered the language during the sixteenth century. It is with items such as these (even though some of them were not to survive) that we see the hard-word dictionary at its most effective in serving the needs of its own time.

7.2.2 (ii) Innovations

Cawdrey had confined his attention almost entirely to the simple explanation of hard words. Bullokar is far more venturesome, diversifying the rather minimalist text of his predecessor to give the user much more than bare meanings.

In the hard words entered in his dictionary there is a clear shift towards more purely technical terms. In entries for words such as *chattell* 'A Law tearme, wherof there be two kinds...', *predicament* 'A terme of Logicke', and *sable* 'In armorie it signifieth blacke...', we may see the beginnings of our modern lexicographical field-labels. The compiler still felt the need to apologize to members of the learned professions for revealing the secrets of their vocabulary to the ignorant, but the comprehensive coverage of such labelled 'Terms of Art' was soon to become an important selling point on the title pages of English dictionaries.

Then, in what is visually the most striking innovation in Bullokar, he uses an asterisk to mark words 'onely used of some ancient writers, and now growne out of use'. These are characteristically Chaucerian words such as **bale*, **eld*, **galiard*, **hent*, and **iwympled*, nearly all of them drawn from Thomas Speght's 1602 Chaucer glossary (Kerling 1979: Chapter 5 and Appendix 5) together with a few Spenserian items. The modern lexicographical practice of including a sprinkling of literary archaisms thus set in very early.

The compiler also occasionally supplements his definition by means of model sentences (at *habit*, for instance), and with an entry for *pseudo* shows at one point a recognition of the dictionary user's need for guidance on word-elements, as well as on words. Under *pseudo* he says 'Note, that words which beginne with Pseudo, signifie counterfet or false, as Pseudo-martyr, a false Martyr...'.

The otherwise largely businesslike text in Bullokar is broken up by a scattering of disproportionately long entries. Thus we are told that a *basiliske* ('Otherwise called a Cockatrise') is the most venomous serpent that exists, and the compiler goes on to describe its size, the colour of its skin and its eyes, where it breeds, how dangerous it is ('If a man touch it but with a sticke, it will kill him') and rounds off the entry with eight lines of verse translated from Lucan. Other somewhat unpredictable items running to a whole column or more include *aspect*, *beaver*, *crocodile*, *divination* (five columns), *eclipse*, *oracle*, and *parallels*. Such readable entries provide the user with resting points in an otherwise rather bleak alphabetical list of words, much after the fashion of the inset panels that have become a distinctive typographical feature of dictionaries in our own day.

7.2.2 (iii) 'This little vocabulary Treatise'

In his *English Expositor* Bullokar thus tries out many things, though without any great regard for consistency. He has a lighter touch than his predecessor Cawdrey, and shows himself to be far more awake to the varieties of meaning, frequency, and current usage: *epigramme* he notes, 'properly signifieth a superscription or writing set upon any thing', but now 'it is commonly taken for a short wittie poeme', and elsewhere, with a near-Johnsonian acceptance of his own ignorance, he says simply of *hide of land* that 'Some affirme it to be a hundred acres'. All this—together with his occasional showpiece entries such as *basiliske*—makes for a more engaging work, and may in part account for the remarkable success of the *English Expositor*. Bullokar died in 1641, but his book went on being published for over 150 years until 1765.

7.2.3 *Henry Cockeram:* The English Dictionarie, *1623*

The first three monolingual dictionaries came out within a period of only twenty years and they had a great deal in common, in size, scope, and intention. Henry Cockeram's *English Dictionarie: or, An Interpreter of Hard English Words* is in some ways the most interesting of them. He was the first of the English compilers to call his book a dictionary, and divided his book into three parts so as to accommodate both the decoding and the encoding needs of less literate readers. His choice of title—*English Dictionary*—was however to prove more durable than this structural innovation.

7.2.3 (i) Part I: Hard words explained

The first part, taking up roughly half of the whole volume, is a hard-word book much in the spirit of Cawdrey and Bullokar and is greatly indebted to them. It contains what the author calls the *choicest* words, presented as an aid to the understanding of 'the more difficult Authors', and the intended readership is much the same as that addressed by his predecessors—'Ladies and Gentlewomen, young Schollers, Clarkes, Merchants, as also Strangers of any Nation'.

Cockeram rightly boasts that his collection contains 'some thousands of words, never published by any heretofore' and it is clear that he turned to the Latin–English dictionaries to supplement what he had found in Cawdrey and Bullokar (Starnes and Noyes 1946: 31–3). The formidable list resulting includes many ghost items such as *famigerate* 'to report abroad', and *floccifie* 'to set nought by', but also a great number of newly current words (*fabulositie*, *facinorous*) and others such as *foliacion* 'budding of the leaves' which seemingly came into use only after his day. The creative potentialities for introducing words from the Latin was overwhelming in the early seventeenth century, and the lexicographer simply lacked the means of knowing for sure which 'hard' words were genuine and which were not. Throwing in everything you could think of was probably not a bad tactic, and there can be no doubt of the general utility of Cockeram's collection.

7.2.3 (ii) Part II: Plain words adorned

The second part of Cockeram's dictionary looks like a reversal (though not a simple reversal) of the first: thus 'Fewnes. *Paucity*' in Part II corresponds to

'*Paucitie*. Fewnesse' in Part I; 'Worldly. *Mundane, Secular*' in Part II takes up the entries for the words *mundane* and *secular* in Part I. Thus whereas Part I appears primarily as a decoding dictionary for readers, Part II may best be seen as an encoding dictionary for writers aspiring to a loftier style, and perhaps also for those who like Sir Andrew Aguecheek felt the urge to lard their speech with affected terms.

For this part of his dictionary Cockeram can be shown to have turned to one of the English–Latin dictionaries of his day, probably John Rider's *Bibliotheca Scholastica* (1589), or one of its later revisions by Francis Holyoke:

(3) **Rider 1589**	**Cockeram 1623**
To Shadowe. 1.Vmbro, adumbro, inumbro, perumbro . . .	to Shadow. *Obumbrate, Adumbrate.*
Sweetnesse. 1. Dulcedo, dulcitudo, dulcitas, suavitas, suavitudo, f. dulcor, m.	Sweetnesse. *Dulcitie, Suavity, Dulcitude.*

Here the sequence of Latin translations provided by Rider has evidently served to put the compiler in mind of equivalent learned terms which existed (or could perhaps exist) in English.

It is a curiously oblique way of devising a list of ordinary English words, and in some cases it is hard to see what function an entry in Part II can have had: *Rarifaction* 'A making thinne of what was thicke' makes good enough sense in Part I, but who is ever going to find the corresponding entry ('a Making of that thinne which is thicke. *Rarifaction*') under the letter M (for *making*) in Part II?

Cockeram was evidently himself aware of the problems of selection which he had created for himself, and in the *Premonition from the Author to the Reader* notes that in Part II he has also included *mocke-words*, 'ridiculously used in our Language', and even *fustian termes* 'used by too many who study rather to be heard speake, than to understand themselves'. This is perhaps the first shot in a campaign that later compilers (Phillips, Kersey, etc.) were to wage against 'inkhorn' words, the excessive Latinity of their age. More cautious than his successors, Cockeram never tells us which ones they are: but with items such as 'to Taste againe. *Regust*' and 'to Walke backe, *Redambulate*', the reader does not have to look far.

This, the most original section of Cockeram's book, thus appears to be in several ways ill thought out in function. As against that, there are many impressively full entries: for the word *strong* he has 'Energeticall, Herculean, Strenuous, Sampsonian, Firme, Atlanticke, Vigorous, Robustious, Doughtie' and *sweet* is 'Mellifluous, Odoriferous, Ambrosiack, Redolent, Aromaticall, Dulcid'. English synonym dictionaries proper were not to appear until the works of John Trusler and Mrs Piozzi in the latter half of the eighteenth century; but the very profusion of equivalents here shows that Cockeram's dictionary will at times have served similar purposes in its day.

7.2.3 (iii) Part III: Names of everything

The third and smallest part of Cockeram's book is 'a recital of several persons, Gods and Goddesses, Giants and Devils, Monsters and Serpents, Birds and Beasts, Rivers, Fishes, Hearbs, Stones, Trees, and the like'. These are arranged, not for quick reference in a single alphabetical list, but in the traditional semantically classified form of the *Nomenclator*, as commonly found in the Latin dictionaries of the day.

Under *Hills & Mountaines* four names are given (Etna, Alps, Ararat, and Chaphareus) and there are six *Men that were Musitians*, including Orpheus; some other categories such as *Women of sundrie qualities* must have been of doubtful utility—this includes Zanthippe, but also Alcippe 'a Woman that brought forth an Elephant' (→ HOARE, Vol. II).

Cockeram thus had his own solution to the compiler's perennial problem of what to do about names in a dictionary: he kept all the linguistically peripheral matter for what amounted to a substantial and perhaps instructive appendix. He was the first to do this, and lexicographers have been shifting the boundaries of lexical and encyclopedic matter ever since.

7.2.4 *Thomas Blount:* Glossographia, *1656*

Blount's *Glossographia* has always been rightly regarded as the classic dictionary of hard words: there are more of them, in greater variety, from a fuller range of (sometimes identified) sources, and they are presented in an altogether more disciplined way. The substantial octavo volume in which they occur was to do much to set a pattern for the physical shape and structured contents of later English dictionaries, and many of Blount's neologisms (e.g. *buxiferous, diventilate, fatiferous, nemorivagant, venustate*) went on to live a life of their own in the works of his successors.

7.2.4 (i) Readership

Thomas Blount was a barrister with literary and antiquarian interests. Coming from a landed Recusant family, he was unable to pursue a career at the Bar, and produced his *Glossographia* during a 'vacancy of above Twenty years' in the

Commonwealth period, with its rigorous anti-Catholic legislation. No wonder, then, that his dictionary stands out above the schoolmasterly products of Cawdrey and Cockeram: no instructions here on how to use the alphabet, and though his book was famously intended for 'the more-knowing Women, and the less-knowing Men', the *Address to the Reader* with its elegant Latin quotations is couched in terms of what every 'Gentleman of Estate' should know.

7.2.4 (ii) Typography and page layout

The complexity of the text also indicates a more sophisticated readership. Each of his three predecessors Cawdrey, Bullokar, and Cockeram had used only two typefaces—respectively, roman plus black letter, italic plus roman, roman plus italic (Luna 2000: 10–14). This was a visual minimum needed to distinguish words from meanings in their simple word lists. But in Blount we find an effective use of all three of these typefaces: with black letter to make the entry words stand out in the column and roman for the basic explanations, italic is available for etymologies, names, and other secondary matter. This display of type is diversified elsewhere by an occasional Greek word in Cyrillic; Hebrew script where it is needed for an etymology (at *Talmud*, for example); and even a Saxon font in the account of better-known words (such as *Gospel*) from Old English.

Blount also introduces illustrations into his text—a couple of woodcuts in entries for the heraldic terms *Canton* and *Gyron*—and the *Glossographia* is the first of the monolingual English dictionaries with headers to help the user to find his word in flicking through the book: following the model of Latin dictionaries of his day, he puts catch-letters at the top of each ruled column on the page (e.g. **FR** above the column of words running from *fortuitous* to *fraction*).

7.2.4 (iii) Sources

Blount is also the first English compiler to provide etymologies for all (or nearly all) the words entered. In scholarly fashion he acknowledges his sources of information: 'I have extracted the quintessence of Scapula, Minsheu, Cotgrave, Rider, Florio, Thomasius, Dasipodius, and Hexams Dutch, Dr. Davies Welsh Dictionary, Cowels Interpreter, &c.' (*To the Reader*, sig. A5r-v), adding 'I profess to have done little with my own Pencil'. This is a far cry from the casually gleaned offerings of his predecessors, though it has been calculated (Starnes and Noyes 1946: 40–2) that some two-thirds of all his entries derive from the Latin dictionary of Thomas Thomas and the 1639 edition of Francis Holyoke's *Dictionarium Etymologicum*.

In about one fifth of all entries in the dictionary Blount identified a contemporary or near-contemporary writer in whose work a word was to be found, including authors such as Bacon, Ben Jonson, Sir Walter Ralegh, and Jeremy Taylor (Osselton 1996: 218). There was precedent in classical dictionaries (for instance, in Scapula) for validating words by attaching the names of authors to them, but Blount was the first English compiler to do this, thus initiating a practice which Johnson was to extend to the whole vocabulary a century later.

7.2.4 (iv) Blount's concern for usage

The *Glossographia* exhibits the vices of the hard-word dictionary (non-existent English words, culled uncritically from Latin dictionaries), but at the same time it celebrates the exuberant vocabulary of the day—Sir Thomas Browne is one of the most commonly cited authors. In his address *To the Reader*, Blount makes it clear that the inclusion of so many learned words did not necessarily mean that he was commending them. But many had now become familiar (even to the vulgar) through use by contemporary authors, and 'to understand them, can be no unnecessary burden to the Intellect'; thus he had added the authors' names 'that I might not be thought to be the innovator of them'. It is for its age a remarkably detached statement of the dictionary-maker's concern for usage and of his duties to the public.

Blount's dictionary was reprinted and considerably enlarged through five editions down to 1681. As the work of Phillips and other successors was to show, 'hard words' had by then become the object of more critical attention and even ridicule.

7.3 THE ENCYCLOPEDIC DICTIONARY

The second half of the seventeenth century saw the production of the first monolingual dictionaries of English in folio: no longer to be seen as learners' aids but rather as handsome books for a gentleman's library. There was thus every reason to make the dictionary readable, putting in more of the generally informative entries of the kind which had been scattered incidentally through Bullokar, and incorporating fully the extensive lists of names which Cockeram had relegated to the back of his book. This represented a clear (but by no means permanent) shift in the view of what an English dictionary should contain.

7.3.1 *Edward Phillips:* The New World of English Words: Or, a General Dictionary, *1658*

Phillips's dictionary, with its grand title modelled on John Florio's Italian–English *Worlde of Wordes* (1598), was the first of the folio dictionaries of English. In five editions down to 1696, followed by the versions revised by John Kersey (1706, 1720) it dominated the big-dictionary market for over seventy years. The handsome volume of 1658 has a rather flamboyant dedication to the illustrious universities of Oxford and Cambridge, and a fine title page with engraved portraits of Chaucer, Spenser, and the antiquaries Lambard, Camden, Selden, and Spelman—all indicating certain pretensions to scholarship which are, however, hardly borne out by the contents.

7.3.1 (i) **Encyclopedic matter**

Phillips's dictionary was published hard on the heels of Blount's smaller work, and was deeply indebted to it, so much so that his 'wholesale thefts' (as well as many errors of fact) were exposed by Blount in a scathing accusation of plagiarism; it has been calculated that two-thirds of all Phillips's word-entries were simply lifted from Blount (Starnes and Noyes 1946: 49–54).

The whole balance of the dictionary is, however, changed by a striking extension of the names and other encyclopedic matter (Roe 1977: 16–17). Even in the earlier, smaller dictionaries of Bullokar and Blount, we have seen that names had been creeping in, but now Phillips makes no bones about admitting into his dictionary 'Proper Names, Mythology, and Poetical Fictions, Historical Relations, Geographical Descriptions of most Countries and Cities of the World...' and boasts on his title page of the 'Arts and Sciences' that he has covered: '*Theologie, Philosophy, Logick, Rhetorick, Grammer, Ethicks, Law, Natural History, Magick, Physick*...'—thirty-one of them in all, including Chiromancy, Curiosities, Merchandize, Horsemanship, and Fishing.

Elaborate title pages doubtless served in the seventeenth century as blurbs, a chief means of promoting sales of your book. But any glance between the covers of Phillips's dictionary shows that the scale of non-verbal and technical matter is indeed impressive. Of the forty entries from *albeito* to *alexipharmac*, twenty-three are names, and, though there is a tailing off through the alphabet, in the dictionary as a whole at least one in every four or five entries may be said to deal with encyclopedic matter of one kind or another. Many such items are lengthy: *Knights of the Garter, Paris* ('son of *Priamus*...'), and *A Vein* ('defined by *Anatomists* to be...') all rank half a column.

7.3.1 (ii) The critical dictionary

Phillips thus shifted the balance of interest in the English dictionary, but his work represented little substantial advance in detailed matters of lexicographical technique: he drops etymology (substituting *lat.*, *Fr.*, *Germ.*, etc., for the etymons given in Blount), and entries for polysemous words remain poorly punctuated. He was, however, the first to introduce into his front matter what amounted to a history of the English language—a practice which was followed by Bailey, Johnson, and many later dictionary-makers.

The most striking innovation in Phillips lay in the treatment of hard words. He took over many, though not all of the ones he found in Blount: for instance, in the sequence of fifteen Latinisms from *obtestation* to *obvolate* he leaves out *obtorted, obvention*, and *obviate*, while adding *obvallation* and *obvarication*. But two of the items †*obticence* 'a being silent' and †o*bundation* 'a flowing against' are prefixed by a dagger symbol as a warning to the dictionary user that these are not acceptable (or not entirely acceptable) words in English. Altogether ninety-five words are thus marked in the dictionary as 'Pedantismes'. More were added in later editions, and in 1678 there is also an appendix of fifty-three affected words 'to be used warily, and upon occasion only, or totally to be rejected as Barbarous'; *circumbilivagination* ('a going round'), *cynarctomachy* ('a Bear-baiting') and *honorificabilitudinity* are fair examples of these.

The introduction by Phillips of this device may be seen to mark the beginning of a clearly prescriptive tradition in the English monolingual dictionary, and during the next hundred years his example was to be followed by Kersey (1706), Bailey ('Vol. II', 1727), and Martin (1749). In these later works the use of the dagger also covered old words (previously marked with an asterisk) and was expanded as a general mark of disapprobation for all kinds of popular forms or spellings (*flower-de-luce, prentice, shagreen*), dialect items (*brock, kirk, rill*), slang (*bamboozle, cit, mutton-monger* 'mulierarius'), and what Johnson was later to call 'low' words (*crack* 'a whore', *to swop, woundy*). Johnson himself is known to have entertained the idea of using such 'marks of distinction' or 'notes of infamy' in his Dictionary, but in the end preferred to put in verbal comments on individual words (Osselton 1958; 2006: 99–105).

7.3.2 Elisha Coles: An English Dictionary, *1676*

In the middle of the Phillips era Elisha Coles, 'School-Master and Teacher of the Tongue to Foreigners', produced a lively and highly original little octavo dictionary, printed in very small type with three columns to the page. It is a book packed with highly concise information on some 25,000 words and names, and aimed no doubt at those whose pockets were too lean to purchase the folio of Phillips.

7.3.2 (i) Character of the word-list

Coles is very heavily indebted to Phillips both for words and for names. On a sample page running from *Misnia* to *modulation* we find a total of eighty-four entries; comparison with the corresponding part of Phillips (third edition, 1671, *misogamy* to *modulation*) shows that only the word *mixture* is omitted, and that forty-five new items have been added, including *misnomer*, *misogynist*, *Miss* ('for *Mistress*'), *miswoman* ('a whore'), *mockel*, *muckle* ('Mickle'), and *mockadoes* ('a kind of stuff'). Definitions are cut down radically, and, though nearly all the names in Phillips are retained, the information given on them is very spare indeed.

7.3.2 (ii) Canting terms

Coles is the first English compiler to take notice of the language of low life: canting terms such as *flog* 'to whip', *fogus* 'Tabacco', *glimmer* 'fire', *grinders* 'Teeth', *nizie* 'a fool', *shoplift* 'one that … steals wares', *witcher* 'silver', are included with the wry apology that they 'may chance to save your throat from being cut, or (at least) your Pocket from being pickt'. Numerous separate glossaries of words from the language of thieves, rogues, and cony-catchers had appeared in the hundred years before Coles. His 217 low-life items (labelled with a 'c') were drawn from *The Canting Academy*, a collection published by Richard Head in 1673 (Coleman 2004: 176–7), and many of them were to pass into the lower end of the accepted nomenclature in general English dictionaries (Johnson marks down *nizy* as a 'low word', and says *grinders* is used only 'in irony or contempt').

7.3.2 (iii) Dialect

The practice of entering a limited number of dialect words in general English dictionaries is also to be dated from this volume by Coles, who derived them from *A Collection of English Words not Generally Used* by John Ray, published in 1674 (Brengelman 1981: 6–7). *Daft* (Norfolk), *geazon* 'scarce, hard to come by' (Essex), *riddle-cakes* (Lancashire), *stunt* 'stubborn, angry' (Lincolnshire) are typical examples. They take up over three per cent of all the dictionary entries in Coles, who set a pattern for Bailey and many later compilers, both in the general character of the words and in the practice of designating them by county name (Osselton 1995: 34–45).

7.3.2 (iv) Lexicographical innovations

For so small a work, Coles's dictionary contains a surprising number of derivatives in groups such as *flammability, flammation, flammeous, flammivomous, flammiferous.* Derivatives have always been, and remain, problematic for dictionary compilers (whether to grant them all full entry status, set them in smaller type, or simply list the semantically less complicated ones). Coles adopts for some of them an ingenious space-saving pattern of concatenated entries:

(4) *Tristifical, l.* which doth
Tristitiate, or make
Tristful, sad, sorrowfull.

This pleasingly jaunty arrangement was however to find no imitators among later compilers.

A more lasting innovation was Coles's list of abbreviations in the front matter. He needed this especially for a compact treatment of dialect items, with abbreviations for county names (*K.* for Kentish, *Sf.* for Suffolk, etc.). But the list also includes abbreviations for Arabic, Syriac, and Persian, as used in some of the more exotic entries, as well as *C.* for *Canting* and *O.* for *Old Word.*

The urge to pack in as much information as the page would bear has led Coles into adopting a jumble of different styles for his entries, from the pithy '*Alexander*, Conquered the world, and was poysoned' or the simple exemplification of 'A buck *Groyneth*, makes that noise' to the three-word whittled down '*Cluni* in Burgundy'. These are typical of what was found in spelling-books of the day. A more successful feature was his introduction of square brackets for the purpose of collapsing two meanings of a word into a single statement, as in *extuberate* '[to cause] to swel or bunch up', and *Lethe* '[a supposed River of Hell causing] forgetfulness'.

7.3.2 (v) 'Here is very much in very little room'

With little substantial change, the *English Dictionary* of Coles went through eleven editions down to 1732. Full of potted encyclopedic information but at times over-ingeniously compact, it can hardly have been in competition with the more expansive Phillips. Coles addressed the needs of less demanding readers who did not mind small print, and would be content with being told simply that *Ajax* was 'A Stout *Grecian*' or that *Hinton* was the name of several small towns.

7.3.3 John Kersey: Revision of Phillips, 1706

For all its somewhat antiquated and eclectic assembly of items, Phillips's dictionary of 1658 saw augmented editions at frequent intervals down to the end of the century (1662, 1671, 1678, 1696) with a growth in the number of entries from 11,000 to around 17,000.

The sixth edition, published in 1706 and reissued in 1720, underwent major revision by John Kersey 'with the Addition of near Twenty Thousand Words'. This is simply a larger book, and represents no great change in lexicographical technique; indeed, with the reintroduction of black letter type for the entry words, the heavily inked pages must have borne the stamp of an earlier age.

In the contents, however, the reviser shows himself to be a modernizer, removing what he calls the 'Poetical Fictions' so dear to Phillips (such as the story of Orpheus, or the legend of Alcyone) and filling up his work with items of more topical interest. By far the greatest expansion has been in the coverage of technical terms: for the word *angle*, for instance, he has forty-nine separate entries, where Phillips had only one. Significantly, there are incidental references in Kersey's text to John Locke (at the word *reflection*: 'according to Mr. *Lock*'s Definition...') and to Robert Boyle (at *animated mercury*: 'so Mr. *Boyle* calls Quicksilver...'). Here, the English dictionary is to be seen quickly catching up on the new science of the post-Restoration world, and in presenting it Kersey can be shown to have made very good use of the recently published *Lexicon Technicum* (1704) by John Harris FRS (Starnes and Noyes 1946: 85–6). To his credit, the compiler also records linguistic extensions in the use of many scientific words: he has a lengthy technical explanation of *eclipse*, ending 'The Word is also us'd in a figurative Sense, as *During the unhappy Eclipse of the Monarchy*', and the entry for *point-blank* (originally a term in gunnery) ends 'Whence it is commonly taken for directly, positively, or absolutely; as *He told me point-blank, he would take it*'.

7.3.4 Glossographia Anglicana Nova, *1707 (GAN)*

The acceptance of the new scientific vocabulary in Kersey's revision of Phillips is taken a step further in the otherwise unimportant *Glossographia Anglicana Nova* (1707, 1720). This derivative little work is something of a throwback to Thomas Blount's *Glossographia* of 1656, and like Blount the compiler takes it upon himself to validate certain words (especially unusual ones) by attaching an author's name to them. But whereas Blount tended to pick on the more eccentric words from Sir Thomas Browne's *Pseudodoxia Epidemica*, the anonymous compiler of the GAN—evidently a scientist himself—typically validates words from recent scientific publications by Boyle, Evelyn, Hooke, Newton, Henry Power, and other leading members of the Royal Society, alongside terms used by contemporary theologians and preachers such as Burnet, Hoadly, and Stillingfleet.

7.3.5 *John Kersey:* Dictionarium Anglo-Britannicum, *1708*

Two years after his revision of Phillips, Kersey went on to produce from it the first abridged dictionary of English. It passed through two further editions in 1715 and 1721. Here, as so often in later centuries (and doubtless for similar commercial reasons), an established dictionary was boiled down to provide a quick look-up reference work for a somewhat different group of users; Kersey defines the readership of his new volume as 'Private Gentlemen, Young Students, Tradesmen, Shop-keepers, Artificers, [and] Strangers'.

Of the two classic ways of producing an abridgement (reducing the number of words or cutting down definitions) Kersey opts firmly for the latter: nearly all the original entries in the 1706 Phillips are retained (there are even some new items), while explanations of them are drastically pruned and sometimes remodelled. The handy octavo volume of the *Dictionarium Anglo-Britannicum* was, surprisingly, for so innovative a publishing venture, the last of the English monolingual dictionaries to use black letter for entry words, and, with two later editions in 1715 and 1721, it must have had a somewhat antiquated appearance in the age of Addison and Pope.

7.4 THE UNIVERSAL DICTIONARY

In the hundred years from Cawdrey the expected (or acceptable) content of the English dictionary had thus expanded way beyond the original target of 'hard words' (often of dubious currency) to include almost every kind of encyclopedic information imaginable: names of English market towns, of Gods and Goddesses, poetic fictions, historical references, dialect, slang, and later even a state-of-the-art scientific terminology. But no set effort had ever been made to provide systematic coverage of the everyday words of the language. Some were inevitably to be found, though often they had been put in only to record a specialized sense. As early as 1616, Bullokar had made the point tellingly: for a word with different meanings, he says, 'one easie, the other more difficult' he would deal only with the harder one, and he then instances *girle*, which duly appears in his dictionary with the single meaning 'A Roe Bucke of two yeares'.

The notion that a monolingual dictionary should record all the generally known words of a language thus became established for English only in the early eighteenth century. Precedent for the inclusion of common words was perhaps to be found earlier in the *Alphabetical Dictionary* incorporated in John Wilkins's *Essay towards a Real Character and a Philosophical Language* in 1668, a work well known to later compilers (Dolezal 1985; → Hüllen, Vol. II). But the alphabetical list printed there was intended primarily as an index to Wilkins's structured analysis of the language; many entries do not offer definitions at all (e.g. '*Buttock.* PG.IV.8', '*Unripeness.* NP.VI.4.D.'), and, though the list of words in it and the information encoded there will yield a wealth of semantic and idiomatic information to the patient user, it can hardly ever have functioned as a dictionary in the conventional sense.

7.4.1 J. K.: A New English Dictionary, *1702*

It was the *New English Dictionary* published in 1702 by J. K. (commonly taken to be John Kersey) that established once and for all the practice of including the everyday vocabulary of English alongside 'harder' words: his letter D begins with *a dab, a dab-chick, a dab-fish, to dabble, a dace,* and *a daffodell,* and at the word *girl* he starts with the common meaning ('A Girl, or *wench*'). This handy little book (like Coles) is in very small print, with three columns to the page, and it runs to some 28,000 entries.

To obtain a suitable alphabetical list of common words as a basis for his work, Kersey turned to bilingual dictionaries with English as 'source' language which (for obvious reasons) had always needed to include them; it can be shown that he leant heavily on the English–French dictionaries of Miège (1688) and Boyer (1699), and on Adam Littleton (1678) or some other English–Latin dictionary of his time (Osselton 1995: 25–33; → Cormier).

One clear by-product of his reliance upon bilingual dictionaries is a far fuller coverage of English compound words and derivatives than had been seen in Phillips, Coles, and the others. After the entry for *wine,* for instance, ten second-element compounds are listed in alphabetical order (*Canary-wine, Claret-wine,* etc.), followed by eight first-element compounds (*A Wine-bibber, A Wine-Cellar,* etc.), with explanations given only when needed (*A Wine conner,* or *wine-taster*). Similarly, derivatives such as *An Adopter, An Adoption, Adoptive* are simply listed after the base word without definitions.

Such lists of compounds and derivatives in Kersey stand as headwords, neither indented nor typographically distinct, and this may leave us with the unfavourable impression of a negligent compiler putting in large numbers of words without definitions. On the other hand, Kersey may be given credit for introducing a highly systematic treatment for a category of words which has bothered lexicographers ever since. Undefined entries were in any case characteristic of eighteenth-century spelling-books, and the compiler may also have had in mind the convenience of learners who would use the dictionary simply to check spellings—on the title page he addresses those 'who would learn to spell truely'.

For learners he silently indicates word-class by putting articles before nouns and the particle *to* before verbs (as in *to adopt*, etc., above). The modern practice of using conventional abbreviations to show the parts of speech of all words entered was to be established only later (1735) in the *New General English Dictionary* of Thomas Dyche and William Pardon, who were also the first compilers to prefix an English grammar to their dictionary.

7.4.2 An Universal Etymological English Dictionary, *1721 (UEED)*

Nathan Bailey equalled John Kersey in output, and his works dominated the English dictionary scene in the first half of the eighteenth century. The octavo *Universal Etymological English Dictionary* appeared in 1721, a handy volume with nearly a thousand pages and 40,000 entries. To this was added in 1727 a so-called 'Vol. II' of similar size, but a hybrid product with two alphabetical lists, the second of which appears as some kind of a bilingualized learners' dictionary with French and Latin equivalents added to the English. Finally, in 1730, his great folio volume *Dictionarium Britannicum* appeared, the second edition of which (1736) is known to have been used as some kind of a base text by Samuel Johnson.

Bailey was not the first to adopt the word 'universal' in a dictionary title (Kersey had slipped it into his revision of Phillips) but in the UEED he uses it advisedly as he here seeks to cover the whole basic vocabulary of English. His word-list is based on Kersey's *Dictionarium Anglo-Britannicum* (1708), but considerably updated: on the two pages from *linseed* to *livery*, for instance, he adds entries for a whole range of common words which would be entered as a matter of course by lexicographers today: *lip*, *to lisp*, *to listen*, *littel* ('small'), *to live*, and *lively*. The coverage of everyday words is, however, still patchy, with entries for the verbs *have* and *be*, but not for *can* and *do*.

There is also a generous selection of marginal terms of the kind that had cropped up in the various works of his predecessors: cant, technical terms, dialect, 'old' words, legal terms, place-name, 'hard' words—for all these the presentation, labelling, and explanation are methodical, matter-of-fact, and admirably concise. Above all, Bailey makes his dictionary usable, accessible: for instance, he devotes much attention to etymology, but he recognizes that this might put off readers with no knowledge of languages, and explains that the etymological information on each word has been put within square brackets 'that they may pass it over without any manner of Trouble or Inconvenience'.

Perhaps the most striking visual innovation in the UEED is the use of capital letters for all entry words. This was to become standard practice in most eighteenth-century English dictionaries; the words stood out well on the page and italic remained freely available for other purposes. In editions from 1731, and earlier in his 'Vol. II' (1727), the accentuation of English words is shown by a stress-mark after the accented syllable, as in CO'FFEE, COGITA'TION, COGNA'TE. His introduction of this system (from a schoolbook by Thomas Dyche) represents the beginnings of recording pronunciation in English dictionaries (Bronstein 1986: 23–4). A further successful innovation was the introduction of a few traditional proverbs ('The Belly has no Ears', 'Proffered Service Stinks'), appropriately highlighted in old-fashioned black letter print. Many more were to be included later in his folio work.

Bailey's weakness lay in the matter of definitions, to which he contributed little (*out* is merely 'Without'; *long* is 'of great Extent'; the meaning of the verb *to come* is given simply as 'to draw nigh, to approach'). But in the UEED he created a well-arranged and eminently usable dictionary; it provides an effective list of the general vocabulary of English, while being pleasantly diversified by less well-known items and out-of-the-way information. No wonder William Pitt the Elder found it worth reading through, nor that it survived well into the Johnson era, to go through twenty-eight editions down to the year 1800.

7.4.3 Dictionarium Britannicum, *1730 (DB)*

With over 700 pages of fine print and some 48,000 entries (almost 60,000 in the second edition) Nathan Bailey's folio *Dictionarium Britannicum* was easily the most comprehensive English dictionary of its day. The whole vocabulary of his earlier dictionary is included, apart from native English names (relegated to an appendix) but it is all greatly enlarged, in range as in treatment.

Making use of the recently published *Cyclopaedia* of Ephraim Chambers (1728), Bailey achieved an impressive enlargement of technical terms (music, printing, cookery, stage plays, painting, hieroglyphs, etc.), and there is almost everywhere a dramatic expansion of the information provided. *Column*, for instance, as an architectural term, had had only a brief, five-line entry in the UEED, but in the DB there are well over fifty separate entries for it, including *Tuscan column*, *Fluted column*, *Rostral column*, etc.; for the word *rhyme* he keeps to a single entry in the bigger dictionary, but the original three-word definition 'Meeter or Verse' is replaced by a whole article on the history of rhyme and blank verse in English, with the opinions of Skinner, Dryden, and Lord Roscommon, and the practice of Shakespeare and Milton.

There is also great expansion in the use of illustrations. The 500 woodcuts of which he boasts occur most often for heraldic items, but also in the explanation of mathematical concepts (nineteen representations at the word *angle*), for chemical symbols (*borax*, *sulphur*), in agriculture (*hurdles*), in military and naval terms (*bombs*, *chain-shot*), and in astronomy (a handsome whole page engraving for *orrery*).

Though it is thus astonishingly rich in contents, the *Dictionarium Britannicum* contains nothing that is new in lexicographical method. The surprisingly numerous self-explanatory derivatives now introduced (including improbable ones such as *eternalness* and *undistinguishableness*) are given full headword status. Where in the bigger dictionary there is a greater complexity of meaning or a wider range of meanings (as for the word *column*) no attempt has been made to structure the information given. In the mammoth sequence of entries to be found for many words in the *Dictionarium Britannicum* the English dictionary may be said to have reached the limits of what mere alphabetic listing could do.

7.4.4 Benjamin Martin: Lingua Britannica Reformata, *1749*

The *Lingua Britannica Reformata* of Benjamin Martin, schoolmaster, mathematician, and instrument-maker, is as remarkable for the 111 pages of its front matter as for the contents of the dictionary proper. The compiler chose to include there his long and erudite *Institutions of Language; Containing, A Physico-Grammatical Essay on the Propriety and Rationale of the English Tongue*, published the previous year and now reprinted with the much-simplified running title 'Introduction to the English Tongue'.

In this he discusses the nature of spoken and written language, the growth of alphabetic symbols from Hebrew onwards, general grammatical principles as exemplified in major European languages, and the evolving structures of English from Anglo-Saxon; the essay ends with a reflective paragraph on the transitoriness of all writings: 'Addison, Pope, and Foster, may appear to our posterity in the same light as Chaucer, Spencer, and Shakespear do to us; whose language is now grown old and obsolete; read by very few, and understood by antiquarians only.'

As the tone here may suggest, it seems likely that Martin was acquainted with Dr Johnson's *Plan of an English Dictionary*, published two years before. This appears even more clearly from the Preface, where he specifies 'the proper Requisites of a Genuine English Dictionary', insisting in particular upon the total exclusion of encyclopedic matter, and the need to distinguish multiple meanings of words: first the original or etymological meaning, then popular uses, followed by figurative or metaphorical senses, humorous, poetical or burlesque use, and finally, the scientific or technical meanings—'no Method but this can give adequate and just Ideas of Words'.

The introduction of numbers for separate meanings marks out Martin's page as something entirely new in English lexicography (the practice was common enough in bilingual dictionaries, and he acknowledges a debt to Ainsworth and Boyer). He is, however, far from consistent or successful in applying the semantic principles he sets out: why should *foot* 'a member of a human body' be number 1, but *foot* 'the paw of a beast' come in only at number 6 after the items for 'twelve inches' and 'infantry'? There are also very many words where numbering would have been welcome (e.g. *consternation*, for both 'terror' and 'astonishment'), and others (such as *construction*) where numbered meanings are given in one entry and additional meanings tagged on in separate entries.

Another useful new lexicographical device is that of putting unassimilated foreign words such as *legerdemain* and *pronto* into italics. This practice (also proposed by Johnson) had become easily workable in the eighteenth century with the introduction of capital letters for entry words.

Martin's dictionary was overshadowed by Johnson and there was only one subsequent edition (in 1754), with the *Physico-Grammatical Essay* left out. He was a major innovator in English lexicography, but promised rather more than he performed.

7.5 CONCLUSION

The emergence of a balanced and usable dictionary of English during the seventeenth and early eighteenth century was a haphazard process, seemingly determined as much by what was marketable as by any reflection upon the true nature of a monolingual dictionary, how it should be structured, and what its function should be.

The original hard-word list clearly served a useful purpose in the first decades of the seventeenth century, when learned books in the vernacular still tended to have English glossaries attached. Demand for the hard-word dictionary (presumably from the least literate) lasted long, with Bullokar's *English Expositor* (1616) lingering on until 1775.

Diversification of the vocabulary was an obvious need if the dictionary was to achieve a wider readership. This was, however, a period of rapid development in dictionaries of specialized terms (Osselton 1999: 2458–65), and in filling out their monolingual dictionaries the English compilers had the convenience of being able to turn to a whole range of useful contemporary works on specialized vocabularies, e.g. for cant, dialect, divinity, heraldry, husbandry, law, and navigation. It is always easier to pillage another man's list than to find the words yourself.

Etymology found a firm place early in the English dictionary (never to lose it), whereas the practice of including everyday words came very late, with meagre entries evidently put in to complete the record or to indicate spelling. Use of a prescriptive obelisk or dagger to mark unacceptable words, always somewhat half-hearted, was a dying episode by the time of Martin. Only two compilers (Blount, and the anonymous compiler of GAN) attempted a methodical validation of words by author's name; where it is a matter of occasional words from Chaucer, Spenser, and Shakespeare, these were mostly drawn from glossaries, not from original texts.

Throughout the seventeenth century, names and all kinds of historical and legendary matter had become a staple feature of the dictionary page in the vernacular dictionary (as they had been in classical dictionaries). In the works of later compilers (Bailey, Martin) there is a shift towards technological information, and they adopt a more narrowly linguistic stance, though the problem of what to do about names in dictionaries would not go away.

In one way or another, the works of the early lexicographers thus came to incorporate much of what we should expect to find in monolingual English dictionaries today. But pronunciation (beyond mere word-stress), the meaning of compound nouns, set collocations, phrasal verbs, particles, abbreviations, idiomatic expressions (other than proverbs), irregular plurals, all kinds of grammatical information—anything like a systematic coverage of these was to be for future generations of dictionary-makers.

8

JOHNSON AND RICHARDSON

Allen Reddick

8.1 INTRODUCTION

SAMUEL Johnson's folio *Dictionary of the English Language* (1755) represents a towering achievement in lexicography and letters, one which immediately captured attention throughout Europe; it remains a source of considerable scholarly interest to the present day, especially for specialists in lexicography, language, literature, history, and culture. In the remarkable *New Dictionary of the English Language*, published several generations later, Charles Richardson made a formidable attempt to reject and supplant Johnson. *A New Dictionary*, of interest and importance in its own right, provocatively illuminates aspects of Johnson's work.

8.2 JOHNSON'S *DICTIONARY*

For over one hundred years before Johnson's *Dictionary* was published, authors and concerned experts had expressed the need to attend to the state of the English language, seen as suffering from luxuriance, indifference, and decay. Many argued for the creation of an English Academy, including the Earl of Roscommon, John Dryden, John Evelyn, William Sprat, Daniel Defoe, Joseph Addison, Jonathan Swift, and Alexander Pope; its function would be to preserve the language and to compile an authoritative dictionary. The Royal Society (1664) set up a committee to monitor and reform the English Language, while Jonathan Swift's *Proposal for*

Correcting, Improving, and Ascertaining the English Tongue (1712) advocated the selection of a group who would establish standards of correctness and enforce them, thus guarding the purity of the language. Johnson's 'Plan of an English Dictionary' (1747) reflected similar concerns. In all cases, the approach was to stress the need for a prescriptive and normative authority, one based on, and rivalling, especially, that of the Académie française (Wells 1973: 31–40).

8.2.1 *Influences of and relation to other dictionaries*

But Johnson's *Dictionary* was certainly not the first monolingual English dictionary: there were important predecessors from which Johnson borrowed or by which he was influenced. Yet Johnson's *Dictionary* surpassed the aims and achievements of other dictionaries of his day, combining the best features of current lexicography in what may be considered the first modern dictionary of English. It was also in certain respects innovative. Johnson's *Dictionary* differed from its predecessors, for example, in the unusual circumstances of its composition and publication, including the two-volume folio format; the unprecedented lengthy 'Preface' to the *Dictionary*, as well as the 'Grammar' and 'History' of the language. There was also the incorporation of thousands of literary and other written quotations, and Johnson's increasing reliance upon empirical written evidence of usage in constructing the word-list and 'explanations'; the relation between the quotations and the definitions in the construction of the entry and attention to historical usage and development; the unprecedented extensive treatment of polysemy and phrasal verbs; and the relation of Johnson's lexicography to the world of letters (Johnson being the only English lexicographer who was a writer of the first rank).

8.2.1 (i) Monolingual and bilingual models

The most popular of all eighteenth-century monolingual dictionaries was not in fact Johnson's but rather, in its various forms, Nathan Bailey's octavo *An Universal Etymological Dictionary* (1721).[1] And it was Bailey's folio *Dictionarium Britannicum* (1730) that significantly raised English lexicographical standards, particularly in the recording and use of etymology. This dictionary (specifically the second edition of 1736) probably originally served as the basis for Johnson's own, and doubtless influenced his practice in a variety of ways (McDermott 2005:

[1] There were at least twenty-eight editions of this dictionary published by 1800. The folio *New Universal Etymological English Dictionary*, published by Joseph Nicol Scott in 1755, is an expansion of Bailey's *Dictionarium Britannicum*, rather than the earlier *Universal Etymological Dictionary*.

1–11). Bailey's and Johnson's folios benefited from the appearance in 1728 of Ephraim Chambers's *Cyclopaedia; Or, An Universal Dictionary of Arts and Sciences*, which provided entries for technical and scientific terms not previously covered. Johnson incorporated many entries direct from Chambers; furthermore, one of his amanuenses had worked for Chambers and presumably shared his expertise with Johnson's team. Johnson took special notice of Benjamin Martin's *Lingua Britannica Reformata* (1748), particularly his plan for defining entries. Martin's dictionary was pioneering in its stated aims of providing definitions of the multiple meanings of words, or their polysemy (perhaps influenced by Johnson's own 'Plan' for his dictionary, published in 1747), yet his ambitious plan collapsed in the performance itself (Reddick 1996: 62, 51–3). The bilingual dictionaries of Abel Boyer—the French–English *Dictionnaire Royal*, first published in 1699—and Robert Ainsworth—the *Latin Dictionary* of 1728 and *Thesaurus Linguae Latinae* of 1736, rev. 1746—were also useful to Johnson, especially in his treatment of the word-list, polysemy, and, most importantly, phrasal verbs. Furthermore, continental dictionaries, such as the *Vocabolario* of the Accademia della Crusca (1612) and the French dictionaries of Richelet (1680) and Furetière (1690), were probably influential on Johnson's method, specifically by providing models for the display of multiple illustrative quotations for word usage.

Johnson composed his dictionary by combining several different characteristics that were beginning to be seen as essential for an authoritative dictionary. He provided lengthy introductory material, including the 'Preface', with a statement of method and a guide to the use of the work, the 'History of the Language', and 'Grammar'. The number of lemmas in his word-list was extensive, though fewer at 43,000 than Bailey's 60,000. However, Bailey had taken no note of the multiple meanings of words or of phrasal verbs (listed by Johnson under the initial verb element); if these are taken into account and considered as separate headings, then Johnson's number of usages in total compares favourably with Bailey's. The length and scope of the definitions, the listing of multiple senses, each with a definition, and the inclusion of written authorities, all extend Johnson's work in comprehensiveness far beyond Bailey's, whose entries are generally brief. As he states in his 'Preface', Johnson omits proper names, many compound words, verbal nouns ending in *-ing*, participles, obsolete terms, 'words now no longer understood' which were current before Sidney, and 'many terms of art and manufacture'. He provided etymologies (usually brief) and some guide to accentuation and orthography. His delineation of multiple meanings of words under each entry follows a stated methodology (often tempered by the contingencies of what he actually found in the printed record), and he included quotations from notable English writers to lend additional authority to word usage and illustration. Of these attributes, the attention to polysemy was unusual in English lexicography, if not literally original with Johnson. Only the adding of multiple illustrative quotations (what he called 'authorities') was a true innovation in England, though it had been practised by the Italian and Spanish academies (1612 and 1729–39, respectively), the French (Richelet, 1680, and Furetière, 1690), and the Germans (J. L. Frisch, 1741).

What has not been sufficiently understood, however, is that Johnson's *Dictionary* was the first English dictionary to attempt, to a considerable degree, to determine its meanings according to word use as it was realized in the works of English authors. This basically empirical practice—privileging use over predetermined categories and models—emerged only after Johnson experienced the futility of fixing or ordering the language according to a settled *a priori* system of defining (or 'explaining', to use Johnson's word). As often as not, the criterion of use trumps prescriptive criteria, such as etymology, semantic rules, or analogy.

8.2.1 (ii) Public linguistic authority

This first full modern dictionary of English was not the work of linguistic academies, as had been the case with the major dictionaries of most other European languages, but rather of one not-yet distinguished author, relying upon assistants and previous models, and sponsored by a consortium of London booksellers. Johnson makes of his necessity a virtue when he claims (in his 'Preface') that the lack of a national linguistic academy is a sign of the free spirit of the English, as against continental (especially French) despotism (nevertheless, Johnson wanted his work to be compared with the activities of the continental academies and exchanged copies of his volumes with the French and Italian academies (Reddick 1996: 15–16)). Its creation instantly became part of English heroic myth. The work was contracted for in 1746, and, in the following year, Johnson published his 'Plan of a Dictionary of the English Language', dedicated to the Earl of Chesterfield, a prominent authority on language. The *Dictionary* was not published until 1755, however, by which point Johnson had renounced Chesterfield's unfulfilled patronage. The title page bears his own name followed by the letters 'A.B.'—a record of his just granted honorary Oxford degree—as well as a list of the publishers, pronouncing a new kind of authority. Unlike his comparable predecessors, Johnson includes no dedication to a patron. The rejection of Chesterfield's patronage has traditionally been considered as signalling the death of aristocratic patronage in England. Because the English dictionary was conceived, and would be perceived by many, as a booksellers' project, its lack of explicit institutional authority necessarily tempers the prescriptive aspects of the book.

8.2.2 *Process of construction of the* Dictionary

8.2.2 (i) Projected semantic structures

Relying upon the examples of several previous dictionaries—notably the *Dictionarium Britannicum* of Nathaniel Bailey (1730), the *Dictionnaire Royal, François-Anglois et Anglois-François* of Abel Boyer (first published 1699), and the *Thesaurus Linguae Latinae* of Robert Ainsworth (1736)—Johnson established very early the outline structure and method for construction of his own text. In particular, he studied the treatment of polysemy in these works, as he constructed his own system for defining, published in the 'Plan', under which all multiple definitions would be sorted and defined. Multiple meanings ('explanations') of particular headwords would be arranged under the following categories: (1) The primitive or natural sense (i.e. that closest to the etymon); (2) the consequential or accidental; (3) the metaphorical; (4) the poetical ('where it differs from that which is in common use'); (5) the familiar; (6) the burlesque; and (7) the peculiar sense as used by a great author. These categories begin with that closest to the etymological root and extend from there. His strategy, based upon previous examples and, most likely, John Locke's discussion (in Book III, 'Of Words', of the *Essay Concerning Human Understanding*) of the use and discrimination of meaning of individual units of language, provided Johnson with a systematic, coherent, and impressive structure on the basis of which he could order and prescribe proper English usage. The incorporation of examples of usage from English writers would provide him with evidence and authority for a coherent structure. Johnson appears to have believed that virtually any example of English usage would fit within his carefully constructed scheme for multiple definitions, and that illustration would be found for most, if not all definitions (Reddick 1996: 25–54).

8.2.2 (ii) Modified procedures

Johnson's prescriptive and normative tendencies, particularly as expressed in the 'Plan' of 1747, were considerably modified in the *Dictionary* of 1755 and in the remarkable 'Preface' to that edition. There, Johnson outlines the history of his project, a profound meditation upon language, lexicography, and (often vain) human endeavour. The elegiac, resigned, and somewhat defensive tone of the 'Preface' replaces the confidence and youthful assurance of the 'Plan' ('these were the dreams of a poet doomed at last to wake a lexicographer' [C^{v}]). In the course of constructing the work, facing 'the boundless chaos of a living speech', Johnson shifted from a prescriptive, normative, and *a priori* procedure to one based chiefly upon written usage. Because parts of Johnson's working papers for the composition and later revision of the *Dictionary* are preserved, it has been possible to trace his procedures and the development of the project. As he attempted to construct the work according to his organizational methods outlined in the 'Plan', he marked tens of thousands of passages in books, having them copied out onto slips and assembled alphabetically under individual lemmas; yet it appears that a crisis, both procedural and philosophical, ensued. The imposition of pre-existing semantic structures onto the wealth of quotations was practically inflexible, theoretically inadequate, and increasingly inconsistent with his philosophy of language use, mirrored in the practical problems of assembling the material.

In late 1749 or early 1750, he abandoned his partially constructed manuscript, altering his procedure to a more empirical approach to the written authorities he had collected and allowing the quotations essentially to determine the word-list and definitions. In a sense, Johnson was overwhelmed by the multiplicity and sheer number of his 'authorities', as well as the unmethodical, often contingent variations in usage. Rather than being simply illustrations of the definitions, they become the groundwork upon which the remainder of the dictionary is constructed. The referential and rhetorical link between quotations, explanations, and notes on usage is considerably strengthened; in extreme cases, the entry functions as a gloss or commentary on the textual example(s) quoted (e.g. 'SIRUPED. *Adj.* [from *sirup.*] Sweet, like sirup; bedewed with sweets. "Yet when there haps a honey fall,/We'll lick the *syrupt* leaves:/And tell the bees that their's is gall." *Drayton's Q. of Cynthia.*') (Reddick 1996: 25–58).

8.2.3 Quotations and 'authorities'

8.2.3 (i) Authors

Most of the quotations Johnson marked and gathered were taken from what he referred to in his 'Preface' as 'the wells of English undefiled'—that is, those authors writing from the time of Sir Philip Sidney in the latter half of the sixteenth century to the Restoration of 1660 (and, in practice, somewhat later). This was the period in the development of the English language, he asserted, before it was considerably influenced by French ('gradually departing from its original *Teutonick* character, and deviating towards a *Gallick* structure and phraseology, from which it ought to be our endeavour to recall it, by making our ancient volumes the ground-work of stile') and yet written after 'a time of rudeness antecedent to perfection', the written language before Sidney. He did stray from this chronological boundary often, however—passages from Dryden and Pope are among the most heavily quoted, Chaucer, Swift, Arbuthnot, William Law, Edward Young, and James Thomson, among many others, are also frequent. Johnson quoted works of poetry and prose, theology and philosophy, history and politics, philology and art history, not to mention technical works and special subjects—on everything from coins to agriculture, to trees, to paints. The specialized sources (often encyclopedias themselves) introduced an often overtly encyclopedic quality to parts of the work. He tended to use encyclopedic sources for words dealing with complicated artefacts (e.g. Chambers under AIRPUMP), with natural objects and phenomena (Arbuthnot on GOUT), and those dealing with human institutions, professions, and fields of learning (John Cowell under ANNUITY), in some cases allowing the borrowed passages to serve as definitions (Lynch 2005: 137; Stone 2005). He also relied extensively upon poetical sources with a specialized vocabulary, such as Thomas Tusser's *Husbandry* or Spenser's *Shepherd's Calendar.*

8.2.3 (ii) Function of quotations

Despite the claim on the title page of the *Dictionary*, Johnson did not necessarily seek examples from 'the best writers': some of the illustrations are 'extracted from writers who were never mentioned as masters of elegance or models of stile; but words must be sought where they are used'. For example, 'in what pages, eminent for purity, can terms of manufacture or agriculture be found? Many quotations serve no other purpose, than that of proving the bare existence of words' [B2^{v}].

This pragmatic strain is evident as well in Johnson's basing of his lexicon on written rather than oral usage. 'No mention is found in books', he writes, of many popular and useful terms, but it would be 'hopeless labour' to attempt to collect them from speech (by 'courting living information'). He expresses some regret for the absence of the spoken and colloquial. His exclusion of dialect words may to some extent reflect his practical reliance upon written sources.

8.2.3 (iii) Rhetorical function of quotations

The function and purpose of the quotations Johnson gathered was primarily to indicate that a particular word was used, whatever his original preferences. Some critics early on accused Johnson of including political writers according to his own stamp, as well as peculiar writers who thought and wrote like him; more recently, it has been claimed Johnson had an 'educational plan' and presented positions and beliefs through the quotations (De Maria 1986). Such an assertion does not take into consideration, however, the nature of the construction of each entry, the rhetoric of the individual entries and their relation to other entries, the manner in which users consult the work, or Johnson's own comments. The decontextualizing of a quotation, partially recontextualized under an entry-heading, acquiring some relation to the other quotations and to Johnson's own authorizing voice, renders it too equivocal to function as either a representative of the author's, or of Johnson's, particular beliefs. How does it function *syntactically* (or *discursively*), we might ask? Furthermore, the user approaches the *Dictionary* very rarely as a codex, to be read from beginning to end, or for long stretches; instead, the user consults it an entry at a time, often to answer a specific question.

There are some occasions, however, especially in the large revision of 1771–73 for the fourth edition, where it appears that Johnson systematically altered his use of certain authorities he had drawn upon before (especially Milton and James Thomson), and added new ones, for the purpose of influencing readers' political and theological views, particularly in relation to current debates (concerning the authority of oaths in Church and state) in Parliament and in the press. Johnson added many quotations from a group of conservative Anglican writers, mainly from the seventeenth century, who had defended the church in its past battles with state authority. Johnson's efforts appear to have been aimed at bringing before his readers names and voices—many of them forgotten—from previous times of strife for use in current disputes (Reddick 1996: 121–69; 1997: 983–1005).

8.2.3 (iv) Dehistoricization

This is an aspect of what should be considered as the *Dictionary's* characteristic 'dehistoricizing' tendency: in this case, the earlier and now forgotten writers are resurrected to speak as contemporaries. In general, Johnson makes no attempt to distinguish the earliest use of a word, despite arranging the quotations in chronological order under each definition, and only occasionally provides explicit reference to diachronic development of word meaning (he gives no dates, for example); and while he often assembles multiple quotations under individual senses, he makes no attempt to be exhaustive or representative. Instead, Johnson's attention is focused more upon specific synchronic occurrences of words in particular (though possibly typical) contexts. (This places its purposes directly contrary to the historical concerns of the *Oxford English Dictionary*.)

The decision to fill his work with citations from authorities of previous generations, indeed previous centuries, setting the *terminus ante quem* at least a generation earlier than the period of compilation, considerably affects the type of dictionary Johnson produces. It was seen by most as a monument to English letters; yet it is *past* written language that is cited. This characteristic of 'preteriteness' or 'pastness' is, on the one hand, characteristic of any dictionary, always attempting to capture the moment in the present which is, however, 'always passing over', as Johnson memorably puts it in the 'Preface'. In Johnson's case, it is overtly contradictory to base *present* usage on *past* examples. In the 'Preface', Johnson thematizes the elusiveness of the present and its tragic overtones of regret, failure, and death. His choices from some prose writers of the seventeenth century, in particular, were derided, and critics satirically aligned Johnson's 'deformities' of style (and person) with his taste for these writers.

8.2.4 Semantics and 'explanations'

Johnson's definitions usually went far beyond those of his monolingual English predecessors, whose definitions often consisted of synonyms, with only a bare reference to genus (or superordinate). (It must be mentioned here that Bailey, especially in the *Dictionarium Britannicum*, not infrequently provided such fuller definitions, and that Johnson, as can be seen in the illustrated examples—see below—often uses synonyms as definitions as well.) He frequently defines by genus and both descriptive and functional differentiae, as in the case of DESK, 'An inclining table for the use of writers or readers, made commonly with a box or repository under it' (Stone 2005: 155). Johnson provided over 1,500 definitions verbatim for the *OED*, and James Murray lauded Johnson as having 'contributed to the evolution of the modern dictionary' by 'the illustration of the use of each word by a selection of literary quotations, and the more delicate appreciation and discrimination of senses which this involved and rendered possible' (Murray 1993: 116; Silva 2000: 79–80). Because the 'definition' serves to 'explain' the use of the word in the quotation, rather than the quoted use simply exemplifying the definition, the elements of the entry may take on a dialogic quality, chiefly between lexicographer and quoted author.

8.2.4 (i) Etymology and meaning

The canonization of etymology as the key to correct assessment of lexical meaning, as we have seen, is much more evident in the 'Plan of the Dictionary' than it is in either the 'Preface' or the *Dictionary* itself. Nothing demonstrates more convincingly Johnson's demotion of the powers of etymology for establishing the true meaning of words than his entries for ETYMOLOGY and ETYMOLOGIST themselves. Their definitions retain little of Bailey's sense of the power of that science. But more revealing are three of the four illustrations under the first sense of 'etymology'. 'When words are restrained, by common usage, to a particular sense, to run up to *etymology*, and construe them by dictionary, is wretchedly ridiculous. *Collier's View of the Stage*'. 'Pelvis is used by comic writers for a looking-glass, by which means the *etymology* of the word is visible, and pelvidera will signify a lady who looks in her glass. *Addison's Spectator*'. 'If the meaning of a word could be learned by its derivation or *etymology*, yet the original derivation of words is oftentimes very dark. *Watts's Logick*'. Two pages earlier in his copy of *Watts's Logick*, Johnson also marked the following illustration of the word: 'But this tracing of a Word to its Original, (which is called Etymology) is sometimes a very precarious and uncertain thing'. These examples display an unmistakable scepticism towards the powers of etymology to determine meaning or usage.

8.2.4 (ii) 'Explanations' and 'examples'

Indeed, Johnson considered semantics to be the most troublesome and controversial aspect of his work: 'That part of my work on which I expect malignity most frequently to fasten, is the EXPLANATION ... since I have not always been able to satisfy myself. To interpret a language by itself is very difficult'. He cites his special concern for phrasal verbs, his distrust of synonyms, and the importance of syntactic context:

> The rigour of interpretative lexicography requires that the explanation, and the word explained, should be always reciprocal; this I have always endeavoured, but could not always attain. Words are seldom exactly synonimous; a new term was not introduced, but because the former was thought inadequate: names, therefore, have often many ideas, but few ideas have many names. It was then necessary to use the *proximate* word, for the deficiency of single terms can very seldom be supplied by circumlocution; nor is the inconvenience great of such mutilated interpretations, because the sense may easily be collected entire from the examples [B2^{r}, emphasis mine].

The word 'proximate' means, in one sense, 'approximate'; but its most applicable meaning is 'near or next' (Johnson defines the word as 'next in the series of ratiocination'). Johnson's use of the term illuminates the elusiveness of semantic precision and the deferral of equivalence between word and definition. Most interesting is his comment that 'the sense may be collected *entire* from the examples', an obvious circularity which perhaps reflects the circularity of defining itself.

Johnson's lingering preoccupation with the relation between the quotations and the explanations and the logical development of the senses of the headword may be clearly illustrated by the changes marked in the working papers for Johnson's revision of the *Dictionary* (fourth edition, 1773). For example, the entries for BLAST. *n.s.* and To BLAST. *v.a.* in the first edition (Fig. 8.1) are altered by Johnson as indicated in Fig. 8.2.

Johnson's manuscript alterations attempt to make the entries more coherent in the fourth edition, by accounting logically for multiple meanings and a precise relation between definition and quotation. He adds the phrase 'the power of the wind' to the definition '1. A gust, or puff of wind', which removes the random or occasional aspect of the definition, supplying instead the idea of a constant and destructive force, necessary for a coherent reading of the two Shakespearian quotations which follow. Johnson inserts a new definition, '2. A particular wind', before the quotation from Dryden's translation of the *Aeneid*, glossing it in terms not of chance gusts but of a determinate and identifiable wind, predictable in its force. He inserts a new illustration from Dryden, 'If envious eyes their hurtful rays have cast,/More powerful verse shall free thee from their blast', to illustrate the existing definition, 'The stroke of a malignant planet; the infection of any thing pestilential', effecting a witty, if hyperbolical, reading of Dryden's couplet. To def. 2 under the entry To BLAST, Johnson adds, 'to wither before the time', more accurately reflecting the usage in, and binding together, the subsequent quotations from *Genesis* and Dryden. He then reverses the order of senses 3 and 4 in order to maintain the continuum of definitions from the literal and graphic to the more metaphorical. In particular, the first three definitions pertain to a force that blights or plagues, especially plants or living and maturing things (especially def. 2 and the reordered 3). For the new def. 4 and the existing def. 5, the effect is more general and impersonal (Reddick 2005: xx, [3E2]^{v}).

8.2.5 *Grammatical concerns*

For the most part, Johnson includes grammatico-semantic derivatives in his word-list, yet indicates their derivation from the root lexeme (e.g. To EMULATE, EMULATION, EMULATIVE, EMULATOR) through the use of cap-and-small-cap, in comparison with the full-size capitals he uses for main root entries. Johnson also uses typography to highlight the relation (of 'conversion') between identical lexemes used as different parts of speech (e.g. 'GENERAL. *adj.*', followed by 'GENERAL. *n.s.*'). He often (but not as a rule) lists compounds as separate lexemes, such as GIDDY. *adj.*, followed in the word-list by GIDDYBRAINED, GIDDYHEADED, GIDDYPACED, typographically distinguished from the root.

A particularly interesting example of Johnson's treatment of grammar is his attention to phrasal verbs, 'too frequent in the English Language', and especially problematic for foreign learners. Johnson used bilingual lexicons, especially Latin–English, as prototypes for the treatment of phrasal verbs. (English monolingual predecessors hardly mentioned them at all, though Robert Cawdrey, in *The Table Alphabeticall*, 1604, uses them from time to time as characteristic of simple

BLAST. *n. s.* [from blæyτ, Saxon; *blasen*, Germ. to blow.]

1. A gust, or puff of wind.

They that stand high, have many *blasts* to shake them;
And, if they fall, they dash themselves to pieces.
Shakesp. Richard III.

Welcome, then,
Thou unsubstantial air, that I embrace;
The wretch that thou hast blown unto the worst,
Owes nothing to thy *blasts*. *Shakesp. King Lear.*

Perhaps thy fortune doth controul the winds,
Doth loose or bind their *blasts* in secret cave. *Fairfax, b.* i.

Three ships were hurry'd by the southern *blast*,
And on the secret shelves with fury cast. *Dryden's Æneid.*

2. The sound made by blowing any instrument of wind musick.

In peace there's nothing so becomes a man,
As modest stilness and humility;
But when the *blast* of war blows in our ears,
Then imitate the action of the tyger. *Shakesp. Henry* V.

He blew his trumpet—the angelick *blast*
Fill'd all the regions. *Milt. Par. Lost, b.* xi. *l.* 76.

The Veline fountains, and sulphureous Nar,
Shake at the baleful *blast*, the signal of the war. *Dryden's Æn.*

Whether there be two different goddesses called Fame, or one goddess sounding two different trumpets, it is certain, villainy has as good a title to a blast from the proper trumpet, as virtue has from the former. *Swift.*

3. The stroke of a malignant planet; the infection of any thing pestilential.

By the *blast* of God they perish. *Job*, iv. 9.

To BLAST. *v. a.* [from the noun.]

1. To strike with some sudden plague or calamity.

You nimble lightnings, dart your blinding flames
Into her scornful eyes! infect her beauty,
You fensuck'd fogs, drawn by the powerful sun,
To fall and *blast* her pride. *Shakesp. King Lear.*

Oh! Portius, is there not some chosen curse,
Some hidden thunder in the store of heaven,
Red with uncommon wrath, to *blast* the man,
Who owes his greatness to his country's ruin. *Addison. Cato.*

2. To make to wither.

Upon this *blasted* heath you stop our way. *Macbeth.*

And behold seven thin ears, and *blasted* with the eastwind sprung up after them. *Gen.* xli. 6.

She that like lightning shin'd, while her face lasted,
The oak now resembles, which lightning had *blasted*.
Waller.

To his green years your censures you would suit,
Not *blast* that blossom, but expect the fruit. *Dryden.*

Agony unmix'd, incessant gall
Corroding every thought, and *blasting* all
Love's paradise. *Thomson's Spring, l.* 1075.

3. To injure; to invalidate.

He shews himself either very weak, if he will take my word, when he thinks I deserve no credit; or very malicious, if he knows I deserve credit, and yet goes about to *blast* it.
Stillingfleet's Defence of Discourses on Romish Idolatry.

4. To cut off; to hinder from coming to maturity.

This commerce, Jeshophat king of Juda endeavoured to renew; but his enterprize was *blasted* by the destruction of vessels in the harbour. *Arbuthnot on Coins.*

5. To confound; to strike with terrour.

Trumpeters,
With brazen din, *blast* you the city's ears;
Make mingle with your ratt'ling tabourines.
Shakesp. Antony and Cleopatra.

FIG. 8.1. Detail from the page containing *BLAST* from Samuel Johnson's *Dictionary*, 1755

man, ſhould venture to own ſuch a villainous, impudent, and *blaſphemous* aſſertion in the face of the world, as this! *South.*

[B]LA'SPHEMOUSLY. *adv.* [from *blaſpheme.*] Impiouſly; with wicked irreverence.

Where is the right uſe of his reaſon, while he would *blaſphemouſly* ſet up to controul the commands of the Almighty? *Swift.*

BLA'SPHEMY. *n. ſ.* [from *blaſpheme.*]

Blaſphemy, ſtrictly and properly, is an offering of ſome indignity, or injury, unto God himſelf, either by words or writing. *Ayliffe's Parergon.*

But that my heart's on future miſchief ſet,
I would ſpeak *blaſphemy*, ere bid you fly;
But fly you muſt. *Shakeſp. Henry* VI. *p.* ii.

Intrinſick goodneſs conſiſts in accordance, and ſin in contrariety, to the ſecret will of God; or elſe God could not be defined good, ſo far as his thoughts and ſecrets, but only ſuperficially good, as far as he is pleaſed to reveal himſelf, which is perfect *blaſphemy* to imagine. *Hammond's Fundamentals.*

BLAST. *n. ſ.* [from blæſt, Saxon; *blaſen*, Germ. to blow.]

1. A guſt, or puff of wind.

They that ſtand high, have many *blaſts* to ſhake them;
And, if they fall, they daſh themſelves to pieces.
Shakeſp. ~~Richard III.~~

Welcome, then,
Thou unſubſtantial air, that I embrace;
The wretch that thou haſt blown unto the worſt,
Owes nothing to thy *blaſts*. *Shakeſp. King Lear.*

Perhaps thy fortune doth controul the winds,
Doth looſe or bind their *blaſts* in ſecret cave. *Fairfax, b.* i.

Three ſhips were hurry'd by the ſouthern *blaſt*,
And on the ſecret ſhelves with fury caſt. *Dryden's Æneid.*

2. The ſound made by blowing any inſtrument of wind muſick.

In peace there's nothing ſo becomes a man,
As modeſt ſtilneſs and humility;
But when the *blaſt* of war blows in our ears,
Then imitate the action of the tyger. *Shakeſp. Henry* V.

He blew his trumpet—the angelick *blaſt*
Fill'd all the regions. *Milt. Par. Loſt, b.* xi. *l.* 76.

The Veline fountains, and ſulphureous Nar,
Shake at the baleful *blaſt*, the ſignal of the war. *Dryden's Æn.*

Whether there be two different goddeſſes called Fame, or one goddeſs ſounding two different trumpets, it is certain, villainy has as good a title to a blaſt from the proper trumpet, as virtue has from the former. *Swift.*

3. The ſtroke of a malignant planet; the infection of any thing peſtilential.

~~By the~~ *blaſt* of God they periſh. *Job*, iv. 9.

To BLAST. *v. a.* [from the noun.]

1. To ſtrike with ſome ſudden plague or calamity.

You nimble lightnings, dart your blinding flames
Into her ſcornful eyes! infect her beauty,
You fenſuck'd fogs, drawn by the powerful ſun,
To fall and *blaſt* her pride. *Shakeſp. King Lear.*

Oh! Portius, is there not ſome choſen curſe,
Some hidden thunder in the ſtore of heaven,
Red with uncommon wrath, to *blaſt* the man,
Who owes his greatneſs to his country's ruin. *Addiſon. Cato.*

2. To make to wither.

Upon this *blaſted* heath you ſtop our way. *Macbeth.*

And behold ſeven thin ears, and *blaſted* with the eaſtwind ſprung up after them. *Gen.* xli. 6.

She that like lightning ſhin'd, while her face laſted,
The oak now reſembles, which lightning had *blaſted*.
Waller.

To his green years your cenſures you would ſuit,
Not *blaſt* that bloſſom, but expect the fruit. *Dryden.*

Agony unmix'd, inceſſant gall
Corroding every thought, and *blaſting* all
Love's paradiſe. *Thomſon's Spring, l.* 1075.

3. To injure; to invalidate.

He ſhews himſelf either very weak, if he will take my word, when he thinks I deſerve no credit; or very malicious, if he knows I deſerve credit, and yet goes about to *blaſt* it. *Stillingfleet's Defence of Diſcourſes on Romiſh Idolatry.*

4. To cut off; to hinder from coming to maturity.

This commerce, Jeſhophat king of Juda endeavoured to renew; but his enterprize was *blaſted* by the deſtruction of veſſels in the harbour. *Arbuthnot on Coins.*

5. To confound; to ſtrike with terrour.

Trumpeters,
With brazen din, *blaſt* you the city's ears;
Make mingle with your ratt'ling tabourines.
Shakeſp. ~~Antony and Cleopatra.~~

BLA'STMENT. *n. ſ.* [from *blaſt.*] Blaſt; ſudden ſtroke of infection.

In the morn, and liquid dew of youth,
Contagious *blaſtments* are moſt imminent. *Shakeſp. Hamlet.*

BLA'TANT. *adj.* [*blatttant*, Fr.] Bellowing as a calf.

You learn'd this language from the *blatant* beaſt. *Dryden.*

To BLA'TTER. *v. n.* [from *blatero*, Lat.] To roar; to make a ſenſeleſs noiſe. It is a word not now uſed.

She rode at peace, through his only pains and excellent durance, however envy liſt to *blatter* againſt him. *Spenſ. Irel.*

BLATTERA'TION. *n. ſ.* [*blateratio*, Lat.] Noiſe; ſenſeleſs roar.

BLAY. *n. ſ.* A ſmall white river fiſh; called alſo a *bleak*, ~~which~~ ~~ſee.~~

BLAZE. *n. ſ.* [blaſe, a torch, Saxon.]

1. A flame; the light of the flame: *blaze* implies more the light than the heat.

They are in ~~a moſt~~ warlike preparation, and hope to come upon them in the heat of their diviſion.—The main *blaze* of it is paſt; but a ſmall thing would make it flame again.
Shakeſp. ~~Coriolanus.~~

Thy throne is darkneſs in th' abyſs of light,
A *blaze* of glory that forbids the ſight. *Dryden's Hind and P.*

What groans of men ſhall fill the martial field!
How fierce a *blaze* his flaming pile ſhall yield!
~~What fun'ral pomp ſhall floating Tiber ſee!~~ *Dryden's Æn.*

2. Publication; wide diffuſion of report.

For what is glory but the *blaze* of fame;
The people's praiſe, if always praiſe unmixt?
Milton's Paradiſe Loſt, b. iii. *l.* 47.

3. *Blaze* is a white mark upon a horſe, deſcending from the forehead almoſt to the noſe. *Farrier's Dict.*

To BLAZE. *v. n.* [from the noun.]

1. To flame; to ſhew the light of the flame.

Thus you may long live an happy inſtrument for your king and country; you ſhall not be a meteor, or a *blazing* ſtar, but *ſtella fixa*; happy here, and more happy hereafter.
Bacon's ~~Advice to Villiers.~~

The third fair morn now *blaz'd* upon the main,
Then gloſſy ſmooth lay all the liquid plain. *Pope's Odyſſey.*

2. To be conſpicuous.

To BLAZE. *v. a.*

1. To publiſh; to make known; to ſpread far and wide.

The noiſe of this fight, and iſſue thereof, being *blazed* by the country people to ſome noblemen thereabouts, they came thither. *Sidney, b.* ii.

My words, in hopes to *blaze* a ſtedfaſt mind,
This marble choſe, as of like temper known. *Sidney.*

Thou ſhalt live, till we can find a time
To *blaze* your marriage, reconcile your friends,
Beg pardon of thy prince, and call thee back.
Shakeſp. ~~Romeo and Juliet.~~

When beggars die, there are no comets ſeen;
The heav'ns themſelves *blaze* forth the death of princes.
Shakeſp. Julius Cæſar.

But he went out, and began to publiſh it much, and to *blaze* abroad the matter. *Mark*, i. 45.

Such muſick worthieſt were to *blaze*
The peerleſs height of her immortal praiſe,
~~Whoſe luſtre leads us.~~ *Milton.*

Far beyond
The ſons of Anak, famous now and *blaz'd*,
Fearleſs of danger, like a petty god
I walk'd about. *Milton's Agoniſtes, l.* 527.

~~Whoſe~~ follies, *blaz'd* about, to all are known,
And are a ſecret to himſelf alone. *Granville.*

But, mortals, know, 'tis ſtill our greateſt pride
To *blaze* thoſe virtues, which the good would hide. *Pope.*

2. To blazon; to give an account of enſigns armorial in proper terms. This is not now uſed.

This, in ancient times, was called a fierce; and you ſhould then have *blazed* it thus: he bears a fierce, ſable, between two fierces, or. *Peacham on Drawing.*

3. To inflame; to fire. This is not a proper uſe.

Pall'd thy *blazed* youth
Becomes aſſuag'd, and doth beg the alms
Of palſied eld. *Shakeſp. Meaſure for Meaſure.*

BLA'ZER. *n. ſ.* [from *blaze.*] One that ſpreads reports.

Utterers of ſecrets he from thence debarr'd,
Babblers of folly, and *blazers* of crime;
His larum-bell might loud and wide be heard,
When cauſe requir'd, but never out of time;
Early and late it rung, at evening and at prime. *Fairy Queen.*

To BLA'ZON. *v. a.* [*blaſonner*, Fr.]

1. To explain, in proper terms, the figures on enſigns armorial.

King Edward gave to them the coat of arms, which I am not herald enough to *blazon* into Engliſh. *Addiſon. Guardian.*

2. To deck; to embelliſh; to adorn.

~~Then~~ *blazons* in dread ſmiles her hideous form;
So lightning gilds the unrelenting ſtorm. *Garth's Diſpenſat.*

3. To diſplay; to ſet to ſhow.

O thou goddeſs,
Thou divine nature! how thyſelf thou *blazon'ſt*
In theſe two princely boys! they are as gentle
As zephyrs blowing below the violet,
~~Not wagging his ſweet head.~~ *Shakeſp. Cymbeline.*

4. To celebrate; to ~~ſet out.~~

One that excels the quirk of *blazoning* pens,
And, in terreſtrial veſture of creation,
Does bear all excellency. *Shakeſp. Othello.*

5. To blaze about; to make publick.

What's

FIG. 8.2. First edition marked by Johnson for revised (fourth) edition, 1773

idiomatic English; foreign language lexicons like Boyer's, on the other hand, paid particular attention to them. In the Latin–English part of a bilingual dictionary, the phrasal verbs, which are translation equivalents, would be scattered and need orderly rearrangement (Osselton 1995: 93–103).) He borrowed synonyms or definitions in many cases. Yet Johnson gathered many more textual examples from printed books than he would have found covered in these dictionaries. He has 'noted with great care' these cases in which 'we modify the signification of many verbs by a particle subjoined'. His *Dictionary* is replete with unprecedented examples, such as those dealt with under the intransitive verb FALL. Johnson provides thirty-six separate definitions of the verb, followed by twenty-eight instances of phrasal combinations: fall *away* (5), fall *back* (2), fall *down* (3), fall *from* (1), fall *in* (2), fall *off* (3), fall *on* (2), fall *over* (1), fall *out* (2), fall *to* (2), fall *under* (2), fall *upon* (3). Each of these, with one exception, is supported by at least one and usually multiple quotations. In a truly astonishing case, Johnson (1773) lists 117 meanings for the transitive verb TAKE, fifty-three of which are phrasal verbs. Under '88. *To* TAKE *off.* To invalidate; to destroy; to remove', he includes a whopping seventeen quotations from a range of sources: Shakespeare (2), Bacon (3), Bishop Sanderson (1), Henry Hammond (1), Sir Thomas Browne (1), Edward Stillingfleet (1), Locke (2), Addison (3), Swift (1), Martha Blount, letter to Pope (1), and Isaac Watts (1). For senses 104, '*To* TAKE *up.* To engross; to engage', and 114, '*To* TAKE *up.* To adopt; to assume', each is illustrated by ten quotations from a similar range of authorities (Bailey, by comparison, lists none). It should be noted that Johnson also includes in the same alphabetical sequence idiomatic combinations with verbs (e.g. take *part*, take *care*, take *oath*, take *place*), not only phrasal verbs in the usual sense.

8.2.6 Prescriptivism: 'Fixing' vs. recording

Johnson acknowledges his earlier hopes that he 'should fix our language, and put a stop to those alterations which time and chance have hitherto been suffered to make in it without opposition'; yet he observes that faced with 'the boundless chaos of a living speech', any attempt to freeze the language is doomed and quixotic: 'to enchain syllables, and to lash the wind, are equally the undertakings of pride, unwilling to measure its desires by its strength' [C2^r]. Johnson's adaptation of Juvenal's satire on Xerxes marks those who would presume to attempt to control language change. Yet his awareness does not deter him from making prescriptive comments throughout the work.

Johnson's pronouncement in the 'Preface' that the lexicographer is one 'who do[es] not form, but register[s] the language; who do[es] not teach men how they should think, but relate[s] how they have hitherto expressed their thoughts', represents a crucial moment in English lexicography: he announces the necessity of a descriptive, documentary policy rather than a prescriptive and normative one. Predictably, Johnson's *Dictionary* was criticized by some contemporaries and successors as insufficiently prescriptive, and his broad descriptive method both too generous and idiosyncratic.

8.2.6 (i) Rules vs. usage

If we examine the extent and kinds of prescriptivism in Johnson's *Dictionary*, we find something of a mixed picture. Johnson's cases of proscription or opinionated commentary on usage are celebrated, yet it is remarkable in practice how often he relies not on rules and prescription based upon etymology or analogy but on the complex evidence of word usage provided by his authorities. There are many exceptions, of course: under ROUNDABOUT. *adj.* Johnson writes, 'This word is used as an adjective, though it is only an adverb united to a substantive by a colloquial license of language, which ought not to have been admitted into books.' His usage notes may comprise the neutral, for example, 'obsolete', 'not in use', or 'a word proper, but little used', as well as the stigmatizing: 'a low word', 'a cant word', or 'a bad word'. In nearly all such cases, the commentary refers directly to the example in an authority he has quoted—the note, as well as the definition, being prompted by the quotation (to prove 'the bare existence of words'). His commentary on an author's peculiar use of a word both records its existence and assists the reader of a difficult, usually older, author (e.g. SUIT *n.s.*, 'In Spenser it seems to signify pursuit; prosecution. "High amongst all knights hast hung thy shield,/ Thenceforth the *suit* of earthly conquest shoone,/And wash thy hands from guilt of bloody field: *Spenser*"'). Unlike his predecessors Edward Phillips (1658), John Kersey (1706), Bailey (1727), Benjamin Martin, and Abel Boyer, Johnson does not use daggers or other graphic marks to indicate disapprobation or alien words.

8.2.6 (ii) Censuring authorial usage

It is noteworthy how frequently Johnson quotes an author—even one as prominent as Shakespeare or Milton—and then censures the way the author uses a particular expression. The fifth sense of 'To MAKE, *v.n.*', the idiomatic phrasal verb 'To Make away with', Johnson defines as 'To destroy; to kill; to make away' (i.e. 'to do away with'), provides an illustration from Addison, then cautions, 'The phrase is improper'. Glossing the adverb NOWADAYS, defined as 'In the present age', Johnson writes, 'This word, though common and used by the best writers, is perhaps barbarous,' and follows it with quotations from Spenser, Shakespeare, Robert South, Tillotson, and Johnson's friend, David Garrick. Because PREJUDICE, to mean '2. Mischief; detriment; hurt; injury', is 'only accidental or consequential... not derived from the original or etymology of the word [then] it were therefore better to use it less .... In some of the following examples its impropriety will be discovered'. He then lists two examples from Shakespeare and one each from Bacon, Locke, and Addison. While this practice is clearly at variance with the role of accepting, as proper language, use as it is found, it also reiterates Johnson's unwillingness to consider the 'best authors' sacrosanct authorities. In cases such as this, he is drawn in opposite directions, retaining two models for judgement: recording usage, yet commenting upon its (lack of) propriety.

Some users were critical that Johnson was not more prescriptive and outspoken. Adam Smith, for example, in an early review in the *Edinburgh Review*, wrote: 'We cannot help wishing, that the author had trusted less to the judgment of those who may consult him, and had oftener passed his own censure upon those words which are not of approved use, tho' sometimes to be met with in authors of no mean fame' (Boulton 1971: 115). Other contemporary critics of the *Dictionary* complained that it was not clear what the 'authorities' were *authorizing*, or the illustrations *illustrating*, specifically concerning proper usage among the passages quoted. For example, Andrew Kippis, the divine and biographer, complained in the 1760s that 'Johnson's Dictionary is rather a history than a standard of our language. He hath shewn by whom words have been used, and in what sense; but hath left the readers to determine what authority they have.' John Pinkerton wrote in 1785: 'The joke is, that with [Johnson] every body is an authority' (Reddick 1998: 70).

Johnson exercises a kind of prescription in limiting the chronological range of written works from which examples would be taken ('the wells of English undefiled'); yet, as we have seen, he does not limit himself to 'the best writers' within this period, as Charles Richardson would, for example. And, in practice, Johnson very often spills beyond the chronological limits he set for himself. The fact that quotations are taken from written rather than oral sources is itself a form of selectivity, yet, whatever the elitist implications, Johnson's reasons for this appear to be largely practical rather than judgemental.

8.2.7 Johnson's Dictionary *and the public*

8.2.7 (i) The common reader

In his general tendency towards non-elitism, Johnson was much more attuned to 'common diction' and the 'common reader' than has previously been assumed (the 'common reader' would be specifically addressed in the Preface to the abridged dictionary of 1756). Several aspects of the *Dictionary* support this conclusion, especially in regard to accessibility: numbered listing of polysemous entries and phrasal verbs, thereby providing explicit and clear references for the reader; pronunciation and orthography determined, for the most part, by analogy with other entries based upon etymological patterns; and non-lemmatization, i.e. providing separate entries for the derivatives of a lemma, distinguished typographically from the root lexeme, rather than grouping these forms under a single headword or leaving them unaddressed (McDermott 2005a: 124). Johnson's providing of 'authorities', as he called them—not 'examples' or 'illustrations'—testified to the basis upon which he made his decisions. His readiness to criticize his authorities is also evidence of appeals to other forms of authority.

8.2.7 (ii) Critiques of language and literature

Johnson's project, with its reconsiderations of the great writings of the past, parallels his *Lives of the Poets*, written twenty-five years later, both philosophically and chronologically (Johnson revised his *Dictionary*, more or less constantly, until his death in 1784). The *Dictionary* constitutes, among other things, the repeated specific unmediated response of this critic to instances of literary discourse through the ages. Nothing else on such a scale exists in the language. His literary-critical writing (including the *Edition of Shakespeare*, 1765, selected *Rambler* and *Idler* essays from the 1750s, and the *Lives of the Poets*, 1779 and 1781) has an identifiable affinity with his lexicographical thinking, and vice versa. While constructing his *Dictionary*, Johnson awakes, in a sense, the critic of literature and—just as Charles Richardson would accuse him of having done—occupies himself increasingly with the contextual existence of words.

8.2.7 (iii) Publication history

Johnson's folio *Dictionary* appeared in six editions in Johnson's lifetime, including the heavily-revised fourth edition of 1773. This revision involved nearly two years of work and constituted certain alterations in procedure, especially concerning the use of quotations. None of the editions of Johnson's folio succeeded in banishing competitors from the market; neither did the many editions of the octavo abridgement, first published in 1756. Nathan Bailey's dictionaries, especially the *Dictionarium Britannicum*, and the *New Universal Dictionary* revised by Joseph Nicol Scott in 1755 to compete with Johnson's folio, continued to sell well, often better than the Johnsonian editions against which they competed head-to-head (Gove 1940: 305–22). In the nineteenth century, Johnson's *Dictionary* was revised and somewhat enlarged by H. J. Todd in four volumes (1818), a version that, in its various editions, continued to prove popular; it was eventually enlarged further by Robert Gordon Latham as late as 1866–70. Only the dictionaries of Charles Richardson and Noah Webster (who both explicitly defined themselves against Johnson) competed effectively during this period with Johnson–Todd (→ LANDAU). Johnson's octavo abridgement was much more affordable and appealed directly to 'the common reader', omitting all quotations, shortening definitions, and leaving out many word-headings. Though outsold by Bailey's octavo, Johnson's abridgement ran through many editions, selling far more copies than the expensive folio.

8.3 CHARLES RICHARDSON'S *NEW DICTIONARY*

Charles Richardson styled his dictionary *A New Dictionary of the English Language*, departing explicitly from Johnson (as would the *OED* from Johnson and Richardson): 'No man can possibly succeed in compiling a truly valuable Dictionary of the English Language,' he wrote in the preface, 'unless he entirely desert the steps of Johnson.' His dictionary was begun as a part of the *Encyclopaedia Metropolitana* (1818–45), the brainchild of Samuel Taylor Coleridge, as an explanatory index for the vocabulary of philosophical keywords in the encyclopedia, intended to be published last. But, instead, the first section of the 'English lexicon' was published as a piece of the first part of the serial publication of the *Encyclopaedia* (Dolezal 2000: 114–15). The complete dictionary was first published in 1836–37.

8.3.1 Criticism of Johnson

Richardson's chief criticism of Johnson's *Dictionary* was based on the remarks by John Horne Tooke, Richardson's mentor and the philosophical father of his work. In particular, it concerned the use of 'authorities'—quotations from earlier writers in English. The central criticism involved Johnson's alleged error of arranging quotations under separate definitions for one headword. He was misled into believing that there were multiple meanings of a word by its different uses in context, while in fact it retained the same original and true meaning. Richardson writes:

> There is one general errour pervading the explanations [in Johnson's entries] . . . imputable to interpreters in general, who, 'are seeking with it the meaning of some other word or words in

the sentence.' This is to interpret the import of the context, and not to explain the individual meaning of the words. And Johnson, by pursuing this method systematically, was led into the accidental but additional absurdity of opposing his authority to his explanation (37).

Furthermore, Richardson accurately observes that Johnson departed from his original procedure of determining multiple meanings systematically:

That Dr. Johnson was impressed with a sense of the paramount importance of this portion of his duty [to explain the meaning of words], is manifest from the earnestness with which he enlarges upon it, in his '*Plan of an English Dictionary*'. . . . If however his professions of performance are compared with the actual state of the work itself, it will be evident, that he must, at an early period of his labours, have abandoned his original design' (37).

'The whole is a failure,' Richardson concludes. 'Had the Dictionary of the English Language been the production of any writer of less name, a period of eighty years would not have been permitted to elapse without the appearance of a rival. And so far the name of Johnson has been an obstacle to the advancement of Lexicography in this country: it has commanded admirers and supporters: and it has deterred competition' (37).

Johnson's procedure, according to Richardson, is based upon the fallacy of 'the signification of the *context* ascribed to the *word*: the number of distinct explanations continued without restriction, to suit the quotations, where any seeming diversity of application may be fancied' (45). Johnson had justified his aims and procedure as follows: 'It is not sufficient that a word is found, unless it be so combined as that its meaning is apparently determined by the tract and tenour of the sentence; such passages I have therefore chosen' ($C1^r$). Richardson claimed, however, that 'each one word has one meaning, and one only; that from it all usages must spring and be derived; and that in the Etymology of each word must be found this single intrinsic meaning, and the cause of the application in those usages . . . one radical meaning' (41). As is only too evident, the lexicographical approaches of Johnson and Richardson concerning the relation of meaning to context are fundamentally divergent.

8.3.2 *Etymology and meaning*

Horne Tooke claimed that the etymology revealed the 'primordial meaning . . . compris[ing] . . . all the senses of the word and those of all its derivations' (Zgusta 1991: 599; 2006: 47); his lexicographic disciple Richardson further insisted, 'when the intrinsic meaning is fixed, every lexicographical object is firmly secured' ('Introductory letter', *Illustrations* p. 6). Richardson's determination to discover the 'literal roots' was founded upon a close (largely erroneous) comparison, based on superficial resemblances rather than systematic comparative analogy and change, across Classical and Germanic (and to some extent Romance) languages (Dolezal 2000: 126). Following Horne Tooke, Richardson also believed that the etymologist's or lexicographer's task is to locate similar words, usually in the same language, from which the full meaning of the word could be derived; these 'etymological extensions', which are to comprise all derivative forms of the root, are thus listed and sometimes explained in Richardson's dictionary. These extensions of similarity (and Richardson's etymologies in general) are often fanciful and impressionistic, frequently ingenious, many originating in Horne Tooke's examples in his *Diversions of Purley.* Murray would later refer to them as 'a fabric of conjectures' (Murray 1993: 118).

8.3.2 (i) Etymology: Johnson and Richardson

Richardson's attention to etymology was not unlike Johnson's original attempt to begin with the meaning of the word closest to the etymon and list metaphorical extensions of the meaning under different senses as he went. Richardson (and Johnson) followed Locke in the belief that words have concrete meanings, only later developing abstract ones; he further insisted that the meaning logically develops new applications through time. Etymology offered an organic theory of language. Johnson, on the other hand, responded more experientially to the authorities he gathered than Richardson, and his etymologies were certainly simpler and less thorough (as well as less fanciful). Johnson's etymologies, as Richardson complains, often consist merely of a Greek or Latin root word, or a root from modern languages, without definition or explanation of how the form(s) developed, often even without telling what the word signifies in the root language, or how it relates to subsequent definitions (e.g. 'ROACH.n.s. [from *rutilus*, Lat. redhaired.] A *roach* is a fish of no great reputation for his dainty taste... *Walton's Angler*'). Johnson also limits his etymologies to those obviously orthographically or orthoepically related, following the tradition of Junius and Skinner. He generally implies a connection between the given root word and the original English usage, yet his definition is rarely arrived at solely by recourse to the etymological root.

8.3.2 (ii) Layout of Richardson's entries

One can best discern the difference in the approach by observing the dictionary page itself. Richardson's own procedure was to make use of a two-column page, like Johnson and other predecessors, but with a visible emphasis on economy and compactness through clustering forms in the one entry of the headword, rather than employing separate main entries. (Richardson relied on Horne Tooke's ideas of grammar and etymology to concentrate or 'abbreviate' entry-headings (the clustering of derivatives and etymological information beneath the principal headword) and definitions.) His *Dictionary* of 1817 was also the first to add white space between entries, reinforcing their boundaries (Luna 2005: 178, 195). The entry-heading consists of a 'root' word, printed in full caps, followed in a vertical list by other forms, in cap-and-small-cap, of the word compounded or derived from this 'root' (including verbs, nouns, adjectives, adverbs, etc.). He follows with an etymology, including classical as well as modern languages, in an attempt to identify a 'literal meaning', one from which all others derive. The definition is worded in a general way to cover the entire derivational group, sometimes followed by a string of approximate synonyms. After commentary on usage, Richardson lists quotations, chronologically arranged, without commentary and, as expected, without separation under individual definitions.

8.3.3 Richardson's quotations

These quotations are selected from the history of English literature, beginning around the year 1300, and ending in the early nineteenth century. Richardson extends the canon very late: Byron starts to be quoted in the *Dictionary* immediately after his death in 1824, from the letter F onwards (Fowler 2004: 57). Yet his primary goal is not to illustrate current usage, rather to demonstrate original meanings of existing words (Osselton 2000: 60). He takes his examples from only 'the best Authorities', criticizing Johnson for not doing likewise. The meaning of the word, Richardson insists, remains the same throughout history, while the different usages, as reflected in the quotations, are merely predictable and recoverable extensions of it. Richardson's quotations are often lengthy and represent a considerable collection of usage over time.

8.3.3 (i) Chronological continuity and development

Richardson's entire procedure emphasizes continuity and similarity between meanings, rather than disparateness, and his quoting of numerous authorities over a wide historical expanse gives the impression of logically developing linguistic practice; it supplied a much wider corpus of usage than Johnson, especially earlier usage. Richardson's failure to date his quotations, however, leads one to question claims regarding chronological development.

8.3.3 (ii) Relation of quotations to entry

It has been insisted that Richardson's quotations and definitions are based upon an empirical examination of existing authorities (Dolezal 2000: 127). It is difficult to accept this position if we consider that the 'root' of the word is already established, and the examples are, to a certain extent, circular confirmations of it. The quoted examples do necessarily determine, however, what notes will accompany the etymology. Richardson claims that the quotations are 'produced for the purpose of exemplifying, confirming, and illustrating the explanations which precede them' (51), although sometimes there is no relevant explanation whatsoever.

8.3.3 (iii) Dialogism

Richardson allows the quotations, for the most part, to speak for themselves, without authorial commentary. Johnson, as we have seen, reserves the right to comment on the quotations, or to respond to and gloss them. Richardson's list of quotations without commentary indeed provides an often glorious collection of usage, a highly readable anthology; however, the extent to which the quotations appear to comment upon, respond to, or stand in some other discursive relationship to one another, perhaps a juxtaposition which may take on ironic rhetorical possibilities, is very slight. Johnson's practice divides the quotations into separate units under individual definitions, retaining the overseeing authority to comment on and arrange; the dialogic possibilities between quoted authorities, whether deliberate or not, as well as between lexicographer and incorporated 'author', are considerably enhanced.

8.3.3 (iv) Readers' accessibility

The practice of listing quotations serially, illustrating the 'root' and its various derivatives, organized only according to chronology, assumed a highly literate readership; indeed, Richardson's quotations leave almost every interpretation to the reader. His practice presupposes that readers will study all the material in an entry to determine specific usage and meaning; yet, by rarely providing commentary on specific quoted examples, and without a division under different definitions, his procedure leads more often to confusion or bewilderment.

However, claims have been made for Richardson's egalitarian tendencies: readers 'are invited to partake of the process' of assessing the documentary evidence presented by the lexicographer (Dolezal 2000: 139). Indeed, the unbroken sections of literary and other quoted texts might encourage a reader to attend to the string of quotations. The recording of multiple examples of usage over time may give the appearance of a descriptive, rather than prescriptive approach, and seem to be offering the reader the opportunity to assess the evidence. However, Richardson's use of quotations is more convincingly described as authoritarian: his insistence on 'the best Authorities' pushes him clearly out of the descriptive camp; and, by insisting upon a linear chronological linguistic development, Richardson forces the reader or user to give tacit assent to the lexicographer's own process and choice. Whatever else Johnson's multiple definitions and comments accomplish, they provide explicit direct commentary, with a more synchronic emphasis, with immediate reference to the attendant quotation(s), and they emphasize the contingent, experiential nature of language use, description, and development. In Johnson's entries, the reader or user can see more transparently the basis and evidence for choices and authority in relation to authorial commentary.

We may also conclude that Richardson's dictionary would be virtually useless for a non-English-speaking person, who requires precision in definitions and discrimination between forms (consider the entry encompassing ABIDE/ ABODE; Fig. 8.3). Richardson's rigorous form of lemmatization—in which inflectional and variant forms of a word (e.g. *Divert, v.* and *Divers* or *Diverse, v.*) are grouped under one headword—requires a level of linguistic competence beyond that of many users. Most users of explanatory dictionaries normally access entries to solve some specific problem of understanding. Grouping derivatives and variants under a given headword makes such access difficult.

8.3.4 Comparative treatments of entries

By departing radically from the established lexicographical tradition of accounting for the individual senses of polysemous words, Richardson is unable to account for various sorts of variation in language use. In particular, his procedure could not explain or display language use that did not reflect a necessary historical development, based on a predetermined diachronic and systematic figurative extension of meaning. For example, there is no mechanism for recording that a word in some authors and in particular geographical regions or professional contexts retains a meaning closer to the 'literal' meaning, despite occurring later than those used in a metaphorical sense. Richardson simply lists all quotations in chronological order. In these cases, chronological 'progression' usurps the logic of actual usage. (Richardson does occasionally allow for this problem with a comment acknowledging a later usage that contradicts his principle.) Johnson's procedure of dividing up explanations into numbered senses allows for parallel, yet possibly divergent, development of meanings or usage according to different senses over time (each numbered sense has a chronological sequence of its own). Johnson's system of accounting for polysemy frees the user or reader to return to a radical use of a word; indeed, considering the conservative, past-oriented nature of Johnson's work (especially the use of

ABI

ABI'DE. Abi'der. Abi'ding. Abo'de. Abi'dance. } A. S. *Abidan, Bidan*; D. *Beyden*, to bide. To stay, or remain; to delay, to tarry, to dwell, to continue, to wait, to expect. To stay under, or support; to bear up against, or endure,—with fortitude, good temper, kindness, hope, or the reverse.

He fley in to the yle of Tenet, he no dorste *abide* no ner.
R. Gloucester, p. 122.

The other were of hem y war, and garkede hem in here syde,
And lette arme here ost wel, batail forto *abyde*.
Id. p. 153.

And the othir day he entride into Cesarie, and Cornelie *abood* hem with his cosyns and necessarie frendis that weren clepid togidre.—*Wiclif. The Dedis of Apostlis*, c. 10.

Lyue sobreli and iustli and piteuousli in this world, *abidynge* the blessid hope and the comyng of the greet God, and of our Sauyour Iesu Crist.—*Id. Tyte*, c. 2.

For men schulen wexe drie for drede, and *abidynge* that schulen come to al the world.—*Id. Luk.* c. 21.

Do grete diligence (saith Salomon), in keping of thy frendes, and of thy good name, for it shal lenger *abide* with thee, than any tresor, be it never so precious.
Chaucer. The Tale of Milebeus.

He [Giovanni Pietro Pugliano] said, "Soldiers were the noblest estate of mankind, and horsemen the noblest of soldiers." He said, "They were the masters of war, and ornaments of peace, speedy goers, and strong *abiders*."
Sidney. Defence of Poesy, p. 1.

The pacient *abyding* of the righteous shall be turned to gladnesse, but the hope of the vngodly shall perish.
Bible. Lond. 1539. *Prov.* c. 10.

There he made his *abode* fortye dayes and as many nightes, still continuing in prayer and fastyng.
Udal. St. Marke, c. 1.

Aut. I cannot tell, good Sir, for which of his vertues it was, but hee was certainly whipt out of the court.
Clo. His vices you would say: there's no vertue whipt out of the court: they cherish it to make it stay there; and yet it will no more but *abide*.
Shakespeare. Winter's Tale, Act iv. sc. 2.

Lor. Sweete friends; your patience for my long *abode*;—
Not I, but my affaires haue made you wait.
Id. Merchant of Venice, Act ii. sc. 6.

When all the earth shall melt into nothing, and the seas scald their finny labourers; so long is his *abidance* [in purgatory].—*The Puritan*, Act ii. sc. 1.

Abating all the rueful consequences of *abiding* in sin, abstracting from the desperate hazards it exposeth us to in regard to the future life, it is most reasonable to abandon it.
Barrow. Ser. vol. iii. s. 17.

When he, whom e'en our joys provoke,
The fiend of nature, join'd his yoke,
And rush'd in wrath to make our isle his prey,
Thy form, from out thy sweet *abode*,
O'ertook him on his blasted road,
And stopp'd his wheels, and look'd his rage away.
Collins. Ode to Mercy.

ABI'E, is very variously written. By Chaucer, *Abegge, Abeye, Abie*; which Tyrwhitt says is Saxon, and means "To suffer for." In Piers Plouhman, *Abegge*. In Gower, *Abeie, Abedge, Abidye*. In Chaucer, are found the participles *Abying, Abien, Abought*. And in Gower, also, *Abought*. Skinner adopts the verb, *To buy* (in preference to the A. S. *Abid-an*, to abide), as the more simple etymology. In Shakespeare (*infra*), *Abide*, thus, should be *Aby*.

In all the examples following, "buy or pay for, dearly, cruelly, sorely," appears to be the meaning.

Turne we thiderward, and delyuer our prisons,
And so it may betide, thei salle dere *abie*
My [mine] that thei hide, my men in prison lie.
R. Brunne, p. 159.

Ac for the lesynge that thow Lucifer, lowe til Eve
Thow shalt *abygge* bitere quath God, and bond hym with cheynes.—*Piers Plouhman*, p. 363.

Ther dorste no wight hond upon him legge,
That he ne swore he shuld anon *abegge*.
Chaucer. The Reves Tale, v. 3936.

Ye fathers, and ye mothers eke also,
Though ye han children, be it on or mo,
Your is the charge of all hir surveance,
While that they ben under your governance.
Beth ware, that by ensample of your living,
Or by your negligence in chastising,
That they ne perish: for I dare wel saye,
If that they don, ye shul it dere *abeye*.
Id. The Doctoures Tale, v. 12034.

ABJ

Quene of the regne of Pluto, derke and lowe,
Goddesse of maydens, that min herte hast knowe
Ful many a yere, and wost what I desire,
As kepe me fro thy vengeance and thin ire,
That Atteon *aboughte* cruelly.
Chaucer. The Knightes Tale, v. 2305.

So goth he forthe, and toke his leue,
And thought anone, as it was eue,
He wolde doone his sacrilege,
That many a man shuld it *abedge*.—*Gower. Con. A.* b. v.

Full ofte er this it hath be seine
The comen people is ouerleyne,
And hath the kynges synne *abought*,
Allthough the people agilte nought.—*Ib.* b. vii.

Which when his brother saw, fraught with great griefe
And wrath, he to him leaped furiously,
And fouly said, by Mahoune, cursed thiefe,
That direfull stroake thou dearely shalt *aby*.
Spenser. Faerie Queene, b. ii. c. viii.

Bar. Fool-hardy knight, full soon thou shalt *aby*
This fond reproach, thy body will I bang.
Beaum. & Fletch. Knight of the Burning Pestle, Act iii. sc. 1.

De. Disparage not the faith thou dost not know,
Lest to thy perill thou *abide* it deare.
Shakespeare. Mid. Night's Dream, Act iii. sc. 2.

ABJE'CT, *v.* A'bject, *adj.* A'bject, *n.* Abje'ctedness. Abje'ction. A'bjectly. A'bjectness. } Fr. *Abject*; It. *Abjetto*; Lat. *Abject-um*, past part. of *abjicere*, (*Ab-jacere*,) to cast, or throw away from; to cast down.
Abject, v. To cast away, to cast off or out, to cast down.

The nouns, adjective, and adverbs, have a consequent application to that which is—

Base, lowly, servile, worthless, despicable, mean, contemptible.

The duches desiring to knowe whiche waye lady Fortune turned her whele, herynge hym to be repudiate and *abiected* oute of the Frenche courte, was in a greate agony, and muche amased, and more appalled.—*Hall. Hen. VII.* an. 7.

For that offence only [disobedience] Almighty God *abjected* Saul, that he shulde no more reigne ouer Israel.
Sir T. Elyot. The Governovr, c. 1.

John the apostle, was now of late in a certaine yle of Licia called Pathmos, exiled for the gospel-preaching, and made a vile *abject* for testifying the name and word of Jesus Christ the onely Saviour of the world.
Bale. Image of both Churches.

The audacite and bolde speche of Daniel signifyeth the *abiection* of the kynge and his realme.
Joye. The Exposicion of Daniel, c. 5.

Jesus calleth thē home frō this affeccion, to ye contemplaciō of his lowe state of *abiecciō* in this world.
Udal. Luke c. 9. fol. 296.

Christ for the time of his pilgrimage here was a most poore man, *abiecting* and casting off all worldly rule and honour.—*State Trials.* 2 *Rich. II.* 1388. *Abp. York.*

The damzell straght went, as she was directed
Vnto the rock; and there, vpon the soile
Hauing herselfe in wretched wise *abjected*,
Gan weepe and waile, as if great griefe had been affected.
Spenser. Faerie Queene, b. v. c. 9. st. 9.

Oh noble Lord, bethinke thee of thy birth;
Call home thy ancient thoughts from banishment,
And banish hence these *abiect* lowlie dreames:
Looke how thy seruants do attend on thee,
Each in his office readie at thy becke.
Shakespeare. Tam. of Sh. Act i. sc. 3.

We are the queene's *abjects*, and must obey.
Id. Rich. III. Act i. sc. 3.

Or in this *abject* posture have ye sworn
T' adore the conqueror? who now beholds
Cherub and seraph rolling in the flood
With scatter'd arms and ensigns.
Milton. Paradise Lost, b. i.

But is it credible, that the very acknowledgment of our owne unworthinesse to obtain, and in that respect our professed fearfulnesse to aske any thing, otherwise than onely for his sake to whom God can deny nothing; that this should be termed basenesse, *abjection* of mind, or servilitie—is it credible?—*Hooker. Ec. Pol.* b. v. § 47.

It *abjected* his [Wolsey's] spirit to that degree, that he fell dangerously sick: such an influence the troubles and sorrows of his mind had upon his body.
Strype. Memorials, b. i. c. 15.

To what base ends, and by what *abject* ways,
Are mortals urg'd, through sacred lust of praise!
Pope. Essay on Criticism.

Nor did he sooner see the hoy approaching the vessel than he ran down again into the cabin, and, his rage being perfectly subsided, he tumbled on his knees, and a little too *abjectly* implored for mercy.
Fielding. Voyage to Lisbon.

ABL

ABJU'RE, *v.* Abjura'tion. } Fr. *Abjurer*; It. *Abjurare*; Sp. *Abjurar*; Lat. *Abjurare*, (*Ab jurare*,) to swear from, to forswear. See the quotation from Hobbs.

To swear—(sc.)

To go away from, or leave: to disown, to disclaim, to renounce (upon oath).

But now was he so obstinate, that he woulde not *abiure* of lōg time. And dyuers daies wer his iudges fayn of their fauour to geue hym with sufferance of some his best frendes and whō he most trusted to resort vnto him. And yet scantly could al this make him submitte himself to make hys *abiuracion*.—*Sir T. More. Works*, p. 214.

In this season were banished out of Southwarke XII Scottes, whiche had dwelt there a long season, and wer conueied frō parishe to parishe by the constable, like men yt had *abiured* the realme, and on their vttermost garment a white crosse before and another behynd them.
Hall. Chron. Hen. VIII. an. 14.

——— For euen now
I put my selfe to thy direction, and
Vnspeake mine own detraction. Heere *abjure*
The taints and blames I laide vpon my selfe
For strangers to my nature.
Shakespeare. Mac. Act iv. sc. 3.

Did not one of them rather leave his inmost coat behind him, than not be quit of thee? Did not another of them deny thee, yea *abjure* thee? And yet thou sayest, Go tell my brethren!—*Bp. Hall. Contemp. The Resurrection.*

Ph. And what is *abjuration*?
La. When a clerk heretofore was convicted of felony, he might have saved his life by *abjuring* the realm; that is, by departing the realm within a certain time appointed, and *taking an oath never to return*.
Hobbs. A Dialogue of the Common Laws.

And thereupon [he] took the oath in that case provided, viz. that he *abjured* the realm, and would depart from thence forthwith, at the port that should be assigned him, and would never return without leave from the king.
Blackstone. Com. b. iv. c. 26.

A Jacobite, who is persuaded of the pretender's right to the crown, cannot take the oath of allegiance; or, if he could, the oath of *abjuration* follows, which contains an express renunciation of all opinions in favour of the claim of the exiled family.—*Paley. Moral Philosophy*, b. iii. c. 18.

ABLACTA'TION. Lat. (of the lower age,) *Ablactatus*. (*Ab-lacte, depulsus*), driven from the milk: applied (formerly) met. to a mode of grafting. See the quotation.

Grafting by approach or *ablactation* is to be performed when the stock you would graft on, and the tree from which you would take your graft, stand so near together that they may be joined.—*Miller. Gardener's Dict. In v. Grafting.*

ABLAQUEA'TION. Lat. *Ablaqueatio*: from *Ablaqueare*, to dig about and lay bare the roots of trees. Evelyn affected such Latinisms.

Now is the time for *ablaqueation*, and laying bare the roots of old, unthriving, and over-hastily blooming trees; stirring up new-planted grounds, as directed in March.
Evelyn. The Gardener's Alm. October.

Ablaqueation now profitable, and to visit the roots of old trees, purge the sickly, and apply fresh mould.
Id. November.

ABLA'TION. A'blative. } Fr. *Ablation*; Lat. *Ablatio*; from *Ablatum*, (See Collate,) taken from—

A taking away, or depriving.

Ablative, that can or may take away.

Prohibition extends to all injustice, whether done by force, or fraud; whether it be by *ablation*, or prevention, or detaining of rights; any thing, in which injury is done directly or obliquely to our neighbour's fortune.
Bp. Taylor. Great Exemplar, p. 2, § 37.

But where the heart is forestalled with misopinion, *ablative* directions are first needfull to unteach error, ere we can learne truth.
Bp. Hall. Sermon. The Deceit of Appearance.

A'BLE, *v.* A'ble, *adj.* A'bleness. Abi'liment. Abi'lity. A'bly. } Goth. *Abal*, strength: and hence the Lat. terminations in *bilis*, and our own in *ble*. See Tooke.
To give force, power, strength; to strengthen, to empower; and, as we now say, to *enable*.

The verb, *to able*, appears to have been in as common usage in ancient writers, as to *enable* is in modern, and with similar applications.

Hable and *Hability* are in the old writers as commonly found as *able* and *ability*.

That if God willinge to schewe his wraththe, and to make his power knowun, hath suffrid in greet pacience vessels of

4

Fig. 8.3. The page containing *ABIDE* from Richardson's *A New Dictionary of the English Language*, 1836

past quotations), the 'primitive' meaning closest to the etymon may be implicitly preferred. Richardson, on the other hand, is strictly positivist, believing in progressive refinement.

An example of the problems caused by Richardson's system can be found in the following entry:

(1) ASH, *n.*
Ash, *v.*,
Ashy, *adj.* } D. *Asche*; Ger. *Asche*; Sw. *Asca*; Goth. *Azgo*; A.S. *Asca*, pulvis; *Asce*, cinis. Dust, ashes. Applied to—
Dust produced by burning any substance–to any similar dust.
Compare Chaucer and Gray.

Philip left his engines withouten kepyng a nyght,
That perceyued the Sarazines, with fire brent tham down right.
For he com on the morowe, assaut he wild haf gyuen,
His engyns fond he lorne, brent & tille *askes* dryuen. *R. Brunne*, p. 176.

If in Tyre and Sydon the virtues hadden be don which han be don in you, sum tyme thei wolden han sete in hayre and *aischis*, & haue doon penaunce.—
Wiclif. Luk, c.10.

For whan we may not don, than wol we speken,
Yet in our *ashen* cold is fire yreken. *Chaucer. The Reves Prologue*, v. 3880.

Ev'n in our *ashes* live their wonted fires.— *Gray. Elegy.*

Tho came this woful Theban Palamon
With flotery berd, and ruggy *asshy* heres,
In clothes blake, ydropped all with teares.
Chaucer. The Knightes Tale, v. 2885.

Ye Troyan *ashes*, and last flames of mine,
I cal in witnesse, that at your last fall,
I fled no stroke of any Grekish swerd. *Surrey. Virgile. Aeneid*, b. iv.

[followed by five quotations from James Howell, Milton, Dryden, Phineas Fletcher, and Cowper.]

Richardson's note ('Compare Chaucer and Gray') seems to recognize the fact that Chaucer's use of the word in the first example is only metaphorically linked to actual ashes, meaning 'dust produced by burning', even though the use precedes chronologically several others invoking the literal meaning of the word. He accurately links the two quotations by inserting Gray's out of chronological order and by calling attention to the juxtaposition; but there is nothing in the etymological material or the definition to account for the fact that the lines are referring not to actual ashes but to human remains, not necessarily cremated. The quotations pun on the relation between fire and ashes, which is necessary for the conceit, yet the transferred meaning of the word (the remains of the human body) is unaccounted for in Richardson's entry.

Johnson's entry reads as follows:

(2) A'SHES. n.s. wants the singular. [asca, Sax. asche, Dutch.]

1. The remains of any thing burnt.

Some relicks would be left of it, as when *ashes* remain of burned bodies. *Digby on Bodies.*

This late dissension, grown betwixt the peers,
Burns under feigned *ashes* of forg'd love,
And will at last break out into a flame. *Shakesp. Henry VI.*

Ashes contain a very fertile salt, and are the best manure for cold lands, if kept dry, that the rain doth not wash away their salt. *Mortimer's Husbandry.*

2. The remains of the body; often used in poetry for the carcase, from the ancient practice of burning the dead.

Poor key-cold figure of a holy king!
Pale *ashes* of the house of Lancaster!
Thou bloodless remnant of that royal blood! *Shak. R. III.*

To great Laërtes I bequeath
A task of grief, his ornaments of death;
Lest, when the fates his royal *ashes* claim,
The Grecian matrons taint my spotless name. *Pope.*

While Richardson's explanation of 'ash' as a kind of dust produced by burning is more precise than Johnson's concrete first definition, Johnson's second sense (adopted almost verbatim by the *OED*) clearly sets out the metaphorical usage common in English, especially poetry and theology. With two different numbered meanings, he can also demonstrate the slight overlapping of the metaphorical with the literal (since Shakespeare's *Richard III* precedes Mortimer's *Husbandry* (1707) chronologically). This clarity is impossible in Richardson, unless one sorts through and analyses the quotations oneself.

8.4 CONCLUSION

Johnson's *Dictionary* influenced the development of the *New English Dictionary* chiefly through its incorporation of multiple definitions, its method of defining, the relation between definitions and authorities, and its extensive treatment of phrasal verbs. Richardson's dictionary was noteworthy for the clarity with which it displayed related words and word families, and was influential on modern lexicography through its attempts to ascertain etymologies. The diachronic listing of quotations marked a major step towards the study of historical semantics. We have seen the ways in which Johnson especially, and Richardson to a lesser extent, moved lexicography towards a more empirical and descriptive orientation. Murray and his colleagues would undertake an increasingly scientific investigation of etymology, and of each word's forms and uses in excerpted quotations, through time (Murray 1993: 120–1; Silva 2000: 78).

9

MAJOR AMERICAN DICTIONARIES

Sidney I. Landau

9.1 WEBSTER'S FIRST DICTIONARY

ON 4 June 1800, newspapers in New Haven, Connecticut, included a statement from Noah Webster declaring that he intended to publish several new dictionaries: a dictionary of the American language and dictionaries for schools, the counting house, and a 'large one' for men of science. Webster was already widely known as the author of the 'blue-backed speller', *The American Spelling Book.* A small book designed for schools, the *Spelling Book* was first published in 1783, reprinted many times, and proved to be one of the most popular spelling books ever produced in the English language; it was also an important source of income for Webster as a lexicographer. Webster's fascination with simplified spelling was to leave a lasting mark on American English, chiefly through his dictionaries; indeed, the orthography used in his dictionaries was to be one of their most controversial aspects, subjecting them at times to scornful criticism. Webster's statement of 1800 was a little premature. In the event, his dictionary of the American language would not appear until 1828, but in 1806 he published his first dictionary, of small size and extent (about 400 pages), called *A Compendious Dictionary of the English Language.*

9.1.1 *Biographical background*

Noah Webster is the most important lexicographer in the history of American lexicography, and his influence on its subsequent course is arguably greater than that of Johnson's on English lexicography. For this reason, a brief discursus to provide some essential biographical facts about Webster may be justified, especially because they help to explain some of his lexicographic policies. Webster was born in West Hartford, Connecticut in 1758 and died in 1843 at the age of eighty-four. Thus his life spanned the war of independence from Britain and the formative years of the new republic. He was an active patriot for independence and while still in his teens briefly served in the Revolutionary army, though he did not see any military action. He graduated from Yale, trained as a lawyer, and engaged in many different pursuits as a young man, among them journalist, schoolmaster, and political writer. He was never shy about introducing himself to people in power, and corresponded with Benjamin Franklin and many others of high station (even briefly with George Washington). For years he campaigned vigorously for federal copyright protection, chiefly to protect his spelling book, at a time when only a few states gave such protection and there were no federal laws to protect copyright. Webster came to lexicography relatively late in life. He published his first dictionary at the age of forty-eight when the average lifespan was about half that of today, and he was seventy years old when his second great work, the *American Dictionary of the English Language*, was published in 1828.

Although the *Compendious* was not the first American dictionary, it was the first of any significance.[1] It was derived, Webster acknowledges, from John Entick's *Spelling Dictionary* of 1764, to which has been added about 5,000 words for a total of about 40,000. There are two columns to a page and definitions are very short so as to fit within a one-column line. No etymologies or pronunciations are given. Stress is indicated by an accent mark in the entry word. As a strange harbinger of the future of American lexicography, even in this first small Webster dictionary, some fifty pages at the end of the book are devoted to appendixes of encyclopedic material including, among others, those listing measures, US post offices, US population, world historical events, and 'remarkable Events' about America, 'intended as the outline of American History'.

The chief importance of the *Compendious* lies in the Preface, twenty-four pages printed in minute type, in which Webster reveals that the present dictionary is just a modest first step in his plan to compile a much larger dictionary, 'a dictionary which shall exhibit a far more correct state of the language than any work of this kind' (Webster 1806: xxiii). Webster uses the Preface as a vehicle to attack Johnson's *Dictionary* as rife with mistakes when that dictionary was still

[1] The first dictionary published in America was *A School Dictionary* (1798) by Samuel Johnson, Jr. (no relation to *the* Samuel Johnson, who died in 1784), a small, derivative work for children. A number of other similar, equally unoriginal dictionaries based on earlier English works were produced through 1804. See Burkett 1979: 3–42, for a detailed description.

the most popular dictionary of the English language. Webster remarks on the omissions of newly formed words, especially in the sciences, such as *telegraph*, and deplores the many inaccuracies in Johnson's etymologies, promising to reveal the true etymology of each word in his own dictionary. He also criticizes Johnson for including many 'inkhorn' terms (difficult words formed from Latin) that are never used, such as *adversable, injudicable*, and *balbucinate* (cited by Friend 1967: 19) and for including vulgar words, which he promises to omit. Webster's intention is nothing less than to replace Johnson as the pre-eminent lexicographer of the English language. For a man who had none of Johnson's elevated status as a celebrated author, essayist, and poet, Webster's ambition was audacious, yet he was ultimately to achieve it.

The main innovation in the *Compendious* was in its recommended spellings. Webster wanted to simplify spelling by dropping out some silent letters and believed that English spelling should reflect its Anglo-Saxon roots (Micklethwait 2000: 143). Thus he dropped the *u* in words like *honour* and *favour*, the *k* at the end of *musick* and *publick*, the *a* in *leather*, and the *e* at the end of words like *determine, discipline, doctrine, examine*, etc. He uses *s* instead of *c* in *defence* and *offence* but does not alter the double consonant in words like *traveller*. A review of 1809 was devastatingly negative, criticizing Webster in particular for 'spreading hurtful innovations in orthography' (quoted in Burkett 1979: 131). Webster's innovations in orthography would be dogged by similar criticisms to the end of his life, yet many of his innovations are now standard in American English. His views on orthography evolved over the years as reflected in his later dictionaries.

9.2 *AN AMERICAN DICTIONARY OF THE ENGLISH LANGUAGE*

By 1800 Webster had begun preliminary work on his magnum opus, *An American Dictionary of the English Language*. He made copious notes in the 1799 quarto edition of Johnson's *Dictionary*, and the character of his notes suggests that he was even then looking beyond the *Compendious* of 1806 to the larger work (Landau 2005: 217–18). The dictionary was published in 1828 in a three-column format in two handsome, large, quarto volumes. It contained about 70,000 entries, and the first printing was 2,500 copies. An edition for the English market was published in 1830–32.

9.2.1 *Webster's debt to Johnson*

A comparison of all the definitions in the letter L of the *American Dictionary* with all those in the 1799 edition of Johnson's *Dictionary* shows a remarkable degree of correspondence, according to one study (Reed 1962). During the actual preparation of the *American Dictionary*, Webster relied chiefly on the revision of Johnson's *Dictionary* of 1818 by Henry Todd, known as the Todd–Johnson. Sledd and Kolb found a close correspondence between the two dictionaries' treatment of entry words, definitions, authorities, and etymologies in part of the letter C (Sledd and Kolb 1955: 198). Of course, Webster was hardly the only lexicographer making use of Johnson's *Dictionary*. As Joseph Worcester (1784–1865) wrote in the preface to his dictionary of 1846, Johnson's *Dictionary* 'from the time of its first publication, has been, far more than any other, regarded as a standard for the language. It has formed substantially the basis of many smaller works, and, as Walker remarks, it "has been deemed lawful plunder by every subsequent lexicographer"' (Worcester 1846: lxiv).

9.2.2 *The Preface and Introduction*

Webster had defiantly named his great dictionary *An American Dictionary* to declare that the English language had developed its own distinctive character in America and was deserving of its own dictionary. Webster was certainly justified in saying that the language had changed since Johnson's day and that many words, particularly in the sciences, were not to be found in Johnson's *Dictionary*. He also drew attention to the different habits, different political entities, and physical differences of the environment between England and the United States, all of which would leave their marks on language. He brashly predicted that 'our language [that is, American English], within two centuries, will be spoken by more people in this country, than any other on earth, except the Chinese, in Asia, and even that may not be an exception'. He estimated the future population of the United States at 'three hundred millions.' One may imagine the amusement such wild speculations must have aroused in many of his compatriots, not to mention British observers. But his prediction proved to be accurate.

Webster concludes his Preface in a style that cannot fail to bring to mind Johnson's Preface, and was doubtless intended to provide a contrast with that of Johnson. Yet in his very eagerness to show his superiority to Johnson, he succeeds only in displaying an unwonted deference. Webster writes:

> I present it to my fellow citizens, not with frigid indifference, but with ardent wishes for their improvement and happiness; and for the continued increase of the wealth, the learning, the moral and religious elevation of character, and the glory of my country.

In the Introduction, Webster expands on the chief faults in Johnson's *Dictionary.* 'Well authorized words' are omitted; the manner of marking how words are accented is unclear; there are inconsistencies in spelling, omissions of participles, a 'want of discrimination' in defining nearly synonymous words, misspellings of words, and numerous mistakes in etymology. The order of definitions ought to show the basic meaning first; and finally, there are a needlessly large number of quotations exemplifying definitions. He asserts that in most cases a single example would suffice, and that some definitions need no exemplification but may be inserted on the authority of the lexicographer. 'Numerous citations serve to swell the size of a Dictionary, without any adequate advantage.' Here Webster anticipates modern practice so far as synchronic commercial dictionaries are concerned.

9.2.3 Etymology in the American Dictionary

As Webster writes in the Preface, he decided, 'after writing through two letters of the alphabet', to postpone further work until he had mastered the science of etymology. He found Johnson's etymologies very inadequate, and resolved to undertake an ambitious comparison of 'about twenty languages' in order to be able to determine more accurately than anyone had ever done before the true origins of the words in his dictionary. For ten years he devoted himself to the study of these languages, and particularly to what he called the consonantal radix (or root) by which affinities could be discovered between languages. He ignored vowels, regarding them as unimportant. Webster was ignorant of the work of Rasmus Rask, Jacob Grimm, and other German philologists who since 1818 had begun to develop the principles of sound change linked to systematic changes of consonants and vowels that would revolutionize the study of etymology. George Philip Krapp concluded that 'Webster's work in etymology illustrates the extreme isolation and provincialism of American scholarship in the early years of the nineteenth century' (Krapp 1966: 365).

Allen Walker Read points out that, because Webster was already a mature man of forty-two when he announced his intention to write dictionaries, his linguistic outlook was that of the eighteenth century, and that French culture, not German, was influential until after 1800 in New England. Read argues that 'Webster made notable advances beyond his eighteenth-century origins, and it was his bad luck that the new German learning followed so soon upon him...' (Read 1966: 163, 166). It was not until his dictionary was virtually complete, in 1827, that he was made aware of the new learning through his assistant, James Gates Percival, a young scholar who knew German and had come to appreciate the importance of the German linguists. Percival urged him strongly to revise the etymologies, advice that Webster regarded as impertinent coming from one so young and untried. Read, taking a more sympathetic view of Webster than many other critics, concludes, 'He has been censured too severely for not adopting the German learning, for at his advanced age he could not be expected to overturn his life's work' (Read 1966: 181). One might add that there were very strong financial reasons for not countenancing any protracted delay in publication. During the years he worked on the dictionary he was frequently hard up for cash and finally had to sell the rights to his spelling book to raise money. Among his personal letters are many appealing for funds to support the dictionary. A delay of a year or more at this point would have jeopardized the entire dictionary and threatened him and his family with financial ruin.

However much one may understand Webster's reluctance to completely redo his etymologies when he was on the verge of completing his dictionary, the fact remains that many of the etymologies are inadequate or wrong, and others erroneously link unrelated words and languages. In 1808, Webster underwent a religious conversion to a fundamentalist Christian view which was to have a powerful effect on his etymological principles and even on some of his definitions. He took the Bible as the literal truth in all particulars. In the Introduction to his dictionary he recounts the story of Adam and Eve, concluding that 'language was bestowed on Adam' and that it was probable that language as well as the faculty of speech were gifts of God. He thought that all the world's languages could be divided into Hamitic and Japhitic, from Noah's sons Ham and Japheth. Furthermore, Webster believed in the existence of a 'single, primitive language', Chaldee, from which all other languages were ultimately derived (Krapp 1966: 363). A good deal of his enthusiasm that carried him through ten years of painstaking work was the result of his belief that he was in a sense doing God's work in tracing the roots of words to their biblical origin before the tower of Babel led to the dispersion of many tongues.

In compiling his etymologies, Webster's working method was to arrange a large number of dictionaries and grammars of different languages on a circular table about two feet wide and walk from one book to the next, taking notes on the graphemic form of a particular word as it appeared, according to his understanding of the likeness of its consonants and the relationship of its presumed primary meaning from one language to another (Warfel 1936: 349; Micklethwait 2000: 161). He was apparently guided by no fixed principle of correspondence between the consonants, but sought to find some pattern of similarity between words sharing some fundamental meaning element. In his assumption that words had a primary meaning and his belief in the importance of consonantal radixes, he was influenced by the theories of John Horne Tooke as expressed in the *Diversions of Purley* (Bivens 1982: 5–6). Webster's etymologies would remain in his dictionaries until they were completely revised by the German scholar, C. A. F. Mahn, for the 1864 edition more than twenty years after Webster's death.

Webster's etymological investigations were originally intended to comprise the third volume of his dictionary, but they were never published. They were eventually compiled as the *Synopsis of Words in Twenty Languages* and left to the New York Public Library, where they remain; they exist in the form of handwritten notes.

9.2.4 *Orthography in the* American Dictionary

Webster's involvement with spelling reform goes far beyond his treatment of spelling in his dictionaries (Krapp 1966: 329–47). Webster had long corresponded with Benjamin Franklin and was influenced by his ideas, but Franklin's proposals, involving a new alphabet, were far more radical than any plan of Webster's. Webster moderated some of the innovations in spelling that he had adopted in the *Compendious*, restoring the *k* in some words ending in *-ic* (such as *frolick* and *traffick*), but omitting it in others, such as *music* and *public*. He continued to omit the *u* in words like *honor* and *humor* and to change the spelling of words ending in *-re* to *-er*, such as *center*, *theater* (although *theatre* is included as a variant), and similar words. He restored the final, silent *e* in words like *determine*, which he had dropped in the *Compendious*, and, though he gave words like *leather* and *feather* preferred status, he retained the simplified forms (such as *lether* and *fether*) as variants in some cases. He also introduced a few new spelling changes on the basis of etymology which strike us today (and which struck many of his contemporaries then) as bizarre, for example, his preference for *bridegoom* over *bridegroom*, *bild* over *build*, and *ieland* over *island* (cited in Krapp 1966: 345). Webster argued that the Anglo-Saxon forms had been corrupted and wanted to restore them, but in so doing he was ignoring centuries of use. Subsequent editions of Webster's dictionaries, beginning with the revision of 1841, ultimately retreated from all of these odd prescriptions.

9.2.5 *Definitions and illustrative quotations in the* American Dictionary

A careful historian of American lexicography, and one not given to overpraising Webster, concludes that Webster's definitions in the *American Dictionary* were 'more accurate, more comprehensive, and not less carefully divided and ordered than any previously done in English lexicography' (Friend 1967: 36). James A. H. Murray, the chief editor of the *Oxford English Dictionary*, famously called Webster 'a born definer of words' in The Romanes Lecture of 1900 (Murray 1993: 118), and any careful comparison of Webster's definitions and use of illustrative quotations with Johnson's or those in any of the earlier dictionaries will confirm that Webster's were a distinct improvement. Although he occasionally lapsed into unnecessarily encyclopedic definitions, in the main his definitions were concise but accurate. Moreover, in keeping with his criticisms of Johnson's too profligate use of quotations, Webster often omitted them entirely, depending on the definition only. Often he cited only the name of an author, such as *Pope* or *Locke*, and when he did include a quotation (which was very often taken directly from Johnson's *Dictionary*), he kept it short. Unlike Johnson, he was not interested in including enough of a quotation to give a flavour of the style or even to convey the sense of the quotation; he gave only enough to illustrate the sense to which the quotation was appended. He also included invented phrases to show the typical context in which some words were used. In so doing, Webster set the pattern for the treatment of definition in commercial lexicography that was to become all but universal and even today seems thoroughly modern.

9.2.6 *Pronunciation in the* American Dictionary

To indicate pronunciation Webster used a few barred letters and a set of diacritical marks over or under the letters of the entry words (or headwords), which were all in capital letters. Syllabic breaks are not indicated apart from the use of a stress mark after an accented syllable. The system was a modest advance over that of the *Compendious*, as well as over Johnson, neither of which indicated vowel quality, but it was far from showing an accurate pronunciation of every word included. It was no match for Walker's popular *Critical Pronouncing Dictionary and Expositor of the English Language*, originally published in 1791 but with many later editions (→ Beal, Vol. II). When Chalmers's abridgement of Todd–Johnson was combined with Walker's pronunciations in the edition of 1827 edited by Joseph Worcester, it immediately achieved high popularity with the American public and was Webster's chief competition. Webster's two-volume *American Dictionary* was, however, much more expensive, selling for $20 (a high price at that time), and it was not until cheaper abridgements became available that any effective inroads could be made into the dominance of the market by Worcester's 1827 edition.

9.2.7 *Critical reception of the* American Dictionary

One contemporary reviewer (of 1835) harshly criticized Webster's dictionary, calling it 'a decided failure' and going on to claim: 'There is everywhere a great parade of erudition, and a great lack of real knowledge...' (quoted by Steger 1913:

53–4 and Burkett 1979: 161). He was particularly critical of the derivation of words and the statement of primary meaning. Some later reviews were considerably more favourable, and in general the dictionary was regarded as an impressive work. In England the reception of Webster's dictionary was on the whole favourable, and the first edition of the dictionary was to sell better there than in Webster's homeland. Most of the criticism of the *American Dictionary* related to Webster's preferred spellings, and this fuelled the conflict between Webster and his publishers and Joseph Worcester and his defenders, discussed below.

9.3 EARLY ABRIDGEMENTS AND REVISIONS OF THE *AMERICAN DICTIONARY*

Webster's publisher, Sherman Converse, quickly realized that if he was to compete effectively with the Todd–Johnson abridgement and other smaller dictionaries, he would have to have a cheaper, one-volume abridgement of the *American Dictionary* to sell, chiefly to schools. Almost every fact involving this abridgement, called *Primary School Dictionary*, which was edited by Joseph Worcester and published in 1829, would eventually be contested in the bitter, long-lasting dispute between Webster and Worcester. But the record supports Worcester's account that he was asked by Webster's publisher to edit the abridgement and at first refused, as he was planning his own dictionary, but when pressed again acceded and agreed to edit the work. Webster was not closely involved in establishing the policies that would govern the abridgement and did not review the manuscript. His son-in-law, Chauncey A. Goodrich, took control of the project and managed it independently of Webster. Webster would later object vigorously to some of the changes made without his permission, such as the addition of new words and revised spellings. But, at the time, he took little interest in the work (Micklethwait 2000: 200–203).

The second edition of the *American Dictionary* was published in two volumes in octavo in 1841. Several thousand words were added, and many scientific terms, edited by Professor William Tully of the New Haven Medical College, were corrected and updated. William G. Webster, Noah's son, also contributed to this revision. Entry words were now shown with complete syllabication rather than showing a simple indication of the accented syllable as in the original 1828 edition, and a 36-page supplement of new words was included at the end of the second volume. This would be the last dictionary that Webster edited, as he died in 1843. The earliest citation in the *OED* of 'Webster's unabridged' is that of 1860, which could apply to this edition but more likely to the one-volume edition of 1847, the first Webster dictionary to be edited and published by the subsequent owners of Webster's dictionaries, the G. & C. Merriam Company.[2]

It is unfortunate that Worcester's own accomplishments as a lexicographer have been overshadowed by his conflict with Webster, relegating Worcester in the minds of many to the status of a minor and forgettable competitor. This is a serious distortion of Worcester's true contribution to American lexicography. He was a major American lexicographer in his own right, producing two major dictionaries of considerable merit and a number of smaller dictionaries. These so worried Webster and his publishers that they took extraordinary steps to disparage his work and malign his character. The so-called dictionary wars consisted of a series of newspaper and magazine articles and pamphlets issued by the principles in this dispute and their supporters, and appearing intermittently over some thirty years, from 1830 to the early 1860s. The publication of Webster's 1864 dictionary, called 'the unabridged', finally ended the dispute. In order to introduce Worcester in his own terms rather than as a foil to Webster, Worcester's major dictionaries will be considered before the discussion of the dictionary wars.

9.4 WORCESTER'S DICTIONARIES

It was natural for Webster's publisher in 1828 to regard Worcester as the best possible editor of the abridgement, for, as noted above, Worcester had just finished editing a revision of the abridgement of Johnson's dictionary. The quick succession in which the Webster abridgement and Worcester's own dictionary, *A Comprehensive Pronouncing and Explanatory Dictionary of the English Language* (1830), appeared ignited the passionate conviction in Webster that Worcester had based his 1830 dictionary on the Webster abridgement with which he was obviously familiar.

[2] Leavitt reports in the G. & C. Merriam's company history that 'soon it [the 1841 edition] became almost universally known by the popular name of *Webster's Unabridged*' (Leavitt 1947: 36). The 1847 edition was also styled 'unabridged', like the 1841 edition, but in respect of having all the words in the earlier editions of Webster's dictionary. The modern sense of 'unabridged' as applied to a dictionary suggests a collection of substantially the whole of the common lexicon of the English language. The first dictionary that fits this description is probably the 1864 edition, known as 'the unabridged'.

9.4.1 Worcester's A Universal and Critical Dictionary of the English Language *(1846)*

Worcester's first major dictionary was *A Universal and Critical Dictionary of the English Language*, published in a one-volume quarto of 1,032 pages, including seventy-six pages of front matter and 120 pages of appendices. Worcester's introductory essays in this, as in his subsequent larger dictionary of 1860, are informed with a sound appreciation of historical scholarship but devoid of pretentiousness or any arrogant sense of superiority such as one sometimes finds in Webster. He discusses in turn the principles of pronunciation, orthography, grammar, etymology, Americanisms, and includes, most originally, a history of English lexicography which includes a catalogue of English orthoepists, English dictionaries, specialized dictionaries, and encyclopedias. About Webster's dictionary of 1828 he says, 'It is a work of great learning and research, comprising a much more full vocabulary of the language than Johnson's Dictionary...; but the taste and judgment of the author are not generally esteemed equal to his industry and erudition' (p. lxv).

In the dictionary proper, headwords appear in capital letters, as was the norm for this period, and are syllabicated with major stress indicated and with diacritical marks above and below indicating vowel quality. A pronunciation key runs along the bottom of every two-page spread, a feature Worcester had introduced in his smaller dictionary of 1830, *A Comprehensive Pronouncing and Explanatory Dictionary.* It is clear that Worcester gave a great deal of attention to pronunciation, responding to a lively public interest and believing that a treatment of pronunciation clearly superior to that of Webster would serve his dictionary well in a competitive marketplace. Worcester acknowledges in the Preface that his pronunciations are largely based on Walker's *Critical Pronouncing Dictionary.* Whereas Worcester's treatment of pronunciation in his introduction consists of a practical description of how English sounds are represented in his dictionary, Webster's was an extended exegesis on alleged inconsistencies in the treatment of pronunciation by the leading orthoepists of his day. In this respect Worcester's treatment foreshadows modern use, whereas Webster's reflects the argumentative tradition of eighteenth-century grammarians.

In orthography, Worcester is a conservative, reluctant to adopt innovations. He writes, 'In adjusting the orthography of this Dictionary,... attention has been paid to etymology, analogy, and usage; and in cases in which good usage is divided, etymology and analogy have been consulted in deciding disputable points. But no innovation has been made with respect to invariable and settled usage' (p. xxvi). Worcester notes the divided usage over the final *k* in words like *musick* and *publick*, but decides that general usage now favours its omission;

hence the *k* is omitted in the representation of these words in his dictionary. With regard to the *-our* ending in words like *colour* and *flavour*, Worcester discusses Johnson's inconsistent treatment (also noted by Webster) and comes down on the side of omitting *u* in all such words because it is the prevailing usage in the United States and because 'it is difficult to fix the limit for a partial omission' (p. xxvii). He prefers the ending *-re* in words like *centre* and *metre*, unlike Webster. In orthography as in every other way, Worcester treads a middle course, sensitive to current usage in America but giving greater weight to traditional usage in England than Webster was ever willing to acknowledge. Worcester completely lacks Webster's lively sense of competitiveness, not to mention hostility, towards Johnson and the British tradition in lexicography.

The headword list and definitions of *A Universal and Critical Dictionary* are largely based, by Worcester's own acknowledgement, on Johnson's Dictionary as revised by Todd, but Worcester has added 'nearly 27,000' new words, such as 'middle-man' and 'serial', and for all but a few the source is given. The definitions are generally short but clear, and authorities, either taken from Todd–Johnson or added, are given for most words. There are, however, few or no actual quotations included, or even invented illustrative phrases. Senses are not numbered and set off in separate paragraphs as in Webster's *American Dictionary* but are run together in a single paragraph separated by semicolons. On the other hand, Worcester has included a number of lengthy usage notes of considerable interest. For example, under *rather* he includes an extended discussion of *rather* and *sooner*, and discusses alternative pronunciations of the former in a most sensitive way, linking a given pronunciation or stress pattern with a particular meaning in a particular social situation. Again, he observes that in Southern states, to *raise* is to *bring up*, as 'The place in which he was raised', citing Jefferson. Thus Worcester demonstrates a high degree of sophistication in discussing regionally restricted usages as well as usages dependent on social contexts at a time when such information was hardly provided in American dictionaries.

In spite of such advances over Webster, Worcester's dictionary cannot match Webster's *American Dictionary* in its vocabulary coverage and in its illustrative quotations. It did satisfy a need for many readers, however, by providing a more traditional approach to spelling than Webster, and by Worcester's reliance on Walker, whose pronunciation system was widely popular. The industrious Worcester, capitalizing on the public interest in pronunciation, expanded on his 1830 dictionary to produce *A Pronouncing, Explanatory, and Synonymous Dictionary of the English Language* in 1855, a dictionary of 565 pages, and then set to work to produce his magnum opus in 1860, *A Dictionary of the English Language*, which, he felt, would be fully competitive with the best that Webster had to offer.

9.4.2 *Worcester's* A Dictionary of the English Language *(1860)*

In the Preface to *A Dictionary of the English Language*, a large quarto of 1,854 pages, including sixty-eight pages of front matter, Worcester says that 19,000 words have been added to the entries in his *Universal and Critical Dictionary* to reach a total of 104,000. Authorities are given for almost all definitions, and illustrative quotations for many. The A–Z text appears in a three-column format, with definitions numbered in separate paragraphs, just as in Webster's dictionaries. Notably, too, the text includes pictorial illustrations, an initiative that Webster's publishers took action to subvert by adding illustrations to their own dictionary and rushing it into print a year earlier, in 1859. (More about this so-called Pictorial Edition below.) In orthography, Worcester, continuing his conservative approach, says that 'the principal American authors differ little from established English usage' (p. iii), and cites the American preference for omitting the *u* in words like *favor* as one of the points of divergence. He also gives considerable attention to pronunciation and claims to have consulted all the major orthoepists in providing the recommended pronunciation for each word. Worcester disputes Horne Tooke's argument that each word has but one meaning and cites a number of common verbs such as *get* and *turn* to show the impracticality of such an argument. 'The original or etymological meaning of many words has become obsolete, and they have assumed a new or more modern meaning; many which retain their etymological meaning have other meanings annexed to them; many have both a literal and a metaphorical meaning, and many both a common and a technical meaning, – all which need explanation' (pp. iv–v). Such an analysis of how meanings change could hardly be improved upon today.

The text of the dictionary is in a readable size, notably larger than that of contemporaneous Webster dictionaries; and Worcester's dictionary uses running heads on each page corresponding to the complete first and last entry, as modern dictionaries do, rather than simply listing the first three letters of each word, as had been the custom prior to this time. (For example, the Webster edition of 1859 has running heads of 'PRO' on each of fourteen consecutive pages—not much help for the user seeking a particular word.) Worcester's dictionary retains a pronunciation key running in a single line along the bottom of each double-page spread. Entry words still appear in capital letters, syllabicated and showing stress and diacritical marks, without respelling. One notices immediately the large number of illustrative quotations as well as the occasional use of invented contextual phrases, as in the entry for the verb *concern*, definition 3: 'To make anxious or uneasy; as, "To be *concerned* for the welfare of friends."' Yet the remarkable fact must be acknowledged that a century after Johnson's dictionary was published, both Worcester's and Webster's dictionaries continued to use many of Johnson's definitions verbatim, and to employ without change, by abbreviating, or by simply citing as an authority, many of Johnson's quotational examples.[3] It is also true that both American lexicographers added many new terms, definitions, and illustrative quotations.

Worcester's dictionary includes about 5,000 synonym discriminations, a feature introduced in the *Universal and Critical Dictionary.* Although the 1859 'Pictorial' edition of Webster's dictionary, revised by Chauncey Goodrich, included a 68-page *Table of Synonyms* by Goodrich, Worcester's synonym discriminations in his 1860 dictionary nonetheless represent a genuine advancement in lexicography and many of them (allowing for some shifts in meaning and register) would not be out of place in a twenty-first century dictionary. Unlike Goodrich's, Worcester's synonym discriminations are scattered throughout the A–Z text under one of the words discussed, as they are in modern dictionaries, and his discussions appear to cover nuances of connotation, application, register, and style, whereas Goodrich's are briefer and deal with plain distinctions of meaning. Worcester also includes numerous notes on questions of usage, as on pronunciation, including differences between American and British pronunciation (as in the entry for *nephew*) and alleged mispronunciations; etymology; and historical uses of particular terms, especially when American use differs from the British (as in the entry for *revolution*).

Worcester's definitions in the 1860 dictionary are on the whole phrased in simpler and more accessible language than those of Webster's contemporaneous dictionaries of 1856 and 1859 edited by Goodrich. In coverage of the words and senses included, both dictionaries are very similar. In etymology, Worcester's dictionary is not distinguished, but neither does it fall into the trap of including false relationships, as Webster does, based on his studies of the world's languages. Clearly, for Worcester, etymology was not a top priority.

9.5 WEBSTER'S ATTACK ON WORCESTER AND THE DICTIONARY WARS OF 1830–1864

On 26 November 1834, Webster publicly charged Worcester with 'a gross plagiarism' in copying material from the Webster dictionaries for use in Worcester's *Comprehensive Pronouncing and Explanatory Dictionary* of 1830. As noted above,

[3] See, for example, the entry for *tooth* and idioms formed with it, in which both Worcester and Webster cite Dryden, L'Estrange, Shakespeare, Young, Shakespeare (again), and Hooker—all cited by Johnson.

Worcester had just before, in a dictionary published in 1829, abridged Webster's 1828 dictionary. Webster felt doubly aggrieved, as he was already under attack by Lyman Cobb for inconsistencies in the spellings used in his dictionaries and for the particular choices he recommended both in his dictionaries and in his spelling book (Micklethwait 2000: 222–5; Friend 1967: 83). While Webster's suspicions were understandable, they were unfounded, but Webster and his publishers, motivated at first by competition for the lucrative market for school dictionaries, and later by the growing market for ever larger, adult dictionaries, persevered in their effort to malign Worcester over the next thirty years.[4] In this they were not, on the whole, successful, but the effort to defend himself nevertheless cost Worcester dearly.

After the death of Webster in 1843, the character of the dispute changed. As Friend remarks, 'What had begun as a personal quarrel in print between rival lexicographers and their partisans was now clearly a fight for the market between publishing firms as well as a linguistic dispute involving regional, class, and academic antagonisms' (Friend 1967: 85). Both publishers exaggerated the differences between the dictionaries and the supposedly different audiences to whom they appealed—Worcester to the anglophiles, Webster to the ordinary American. As might be expected, some of Worcester's defenders went on the attack and disparaged Webster's treatment of spelling. Many of the Merriam accusations were anonymous, and pamphlets and newspaper articles on both sides frequently appeared under pseudonyms. Webster's publishers used various stratagems in an effort to discourage bookshops from stocking Worcester's dictionaries and his geographies (which Worcester had also edited) (Burkett 1979: 222 ff., especially 226).

In 1853, a British edition of Worcester's *Universal and Critical Dictionary* appeared under a title that included '*Compiled from the Materials of Noah Webster, LL.D.*' yet with Worcester listed as the editor. Years before, Worcester's publishers had authorized their agent to explore the sale of the British rights to Worcester's dictionary. Subsequently they sent a set of plates to the agent, and these apparently were later used without their authorization by Henry G. Bohn, a British publisher, who changed the title to introduce Webster's name and omitted Worcester's remark in his preface that he had not used 'a single word, or the definition of a word' from Webster's dictionary. All of this was unknown to Worcester, who was at the time virtually blind owing to cataracts in both eyes. His publishers, who realized they could be considered complicit or at least negligent in the deception, even though they had not profited from it, concealed the

[4] The most detailed descriptions of the charges and countercharges made by Webster and Worcester and their supporters over the years may be found in Burkett 1979: 221–57 and Micklethwait 2000: 225–33, 279–85. Friend 1967: 82–8 gives an excellent summary and overview.

existence of the contraband edition from Worcester for two years, until the time when his sight was sufficiently restored and he read a letter in a Boston newspaper from the G. & C. Merriam Company calling attention to it, with the implicit suggestion that Worcester or his publishers were somehow involved in the deception. In his defense, Worcester published a pamphlet in 1854 entitled, *A Gross Literary Fraud Exposed; relating to the publication of Worcester's Dictionary in London.* Who exactly was responsible for this fraud remains somewhat murky. It is not unprecedented in the history of lexicography, nor in modern business practice, for publishers to make exaggerated, unsubstantiated, and even false claims about their dictionaries. It seems likely that Bohn's ethical standards were severely compromised, and that Worcester's publishers were quite uncommonly inept, even for dictionary publishers.[5] As noted earlier, the battle between the two publishers continued sporadically until 1864, when the Merriams published a newly revised edition by Chauncey Goodrich and Noah Porter that featured new etymologies by the German scholar, C. A. F. Mahn. Called the 'Webster–Mahn', or 'the unabridged', the new edition succeeded in capturing most of the market for a large dictionary and relegated Worcester's 1860 dictionary to a secondary status. Worcester never produced another dictionary and died in 1865. Like Webster, he was extraordinarily productive, not only editing the dictionaries described here but compiling many other valuable reference works in geography and biography, most of them for students. He is a major figure in American lexicography and in any just appraisal of lexicographical quality must be reckoned Webster's equal. The only arena in which he proved deficient was in commercial success.

9.6 WEBSTER DICTIONARIES FROM 1847 TO 1890

Following Webster's death in 1843, his heirs sold the rights to his dictionary to George and Charles Merriam. They also acquired unbound sheets to revisions of the 1841 edition and, beginning in 1845, bound them in two volumes with their own imprint on the title page and offered them for sale. They resolved to publish a revised edition of Webster's dictionary in one volume by reducing the size of type, and offering it for sale at a low price that would make it broadly

[5] Micklethwait makes some fascinating speculations about Bohn, who he says must have been the Merriams' licensee in London for a Webster dictionary in 1848, though in pamphlet exchanges the Merriams 'never admitted to having any dealings with him at all...'. He does not accuse the Merriams of having instigated the fraud, but he does say, 'Somewhere in there, one smells a rat' (Micklethwait 2000: 283–4).

affordable to compete with Worcester's *Universal and Critical Dictionary* published in 1846.

9.6.1 *The* American Dictionary *of 1847*

Retaining Chauncey Goodrich as chief editor, and enlisting the aid of Noah Porter, William G. Webster, and Professor William Tully (for scientific entries), the Merriam brothers managed to publish Webster's dictionary, containing 85,000 entries, in one volume in 1847, priced at six dollars. It was an immediate success.

The preface emphasizes the importance of keeping abreast of the latest scientific nomenclature, and cites the inclusion of many specialized terms in botany, medicine, etc., as well as in the arts, religion, philosophy, and law. Many consultants are listed. The preface includes this adjuration regarding neologisms: 'There is, at the present day, especially in England, a boldness of innovation of this subject [new words], which amounts to absolute licentiousness. A hasty introduction into our dictionaries, of new terms, under such circumstances, is greatly to be deprecated.' By contrast, every modern dictionary trumpets its inclusion of the very latest new words as a major attraction.

The title page says that this edition of *An American Dictionary of the English Language* contains the whole vocabulary of the first edition along with the corrections and improvements of the second edition (of 1841 and its revisions). These revisions are not extensive and the text is substantially the same as that of 1841. Indeed, a note by the publishers in the first of the *International* dictionaries (of 1890), states that the first revision of 1847 'was little more than the original work of 1828 brought from two volumes into one, pruned of some excrescences, and with moderate additions'.

9.6.2 *The* American Dictionary *of 1859, 'the Pictorial Edition'*

When the Merriam brothers became aware that Worcester's new enlarged dictionary of 1860 would include pictorial illustrations, they managed to insert at the last minute a section of 1,500 pictorial illustrations before the A–Z text in an edition of the 1847 *American Dictionary* and publish it in 1859 just before Worcester's dictionary. This edition is accordingly known as 'the Pictorial Edition'. An introductory note explains that many of the illustrations in the 81-page section were taken from an English dictionary, John Ogilvie's *The Imperial Dictionary*, which, the note says, was 'a reprint (almost verbatim) from an earlier edition of the *American Dictionary*', that is, from an edition previous to the 1847 revision. Having made such free use of the Webster dictionary, owing to the lack of any international copyright restrictions at the time, Ogilvie could scarcely complain of the subsequent use of many of *his* illustrations for the Webster dictionary of 1859 (Micklethwait 2000: 272–8, 298). The illustrations are mainly wood engravings, though in some cases line drawings are used. Generally of good quality, they are categorized by subject, for example, architecture, geology, heraldry, mythology, insects, quadrupeds, reptiles, and races (of man).

Altogether it may be said that the 1859 edition is significant chiefly as a pre-emptive marketing response to the big Worcester dictionary of 1860. Its new features were reactive rather than innovative. It is an example of the keen competitive instincts of the Merriam-Webster enterprise throughout its history.

9.6.3 The American Dictionary *of 1864, the 'Webster–Mahn'*

Chauncey Goodrich and the Merriam brothers had long been aware of the deficiencies of Noah Webster's etymologies, and in 1854 the publishers contracted with a prominent Prussian linguistic scholar, C. A. F. Mahn, to revise the etymologies thoroughly. He reviewed every etymology and made numerous changes and improvements. The early Webster was not always wrong, but even when not wrong his terminology was frequently archaic or eccentric. Mahn consistently gave a more modern aspect to the etymologies by using more acceptable terminology, discarding the citations of Saxon, Armenian, and Gothic, for example, and instead tracing the origin of words to Old French, Old English, and Latin, etc., as modern dictionaries do. Many etymologies are obviously improved, and, accordingly, this edition is widely known as 'the Webster–Mahn'.

The 1864 edition of *An American Dictionary of the English Language* was published in one large, quarto volume under the editorship of Chauncey Goodrich and Noah Porter. Goodrich had begun the new edition but died in 1860, and Noah Porter, a professor at Yale College and later to become president of the college, took over and completed it. The pictorial illustrations which in the 1859 edition have been gathered in a separate section are now distributed individually throughout the text, each next to its appropriate dictionary entry, and in number they have increased to three thousand. In addition, at the back of the book, the illustrations are collected together by category, with references to their position in the text. Goodrich's table of synonyms has now been split up into separate paragraphs within the main dictionary text and linked to the particular words discussed. Following Worcester's innovation of 1860, the running heads now consist of full entry words rather than just the first three letters.

The dictionary is substantially larger than previous editions, containing about 114,000 entries in some 1,840 pages, and was the first dictionary commonly referred to as 'the unabridged'. There is evidence of significant changes in the definitions and illustrative quotations as compared with previous editions. Pronunciations have also been improved, with entry words syllabicated, separate respellings after each word, and a pronunciation key running along the base of each two-page spread.

The publication of the Webster–Mahn of 1864 effectively marks the end of the 'dictionary wars' begun by Webster in 1830 and carried on intermittently by his publishers thereafter. The 1864 Webster was a major step forward in the trend towards larger and larger dictionaries, with greater attention given to pronunciation and to the scientific and technical vocabulary. Reader interest was solicited by the inclusion of extra features: pictorial illustrations and synonym discussions, and various appendices relating to biblical names, Latin expressions, the pronunciation of place-name, etc. The idea implicit in all of these supplementary items was to make 'the dictionary' the most useful all-round book any family could own. The idea was to instil in the minds of more and more Americans that, apart from the Bible, a big dictionary was the one book they must have. In this strategy the Webster publishers were immensely successful, but they were aided by the broader intellectual and social climate of the latter part of the nineteenth century that encouraged massive compilations of knowledge and of language. It was an era of the democratization of learning, and the drive to acquire a complete record of the world's knowledge and of the English language by way of multivolume encyclopedias and ever grander dictionaries was about to begin.

9.6.4 Webster's International Dictionary of the English Language *(1890)*

Although there were new editions of Webster's *American Dictionary* in 1879 and 1884, it was not until 1890 that G. & C. Merriam & Company (as it was now called) published the first of its distinguished line of *International* dictionaries, finally changing the name of its standard-bearer and dropping *American* from the title. The new dictionary was much larger than any of the previous Webster editions, with 175,000 entries, and was called *Webster's International Dictionary of the English Language.* The title page was the first to bear the familiar Merriam-Webster colophon, of an elaborate 'W' encircled by a wreath, which would appear in every subsequent Webster dictionary. It was this dictionary that inaugurated the great age of the unabridged dictionary in America.

The chief editor of the 1890 edition was Noah Porter, who had completed the job of editing the 1864 edition after the death of Goodrich. The Preface traces the history of earlier editions of the *American Dictionary* and mentions Professor

William Dwight Whitney, later to become the editor of *The Century Dictionary*, as among those who had revised the definitions for the 1864 edition. The 1890 edition, the Preface says, gives particular attention to scientific, technological, and zoological terms. 'While we sympathize with their regret [i.e. of critics] that so much space is given to explanations and illustrations that are purely technical rather than literary, we find ourselves compelled to yield to the necessity which in these days requires that the dictionary... should carefully define the terms that record the discoveries of Science, the triumphs of Invention, and the revelations of Life.' Such a statement could well find a place, even more fittingly, in more recent dictionaries of the late twentieth and early twenty-first centuries, but none is given, as the pre-eminent status of science and technology is now so well established that devoting a huge amount of space to specialized terms is deemed unworthy of apology. The trend to devote a greater and greater proportion of dictionary space to science and technology began in the mid-nineteenth century and continues to this day (Landau 1974). Illustrations are included throughout the text and are also gathered in an 84-page section at the end of the book classified by category, with cross-references to the page in the A–Z section where they appear. The etymologies have been recast by Professor Edward S. Sheldon of Harvard. Various specialists are listed for scientific, technological, and other subject fields. The front matter includes for the first time phonetic diagrams of articulation of the vocal organs, with explanations for the production of each sound used in speech. Also included are a memoir of Noah Webster by his son-in-law Chauncey Goodrich and the prefaces to the 1828, 1847, and 1864 editions. Clearly, the publishers saw this dictionary as a great moment in the history of the Websterian tradition or they would not have devoted so much space to the predecessors from which it developed.

The bulk and size of the book—the A–Z section is 1,681 pages set in a three-column format—immediately calls to mind the appearance of later unabridged dictionaries that would remain the gold standard of American lexicography into the 1960s. The dictionary is about five inches thick, and the ends of the pages have indented cuts for thumb indexing, one of the earliest (if not the first) to have this feature. The size of type, the arrangement of entries on the page, and the pronunciation key running along the base of the pages are all very similar to the style of presentation that would become familiar to generations of Americans in the years ahead. Entry words remain capitalized (the one retrograde feature of this edition), but are syllabicated, with primary stress shown, and occasionally secondary stress (probably an innovation, but inconsistently applied) and are immediately followed by respellings for their pronunciation, using the familiar diacritics that would remain more or less constant in American lexicography for the next half-century. Following the pronunciation comes the part-of-speech label and the etymology. Definitions are identified by boldface numbers and each number is set off in a new paragraph, as in later unabridged dictionaries. Most definitions are followed by a cited authority or by a quotation. A list of synonyms or a synonym discrimination completes the entry paragraph. There appear to be no run-on derivatives; all entries, even rare ones (e.g. *abortively*, *abortiveness*) are given main-entry status. The emphasis on science and technology is reflected in the frequency of field labels, such as *Astron.*, *Opt.*, and *Physiol.*, though others such as *Law* are also common. Here is a typical entry:

(1) **Cog'nize** *v.t.* To know or perceive; to recognize. 'The reasoning faculty can deal with no facts until they are *cognized* by it.' *H. Spencer*

In spite of the unusual length and attention to detail in the Preface to this edition, there is no explanation given in it for the change in title from *An American Dictionary of the English Language* to *Webster's International Dictionary of the English Language*—surely a considered decision. One has to notice, at the very end of the dictionary, a 'Statement by the Publishers of Webster's International Dictionary of the English Language', signed 'G. & C. Merriam & Co.' It bears no page numbers and appears at the end of all the supplements and appendixes, suggesting that it may have been tipped in (inserted separately) rather than printed and gathered with the rest of the text. This extraordinary statement has already been alluded to in connection with its honest depiction of the 1847 edition as only modestly changed from the 1828 edition. Here, finally, the change in title is addressed. 'The present substitution of "International" for "American" ', the statement says, 'marks an accomplished change in the relations of the English speaking peoples. It is not their separation, but their community, which is now emphasized by the best thought and feeling in every department of life and literature.' They now wish to call the dictionary 'International' because English is used around the globe and because the common vocabulary and unity of structure renders local variations too trifling. How different language scholars feel about the uses of English today! It may be doubted that the vocabulary and structure of English as used throughout the world were ever as unified as here represented, but such, then, was the common assumption. The dictionary, the publishers concluded, must be serviceable to Britain, the United States, Canada, and Australia, and to the English-speaking population of India and South Africa. One can only speculate as to why such a signally important change from the historic title given by Webster himself to his dictionary in 1828 is explained not in the Preface, as one would expect, rather than as a kind of afterthought by the publishers buried at the end of the book. One thing is clear. The use of *American* was seen as parochial and limiting, and had to be jettisoned. The change in title was a considered marketing decision intended to expand the acceptance of Webster's dictionaries throughout the world.

Though in many ways a forerunner of the modern unabridged dictionary of the twentieth century, in its sense divisions and choice of illustrative quotations *Webster's International* was still modelled on an earlier tradition going back to Johnson. Indeed, some of the illustrative quotations can be traced originally to Johnson, are adapted by Webster, and retained nearly a century and a half later in *Webster's International*.[6] In some respects, therefore, the *New International*, in spite of its modern appearance, is old-fashioned, oriented towards the historical treatment of meaning and giving priority in its illustrative quotations to the classical literary sources drawn upon by Johnson. The first dictionaries to depart significantly from this model were the Funk & Wagnalls dictionaries, which are discussed below.

9.7 THE CENTURY DICTIONARY (1889–91)

In the history of American lexicography, *The Century Dictionary* is a dictionary *sui generis*.[7] There had been nothing like it before and there has been nothing like it since. *The Century Dictionary* was not a historical dictionary like the *New English Dictionary* (later to be called the *Oxford English Dictionary*) then under way in Britain, but it was a multivolume dictionary of comparable scale, and was seen to be competitive by James A. H. Murray, who attacked it with remarkable acerbity in a letter to a journal in 1890 soon after its initial volume appeared.[8] He evidently feared that the *Century* was making use of the early fascicles of the *New English Dictionary*, and, indeed, the editor of the *Century* acknowledges consulting *A* and *B*, the only two letters available before the *Century* was completed. In the long run it is likely that the editors of the *New English Dictionary* made more use of the *Century* than its editors did of the *NED*.

[6] For example, definition 3 of the verb *regard* cites Shakespeare: 'If much you note him, You offend him;...feed, and regard him not.' The *Century* also quoted this, but more fully, and with exact reference (from *Macbeth*); it appeared originally without the ellipsis in Johnson.

[7] I have been greatly assisted in the writing of this section by the special issue of *Dictionaries: Journal of the Dictionary Society of North America* in 1996 commemorating the centennial of the *Century Dictionary*, organized by Richard W. Bailey. Specific acknowledgement is given of particular articles.

[8] The putative reason for Murray's letter was to challenge the etymology for *cockney*, but the tone and substance of his letter were clearly intended to disparage Professor Whitney and the standing of the *Century Dictionary* as a work of scholarship (Liberman 1996: 40–8; Murray 1977: 266–7). Liberman discusses in detail the history of various explanations for the origin of *cockney*.

The *Century* was issued in parts beginning in 1889 and was completed and bound in six volumes at the end of 1891. The price was $120, a cost that put it beyond the means of most individuals. The dictionary contained 215,000 entry words, about 500,000 definitions with many thousands of illustrative quotations, and 8,000 pictorial illustrations.

9.7.1 Origins of The Century Dictionary

The driving force behind *The Century Dictionary* was Roswell Smith, who, with Josiah Gilbert Holland, had launched a new magazine of the arts and letters, *Scribner's Monthly*, in the early 1870s. In 1881, the two men founded The Century Company and began publication of *The Century Magazine*, which was intended to showcase the highest standards of design, illustration, and printing (Bailey 1996; Metcalf 1996). It was printed by the De Vinne Press of New York, which had become famous for the exceptional quality of its work. Ogilvie's *Imperial Dictionary* (1850) has already been mentioned as the primary source for the illustrations in Webster's Pictorial Edition of 1859. Ogilvie's dictionary had in turn been largely based on the 1841 revision of Webster's *American Dictionary*. When Charles Annandale substantially revised the *Imperial Dictionary* and brought it out in four volumes in 1883, Smith acquired the American publication rights, but it was still a British dictionary, and Smith had determined a year earlier to produce an American one based on it. Accordingly, he sought out William Dwight Whitney, a professor of philology and a Sanskrit scholar at Yale who had already worked as a lexicographer for Noah Porter on the Webster–Mahn edition of 1864. He had also written a highly regarded descriptive English grammar in 1877. Richard Bailey has called him 'the greatest American philologist of the 19th century' (Bailey 1996: 6). For managing editor Whitney signed up Benjamin Eli Smith (a relative), who became editor-in-chief upon Whitney's death in 1894. B. E. Smith was responsible for the Cyclopedia of Names, added in 1894 and later combined with an atlas of maps to make up the last two volumes in the ten-volume set published in 1896. At this time the title was changed to *The Century Dictionary and Cyclopedia*.

9.7.2 Outstanding Features of the Century

What truly distinguishes the *Century* from other dictionaries before or since are the extraordinary care taken to produce a well-crafted, handsome set of books, with clear, legible, and attractive type printed on good paper and, related to that, the large number of very fine wood engravings and other pictorial illustrations, many composed by the best nature artists, such as Ernest Thompson Seton. Also impressive were the lavish attention and space given over to etymologies, which were the responsibility of Charles P. G. Scott; and lastly, the coverage given to encyclopedic material, particularly in the sciences and technology, but extended also to cover names of all kinds (biographical, geographical, literary and mythological characters, etc.) in the Cyclopedia of Names.

Including encyclopedic material in dictionaries was nothing new, but in Webster's early dictionaries (as in earlier British dictionaries) the choice of encyclopedic material was unpredictable and even eccentric; by contrast, the scope and systematic nature of the *Century*'s coverage of science, technology, and other encyclopedic terms was unprecedented in American lexicography. It did not just define *cog-wheel*, for example; it included an illustration of it, and its definition explained how it transmits motion and directed the reader to several particular types of cogwheels, all included in separate entries within the dictionary. The noun *count* was not only defined as a title of nobility; in smaller type a short essay described the history of the uses of the term, beginning in the Roman republic and continuing into feudal times.

Given the space and attention devoted to pictorial illustrations in the *Century*, it is remarkable how little Whitney says about them in his Preface. He says that, though they have been selected to be subordinate to the text, they have considerable independent merit and artistic value. W. Lewis Fraser, manager of the Art Department of the Century Company, which produced the Century Magazine (and from which some of the illustrations were taken) was the person responsible for them. A very large number of them are of animals and insects, and they are exquisitely drawn, mostly reproduced from wood engravings. Some of the illustrations are line drawings and a few, according to Michael Hancher, are half-tones, a relatively innovative process in 1889, but one that would become a mainstay in published books for the next century (Hancher 1996: 88).

The *Century* was printed in three columns with running heads at the top and with no pronunciation key at the base. The type, designed by Theodore Low De Vinne, was unusually readable for its size, and from it a number of modern typefaces have been derived (Metcalf 1996). Entry words appear solid, without syllabication, and (unlike *Webster's International* of 1890) are not capitalized unless they are names, a practice now standard in lexicography. The pronunciation, following the entry word, is based on a respelling system employing few diacritics. The pronunciation system is not very sophisticated or innovative, but is serviceable. Following the part-of-speech label is the etymology, enclosed within square brackets. Some of the etymologies in the *Century* are immensely long. For example, the etymology for *man* is fifty-eight column lines long. After the proximate etyma (comparatively recent forms from which the current word was derived) are given, the note speculates about the ultimate origin of the word as relating to the meaning of 'thinker', but then dismisses the idea of primitive men as thinkers as 'quite incredible'. It then goes on to consider other theories. Even relatively uncommon words receive detailed and lengthy etymologies. The etymology for *akimbo* runs to thirty-three column lines, whereas the rest of the entry devotes about half as much space (seventeen lines) to its definitions and illustrative quotations.

The coverage of science is notable in many areas, such as electricity, then of intense and growing interest in the modern world. The entry for *electricity* consumes over a full column of small type. The word *electric* takes up, with its derivative phrases and three illustrations of electrical apparatuses, more than a page. The combining form *electro-* introduces well over one hundred compounds, from *electroballistic* to *electrovital.*

9.7.3 *Lack of a legacy*

The critical reception given the *Century* was overwhelmingly positive, and it was even compared favorably with the Oxford dictionary then in progress. Yet the high cost of the *Century* kept it from being accessible to a wider public. In 1927, an abridgement, the *New Century Dictionary,* was published, initially in three volumes, then in two, in which form it remained in print for many years. Eventually the *New Century* would form the basis of the *American College Dictionary* (1947) and the *World Book Dictionary* (1963) (Barnhart 1996). Yet the *Century Dictionary* failed to sustain a continuing programme of research and revision, although editions appeared as late as 1911 and 1914, and it could not compete effectively against the new series of unabridged dictionaries of Funk & Wagnalls and G. & C. Merriam that appeared from 1893 to 1913 and were much cheaper in price. As the years passed and the *Century* began to show its age by not keeping abreast of the latest popular and scientific words, the *Century* fell into the role of a relic—beautiful, to be sure, like an old Bible printed on parchment paper—but regarded more as an object of veneration than as a commonly used dictionary. So it remains. Yet its comparative neglect is regrettable, as it is a superb dictionary in many respects and still has much to offer to those interested in the vocabulary of its period. It was from the beginning a quixotic venture (as many new dictionaries are), and it occupies a singular place in American lexicography for its attempt to marry the highest form of the printer's art with dictionary-making. In this it succeeded. But as a dictionary that would endure to make a lasting mark on American intellectual life, it cannot be said to have succeeded. The unforgiving demands of the commercial marketplace led dictionary publishers in another direction: towards the creation of ever-larger, single-volume or two-volume unabridged dictionaries that could be sold at an affordable price.

9.8 FUNK & WAGNALLS' UNABRIDGED DICTIONARIES (1893–1913): THE *STANDARD* AND THE *NEW STANDARD*

Following the publication in 1890 of *Webster's International Dictionary*, the next major dictionary to be published was the first of Funk & Wagnalls' unabridged dictionaries, the *Funk & Wagnalls Standard Dictionary of the English Language*, in two volumes; the first volume was published in 1893, the second volume the following year, and the two-volume set in 1895. The *Standard Dictionary* reportedly covered 304,000 terms, a vocabulary almost fifty per cent larger than the *Century*'s and nearly seventy-five per cent larger than that of *Webster's International Dictionary*. Although the *Standard Dictionary* was very different from the *Century*, it too vaunted its coverage of science and technology.

In 1913, a new edition, the massive *New Standard Dictionary of the English Language*, containing 450,000 terms, was published in a single volume. The *Funk & Wagnalls Standard* and the *New Standard* thus continued the relentless growth of dictionaries to ever-larger and more comprehensive size, a pattern originally established by *Webster's American Dictionary* of 1847, which might be summarized as, 'Give them more for less', i.e. increase the coverage of vocabulary and package the book so that it can be sold cheaply. (The *Century* is the notable exception to this trend.) The A–Z text of the *Standard* runs to 2,100 pages, and of the *New Standard* to 2,757 pages. The prestige of owning an immense, unabridged dictionary, representing in its solid, blocklike weight the stability and power of the whole of the English language, as the Bible represented faith in God, was a powerful argument for purchase.

Krapp observes that the *Century*, the *Standard*, and the *New International* (referring to the edition of 1909) 'illustrate the disappearance of the individual in the making of modern dictionaries, and the emergence of what may be called the syndicate or composite dictionary' (Krapp 1966: 375). It is true that this period marks a shift away from the idea of the dictionary as a book having an author worthy of identification to one of the dictionary as the product of a company. Yet not until *Webster's Third* of 1961 would any other unabridged dictionary be so completely controlled by one man as was the *Standard* of 1893 by Isaac Funk.

Isaac Kauffman Funk was a minister of the Lutheran church who later became a newspaperman. He founded and edited various publications designed to assist preachers prepare sermons, and in 1877 joined Adam Willis Wagnalls in a partnership to form the publishing company (incorporated in 1890) as Funk & Wagnalls. Wagnalls was involved purely as the principal investor and never played an editorial role. In 1890, Funk planned and launched *The Literary Digest*, which would prove to be a very successful magazine in its day. Producing the *Standard Dictionary* was an enormous enterprise, yet it was completed in less than four years. A very large staff would have been employed; Frank Vizetelly, managing editor of the *New Standard*, wrote that that dictionary employed a staff of 250 and engaged more than 530 readers for quotations[9] (Vizetelly 1923: 22).

Whereas Whitney had been a professor at Yale, Funk, as we have seen, had been a newspaperman and preacher. He was no academic, and he emphasized practicality rather than scholarship in his dictionaries. Convenience, he said, was more important than tradition. He wanted his dictionaries to be easy to use, and accordingly he introduced a number of innovations. Taken together, these were profoundly influential in moving American lexicography away from the English tradition begun by Johnson and continued with various modifications by Webster and Worcester. First, Funk decreed that the commonest meaning, not the earliest in historical terms, should come first in the sequence of definitions. He did not believe that the typical dictionary user was most interested in the earliest use of a word when this use might be rare or obsolete at the present time. Indeed, he argued that it would be confusing. Next, and at the opposite pole from Whitney, Funk deemed etymology of lesser importance and placed it after the definition at the end of the dictionary entry rather than before the definition. In his view, people looked up words for meaning, spelling, and pronunciation, but seldom for etymology. The etymology for *man*, which occupied fifty-eight lines in the *Century*, consists of '< AS. *man*' in the *Standard*. Most of the etymologies are very brief, going back immediately, or, sometimes, with an intermediate step or two, to the earliest known form and giving no cognates in other languages. Another innovation of the *Standard* was to introduce what Funk called 'run-in words', but which are now more commonly called 'run-on derivatives', i.e. derivatives (usually undefined) that are tacked on at the end of the basic entry with which they are associated. For example, *attributively* and *attributiveness* appear, fully syllabicated but without definitions, at the end of the entry for *attributive*. This practice saves space and allows the publisher to claim the inclusion of more entries than would otherwise be possible. It was soon adopted by almost every dictionary.

Definitions in the *Standard* are considerably stronger than its etymologies and are comparable to those of *Webster's International*. The definitions in the *Stand-*

[9] The context in Vizetelly's book, which is really a promotional publication for the *New Standard*, is ambiguous as to whether these numbers refer to the *Standard* or the *New Standard*. Photographs accompanying the text show a large editorial staff for the *New Standard*, and it is likely the staff numbers he used referred to that dictionary.

ard and *New Standard* are more usually illustrated by invented phrases than by quotations. Phrases take up less space and they do the job of showing a typical collocation or pattern of use. The *Standard* and *New Standard* contain far fewer illustrative quotations than *Webster's International* or the *Century*, and those they do include are largely cited from books of the last few prior decades. Gone are the quotations from Milton, Dryden, and Shakespeare that abound in the Webster and Worcester dictionaries and that were still common in *Webster's International*. Funk was never part of the Johnsonian tradition. Although Webster had talked a great deal about being American, it was Funk who really departed from the English tradition in lexicography in America.

Funk's introduction immediately declares that the aims of a dictionary are to be comprehensive, accurate, and simple. Comprehensiveness and accuracy are surely unsurprising goals, but simplicity is new, and the innovations in the Funk & Wagnalls dictionaries were designed to simplify the process of looking up a word, finding the appropriate definition, and understanding it once it was found. Funk, like many of the linguistic authorities of his day, was interested in spelling reform; the goal was to make spelling more rational and simplify it. It is important to recognize that the programme to simplify spelling then was most emphatically not the crackpot enterprise of a few impractical visionaries. Among those in favour of simplified spelling were Francis A. March, who was a consultant to Funk and who had earlier helped Murray secure American readers for the *New English Dictionary*; William Dwight Whitney, editor of the *Century Dictionary*; the distinguished philologist Max Müller; James A. H. Murray himself; the eminent English phonetician Henry Sweet; Melvil Dewey, who was a founding member of the American Library Association and the originator of the Dewey decimal system; and Charles P. G. Scott, the etymologist of the *Century* and a leader in the spelling reform movement. The major professional philological association in America endorsed simplified spellings for 3,500 words, and these were duly included in the *Standard*, though not as main entries but as alternate spellings, with cross-references to their traditional spelling.

Despite the fact that Funk was a minister, he was not, like Webster, at all in favour of spreading the word of Christianity by means of his dictionaries. Near the beginning of his introduction he says that the function of a dictionary is to record usage, not create it, and later cautions his definers against colouring their definitions with their own theories, opinions, or beliefs. 'The work of a dictionary is to define, not to advocate'. If etymology was comparatively neglected, spelling and pronunciation were accorded a great deal of attention. The *New Standard* employed two pronunciation keys, which are displayed, in another of Funk's innovations, at the top of every page rather than at the base. Every word is given two numbered pronunciations. One is keyed to a system called the Revised Scientific Alphabet (a forerunner of the International Phonetic Alphabet), while the other refers to the system of phonemic respelling found traditionally in American dictionaries. It is hard to reconcile the use of dual pronunciations with the overriding object to be simple, but such is the case.

Entry words in the *Standard* and in the *New Standard* appear in lower case and in boldface, as was customary, and are syllabicated with primary and, if called for, secondary stress, as in **o″cean-og′ra-phy**. Although *Webster's International* had sometimes indicated secondary stress, it was inconsistent in its application and rarely employed it; the *Standard* appears to be more rigorous. There are numerous pictorial illustrations of relatively good quality and tipped-in colour plates of birds, medals ('decorations of honor'), flags, gemstones, and so forth, as well as full-page black-and-white plates. There are also numerous synonym discriminations and lists of antonyms. Though not elegant or as legible as the *Century*, the *Standard*'s and *New Standard*'s design is clear and straightforward, and easy to negotiate, as the headwords are set off and made prominent. The volumes are handsomely bound and are thumb-indexed.

An enlarged edition of the *Standard* appeared in 1903, and a separately bound *Supplement* in 1904, containing an addenda section of 13,000 new words as well as new colour and black-and-white plates. The *New Standard* remained in print for many years, well past mid-century, and although it was updated in minor ways—enough to receive new copyrights—it was never thoroughly revised and remained essentially a 1913 dictionary.

Although the Funk & Wagnalls *New Standard* had become *passé* by the 1940s, for nearly fifty years prior to that the unabridged Funk & Wagnalls dictionaries had competed head-to-head with G. & C. Merriam's Webster dictionaries, from the *International* of 1890, the first *New International* of 1909 to the great Second Edition of 1934. During all this period, the Funk & Wagnalls dictionaries were widely considered on a par with the Webster dictionaries, and the competition between the two companies was just as fierce as the rivalry of an earlier time had been between Noah Webster and Joseph Worcester and their supporters, although it was not so public and was fought by the companies' respective marketing staffs rather than by their editors. Gradually, after the publication of the Webster Second Edition in 1934, when there was no response from Funk & Wagnalls in the form of a new edition of its unabridged, the Webster dictionary began to have the field to itself, and, in spite of the publication of a number of new smaller dictionaries in the 1950s and 1960s, the Funk & Wagnalls Company never recovered and indeed struggled to survive as a dictionary publisher.

9.9 *WEBSTER'S NEW INTERNATIONAL DICTIONARY OF THE ENGLISH LANGUAGE* (1909)

Following the Funk & Wagnalls publication of its *Standard Dictionary* in 1893–95, the Merriam company was put on notice that it had a new, serious competitor to its position of pre-eminence in American lexicography. The *Standard* challenged the 1890 *Webster's International*, though its two-volume format may have put it at a slight disadvantage. Word would surely have got out that Funk & Wagnalls was working on a new and even larger edition, and the Merriams knew they had to respond. *Webster's New International Dictionary of the English Language*, based on the 1890 dictionary and amalgamating the extensive supplementary section of the 1900 edition, was their answer. Published in a single volume in 1909, the *New International* broke new ground in several areas, though at the same time it is recognizably in the tradition of the older Webster dictionaries.

Most importantly, the *New International* claimed to include 400,000 entries, substantially more than the *Standard* and more than twice as many as the *International* of 1890. It initiated the practice of dividing the page horizontally in order to encompass more entries; to quote the preface, the upper section contains the main words of the language, and the lower section, 'in a somewhat smaller type and narrow columns', contains 'various minor words, foreign words and phrases, abbreviations, etc'. This feature, an innovation in 1909, would become much beloved by some users of the Second Edition of 1934, which perpetuated the practice, but it is difficult to justify the inclusion, even in very small type, of many of the items below the dividing line, and it is difficult to understand on what basis some words were considered minor and others major. Nonetheless, the practice enabled the publishers to fit 400,000 entries into an alphabetic section of 2,373 pages and to keep the dictionary in one volume.

Another innovation of the *New International* is its vastly expanded coverage of encyclopedic material, including a section of about 140 pages called *A Reference History of the World*, a chronological history from 6000 BC to the present time, a feature the *Funk & Wagnalls New Standard* of 1913 would later imitate. In the *New International*, this section is replete with full-page plates of illustrations, many in colour. (This section, brought up to date and enlarged to 360 pages, would be included in some editions of the Second Edition of 1934, but did not appear in the Third Edition in 1961.[10]) Within the A–Z text, too, encyclopedic material is

[10] By email communication from Joanne Despres of Merriam-Webster in response to my inquiry. I am indebted to her and to Steve Perrault and Ward Gilman, also of Merriam-Webster, for their kind assistance.

afforded expanded treatment. For example, under *machine* there is an extended description of types of machines operated by motors. *Spinal* includes a veritable anatomical essay on the spinal nerves, taking up more than two-thirds of a column of very small type, and complete with an illustration of the cross section of the spinal cord. Another aspect of encyclopedic content is the expanded use of pictorial illustrations, which have been increased in number to 6,000, nearly half of which are new to this edition. Most of the illustrations within the alphabetic section are small and not of any outstanding quality, but they are numerous and they do succeed in breaking up the type page and making it more readable. There are also a number of glossy plates embedded in the alphabetic section. Another notable quality of the *New International*, allied to its greater attention to encyclopedic material, is its more common use of qualifying field labels in definitions. Many specialists are listed as consultants in fields ranging from agriculture to zoology, and the text is larded with entries labelled *Org. Chem.* (for organic chemistry), *Micrometal.* (for micrometallurgy), *Min.* (for mineralogy), *Naut.* (for nautical), etc.

The use of illustrative quotations in the *New International* represents a particularly intriguing departure from earlier tradition. The editors make no mention of illustrative quotations except with reference to their use in newly fashioned synonym discriminations. Goodrich's earlier synonymies, numbering about 600, were nearly all rewritten, and the total has been increased to more than 1,400, with 6,000 illustrative quotations. The new synonym discriminations were written by Professor John L. Lewis under the direction of Professor George Lyman Kittredge of Harvard, and they are indeed much superior to Goodrich's, and well illustrated with quotations, mainly from literature. However, to make room for the expanded synonymies, the great addition of new entries, and the enlarged encyclopedic material, the use of illustrative quotations in the main dictionary text has been cut back. There are markedly fewer than in the *International* of 1890. The editors claim to have reviewed and revised the definitions and rearranged them more rigorously according to the historical principle, and there is ample evidence that many such changes were indeed made.

In other respects, the *New International* perpetuates the established policies of earlier Webster dictionaries. Its pronunciations employ the same 'textbook' system of respellings as in the *International.* The *New International* does, however, include an extensive guide to pronunciation with a section on phonetic principles, a description of the organs of speech, and an analysis of the articulation of the sounds used in English speech, which, for its time, seems extraordinarily up to date. It was evidently prepared by its pronunciation editor, Paul W. Carhart.

The etymologies are said to have been revised, but are not a feature to which much attention is given. In spelling, the *New International* adopts a conservative approach, listing first, as a matter of course, the more established American spellings: *center, traveled, skillful*, for example. But the corresponding British spellings—*centre, travelled, skilful*—are nevertheless also given, and without any indication that they are especially British. The editors reject many of the recommendations of the Simplified Spelling Board and other professional organizations, though, when usage is divided, they opt for the simpler form, for example, *program* over *programme*.

On balance, it seems clear that the emphasis in the *New International* on encyclopedic and pictorial material is in large part a response to the *Funk & Wagnalls Standard*, which trumpeted its practicality and its attention to the latest scientific and technical advances. Like the *Standard*, it de-emphasized etymology. In 1913, the massive *Funk & Wagnalls New Standard*, with 50,000 more entries than *Webster's New International*, appeared in a single volume. The battle was joined. The Merriam company knew it had to take some decisive action to set its next unabridged dictionary apart and establish its supremacy.

9.10 *WEBSTER'S NEW INTERNATIONAL DICTIONARY OF THE ENGLISH LANGUAGE, SECOND EDITION* (1934)

Webster's New International Dictionary of the English Language, Second Edition, much beloved of a whole generation of Americans and revered to this day, is a massive book, nearly five inches in bulk and so heavy that it is best set out on a sturdy dictionary stand and consulted *in situ*. The main vocabulary section alone is only slightly less than 3,000 pages, and, with front and back matter, the total comes to nearly 3,300 pages. It was the largest, single-volume dictionary yet produced, with a vocabulary section containing more than 550,000 words. The Second Edition covers all words in the modern period beginning with the year 1500, and, exceptionally, also covers Chaucer's language before that. If the gazetteer and biographical section entries are included, the total exceeds 600,000. Many reviewers, especially from the academic world, regarded it as not only the biggest one-volume dictionary ever produced but the best. They judged it the most comprehensive, the most up-to-date, and the most authoritative. It was commended for explaining the common usage, according to one scholar, who quotes from a number of laudatory contemporary reviews (Laughlin 1967).[11] The Merriam Company cranked up its publicity apparatus to spread the word through print advertisements and by the efforts of its large and aggressive sales force. As Funk & Wagnalls faded from the scene, the Webster line of dictionaries gained an unparallelled dominance, and at the top of the line was the famous Second Edition. It soon became the most prestigious dictionary in America, an achievement of linguistic excellence on a grand scale, and it would maintain that position for over twenty-five years until the *Third New International* appeared in 1961. Some influential critics publicly disparaged the *Third* and asserted that they would continue using the Second Edition, thus elevating it to the status of a cultural icon. More than forty years after the publication of the *Third*, near the end of the year 2005, the New York Public Library's huge main reading room displayed three times as many copies of the Second Edition on its lecterns than of the *Third* (nine of the former to three of the latter).

Was the Second Edition ever as good as its admirers believed? The *Oxford English Dictionary* was the only other dictionary of comparable extent, but it was a historical dictionary intended for the literary and linguistic scholar. It was devoted almost exclusively to British English, contained no encyclopedic material at all and no pictorial illustrations, and provided little vocabulary coverage of scientific and technical terms. Appearing in many volumes, it was also expensive. Judged in its own terms, the Second Edition was in a class by itself, although one of the main reasons the Second Edition *was* so good is that it had the *Oxford English Dictionary* as a source. Since the *OED* was completed in 1927—the Supplement appeared in 1933—it was fully available to the editors of the Second Edition. They do acknowledge their debt to the *OED*, probably not sufficiently, but at least it is there in print.

The Second Edition is justly regarded as a great achievement, but the policies that informed it were essentially the same as those governing earlier editions. The Second Edition made use of 1.6 million citations and examined about two million others in other dictionaries. 'In conformity with the traditional principle of Merriam-Webster Dictionaries,' the Introduction states, 'that definitions, to be adequate, must be written only after an analysis of citations, the definitions in this new edition are based on citations . . . . It cannot be emphasized too strongly that the reason for the fundamental and thorough soundness of the Merriam-Webster Dictionary is that it is a "Citation Dictionary".' In other words, all definitions are based on the record of actual usage as documented by citations. Nowhere in the Second Edition is any mention made of prescribing correct usage or expunging

[11] It is a curious reflection of changing public tastes that a quarter of a century later the Third Edition was especially criticized for giving too much attention to common usage.

slang or jargon from the covered vocabulary. Indeed, the Second Edition was praised for its coverage of new uses and slang. There is no section either in the Introduction or in the Explanatory Notes dealing with usage questions. Whatever attention is given to usage is covered within the synonymies, some of which distinguish between words that are 'improperly confused'. With respect to the synonymies, the editors say, following a tradition that goes back to Johnson, 'The citations have been drawn from writers . . . whose works exemplify the best modern usage, . . . [especially] those authors who combine idiomatic freedom of style with correctness.' No such statement is made with respect to citations used to illustrate definitions in the vocabulary proper, and it must be assumed that no such standard was applied, as the object of citations within definitions is not to illustrate good usage but to exemplify meaning or collocation.

The editor-in-chief of the Second Edition was William Allan Neilson, who was president of Smith College; Thomas A. Knott, a former professor at the University of Iowa, was general editor; and Paul W. Carhart, who had been the pronunciation editor of the 1909 *New International*, was managing editor and pronunciation editor. How much work on the actual pronunciations Carhart did is a matter of speculation, as John S. Kenyon, the distinguished phoneticist, was the consulting editor and is said in the Introduction to have been 'a constant adviser on all matters of policy and on their application in detail'. Kenyon also entirely rewrote the nearly 60-page guide to pronunciation, by far the most complete, authoritative, and up-to-date description of the principles of phonetics to be found in any dictionary. The etymologist was Harold H. Bender, professor at Princeton, who revised the work of Sheldon and Wiener of the previous edition. The etymologies, though based on Mahn and Sheldon, were completely overhauled. The synonymies of John Livingston Lowes were retained with few changes. The dictionary is illustrated throughout with many pictures, and contains eight plates of illustrations.

The order of definitions is historical, as in past editions, and here again the *OED* had been invaluable in determining the sequence of definitions. In the Second Edition, the definitions of some very long entries, such as *body*, *block*, and *set*, are subdivided with roman numerals into different sections. Following the initiative of Funk & Wagnalls, the Second Edition also introduces lists of undefined words having the same prefix or combining form, such as words beginning with *color-* or with *anti-*. The famous lower section of the page—that part of the page below the line—still exists, but is much reduced and extenuated, occupying only a small fraction of the page and on some pages absolutely disappearing. One senses an unwillingness in the editors to expunge the feature completely, but something less than a whole commitment to its utility.

A feature certainly novel in Webster dictionaries up to this time is a page entitled *The Editorial Staff*, with a complete listing not only of the top editors but of the assistant editors, proofreaders, and editorial assistants, followed by a number of paragraphs providing details about which subjects particular editors were chiefly responsible for. In the *New International* of 1909, the only acknowledgement of the editorial staff—and this only of the top people—was tacked on at the end of the preface after the special-subject editors (the outside consultants) were recognized. Historically, dictionary staffs were generally not acknowledged at all, or, if acknowledged, allotted begrudgingly small type in a place as obscure as could be found. The Second Edition breaks new ground among commercial dictionaries in giving proper credit to its staff, and not just to its senior staff. It may have been influenced in this by the *OED*, which scrupulously listed its contributors, sub-editors, assistants, and proofreaders.

Perhaps the most far-reaching innovation of the Second Edition was that it was one of the first dictionaries to address the needs of dictionary users by explaining the features of the dictionary. In most previous dictionaries, there were no explanatory guides addressed to readers, or, if there were, they were brief, inadequate, and put into type so tiny they could scarcely be read. In his decision to devote five full pages in relatively large, legible type, with generous spacing between the lines, to all the various features of the dictionary entry, Neilson took a giant step forward in educating the ordinary dictionary user. The guide even had—again for the first time—an explanatory two-colour chart showing an actual column from the vocabulary section of the dictionary, with various individual features encircled in red and with leaders extending to the margins where each feature is identified; a reference is given to the numbered paragraph in the pages following where a full description of that feature is provided. Such an explanatory chart, often utilizing a second colour, would become a standard feature of college dictionaries for the next fifty years.

Neilson says that the dictionary cost $1.3 million—an enormous sum in the 1930s—and employed a staff of 250 editors and editorial workers. This huge investment in both money and labour marked the culmination of the age of the unabridged dictionary in America, and the succeeding decades would witness the gradual but irreversible decline of this genre, so by the time *Webster's Third* was published in 1961, even before the final insult of computer storage of vast files made very large print dictionaries obsolescent, the unabridged dictionary was already in a most vulnerable condition from which it would probably not have recovered in any case. The collapse of the stock market in 1929 and the onset of the great depression meant (for those who could raise the capital) that labour was plentiful and cheap. But after the great depression ended in the latter part of the

1930s, the cost of living increased, and the war years of 1941–45 and its aftermath saw rapid growth in wages and prices even in the face of rises in productivity. The cost of assembling a large staff of trained editors in the 1950s, along with the much higher costs of typesetting, paper, printing, and binding, would make any new project of the scope of the Second Edition prodigiously expensive and, given the hard facts of commercial success in publishing, difficult to justify from a business point of view. That explains why Funk & Wagnalls never revised its *New Standard* of 1913. Only a company with such a long and distinguished history in dictionary publishing as G. & C. Merriam—it later changed its corporate name to Merriam-Webster—could muster the will and the means to produce a new unabridged dictionary during this period. To some extent Merriam was insulated from high costs because it operated in the small city of Springfield, Massachusetts, where it owned the building housing its editorial offices and where staff and other expenses could be readily controlled. Even so, the commitment to produce a completely revised Third Edition of its unabridged dictionary represented a huge investment for Merriam-Webster.

9.11 *WEBSTER'S THIRD NEW INTERNATIONAL DICTIONARY* (1961)

The *Webster* unabridged dictionaries published by G. & C. Merriam had typically had as editor-in-chief a distinguished academic person such as William Allan Neilson, president of Smith College, of the Second Edition. According to Herbert C. Morton, the publishers originally sought to make a similar appointment for the Third Edition, but, although they received valuable help in planning for the new dictionary from prominent academic people, none was willing to assume the editorship, and in the end the publishers turned to an in-house editor, Philip Babcock Gove. To be sure, Gove had done postgraduate work on Johnson's dictionary and had earned a doctorate on a literary subject from Columbia University, but he was not in the firmament of academic superstars.[12] Neilson and his predecessors had been far more than mere figureheads, having had a

[12] I am indebted to Herbert C. Morton's *The Story of Webster's Third: Philip Gove's Controversial Dictionary and Its Critics* for information about Gove and much else concerning the Merriam Company's publicity campaign and Gove's response to the criticism levelled against his dictionary. An in-depth discussion of the controversy over this dictionary, recounted with admirable balance and discernment, is contained in pp. 153–264.

hand in many major decisions involving policy, but they did not systematically edit or review the editing of the dictionary text as a whole. That was the role of the general editor. Gove was appointed general editor in 1951; no one was appointed editor-in-chief until ten years later, the year of publication, when Gove was officially given that title. *Webster's Third* is very much Gove's dictionary in the sense that all the important policies were essentially his, and their implementation was closely monitored by him. His was the major voice in determining what entries to include and to omit; the style of definitions; the attention paid to pronunciation; the use of illustrative quotations, usage labels, and subject labels; and many other decisions which would provoke strong criticism in the years following publication. It is remarkable that, though *Webster's Third* has by all accounts sold very well over the years, especially internationally, it has never been as widely accepted among professors and teachers in the humanities as has the Second Edition, owing in large measure to the enormous controversy that greeted the *Third*'s publication in the years following its publication. It is therefore necessary to examine what the features of the *Third* were that elicited so much contention.

9.11.1 Controversial features of Webster's Third

Although the Merriam company had always emphasized its traditional pedigree, leading back in a straight line of descent of distinguished dictionaries to Noah Webster's first great dictionary of 1828, Gove's preface emphasizes in the opening sentence that the *Third Edition* is 'completely new', and for good measure repeats it in the next sentence, which reads: 'Every line of it is new.' The rest of the paragraph deals summarily with the original Webster dictionary of 1828 and the first Merriam dictionary of 1847. All the other great unabridged dictionaries—of 1864, 1890, 1909, and 1934—are relegated to a footnote. So much for tradition!

The *Third Edition* does indeed differ more from the Second Edition in many important particulars than the Second did from First. In order to keep the dictionary within manageable size and limit it to one volume, especially in view of the necessity of adding thousands of new terms and definitions, many of the 600,000 entries of the Second Edition would have to be cut. Words obsolete before 1755 were omitted, and almost all of the rare words found below the line in the pages of the Second Edition. The *Third Edition* abandoned the divided page. More significantly, all encyclopedic entries, and the historical reference material which had been featured in the back sections of the two earlier *New International* dictionaries, were cut. *Webster's Third*'s omission of all biographical and geographical entries was especially challenged by critics. It is difficult to avoid the conclusion that Gove regarded the omission of encyclopedic material as a convenient exigency: it would at once rid his dictionary of extraneous matter and enable him and his colleagues to create a purer model of what a dictionary should be. Gove was hardly a radical, but he was bold and confident enough to respond to linguistic trends that broke significantly with the *Webster* tradition, and to introduce innovations that could be justified on theoretical grounds but that would exasperate many conservative critics and even some sympathetic observers who generally praised the dictionary. He clearly hated to make exceptions, even when the failure to do so created the occasional absurdity, ambiguity, or obfuscation.

As Morton shrewdly observes, *Webster's Third* unfortunately appeared just at the time when linguists and humanists in universities were most at odds (Morton 1994: 2). At the time, the new study of structural linguistics had trouble finding a home for its scholars. They were often lodged within English Departments, but the marriage between the younger, statistically minded linguists, who regarded themselves as scientists, and the cadre of professors who taught Shakespeare, Milton, Wordsworth, Shelley, and the flowering of the modern novel was not a happy one. Each side mistrusted the other, but the traditional faculty certainly had the upper hand. The linguists were seen as arrogant and self-deceived upstarts, ignorant of and often indifferent to the cardinal creations in English literature.

It was in this environment that Gove described the central tenets of structural linguistics in a Merriam publication called *Word Study*, shortly after *Webster's Third* was published. Quoting from a 1952 statement published by the National Council of Teachers of English, Gove listed the principles as follows: (1) Language changes constantly; (2) Change is normal; (3) Spoken language is the language; (4) Correctness rests on usage; (5) All usage is relative (Morton 1994: 206). Though Gove was clear in saying that recent developments in linguistics had had little or no influence on *Webster's Third*, with the exception of its treatment of pronunciation, some critics—notably Dwight Macdonald in *The New Yorker*—interpreted Gove's admiration for structural linguistics as an admission that he advocated the abandonment of traditional lexicographical restraints in describing modern usage.[13] Although Macdonald reads far too much into Gove's educational article, it seems fair to presume that Gove's attitudes towards language were shaped by his understanding and acceptance of the principles he

[13] Macdonald's article, entitled 'The String Untuned', appeared in *The New Yorker* of 10 March 1962. It was reprinted, along with favourable reviews and other critical ones, including the often-quoted review of Wilson Follett's in *The Atlantic* of January, 1962, entitled, 'Sabotage in Springfield', in Sledd and Ebbitt (1962), an invaluable resource for the *Webster Third* controversy.

elucidated in this publication. As such they could have influenced some policies adopted in his dictionary, and, indeed, in some respects, this influence can be detected. For example, *Webster's Third* most remarkably capitalizes no entries except *God*. Up until the first *New International* of 1909, all entries were capitalized in *Webster* dictionaries. *Webster's Third* professed to contain no encylopedic entries, and so theoretically would have no need to capitalize anything, but in fact it contains many entries derived from names (such as *new yorker*), and many names of materials (*african teak*), flora and fauna (*japanese cedar, russian wolfhound*), and other entries having geographical or biographical elements (*swedish massage, einstein equation*). All of these entries include some italicized usage label signifying that the entry is usually or always capitalized, but it remains a puzzle why the editors did not simply capitalize them. The answer may be in Gove's acceptance of the primacy of the spoken language, which may also account for the extraordinary attention and space devoted to exacting transcriptions of pronunciations, which will be considered below. The failure to capitalize has been criticized almost universally, even by those with generally positive views of the dictionary (Chapman 1967).

The *colloquial* or *informal* label was dropped completely, and *slang* is used very sparingly. In America, an informal style of language had become all but universal by the 1950s, as Bergen and Cornelia Evans observed in their guide to usage (Evans and Evans 1957: vii). There was also the question of the class of people to whom a particular usage was informal. Earlier unabridged dictionaries were addressed to a somewhat restricted, educated class, but, by 1961, with the huge increase in college and university attendance following the Second World War, and with the vast expansion of mass communications by radio and television, the prospective market had grown immensely and changed demographically. One sympathetic critic argued, only slightly tongue-in-cheek, that the old *Informal* label actually had come to mean 'informal for those of a higher social class, especially older, well-educated authors and professors in the humanities' (Landau 2001: 258). Some within the group thus disempowered were outraged; they attacked the dictionary for abandoning all standards simply because it had abandoned theirs. There is less justification for the sharp reduction in the use of the *slang* label. The Explanatory Notes contain this confusing comment: 'No word is invariably slang, and many standard words can be given slang connotations or used so inappropriately as to become slang.' Although meant as a justification for seldom using *slang*, it is irrelevant. In deciding what to label, as in everything else, the lexicographer is guided by the preponderance of the evidence. The possibility of limitless variation is no warrant for the failure to label words as slang.

Apart from all of these changes, the new defining style of the *Third* set it apart most dramatically from the Second and from all earlier *Webster* dictionaries. The style avoids commas except to separate items in a series, proscribes semicolons entirely, and relies on a single unbroken description with embedded phrases and clauses following directly upon each part of the definition they modify (very like the second half of this sentence). In most definitions, particularly verbs, the stylistic change is hardly noticeable, as is also the case with many common words, which are defined simply and clearly with brief definitions. The style is most conspicuous when applied to scientific terms. Here is the definition for *iridium*: 'a silver-white hard brittle very heavy chiefly trivalent and tetravalent metallic element of the platinum group that occurs usu. as a native alloy with platinum or with osmium in iridosmine, is resistant to chemical attack at ordinary temperatures, and is used esp. in hardening platinum for alloys suitable for surgical instruments, electrical and other scientific apparatus, jewelry, and the points of gold pens.' This is not exactly standard English, but it is a superbly crafted definition for getting across an amazing number of facts economically, that is, if the reader can stay with it till the end without losing focus. It contains all of the most important facts given in the much longer definition of the Second Edition, and in much less space. By and large, the new defining style works well, but it takes some getting used to, and sometimes it sacrifices clarity for economy of expression. It is not necessarily more logical than more traditional methods of defining, but Gove evidently admired its straightforward linear drive, like a car in smooth acceleration.

As the *iridium* definition quoted above suggests, one of the few areas in which *Webster's Third* did follow the tradition of the Second was in giving extraordinary attention to scientific and technical entries, although it did not label them. Indeed, it can be argued that this edition lacked discrimination in its coverage of scientific and technical terms, devoting an excessive amount of space to them.

Another area for which the *Third* was widely attacked, even ridiculed, was its choice of selection of illustrative quotations. Given the vast changes in the lexicon and in new senses since the Second Edition, the editors of the *Third* expanded their collection of citations to six million, adding about 4.5 million to those they had inherited, and a large percentage of the new citations was from recent literature, newspapers, and magazines. Many of the illustrative quotations used were from contemporary sources, for which the *Third* was attacked by those who defended an older tradition of citing, wherever possible, exemplary users of the language to illustrate good usage. Such had been Johnson's plan in 1755, but even Webster's first great dictionary of 1828 abandoned that model, and subsequent unabridged dictionaries published by the Merriams and by Funk & Wagnalls from the 1890s on rejected the idea that only the usage of esteemed writers of literature was worthy of being quoted; any contemporary source that clarified the sense of a word was worthy of being cited. Furthermore, it simply is not true that great literary figures of the past were ignored; they are quoted extensively throughout the dictionary. Nonetheless, *Webster's Third* was ridiculed for quoting radio show talk hosts and musical comedy actresses, among others, to illustrate current usages. Such criticism seems particularly ill-informed and transparently snobbish. With respect to the charge that *Webster's Third* had abandoned its sacred role of representing the correct use of English, some of the responsibility must be attributed to the past advertising of Merriam's unabridged dictionaries as 'the ultimate authority', which encouraged the conviction that *Webster* dictionaries were guardians of the English language. The unfortunate emphasis on newness both by Gove and the publicists hired by Merriam to manage the initial marketing of *Webster's Third* also contributed to the idea that this dictionary was a radical departure from the sensible, traditional policies of the past (Morton 1994: 168–70).

9.11.2 Pronunciation in Webster's Third

The treatment of pronunciation, under the guidance of Edward Artin, also came in for some criticism, on the grounds of its complexity and overelaboration (Chapman 1967). To save space, Gove dropped the pronunciation key that traditionally ran along the base of the pages, so that readers had to refer to the explanations for the symbols in the front matter. Many reviewers objected to dropping the key. Nevertheless, compared to other aspects of the dictionary, pronunciation escaped heavy criticism, mainly through neglect. It deserved better.

The pronunciations in *Webster's Third* represent a considerable advance over any earlier English dictionary, including the *Oxford English Dictionary.* The system employed, while retaining many of the familiar phonemically based alphabetic symbols and diacritics, introduces a few characters of the International Phonetic Alphabet (IPA). Though the schwa ([ə]) had been introduced in dictionaries by the *American College Dictionary* in 1947, the system used in *Webster's Third* employs it in a variety of novel ways, in both stressed and unstressed environments, and defines it with rigorous specificity in many different contexts in an explanation that runs to nearly four pages in the Guide to Pronunciation. Whereas John Kenyon's guide in the Second Edition included a phonetic description of the sounds of English, Artin's in the *Third* confines itself to describing the symbols used in its dictionary pronunciations. Within these limits it is quite expansive; for example, the syllabic consonant used by many speakers in words like *kitten* is analysed at length, beginning with Webster's 1828 dictionary and including every major *Webster* dictionary since. Adopting the IPA's method of indicating primary and secondary stress, the *Third* uses a short, boldface, vertical line preceding the stressed syllable, raised if the stress is primary, and dropped to the base of the line if the stress is secondary. Both marks appear before a syllable that can be either primary or secondary, usually in compounds. Thus in *home-made*, the pronunciation is given as 'hō:mād, indicating that the word may be pronounced with primary stress on the first syllable or with equal stress in both syllables.

The system used is no more complicated than it needs to be to render the variety of sounds to be represented. Very few of the criticisms of the pronunciations alleged any inaccuracy or incompleteness of treatment. The criticisms mainly address the difficulty of understanding the pronunciations when, to avoid repeating the same pronunciation in a string of words, various symbols such as the equals sign are used to represent part of a preceding pronunciation. Allied to this criticism is the charge that too many variations are given, so that, combined with the shortcuts used, comprehending all the varieties is a formidable challenge. There is some justice in each criticism, but both, especially the latter, are exaggerated.

9.11.3 Etymology in Webster's Third

The etymologies, under the supervision of Charles R. Sleeth, are among the few features of *Webster's Third* that were not attacked and, if mentioned at all, were generally praised. Innocent of any relevance to the issues of correctness in usage that so exercised the critics, the etymologies seemed to be the one reliably old-fashioned aspect of the dictionary. In some ways this was true, as the purpose of tracing the origin of words as far back in English as possible, or showing in what form they came into English and from what source, was the same as in previous editions. A comparison with the Second Edition confirms that the earlier work's etymologies were thoroughly re-examined and improved.

The one major innovation in the treatment of etymology is the introduction of an abbreviation, ISV, for International Scientific Vocabulary. ISV is used in etymologies for those technical words or parts of technical words which are used in languages other than English and which may have been coined in one of those languages rather than English. Because of the international character of scientific vocabulary and the rapidity with which any new item is adopted in different languages, often in slightly altered form, it is often impossible to establish the language of origin. In the past, many dictionaries had designated most such terms as New Latin if the words were formed from Latin roots, as they usually were. But etymologists had long been dissatisfied with this designation, because New Latin is a completely artificial construct invented to describe scientific terms whose actual origin is unknown. ISV was created because it was deemed more honest, and reviewers generally endorsed the innovation as a sensible way to deal with the problem.

9.11.4 Assessment of Webster's Third

Although Gove asserts near the beginning of his preface that the dictionary is not just for the scholar or professional but for the general user without any advanced preparation, the style frequently employed in the dictionary does not support such a claim. Users did not understand why even entries including names are not capitalized. The pronunciations, though of high quality, are far from simple. Readers were apt to be puzzled and occasionally misled by the reluctance to use subject labels for technical definitions, such as *Astronomy* or *Engineering*, labels used liberally in the Second Edition but extremely sparingly in the *Third*. Gove's sole justification for this major change is delivered in the preface by the simple announcement that '... this edition uses very few subject labels. It depends upon the definition for incorporating necessary subject orientation'. Sometimes this is true and sometimes not. In any case it places the responsibility on the user to divine, often from an illustrative quotation rather than the definition, the specialized nature of a definition. To do so often requires specialized knowledge which the user may not have. In many respects *Webster's Third* is a great dictionary, but it is not user-friendly.

Gove placed too much reliance on definitions to provide context of subject, and too much reliance on illustrative quotations to provide guidance for level of usage. The virtual absence of subject labels and the begrudgingly rare use of *slang* are defects, as is the absurd absence of capital letters in words that are invariably capitalized. Thus some of the criticisms arguing that *Webster's Third* had abandoned its responsibility to guide the reader have a modicum of merit, but the expectations of the critics were sweeping and unrealistic. It is unfortunate that some of Merriam's own advertising contributed to such misapprehensions, but it was mainly Gove's lack of empathy with the user—perhaps also his lack of sympathy with the user—that made him so inflexible in applying his sets of criteria governing the presentation of his dictionary. The policies Gove promulgated and saw through seemed designed to improve the art of lexicography rather than to produce a fine commercial dictionary. That they did both, in spite of some of the lapses of *Webster's Third*, is a testament to the quality of the Merriam staff and to Gove's integrity and assiduity as a lexicographer.

9.11.5 *The end of the era of the unabridged dictionary in America*

Although no one knew it at the time, *Webster's Third* marked the end of the era of the unabridged dictionary in America, a period of nearly a century beginning with the Webster's dictionary of 1864 and reaching its highest level from the 1890s to the 1930s, when readers had a choice of three major works: the *Century Dictionary*, Funk & Wagnalls' dictionaries, and Webster's.

Before the advent of computer technology, the editorial costs of producing a dictionary, though high, were relatively small compared to the cost of typesetting and the continuing high cost of printing and binding. In order to market each new edition successfully, the publisher had to have the dictionary thoroughly revised. This required a large editorial staff. But with the development of computer technology, publishers feel they can market new electronic editions on the basis of continuous updating limited to adding new words and new senses. They incur no great costs in the distribution of electronic dictionaries, so they see no justification for the expense of a considerable editorial staff. They thus save a great deal of money, but the dictionary text is essentially unrevised. Definitions from past editions whose meanings have changed in subtle ways, or which are used in different contexts or in different collocations, or which have changed register to become more or less formal or changed frequency to become more common or rarer, are seldom recorded. Likewise, scientific entries which have become general in usage are not accurately represented, nor are slang words and expressions which have gained currency among the general population and are no longer slang. It is also noteworthy that the audio feature used for pronunciations (in CDs packaged with printed dictionaries or heard as a feature of online dictionaries) rarely includes variants. Only a thorough re-examination by a competent staff of every definition and its illustrative quotations and of every pronunciation and etymology within each entry can produce a new edition, but publishers of electronic dictionaries have no financial motivation to pay for such a re-examination, at least not on the scale required to prepare an unabridged dictionary.

9.12 OTHER LARGE DICTIONARIES AFTER *WEBSTER'S THIRD*

This account will conclude with descriptions of other large dictionaries published after *Webster's Third*—in the latter part of the twentieth century and in the first few years of the twenty-first. Though all are considerably larger in extent than the American college dictionaries, and though at least one calls itself unabridged, none are truly comparable to the great unabridged dictionaries of the 1880s to 1961. Each has its distinct merits, but none provides the scope and depth of coverage of the earlier unabridged dictionaries.

9.12.1 World Book Dictionary *(1963)*

Clarence Barnhart had long been a major figure in American lexicography, and was one of the few dictionary publishers to have his own large citation file. Barnhart was best known for the series of children's dictionaries published under the Thorndike–Barnhart rubric. These were the successors to earlier children's dictionaries based primarily on the *New Century Dictionary*. In 1958, Barnhart was invited to prepare a very large new dictionary that would be sold with the *World Book Encyclopedia*, one of the best-selling encyclopedias in the United States (Barnhart 1996: 124). The new dictionary, like the encyclopedia, was designed for students at the upper-grade school and high-school levels. It would be published in two volumes in 1963 as the *World Book Dictionary*, and was sold both with the encyclopedia set and separately by the encyclopedia publishers.

Edited by Clarence L. Barnhart and his son, Robert K. Barnhart, the *World Book Dictionary* originally contained about 170,000 entries, in later editions at least 225,000. Because it was meant to be compatible with the *World Book Encyclopedia*, it did not include biographical or geographical entries, nor did it include any detailed encyclopedic material. In light of its intended readership, the definitions are written simply whenever possible. Although the dictionary omits excessively technical terms along with most obsolete and rare words, it does cover a wide range of scientific and technical vocabulary. Perhaps the most distinctive feature of the *World Book Dictionary* is its use of illustrative quotations to exemplify its definitions. Drawing upon the Barnharts' own extensive citation file, the editors have liberally included quotations, generally in complete sentences, with the author identified. Few, if any, other dictionaries designed for students include authentic quotations.

The presentation and typography employed in the *World Book Dictionary* also set it apart from most other dictionaries. A sans serif type is used in the three-column dictionary page, and a ragged right (unjustified) style is used for end-of-line breaks. The editors explain that this style is believed to be easier for younger users than the more traditional page layout. The pronunciation guide is based on a phonemic approach commonly used in American dictionaries. Etymologies are also included, in appropriately simplified form. Some 3,000 pictorial illustrations supplement the text.

9.12.2 The Random House Dictionary of the English Language *(1966, 1987)*

The distinguished American publishing firm of Random House entered the dictionary business in 1947 by publishing the trade edition (for the general public) of Clarence Barnhart's *American College Dictionary.* (Harper & Bros. published the text edition for students.) A succession of Random House college dictionaries followed, and, in 1966, no doubt in order to capitalize on the heavy criticism given *Webster's Third, The Random House Dictionary of the English Language* appeared. The dictionary certainly looked like an unabridged in size and bulk, but it was a different animal in many ways from *Webster's Third.* In conception and design it explicitly rejected almost all of the policies implemented in *Webster's Third.* It embraced encyclopedic terms, including biographical and geographical ones—even including the titles of literary works and given names—in its main alphabetic section. It included nearly four hundred pages of supplementary material, including concise dictionaries of French, Spanish, Italian, and German, and a 32-page full-colour atlas of the world, all of which was retained in the Second Edition of 1987 but later unceremoniously dropped. The First Edition's preface explicitly rejected 'novelty in the guise of innovation' and had no scruples to prevent it from capitalizing all words usually capitalized. It employed the standard roster of usage labels, not just *slang*—which it used much more liberally than *Webster's Third*—but *informal* and many others. More to the point, the preface, written by Jess Stein, the editor-in-chief, eagerly endorsed the position—almost in paraphrase of some of the critics of *Webster's Third*—that the responsibilities of lexicographers did not end with merely recording usage; they needed to report also the social attitudes reflected in many words and expressions. Usage labels were included 'to guide the reader to effective and appropriate use of words'.

Based upon the latest Random House college dictionary, the first edition of the unabridged dictionary added thousands of entries of various kinds, many scientific and technical, many encyclopedic, and long lists of undefined words beginning with a particular prefix, such as *un-*. Any close comparison of the treatment of a sequence of entries in any edition of the *Random House Dictionary* and *Webster's Third* clearly shows that *Webster's Third* displays finer sense discrimination, often with additional subsenses, and more authentic illustrative quotations. Two areas in which Random House dictionaries have always excelled are in their coverage of new words, especially slang, and of scientific and technical terms, and the *Random House Dictionary* carries on that tradition. No other features of the *Random House Dictionary* stand out as exceptional, though a secure level of competence can be assumed. Its pronunciations and etymologies are less complex than those of *Webster's Third*, similar to those found in a college dictionary.

Because of the efforts of Laurence Urdang, the managing editor, the *Random House Dictionary* was one of the first dictionaries to make use of data processing systems, the forerunner of modern computer technology, in some phases of its editorial preparation and in its production. Such technology was used to sort dictionary entries to facilitate their distribution to subject specialists and consultants, and innovative methods for the time were used to produce typeset text including the required mark-up for styling (italic, boldface, etc.) before it was turned over to the compositors for typesetting.[14]

In summary, the 1966 *Random House Dictionary* was offered to the public as a distinct alternative to *Webster's Third*. Although calling itself *Unabridged Edition*, the original *Random House Dictionary*, with about 260,000 entries, was not nearly as comprehensive as the *Webster* and *Funk & Wagnalls'* unabridged dictionaries. Twenty-one years later, in 1987, the Second Edition of the *Random House Dictionary* appeared, with a vocabulary enlarged by nearly twenty per cent for a new total of 315,000 entries. The editor-in-chief was Stuart Berg Flexner, and the managing editor, Leonore Crary Hauck. The strengths and comparative deficiencies of the First Edition remain evident in the Second Edition. As the tribulations of *Webster's Third* had by then receded from the public consciousness, the new preface places less emphasis on the lexicographer's responsibility to report prevailing social attitudes and more on its coverage of new terms and international usages previously neglected.

In 1993, an updated edition renamed *Random House Unabridged Dictionary* still retained the hundreds of pages of supplementary material, but in 1997 almost all the supplementary material was dropped. The new edition, timed to coincide with the publication of the second edition of the *Random House Webster's College Dictionary*, was renamed once more. *Webster's* was added to the title, and it was reborn as *Random House Webster's Unabridged Dictionary*.

9.12.3 Intermediate-sized dictionaries

In the last decades of the twentieth century, the two largest American dictionaries were *Webster's Third*, updated with supplements of new words, and the two

[14] Personal communication from Laurence Urdang, 19 January 2006.

editions of the *Random House* dictionary, but near the end of the century a new type of dictionary appeared, of intermediate size, smaller than the *Random House* but perhaps fifty per cent larger than college dictionaries. These dictionaries are in large format and contain about 2,000 pages. Two of them have been produced in closely coordinated stages by freelance teams of British and American lexicographers to create regional editions. These are the *New Oxford American Dictionary* (Second Edition 2005), allied originally to the *New Oxford Dictionary of English* (1998), and *Encarta Webster's Dictionary of the English Language* (Second Edition 2004), an offshoot of the *Encarta World English Dictionary* (1999), which was represented as covering all national varieties of English. The new *Encarta* dictionary has abandoned that idea and gives primary attention to American English. A third dictionary of this class is *The American Heritage Dictionary of the English Language* (Fourth Edition 2000), which was produced only in American English.

The freelance lexicographers who edited *Oxford* and *Encarta* dictionaries were widely dispersed but had access to secure websites containing the dictionary text. Indeed, many other dictionaries, especially large foreign-learner dictionaries, are produced in this way. The degree of access varies according to the editors' responsibilities, but, so long as they have the appropriate equipment and software, they can work in their homes on their own schedules. Even those publishers which still have in-house staffs rely on freelancers for many aspects of the dictionary's preparation. Through regular email correspondence the managers of the dictionary stay in touch with the freelancers and supervise their work. This modus operandi seems to herald a permanent change in the way large dictionary projects are handled. Even with this cost-saving manner of editorial preparation, the future of large dictionaries as a genre remains uncertain. Whether they provide enough additional information compared with college dictionaries to justify their higher prices is open to question. Whether they will endure as a dictionary genre or disappear, it is too early to say, but in general the outlook for large dictionaries in print is anything but secure.

10

THE *OXFORD ENGLISH DICTIONARY*

Lynda Mugglestone

It is with no disparagement of the lexicographical labours of the many scholars who, since the appearance of the tiny 8vo. of Henry Cockeram in 1623, have built each on the structure of his predecessors, and laboured to perfect the fabric of English lexicography (including as they do such eminent names as Blount, Bailey, Johnson, Richardson, Todd, Webster, and Worcester) that this work seeks to do for English words something different from what their cumulative labours have effected (MP/18/10/83).

10.1 A NEW ENGLISH DICTIONARY

JAMES Murray's words stand as eloquent testimony to the distinctiveness of the work which he was to edit for the next twenty-one years. Defined by its refusal simply to appropriate the evidence of existing English dictionaries, the *New English Dictionary* (later the *Oxford English Dictionary*)[1] was, as Murray indicates, characterized by a spirit of genuine critical enquiry—and an emphatic desire to return to first principles in the collection and examination of data. The 'newness' extolled by its original title (which remained in use until 1933) was, in this sense, by no means rhetorical; in its scale and detail, as well as in its principles of inclusiveness and descriptive rigour, the *OED* would regularly transcend

[1] The history of the dictionary's title is by no means straightforward. *A New English Dictionary* appeared on the title pages of the various parts and sections throughout the first edition 1884–1928 though its designation as the *Oxford English Dictionary* was also established from 1895 on the covers and wrappers of the individually published parts. The 1933 corrected re-issue, with *supplement* by Craigie and Onions, maintained the *OED* title.

previous lexicographical achievement in English. Distinctive too was its historical vision and, by extension, the theoretical model on which it was founded. While Johnson (1755: B2^{v}) had seen barrenness in philology (which needed to be enlivened by 'verdure and flowers'), for the *OED* this was fertile terrain, enabling new and critical understanding of lexical and semantic developments in the English vocabulary on fully formed 'historical principles'. It was therefore to 'pre-scientific' philology (and an era when 'real analogies were overlooked, and superficial resemblances too easily seized') that Murray consigned Johnson (MP/4/10/83: 4). The *OED*, in contrast, was to emblematize the philological advances of a new epoch in lexicography: 'It is because of the novelty of its aims, the originality of its method, the fresh start it makes from materials never before collected, that it claims in a distinctive sense to be A NEW ENGLISH DICTIONARY' (MP/8/10/83).

10.1.1 *The Dictionary and the Philological Society*

The first edition of the *OED* has a long history. Public disquiet about the lexical record supplied by existing dictionaries was evident within a few years of Johnson's death. Samuel White in 1788 had already proposed writing *An Universal Dictionary of the English Language* which, unlike Johnson's *Dictionary*, would take in 'the whole scope' of English. However, as *The Times* observed with some prescience in reporting White's scheme, 'Of course this *dictionary* will be vastly greater, and more useful than that of JOHNSON – but will require many *years* to render it perfect'.[2] White's projected work remained unpublished and letters to contemporary newspapers and journals continued to exhibit marked frustration with the limitations of English lexicography. Readers sought information on unrecorded words such as *distord* and *sinage* (H. W. 1851: 6). Similar was F. B. Relton's quest for *stickle* as used in William Browne's *Pastoral* ('Patient anglers, standing all the day// Near to some shallow stickle, or deep bay'). While Relton (1851: 209) deduced that *stickle* signified a pool of some kind, he desired more detail on its history and use: 'Is it ever so used now, or has that meaning become obsolete? I do not find it in Richardson's *Dictionary*', he asked his fellow readers of *Notes and Queries.*

The publication in 1852 of the first part of the *Deutsches Wörterbuch* exacerbated these perceived deficiencies. Edited by Jacob Grimm, it already demonstrated the advantages of the philological method. Scientific research on etymology, on historical development, and on sense-relationship placed the German dictionary

[2] 'A New Dictionary', *The Times* 22 March 1788: 3.

far above its counterparts in English. Grimm had been elected as the first Honorary Member of the London Philological Society in 1843, and his work encapsulated the new linguistic ideals of the age. His early support for the endeavours of the Society (formally founded in the previous year)[3] was justly recorded with pride (see Wilson 1843: 13). The stated aims of the Philological Society ('to investigate and promote the study and knowledge of the structure, the affinities, and the history of languages') deliberately removed it from the subjective appraisals of language (and the prescriptive metalanguage) which continued to characterize much popular language comment in Britain at this time. The papers delivered at its early meetings (on Anglo-Saxon, on Sanskrit, on Greek, or on the structure of the Russian verb) signalled an appropriate breadth of linguistic inquiry, and a commitment to the new discourses of science and empiricism. F. H. Trithen (1843: 101), for example, concluded a paper on Russian by stressing the importance of contemporary research into cognate languages 'which will no doubt enable us to carry still further those laws and analogies, the discovery of which has already given to Philology the character of a science'. In etymology, Hensleigh Wedgwood (1844: 2) likewise emphasized that only facts with undeniable 'scientific value' should merit consideration in dictionaries (a principle which, for him, exposed the weakness of Johnson in deriving, say, *curmudgeon* from *cœur méchant*, or *helter-skelter* from *hilariter celeriter*).

By the 1840s the Society was already seen—as by Wedgwood—as an appropriate body for a wider collective project in the history of words. 'We might perhaps be the means of preserving much valuable knowledge, and might gradually accumulate materials for an etymology of the English language, for which, at the present day, we have little to show beyond the uncertain guesses of Junius and Skinner', he argued (1844: 2). Other members concurred and the politician and philologist George Cornewall Lewis drew the attention of the Society's Council to 'a subject of great importance, namely, the compilation of a dictionary devoted to the archaic and provincial terms of the English language'.[4] In spite of some initial caution,[5] the appeal of the grand collective endeavour remained. Another lengthy debate took place at a meeting on 20 February 1852. As this made plain, 'an organization of labour... promised advantages that could

[3] The Society had existed in an earlier form at University College, London from *c.*1830.

[4] The letter was reported at the opening of the meeting of the Philological Society held on 26 January 1844. See Wilson (1844: 169).

[5] See Wilson (1844: 169) when (as President) Wilson acknowledged that the Society 'possessed within itself facilities for carrying such an object into effect, which were probably not at the command of any single individual' yet also concluded that 'the Council would not commit themselves to the recommendation of any specific plan without the most mature deliberation'.

not be expected from the isolated efforts of individuals'. As the notes of the meeting further record, the impression now 'seemed very general, that a more systematic investigation of our language might lead to a much more satisfactory knowledge of its peculiarities'.[6] It was this 'organization of labour' which took specific shape some five years later with the introduction of the project that would ultimately become the *OED*.

10.1.2 *Early Plans*

Discussions in early 1857 focused on a scheme by which the Philological Society might produce a supplemental list of words to remedy omissions in the lexical and semantic record provided by existing dictionaries. Stressing 'the deficiencies of the two standard Dictionaries of Johnson and Richardson, both as vocabularies of the language and as philological guides' ('Proposal' 1857: 81), a *Proposal for a Complete Dictionary of the English Language* was sent as a circular to newspapers, journals, and other interested parties in July. As its title indicates, completeness of coverage was already seen as an important issue, affirmed also in the ideal of the '*Lexicon totius Angliticatis*' which was here set out for the first time. At this point, however, even if the *Lexicon totius* was regarded as a legitimate aspiration, it was also seen in terms of the specific gathering of evidence on hitherto unrecorded words and meanings. It did not, as yet, suggest the need to rewrite the dictionary in entirety.

Within the Philological Society, energies were initially directed to the work of a Special Committee consisting of Frederick Furnivall, Herbert Coleridge, and Richard Chenevix Trench. Established 'for the purposes of collecting words and idioms hitherto unregistered', its specific remit over the summer of 1857 was to gather as much evidence as possible before a formal report was made to the Society in the autumn. The collection of data was moreover to involve not only the members of the Committee and the Philological Society but also (here following precedents established for the *Deutsches Wörterbuch*) to depend on interested sections of the populace as a whole. Made explicit in the later *Proposal for the Publication of a New English Dictionary by the Philological Society* ('We do but follow the example of the Grimms, when we call upon Englishmen to come forward and write their own Dictionary for themselves' ([Phil.Soc.] 1859: 8), this principle was being actively tested by August 1857. An extensive list of books to be read for the purposes of gathering citations (and thereby empirical evidence on English usage and development) was reproduced in journals such as the *Athenaeum* and *Notes and*

[6] Meeting of the Philological Society held on 20 February 1852, *Proc.Phil.Soc.* (1852, V: 142).

Queries.[7] Readers were thereby encouraged to play their own part within this national philological endeavour by contributing quotations which illustrated the many words and senses still unrepresented in existing dictionaries. *Notes and Queries*, in particular, emerged as a forum in which early results could be debated and discussed. R. W. Dixon (1857: 208–9) argued, for example, that *fore-elders* in the sense 'fore-fathers' was clearly one of the absences which the proposed new dictionary could remedy, given the silence of both Johnson and Richardson in this respect.

10.1.3 *Richard Chenevix Trench*

The promised report was delivered to the Philological Society by the scholar and theologian Richard Chenevix Trench in the form of two lectures, the first given on 5 November and the second two weeks later.[8] Trench's *On some Deficiencies in our English Dictionaries* was to become one of the seminal documents in the history of the *OED*. Here he described not only the weaknesses of existing lexicographical texts but he also outlined the components—and the theoretical approach—of an entirely new dictionary. Trench's earlier work on language had established his interest in the flux of language through time, and the historical significance of words. As he had contended (1855: 3), 'If we would understand this language as it now is, we must know something of it as it has been; we must be able to measure . . . the forces which have been at work upon it, moulding and shaping it into the forms which it now wears'.

While his earlier publications had often placed the history of words in a popular format (and, at times, with a conspicuously theological slant),[9] Trench's 1857 lectures to the Philological Society provided a rigorous critique of the historical and linguistic fallibilities of English lexicography as it then existed. A series of maxims isolated core areas of weakness ('Obsolete words are incompletely registered; some inserted, some not', 'Families or groups of words are often imperfect, some members of a family inserted, while others are omitted'; 'Much earlier examples of the employment of words oftentimes exist than any which are cited'; 'Important meanings and uses of words are passed over; sometimes the later alone given, while the earlier, without which the history of

[7] See 'Notes on Books, etc.', *Notes and Queries* (Second series.) IV (1857: 139–40).

[8] Appointed as Dean of Westminster in 1856, Trench's work for the Philological Society was structured around the range of commitments which this imposed.

[9] See, for example, his conviction that 'words often contain a witness for great moral truth – God having impressed such a seal of truth upon language, that men are continually uttering deeper things than they know' (Trench 1851: 8).

words will often be maimed, are unnoticed' (Trench 1860: 3)). Trench likewise drew attention to the fact that 'Our Dictionaries pay comparatively little attention to the distinction of synonymous words', as well as pointing out the ways in which a full corpus of illustrative citations—as the activities of the summer had already proved—might be systematically employed to document a word's usage and sense-differentiation. Nevertheless, as Trench noted at the outset (1860: 2), 'the fact that the vocabulary of our Dictionaries is seriously deficient can only be shown by an accumulation of evidence, each several part of which is small and comparatively insignificant in itself; only deriving weight and importance from the circumstance that it is one of a multitude of like proofs'. As a result, while Trench's lectures examined lexicographical practice *per se*, his iterated emphasis on 'proof' also meant that the assembled evidence was to provide an unassailable case for a new dictionary entirely.

The unsystematic and haphazard way in which English and its lexical history had hitherto been recorded is the shared theme which unites, say, Trench's condemnation of the inconsistent recording of *snag* and related forms in existing dictionaries, his equally negative comments on the wholesale omission of various categories of words, and his outright censure of Johnson's precept that 'Obsolete words are admitted when they are found in authors not obsolete, or when they have any force or beauty that may deserve revival' (Trench 1860: 10). As Trench argued, the perceived merits (or otherwise) of unrecorded words such as *mirificent* or *septemfluous*, both used by Henry More, were entirely irrelevant. Trench himself, he noted, could make a convincing case for *mulierosity* (another word unnoticed by lexicographers and also used by More). Signifying 'excessive fondness for women' as the *OED* would record, it expressed 'what no other word in the language would do' (1860: 7). Yet, as Trench insisted, for the historian of language it was the verifiable facts of a word's existence—its birth, life, and (where relevant) its death—which were pre-eminent, irrespective of any language attitudes to which lexicographers might find themselves disposed. In Trench's vision of a reformed lexicography, the maker of dictionaries would therefore no longer act as a critic of words. He would instead be a historian, responsive to the facts of language alone. Just as the philologist Franz Passow in Germany had earlier stressed the need for a word to 'tell its own story',[10] so, for Trench, a new emphasis on evidence-based lexicography was depicted as the means by which the dictionary might present the life-history of each word, tracing its changing forms and meanings through time with impeccable objectivity.

[10] See Passow's 1819 revision of J. G. Schneider's *Kritisches griechisch–deutsches Handwörterbuch*. This was translated into English by Liddell and Scott in their *Greek–English Lexicon* of 1843.

Supplementation of existing dictionaries was now rejected; a few months' work had revealed the scale of error and omission which characterized earlier works. What was needed was 'a new garment entirely, no patch upon old garments'. In particular, the dictionary so constructed should be 'an inventory of the language' (Trench 1860: 4). Explicitly rejecting the principles of selection which had characterized Johnson's earlier work (by which 'modes of expression' were to be 'rejected or received'), the image of the inventory (and the impartial and thorough listing of the contents of the English language which this implied), was, Trench wrote, the only model of lexicography which 'seemed capable of being logically maintained'. Significant too was the denial of subjectivity which the 'inventory' also suggested. 'It is no task of the maker of [the dictionary] to select the good words of the language', Trench stressed (1860: 4). The very activity of 'picking and choosing' was antithetical to the wider lexicographical remit which was now kept firmly in view. As he stressed in a further maxim for modern lexicography and the future *OED* (1860: 5), it was imperative for the lexicographer to bear in mind that 'the business which he has undertaken is to collect and arrange all the words, whether good or bad, whether they do or do not commend themselves to his judgment'.

10.1.4 First Steps

Trench's lectures articulated a number of the founding ideals of a work which would, as James Murray later affirmed, indeed be 'a NEW ENGLISH DICTIONARY'; objectivity, inclusivity, a respect for the historical record, and a commitment to original research were all constituted as newly canonical precepts. The formal *Proposal for the Publication of a New English Dictionary by the Philological Society*, together with the *Canones Lexicographici; or Rules to be Observed in Editing the New English Dictionary* (drawn up over five meetings between December 1859 and May 1860) provided a detailed outline of the 'lexicographical creed' of the project ([Phil.Soc.] 1859: 2) in ways which confirmed the influence of Trench's lectures ('the first requirement of every lexicon is, that it should contain *every word occurring in the literature of the language it professes to illustrate*', 'We entirely repudiate the theory, which converts the lexicographer into an arbiter of style'). The next stage of the enterprise—the gathering of the illustrative material (and vital evidence) from 1250 onwards—was also clarified. Three historical periods (*c.*1250–1526, 1526–1674, and 1674 onwards) were established, each provided with a 'Basis of Comparison' which documented the word forms already known to exist (the first was founded on Coleridge's own *Glossarial Index to the Printed Works of the Thirteenth Century* which, as Coleridge (1859: iii) noted, 'may be considered as the foundation-stone of the Literary and Historical portion of the Philological Society's proposed English Dictionary'. The second was defined by the words listed in the Concordances to the Bible and Shakespeare, and the third was based on a projected index to the language of Burke. Using these in parallel with their own reading, volunteers were therefore directed to submit quotations for all words and meanings for which the Bases possessed no record. By this means, information on forms recognized as obsolete or 'remarkable', or which seemed in other ways new or worthy of note, could be collected as work on the dictionary began in earnest.

The resulting reading programme (and creation of the underlying corpus for the dictionary) again relied for its success not only on the members of the Philological Society but also on the recruitment of a wider volunteer base. As the *Proposal* noted ([Phil.Soc.] 1859: 6), this already extended to America. An accompanying list of books also confirmed a ready participation in the project; many texts were asterisked, signifying that reading was already in progress. Coleridge undertook a range of works (particularly within the earlier period), as did Furnivall. Trench read Henry More's *Mystery of Iniquity* and Roger's *Naaman the Syrian. A Treatise on Infant Baptism* was being read 'By a Lady', as was Butler's *Hudibras* (and Glanville's *Evidence Concerning Witches*). Correspondence columns in contemporary journals and newspapers likewise confirmed an enthusiastic engagement with what this new dictionary promised to provide. 'J. M. N.' (1859: 144) described his reading of Samuel Harsnet's works, 'gone through *paginatim* for the Philological Society'.[11] Likewise, an article on Bishop Wetenhall commented on the latter's use of *diverb* in the sense 'a proverb, byword, a proverbial expression' ('Eirionnach' 1859: 273). The accompanying quotation ('...What do we mean by the usual diverb, the Italian Religion?') later appeared in the *OED* entry for this word.

A spirit of marked confidence was therefore well in evidence in the initial years of the dictionary project. Advertisements for its forthcoming publication (envisaged as a work in four volumes) were placed by mid-1859. Coleridge, who had assumed the role of editor, worked assiduously at collating the material which had been sent in, and even began to draft some of the early entries. A single specimen page (*Affect–Affection*) was printed. Confidence too pervaded attitudes to the vital collection of quotations; a letter sent to Trench by Coleridge in May 1860 records the participation of 167 volunteers and, though just fifty of these

[11] J. M. Norman joined the Philological Society in 1858 and is specified as the reader of three of Harsnet's works in the *List of Books Already Read, or Now (July 12, 1861) Being Read for the Philological Society's New English Dictionary* circulated by Frederick Furnivall.

were really 'first-rate', this was, Coleridge pointed out, considerably better than the experience of the Grimms (whose collective exercise for the *Deutsches Wörterbuch* had so far depended on just six 'satisfactory' readers). 'I believe that the scheme is now firmly established, and is so regarded by the public, [that] I confidently expect, unless any unforeseen accident should occur to paralyse our efforts, that in about two years we shall be able to give our first number to the world', he concluded (1860: 78).

10.2 INTERREGNUM

Within two years, however, unforeseen circumstances had indeed materialized. Coleridge's own death, from consumption in the spring of 1861, was not the least of these. It was Frederick Furnivall who instead assumed the role of editor, guiding the dictionary through the 1860s and through much of the following decade. One of the 'scholar adventurers' of the nineteenth century (see Benzie 1983), Furnivall has often been characterized by his consummate energy and industry. Certainly both were in evidence in the early years of his editorship. As well as organizing the dictionary, corresponding with readers and sub-editors (and acting as sub-editor of A), he also served as Honorary Secretary of the Philological Society from 1862. Recognizing moreover that accurate citations for the dictionary (and, in turn, the accuracy of the historical record the dictionary sought to establish) depended on the provision of equally accurate source texts, Furnivall founded the Early English Text Society (EETS) in 1864. A flow of authoritative and scholarly editions (over 250 within Furnivall's lifetime) began to appear. With a similar remit, if for different writers and periods, Furnivall initiated the Chaucer Society, the Ballad Society (in 1868), and the New Shakspere Society five years later. As the phonetician Alexander Ellis later noted in his role as President of the Philological Society (Ellis 1873: 245), this too was part of 'a new era in philology'.

10.2.1 *The Dictionary in the 1860s*

From the beginning, Furnivall was, however, less sanguine than Coleridge had been about the speedy appearance of the dictionary. Self-evident gaps in the assembled material, he argued in September 1861, meant that at least two further years would be necessary to provide thorough (and newly revised) Bases of Comparison. A *Vocabulary of Words beginning with the Letter B* was published in 1863 (by William Gee, the volunteer sub-editor of this portion of the alphabet); another for N appeared two years later. Though the Bases were later condemned by Murray (1879b: 571) as being fundamentally misguided in both approach and execution ('In my own opinion, [they] . . . were a mistake, and detrimental to the work which they were designed to serve'),[12] it was nevertheless largely to this end that the energies of the Dictionary's readers were directed over the course of the 1860s.

After Coleridge's death, publication was, however, also formally deflected from what was now often referred to as the 'Big Dict^{y}' or the 'Full Dictionary'. Instead plans were made for what seemed a more realistic and immediate aim—the publication of a *Concise Dictionary* which would 'serve as a new and revised Basis of Comparison' for all three periods previously specified by the *Proposal.* Approved by the Philological Society early in 1862, this condensed version of the original dictionary project was, Furnivall stated (1862: 328), intended to work as 'an abstract of what the larger Dictionary should be'. Meanwhile the contract for 'the big Dictionary' remained in place on the assumption that this would be published some three years after its shorter counterpart.

Progress was initially encouraging. The volunteer principle remained active and some 230 readers had produced material for the dictionary by February 1862, reading a total of 756 books. Between 25 October 1862 and 15 October 1864, 619 packets of words were received—'more than a packet a day, excluding Sundays', Furnivall noted (1864: 4). Books to be read were despatched to contributors on a regular basis though, given Furnivall's anxieties about accuracy, contributors were advised to clip out the desired citations wherever possible rather than run the risk of introducing inadvertent error through mistranscription. Copies of John Maplet's *A Greene Forest* (1567), Sandys' *Survey of Religion* (1599), and Pagitt's *Christianographie* (1630) were all offered under this head in 1864, along with a range of other texts. It is therefore not unusual to find, on the extant proof sheets of the first edition of the *OED*, appended slips bearing excised sections from these original texts, as in the two-line section from Latham's 1615 *Falconry. The Terms of Art Explained* which appears on a slip pasted onto the first revise of *Gorge.*

By the latter half of the decade, however, it is clear that the dictionary had begun to lose the momentum of the earlier years. A letter in *Notes and Queries* publicly

[12] As Murray also pointed out (1879b: 571–2), 'Their most obvious result, to one who examines the material, is, that while rare, curious, and odd words, are well represented, ordinary words are often most meagrely present; and the editor or his assistants have to search for precious hours for examples of common words, which readers passed by because they happened to find them put down in their "Basis" as occurring in the Bible or in Burke'.

indicated dissatisfaction with a work for which a collective—and indeed national—response had been asked, and for which evidence had duly been contributed, though as yet without any sign of publication. 'I am very anxious to gather some fruit from these labours', as L.L.L. asserted (1867: 169); 'Will someone who has authority in this undertaking report progress?'). It was the Cambridge medievalist Walter Skeat (a member of the Philological Society since 1863) who replied, offering reassurance that the dictionary was in fact 'being pushed on *now* as vigorously as ever'; the collection and arrangement of material, he added, was 'practically, in not a very incomplete state'. Likewise, in terms of the critical 'digestion and compilation from the material', Skeat stressed that 'parts of most of the letters are nearly ready for press' (Skeat 1867: 256). A close reading of Skeat's words (especially given the proliferation of negatives and qualifiers) serves nevertheless to confirm that progress on the dictionary was by no means as advanced as it should be. The *Concise Dictionary* had been promised to the publishers for early 1866 and, while Furnivall's *Circular* (1865: 3) had noted some inevitable delay, almost two years later it remained unpublished. Moreover, given that publication of the 'Full Dictionary' depended upon the prior appearance of the *Concise*, this made the eventual realization of the *OED* itself still more doubtful.

L.L.L. was in fact to prove remarkably prescient in the anxieties he expressed. As plans for publication lapsed, the volunteers on whom the work depended lost enthusiasm for a project which seemed to have no end in sight. Activities for the dictionary had so diminished by 1872 that no annual report was deemed necessary. As the phonetician Alexander Ellis stated two years later in his Presidential Address to the Philological Society, the dictionary 'remains, and may for some time remain, merely one of the things we have tried to do'. As he added (1874: 354), 'Several things, indeed, make me inclined to think that a Society is less fitted to compile a dictionary than to get the materials collected'.

10.3 REVIVAL AND RESURGENCE

Over the next few years, the dictionary project was, however, to receive new impetus and direction, derived in part from the presence of a new editor and in part from a new and firm commitment to publication. The editorship of the dictionary had been seen as problematic for some time; Furnivall's energies were increasingly dissipated among the range of activities to which he had committed himself. A single editor, prepared to work single-mindedly at the dictionary, was preferable. Moreover, as James Murray later commented (MP/19/6/82), the real problem of Furnivall's editorship lay in the fact that he 'never "edited" one word—he merely superintended the Reading'.[13]

By 1876, it was Murray who had emerged as a promising candidate. A schoolmaster at Mill Hill School in London, Murray had joined the Philological Society in 1868, swiftly establishing himself at the forefront of scholarly activity. His editions of the poems of Sir David Lyndesey, of *The Compleynt of Scotland* and of *The Romance and Prophecies of Thomas of Erceldowne*, all published for Furnivall's EETS, were impeccably researched and textually precise; his work on *The Dialect of the Southern Counties of Scotland* (1873), was, as Henry Bradley noted, a landmark in linguistic scholarship which 'may be said to have laid the foundations of the scientific study of the local varieties of English speech' (Bradley 1917: 546). Its 'insistence on the true spirit of philological inquiry' further consolidated Murray's academic reputation, as did his evident facility in languages.

Though reluctant to commit himself to becoming editor when initially approached by Skeat (and by Furnivall) in early 1877, it was Murray rather than Furnivall who played the prominent role in discussions of the dictionary project with Oxford University Press. OUP had been contemplated as a possible publisher by Skeat in 1876 though, until a replacement for Furnivall had been found, it was, to his mind, advisable to wait. It was therefore not until April 1877 that a formal approach was made by the phonetician Henry Sweet (then President of the Society). With persuasive confidence, Sweet's letter detailed a proposal of mutual advantage for Press and Society alike. Emphasizing the philological value of the 'mass of materials' which had been collected (the product of nineteen years of industry), he depicted a project well on the way to realization with over half the alphabet having been sub-edited and the remainder consisting of 'sorted slips'. He stressed too the significance of lexicography in both national and international contexts. Just as Johnson had vaunted the fact that, by his dictionary, Britain would 'no longer yield the palm of philology' to France, so too did Sweet emphasize the potential—and the need—for similar achievement in the nineteenth century. The 'conditions of a good dictionary' had been completely changed by 'the great advance of Philology', Sweet pointed out; 'What is now required is fullness of citations and historical method' as well as the treatment of pronunciation and etymology 'according to the latest results of linguistic science' (MP/20/4/77).[14] All this the proposed dictionary could deliver.

[13] Murray's criticism also extended to 'the sufficiency of [Furnivall's] scholarship' (MP/19/6/82). Furnivall's maverick and at times volatile personality was, as by Skeat, also seen as an impediment to the dictionary's success.

[14] Reprinted in Murray (1977: 342–6).

Friedrich Max Müller, one of the foremost philologists of the later nineteenth century as well as one of the Delegates of the Press,[15] endorsed both the dictionary and the sense of linguistic patriotism advanced by Sweet: 'In an undertaking of such magnitude, in which one might almost say the national honour of England is engaged, no effort should be spared to make the work as perfect as possible' (Müller 1878). He was confident too of its commercial success. Given Müller's encouraging response, negotiations continued. Detailed specimen entries were drafted (again with Murray in charge); as indicated in Sweet's letter, the expectation was, however, that Murray would edit not merely the specimens but the dictionary as a whole. This was, moreover, made salient to the Delegates' acceptance of the project. With Murray as editor, the terms could be agreed; without him, they could not. As Murray later wrote of the ultimatum which, in effect, he came to face on behalf of the Philological Society, 'it was a question whether the Dictionary should be done or not, and having with much trouble got it to the point, that the Delegates would accept it with me as Editor – but would hold all that had been done as cancelled, if I declined, I could only agree to it. I hope I did wisely; I think I acted loyally, but I do not see my way through it pecuniously' (MP/JAHM/[?5]/81).

10.4 REASSESSMENT

The formal contract with Oxford University Press was signed on 1 March 1879, specifying the completion of the *Dictionary* within ten years and in four volumes. Murray had made his own promise to Bartholomew Price, the Secretary of the Delegates, some months earlier: 'The time estimated for the preparation of the Dictionary (with due assistance) is 10 years, & I agree to complete the work within that time, as far as it shall be found to be possible' (MP/25/11/78). What was possible was, however, to be subject to a number of reappraisals (as, in fact, were some of Trench's founding ideals). While Murray had endeavoured, in the specimens, to edit a fraction of the assembled materials, he had no idea at that point of their real extent. Skeat had written extolling their worth ('it has taken 10 to 15 years to get the results together: & they only want arranging in some places. There are *gaps*, I firmly believe; I believe that perhaps even a whole letter may be

[15] The Delegates are appointed from the senior academic staff of the university and are actively involved in the publication processes of the Press; their approval is necessary before any book is accepted for publication.

missing: but *what there is is of the highest value*' (MP/6/4/76)); Furnivall had likewise maintained his habitual confidence in what had been achieved. The one and three quarter tons of material delivered to Murray after the formal signing of the contract certainly confirmed early estimations of the scale of the material. Together with two assistants (and alongside his work as a schoolmaster), Murray began the laborious task of taking stock.

'There are some cruel jokes in your reports G "done", "nearly done", "will be done in 1872" ', Murray berated Furnivall (MP/10/5/79); the statement that *Pa* was 'part done' seemed equally unfounded. 'We can find no clue', Murray wrote;[16] *Q* presented similar problems. Though some sections—such as F and K—were admittedly in 'excellent order', most were not. Rather than editing a corpus which, according to Skeat, was '*simply invaluable*' (MP/6/4/76), Murray instead found himself facing 'an incubus of rubbish & error' (OED/MISC/13/24). Though Furnivall was able to inform Murray that he had just found the words in *X* in his Dictionary cupboard (and thought that *H* might be in Rome with the American scholar George Perkins Marsh), it was nonetheless evident that Murray was in an essentially untenable position within two months of signing the contract with OUP. The first part of the dictionary was due for submission in 1882 but *A*, sub-edited by Furnivall, was as weak as the rest. The 'original materials' are 'rarely to be trusted', Murray concluded (OED/MISC/13/24); fewer than one sixth would make their way into the published text. Launching a new appeal for citations, the collection of material for the dictionary was, in effect, to begin anew.

10.4.1 *The creation of a new corpus*

Murray's *Appeal to the English-Speaking and English-Reading Public* was published in May 1879 with further versions following in June and in January 1880, each with accompanying desiderata in terms of words to be traced and books to be read.[17] It was to be vital to the success, and the scholarship, of the dictionary as eventually published. Circulated widely in journals and newspapers, it received a prominence—and response—which dwarfed that of the Philological Society's circulars of twenty years earlier. Some stalwart readers of course remained from these early days; Henry Hucks Gibbs, for example, had contributed to the dictionary as a sub-editor and reader in the early stages of the project under

[16] *Pa* remained elusive. A note sent over a year later by Furnivall (MP/3/11/80) recorded that he had just found 'the address of the *Pa* man's brother'. *Pa* was eventually traced to Ireland where all but a small section had been used for lighting fires.

[17] Other lists of desiderata continued to be issued at regular intervals. See, for example, 'Word Lists'. *Notes and Queries* (Sixth series.) (1882: 86, 107, 146, 167).

Furnivall and Coleridge, and continued as a valued critical reader under Murray's editorship. But the wider aim, as Murray stressed (1879b: 570), was to gain the attention of a 'new generation' who 'had arisen since 1857 [and] had never heard of the Dictionary'; the 290,000 citations delivered to Murray's scriptorium (and the 691 books read with a further 881 in progress) by March 1880 confirmed the significance of this new *Appeal.* By May, as Murray informed the Philological Society, 754 readers had contributed 361,670 citations. Over 1,000 quotations a day would be delivered in 1882; within three years over 1,300 readers had contributed a million additional quotations derived from the careful scrutiny of over five thousand writers.

The *Appeal* (and its results) gave practical reality to Murray's axiom that 'the perfection of the dictionary is in its *data*' (Murray 1880: 129). This represented a genuine advance in the kind of evidence-based lexicography advocated by Trench. In other respects, however, it exacerbated the problems which Murray faced. In December 1880, for example, though Murray now possessed some 2,500,000 citations, these were, he admitted (MP/n.d./12/80) 'only partially brought into alphabetical order, & scarcely at all into chronological order under each word'. With each new consignment, such problems increased, necessitating renewed and sometimes strikingly different arrangements of sense-development and meaning for the slips which had already provisionally been sorted. By 1882, Murray was explicit that the 'very shortest period' needed to complete the dictionary was seventeen years—and even this relied on the optimistic premise that thirty-three words could be completed each day (MP/12/2/82). Yet even drafting the single word *approve* had taken almost a whole day; the entry for *do* would take over six months. Over twenty years later, Murray would comment that, for certain words such as *penguin* and *pelican,* he 'could have written two books with less labour' (MP/24/12/04).

10.4.2 *Gains and losses*

This revised timescale, leading to a putative completion date of 1896, also failed to include provision for the correction of the proofs and revises—an activity which took some six hours a day. The proofs were in fact to be salient to Murray's working methods and the habits of wide-scale revision which he (and later his co-editors) implemented at this stage. The entry for *art,* for example, had been laboriously constructed over several weeks in 1884 yet, as Murray (1884: 509–10) noted, once he saw the proofs, 'the renewed consideration of it in print, with the greater facility of reading and comparison which this afforded, led to the entire pulling to pieces and reconstruction of the edifice, extending over several columns of type'. The still extant drafts of the first edition (see Mugglestone 2005) offer countless illustrations of this process during the lengthy production of the dictionary (see Fig. 10.1).

Murray's editorial perfectionism brought, of course, self-evident advances. Each fascicle of the dictionary was calibrated against corresponding sections in earlier works. Between *Horizontally* and *Hywe*, the *OED* included 4,371 entries (against the 403 in Johnson's *Dictionary*); these were supported moreover by the evidence of 15,160 quotations (930 had sufficed for Johnson). Similarly striking figures were in evidence for each successive fascicle and volume; for O and P, Johnson's 4,485 entries were dwarfed by the 48,870 entries of the *OED* (accompanied in the latter by 38,365 illustrative citations). As the Delegates came to realize, the 'fullness of material' and scientific rigour of the new lexicography promised by Sweet came at a cost in terms

speech in grammar.
1593 G. HARVEY *Pierces Supererog.* Wks. (Grosart) II. 246 When I am better grammered in the Accidents of his proper Idiotisme. *a* 1616 BEAUM. & FL. *Laws of Candy* II. i, *Erot.* *I can, I doe, I will.* *Gose.* *She is in her Moods and her Tences: Ile Gramer with you.* And make a triall how I can decline you. 1682 BUNYAN *Holy War* 32 These two .. did much more Grammer and settle the common people in hurtful ways. 1883 R. H. BUSK in *N. & Q.* Ser. VI. VIII. 51 Groups of phenomena which have been gathered, and grammared, and ranged into sciences.

Grammarian (grămēə·riăn). Forms: 4–5 gramarien, 4–7 gramarian, (4 gramariene, gramarion, 5 gramaryone, -oun, grammaryan, -on, 6 gramaryen, grammarien), 6– grammarian. [a. OF. *gramarien* (F. *grammairien*), f. *gramaire* GRAMMAR: see -AN.]

1. One versed in the knowledge of grammar, or of language generally; a philologist; often signifying also a writer upon, or teacher of grammar.
c 1380 WYCLIF *Serm.* Sel. Wks. I. 376 Gramariens and devynes. 1387 TREVISA *Higden* (Rolls) V. 161 Donatus þe gramarian. 1412–20 LYDG. *Chron. Troy* II. x, To sewe his style in my translation Worde by worde like the construction After the maner of gramariens. 1509 BARCLAY *Shyp of Folys* (1570) 105 The great Gramarians and pleasaunt Oratours. 1583 T. WATSON *Poems* lxviii. (Arb.) 104 Suidas mentioned an other Telephus, an excellent Grammarian of Pergamus. 1600 O. E. *Rep. Libel* I. i. 9 Not vnlike hungrie Grammarians, that are descanting still of the calamities of Troie, and yet see not their owne domesticall miseries. 1643 SIR T. BROWNE *Relig. Med.* II. § 8, I have seene a Grammarian toure, and plume himselfe over a single line in Horace. 1681 NEVILE *Plato Rediv.* 123, I know some Criticks, who are rather Grammarians than Lawyers, have made a distinction between *elegerim* and *elegero*. *a* 1704 T. BROWN *Sat. Antients* (1730) I. 22 They have commented upon him like grammarians not philosophers. 1727–41 CHAMBERS *Cycl.* s.v., The denomination grammarian is, like that of critic, now frequently used as a term of reproach; a mere grammarian; a dry, plodding grammarian, etc. 1771 SMOLLETT *Humph. Cl.* 19 May, They serve only as exceptions; which, in the grammarian's phrase, confirm and prove a general canon. K. WHITE Or stiff grammarians quaintly teach. 1861 HOOK *Lives Abps.* (1869) I. vii. 436 The homilies of Elfric the Grammarian. 1876 JAS. GRANT *Burgh Sch. Scotl.* II. xiii. 359 *note*, He educated a Grammarian not inferior to himself.

†2. A pupil engaged in the study of grammar; a grammar-school boy, or one qualified for that position. *Obs.*
1571 *Vestry Minutes St. Olave's, Southwark* in *Lett. Lit. Men* (Camden) 65 He should have twentye marks by the yere .. to teache so many gramaryens as we think shall be found meet for the same. 1607 in *Hist. Wakefield Gram. Sch.* (1892) 71 Because this schole is not ordained for petties but for grammarians.

3. *attrib.* and *Comb.*
1586 WARNER *Alb. Eng.* v. xxvii. (1589) 119 Grammarian-like, in order words significant to speake. *a* 1853 WHEWELL in Todhunter *Acct. W.'s Writ.* (1876) II. 376 The absurd injustice of our grammarian critics.

Hence **Gramma·rianism** [see -ISM], the principles or use of grammar.
1846 in WORCESTER, quoting *Ch[ristian] Ob[server]*. Hence in later Dicts.

Grammarie, var. of GRAMARYE.

†**Grammariour.** *Obs.* [f. as prec. + -*our*, -OR.] = GRAMMARIAN 1.
1536 BELLENDEN *Cron. Scot.* (1821) I. 231 About this time war mony clerkis profound in every science: as .. Donatus, grammariour; .. with mony otheris. 1597 LOWE *Chirurg.* (1634) 34 Speaking of Antioch mediciner, and Telephus grammariour. 1617 *Sc. Acts Jas. VI* (1816) IV. 576/1 With

First Revise. B 11

a gramer scole. 1454 *E. E. Wills* (1882) 133 For to fynde to gramer scole my cosyn, his sone William. 1523 FITZHERB. *Husb.* § 147, I lerned two verses at grammer-schole. 1593 SHAKS. 2 *Hen. VI*, IV. vii. 37 Thou hast most traiterously corrupted the youth of the Realme, in erecting a Grammar Schoole. 1616 R. C. *Times' Whistle* ii. 845 The foole Was never farther than the grammer schoole. 1647 *Laws Massachusetts* (1672) 136 Where any Town shall increase to the number of one hundred Families .. they shall set up a Grammar School. 1711 STEELE *Spect.* No. 157 ¶ 1 The many Heart-aches and Terrors, to which our Childhood is exposed in going through a Grammar-School. 1809 KENDALL *Trav.* III. lxxvii. 197 It differs therefore in nothing from the other grammar schools, called academies. 1858 DE QUINCEY *Autobiog. Sk.* Wks. II. 268 At the little town of Hawkshead .. a grammar-school (which, in English usage, means a school for classical literature) was founded. 1874 GREEN *Short Hist.* vi. § 4. 305 The grammar schools of Edward the Sixth and of Elizabeth .. had changed the very face of England. 1876 BANCROFT *Hist. U. S.* V. xxii. 577 They provided for a school in each town, a grammar-school in each county, and a university in the state.

attrib. 1826 SYD. SMITH *Wks.* (1869) 529 An Hamiltonian makes, in six or seven lessons, three or four hundred times as many exchanges of English for French or Latin, as a grammar schoolboy can do. 1898 J. K. JEROME *Second Thoughts of Idle Fellow* 266, I like to think of him [Shakespeare] as village ne'er-do-well, denounced by the local grammar-school master.

2. *U.S.* 'In the system of graded common schools in the United States, the grade or department in which English grammar is one of the subjects taught' (*Cent. Dict.*).
1860 WORCESTER, *Grammar-School* .. 2. A school next in rank above a primary school and below a high school. (U.S.) 18 .. *Amer. Cycl.* VI. 424 (Cent.) After passing through the primary grade .., the pupil enters the grammar school.

Grammarye, var. of GRAMARYE.

†**Grammates**, *sb. pl.* *Obs.*[−1] [? ad. Gr. γράμματα, pl. of γραμμα letter.] Rudiments; first principles.
1633 FORD *Broken Hrt.* I. iii, These apish boys, when they but taste the grammates, And principles of theory, imagine They can oppose their teachers.

Grammatic (grămæ·tik), *a.* [ad. L. *grammatic-us*, ad. Gr. γραμματικ-ός, f. γράμμα letter.] = GRAMMATICAL *a.*
1599 H. BUTTES *Dyets drie Dinner* E viij, Other expound it mystically, and not according to the grammaticke sense. 1644 MILTON *Educ.* Wks. (1738) I. 136 They [Novices] having but newly left those Grammatic Flats and Shallows .. do for the most part grow into hatred and contempt of learning. *c* 1645 HOWELL *Lett.* I. II. § 5 xxvii. (1650) 164 To frame Grammatic toiles to curb her. 1762 WARBURTON *Doctr. Grace* I. viii. Wks. 1788 IV. 575 What was thus inspired was the terms together with that grammatic congruity in the use of them, which is dependent thereon. 1814 W. TAYLOR in *Monthly Rev.* LXXIII. 455 Grammatic studies were understood at Alexandria to comprehend all that we call philology. 1829 *Blackw. Mag.* XXVI. 504 True wisdom all grammatic stuff disowns. 1884 *Science* III. 794/2 To judge from their lexical and grammatic character, the [Maya] dialects have evolved in the following historic order from the parent language.

Grammatical (grămæ·tikăl), *a.* [f. as prec. + -AL.]

1. Of or pertaining to grammar.
1530 PALSGR. The accidentes .. and other preceptes grammaticall. *a* 1586 SIDNEY *Arcadia* II. (1633) 122 The beautie of vertue .. taught them with far more diligent care, than grammatical rules. 1591 PERCIVALL *Sp. Dict.* Gram. B, I haue taken in hand to deale with this Grammaticall treatise. 1603 FLORIO *Montaigne* II. xii. 305 Most of the occasions of this worlds troubles are Grammatical. Our sutes and processes proceed but from the canvasing and debating the interpretation of the Lawes. 1620 GRANGER *Div. Logike* 127 Grammaticall comparison: which hath two degrees, comparative, and superlative. 1644 BULWER *Chiron.* 98 Glancing at the same Grammaticall expressions. 1781 WARTON *Hist. Eng. Poetry* Diss. iii. (1840) I. p. cciv, Berchorius probably compiled this work for the use of his grammatical pupils. 1804 BP. HORSLEY *Serm. on Christ's Descent* 13 It is of great importance to remark, though it may seem a grammatical nicety, that 1841 BORROW *Zincali* II. II. iii. 140 The pure Gypsy language,

First Revise. B 12

(*Continued*)

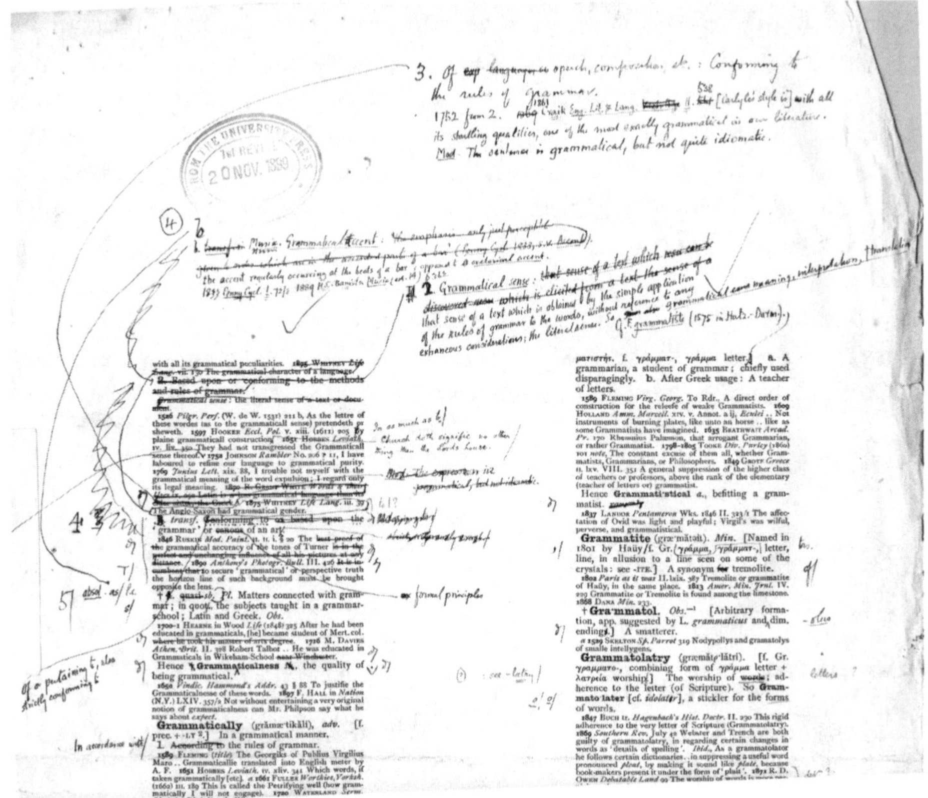

FIG. 10.1. Extant proofs of *The Oxford English Dictionary*, dated November/December 1899

of time as well as money. As a result, while the first fascicle of the dictionary, *A–Ant*, was published to wide acclaim in 1884, followed by *Ant–Batten* in 1885, it was not in fact until April 1928, thirteen years after Murray's own death in 1915, that the final fascicle would pass through the press. By that time, the dictionary consisted of twelve volumes rather than the four agreed in the original contract; it also encompassed 15,488 pages (rather than the 6–7,000 stated in 1879), 178 miles of type, 50,000,000 words, and provided some 500,000 definitions. Had he been alive to see its completion, Müller would undoubtedly have agreed that the *OED* was, precisely as he had desired (Müller 1878), 'no unworthy rival' to the work of Grimm and Émile Littré—specially since the *Deutsches Wörterbuch* still remained incomplete.[18] His early confidence in its financial success, on the other hand, would prove entirely

[18] Publication of Émile Littré's *Dictionnaire de la Langue Française* began in 1863 and was completed ten years later. The *Wörterbuch* would not be completed until 1960.

misplaced. Even by 1914, the dictionary involved 'a dead loss of some £100,000' (MP/10/7/14). By 1928, this had risen to £300,000.

10.5 'A NEW GARMENT THROUGHOUT'

The decades expended upon the first edition of the *OED* saw the painstaking evolution of one of the great works of modern scholarship. Trench's early insistence that the dictionary should be a 'new garment throughout' remained at the heart of its originality. Where earlier lexicographers had been content to accept the authority of their predecessors in including, say, entries for words such as *abacot* ('a Cap of State, made like a double Crown, worn anciently by the Kings of England', as Nathaniel Bailey had stated in his *Universal Etymological English Dictionary* of 1721), the 'patient induction' of facts which Murray advocated (MP/JAHM/83) led to some striking reassessments. *Abacot*, a word given in the desiderata accompanying Murray's first *Appeal*, proved to be a mistranscription of *bycoket*, a different word entirely (even if one which did legitimately signify 'a cap or headdress'). *Adventine*—a misprint for *adventive* ('an immigrant, a sojourner')—had appeared as an independent entry in Johnson and a range of other dictionaries. This produced another necessary corrective in the *OED*, as did the entry for *compasture*. Defined by Bailey as 'large Tracts of Pastures or Pasture Grounds, lying together', the word was, however, properly *composture*. It signified 'compost, manure', as in its use in Shakespeare's *Timon of Athens* ('The Earth's a Theefe, That feeds and breeds by a composture stolne From gen'rall excrement') from where the original mistranscription—and misassignment of sense—had arisen.

The identification of 'ghost-words' of this kind (a term coined by Skeat (1886: 350–74)) manifested the value of the 'original work' for the dictionary (MP/24/6/86). Nevertheless, the research which underpinned discoveries of this kind was, as Murray acknowledged, both time-consuming and unpredictable. Murray's extant letters record countless quests for hitherto unknown information—in August 1881 he wrote to try and verify the history of *anaconda*, in October 1884 he was preoccupied by *augmentation*, in February 1889 by *chorograph*; *collocate* and *collocation* (in the legal sense) were the subject of a number of letters in 1890. This represents a tiny fraction of the correspondence despatched on a daily basis in order to elicit the information on which the dictionary was based. 'It pleases me, at any practicable amount of work, to get at the facts, and force them to yield their secret', Murray confessed (MP/24/12/04). Letters were sent to 'astronomers, mathematicians, geologists, zoologists, botanists, chemists, lawyers, historians, theologians, [and] philosophers' (MP/JAHM/1912); Murray's early search for specific details about *anaconda*, for example, originally written to James Britten, was passed on to the British Museum Zoological department from where Stuart Ridley later replied (MP/31/8/81). A perplexed letter from the historian Edith Thompson (a volunteer for the dictionary from 1884 until its completion) notes her own uncertainties on *castor* in response to another request from Murray in 1888: 'Neither my father nor I know *castor* in the sense wanted. In fact, we cannot remember that we ever called those wart-like things on a horse's legs by any name. As they are of no practical use, & (as far as I know) are not subject to disease, one may live one's life without having occasion to think of or mention them' (MP/23/3/88).

For the dictionary, however, such items had to be named and in turn equipped with a full sense-history, etymology, and pronunciation. Endeavours of this kind, with their painstaking concern for detail and accuracy, characterized the *OED*. Entries such as those for *penny* and *parson* were, Murray stated, 'masterpieces of patient industry and constructive genius', involving the slow piecing together of disparate facts and historical evidence (MP/JAHM/96). For Oxford University Press, however, it was conversely all too clear that they also slowed down progress in terms of publication, and actively increased the costs of production. 'The work is *wanted* by students *now*', Murray was informed in 1887; 'The Delegates are as fully impressed as it is possible to be with the necessity of keeping up to the highest standard of *quality* and accuracy; still; they beg you to consider... that it would be in vain if the pursuit of an unattainable standard in particular minutiae were to end in the non-completion of the dictionary' (MP/31/1/87).

10.5.1 *Pioneers*

The pressures to complete the dictionary led to the appointment of a second editor, Henry Bradley, in 1888, and a third editor, William Craigie, who was appointed in 1901 after having worked for four years as a member of Bradley's staff; a fourth editor, Charles Onions, was appointed in 1914 (after almost twenty years of working on the dictionary). Each editor was responsible for separate fascicles, aided by his own teams of assistants, and by a set of volunteer sub-editors, readers, and critical readers who made their own comments on the proofs. In early 1910, for example, Murray worked at completing P, Bradley continued to make his way through S, and Craigie was at work on the final section of R. The dictionary ultimately attained a regularity of appearance with which the Delegates had to be satisfied.

The question of what precisely was to be 'attainable' (in time, scale, as well as finances) in a dictionary such as the *OED* nevertheless remained problematic, leading to a number of conflicts between dictionary and Delegates on the limits of inclusion. The image of the 'ideal dictionary' had inspired both Murray and Trench, together with the desire to translate this into practice in terms of modern linguistic scholarship and scientific principles. Murray rightly saw himself as a pioneer. 'I am absolutely a pioneer; nobody exc[ept] my predecessors in specimens of the Dict^{y}. has yet tried to trace out historically the sense-development of English words', he had written to Sweet in 1882: '. . . I shall have to do the best I can at defining probably 80,000 words that I never knew or used or saw before' (MP/29/3/82). This pioneering status is, for instance, succinctly confirmed by the terminology which Murray needed to create as he began his work as editor. 'One of the commonest phenomena in the history of English words is the dropping of an initial toneless vowel', he noted, adding that this process currently lacked any designation in English. 'We want a name for this phonetic phenomenon, and especially a descriptive adjective for these shortened forms' (MP/30/2/81: 39). He was forced to settle on his own coinages of *aphesis* and *aphetic* (the terms still used for these phenomena). Likewise no precedents existed for terms such as *back-formation* and *nonce word*. 'An *appropriate* English name is greatly wanted for the latter', Murray added, pointing out that French possessed *mot d'occasion*, which signified exactly the sense required.

Etymology too was part of the 'untrodden forest' in which he saw himself working. 'One does not look in Johnson for Etymology, any more than in 18th c. writers for biology or electricity. Etymology began about 1850 in England', Murray declared (MP/20/12/06). The science of philology, as Wedgwood had early indicated, brought incalculable advantages to the historical record, resolving traditional uncertainties about the origin of words such as *hurricane* and *Huguenot*, or *caterpillar* and *betwixt*. Even if etymologies in Johnson possessed a certain charm, they could also be inconclusive or even, as Wedgwood had pointed out on Johnson's entry for *curmudgeon* (see 10.1.1.), downright wrong. Johnson's *Dictionary* merely makes a tentative guess at the etymology of *bustle* (v.): 'perhaps from *busy*'. Murray's entry in the *OED* provided seven variant forms and probed its origin in Middle English, its links to *buskle* (in the sense 'To agitate, shake, toss'), and its debt to possible cognate forms in Old Icelandic. Letters between Bradley and Murray on words such as *battels* and *bullion* record the slow search for resolution of etymological cruces. European scholars such as Eduard Seivers also added their own detailed annotations to the proofs in this context, as did Walter Skeat (whose *Etymological Dictionary* was published in 1882). The 'combined action' advocated by Trench (1860: 70) remained fully in evidence.

The representation of pronunciation likewise gained an entirely new format; the complex numerical diacritics and respellings devised by John Walker and

Thomas Sheridan in their pronouncing dictionaries of the eighteenth century (replicated in various ways over the nineteenth) were jettisoned. A new—and descriptive—system was devised, intended to represent 'the actual variety of existing English usage' rather than encode a normative ideal. The question of an appropriate mode of transcription remained a major concern in the early 1880s, as Murray reported to the Philological Society (1881: 268). Again he appealed to the sense of collective endeavour: 'I should be very glad . . . to be helped to a solution of the best mode of marking the pronunciation; the prospect of doing this by any mode of practically reformed spelling seems to recede before me'.

While personal predilections could at times still intervene, the overarching tenor of the dictionary was one of intended neutrality. As Ellis had indicated to Murray in 1883, while he—and no doubt Murray himself—disliked new words such as *reliable*, 'there is no doubt it is used' (MP/5/1/83). As such, it had to be included. This encapsulated the guiding premise of the *OED*, precisely in line with Trench's separation of the roles of historian and critic for the lexicographer, and the status of the dictionary as impartial inventory. As a result, if the critic occasionally makes his presence felt in entries for words such as *enthuse* (condemned by Bradley as 'an ignorant back-formation from *enthusiasm*') and *enormity* (where Bradley resisted change in progress in the form of the newer meaning 'Excess in magnitude; hugeness, vastness'),[19] it is the historian who dominates in the scrupulous—and objective—editing of countless other words, carefully defusing the language attitudes which informed more popular works on language. While Alford in *A Plea for the Queen's English* (1864: 109) hence condemned the nineteenth-century coinage of *talented* as a 'newspaper word' which was 'about as bad as possible', the *OED* impartially engaged with historical development and the realities of usage, locating its first use in 1827 (in Bulwer Lytton's *Falkland*). Samuel Taylor Coleridge's prescriptive sensibilities on this matter ('I regret to see that vile and barbarous vocable *talented*, stealing out of the newspapers into the leading reviews and most respectable publications of the day') were moreover deftly inserted as empirical evidence for the usage and incontestable status of the word.

10.6 PROOF AND PROCESS

This meticulous attention to citational evidence (and its rightful interpretation) was another factor which underpinned the slow evolution of the dictionary. The

[19] See further Mugglestone (2002a: 189–206) and Mugglestone (2005: 143–78).

quotations for entries such as *silly* spanned twelve centuries; the entry for *set* occupied over eighteen pages, anatomizing 154 sense-divisions and 83 phrasal combinations such as *to set off*. The citations for *wit*, edited by Craigie in 1928, began with *Beowulf* and ended with the Prime Minister, Stanley Baldwin, writing in the *Morning Post* in 1926 ('Men ... who ... had formed his Majesty's Government ... and who had the wit to understand what the challenge meant'). While the Delegates made repeated attempts to tether the dictionary to a scale based on Webster's 1864 *Dictionary* (initially on a basis of 1 page of Webster to 6 of the *OED*, though this was later relaxed to a ratio of *c*.1 : 8), in practice the dictionary would regularly exceed all formal limits placed on it. A ratio of 1 : 11 was, for example, in evidence in October 1900; Craigie temporarily moved to a scale of 1 : 19 in 1902. Trench's 'inventory', while not being realized in entirety, remained an active principle. Indeed, in some respects, the dictionary deliberately moved beyond what Trench had contemplated. The diction of science and technology, was, for instance, proscribed by Trench ('purely technical words ... are not for the most part, except by an abuse of language, words at all, but signs') (1860: 57–8) and formally excluded from the 'Main Dictionary' in the 1859 *Proposal*. By 1880, Murray was instead asking readers to 'devote themselves to the examination of scientific and technical books, and special treatises of any description' (1880: 9). His self-professed status as a scientist of language—and his insistence on the 'scientific spirit' of the nineteenth century which, to his mind, had 'rendered [the *OED*] possible' (1900: 51)—served to make these early restrictions untenable. The discourses of Darwinism and evolution, of engineering and chemistry, and of the wide-ranging discovery processes of the nineteenth and early twentieth centuries are all represented in the published text (even if the inclusion of vocabulary of this kind was perhaps ultimately less extensive than that once drafted in the extant proofs).[20]

The crafting of the dictionary took place slowly, in a pre-computer age. Words were carefully anatomized into their senses which were, in turn, ordered in terms of their historical development; at each stage, dated citations provided empirical evidence of usage through time (see Fig. 10.1). While volunteer sub-editors provided provisional arrangements (and tentative definitions) for each entry, the whole could be cast aside and redone once the material arrived with the editor of the fascicle in question. Drafted in longhand, the dictionary was, as we have seen, often set into type only to see the process of revision begin again. The extant proofs and revises of the first edition therefore perhaps reveal with greatest clarity the real

[20] Mugglestone (2005: 110–42) presents a detailed examination of the challenges faced by the *OED* in attempting to record the language of science and technology.

challenges involved in making the *OED*, readily illustrating the conditions of temporality which, much to the Delegates' frustration, characterized the ongoing process of composition and critical reassessment. The unpredictability of the material sent in to the dictionary was an important part of this; entries which appeared to have attained their final form could suddenly be disrupted by the arrival of a new citation confirming an earlier use (and hence, as in Trench's original model, an earlier date for the 'birth' of a given word or meaning). This can be seen with *grotesquerie* which, given as a late nineteenth-century coinage in the first proof, unexpectedly gained a 1654 quotation from Roger Orrery's *Parthenissa* which appears as a hand-written addition in proof (duly being incorporated in subsequent versions of the text). *Linnet-hole* (a specialized term in glass-making) was another late revision of this kind, a newly arrived citation being sent to the printers on a separate memorandum by Bradley on 4 June 1902. Its importance, however, meant that it had to be included, not least because it supplied a corrected reading which proved the first element of the word to be a variant of *lunette* (in the earlier proofs, it had been provisionally defined as 'a hole connecting the glass-making furnace with the arch'). Still more critically, this new information provided an antedating of over two hundred years, locating first usage in 1662 (rather than 1875).

Historical lexicography (and the *OED*'s own history, not least in terms of the contributions of volunteer readers) therefore frequently imposed its own imperatives upon the writing—and rewriting—of the text. Evidence on unrecorded items of lexis could appear at the last minute, necessitating inclusion (and occasionally a complex process of symbiosis as other elements were excised in order to accommodate them). Words such as *glossomachiall* ('given to wordy strife') and *goosified* ('affected with "goose-flesh" '), a nonce-word used by J. H. Newman, first appear as hand-written annotations in the margins of the proofs; both represent this last-minute gathering of hitherto entirely unknown words. Yet, in terms of the published inventory, gain could not always exist without loss. Even for a work such as the *OED*, space was finite, as Murray and his co-editors were often reminded; for pragmatic reasons alone, the dictionary could not in reality encompass all words or all possible citations. As Murray made explicit in the 'General Explanations' of the *OED* (1888: p. v), even if 'Nature' had failed to draw a neat dividing line around the language, one had to be imposed by the lexicographer. As a result, it was comprehensiveness—albeit on a hitherto inconceivable scale—rather than Trench's *Lexicon totius Anglicatitis*, which best characterized the *OED*. Words such as *lunching*, *limeade*, *glou-glou* ('the sound made by a liquid when being poured out of a bottle', used in *Good Words* in 1883), *lericompoop* (a verb with the meaning 'to hoax' or 'delude' used by the poet and dramatist, Thomas D'Urfey (1653–1723)), *landlord* (used as a verb), *landscaping*, as well as *lexicographing* ('the art of making dictionaries') were, for a variety of reasons, all excised, together with many others, during the process of making the dictionary.[21] If the rhetoric of completeness could remain ('[the dictionary] seeks . . . to record every word that has been used in the language for the last 800 years', as Murray affirmed in his Romanes lecture (1900: 47)), behind-the-scenes compression and adjustment came at times to offer an alternative—if necessary—reality. 'One must contrive to end near the bottom of the second p[age] of a leaf, and that requires usually much measuring, adjusting, contracting & expanding', as Murray explained to Henry Hucks Gibbs, one of the most stalwart volunteers on the dictionary (OED/EP/ALD/1/2.i.). The drafted entries for countless words, as well as many thousands of citations (particularly from popular sources of evidence) as originally given in the proofs, were all casualties in this inevitable process of contraction. Other words—particularly those denoting aspects of human sexuality, anatomy, and contraception—were deemed unacceptable in a wider cultural sense. Here the inventory was deliberately kept in check, as in the exclusion of *cunt*. Where senses which challenged decorum were included, they were often proscribed via morally weighted definitions such as 'the action or practice of self-abuse' (for *masturbation*) or 'A woman who practices unnatural vice with other women' (*tribade*). 'Of women: The offering of the body to indiscriminate lewdness for hire') states the definition of *prostitution* in *OED1* (see Mugglestone 2007).

10.6.1 *The gentle art of lexicography*

The extant proofs can therefore often act as a compelling witness to this 'redrawing' of the lexicographic line—for words, senses, and citations—in a variety of ways. They also illustrate with particular clarity other important aspects of the writing of the dictionary. The art of definition regularly imposed its own challenges throughout the making of the *OED*. The apparently watertight clarities of the published text were, as the various drafts of the fascicles confirm, often achieved only by means of a cumulative process of revision. It was, for instance, at proof stage that the initially verbose definition of *length* ('The quality of having considerable longitudinal extent') was subject to renewed scrutiny, being rewritten by Bradley to provide the more succinct 'The quality [or] fact of being short; opposed to shortness'. The ambiguities of *locative* ('pertaining to the location of the position of land by means of some object') were likewise resolved only in the second revise when a new form of words ('Serving to locate or fix the position of something') appeared as an annotation in the adjacent margin. Similar was

[21] See Mugglestone (2005: 70–109) for a detailed discussion of this process.

German, for which critical rephrasing continued until the very final stages of production. The undeniably cryptic 'Of a cousin: That has a parent who is own brother or sister to the parent of another person' (originally given for sense 2 of this word) was displaced by a definition which came much closer to the required sense.[22] As here, rephrasing and the art of definition was an active process which could continue almost until the moment of publication.

Other aspects of the proofs illustrate the unremitting attention to detail which also featured in the making of the *OED*. Tracing the historical record was far from easy. The definition of *gimbal*, for example, initially appeared with a critical confusion of *horizontal* and *vertical*. 'A contrivance by means of which articles for use at sea (esp. the compass and the chronometer) are suspended so as to keep a vertical position', the original definition proclaimed. 'A compass is in a horizontal position', Walker Skeat emended in the margin, obviating a similar error being perpetuated in the published text. Similar was *gliriform*. Its first sense ('Resembling a dormouse in shape') was apparently unexceptionable as well as fully supported by the accompanying, and eminently scientific, quotation ('The masseter in this gliriform Marsupial is single'). The definition given in proof to its second sense ('Resembling the teeth of a dormouse') was, however, seriously awry. Henry Hucks Gibbs in his role as critical reader corrected the self-evident confusion of both sense and interpretation. 'The marsupian does not "resemble the teeth of a dormouse"', he stressed in the adjacent margin (even if 'the masseter resembles a certain muscle of the beast'). The sense duly disappeared, leaving no trace in the entry as finally published.[23] As here, the comments of critical readers punctuate the drafted text, aiding in the process of critical composition and eliminating infelicities by which *ground-floor* was (at least at first) erroneously defined as 'The lowest set of rooms in a building, having their floors more or less level with the ground outside' (a sense countered by Gibbs in the marginal comment that 'The basement rooms are lower'). A revised definition as 'The floor in a building which is more or less on a level with the ground outside' appeared in the published text. Similarly problematic was Bradley's original definition of *greasy-pole* (as 'A pole rubbed with grease to make it harder to climb or cling onto') which, as Murray pointed out, inadvertently managed to suggest that 'people were so keen on climbing poles that they had to be kept at a

[22] 'Closely akin' ... 'That is the child of a 'german' brother or sister of either of (one's) parents; = 'first' or 'own' (cousin). *Obs.* exc. in COUSIN-GERMAN'.

[23] For examples of similar revisions, see Mugglestone (2005: 57–64). Interestingly, a further note on the proofs (in Bradley's hand) states that the erroneous sense of *gliriform* had been taken from the *Century* dictionary. As always, it was the 'original work' vaunted by Murray which proved the best course.

distance by the use of grease'. Again, the published text was to gain in both explicitness and precision: 'a pole rubbed with grease to make it harder to climb or walk upon (commonly used as an object of diversion at fairs or village sports).

Words such as *garrot* and *garrub* (for which definition was entirely absent in the early proofs) further illustrate the difficulties of undertaking a work for which no precedents existed in English. '? Definition & origin', Skeat prompted for both in the margin of the relevant proofs. Definitions were derived by a process of inductive methodology, yet the accompanying quotations for these entries ('For the garrott: plucke away the flesh that is dead with a sharpe instrument'; 'There is Silk Romals, there is Romals Garrub and Cotton Romals... The Garrub is the most deceitful of any, for they for the generality wear like Dirt')[24] reveal just how problematic induction of this kind could be. Skeat likewise contested the opacity of the only definition which (at proof stage) Bradley had been able to devise for *Germantown* (as 'Some kind of vehicle'). 'Can we not learn what?', Skeat demanded in the margin. Again induction could only go so far (though newly imitated quests for information in this instance led to the much-improved 'A one-horse covered vehicle used in country districts: more fully **Germantown wagon**' by the time the text was published). Unwarranted bias (and an uneasy slippage between the roles of historian and critic) could also be cause for comment. Skeat rightly queried the drafted definition for *gitano* as 'A gypsy fellow'. 'Why *fellow*?', Skeat demanded; 'why not "a nobleman of the gypsy persuasion?"' The definition was revised to read 'a male (Spanish) gypsy'.[25]

When it came to definition, however, even common words could present problems. *Handsome*, for instance, perplexed Murray for weeks. It 'is a desperately difficult word to grasp', he wrote to another valued critical reader; 'I find it impossible to formulate the differences between current & many obsolete senses'. Having consulted his assistants, Murray moreover found that 'we none of us quite agree in our notion of the actual sense of "handsome" '. 'If you can send us a definition it will be lovingly considered', he added (OED/MISC/13/17). As here, semantic resolution relied not merely on the presence or absence of the relevant linguistic facts but on the potentially fraught issues of interpretation.

Historicism suggests the seamless translation of the historical record to the printed page (as in Passow's ideal that each word should 'tell its own story'). Nevertheless, the role of the lexicographer as the critical interface between the raw information at the dictionary's disposal and the means by which it was to be

[24] These derive respectively from Richard Surflet's *Maison Rustique, or the Countrie Farme* (as augmented in G. Markham in 1616) and J. F.'s *The Merchant's Ware-House Laid Open* (1696). *Garrub* remained without definition in the published dictionary.

[25] For other examples of bias and ideology in *OED1*, see Mugglestone (2005: 163–8).

presented necessarily intervenes in a variety of ways. Labelling is a case in point. Bradley, for example, had noted that *glister* ('to sparkle; to glitter') was obsolete; Gibbs, surveying Bradley's evidence in proof, countered that he 'would certainly have used it without conscious reminiscence'. In a parallel manner, Bradley labelled *gripe* ('a ditch') as 'dialectal' only to have it firmly deleted when Gibbs read the proofs. 'In common use everywhere', Gibbs added in justification.[26] Editors were equally free to reassess their own earlier decisions so that Bradley, for example, assigned in proof the designation of *nonce-word* to Thackeray's use of *giftling* ('a little gift')—a sense previously left unmarked. A similar process can be detected for *grudgekin* ('a little grudge') which, again used by Thackeray, was reassigned as a *nonce-word* rather than merely *rare* (the status it had previously had in the proofs).[27] Even in their role as part of the historical record, the facts could, in each case, prompt different—and conflicting—interpretations at different points of the text's evolution.

Perhaps the clearest illustrations of the difficulty involved in crafting the historical record of English are revealed by those instances in which one of the editors inadvertently used a given word in drafting a definition which, according to the dictionary's own authority, had formally been declared obsolete. Bradley, for example, defined *grievesomeness* as 'the quality or condition of being griefsome'. Yet the earlier entry for *griefsome* had located the obsolescence of the word in the mid-seventeenth century. Its apparent resurrection two centuries later by an editor of the dictionary clearly had to be rectified (not least given Trench's canonical strictures on the need to ascertain as accurately as possible the date of a word's death). Here the definition of *grievesomeness* was cut and the temporal—and linguistic—anomalies eliminated. Similar was *fray* which, for Murray, was the ordinary word for the action of scaring away birds. As he noted, he had therefore naturally used it to define *huff* (as 'to fray') in a sense which now appears as 'to frighten or scare away'. In an earlier fascicle, however, *fray* had already been labelled *obsolete* by Bradley, a statement markedly at odds with Murray's newly drafted definition of *huff*. While the relevant sense of *huff* was swiftly rewritten, the underlying conflicts of evidence and explication remain. In the later nineteenth century, was *fray* obsolete (as Bradley thought) or current, as in Murray's own usage in a now cancelled section of the dictionary?[28]

'How can there be a true History, when we see no Man living is able to write truly the History of the last Week?', Sir William Belford demanded in Thomas Shadwell's play *The Squire of Alsatia* (a quotation tellingly included

[26] Bradley, as editor, had the last word. *Gripe* retained its regional designation in the published text and Gibbs's emendations were disregarded.

[27] For the flux of labels and (re)interpretation at this stage, see also Mugglestone (2000: 27–36).

[28] See Mugglestone (2002a: 200).

under the *OED*'s own entry for *history*). In the flux of labels, pronunciation, or meanings, the proofs act as a compelling witness to the difficulty—and at times near-impossibility—of determining the 'true history' of words and their development. Judgement, after all, is an inevitable part of the lexicographic process. As a result, while the descriptivism of the *OED* functioned as a salient part of its *raison d'être*, judgements, and conflicting judgements—still manifest on the extant proofs—record the process of a complex set of decisions about labelling, pronunciation, definition, and etymology, or the number of senses any word should rightly possess. *Greatness*, for example, entered with the first revise with eight senses, and ended with six; deletions and revisions in Bradley's hand litter the surviving draft. Acts of interpretation, and reinterpretation, framed the day-to-day editing of the dictionary in the search to establish the facts of the historical record (and the individual editor's sense of their rightful presentation). The insights afforded by the proofs into the reality of these working processes therefore remain of critical importance for understanding the complex challenges of each and every entry in the first edition of the dictionary.

10.7 DEFICIENCIES ONCE MORE

'This year, whatever else it may be, is the Year of the Dictionary', wrote C. T. Onions in *The Times* (1928: 10) in an article celebrating the completion of the *OED*. The publication of the final part of the *OED* on 19 April 1928 was an event of 'outstanding importance to all who speak or use or understand the English language and to philologists the world over', *The Times* had extolled; it was the end of a 'story... of unremitting labour and unflagging concentration, consuming the best energies not of one man but of many during the best years of their lives' ('The Oxford English Dictionary' 1928: 11). This litany of praise was widely endorsed: it was 'a great national dictionary', the *Guardian* wrote in early March. It will 'rank in the world of philology as a unique monument to British learning and enterprise', King George V affirmed on being presented with the dictionary's final part, 'beautifully and specially bound for the king's acceptance' ('The King's Congratulations' 1928: 73). Yet, as the *Guardian* perceptively added some months later, 'Truly our dictionary-makers are toilers at a Sisyphean task—just as soon as they have got "Z" neatly caged an enlarged and adipose "A" has broken loose at the other end of the menagerie' (OED/MISC/60/1/2). Even in the early days of the dictionary, correspondents had written to Murray commenting on, say, the inadvertent omission of *bondmaid* or the decision not to include *bounder*.[29] Other letters had commented on the absence of *anaerobic*, *ansire*, and *nitrary* (among many other perceived gaps). As Murray acknowledged, the material for the dictionary could, in practice, have filled a hundred volumes; only the need to filter and reduce had kept it within publishable limits. Nevertheless, while the main dictionary slowly came into being, material for a *Supplement* was being filed away, stored for another and future publication. 'The collection and arrangement of material for the Supplement . . . steadily flows on', Murray stated at the Philological Society's Annual Dictionary Evening in 1908. Seven years later, he commented on the '*shelves* of material' which had already accumulated. After Murray's death in 1915, this pattern of research continued—the crafting of new and hitherto unpublished sections of the alphabet took place alongside the gathering of material on words and senses which, for whatever reason, had been omitted, or which had themselves become part of the shifts of history. The dictionary's own lengthy gestation provided appropriate illustration of the import of the historical principles on which it had been founded; definitions given for words such as *aeronaut* ('one . . . who makes balloon ascents') or *aerodynamic* ('pertaining to the forces of gases in motion') which appeared in the first fascicle of 1884 were strikingly out of date by the time the dictionary was completed. *Aviation* (and related words) were entirely absent. 'The whole terminology of aeroplanes and aeronautics is wanting', Murray had noted (MP/JAHM/1912). The entries in C had, by virtue of history itself, revealed nothing of the *cinema* or *cinematograph*. Entries such as *projectile* further revealed the divide which time had wrought; the *OED*'s statement that these were fired from cannons no longer matched the realities of usage introduced in the First World War. 'New knowledge accumulates, and new Editors enter on the task of the old, with advantages due not to themselves, but to time', Murray had written in the early days of the first edition (MP/JAHM/1883). By 1928, another new era for the dictionary had begun.

REFERENCES

Unpublished Sources

Murray Papers, Bodleian Library, Oxford
MP/6/4/76. W. W. Skeat to J. A. H. Murray, 6 April 1876.
MP/20/4/77. H. Sweet to B. Price, 20 April 1877.

[29] Murray regarded this as 'undergraduate slang', deciding that it should not be included in the first edition of the *OED*. See Mugglestone (2002b: 10 n).

MP/25/11/78. J. A. H. Murray to B. Price, 25 November 1878.
MP/10/5/79. J. A. H. Murray to F. J. Furnivall, 10 May 1879.
MP/3/11/80. F. J. Furnivall to J. A. H. Murray, 3 November 1880.
MP/n.d./12/80. Draft of a letter from J. A. H. Murray to Mrs H. Pott, December 1880.
MP/8/1/81. H. Nicol to J. A. H. Murray, 8 January 1881.
MP/JAHM/[?5]/81. Ms draft of letter by J. A. H. Murray [? to H. H. Gibbs].
MS/30/2/81. Annotated proof of 'Philological Society's Dictionary Wants'.
MP/31/8/81. S. Ridley to J. Britten, 31 August 1881.
MP/12/2/82. J. A. H. Murray to H. H. Gibbs, 12 February 1882.
MP/29/3/82. J. A. H. Murray to H. Sweet, 29 March 1882.
MP/19/6/82. J. A. H. Murray to B. Price, 19 June 1882.
MP/JAHM/83. Proof of drafted *Notice of Publication* for *A New English Dictionary on a Historical Basis.* Part 1. A–APO.
MP/5/1/83. A. J. Ellis to J. A. H. Murray, 5 January 1883.
MP/4/10/83. Proof of drafted *Preface to Part I* for *A New English Dictionary on a Historical Basis.* Part 1. A–ANT. [Annotations by J. A. H. Murray].
MP/8/10/83. Proof of drafted *Notice of Publication* for *A New English Dictionary on a Historical Basis.* Part 1. A–ANT.
MP/18/10/83. Proof of *Notice of Publication* of *A New English Dictionary on a Historical Basis.* Part 1. A–ANT.
MP/24/6/86. J. A. H. Murray to P. L. Gell, 24 June 1886.
MP/31/1/87. P. L. Gell to J. A. H. Murray, 31 January 1887.
MP/23/3/88. E. Thompson to J. A. H. Murray, 23 March 1888.
MP/JAHM/96. Ms Notes for Annual Dictionary Evening at the Philological Society.
MP/24/12/04. J. A. H. Murray to E. Arber, 24 December 1904.
MP/20/12/06. J. A. H. Murray to W. Jenkinson, 20 December 1906.
MP/JAHM/1912. Ms Notes for Annual Dictionary Evening at the Philological Society.
MP/10/7/14. I. Bywater to J. A. H. Murray, 10 July 1914.

OED Archives at OUP

OED/EP/ALD/1/2.i. J. A. H. Murray to H. H. Gibbs, 7 December 1900.
OED/MISC/13/17. J. A. H. Murray to F. Hall, 6 April 1897.
OED/MISC/13/24. J. A. H. Murray to F. Hall, 11 April 1899.
OED/MISC/60/1/2. 'Language in the Making', *Manchester Guardian*, 29 December 1928.

11

THE *OED* SUPPLEMENTS

Charlotte Brewer

11.1 FIRST SUPPLEMENT: PUBLICATION, RECEPTION AND EVALUATION

THE necessity for eventual supplementation of the *Oxford English Dictionary* had been recognized in the terms under which the Philological Society handed over the dictionary to Oxford University Press in 1879, and had been kept in view since the publication of the first instalment in 1884. By the 1920s, the lexicographers had amassed 'a collection of closely-packed slips occupying some 75 linear feet of shelving',[1] containing the accretions of fifty years for the letters *A–B*, compared with only five years or so for *X*, *Y*, and *Z*. On the basis of this material, the first *Supplement* was produced relatively swiftly in 1933, along with a re-issue of the parent dictionary (Murray *et al.* 1933). Edited by the two surviving senior members of the previous team, Craigie and Onions, its publication was a chief item on the BBC news and was treated as a major literary event of the day.

The post-Victorian era, together with the enormous social changes wrought by the First World War, the beginnings of social democracy, and many other cultural factors—modernism, increasing exposure to American culture, the development of new sciences and industries—had thrown up vast numbers of new terms. The peculiar fascination of the 1933 *Supplement* seems to have been the reflection in its pages of this crowded and turbulent period of social, political, cultural, and intellectual history. In their Preface, Craigie and Onions made it clear that such social and historical relevance was what they had aimed for, seeking in particular to record the burgeoning volume of technical language relating to both arts and sciences (e.g. 'biochemistry, wireless telegraphy and telephony, mechanical transport, aerial

[1] Preface to *Supplement* in Murray (1933:v).

locomotion, psycho-analysis, the cinema'), and also 'the varied development of colloquial idiom and slang, to which the United States of America have made a large contribution, but in which the British dominions and dependencies have also a conspicuous share'. This topicality was seized on with delight by reviewers, who greeted the *Supplement* with almost universal approval. 'We found this volume of absorbing interest', reported *Notes and Queries* (1934: 51), explaining 'There is a sense in which it may claim to be the most massive, comprehensive, enduring monument in existence of the last eventful thirty years, encompassing the very life of them, which we see, as it were, captured and pinned down in its pages'.

Scientific and technical language on the one hand, and slang and colloquialisms on the other, were the two features picked up by the President of Magdalen College, Oxford, G. S. Gordon, in his address to the guests assembled for *OED*'s celebratory lunch of 21 November 1933. The *Supplement*'s pages contained, he said, 'the whole riotous, "riproarious", linguistic wealth of the industrial, scientific, artistic, literary, and social and colloquial life, not only of England, but of all the English-speaking countries, during the last half-century'.[2] Although the later volumes of the original dictionary had had their fair share of contemporary words, these were buried among many other much older ones, so when readers browsed a typical page of the first edition they would see a preponderance of historical material. The *Supplement* was a different matter altogether. It included a smattering of mid-nineteenth-century and earlier vocabulary, but its pages teemed with more topical and everyday usages, often colourfully colloquial, that had escaped entry to the parent volumes.

It was clear to contemporaries that recent years had seen a 'rapid and luxuriant growth of popular idiom and phraseology', a principal motive being 'impatience with propriety of speech, and the desire to find intentionally undignified substitutes for it' (*Periodical* 1934: 20). Presumably all ages feel the same; what may have made the first thirty-odd years of the twentieth century different from earlier periods was the increasing acceptability of informal language, colloquialism, and slang in printed sources, which had previously censored such usage. This meant that many more spontaneous, up-to-the minute coinages and bouncy informalities were widely published and therefore available for record in the *Supplement*, and they lent its pages an enchanting immediacy and social relevance. It may also be that the appetite for colloquialism had recently increased in classes previously resistant to it. 'Even among persons of riper years', Henry Bradley (who died in 1923) had 'demurely' said, 'there are many to whom ceremonious speech is

[2] *Periodical* 1934: 18; the *Supplement* had antedated *OED1*'s entry for *riproarious* to 1840 (subsequently further antedated, to 1830, in the second *Supplement*).

unwelcome'. 'All ages and classes are in this conspiracy', Gordon believed, and he pointed the finger at American culture, faithfully investigated and recorded for the *Supplement* by Craigie—who had held a chair at Chicago since 1926 and was simultaneously compiling the *Dictionary of American English*—as particularly influential in this respect (→ BAILEY). *The Times* agreed, quoting 'Mr Dooley'—the fictional author of a nationally syndicated newspaper column in the USA—as saying 'When we Americans are done with the English language, it will look as if it had been run over by a musical comedy' (*Periodical* 1934: 20).

It takes only a glance through the pages of the *Supplement* to see Mr Dooley's point. Yet, as Gordon also noted, 'when you examine the culprits, how almost irresistible at any rate the best of them are! They are so frank, so fresh, so Topsy-like, so impudently expressive and near the truth, that it is hard to deny them a place in any honest lexicon of English', even though 'Dr Johnson would doubtless have rejected them all as low, as "not yet refined from the grossness of domestic use"'. Gordon lists some of his favourite Americanisms, many of which have proved long-lived—*graft, O.K., the once-over, dope* (v.), *fool proof,* and *step on the gas.*

Other notable *Supplement* inclusions, scooped by Gordon out of what he described as a 'prodigious lexicographical lucky-bag', were *apache, automobile, cubism, futurism, robot, pacifist, radium, movies, screen, talkies, sabotage, tank, hooligan, broadcasting, loud-speaker, League of Nations, lip-stick, relativity, slimming,* and *psycho-analysis.* An 'odd jumble', he called them, amounting to 'a rude and crude epitome of the very strange generation we belong to or from which we are emerging'. Nevertheless, 'with their definitions and attendant quotations, their approximate birth-dates and genealogies', they were 'perhaps the most fascinating type of history there is'. Many reviewers copied both Gordon and *The Periodical* (1934: 12–14) in simply listing a selection of terms with attached dates (e.g. 1885 *silk, artificial*; 1886 *appendicitis, crook, damfool, gadget, zoom,* etc.).

But how were either editors or reviewers to judge whether such items were comprehensively or appropriately included? Craigie and Onions were well aware of the problem. On the vexed question of inclusion or omission of 'the more esoteric scientific terms' and of foreign words, they admitted that 'it cannot be hoped or pretended that this problem has been solved in every instance with infallible discretion'. They appeared more confident in their treatment of 'temporary or casual uses', which were recognized 'only in so far as they marked stages in the recent history of scientific discovery, invention, or fashion, or illustrated the progress of thought, usage, or custom during the half-century under review'. Criteria for identifying such 'stages' were not revealed.

Papers preserved in the OUP archives witness much discussion, sometimes acrimonious, over what to embrace and what to rule out. Through a combination of variable circumstances, some worthy candidates did not make the grade, for example *putsch*, or *lesbian* (discussed below), while the editors may simply have missed perhaps hundreds of others subsequently entered in the second *Supplement* with evidence dating back well before 1933 (as *snide*, *snoop* (noun), *soap-box* (fig.), *social work(er)*, etc.). Conversely, many less eligible candidates were recorded: linguistic ephemera (as *sosh*, US slang for 'a person having social polish and little else'; *sourceful*, 'acting as a source'; *spadassin*, 'a swordsman'; *spalt*, 'a section of log') that no doubt seemed promising to contemporaries but proved in the longer run less durable. The first *Supplement*'s fiercest critic in this respect was the editor of the second, R. W. Burchfield (see 11.3 below); but such judgements are always more easily made with hindsight.

11.2 BETWEEN SUPPLEMENTS

After what was recognized, with some relief, as a *tour de force*, the publishers hoped to close the *OED* enterprise down. 'It is not thought practicable to provide further supplements', the Secretary to the Press, R. W. Chapman, wrote in May 1933, 'so that we are saying *finis coronat opus* ... the New English Dictionary on Historical Principles does necessarily come to an end, and it may be doubted if such a comprehensive work, attempting to cover the whole vocabulary from the beginnings, can ever again be attempted'.[3] The dictionary staff and operations were broken up and dispersed; unused slips, later counted as 140,000 in all, were packed into storage; and, in 1935, Chapman's Deputy, the New Zealander Kenneth Sisam, wrote to an inquiring correspondent (William Empson, seeking elucidation on how *OED1* had differentiated the senses of complex words, and asking to look through the original slips) to say that 'the reserve material for the *OED* is not now available for consultation, as the work has been closed. Part of it is warehoused in cases and is not easy to get at; some of it was lent to America for use in the new "period" dictionaries that are being undertaken there' (→ ADAMS).[4] Nevertheless, many scholars and others continued to send in information about new words and senses and about omissions or errors in the printed dictionary. This material was filed away and occasionally reviewed: as the archives reveal, up to the mid-1950s the publishers revisited again and again the question whether they should produce a further supplement, or instead undertake a full re-working of the original dictionary and incorporate new words and senses as they did so.

[3] OED/B/3/2/22, 31 May 1933. [4] OED/B/3/2/24, 3 July 1935.

Both Craigie and Onions continued to work on lexicographical projects related to *OED*. Craigie returned from Chicago to Oxfordshire in 1936, on the completion of the *Dictionary of American English*, to pursue his Icelandic dictionary and the *Dictionary of the Older Scottish Tongue*, while Onions toiled away for OUP on successive editions of the *Shorter Oxford English Dictionary* and on his long-gestated etymological dictionary (completed posthumously in 1966). Albeit desultorily, Craigie in particular continued to amass material for the main dictionary, reporting in 1945 to Sisam, now Secretary to the Press, that he had 'taken stock of the supplementary material to *OED* which I now have in hand', for which he estimated there were altogether 13,000 slips by him and 4,000 by St Vincent Troubridge (many relating to theatre).[5] A third significant contributor, H. E. G. Rope of Shrewsbury—who had joined the *OED* in summer 1903—was also steadily at work, while R. W. Chapman was also recording quotations for use in a future revision or supplement to the original dictionary, despite his earlier view (Burchfield 1961: 37 n.8).

What was the Press to do with this? An important consideration was the relationship between the *OED*, which had stood still since 1933, and the subsidiary Oxford dictionaries. By the early 1950s, these dependent offshoots—the *Shorter*, *Concise*, and *Pocket*—had all prospered and been re-edited, mostly out-of-house. While these dictionaries did their best to register what Chapman (1946) called 'an Elizabethan riot of verbal invention', inspired once more by war and by enormous changes in culture and society, it was extraordinarily difficult for them to keep up with (in Chapman's words again, using terms notorious from reviews of the 1933 *Supplement*) the 'riproarious macédoine' of new vocabulary pouring into the language, given the absence of properly funded and directed lexical research conducted by trained lexicographers in Oxford.

This factor—the need to update the *OED* in order to breathe new life into the lesser dictionaries, thus staving off competition from rival publishing houses such as Merriam-Webster in the US, whose dictionary departments (→ LANDAN) were better resourced—was brought into sharp focus by the second main reason the publishers had to rethink the question of revision. Stocks of the 1933 reprinting of the *OED* were running dangerously low, and, by 1954, had dropped under 3,000. It would soon become necessary to undertake the massive and expensive job of reprinting. By then—1962, perhaps—the first edition of the dictionary would look unequivocally out of date. Should the publishers undertake a wholesale revision? Or supplement the 1933 *Supplement*? In favour of the first plan was the knowledge, increasingly borne in on them as time went on, that the first *OED* had

[5] OUP/BoxOP1713/PB/ED/012869, 17 January 1945.

many defects, or, as Onions put it to them, 'hosts of wrong definitions, wrong datings, and wrong crossreferences'.[6] But in favour of the second plan was the cost of a complete revision, which, if adequate, would require the Press to invest phenomenal quantities of time, labour, and money.

The advice of Sisam was crucial. Writing to the Press from retirement in the Scilly Isles, he was clear that wholesale revision would be institutional suicide.[7] He strongly urged supplementation, conducted under rigorous management by the Press, and, from 1955 onwards, the publishers undertook the search for an editor of a second *Supplement*. Several candidates were identified but only one stayed the course: Robert W. Burchfield, who was, in his own words, a member of 'the New Zealand mafia', a lecturer in English language at Christ Church College who had originally come to Onions' college, Magdalen, on a Rhodes Scholarship in 1949. Onions and other sponsors—chiefly the medievalist Norman Davis, another New Zealander who had earlier turned down the job—recommended him to the Press, and he took up his appointment in 1957 (Brewer 2007: ch. 5).

11.3 SECOND SUPPLEMENT: INITIAL STAGES

'My recollection of the time', Burchfield wrote later (in terms perhaps recalling Murray's description of himself and his assistants as colonizing 'pioneers, pushing ... experimentally through an untrodden forest, where no white man's axe has been before us'), 'is that I felt like a pioneer arriving in a new colony and finding a log cabin to house me but no other resource except a rather superior Man Friday [the temporary editor R. C. Goffin] to assist me' (Burchfield 1984: 16; Murray 1882–84: 509). On his first day, he 'reported to the Oxford University Press', expecting to be told 'how to go about compiling a large-scale dictionary on historical principles. It quickly dawned on me that I would simply need to organize the whole project myself from scratch. There were no courses, no conferences, no seminars, no handbooks or manuals of lexicography'. So Burchfield started instead by reading through his copy of *The Times*, and systematically comparing its entire contents, from first to last page, against the parent dictionary and its *Supplement*. 'The results', he found, 'were a revelation':

[6] SOED/1951/14/3, 14 March 1951.

[7] OUP/BoxOP1713/PB/ED/012869, memorandum entitled 'September 1952'.

> The *OED* was shown at once to be a product of the Victorian and Edwardian period, and not up-to-date at all. The reigns of George V and George VI had witnessed wars, scientific discoveries, and social changes of immense importance, but these were very poorly reflected in the *OED* and its 1933 *Supplement*: *body-line bowling*, *Bolshevism*, *questionnaire*, and such unmissable terms apart ... the language that had come into being in the period since 1879 (when J. A. H. Murray undertook the *OED*) had been collected and dealt with only in the manner of a Sunday painter. Subject for subject, word class for word class, the first *OED* Supplement of 1933 was a riffraff assemblage of casual items, in no way worthy of the magnificent monument to which it formed an extension (1989: 190–1).

To understand the force of this damning criticism, one needs to bear in mind *OED*'s own definition of *riff-raff* (*s.v. riff-raff*[1]3b): 'Of things: Worthless, trashy'. Burchfield was the scholar best placed to judge the work of his predecessors, but how would he ensure that the second *Supplement* would provide a better record of contemporary usage than the first?

In some respects, Burchfield exaggerated the absence of any form of lexicographical or institutional guidance. Sisam had corresponded regularly with the publishers over plans for the new dictionary, and many papers were stored in the OUP files detailing his recommendations on timescale, choice of vocabulary, use of volunteers and assistants, and office systems (in particular, the importance of restraining assistants from 'endless research' in Bodley). To make sure Burchfield fully absorbed this advice, Davin packed him off to the Scilly Isles for four days in August 1957 to receive instruction from Sisam in person. Burchfield himself later described Sisam's counsels (1984: 116–17). He was to set himself a time limit of seven years, stick to one volume of about 1,275 pages, base his dictionary on 'the English of educated people in England' (no colonialists), and exclude the terminology of science and technology except for those words which 'could be explained to an intelligent layman'.

One way or another, Burchfield defied all these directives. Inevitably, it proved impossible to keep to either the scale or the timetable proposed. He eventually produced four volumes, totalling 5,732 pages, and completed his work in 1986, nearly thirty years after his visit to Sisam. Part of the delay was due, no doubt, to the difficulties inherent in setting up the new project from scratch, instituting reading and editorial procedures, and devising appropriate criteria for inclusion and exclusion (though in many respects the main lines of procedure were already well established by the parent dictionary). A further cause was the Press's updating its flotilla of smaller dictionaries and centralizing their production in Oxford, in accordance with Sisam's prescription that the 'lesser dictionaries' should suck dry the new material prepared for the *Supplement* 'before it appeared in print as a quarry for competitors' (note 7 above). Although this provided 'funds for the survival of

OUP and its scholarly publishing programme', it siphoned off Burchfield's time and energies and was 'a distraction and encumbrance of indescribable proportions' (Burchfield 1984: 118). The most important delaying factor, however, seems to have been Burchfield's determination to avoid the judgement he himself was to mete out to Craigie and Onions. In this respect, the publication of *Webster's Third New International Dictionary* in 1961 was a highly significant event. As he himself described, 'the sheer quantity of words included in it made it apparent at once that I had seriously underestimated the task of collecting modern English vocabulary wherever it occurred. The whole editorial process had to be delayed—in the event by several years—until my editorial assistants and outside readers had assembled evidence on this majestic scale' (1984: 117).

11.4 ANALYSIS AND EVALUATION

Analysing and evaluating Burchfield's contribution to the *OED* is not a straightforward task. He absorbed most, but not all, of Craigie and Onion's material into his own four volumes, and these were subsequently merged with the first edition of the *OED* to create the second edition (*OED2*).[8] The resulting amalgamation of Burchfield's *Supplement* with *OED1* is electronically searchable both on CD-ROM and online, but its separate components cannot now be systematically distinguished from each other. Electronic investigation of specific categories of vocabulary added or enhanced by Burchfield, or editorial comment, or quotations, attributable to him rather than his predecessors, must therefore be carefully handled if it is to yield reliable information about Burchfield's portion of the *OED* rather than that of his predecessors (or vice versa). As we have seen, Burchfield's job was strictly to update rather than revise the dictionary, and this meant leaving the bulk of existing entries untouched.[9]

[8] Burchfield (1958: 229); criteria and statistics for exclusion of material from the 1933 *Supplement* are nowhere stated.

[9] In an apparently small number of instances, discoverable only through manual comparison of *OED1* with the 1972–86 *Supplement*, Burchfield did incorporate entries covering earlier material (e.g. a quotation dated 1639 for *novel*, 1770 for *tollent*, 1779 for *valedictory*). It is not clear why these slipped in given the enormous number of equally or more deserving candidates and the general policy stated in Vol. 1 (xv): 'It was also decided to exclude, in the main, pre-1820 antedatings of *O.E.D.* words or senses from general English sources, since the systematic collection of such antedatings could not be undertaken at the present time'.

What were Burchfield's editorial policies and what sort of dictionary did they produce? Burchfield himself discussed and reviewed his procedures and practice both in the Prefaces to his four *Supplement* volumes and in numerous articles published elsewhere. Reading these in sequence, along with the archival documents, exposes a number of inconsistencies, no doubt inevitable over the thirty years which he spent on the work. Further equally inevitable inconsistencies appear in the *Supplement* itself, some of which I discuss below. All should be seen in proportion to Burchfield's achievement as a whole. As one of the reviewers of *OED1* observed, 'It must be highly doubtful if any dictionary has received a tithe of the compliments paid to [this dictionary] in the way of errata and addenda', given that the *OED* itself supplies critics 'with their standards and many of their materials' (Brodribb 1928: 277), and the same is also true of the second *Supplement*.

In the Introduction to the first volume of the *Supplement*, under the heading 'Editorial Policy', Burchfield declared, 'Our aim has been first and foremost to ensure that all "common words" (and senses) in British written English of the period 1884 to the present day (of those not already treated in the Dictionary) are included'. He went on to specify the three areas of vocabulary earlier identified by Sisam, namely, literary language, World English, and scientific and technical English, along with a fourth, 'colloquial and coarse expressions referring to sexual and excretory functions'. Whereas it is possible to examine, in some reasonably systematic way, samples of these subsidiary categories of vocabulary (and I shall do so in 11.5–11.8 below), it is scarcely feasible to evaluate Burchfield's success in treating 'all "common words" (and senses)'; the quotation marks round 'common' point to the difficulty of definition and consequently of assessment.

Entry after entry of the vast bulk of the dictionary prepared under Burchfield's hand evidences painstaking research through a massive range of sources, with banks of quotations skilfully analysed to yield lucid, polished, and apt definitions, and meticulous updatings of *OED1* material where appropriate. Unsurprisingly, given the magnitude of his task, it is also comparatively easy to find items which should have been brought up to date and were not. A striking example is the failure in the *A–G* volume, published in 1972, to update *OED1*'s reference to the Conservative Party as 'one of the two great English political parties' (s.v. *conservative*, 2a), the other, evidently, being the Liberal Party (cf. s.v. *liberal*, 5). *Labour Party* fared little better in 1976 (Vol. 2): having been omitted from *OED1*—understandably given that the *l–leisurely* fascicle appeared in 1902—the term was treated by Craigie and Onions in the 1933 *Supplement*, who placed it in the ragbag category of attributive uses of *labour* and provided six quotations dated between 1886 and 1922. Burchfield reproduced their definition, added four more quotations, and kept the term in the same minor position (sandwiched between *labour-pains* and *labour-relations*).[10] Such aberrations appear minor beside the wealth of updated material but are notable nevertheless.[11]

11.5 'A LITERARY INSTRUMENT'?

The treatment of literary vocabulary in a contemporary dictionary of English may seem a relatively minor matter. In the case of the *OED*, the significance of literary words in relation to the lexicon as a whole takes on an entirely different aspect. The first edition had been unproblematically conceived as a repository of great writers, in accordance with the then conventional views expressed by one of its early contributors, G. P. Marsh (1860: 17–18): 'The importance of a permanent literature, of authoritative standards of expression, and, especially, of those great, lasting works of the imagination, which, in all highly-cultivated nations constitute the "*volumes paramount*" of their literature, has been too generally appreciated to require ... argument or illustration'. In this intellectual and cultural climate, the statement on the first page of Volume 1 of *OED* (*A–B*) in 1888, that 'all the great English writers of all ages' were the first port of call for quotations, seemed perfectly natural, and source studies of *OED1* plainly indicate the literary preferences of the first lexicographers (Schäfer 1980; Brewer 2005–).

Very much in the spirit of his predecessors, Burchfield began with a strong sense of the centrality of literature both to language and to the *OED*. Reporting to the Delegates in 1962, five years into editing the *Supplement* and ten years before the first volume appeared, he put 'The main literary works of the period 1930–1960' at the head of his list of sources tackled by readers for the new dictionary. Scientific sources came next, followed by newspapers, 'the main Commonwealth sources', and finally 'as many literary works of the period 1884–1930 as could be managed in the time available'—this last item in order to remedy, so far as might then be possible, the failings of the first *Supplement*.[12] In Burchfield's view, the earlier volume had 'suffered from the defect, in a literary instrument, of not being based on a proper reading of the literary works of the period 1884–1930 ... Kipling, Conrad, Henry James, Shaw, Arnold Bennett, and other writers who flourished after 1890 are hardly represented at all ... and the poets are ignored'. Burchfield preserved to the last this

[10] Burchfield (1987: 18) identified attributive uses of common words as one of the main areas of vocabulary expanded in the Supplement; countless entries with long tails of compound examples attest to his success.

[11] For further 'blackheads on the brow of Nefertiti', see Barnes (1982), Strang (1974, 1977), Baker (1988).

[12] OUP/BoxOP1713/PB/ED/012869, 'OED Supplement: New Edition'.

determination to quote from 'great writers', on occasion expressing a strong sense of embattlement against the destructive practices of 'scholars with shovels intent on burying the linguistic past and most of the literary past and present'. To ignore 'our greatest living writers' left one, he felt, 'looking at a language with one's eyes partly blindfolded' (Vol. 4: x).

Burchfield emphasized many times (e.g. Vol. 1: xiv) his fondness for inclusion of the *hapax legomena* and eccentric usages of major literary writers (Beckett's *athambia*, Joyce's *peccaminous*, Woolf's *scrolloping*, Edith Sitwell's *Martha-coloured*, etc.). Quite how and why these usages (especially *hapax legomena*) contributed to the language is never made clear, though the analysis would be a valuable one. As countless scholars have investigated, literary writers often choose to express themselves by deviating from 'ordinary language' rather than merely exemplifying it; Burchfield's contention that the presence of such usages in his volumes were 'mere golden specks in the whole work' (1989: 12) suggests he saw them as peripheral to general usage rather than influencing it in any substantial way.[13] In the event, several critics complained that the coverage and treatment of literary language was insufficient: Geoffrey Hill, for example, resented the inclusion of words like *tofu* at the expense of adequate treatment of Hopkins's language, in particular the exclusion of *unchancelling*, asking 'is the name of an easily analysable substance which has appeared on a million menus more real than a word, peculiarly resistant to analysis, which has lodged itself in a few thousands of minds?' (Hill 1989: 414). Such a question indicates the impossible burden of expectation that the *OED* has to bear. It would be out of the question to provide a comprehensive record of the usage of all literary writers (or even the most distinguished); to attempt to do so at the cost of documenting the general lexicon would be regarded by many, perhaps most, users as unacceptable.

Burchfield also wrote that 'the entire works of writers like Eliot, Auden, Joyce, Lawrence, and many others, needed to be indexed in the manner that the readers of sources drawn on for the *OED* had indexed the works of Chaucer, Malory, Marlowe, Shakespeare, Milton, Johnson, and all the other famous writers of the past', and recounted his battle to retain the quotation from T. S. Eliot's 'East Coker' under *loam* ('Lifting heavy feet in clumsy shoes Earth feet, loam feet, lifted in country mirth') when he submitted sample pages for review to the Press and academic readers in 1962 (1989: 8, 11–12). But there is no indication that indexing of this sort occurred; indeed, in the Introduction to Volume 1, Burchfield apologized for his policy of 'liberally representing the vocabulary of such writers

[13] Although a small proportion of these terms, used by famous writers such as Tolkien (e.g. *hobbit*), have become widely recognized.

as Kipling, James Joyce, and Dylan Thomas', as against the *OED*'s 'policy of total literary inclusiveness for the earlier centuries [of] all the vocabulary, including *hapax legomena*, of such authors as Chaucer, Gower and Shakespeare'. This last remark is baffling. Any regular user of the parent dictionary can attest that the *OED* did not remotely achieve 'total literary inclusiveness', and nor did it in practice aim for such a thing (except in the case of Shakespeare's lexicon).

Inconsistency was unavoidable in a policy such as this, and Burchfield freely acknowledged that he changed his mind as he went along, for example deciding in 1973—after the publication in 1972 of his first volume, treating the letters *A–H*—to include all rather than just some Jabberwocky words, with the consequence that, of this group of words, only *borogove*, *callay*, *callooh*, *frumious*, and *gimble* are omitted from the *Supplement* (1974: 13). The question of how to identify the best writers was one Burchfield never addressed, though he did point out that 'the pattern of admission was governed as much by the choice made by the readers as by any abstract principles adopted by the editors. If a reader made a slip for such an item it was likely to be included, with small regard for consistency in comparable words, or in words drawn from other writers, in other parts of the Dictionary. Conversely a word that was not copied by a reader had little chance of inclusion since the editorial staff would almost certainly be unaware of its existence' (1989: 89; cf. similar remarks 1989: 13, 84).

The results can be seen in any *Supplement* author whose works are checked in detail against the dictionary itself. A typical case is that of Auden, named several times by Burchfield as a well-mined source, with around 750 quotations altogether. Some of his poems were not cited at all, despite the fact that they appeared in volumes listed in the *Supplement* bibliography, and contained many words and usages just as unusual and notable as ones which the *Supplement* did record. In any one poem, some of the unusual words got into the dictionary and some did not (*semble*, but not *rundle*, was recorded; they occur six lines apart in 'Thanksgiving for a Habitat' (1965); *ubity* and *videnda*, but not *flosculent* and *maltalent* (n.), were recorded; they occur a few pages apart in the same work).[14] When such words were cited by the *Supplement*, they were variously, and apparently inconsistently, labelled as *poetic*, *archaic*, *isolated later example*, *rare*, with no indication how these labels were assigned or what the distinction between them is.[15]

[14] *maltalent* has recently been treated in *OED3*, with this example from Auden printed as an illustrative quotation.

[15] Examples from Brewer (1993); for more on labels see Stein (1983), Brewer (2004).

Electronic searching of *OED2* discloses interesting data on the respective numbers of quotations from literary authors. In the event, where male-authored sources were concerned, Burchfield favoured a more or less traditional canon, most frequently citing Shaw, Kipling, Joyce, Wodehouse, Lawrence, Twain, Aldous Huxley, and Auden (in that order, from around 2000 down to 750 quotations). But he chose differently from female-authored sources, quoting, in far fewer numbers, the New Zealand crime writer Ngaio Marsh, together with Dorothy Sayers and Agatha Christie, at around 450 quotations each, followed at some distance by more literary writers such as Elizabeth Bowen and Woolf (around 340 and 230 respectively).[16]

These figures and ratios reflect the reading preferences of Burchfield, his staff, and his volunteers (who included the indefatigable contributor Marghanita Laski, an enthusiastic reader of crime novels). They do not tell us about the relative contribution such writers made to the English language, however tempting it may be to hope that electronic searches of the *OED* will yield such information.

11.6 WORLD ENGLISH AND FOREIGN LOAN-WORDS

In 1961, Burchfield recorded that 'No systematic treatment of Commonwealth sources is being attempted [in the *Supplement*] but Australian, New Zealand, and South African words already in *OED* will be joined by a relatively small number of additional words and senses which now seem to deserve a place ... pending the preparation of regional dictionaries of various kinds of English ... .A few words from other Commonwealth countries [than those mentioned] will also be included, as *bhoodan* and *gramdan* from India, *calypso* from the West Indies, and so on' (1961: 48). By the time the first volume appeared, in 1972, this policy too had changed, and the editor was making 'bold forays into the written English of regions outside the British Isles, particularly into that of North America, Australia, New Zealand, South Africa, India, and Pakistan' (Vol. 1: xiv–xv). In 1975, he explained why: 'it is now [as opposed to in Murray's time] a legitimate function of a historical dictionary, even one prepared in Britain, to record and treat overseas words that are virtually unknown in this country' (1975: 352, instancing Austr. *to lob in*, 'to arrive in', NZ *marae*, 'a space in a Maori settlement set aside for social functions', SA *lappie*, 'a dish cloth, a small rag'); in 1984, Burchfield declared, 'English is English wherever it is spoken and written as a first language, and the natural repository for all of it, subject

[16] Figures from Brewer (2005–); on *OED* and gender see Baigent *et al.* (2005).

only to the physical difficulty of collecting it, was the *Supplement to the OED*' (1984: 117).[17] The result of this change in policy was that words and usages from 'countries such as the West Indies and even Scotland ... have better coverage in the range H–P [Vol. 2] than ... in A–G [Vol. 1]' (1975: 355).

It seems right that Burchfield jettisoned the 'unblushingly "Britocentric"' views of Murray, and later Sisam, understandable though both had been at their time (Weiner 1990: 500). Equally it seems surprising that no policy was ever stated, or perhaps formulated, for systematically discriminating the items suitable for inclusion, given that total coverage of World Englishes would have been both impossible and (in view of the proliferation of dictionaries of regional English from Oxford and elsewhere) unnecessary. It is not easy to use electronic searches to identify uneven coverage of the sort Burchfield does identify—i.e. over alphabet-range; for example, the provenance of words is sometimes indicated in etymology text, sometimes in definitions text, while it is not possible to distinguish between searches for *Sc.*='Scottish', and *sc.*='*scilicet*'. One imbalance is notable, however: the threefold increase in words of Chinese origin added to the *Supplement* after Burchfield's own visit to China in 1979 (e.g. *pipa, pyotonghua, Little Red Book, running dog, scorched earth*).[18]

Burchfield's treatment of the many hundreds, perhaps thousands, of foreign terms is additionally difficult to investigate since it is not possible to search electronically for the vertical parallel lines, or 'tram lines', that are used to indicate 'alien' or not yet naturalized words, with which Burchfield often—but not always—marked these terms. Of his examples quoted above, the two Hindi words *bhoodan* and *gramdan* are thus marked, but *calypso* is not; other Hindi words, however, are unmarked, for example *dhoon, dhoona, dhrupad, dhyana*. On the same page, *diable*, and *diable au corps* are 'tram-lined', but *diabolo* is not; a theory that words that seem to require (for native English speakers) difficult pronunciation is scotched when one sees that *déjeuner* and *déjà vu* have no tram lines either. There is no clearly discernible policy here, and nor do the quotations offer any further help, as there seems to be no consciousness of foreignness in the quotations themselves (rendering a word in italics, for example) that correlates with the presence of tram lines.[19]

[17] In fact, standards of spoken and written English, in countries such as India, that approximate most closely to British norms are achieved by people for whom English is a second language; see, for example, Quirk (1982), contemporary with Burchfield's comment quoted here.

[18] Vol. 4: viii. Searching *OED2* 'Entries' for '1928–' in quotation date and 'Chinese' in etymologies produces twenty results for A–G (Vol. 1), thirty-two results for H–N (Vol. 2), thirty-two results for O–Scz (Vol. 3) and a hundred results for Sea–Z (Vol. 4).

[19] Tram lines were not used in the 1933 *Supplement*, as first observed by Ogilvie (2004).

11.7 SCIENTIFIC AND TECHNICAL VOCABULARY

In 1884, the Delegates had urged upon Murray the principle that 'slang terms and scientific words should both be limited to such as were found in literature' (Murray 1977: 221). Burchfield seems to have begun with much the same aim. So, in 1972, justifying his inclusion of unusual vocabulary in the *Supplement* (scientific terms, poetic *hapax legomena* such as Edith Sitwell's *Martha-coloured*, technical vocabulary and trade names), he explained that 'Many rose- and pear-names—*Gloire de Dijon*, *Maréchale Niel*, *Marie Louise*, and the rest—will owe their presence in the dictionary as much to their appearance in the works of Charlotte Yonge or Oscar Wilde or John Galsworthy as to their place in the hierarchy of trees and fruits' (1975: 351).[20] The implication is that it is use in literature that guarantees a place in the dictionary.[21] However, by 1977, as Burchfield reported in a discussion at a lexicography conference, he had categorically dropped the 'literature criterion': 'we have decided ... that it is unworthy to treat scientific and technical vocabulary only in respect of those words which make their way into the common language and into fiction .... We are attempting to treat with consistency the central vocabulary of psychology, sociology, physics, chemistry, and so forth' (1980: 316). One of his interlocutors pointed out, 'I must say there is some difficulty in deciding what is meant by the central vocabulary', and it is also difficult for anyone who is not an expert in a particular field to determine exactly how well Burchfield fulfilled this formidable aim. It is readily apparent from a rough scan of his four volumes that scientific and technological terms form a sizeable proportion of new items (there is no systematic way of searching for them), and Burchfield broke new ground by employing science consultants on the *OED* staff, which, as he describes, was 'a radical departure from the policy adopted by the editors of the main Dictionary', influenced by his visit to North American dictionary departments in 1968.[22] As noted by approving reviewers, the abundance of new senses recorded on his pages indicated the quality of scientific advice his staff supplied. He was criticized, however, for more patchy treatment of technical vocabulary relating to non-scientific subjects—horse-riding, cookery, pottery, sports (with the exception of cricket, whose terminology was fully covered; see Strang 1974, 1977; Baker 1988).

[20] *Maréchale Niel* was not in the event included, though the term occurs in a quotation from Galsworthy s.v. *Gloire de Dijon*.

[21] Cf. Burchfield (1974: 16): 'literary currency...is the governing factor in the admission of proprietary terms to the *OED*'.

[22] Vol. 1: xiv; Burchfield (1989: 7). *OED1* had of course regularly consulted scientists for help, as detailed in the prefaces to the original fascicles of the work.

11.8 SEXUAL AND 'COARSE' WORDS AND EXPRESSIONS; RACIST AND OTHER OFFENSIVE TERMS; SLANG, COLLOQUIALISMS, CONTENTIOUS USAGES

In these areas, Burchfield confidently and boldly changed *OED1* policy. In a review of the first *Supplement*, the linguist A. S. C. Ross (1934: 129) had criticized that dictionary's 'definite policy of omission' of obscene words, principally *cunt* and *fuck*, along with some items of modern slang, commenting 'It seems regrettable that the perpetuation of a Victorian prudishness (inacceptable [sic] in philology beyond other subjects) should have been allowed to lead to the omission of some of the commonest words in the English language'. Alluding to this criticism, in a leading article in the *TLS* entitled 'Four-letter words and the *OED*', published to coincide with the appearance of the *Supplement*'s first volume in 1972, Burchfield explained that, in common with other English language dictionaries, the *OED* was now opening its doors to vocabulary previously shunned on grounds of taste or obscenity. The words *come* (verb), *condom*, *cunnilingus*, *fellatio*, *French letter*, *frig*, *frigging*, among 'numerous others', were now included, fully supported by etymologies and quotations (which in many instances had long been on file in the *OED* offices; see Murray 1977: 195).

Burchfield's treatment of these terms varies: *come* is said to be 'slang', *bugger* 'coarse slang', whereas *frig* and *frigging* are unmarked; as we shall see, consistency and transparency of labelling in the *Supplement* seems to have raised insuperable problems. More significantly, the handling of one of the newly included words, *lesbian*, together with that of its older predecessor, *Sapphism*, belies in at least one respect Burchfield's implied rejection of 'Victorian prudishness'. *Sapphism* had been included in *OED1* (defined as 'unnatural sexual relations between women'), with a reference to a medical dictionary of 1890 and a single illustrative quotation from the *Lancet* (1901): 'As yet in this country the novelist ... has not arrived at the treatment in romance of excessive morphiomania, or Sapphism, or vaginismus, all of which diseases will be found in French novels'. Burchfield left this untouched—it was one of the tiny number of existing items to be changed in *OED2*, which substituted 'homosexual' for 'unnatural' in the definition—but was able to consult existing files on *lesbian*, which *OED1* had defined simply as 'Of or pertaining to the island of Lesbos'; the term had been discussed, and on Craigie's insistence rejected, in 1930. Burchfield's definitions for both adjective and noun are unproblematic, but his choice of quotations is another matter, particularly for the noun; they include Aldous Huxley: 'After a third-rate provincial town, colonized by English sodomites and middle-aged Lesbians, which is, after all, what Florence is, a genuine metropolis will be lively'; and C. Day Lewis: 'I shall never write real poetry. Women never do, unless they're invalids or Lesbians or something'. Were such examples the only ones available to him? Or do they illustrate a personal, or perhaps more general, societal, view? Here it is instructive to compare the quotations for *homosexual*, another term new to the *Supplement*, which are almost all neutral (e.g. Stella Gibbons: 'There were many homosexuals to be seen in Hyde Park', or the *Daily Telegraph*: 'Homosexuals and lesbians make up a sizeable minority of the population').[23]

Where racist terms were concerned, Burchfield took justifiable pride in establishing the claims of descriptive lexicography. Not only did he insist on including all offensive terms, suitably labelled, if they were to be found in common use, but he also determined, 'in order to avoid misunderstanding and consequent hostility, that the historical record of words like *Jesuit*, *Jew*, *Negro*, *nigger* and others already entered in the *OED*, should be brought up to date [in Volumes II and III of the *Supplement*]' (Vol. 2: vii; Burchfield 1989: 109–15). As ever, this admirable policy was difficult to sustain with consistency. By the time Burchfield had reached this view, his first volume (*A–G*) had already appeared, which meant that words such as *bogtrotter*, *bohunk*, *blackie*, *darkie*, and no doubt others, unidentified as racist or derogatory in *OED1*, continued similarly unidentified in the *Supplement*. In addition, a number of other racist definitions, labels, and usages in *OED1* from *H* onwards, unexceptionable at the time they were written, somehow escaped the process of updating (e.g. the reference to 'wild or savage races' s.v. *hubbub*, or the definition of *white man* as 'a man of honourable character such as one associates with a European (as distinguished from a negro)'), while Burchfield actually introduced a racist formulation under *interlocutor*, viz. 'the compère in a group of nigger minstrels'.[24]

Owing to the difficulties of producing so substantial a piece of work over so long a period of time, Burchfield seems never to have settled on a standard procedure for treating both these and other contentious items.[25] Sometimes he uses definition alone (*nig-nog* is unlabelled but defined as 'A coarsely abusive term for a Negro'); sometimes label alone (*coon* is labelled '*slang.* (Derog.)' but defined simply as 'a Negro'). In rather more cases, he labels the word simply 'slang', but indicates its offensiveness in the definition (as with *kike*, defined as 'A vulgarly offensive name for a Jew'; *wog*, defined as 'A vulgarly offensive name for a foreigner, esp. one of Arab extraction'). Sometimes the warning or comment

23 Both terms were further edited in *OED2*.

24 *OED2* rewrote the definition for *white man* but retained those for *hubbub* and *interlocutor*.

25 See further Brewer (2005), from which some of the following material is taken.

appears as a note separate from both label and definition (as, for *honky*, 'Disparaging in all applications'; *wop* 'Now considered *offensive*').

Burchfield had from the beginning retained *OED1*'s use of the paragraph mark to indicate 'catachrestic and erroneous' usages (e.g. of *data* with a singular verb), but his addition of usage notes was a newly enunciated policy, again introduced part-way through the *Supplement* (possibly influenced by his recent undertaking to re-edit Fowler's *Modern English Usage*, one of the bibles of linguistic prescriptivism, (→ ALLEN, Vol. II). So in Vol. 3 (v–vi) he noted the recent prescriptivist backlash to the 'markedly [sic] linguistic descriptivism of the post-war years', and commented, 'One small legacy of these great debates is that here and there in the present volume I have found myself adding my own opinions about the acceptability of certain words or meanings in educated use. Users of the dictionary may or may not find these editorial comments diverting: they have been added (adapting a statement by John Ray in 1691) "as oil to preserve the mucilage from inspissation"'.

Such a departure from the stated principles of the parent dictionary comes as a surprise, but in fact Burchfield had already entered comments of various kinds in the earlier volumes—for example that use of the plural form *agenda* with a singular verb was 'now increasingly found but avoided by careful writers', or that *nite* was 'A widespread vulgarism'. Assertions of personal taste, like the latter, were often curiously out of step with the quotation evidence Burchfield also printed, seeming to indicate that the editor was turning his back on the duty, identified by Trench, to be historian rather than critic (→ MUGGLESTONE, 10.1.3; 10.5.1). Comments of this type were, however, few. In the transition to *OED2* some were removed, or marked with the distinguishing label 'RWB', while in *OED3* they are being altogether excised.

11.9 CONCLUSION

The *Supplement* volumes represent a substantial and significant achievement by their editor. Burchfield's definitions are precise and lucid, and he treats an extraordinarily wide range of words with admirable thoroughness. Constrained by the aims of its publishers, the second *Supplement* was far less ambitious than its predecessor, and the typographically seamless combination of the two into the so-called second edition of the *OED* produced an unhappily uneven result (Stanley 1990, Brewer 1993). Inevitably, Burchfield's re-thinking of aspects of the project as he went along gave rise to inconsistencies and imperfections. Nevertheless, his contribution to *OED* valuably extended the range of this great dictionary, establishing a solid basis for his successors.

I am grateful to Beverley Hunt for help with the *OED* records and to Peter Gilliver for his valuable comments on this piece; all responsibility for views expressed remains my own. The material introduced here was later freely developed into a full-scale history of the *OED* Supplements (Brewer 2007).

REFERENCES

Unpublished sources

OED Archives at OUP

OUP/BoxOP1713/PB/ED/012869.

SOED/1951/14/3.

OED/B/3/2/22.

OED/B/3/2/24.

12

NATIONAL AND REGIONAL DICTIONARIES OF ENGLISH

Richard W. Bailey

Languages declare their independence by creating dictionaries.

12.1 INTRODUCTION

WITH a dictionary, a language (or language variety) is no longer a dependent or derivative, no longer insufficient and inadequate. In the sixteenth century, a sense of the inferiority of English prevailed among learned people: English was a poor language, and they bemoaned its shortcomings. It was not sufficiently copious—other languages had more words and hence could express more concepts. It was corrupt and impure in that it was a mingle-mangle or gallimaufry (to use two terms from the era) of borrowings from other languages. It was unattractively formed, clotted with consonants, marred by monosyllables. It had no dictionary.

In the last quarter of that century, opinions shifted. The great schoolmaster, Richard Mulcaster, defended English against the carpers: 'I do not think that anie language, be it whatsoeuer, is better able to vtter all argumēts, either with more pith, or greater planesse, then our *English* tong is'. In the margin of this argument, Mulcaster wrote: 'A perfit English dictionarie wished for' (quoted by Starnes and Noyes 1991: 10).

English monolingual dictionaries began to appear in the seventeenth century but they were not at first designed to remedy any of the problems bequeathed by the prior century. They were merely to help those unskilled in literacy. Yet as dictionaries grew and grew, they incorporated more and more words—not just the hard ones—and English came to be seen as a rich language rather than an impoverished one. These new dictionaries were not the cause of changing opinion but a symptom of the new ideology: that English was not a language inferior to Latin; that it was not less valuable as an instrument for thought than French.

A pattern in the evolution of dictionaries began to establish itself. First, dictionaries contained words that were 'hard' (like Cawdrey) or 'bad' (like the cant glossaries) or 'dialectal' (like Ray's 'collection of words not generally used'). Then these words were absorbed into larger dictionaries. Finally distinct regional varieties of English would begin to be discerned—first as departures from a norm, and then as usage worthy of respect. Dictionaries became comprehensive, with the small wordbooks being swallowed by the larger ones. Eventually they tend to be comprehensive (for instance, the whole of Australian English) and eventually global (as in the emerging third edition of the *Oxford English Dictionary*). The movement of the lexical culture is ever from the despised to the celebrated, the part to the whole.

Two centuries would pass before a variety within English would begin to assert its independence. That revolution began in Scotland with John Jamieson's *Etymological Dictionary of the Scottish Language* (1808) (→ DAREAU AND MACLEOD). An ardent patriot, Jamieson felt a sense of loss at the gradual disappearance of Scots as a national language. (This was a view shared by the novelist Walter Scott, among many others.) Of course Jamieson's work would serve the needs of antiquarians, but he had something more ambitious in mind: 'Without entering at present into the origin of the [Scottish language], I am bold to affirm, that it has as just a claim to the designation of a peculiar language as most of the other languages of Europe' (vii). For Jamieson, its apparent similarity to the English of south-east England was merely accidental: 'There is no good reason for supposing that it was ever imported from the southern part of our island' (viii).

National and regional dictionaries of English began to appear at the same time as revivalist movements stirring in Scotland were asserting the independence of Norwegian, Czech, modern Greek, and other European languages where the connection of language and nationhood, so strongly endorsed by Jamieson, began to be felt. New 'standards' were created for these languages, and grammars and dictionaries were produced to support their independence.

In organizing this chapter, I present the emergent regional and national varieties in the order in which dictionaries were published to assert their independence.

12.2 AMERICAN ENGLISH

Outside Britain, the first stirrings of linguistic autonomy were discerned in the United States. Of course words from America had appeared in English dictionaries: *cannibal* (in 1616), *tobacco* (1623), *canoe* (1658), but words like these were imported into English and not seen as harbingers of revolution.

In 1789, swept up in his enthusiasm for the newly ratified constitution, Noah Webster predicted that 'several circumstances render a future separation of the American tongue from the English, necessary and unavoidable' (quoted in Bailey 1991: 104). He had even conceived a 'Federal Language' and composed an elaborate crest for it with flanking allegorical figures (Read 1934). Yet his ardour was premature. Few travellers—whether Britons in America or Americans in Britain—could detect differences in accent. The few distinctions were barely noticeable, though John Witherspoon, a Scot who had been named president of Princeton University, coined the term *Americanism*, in 1781, to describe them.

Remarks like Webster's were preparatory for a dictionary, even though those making them were not at first aware of their tendency. In 1800, John Pickering, son of Washington's Secretary of State, wrote to his father from London: 'I find we use several words in America which are not in use here & for which *there is no authority*' (quoted by Read 2002: 16). For words to have *authority*, in Pickering's view, there must be found some respectable precedent in British usage. Purely American innovations were lacking in authority, he believed, and he gave three examples of unworthy American innovations, one an adjective (*lengthy*) and two verbs (*advocate* and *progress*).

At the same time that Pickering wrote this letter, Noah Webster was making a far more radical proposal in letters to American newspapers in which he announced the composition of two dictionaries, a small one for schools and the 'counting house' and a larger one for 'men of science'. The need for such works seemed to him urgent:

> It is found that a work of this kind is absolutely necessary, on account of considerable differences between the American and English language. New circumstances, new modes of life, new laws, new ideas of various kinds give rise to new words, and have already made many material differences between the language of England and America (Webster 1800: 3).

When he published his *Compendious Dictionary* in 1806, however, Webster did not devote much attention to these 'differences'. Reformed spellings and the inclusion of local words in this volume provoked savage attacks. One reviewer took solace in the fact that 'a single writer' could not damage English, but he saw

Webster as a subversive: 'insinuating suspicions of the definitions of Johnson, justifying ridiculous violations of grammar and spreading hurtful innovations in orthography' (quoted by Burkett 1979: 131). The case for a distinctive American language was postponed.

On his return to America, John Pickering presented a paper to the American Academy of Arts and Sciences in 1810, and in 1816 he produced a substantial book: *A Vocabulary; or Collection of Words and Phrases which have been supposed to be peculiar to the United States.* Nearly all of them were usages that had been derided by British critics, and Pickering set out to show that many of them had good pedigrees in British English though perhaps not used so frequently there as formerly. Others, lacking such authority, should be used cautiously by American writers.

Pickering was a learned philologist, having acquired a deep knowledge of Hebrew, Greek, and Latin, as well as the modern languages of Europe. He was especially interested in the languages of America, proposing a 'uniform orthography for the Indian Languages' in 1820, preparing a grammar of Cherokee, and organizing the materials for Abenaki produced by a Jesuit missionary a century earlier. The auction of his books following his death in 1846 revealed what must have been the richest private collection of philological books in the United States (Pickering 1846.) Unfortunately, he is remembered mainly as the target of Noah Webster's wrath.

Reading Pickering's *Vocabulary*, Webster published a letter attacking his insufficiently ardent patriotism and sneering at his willingness to toady to British opinion. 'There is nothing which, in my opinion, so debases the genius and character of my countrymen, as the implicit confidence they place in English authors, and their unhesitating submission to their *opinions*, their *derision*, and their *frowns*' (Webster 1817: 59). Socially and intellectually of more consequence than Webster, Pickering ignored this attack. Most of his correspondents and the published reviewers of his book supported his efforts to identify Americanisms so authors might be prepared for an adverse reaction by British critics (Burkett 1979: 86–91).

As Webster laboured in preparing his great dictionary of 1828, he became less persuaded of the depth of the schism between American and British English. When he completed his manuscript, he was living in Britain and had been taken up socially by the dons at Cambridge. He even sought an English publisher for it, but was obliged by British indifference to seek one in New York. *Advocate*, *lengthy*, and *progress* were all entered with no commentary about the dispute that Pickering had identified. Even the entry for *Americanism* stepped back from Webster's earlier advocacy of his country:

(1) AMERICANISM n. The love which American citizens have to their own country, or the preference of its interests. *Analogically*, an American idiom.

All of the distinction between 'the American and English language' had vanished. In his entry for *English* (sense 2), Webster wrote: 'The language of England or of the English nation, and of their descendents in India, America, and other countries.' England is the parent; the Americans are children. Pickering must have smiled when he saw that Webster's opinion had shifted so close to his own.

In the *American Dictionary*, Webster explained American institutions (like *congress*) but never defends an American usage. In defining *creek*, for instance, he declares: 'In some of the *American States*, a small river. This sense is not justified by etymology . . . '. Since English people limited *creek* to an inlet from the sea, American writers who extended the meaning to freshwater rivulets were 'not justified' even though their usage was documented in American writers of the seventeenth century.

Far less dependent upon British opinion, John Russell Bartlett published his *Dictionary of Americanisms* in 1849. His purpose was, primarily, to record 'the class of words which are purely American in their origin and use' (1989: v), and he cast a wide net, drawing in expressions from the flowering of American dialect humour so popular in the second quarter of the century. He was eager to admit them, seeing corruption in English as particularly vexatious among the educated, especially the clergy to whom he attributed such innovative verbs as *fellowship*, *difficult*, *eventuate*, *doxologize*, *happify*, and *donate* (1989: xviii–xix). His citation of *fellowship* comes from 1813: 'We considered him heretical, essentially unsound in the faith; and on this ground refused to *fellowship* with him' (s.v. *fellowship*). He has nothing critical to say about *sockdolager* 'a patent fish-hook'. (Subsequent lexicographers have traced this usage to 1830; the gloss 'a decisive blow' shows the source of the fish-hook, spring-loaded to open violently in the mouth of the fish.) For Bartlett, *fellowship* (v.) was a 'barbarism'; *sockdolager* is an exuberant Americanism.

Bartlett was not reluctant to provide usage advice. *All-fired* 'very' was, for him, 'a low American word'. *Big-bugs* (like *big-wigs*) 'people of consequence' was merely an expression of American dislike of rank and hierarchy. *Grit*, 'courage, spirit', was Bartlett's idea of a welcome Americanism. (Successor dictionary-makers found the first use of *grit* in this sense in an American writer of 1825.)

Bartlett's *Dictionary of Americanisms* was not a complete dictionary of American usage, of course, but a specialized collection of distinctive national usages. What happened in the decade in which it was published was to shift lexicography away from questions of taste and propriety, to diminish the importance of usage by elites, and to depart from a concern for lexical origins. All of these aspects of lexicography remained important, of course, but new forces drove the composition and sales of dictionaries.

By the 1850s, American dictionaries were comprehensive, inclusive of Americanisms, and indifferent to opinions of Britain. Webster's linguistic patriotism, which had aroused such ire sixty years earlier, was now fulfilled in the encyclopedic dictionaries published in Webster's name—he had died in 1843—and by Joseph Emerson Worcester (→ LANDAU).

The compilation of big dictionaries, however, did little to discourage enthusiasts for Americanisms, and several collectors compiled and published dictionaries dealing with its exotica. Among the most interesting was *Americanisms, Old and New* (1889), by John S. Farmer, an English scholar scraping by with all sorts of literary projects, including *Slang and Its Analogues* (1890–1904). Farmer never left England and gathered his materials only through reading. Yet, however reluctantly, mainstream English lexicographers began to encompass American usage. This trend was rapidly accelerated with the publication of William Dwight Whitney's *Century Dictionary* (1889–91), a work unashamedly plundered by Murray and his co-editors for the *OED*.

12.2.1 Scholarly dictionaries of Americanisms

In 1900, James A. H. Murray wrote to a librarian in Greenock discussing the cry that he include yet more words in his dictionary:

> It is a cheap pleasure evidently which we have given our 'philological time fellows', and one that they need never be without, since every newspaper contains South African Dutch, Malay, Patagonian, Alaskan, Samoan, or Chinese words 'new to Murray' who confesses ignorance of all these far-off languages, and is merely a Little Englander in lexicography. The bolder notion of an Imperial Dictionary or Pan-Lexicon, to include all the languages with which Englishmen have & have had dealings, belongs to 'the new Imperialism' no doubt. It will be a big order; we find the language of Little England enough for us (MS 3219.f158. National Library of Scotland.)

In these claims, Murray was somewhat disingenuous since it is hard to find words used in English that are not included, however distant their sources. From Azerbaijani, the *OED* supplies three words, hardly of great currency in 'Little England': *kazak*, *kuba*, and *soumak*. Murray treated them in detail.

Political disputes between 'Imperialists' and 'Little Englanders' were especially common in discourse about the Boer War. (The imperialists wanted to put down what they saw as a rebellion in South Africa; the little Englanders wanted military force kept close to home.) In lexicography, Murray claimed to be an isolationist, only interested in the world of English in England, but in his practice he scoured English writings for expressions from faraway places. For all his disclaimer in that letter, he was very much a lexical imperialist.

In his 1919 address to the Philological Society, William Craigie outlined the period and regional dictionaries needed to supplement the coverage provided by the *OED*. With the parent and daughter dictionaries taken together, the great 'pan-lexicon' foreseen by Murray in 1900 would be realized.

The *Dictionary of American English* (*DAE*) was the first of these to be completed; it was published in parts by the University of Chicago Press (1938–42). In defining the scope of the work, Craigie, its co-editor, first imagined a dictionary that would include 'every word which has been current in the spoken or written language' (Craigie and Hulbert 1938–42: v). Such a dictionary would have no explicit connection to English used in other countries; it would record, on historical principles, the whole of American English.

In the interests of practicality, Craigie narrowed the scope to material that would distinguish American English from usages employed in 'the rest of the English-speaking world'. Even with this limitation, Craigie's scope was broad.

> [The dictionary includes] not only words and phrases which are clearly or apparently of American origin, or have greater currency here than elsewhere, but also every word denoting something which has a real connection with the development of the country and the history of its people (Craigie and Hulbert 1938–42: v).

Thus *boat* is included, not because it did not exist in English before the arrival of the first settlers in North America: it did. But in order to understand the American coinage *boat-yard* one must begin with the meaning of *boat*. Such a policy of inclusion expands the size of the *Dictionary of American English* far beyond the scope set by Bartlett and his successors.

One of the assistant editors from *DAE*, Mitford M. Mathews, went on to edit a successor to it: *A Dictionary of Americanisms on Historical Principles* (*DA*) (1951). Craigie had set a terminal date for *DAE* at 1900 for first usages, and Mathews was eager to bring twentieth-century evidence forward. More important, however, was his limitation of entries to 'a word or expression that originated in the United States' (1951: v). All the words in *DAE* with merely a 'connection' to the history of the country were excluded unless there was some American innovation about them. Exemplifying the laxity of prior scholarship, Mathews pointed out that *drummer* 'commercial traveller' was listed as 'U.S.' in the *OED* even though the first citations were from Walter Scott. All such false attributions needed to be cleared away and evidence minutely sifted. Thus *blizzard* 'a violent snow storm' was likely to be of English rather than American origin, though Mathews gives both citations of usage and sources of scholarly dispute treating the question.

Mathews's *DA* was the last of the substantial dictionaries to focus on Americanisms alone. Two other dictionaries, mentioned in Volume II, constitute supplements to *DAE* and *DA*, however. The *Dictionary of American Regional English* (*DARE*) does not encompass all the vocabulary defined in the earlier works, but, where entries appear for words listed in the *DAE*, the dictionary supplies antedatings or significant new citations. Likewise the *Historical Dictionary of American Slang* (*HDAS*) adds more information when it is available. For the word *hobo* 'migrant worker', *DAE* declares it to be an Americanism and gives a first citation to 1891. *DA* gives more citations, the first to 1889. *DARE* has no entry for *hobo* since it is not regional in the specialized sense of *regional* used in that work. *HDAS* has the most abundant citation of etymological speculation and offers as a first use one from 1885. *HDAS* acknowledges that *hobo* is now used in respectable English but treats it because it was formerly slang. In short, for the definitive account of *hobo* in American English, one must consult all of these dictionaries.

In addition, subdivisions of American English have acquired dictionaries 'on historical principles' that celebrate the independence of the varieties. In his *Dictionary of Alaskan English*, Russell Tabbert gave citational evidence for words 'distinctively characteristic' of that state. Typical of borrowings from the first languages of Alaska is *oosik*: 'The penis bone from the walrus is polished, decorated, and sold as an Alaskan souvenir' (Tabbert 1991: 260). Less exotic expressions with special Alaskan meanings are also treated: *ice bridge*, *ling cod*. In the *Dictionary of Smokey Mountain English*, Michael Montgomery and Joseph Hall show the connection of the English of this region (a part of the Appalachian chain of mountains in Tennessee and North Carolina) in defining such phrases as *redd up* 'clean up, tidy' (as in 'redd up a room'). In addition to citations collected locally, Montgomery and Hall draw connections from the American usage to its source in Scots and the northern dialects of English. Exact references to the *OED*, the *Scottish National Dictionary*, and the *Concise Ulster Dictionary* deepen understanding of the linguistic history of *redd up*.

12.3 SOUTH ASIAN ENGLISH

In the heyday of the British Empire, conditions were far from auspicious for the development of an autonomous variety of English in India. Macaulay's policy paper in 1835 had raised English above the classical languages of the region—Sanskrit and Persian—and set as a goal the creation of a new class. 'We must at present do our best to form a class who may be interpreters between us and the millions who we govern, a class of persons, Indian in blood and colour, but

English in taste, in opinions, in morals, and in intellect' (quoted by McArthur 1992: 505). In the course of the nineteenth century, this policy was largely successful among Indian elites, and not until the twentieth did Gandhi (among others) point to English used by Indians as a sign of cultural subordination.

The first dictionary of *Anglo-Indian* appeared in 1885 as the result of a decade of work by an official in India, George Clifford Whitworth. He saw it as a 'supplement to the English dictionary': 'An Anglo-Indian Dictionary should contain all those words which English people in their relations with India have found it necessary or convenient to add to their own vernacular, and should give also any special significations which pure English words have acquired in India' (Whitworth 1885: vii). Though not a citation dictionary (like its more famous successor, *Hobson–Jobson*), it is an excellent work mostly devoted to loan-words from Indian languages like *sari* or *stupa.* Distinctive English usages are also treated (e.g. *serpent race, settlement, state railway* [vs. *guaranteed railway*]). It was cited sixteen times in the *OED* and provided the first evidence for three loan-words subsequently documented in the language (for instance, *desi* 'native, indigenous' later used by Kipling and by twenty-first century Indian journalists).

Newly discerned linguistic prejudices were exported from Britain with each wave of teachers and administrators to arrive in South Asia. Further, ridicule of emergent speechways placed an obstacle to the development of a *desi* standard. Specimens of faults and eccentricities were a staple source of humour in India and in Great Britain, most notably in the book-length treatment by Arnold Wright, *Baboo English as 'tis Writ* (1891).

Into this cultural mix came a remarkable volume celebrating Indian English: *Hobson–Jobson: A Glossary of Colloquial Anglo-Indian Words and Phrases* (1886) by Henry Yule and A. C. Burnell. Here was a work of profound scholarship with precisely identified quotations from a copious bibliography showing the evolution of expressions in the subcontinent. James Murray was an enthusiast of the work and cites it nearly five hundred times in the *OED*—for instance in the etymology of so English a word as *elephant.* The compilers were broadly interested in words that had entered English from the region and more particularly concerned with 'the common Anglo-Indian stock' in commercial and administrative use. Many of these were well established in British English: *curry, toddy, veranda, cheroot.* Others were more specialized and had retained connotations of their origin: *pukka, mahout, nautch.* The compilers were further interested in new senses of English words acquired in the region: *bearer, cot, belly-band, college pheasant, chopper, summer-hand, eagle wood, jackass-copal, bobbery* (xxi).

Ambivalence about the role of English after independence did not lead to consequential lexicography of distinctive uses of English in the region. Collectors still publish lists of borrowings (like *loofa* for the product of the vegetable sponge vine) and innovative senses (like *denting* for smoothing of dents in automobile bodies). (For an example of a dictionary of this type, see Hankin 2003.)

As the example of Pickering reveals in the American context, recognition of distinctive English may begin with a treatment of differences between the superordinate and the subordinate variety. A rich example of this practice in India was provided in the usage dictionary by Nihalani and his collaborators. Most entries are designed to alert users to differences (for instance, *jotter* 'ball-point pen'). But some innovations, the compilers believe, deserve respect in their own right and beyond south Asia:

> The pages which follow will demonstrate how users of English in India have shown considerable ingenuity, not only in the way in which they have used the linguistic resources of English to represent Indian reality, but also in the creation of new English forms, some of which deserve to be of wider application (Nihalani *et al.* 2004: 6–7).

Expressions of this sort include *batch-mate* 'fellow-student', *soft corner* 'soft spot' ('I've always had a soft corner for her.'), *foot* 'walk' ('The bus is gone—we'll have to foot it.').

Though the earlier edition of this work was also descriptive, it was far more tentative. In the preface, an eminent professor regarded the work much as Pickering had viewed his collection: 'Indian users of this book will do well to note the peculiarities in their English and avoid those which may damage communication with other speakers of the language' (Nihalani *et al.* 1979: viii).

Conditions for the production of dictionaries on historical principles have not been auspicious in India, Pakistan, Bangladesh, and Sri Lanka. Malaysia has adopted Bahasa Malayu as the 'national language' and marginalized the use of English for some purposes, so conditions for such work are hardly any better there. In Singapore, government action has discouraged the recognition of a distinctive Singaporean English. Nonetheless, an edition of the *Chambers Dictionary* designed for Malaysia and Singapore contains an appendix of borrowed words in common use (for instance, *ang moh, Mat Salleh, orang putih,* all three expressions used to designate a Caucasian person). Within the main alphabet there is a category for Singapore-Malaysian English 'informal English', as shown in this entry:

(2) **lamp post**

2. (*SME informal*) You might be called a **lamp post** if you are in the company of two people who would rather be alone together. *Wei Ming, I don't want a lamp post around when Mei Ling comes afterwards, all right* (Seaton 2002, *s.v. lamp post*).

These varieties—known as *Manglish* and *Singlish*—are as revealing of their history as any of the other national kinds of English. Thus *gostan* 'move backwards, go slow' is derived from *go astern* and *zap* 'to photocopy' from international English. Only very recently has the power of the Internet allowed word enthusiasts, despite official indifference, to create ambitious citation dictionaries designed on historical principles. (See http://www.singlishdictionary.com/Tsen-Ta Lee 2004.)

12.4 SOUTH AFRICAN ENGLISH

A rage for words swept through Anglo-American culture in the third quarter of the nineteenth century. Ambitious dictionaries like the *OED* in Britain and the *Century* in the United States required huge investments in money and in time. Dictionary-making had become a growth industry in both Britain and the United States, and individuals elsewhere clamoured to see words from their part of the world included.

In the early days of exploration, visitors to distant lands made lists of the plants and animals found in them. Now, in the last quarter of the nineteenth century, visitors made lists of words. On the day of his arrival in Cape Town in 1876, Charles Pettman began to jot down unfamiliar words in a notebook. As his collection increased, Pettman studied the work of other scholars, and was surprised to find that 'by some strange oversight' Murray's slowly emerging dictionary was deficient in representing the usages of Southern Africa (Pettman 1968: v). Works by W. W. Skeat and Yule and Burnell's *Hobson–Jobson* provided models for his local work. For the most part, he limited his entries to *Africanderisms*: 'Dutch words and idioms and use in South African English are thus designated.'

Though most of Pettman's entries come from Afrikaans, he recognizes that English words have acquired African meanings: *good-for* meaning 'IOU', for instance. To say that a river is *down* is to indicate that it is in flood and likely to overspill its banks. *Tailings*—the residue of earth from which gold had been extracted—though he did not know it—had come to South Africa from the gold fields of California by way of Australian miners. For the most part, however, he was interested in borrowings:

> The following list contains a very small proportion only of the words which have been thus annexed by the English colonist from his Dutch neighbour. They are many of them quite unknown to the great Oxford Dictionary, but the English colonist would find

himself sadly hampered every day had he to do without them: *baas, banket, biltong, brak, erf, hamel, hok, kloof, kranz, lager, inspan* and *outspan, moregen, muid, nek, poort, schans, schlelm, schimmel, schut, slut, spruit, trek, tripper, veld, vlei*, etc. (Pettman 1968: 15).

Pettman was a careful scholar. The current edition of the *OED* has not been able to improve on his first citation for *trek* 'a journey by wagon'.

As a minority language community, English-speaking South Africans were not confident of their linguistic tastes, and the view held by Pickering—that one would wish to know usages departing from those of south-east England—was frequently articulated. Attempting to provide for South Africa a usage guide to rival those of Fowler (in England) and Follett (in America), Douglas R. Beeton and Helen Dorner created a journal, in preparation for their dictionary of 1975, to solicit opinions—a procedure almost guaranteeing that someone would object to any usage nominated for acceptance. They gathered from their contributors both 'local vocabulary and idiom' (like *biltong* 'strips of raw, salted, dried venison or beef') and 'mistakes and problems' (1975: iv) found in English worldwide and, especially, in South Africa (like *busy* in 'They were busy to eat'). Some of these provide insight into the culture of the nation in the apartheid era. The borrowing from Afrikaans, *taal* 'the Afrikaans language', might appear 'derogatorily': 'He thinks that just because he speaks *the taal* he is better than we are' (s.v. *taal*).

The terrifying history of South Africa played out in the second half of the twentieth century was mirrored in its English. The zest for new words characteristic of Pettman and the desire for gentility expressed by Beeton and Dorner stimulated the creation of far better dictionaries. Jean Branford compiled the first modern compilation of 'South Africanisms'. Her hope was 'to smooth the hackles or allay the alarms of the purists' (Branford, J. 1987: xvi).

In the successive prefaces to her *Dictionary*, Branford expressed dismay at the changing image of English in South Africa. The old pioneer words like *trek* and *biltong* were being supplemented by more sinister vocabulary:

> Since this was written [in 1980] conflict of a different and closer kind impinges on the daily life of most black and many white citizens of this country. Military vehicles no longer patrol only our borders but are a common sight in townships and cities. Internal civil struggle between group and group, citizen and citizen, has brought with it an explosive vocabulary of another kind—*necklace, impimpi, Viva, Casspir, mellow-yellow, witdoek, father, helicopter, kitscop, a sneeze-machine, green flies, toyi toyi* ... (Branford, J. 1987: xvi).

One of these innovations can represent the rest:

(3) **necklace** *n., n. modifier* and *vb.* A method of killing, usu. but not always politically-motivated, practiced upon those thought to be informers or *sellouts*

(q.v.) in which a motor tyre filled with petrol is placed round the neck and shoulders of the victim and ignited.

Though there was little reason for optimism when she wrote, Jean Branford and her husband William in 1969 had established a 'dictionary unit' at Rhodes University in Grahamstown but there were few staff and little money. Nonetheless, they persevered and their first effort brought authoritative information to a wide public: *A Dictionary of South African English* (1978). In 1985, the national government provided funding, partly because the Delegates of the Oxford University Press had expressed interest. Finally, in 1991, a contract was signed for an entirely new dictionary, and Penny Silva became editor. Editing—for which the Internet proved invaluable—was undertaken at an energetic pace, and the remarkable speed with which the dictionary was completed must be attributed to the excellent collecting and preliminary editing undertaken over the previous two decades.

In 1996, the finished work appeared: *A Dictionary of South African English on Historical Principles* (*DSAE*). Collaboration with the editors of the second edition of the *OED*, John Simpson and Edmund Weiner, ensured a uniform plan with the parent dictionary, then in the process of revision. The purpose of the *DSAE* was 'to map and illustrate that variety of English which is particular to South Africans—words borrowed from the many languages of South Africa, English words which have acquired particular senses here, and words coined for local phenomena' (1996: vi). As was Craigie's practice in the *DAE*, words are included that are not of South African origin but which have a 'particular significance' for the country. Despite some residual belief in South Africa that only the prestige English of south-eastern English is 'the standard', the dictionary takes the view that 'the future of English within South Africa is not so much a question of what variety of English will emerge, but rather of whether an appropriate learning context can be constructed which enables English to be a language of access and empowerment' (xix).

From a commercial perspective, the value of *A Dictionary of South African English on Historical Principles* lies in the authority derived from it in the production of shorter and more popular works. William Branford's *The South African Pocket Oxford Dictionary* drew upon Jean Branford's 1978 dictionary for 1,500 main entries and 570 compounds that were deemed necessary for South African users (Branford, W. 1986: xiii). Following the publication of *DSAE*, as it had done elsewhere in the world, Oxford University Press published a variety of affiliated dictionaries—concise, school, pocket, mini—that gain authority from the parent dictionary and, incidentally, to lend prestige to South African English.

From a linguistic perspective, this dictionary on historical principles arrived at just the right time. Under the previous régime, English was one of two official languages of the country. Under the constitution adopted in 1996, eleven languages were declared 'official' and eight more 'non-official' but deserving of public support in some domains. External norms will continue to diminish in importance, and more speakers of languages other than English will become stakeholders in the future of the language. The *DSAE* will thus provide a baseline against which to measure future developments.

12.5 AUSTRAL ENGLISH

For Australia and New Zealand, the foundational volume was *Austral English: A Dictionary of Australasian Words, Phrases and Usages*, published by Edward E. Morris in 1898. Morris had been approached by Murray to gather material for the *OED*, and, addressing a learned society in Melbourne in 1892, he had declared: 'It might even be possible, with sufficient cooperation, to produce an Australian dictionary on the same lines as the *New English Dictionary* by way of a supplement to it' (x). But 'sufficient cooperation' was not forthcoming, though Morris himself continued to gather materials. Failure to influence dictionaries published abroad to include entries for Australia and New Zealand persuaded him 'of the necessity for a special book on Australasian English' (xi).

Morris took as his territory Australia, Tasmania, and New Zealand, and he rejected the idea that distinctive usages of English found there were mainly 'slang'. Many of the words were borrowings from Aboriginal languages and Maori, and these were frequent in the names for plants and animals—*puriri* 'a tree of New Zealand' (< Maori), *kookaburra* 'a bird of Australia' (< Wiradhuri). In addition to supplying quotations for both words, Morris illustrated the way in which early Australians drew upon metaphor. From the sound of the bird's cry, the kookaburra was early called the *laughing jackass* or simply *jackass*. In a lengthy note, he raised the idea, proposed by others, that the name *jackass* comes from a French word *jacasse* (allegedly from French *jacquot* 'a name for parrots or magpies'). After reviewing the etymology, Morris dashes its claims in favour of the simpler explanation that *jackass* is merely English. In expansiveness, the entry rivals those of *Hobson–Jobson*, a work much admired by Morris. Though he presented many borrowings, he saw the most common source of Australasian English words as 'the turning and twisting of an already existing English name' (xii–xiii).

Morris's excellent dictionary did not immediately establish successor books devoted to the English of the region. In 1945, Sidney J. Baker published *The*

Australian Language, a conscious imitation by a journalist of H. L. Mencken's *American Language*. Though not a scholar, Baker popularized interest in Australian English, particularly in the slangy part of the lexicon. One of the major figures in Australian lexicography, W. S. Ramson, found the book 'tendentious, often idiosyncratic, frequently exasperating' (quoted by McArthur 1992: 95). Nonetheless, *The Australian Language* was popular and influential, even though it repeated the French etymology for *jackass* discredited by Morris half a century earlier.

The great milestone for English lexicography in Australia was *The Macquarie Dictionary* (Delbridge 1982). A substantial volume, the book had embossed on the cover 'An Australian Achievement' and the publisher thought it necessary to introduce into the front matter a series of testimonials to its excellence by Australian journalists. Some flavour of the patriotic vaunt can be grasped from the conclusion of the foreword: 'What the Oxford is to the British and what Webster's is to the Americans, the Macquarie is to all Australians—the first book to make us independent of any outside culture when it comes to the interpretation, understanding and use of our own language' (10). Presuming a need for justification, the editor, Arthur Delbridge, provided a prefatory essay on 'The Need for an Australian Dictionary'. Using a British dictionary (Hanks and Simon, 1971, based on Barnhart's *American College Dictionary* published in 1947), the editors weeded entries with connections to British and American social practices and, based on a reading programme, collected citations so that they might 'Australianize' the base dictionary to produce something completely new: 'a reflection on linguistic terms of modern Australian society' (Delbridge 1981b: 1; see Burchfield 1991: 147–65.). Regional labels for dialects within Australian English were provided; *peanut paste* 'peanut butter' is found in Queensland and South Australia. Varieties of English used outside Australia have carefully nuanced labels. *Traffic circle* is *U.S.* for 'roundabout'; *traffic warden* is *Brit.* for 'parking policeman'.

Wishing for the *Macquarie* to reach the widest audience, the editors departed from the lexical to the encyclopedic in providing, among other things, a full-page illustration of 'Australian Standard Meat Cuts' (2045). Encyclopedic information was also provided for distinctively Australian words—for instance, a typology of *kangaroos*. Under *kookaburra* was arrayed both the expected zoological description and a thesaurus of names by which the bird is known: *giant kingfisher, ha-ha duck, laughing jackass, settler's clock.*

The *Macquarie* was immediately successful and smaller works were hived off from it, one dealing with colloquialisms (*Aussie Talk* 1984) and another listing words of Aborginal origin (Thieberger and McGregor 1994). More consequentially, however, it showed the potential for the even more distinctive Australian dictionary which the editors of the *Macquarie*, among others, were ready to undertake.

In 1978, scholars began collecting in earnest for a dictionary on historical principles, and the success of the Macquarie helped spur popular (and financial) support for the endeavour. A bibliography of source texts (and paid readers to select from them) and a file of 250,000 citations were compiled. W. S. Ramson, the editor, was thoroughly acquainted with the international history of regional lexicography, and he drew on the successful practices of Craigie and Hulbert, Mathews, and others to create *The Australian National Dictionary* (*AND*) (1988). Following their practices he echoed their language:

> For the purpose of this dictionary an Australianism is one of those words and meanings of words which have originated in Australia, which have a greater currency here than elsewhere, or which have a special significance in Australia because of their connection with an aspect of the history of the country (1988: vi).

Remarkably, the editing occupied only three years, abetted by the use of the Internet to exchange information, consult specialists in science, and gain from the guidance of the *OED* lexicographers in Britain. Some 9,000 entries were prepared, and the entries show filiations with innovative uses in other varieties of English around the world—for instance, pointing out that *cradle* 'gold-mine apparatus' appeared in a Sydney newspaper in 1851, likely derived from an American usage traced in the *DA* to 1824. The liveliness associated with Australian English was put fully on display: candour about usages that are (or were) elsewhere thought taboo (*shag* and *shag wagon* have no restrictive usage labels); cultural practices (see *mateship*); and a fondness for shortening (see *sambo, sambie* <sandwich). An anthropologist would find sufficient matter for a monograph in the entry for *wowser* ('an obnoxious person'; a prude) and its related forms *wowserdom, wowserish, wowserism, wowseristic, wowserly, wowsery,* and *wowsey.*

In 1988, consequent on the publication of the *AND*, the Australian National Dictionary Centre was established in Canberra to conduct research and to produce dictionaries and other wordbooks (e.g. Jauncey 2004). The most important of these is a dictionary of 100,000 words: *The Australian Oxford Dictionary* (Moore 2004). Responding to what was seen as a demand in the marketplace, the editors have added usage notes (for instance, explaining uses of *shall* about which there is alleged to be 'considerable confusion') and status labels (so the expressions *shag* and *shag wagon* are described as 'coarse colloq'). As in the *Macquarie*, Australian usage was taken to be normative and phrases like *traffic circle* and *traffic warden* are labelled as *U.S.* and *Brit.* respectively. (See Australian National Dictionary Centre in the online references.)

If Oxford and Webster are important names in lexicography elsewhere, the great name in New Zealand dictionary-making is H. W. Orsman. He began with a Ph.D. dissertation, 'The English Language in New Zealand', in 1951 and continued with *hard yacker* for the rest of his life (*yacker* 'strenuous work' <Australian Aboriginal *yaga* entering English there as *yakka* in 1888 before arriving in New Zealand in 1905). Inspired by the treatment of New Zealand in Sidney Baker's account of 1945, Orsman soon 'settled down to a long stretch of scanning methodologically everything which looked promising in my bibliography or, as opportunity offered, on library shelves' (Orsman 1997: vii). An editor of two short dictionaries with New Zealand content (see Orsman 1979 and Orsman and Orsman 1994), he prepared for the reception of a more ambitious dictionary.

Thirty years into collecting, Orsman was encouraged by the example of W. S. Ransom and his work towards the *Australian National Dictionary.* They corresponded and thus discovered the relation of innovations in English in their respective countries—*yacker,* for instance. Support from Victoria University and from the New Zealand lottery board provided funds for staff, and Ransom agreed to scrutinize the draft. The result was *The Dictionary of New Zealand English (DNZE),* a work on historical principles containing 6,000 main entries and 9,300 sub-entries. Naturally enough there was a substantial representation of borrowings from Maori. Like the other dictionaries of its kind, it treated 'the history of words and particular senses of words which are in some way distinctively or predominantly, though not always exclusively, "New Zealand" in meaning or use' (Orsman 1997: vii).

The Dictionary of New Zealand English is, like its Australian counterpart, a work of remarkable scholarship. Long-standing English words acquired new senses in New Zealand: *lagoon* 'shallow freshwater lake'. Morris had already noticed that *laughing jackass* in New Zealand was not a kingfisher (as in Australia) but an owl (referred to by its Maori name as *whekau*), and Orsman provided citations to document these facts. New Zealand terms for sheep mustering are common: *dagger, fadge, to kilt,* and *run-off* (as in *to take a run-off* of 'a group of sheep drafted from the main mob'). Recent innovations are also covered (for instance, *dairy porn* [1993] < *dairy* 'a small, mixed grocery store'). Culturally important terms of all kinds are treated. *Pakeha Maori* (1832) is a European-descended person who behaves like a Maori; *Maori Pakeha* (1867) is the reverse.

Following the publication of the *DNZE,* the New Zealand Dictionary Centre was established at Victoria University in 1997. Orsman's citations were entered into machine-readable form and continuous collecting brought expressions new to dictionaries to the attention of lexicographers. The result was *The New Zealand Oxford Dictionary* (Deverson and Kennedy 2005) and abridgements parallel to those in South Africa and Australia: little, school, mini, and others.

While closely resembling its Australian counterpart, the *New Zealand Oxford* gives special prominence to local coverage. For *laughing jackass*, the *Australian Oxford* offers merely the kookaburra; the *New Zealand Oxford* distinguishes the Australian and New Zealand usage. The *shag wagon*, a vehicle perhaps unknown in New Zealand, is not entered.

12.6 CANADIAN ENGLISH

Lexicography in Canada arrived late, in part because Canadians felt caught between Yankee schoolmasters and British remittance men.

(4) **Remittance man** *Derog.* a person living in Canada on money remitted from his family in the Old Country, usually to insure that he did not return home to become a source of embarrassment (first cited in 1896; Avis *et al.* 1967).

While other nations suffering from the colonial cringe have viewed their distinctive usages as *slang* or *nonstandard*, Canadians have been discouraged by the view that their English is merely an amalgam of American and British expressions and, hence, a mongrel dialect.

The first substantial collection of Canadian expressions, upon which this idea of inferiority was founded, was gathered by A. C. Geikie in the mid-nineteenth century to illustrate the horrors of innovation. Concluding his list, Geikie warned of 'a corrupt dialect growing up amongst our population, and gradually finding access to our periodical literature, until it threatens to produce a language as unlike our noble mother tongue as the negro patua, or the Chinese pidgeon English' (Geikie 1857: 353). Not until well into the twentieth century was there an expression of a contrary view along the lines of those found in Pettman, Morris, Baker, or Mencken.

Only as the centenary of confederation of the provinces approached was an effort made to show the evolution of Canadianisms, and the anniversary was marked by the publication of *A Dictionary of Canadianisms on Historical Principles* (Avis 1967). Given the climate of opinion on the very subject of Canadian English, it is no wonder that its relation to American and British English was the subject of the first sentence of the introduction:

> That part of Canadian English which is neither British nor American is best illustrated by the vocabulary, for there are hundreds of words which are native to Canada or which have meanings peculiar to Canada (Avis 1967: xii).

Collecting by a group of scholars scattered across the country led to a slow accretion of evidence, but the belated interest of a Toronto publisher in issuing a centennial volume required rapid completion, and it appeared just in time for the centenary in 1967. Handsomely produced, the dictionary had abundant pictorial illustrations—a relatively uncommon feature of dictionaries of this sort. For instance, the line drawing under *motor toboggan* (1948) is the locus for a set of synonyms for the vehicle: *autoboggan, motorized sled, motorized toboggan, power toboggan, skidoo, ski-scooter, ski-sled, snow-bug, snow-buggy, Snow Cruiser, snowmobile, snow scooter,* and *toboggan.* Given the predisposition of the editors, terms from early Canada were abundantly represented, particularly ones associated with members of the First Nations: **midewewin** < Algonquian, Ojibwa 'an affiliation into lodges, *Grand Medicine*'. Terms associated with early settlement were also treated in detail: *Red River cart* 'a two-wheeled cart drawn by an ox' in a *brigade* 'train' of westering migrants.

Marketing for subsequent general-purpose dictionaries revealed a gradually strengthening confidence in Canadian English. *The Penguin Canadian Dictionary,* for instance, has a seal on the front cover saying '100% Canadian Content', while on the back large letters proclaim 'The only dictionary based on a fully Canadian database' (Paikeday 1990). Unfortunately, *Red River cart* does not find its way into the dictionary; *snowmobile* carries the *Can.* label though the first citation of it appears in an American account of an expedition to the South Pole (see Hince 2000).

Consequent on a bequest to Queen's University in Kingston was the production of a *Guide to Canadian English Usage* (Fee and McLain 1997). Though not a dictionary of Canadianisms, the *Guide* gives dated citations supporting interpretations of Canadian practices. Thus *program* is 'the usual Canadian spelling' as is *programmed* and *programming.* 'Canadian and British writers prefer *ketchup*' (rather than *catsup*). Trends in pronunciation are also explained: 'Sociolinguistic studies indicate that the *ski* pronunciations [for *schedule*] are by far preferred by Canadian speakers of all ages and backgrounds, and that *SHEH jole* is on the decline.'

Another general-purpose dictionary appeared in 1998: *The Canadian Oxford Dictionary* (Barber 2001). Its dust jacket carried several patriotic appeals: 'The foremost authority on current Canadian English'; 'Defining Canadian English'; 'The Official Dictionary of The Canadian Press'. Behind these words was a schematic red maple leaf, the national symbol. In the dictionary, *Red River cart* was designated as *Can hist.* and appropriately defined. *Snowmobile* was (correctly) listed without being identified as Canadian. A list of pronunciation variants was provided for *schedule* without any notice of their distribution.

Two regions in Canada have been provided with dictionaries on historical principles. *The Dictionary of Newfoundland English* (*DNE*) treated one of the most independent varieties of English in the Western Hemisphere (Story, Kirwin, and Widdowson 1980). Not a province of Canada until 1949, Newfoundland (incorporating Labrador in 1964) was the site of the earliest North American settlement of Europeans and among the first places to receive English settlers. Connections with Ireland and the West Country of England (through the Grand Banks fishery) have given it a distinctive set of cultural practices and a variety of English showing transatlantic influences. Larger than the *Dictionary of Canadianisms*, the dictionary had a wealth of quotations and many cross-references to other historical dictionaries. Like other regional lexicographers, its editors were reluctant to rule anything out that has a local connection:

> Rather than attempting to define a 'Newfoundlandism' our guiding principles in collecting have been to look for words which appear to have entered the language in Newfoundland or to have been recorded first, or solely, in books about Newfoundland; words which are characteristically Newfoundland by having continued in use here after they died out or declined elsewhere, or by having acquired a different form or developed a different meaning, or by having a distinctly higher or more general degree of use (1980: xii).

Users of the *DNE* will especially value the references to other dictionaries. For instance, *baccalao* 'salt cod' is among the first words connecting exploration and North America. In addition to information found here, readers were invited to see how the word has been treated in the *OED*, the *Dictionary of Jamaican English*, and the *Dictionary of Canadianisms*.

The second of these regional dictionaries concerns the smallest of Canadian provinces, an island in the Gulf of St. Lawrence: the *Dictionary of Prince Edward Island English* (Pratt 1988). Documentary evidence was supplemented by a questionnaire sent to island residents and by an archive of recorded interviews. Entries were chosen in part for their affiliation with other language groups, so, for instance, *groik* 'an awkward or clumsy person' is ultimately from Scottish Gaelic and is cross-referenced to the *Scottish National Dictionary*. There are 873 main entries.

In 2006, an advisory committee was formed to assist in the preparation of a second and much enlarged edition of the *Dictionary of Canadianisms on Historical Principles*. A publication date has been set for the book to appear in 2012. Its offices will be at the University of British Columbia in Vancouver.

All of these efforts are designed to foster national pride and cultural independence. As a recent writer on the subject has declared: 'We have created unique Canadian words and sayings that belong strictly to us. Both help make us

Canucks, not Yanks' (Casselman 2006: xxvi). Nor Brits either, he might have written.

12.7 ENGLISH IN THE REPUBLIC OF IRELAND

Because English has been seen as the language of oppressors in the Republic of Ireland, there have been few dictionaries devoted to its distinctive local flavour, especially in comparison to the number of dictionaries compiled for Northern Ireland (but see Ó Muirithe 2002, 2004). Beginnings for study are found in works devoted to the Irish flavour of the country's great literary figures—particularly the study of James Joyce's English and the usages of other Irish writers (see Wall 1987, 1995). Words deriving from Irish Gaelic are given special attention but so are works from sources abroad—for instance, *quare* 'strange, odd, peculiar, memorable, queer' from eighteenth-century English. Many readers will have encountered the word in the title of Brendan Behan's 1956 play, *The Quare Fellow.* Since there is little explicit connection between Wall's *Dictionary and Glossary for the Irish Literary Revival* and other dictionaries, the reader does not discover from him that the first recorded instances of *quare* (also spelled *queer*) in this sense appear in sixteenth-century Scots poets or in so American a work as Edward Eggleston's *Hoosier Schoolmaster* (1871). This information is abundantly displayed in the *OED.*

A work not so tied to literary sources is Terence Patrick Dolan's *Dictionary of Hiberno-English* (1998). Dolan sought to 'make accessible the common word stock of Hiberno English in both its present and past forms, oral and literary' (xix). The focus of the entry for *queer* (also *quare*) narrows the definition to 'great', omitting the idea that 'memorable' or 'peculiar' are part of the meaning. Quotations from imaginative literature (with undated but particular references) show a range of uses including one that shows that *quare* can be an intensifier: 'He's trainin' queer hard.'

Productive word-formation suffixes are given special attention in Dolan's work—for instance, the diminutive *-een* in *girleen, maneen, priesteen, stooleen* which derives from Gaelic *-ín.* The entry words include cultural practices in wide use outside Ireland—for example, *curate* 'a priest assisting a parish priest', *curse* 'swear word', *strand* 'beach'. Usages associated with particular counties in the Republic are noted—for instance, *fear* 'a man' (< Irish *fear tí* 'man') used in Kerry. One may hope that this work will inspire more comprehensive successors.

12.8 ENGLISH IN ENGLAND

Intellectuals in south-eastern England have long assumed that there is no such thing as a *Briticism*, though citations in the *OED* show usages of the term beginning in 1868.

(5) **Briticism.** A phrase or idiom characteristic of Great Britain, but not used in the English of the United States or other countries. (*OED2*)

Advocacy for such an idea came, as the *OED* notes, from the United States. In 1881, an American visitor astonished his audience by claiming that he spoke the English of Chaucer and Shakespeare and that 'innovations' tending to 'corrupt "the well of English undefiled" originated' in England. Amplifying this audacious claim, he lambasted the English for abandoning the speech of 'our' Saxon and Norman ancestors (see Bailey 1991: 154–6).

Briticisms exist, though the first edition of the *OED* did not acknowledge them. The current *OED* (in progress) has begun to show the *Brit.* label in definitions: for instance, **Accident and Emergency** (or **A and E**) 'emergency room in a hospital' is described as chiefly Brit. and N. Z.; **mucker** 'close companion or friend' is simply Brit. One example of Briticisms that remain unlabelled is the verb *maffick* 'to celebrate uproariously, rejoice extravagantly' (1900). Coined in newspapers to describe the celebrations following the lifting of the siege of Mafikeng (as it is now spelled) in the Anglo-Boer War, *maffick* appeared just in time for Henry Bradley to include it in the fascicle of the *OED* published on 1 April 1906. Journalists were delighted by the new word: 'It was terrific as they passed about two thousand maffickers, mafficking as hard as they could maffick' (*OED*, 1900). The verb, an undoubted Briticism, is sustained only by the fact of its appearance in the *OED* and in the reference works influenced by it.

In 1938, an American Rhodes Scholar who had studied with C. T. Onions in Oxford—Onions was the most junior of the four editors of the original *OED*—proposed a dictionary of Briticisms (Read 1938, 1987). A former assistant editor on Craigie's *Dictionary of American English*, Allen Walker Read was well prepared by training and aptitude to undertake this work, and he amassed substantial numbers of citation slips. With the outbreak of the Second World War, Read found his attention diverted to war work in New York, and, though he prepared copy, he never brought the dictionary to completion. In old age, he told a reporter: 'I was looking forward to a bit more perfection than I could ever hope to achieve' (Read 2002, xx).

12.9 CONCLUSION

In 1900, James Murray contemplated a 'pan-lexicon' of all varieties of English, and he was right in thinking that editing such a work would be 'a big order'. How astonished he would be could he examine the dictionaries described in this chapter, nearly all of them built on his idea of 'historical principles'—the most enduring of his many lexicographical ideas. In the twenty-first century, we have the technical capacity to make this pan-lexicon all one work, and the whole could be stored on a tiny silicon chip.

Work remains to be done. Important English-speaking communities in Africa have hardly been studied at all (but see Asomugha 1981), and there are many other places in the world with a history of assimilating English and developing local standards.

In 1999, the Australian National Dictionary Centre mounted a conference with a provocative title: 'Who's Centric Now?' (Moore 2001). John Simpson, Murray's successor as editor of the *OED*, answered the question cleverly: 'If everything is a variety, is there really a centre?' (282). He followed his rhetorical question with a joke: 'Does the Queen of England really just speak Australian English with a funny accent?'

The dictionaries imply something far more democratic than the 'Queen's English'. The Queen speaks one variety of English, not one better or worse than any of the other ones. As the dictionaries surveyed in this chapter show, there are now many centres for English and likely to be more.

ONLINE REFERENCES

http://www.anu.edu.au/ANDC/ Australian National Dictionary Centre. (Accessed 23 June 2006.)

http://www.singlishdictionary.com/ Tsen-Ta Lee, J. (2004). *A Dictionary of Singlish and Singapore English.* (Accessed 22 June 2006.)

13

DICTIONARIES OF SCOTS

Margaret Dareau and Iseabail Macleod

13.1 INTRODUCTION

SCOTTISH lexicography forms a distinctive and very important strand in the lexicography of national and regional varieties of English. Scots is descended from Old Northumbrian and the Anglo-Danish which developed in the north of England, before and after the Norman Conquest. It had become, by the late fifteenth century, 'the principal literary and record language of the Scottish nation' (A. J. Aitken in *CSD*: x). During the sixteenth and seventeenth centuries, the language came increasingly to be influenced by Standard (southern) English, as part of a process usually referred to as Anglicization. This gathered pace after the Scottish Reformation in 1560 through the use of an English Bible, and was enhanced by the Union of the Scottish and English Crowns in 1603 and the Union of the Scottish and English Parliaments in 1707. By that date, English had become the language of formal writing in Scotland, and of the speech of the upper classes. 'This was now the language of social pretension, of intellectual discussion and of formal speech ... forms of speech which mostly favoured traditional Scots usages were identified with conservatives, eccentrics and, especially, with the common people' (A. J. Aitken in *CSD*: xi).

Gavin Douglas, in his early sixteenth-century translation of Virgil's *Aeneid*, made two important assertions about the Scots language: firstly, he claimed it as his own and affirmed that he would use it as the medium of his translation, despite any shortcomings it might have—he might indeed have to borrow from other languages where it was lacking—and, secondly, he was one of the first to call the language *Scottis* rather than *Inglis* (i.e. English). This awareness of the distinctness of Scots which arose in the sixteenth century was gaining expression just as it was beginning to suffer these assaults, and from the eighteenth century the awareness transformed into concern, among some for the continued existence of the language, among others for the suppression of what was seen as a hindrance to advancement.

These concerns are inseparable from a sense of Scots as a national language. 'The unique characteristics of Scots ... its individual history, its own dialect variation, its varied use in a remarkable literature, the ancient loyalty of the Scottish people to the notion of the Scots language, as well as the fact that since the sixteenth century Scots has adopted the nation's name—all of these are attributes of a language rather than a dialect. Manifestly Scots is to be seen as much more than simply another dialect of English' (A. J. Aitken in *CSD*: xiii). Consequently, lexicography itself became of particular interest in Scotland, and Scottish influence on the lexicography of English is much wider than is suggested by the Scottish dictionaries alone. Mention need only be made of Sir James Murray, a Border Scot from Hawick, one of the most eminent of all lexicographers of English (→ MUGGLESTONE). The Glasgow publisher Blackie's *Imperial Dictionary* (1850, 1882), compiled and revised by two Scots, was a major contribution to nineteenth-century lexicography, and the publishers Chambers in Edinburgh and Collins in Glasgow have played a leading part in the production of popular dictionaries up to the present day.

13.2 SIXTEENTH TO NINETEENTH CENTURIES

13.2.1 *Glossaries to individual works*

Two small works from the 1590s are the earliest known examples of Scottish lexicography: The *Appendix Etymologiae ad copiam exemplorum, una cum indice interprete* (1595), by Alexander Duncan, rector of the grammar school of Dundee, contains an index to his Latin grammar with the Latin glossed in Scots. Consider, for example: **expiro** to blawe out; to gif up the ghaist. This work was closely followed (1597, 1599) by John Skene's *De Verborum Significatione. The Exposition of the Termes and Difficill Wordes, conteined in the Foure Buikes of Regiam Majestatem*, ... (a body of laws used in Scottish medieval legal practice). Its terminology is explained, for example, *Serplath* ... conteinis foure score stanes, (and reference made to the Latin version of the work).

By the eighteenth century, glossaries were being produced of terms in Older Scots texts and later literature, especially as part of a movement which became known as the Vernacular Revival, a reaction against the Anglicizing influences following the Union of 1707. One of the earliest and most distinguished of these was Thomas Ruddiman's glossary to his 1710 edition of Gavin Douglas's translation of the *Aeneid*, mentioned earlier. It is described as 'A Large Glossary, Explaining the Difficult Words: Which may serve for a Dictionary to the Old Scottish Language'. Ruddiman not only explains words, with references to the text, and provides etymological information, but from time to time also adds notes on the Scots usage of his day, including references to his own North-East dialect, for example:

(1) Fillock, *a young mare*, equula, Scotis Bor. *filly*, and in a derisory way for *a young woman or girl*: ...

The poet Allan Ramsay added glossaries to his own poetry, and these are regarded as having influenced the somewhat Anglicized Scots spellings widely used to this day (Ramsay Vol 1.: 247–63; Vol. 2.: 291–306). Robert Burns appended a glossary to the Kilmarnock edition of his poems in 1787.

13.2.2 *Glossaries of Scotticisms*

Awareness of the impropriety of 'Scotticisms' was an important aspect of attitudes to Scots in the eighteenth century. It is first noted in the late seventeeth century in *Ravillac Redivivus*: 'that you would ... faithfully admonish me of all the Scoticisms or all the words and phrases that are not current English ...' (Hickes 1678: 77).

Post-Union Anglicization was encouraged as English became the language of formal writing, administration, and polite society. Efforts of the upwardly mobile to rid their speech and writing of Scottish features included the production of glossaries of Scots words to help in their avoidance. The earliest of these was appended by David Hume to his *Political Discourses* (1752). Probably the best known was by the North-East poet and philosopher James Beattie (1735–1803): *A List of Two Hundred Scoticisms* (1779) and *Scoticisms, arranged in alphabetical order, designed to correct improprieties of speech and writing* (1787). An interesting aspect of these lists is that quite a few of the usages then condemned as provincialisms to be avoided are now ordinary English. For example, the Scotticism 'To play cards' was to be rejected in favour of 'To play at cards'.

Sir John Sinclair of Ulbster, editor of the *Statistical Account of Scotland* (1791–98), published, in 1782, *Observations on the Scottish Dialect*. 'It was the full persuasion that a Collection of Scoticisms could be of use to my countrymen, not the vanity of being thought an Author, which gave rise to the following Publication' (Sinclair

1782: iii). Another list, *Scotticisms, Vulgar Anglicisms and Grammatical Improprieties corrected, with reasons for the corrections* ... was published in Glasgow in 1799 by Hugh Mitchell, 'Master of the English and French Academy' there.

13.2.3 *Jamieson's* Etymological Dictionary of the Scottish Language

Jamieson's *Etymological Dictionary of the Scottish Language*, first published in 1808, was in its various editions the key lexicographic text of the Scots language in the nineteenth century. It has been described by A. J. Aitken as '... the first completed British dictionary to substantiate its definitions with accurately referenced quotations, usually in chronological order, and therefore the first dictionary on historical principles of any variety of English. In its original form or in re-editions or abridgements ... Jamieson's *Dictionary* was consulted as the authority on Scots vocabulary long after it had been superseded by the *Oxford English Dictionary* in 1928' (Aitken 1992: 902).

John Jamieson (1759–1838) was a minister of the Secession Church, first in Forfar, then in Edinburgh. In Forfar in 1787, he met Grímur Thorkelin (1752–1829), professor of antiquities in Copenhagen. Thorkelin convinced Jamieson of his view that the Scots language, in which he found many echoes of his native Icelandic, was derived not from Old English but from Old Norse, which he called Gothic. As a result, in his etymologies Jamieson tends to favour Norse etymons. Following this encounter, Jamieson abandoned his previously held opinion 'that the language, spoken in the Lowlands of Scotland, is merely a corrupt dialect of the English ...' (Jamieson 1808: 1). He realized also that the disappearance of the language was hindering understanding of Scotland's past. 'It is surprising, that no one has ever attempted to rescue the language of the country from oblivion, by compiling a Dictionary of it' (Jamieson 1808: ii). He began to collect words from printed sources and from the spoken language of his day, from many parts of Scotland, 'often as a relaxation from professional labours, or studies of greater importance ... ' (Jamieson 1808: vii). The first edition was published in 1808, by subscription, in two quarto volumes. The following is part of a typical entry:

(2) To RED, REDD, REDE, RID, *v. a.* 1. To clear
to make way, to put in order, S.
... Thare he begowth to *red* a grownd,
Quhare that he thowcht a kyrk to found.
Wyntown, v. 12. 1180.

> *To red*, or *red up a house*, to put it in order, … 'Your father's house, –I knew it full well, a but, and a ben, and that but ill *red up*.' Statist. Acc. xxi. 141. N.
>
> *To red up*, also signifies, to put one's person in order, to dress.
> Right well *red up* and jimp she was, …
> *Ramsay's Poem's*, i. 273
>
> 2. By a slight obliquity, to separate, to part combatants …
> 'Gif it sall happen ony person … to be hurt … in *redding*, and putting sindrie, *parties* meetand in armes … ' Acts Ja. VI. 1593.
> c. 184. Murray …
>
> The *v.*, as here used, may be immediately allied to A.S. *ge-raed-ian*, Su.G. *red-a*, Isl. *reid-a*, Belg. *reed-en*, Germ. *be-reit-an*, to prepare; Isl. *rad-a*, … As E. *rid*, however, also signifies, to clear, it is questionable whether our *red*, in this sense, should not, rather, be traced to A.S. *hredd-an*. …

Entries are systematically organized and listed alphabetically, often with information on dialect, e.g. DINMONT, … This is pronounced *dummond*, Tweedd., *dummott*, Berw.

Some speculative commentary is inserted into the entries, but the definitions are substantiated by the fully referenced quotations, and thus most of the apparatus of a modern historical dictionary is present.

The dictionary met with great acclaim and Jamieson was encouraged to continue the work both by its warm reception and by help and contributions from many, including Sir Walter Scott and James Hogg. In 1825, a 'Supplement' was published, not a modest body of addenda but equal in length to the 1808 edition, so that it is often mistakenly referred to as the second edition. Apart from his own abridgement in 1818, these were the only versions of the dictionary published in Jamieson's lifetime, but it went into many more long after his death. The longest, begun by John Longmuir and completed by David Donaldson, was published between 1879 and 1882 in four volumes, with a supplement (this time of slighter bulk) in 1887; a considerable amount of new material was added—marked by square brackets—and earlier errors were corrected. Reprints of a shortened version were produced right into the twentieth century.

Like Sir Walter Scott, Jamieson is a major figure of the latter part of the Scottish Enlightenment, giving, with the *Dictionary*, crucial support to the Scottish tradition as well as to the beleaguered language. As well as contributing to many later dictionaries, it provided, in the early twentieth century, a major linguistic source for the poets of the Scottish Renaissance—in particular Hugh MacDiarmid—in their work to extend the use of the Scots language. His achievement is inestimable.

13.2.4 *Other nineteenth- and early twentieth-century dictionaries*

Other Scots dictionaries of the nineteenth and early twentieth century are slight in comparison with Jamieson. Ebenezer Picken's *A Dictionary of the Scottish Language* is a brief glossary published anonymously in 1818. Captain Thomas Brown's *A Dictionary of the Scottish Language* (1845) does include quotations and claims to include 'all the words in common use in the writings of Scott, Burns, Wilson, Ramsay, and other popular Scottish authors'. Another little glossary, A *Handbook of the Scottish Language*, published in 1858 under the pseudonym of 'Cleishbotham the Younger', was drawn straight from Jamieson. A more discursive treatment is found in Charles Mackay's *A Dictionary of Lowland Scotch* (1888), with etymological notes, anecdotes and quotations (not fully referenced), as well as a long introduction and an appendix of Scottish proverbs. Alexander Warrack's one-volume *Scots Dialect Dictionary*, later retitled *Chambers Scots Dictionary*, was published in 1911 and reprinted without alteration until the 1990s. Warrack had been a contributor to Joseph Wright's *English Dialect Dictionary*, which included large amounts of Scottish material (→ PENHALLURICK, Vol. II).

13.3 *DICTIONARY OF THE OLDER SCOTTISH TONGUE* (*DOST*) (1931–2002)

13.3.1 *Beginnings*

From at least as early as 1916, William Craigie[1] had begun planning a dictionary of Older Scots, to be edited on historical principles, with quotations used to support the definitions, in the style of the *Oxford English Dictionary* (*OED*). In 1919, as the *OED* was drawing towards completion, he proposed to the Philological Society a

[1] Sir William A. Craigie (1867–1957), graduate of St Andrews and Oxford Universities, worked on the *OED* from 1897, becoming co-editor with James Murray and Henry Bradley in 1901.

number of supplementary dictionary projects (Craigie 1926: 9). He considered such a series of dictionaries necessary to allow comparisons to be made relating to the changing character of English over the centuries. Specifically mentioned were dictionaries of Old English (OE), Middle English (ME), Early Modern English (EME), and 'the older Scottish'. Craigie described the different character of the Scots element in the *OED* thus: 'While the older Scottish tongue has thus received very generous treatment in the Dictionary (*OED*), the appearances it makes there are necessarily scattered and to a great extent subject to accident. At the best, it is submerged in a great mass of earlier, contemporary, and later English with which it has little in common. Considered by itself it is a very definite thing, beginning with the fourteenth century, flourishing as a literary medium from about 1375 to 1600, and maintaining a precarious existence in writing till towards the close of the seventeenth century, when a new period definitely sets in and continues unbroken down to the present day' (Craigie 1926: 9).

That he chose to edit the dictionary of Scots himself indicates Craigie's deep attachment to his Scottish roots, but *DOST* was part of his programme for the history of English, as were the dictionaries mentioned above and proposed in his original talk,[2] and those added in the published version, the *Dictionary of American English* (*DAE*) and the *Scottish National Dictionary* (*SND*). Craigie was a proponent of a separate dictionary for the modern era (1700–), but expressed the hope that the editing would facilitate comparisons between the earlier and later periods.

13.3.2 *Coverage*

Craigie's plan for the coverage of *DOST* was to take in the whole wordstock to 1600 and 'to continue the history of the language down to 1700, so far as it does not coincide with the ordinary English usage of that century. Words not found before 1600 are also included when they are not current, or are not used in the same sense, in English of the period, or when they have some special bearing on Scottish history or life. The closing of the record with 1700 rests on the practical ground that after that date few traces of the older literary language remain, and Scottish survives only as a dialect, differing so much both in form and vocabulary from the earlier standard that the two periods can be fully and consistently treated only in separate dictionaries. The full vocabulary of the language throughout this older period is included, because any attempt to limit it to words or senses entirely or specially Scottish would (in the lack of complete

[2] Holograph copy in *DOST* Archives, Edinburgh University.

dictionaries of Middle and Early Modern English) constantly render selection difficult or arbitrary, and would also fail to exhibit fully the relationship between the languages of Scotland and England during the period when they were most distinct from each other' (*DOST* Vol. I: vii). Craigie's view was influenced by his time—the heyday of the British Empire—into which Scotland had been successfully incorporated; and by the suppression of its language on a formal level. Later editors took the view that, although Scots fell into disuse for formal functions, it was used informally by many sections of society and never became merely a collection of dialects.[3] Because the two-dictionary solution was chosen, the vast number of continuities between the two periods are less evident than they might have been if the focus of the two dictionaries had been the same.

The cut-off date of 1600 was less rigorously applied by Craigie's assistant and eventual successor, A. J. Aitken.[4] If a word was included as an entry at all its whole history up to 1700 was covered, and all words originating prior to 1600 were included. Thus only words appearing after 1600 and in every way coinciding with English usage would be considered for exclusion. This too was James Stevenson's policy.[5] Margaret G. Dareau[6] and Harry Watson[7] included all words evidenced in the dictionary's citation slips, regarding the fact that a word had been borrowed into Scots during the seventeenth century as in itself of interest. However, excerpting of seventeenth century sources was less rigorous than for earlier centuries and few texts were excerpted after the 1970s, so attestations of shared vocabulary beginning in the seventeenth century were largely unavailable, with the result that from Aitken on there is little variation in coverage.[8]

13.3.3 *Collection of citations*

Craigie had had *OED*'s used and unused Scottish slips assigned to *DOST*. A further collection was added by him in the 1920s and another by Aitken in the 1950s and 1960s. The collections made or acquired by Craigie covered the most readily available sources (*DOST* Vol. I: iii–xi and List of Additional Titles, *DOST* Vol. II),

[3] See also 13.4.1 p. 316 and 13.4.4, p. 319.

[4] Adam J. Aitken (1921–98), graduate of Edinburgh University, combined work on *DOST* with teaching Scots language at Edinburgh University.

[5] James A. C. Stevenson (1917–92), graduate of Edinburgh University, came to *DOST* from teaching in 1966.

[6] Margaret G. Dareau (1944–), graduate of Edinburgh University, *DOST* Senior Editor (1988–97), Editorial Director (1997–2001).

[7] Harry Watson (1946–), graduate of Edinburgh University, Editor-in-Chief (1985–88), Senior Editor and Director (1988–2001).

[8] Recent research suggests that much more Scots continued to be used in seventeenth-century private materials (letters etc.) than had been realized or was available to *DOST*.

to which Aitken added material from less accessible printed sources and manuscripts that more than doubled the number of volumes listed (*DOST* Vol. III: xiii–xxxii). Excerption depended on volunteer readers and the editors themselves. The corpus eventually covered every available printed source and most manuscript sources: cartularies, rentals, and tax-rolls of religious institutions; parliamentary, treasury, burgh, trade, and church records; collections of laws and legal writings; testaments, family papers, account books, inventories; literary prose, history, polemic, and poetry; as well as a miscellany of other material from heraldic tracts to grammars and traditional lore—in total around two million citation slips. Aitken was also responsible in the early 1960s for the electronic Older Scottish Textual Archive,[9] from which listings of words were made available to the dictionary's editors; in this he was a pioneer in the use of computers in lexicography (Aitken 1971, Aitken and Bratley 1967, Hamilton-Smith 1971).

13.3.4 *Scale*

Problems of scale dogged Craigie's editorship. While still at the University of Chicago, he had negotiated the publication of *DOST* with the University Press. The agreement of 1929 stated that the dictionary would be completed in twenty-five parts of 120 pages each (3,000 pages in all; *DOST* in fact runs to 8,000 pages). Craigie found it impossible to keep within these limits, but Chicago found funding the publication increasingly difficult. Abandonment of the project was a real possibility. By 1950, the situation had reached the point where Professor Angus McIntosh[10] suggested that the project be managed within the environs of the Scottish universities. Aitken, who had become Craigie's assistant in 1948, was based in Edinburgh. The *SND* was also in financial difficulties, so a Joint Council for the Scottish Dictionaries was set up in 1952 to support both dictionaries, with funding from the Universities of Edinburgh, Glasgow, Aberdeen, and St Andrews (later joined by the new universities of Stirling and Dundee) as well as from the Carnegie Trust for the Universities of Scotland. When, in 1955, Aitken took over editorship, this development of the infrastructure for funding and academic support led to an expansion of the project as a whole. The size of the staff increased, though never to more than seven or eight and mostly far fewer. Aitken was joined in 1973 by Stevenson, who succeeded him as main editor in 1983. Through the 1960s and 1970s, under their leadership, the pressure to produce

[9] With Paul Bratley and Neil Hamilton-Smith of the Edinburgh University Computing Service. A copy of this archive is held by the Oxford Text Archive as 'Older Scottish texts: the Edinburgh DOST corpus'.

[10] Professor of English Language and General Linguistics in the University of Edinburgh.

copy that Craigie had suffered under abated and the project became much more a matter simply of scholarship. Aitken was central to the upsurge of interest in Scots from the 1960s and his influence in Scots-language studies continues worldwide, a decade after his death.

Whereas Craigie limited the scale of entries where Scots seemed to differ little from English and was apparently already fully covered by the *OED*, Aitken, aiming to create a full record of Older Scots, widened the scope of the editing. For instance, **Ga** *v.* and **Go** *v.* 'to go' cover barely four columns in *DOST*, in comparison to thirty-five columns of **Go** *v.* in the *OED* (*DOST* having two columns to the page where the *OED* has three), whereas **Lay** *v.* and **Ly** *v.*, under Aitken, cover fourteen and nine and a half columns respectively, to *OED*'s twenty-four and thirteen and a half. Further, Aitken refined sense analysis and developed the illustration of usage, both of which increased the number of citations, and, wherever possible, he added notes of an encyclopedic nature. He and Stevenson regarded the cultural information available in the dictionary entries as one of its great glories. **Lord** *n.*, for example, runs to thirty-two columns (**Lord** *n.* in the *OED* occupies just short of eight columns), with thirty-four main senses illustrating Scottish usage of the word in immense detail:

(3) **Lord**, *n.* ...

7. *plur.* The nobles or lay magnates of a kingdom (commonly, the Scottish kingdom) ...

Also **b.** applied to specific sections or factions of the nobles, *Lordis of (the) Congregatioun*, ...

8. *spec.* A 'lord of Parliament'.

a. A member of the class of great landowners, as dukes, earls ...

b. Further *spec.* An important baron below the rank of earl ...

Such 'lords' thus constituted a new rank of the titled nobility of Scotland, ... above the lesser barons or 'lairds' ...

II. ... Applied ... to members of Parliament or General Council or of the sovereign's Council ...

In these senses frequently embracing persons who were not 'lords' ... such as commissioners for the burghs in Parliament, or ... members of the Privy Council who were not noblemen.

13.3.5 *Structure of entries*

One characteristic of *DOST* is the appearance of several entries depending on minor differences in spellings and sources, e.g.:

(4)a **Firlot,** *n.* ... [Var. of FERLOT. See also FORLOT and FURLOT.]
1. The fourth part of a boll ...

b **Ferlot,** *n.* ... [Reduced from *ferthelot*, 'fourth part'. Cf. FIRLOT and FURLOT.]
1. The fourth part of a boll.

c **Furlot(t, Furlet(t,** *n.* ... [Var. of FIRLOT. Cf. FORLOT, FOURLOT.]
1. A firlot or bushel.

d **Fourlet, -lit,** *n.* ... [Var. of FIRLOT, FORLOT.] A firlot.

e **Forlot,** *n.* ... [Var. of FIRLOT. See also FOURLET, FURLOT.] A firlot.

This is typical of Craigie's style. Aitken and Stevenson continued with the method, though in a less extreme way, restricting such multiple entries to cases of genuine phonological distinction, e.g. 'Scottish variants', such as **Mar(e** *adj*, as against **Mor(e** *adj*, 'more'. Dareau and Watson reversed the policy, producing single entries for such groups of variant spellings: 'The rationale behind our new method is ... based on the premise that semantic rather than phonological variation should have priority in the organisation of our material' (*DOST* Vol. VII: vi).[11] For example:

(5) **Thesaurar(e, -er(e, Tresaurar, Thresaurar,** *n.* Also: **thessaurer, ... theassurer; tresorare, ... thres(o)urer,** ... [ME and e.m.E. *tresurer* (*c*1290), *thresorer* (1292), ... OF *tresor(i)er*, late L. *thesaurarius*.]

The Craigie entries, as can be seen from the examples above, are not highly detailed, though sufficiently so, considering the scale on which he was expected to work. Sometimes, further information is added:

(6) **Boll, Bow,** *n.* ... [Only Sc. and (late) northern English, perhaps repr. OE. *bolla* or ON. *bolle*, *bolli* bowl.] A measure of capacity for grain, malt, salt, etc., or of weight, varying for different commodities and in different localities.
Bolla occurs freq. in Latin documents and acts from 1240 onwards.

From Aitken onwards such Latinized examples are illustrated by quotations.

[11] See also 'A re-editing of GIF' in Macafee and Macleod (1987: 25–57).

Under Aitken and Stevenson, in spite of the inclusion of much encyclopedic material, the structure of entries is still intrinsically linguistic. Aitken was especially interested in phonological relationships, for example:

(7) **Lippie, Lepy, Leipie,** *n.* ... [Origin doubtful.
Appar. confined to the northern and eastern half of
the country, from Caithness to the Forth. Also in the
mod. dial. of the same region, in the form *lippie* (occas.
leppie) only. ...
Perh. a dimin. of ME. *lepe, leep,* (north.) *leippe* (1495–6),
e.m.E. *leap,* OE. *léap,* a (large) basket, ... There appears however to be no certain
trace of the simple *lepe* ... in Scots, ... the form
lepy, leipie would [appear to] be the orig. one and the surviving *lippie*
would represent a variant of this with late vowel-shortening.]

Stevenson was especially interested in syntactic and semantic analysis. The definitions remained similar in level of information to those of his predecessors but he divided the text into numerous paragraphs illustrating syntactic or semantic features, for example:

(8) **Pint, Pynt(e,** *n.* Also: **pinte,** ... ; POINT, PUNCT; PUNT. [ME.
and e.m.E. *pynte* (1432), ...
F *pinte* a liquid measure (13th c.) Cf. MDu. *pinte*
(1338) a liquid, or granular, measure. Of doubtful
ulterior origin.] A pint, in the usual senses and
collocations.
a. The measure of capacity for, chiefly, liquids; this
amount (*of*) the liquid, or other substance, specified.
Varying in amount according to time and locality.
Also, once, *pl.* without inflection.
Also, in *fig.* context.
(1) Et j pynt vini; ... Foure pynts tar ... For 17 pynts acavite ...
(2) ... For a pynt now mon [we] pay ... Ande ilk pynt ...
For ij s. the pynt ...
(3) That euerie salmond barrel ... sall contene twelf gallounis
of the Striuiling pynt; ... The pynt of Stirling ...
The Scottish pinte ...
b. A vessel or measure containing a pint ...
c. *attrib.* and *comb* ...

Dareau considered encyclopedic information a key element, as here:

(9) **Stan(e** *n.* ...
III. 26 A unit of weight for goods in bulk, considered as comprising a set number of pounds (latterly 16), the multiplier depending to some extent on the period and the type of produce weighed, which also determined the appropriate pound unit.
First defined in the Assize attributed to David I as 15 pounds, where the pound is 15 Cologne ounces, ...
The stone of the 1426 Assize is of 16 merchant or 'Scots' pounds of 16 Cologne ounces ... and of 16
French or Flemish 16-ounce trois pounds from 1563. ...

Contact with the rest of the community of scholars interested in Scottish studies in its widest application—literary scholars, historians, and antiquarians, dependent on *DOST* for aspects of their research—led through the 1980s and 1990s to a two-way exchange of information that caused Dareau and Watson to alter the layout in accordance with content. Much earlier H. H. Meier (1962: 445) said: 'Under Aitken, *DOST* has become more fully than ever an encyclopaedia of older Scottish culture and a first class reference book for Scottish historiography'.

13.3.6 *Etymology*

Craigie's etymologies, depending on the date of the first Scots example, supply comparative examples from ME or from EME, and occasionally from both, then from any anterior source or cross-reference as appropriate:

(10)a **Futeball** ... [Late ME. *fotebal* (1486).] **a.** The game of football. ...
... that na man play at the fut ball vnder the payne of iiij[d]; 1424 *Acts* II. 5/2.

b **Fraction** ... [e.m.E. and F. *fraction, L. fractio.* The sense appears to be peculiar to Scottish.]
a. A proportional payment ...

Aitken systematized the presentation of material, supplying comparative examples from both ME and EME, where they were available, and organized information intricately according to its closeness in location and dating to the Scots:

(11) **Mister,** *n.* ... [North. and midl. ME. *mister(e* (Cursor M.), *myster, -re, mester* (14th c.), *-ire, maistur* (c. 1400), need, necessity, but after the

15th c. appar. only Sc., ME. and e.m.E. *mister, mystere, mestier*, early ME. *mester* (Ancr. R.), craft, employment, art, OF. *mestier, mester* (F. *métier*), (1) service, office, occupation, (2) instrument, made-up article, (3) need, necessity.] …

The density of detail, given the complexity of the etymology, is typical.

The policy of Dareau and Watson was 'to regard the etymological section as simply a record of all the material available to us in related languages which *may* be of relevance to the source or development of the word … this material will normally be ordered in the standard fashion ME, e.m.E, OE, ON, MDu., MLG, or F., L., or other anterior source; unless there is clear-cut evidence that the Scots word has come direct from one of the continental languages' (*DOST* Vol. VII: vi). A level of information appropriate to the etymon was still supplied; for example:

(12) **Tartan(e**, … *n.* … [OF *tiretaine* (1247) a sort of cloth half wool, half some other yarn (Godefroy Comp.), stuff of which the weft is wool and the warp linen or cotton (Wartburg), *tridaine* (?14th c., toile de fil et de coton bleu et rouge), *tyretenne, tirtaine* (1449–1501), … Cf. also ME *tartaryn* (1343), *tartryn* (1339), *tartyn* (1454, E.E. Wills 133/2 'the testour & canape ther-to palid tartyn white and rede': MED suggests ?read *tartaryn*), … Cf. TARTAR n.]

13.3.7 *Headword*

Craigie gave the 'more etymological' of two or more forms as the first headword, thus **Abade** not **Abaid** (*DOST* Vol. I: viii). This approach continued throughout, thus **Stur(e, Stuir**, but in the final volumes this rule was applied less rigorously, with other criteria being taken into account, with, for example, the more typically Scottish form coming first, thus **Thirl(l, Thrill, Thral(l**, or, the commonest, thus **Tym(e, Tim(e**. Other common and/or phonologically distinct forms are given as secondary headwords. Thereafter all attested forms are listed. Sometimes unattested forms are used, for instance (**Pultryman,**), to help readers to locate related entries together in the strictly alphabetical listing. Brackets are used freely to indicate multiple spellings as economically as possible, for example, **Prof(f)it(t)abil(l**; the final set of brackets is not closed. To the same end, part-words are allowed, and even in some volumes used as the first headword, e.g. **Proced-, Proceiding, … proseding, -ynge.**

13.3.8 Conclusion

Funding crises occurred in 1950 (see 13.3.4), in 1981, and in 1993, when the six Scottish universities supporting the project, and the Carnegie Trust, agreed that their support would terminate in 2000. The editors Dareau, Watson, and Lorna Pike,[12] agreed to completion according to this timescale, with the proviso that the volumes of *DOST* published thereafter would maintain the quality of those already published. Time was to be saved on production by employing electronic means and the whole editorial process was rethought with the aim of completion in mind. The final three volumes of *DOST*, begun in 1994, were completed in 2001 and brought to publication in 2002.

13.4 *SCOTTISH NATIONAL DICTIONARY* (*SND*) (1931–76)

13.4.1 Beginnings

As well as being editor of *DOST*, William Craigie also played an important role in the creation of the dictionary for the modern period. In December 1907, he gave a lecture in his native Dundee to the Scottish Branch of the English Association on 'what steps should be taken to secure co-operation of members in collecting Scots words, ballads, legends, and traditions still current'. In response, William Grant,[13] a lecturer in Aberdeen, took steps to set up the Scottish Dialects Committee (SDC), with himself as convener. By 1909 the SDC had determined on a programme of 'investigation into the present condition of the Scottish dialects', and agreed that 'the record of the language should be as full as possible'.[14] Although the dictionary was thus begun by a group with a particular interest in dialectology, and therefore with a particular focus, the material collected covered written sources—literary, formal, and informal—as well as spoken dialect material (see 13.4.2). While Scots had lost its formal status, in informal use it still had a substantial level of uniformity, pinpointed as Sc. or Gen.Sc. (for General Scots) in the Dictionary, indicating use countrywide. (See also 13.1 and 13.3.2.)

[12] Lorna Pike (1956–), graduate of Edinburgh University, is Project Manager of *Faclair na Gàidhlig*, the historical dictionary of Scottish Gaelic.

[13] William Grant (1863–1946) teacher in Aberdeen of English, classics and modern languages, and phonetics.

[14] Reported in the minutes of the Scottish Branch of the English Association, 29 March 1909.

In 1924, Craigie lectured in Edinburgh on 'The Study of the Scottish Tongue', aiming 'to enlist volunteers for the preparation of a new Scottish Dictionary ... based upon the historical principles of speech sound and the careful examination of quotations illustrating the first and last appearance, and every notable point in the life-history of every word' (reported in the *Scotsman* 1924: 1 Oct.).

The Scottish National Dictionary Association Ltd (SNDA) was incorporated in 1929 to undertake the production and publication of a modern Scottish dictionary. Grant was appointed as Literary Director and Editor, with the assistance of a Representative Executive Council and of a Dialect Advisory Committee. A title, 'the Scottish National Dictionary' was determined upon, though some controversy attaches to this decision; Craigie in particular disliked the use of the word 'National' as he considered that it would be appropriate only for *DOST* and *SND* together. However, the Dictionary was aimed at a general as well as an academic readership, claiming to present 'a kaleidoscope of dissolving views of Scottish life and character, and thus makes a direct appeal to all Scots or folk of Scottish descent who take a pride in the language and history of their country' (*SND* Vol. I: i). It was seen to be a truly national enterprise, confirming the unspoken attitude of Scottish people that, despite efforts to erase it, Scots was still, as it always had been, their language: their feelings were deep and heartfelt, and 'National' resonated with those feelings. Publication began in 1931 with the first part and Volume I appeared in 1933, Volume II in 1941. David Murison[15] became Editor in 1946 and Volume III, the first under his regime, was published in 1952. In 1954, the SNDA joined *DOST* in offices in the University of Edinburgh, alongside the recently founded School of Scottish Studies and the Linguistic Survey of Scotland. To secure its future, the SNDA, like *DOST*, came under the supervisory control of the Joint Council for the Scottish Dictionaries, with support from the member universities and the Carnegie Trust. Each volume gives evidence, however, of further fund-raising efforts, with lists of patrons and other large donors.

13.4.2 *Collection*

Scotland was divided into dialect areas according to pronunciation: these are demarcated on the map in Volume I of *SND*. The areas are further divided by pre-1975 county boundaries, listing roughly north to south, from Shetland to Galloway, and including Ulster. Correspondents, provided with lists of words

[15] David Donald Murison (1913–97), graduate of Aberdeen and Cambridge Universities. He taught Scots language in the Universities of St Andrews and Aberdeen, and later Glasgow. At this time too he published *The Guid Scots Tongue* (1977), a lively and readable as well as authoritative short history of the language.

from written sources and printed slips for new words or meanings, collected material in the different dialect areas. The *Transactions of the Scottish Dialects Committee* appeared thereafter in four booklets between 1913 and 1921 and formed the beginnings of a dictionary. The spoken language represented in the collections of *SND*, in effect largely that of the middle of the twentieth century, is represented by quotations and supported by numerous references, pinpointing the time and place where a word or meaning was recorded in current use. For instance, a county abbreviation, such as Abd., Per., Kcb., indicated that the word or usage was known in that county, and a broad-area label (such as m.Sc. for central Scots), that it was known in all the counties within that wider area. From Volume III onwards (under Murison), questionnaires listing items from written sources were sent out to contributors, who marked them with local information, sometimes noting the local word for a concept if the word given was unknown.

13.4.3 Corpus

The written quotations excerpted by volunteer readers came from a large number and variety of works, including many of the same types of source used for *DOST*, except for official records, which were written mainly in English after the Union of 1707. Murison greatly increased the number and range of written sources, reading many of them himself. The list of over 6,000 works cited in Volume X covers 'books, periodicals, newspapers and other printed sources, as well as MSS' (*SND* Vol. X: 537). These and the definitions they support provide not only a record of the language of their time but also a vivid picture of Scottish life over the past three centuries.

Other reference works were used, not least Jamieson's *Etymological Dictionary*. Regional dictionaries and glossaries were also a valuable source. John MacTaggart's *The Scottish Gallovidian Encyclopedia* (1824) covered the south-west, while Jakob Jakobsen's *An Etymological Dictionary of the Norn Language in Shetland* (first published in Danish in 1908, and only in 1928 in English), and Hugh Marwick's *The Orkney Norn* (1929), treated the far north. Rev. Walter Gregor's *The Dialect of Banffshire with a Glossary of Words not in Jamieson's Scottish Dictionary* (1866) dealt with the north-east and George Watson's[16] *Roxburghshire Word Book* (1923), the

[16] George Watson (1876–1950) worked on the *OED*, then on the *DAE*, and on the early editing of *DOST*. He also made a considerable contribution to the planning of the new modern Scots dictionary, corresponding with Grant on detailed points of style and content, as well as on more general policy. In fact, in 1916 Craigie had suggested Watson as a possible editor of *SND*. His contributions to lexicography have not been sufficiently acknowledged; see Mathews (1985).

south-east, the last being an excellent account of his native dialect by an important contributor to Scottish lexicography.

13.4.4 Coverage

Grant noted in his early plan that the dictionary was to contain: '(1) All the words used in the language from the present time as far back as our literary records go; (2) the meanings and usages of these words, defined by phrase or quotation; (3) their pronunciation; (4) their etymology'.[17] The content of *SND* was in fact limited in two ways: its start date is 1700, beginning where *DOST* ends; and, whereas *DOST* deals with the whole language, including what is shared with English, *SND* deals only with words, meanings, and expressions which are distinctively Scottish. It thus excludes what is shared with Southern Standard English, but includes much that is shared with other varieties of English, especially Northern English, with which Scots has a common ancestry. Ulster Scots is included as a dialect of Scots, its development being one result of large-scale Scottish emigration there, especially in the seventeenth century.

The dictionary covers urban and, especially, rural vernacular speech of less formally educated people, for instance, *gallowses* (trouser braces), *fail* (a turf), and it includes a great variety of regional words and expressions collected throughout Scotland, for example, Shetland *shalder* (oystercatcher), North-East *tyauve* (struggle, work hard). The formal language of Scots law, education and the Church of Scotland—those areas of public life excluded from incorporation into Great Britain by the Treaty of Union—give us *advocate* (a barrister), *reset* (receiving stolen property). There is also technical vocabulary: *astragal* (a glazing bar), *pirn* (a spool). Finally, there are the many words and usages which are widely used by Scots, for example, *ashet* (a large oval plate), *outwith* (outside, beyond), *dreich* (miserable). These form a substantial portion of the total. It must be added that the vocabulary known throughout Scotland is somewhat obscured in the dictionary text, such is the wealth of regional material. Nonetheless, the element of common-core vocabulary, indicated by the label Gen.Sc. or Sc., is substantial, as witness:

(13) PLOWTER *v., n* . . . .

I. *v.* 1. *intr.* (1) To dabble . . . (Sc. 1808 Jam.; Bnff. 1866 Gregor *D.Bnff.* 129, *plleuter;* Rxb. 1923 Watson *W.-B., plouter*; Ork. 1929 Marw.,

[17] Reported in the minutes of the Scottish Branch of the English Association, 29 March 1909.

> *pulter*); 'to walk feebly' (Sh.1908 Jak. (1928)). Gen.Sc.

13.4.5 *Entry structure*

Entry structure in *SND* differs in a number of ways from that of *DOST* (or indeed from *OED*, which *DOST* largely followed). One of the problems common to *SND* and *DOST* is the lack of standardized spelling, leading to a large number of variant spellings. These are listed in the early letters with the main form or forms in capitals following the headword, followed in turn by the less common in small capitals, thus: BRITHAL, BRYTHAL, Brydal, Briddal. Later, only the commonest form is given in capitals, followed by others in italic (see (14), below). Source references are not infrequently given within the list of variant forms, as here:

(14) MERCAT, *n.* Also *mercatt, mercate, mercet, mercket, merkat, -et, -it* (Sc. 1712 J. Arbuthnot *John Bull* II. iv.; Abd. 1768 A. Ross *Helenore* (S.T.S.) 35; Rxb. 1926 *Kelso Chron.* (18 June) 4); *mairket; marcat* (Ork. 1766 P. Fea *MS. Diary* (18 June)); *markeet.* Sc. forms and usages of Eng. *market* (Sc. 1825 Jam.). Vbl.n. *mercating,* marketing (Lnk. 1710 *Minutes J.P.s* (S.H.S.) 97). [m. and s.Sc. Amɛrkət]

The same method is used to exemplify forms in subsequent word-class sections (*v., pa.t., pa.p.*, etc.). Sometimes these are clearly numbered, as in LAT *v.*, but other entries, such as LEAVE, *v.*[1], have one long list from which the user is left to pick out the word-class labels near its end.

The pronunciation, in the International Phonetic Alphabet (IPA), concludes the headword section, except where 'the headword spellings clearly indicate the word's pronunciation by normal English conventions, . . . ' (*CSD* xxi), in which case no pronunciation is given. Usually the General Scots pronunciation is given first, with dialectal pronunciations following, as in, POUT . . . [put; Kcd., Ags., Arg. p&uv.ut]. Grant's 'Phonetic description of the Scottish language and its dialects' (*SND* Vol. I: ix–xlv) is still one of the best surveys of spoken Scots.

The senses generally begin with a reference to how the word relates to English:

(15)a MISERABLE, *adj.* Sc. usage: mean, stingy, miserly. Gen. Sc. Dial. in Eng.

b TAE, *n.*[1] ... Sc. forms and usages of Eng. *toe* ...

c THIN ...

I. *adj.* 1. As in Eng. Phrs.: *thin o' claise*, poorly or scantily dressed. *Cf.* obs. Eng. *to go thin*, to be thinly clad; ...

The senses thereafter are those exclusively Scots:

(16) THIN ...

2. Of a shot in *bowls* or *curling*: narrow, not having enough bias, (Fif., Lth. 1926 Wilson *Cent. Scot.* 270). Gen. Sc. ...

4. Piqued, ... ; unfriendly (Abd., Ayr. 1972). Hence *thinness*, n., a quarrel ...

Derivatives, compounds, and phrases are generally listed in a separately numbered section with each derivative, compound, or phrase further numbered and subdivided as necessary:

(17) THIG ...

5. Derivs. and phrs.: (1) *thigger* ... a kind of beggar ... (Sc. 1825 Jam.; ne.Sc. 1972, *hist*) ... Phr. *thigger and sorner*. See also SORN, *v.*, 1.; (2) *thigging*, †*thigeing*, vbl.n., (i) the practice of begging or soliciting gifts ... ; (ii) the gift or contribution so obtained (Per. 1825 Jam.), also comb. *thigging bit*, id.; (iii) phr. *to go a thigging* ...

In other cases they are added to the appropriate category or sense, as in *mercating* and *thinness* at (14) and (16) above. Some definitions include information on register, as in MANTEEL ... Obs. in Eng. Now only *liter.*

As *DOST* and *SND* contain more encyclopedic information than most historical dictionaries, the reader fills out the picture of Scottish life as reflected in the language. For example, SAINT appears in thirteen combinations, including:

(18) ... 12. *Saint Mungo*, a name for the city of Glasgow of which St Kentigern or Mungo

is the patron saint. Phr., *St Mungo's knot*, appar. a kind of knot tied on the tails of cattle, to avert witchcraft;

In the later volumes, density of information was increased by providing fewer headwords and more sub-entries. In the early letters of the alphabet many derivatives and compounds, such as BIENLY and BACKSPANG, are separate entries, whereas such forms are later subsumed under a main headword. The headword BLACK is followed by over a hundred headwords for complex and compound forms, beginning with:

(19)a BLACK-AIRN, *n.* . . .
b BLACK-A-VICED, -VISED, -VIZED, *adj.* . . .
c BLACK-BACK, *n.* . . .

But REID (red) has eighty numbered compound forms in section *adj.* 1., beginning thus:

d . . . (1) *red-aiten*, . . . ; (2) *red-arsie*, *-ersie*, . . . ; (3) *red-avised*, . . . ; . . .

Up to the end of letter D, quotations were listed in geographical order, reverting, from E on, to chronological order. The geographical areas are listed from north to south (*SND* Vol. I: xlvii–xlviii), and the quotations follow this list, with chronological order being used where there is more than one quotation from the same area.

The formal etymology comes at the end of the entry. It traces the history of the word back to the main origins of Scots in Old English, Old Norse, Old French, and Gaelic/Old Irish. Especially in later letters, dated Older Scots forms are included, most of them extracted from *DOST* files for then unpublished volumes, as here:

(20) THRAPPLE . . . [O.Sc. *throppill*, the windpipe, 1375; . . .].

However, not infrequently, the relationship of the Scots word to English stated in the headword section, or in the first sense, as described above, is the only etymological information provided.

Typefaces are of generous size throughout, a feature which made it easy to produce a Compact Edition in 1987—supplied with a small magnifying glass, but capable of being read without aid by anyone with normal eyesight. Choice of typefaces also made possible the data capture of the text by Optical Character Recognition (OCR) which produced the electronic version in 2004; see below 13.5.2.

13.4.6 *Conclusion*

Murison, like Grant before him, was supported by varying numbers of assistant editors—more from the mid-1950s, when funding became available from the Joint Council. With a great struggle, the work was completed in 1975, with Vol. X being published in 1976. Murison had an important role in enhancing the prestige and acceptance of Scots in the latter part of the twentieth century. Along with his unceasing devotion to the *Dictionary*, he supported the study of Scots with numerous articles and talks throughout the country; its debt to him is incalculable. He was responsible for Volumes IV to X, and for the completion of Volume III. Grant's contribution in the early years of word collection, and his persistence in the face of many obstacles, should not, however, be forgotten.

13.5 TWENTIETH—TWENTY-FIRST CENTURIES

13.5.1 Concise Scots Dictionary (CSD)

As *SND* approached completion, the SNDA found itself at a crossroads. Some thought it should close down and donate its residual funds to *DOST*. (These were considerable, owing to a large anonymous legacy which arrived too late to support work on the final volume of *SND*.) The view that research and compilation should cease partly reflected a belief that Scots was a dying language which had been recorded just before its disappearance, and that the future would offer nothing else worth recording. This belief has of course not been borne out and Scots, in a period of greater political self-confidence, is flourishing. Others were optimistic and felt that more should be done to encourage Scots. A one-volume dictionary designed for a wider public was agreed upon, and the *Concise Scots Dictionary* (*CSD*) began production with a new team of editors under the direction of Mairi Robinson,[18] and with Aitken as editorial consultant.

CSD is essentially a digest of *SND* and *DOST*: its headword, for instance, is that used in *SND* or *DOST* and its content closely shadows that of *SND*, with the addition of uniquely Scottish material from *DOST* for the earlier centuries. For the letters (R–Z), where *DOST* was not yet in print, it drew on the *OED* and a

[18] Mairi Robinson (1945–), graduate of Edinburgh University, assisted Murison on *SND* from 1966 to 1973—from 1972 as Senior Editor.

number of glossaries. Forms and senses are dated and, as in *SND*, pronunciation and geographical distribution are included. An informative Introduction includes an excellent short History of Scots by Aitken. The volume was a best-seller when it came out in 1985 and continues to sell well.

Scottish Language Dictionaries (SLD), the organization set up in 2002 to carry on the work of SNDA and *DOST*, is preparing a new edition of *CSD*, with updating from the continuing data collection, as well as the *DOST* material unavailable for the first edition. The new edition will use modern Scots spellings for the headwords, and will give emphasis to the modern language as regards the layout of senses, but will nonetheless include the historical material that explains the language's past.

13.5.2 Dictionary of the Scots Language (*DSL*): *www.dsl.ac.uk*

In the 1980s, following the computer-typesetting of *CSD*, an electronic system was set up for the storage and retrieval of the SNDA's new data collection, based as before on both written and spoken sources.

From 2001 to 2004, an electronic version of *DOST* and *SND*, based on the version of *SND* already begun by SNDA, was produced in the University of Dundee. It was followed in 2005 by a *New Supplement* to *SND*, produced by SLD, with new material from the data collected since the 1980s. The former was created with funding from the Arts and Humanities Research Board (as it then was) and the latter with the help of a grant from the Heritage Lottery Fund; the funding bodies ensure that these resources are available free of charge to anyone. The Internet site www.dsl.ac.uk hosts *DOST* and *SND*, their Supplements as they exist in their printed versions, and the uniquely electronic *New Supplement*. It is a long-term ambition of SLD to undertake a major revision of all of these. Until that time comes, some of the elements required in such a revision are being created in the database that will underpin the revision of *CSD*.

13.5.3 *Small Scots dictionaries*

Smaller dictionaries have also been produced, especially with the aim of supporting the teaching of Scots in schools: notably the *Essential Scots Dictionary* (Macleod and Cairns 1996), with Scots–English and English–Scots sections. On a similar scale were William Graham's *Scots Word Book* (1977) and the *Collins Scots Dictionary* (1995).

13.6 CONCLUSION

The resources available now, and in the near future, for a language whose demise has frequently been announced are impressive. The electronic dictionaries allow the would-be user access to all the most important dictionary texts while the new *CSD* will offer the linguistic structure and spelling system frequently missing from descriptions of a language of minority status. We began this survey with the words of Gavin Douglas. We are, as lexicographers and as Scots, content that his attitude is still shared by Scotland's writers and poets in the twenty-first century. The lexicographers of Scots have almost all been Scottish and for many, probably most of them, a passion for lexicography has been combined with a passion for their native language and culture. They have been inspired to create the great dictionaries that are now so easily accessed by anyone with a computer from Aberdeen to Arkansas, for although Scots seems so much a matter for the Scottish people, it is a language that is studied and whose great writings are appreciated worldwide. In the twentieth century, Aitken and Murison were central to the Scottish lexicographical story, but, if Aitken is right in his judgement that the establishment became less inimical to vernacular Scots early in the nineteenth century and that 'We may perhaps associate this change of heart with the publication of John Jamieson's *Etymological Dictionary of the Scottish Language* in 1808 ... ' (*CSD*: xii), then perhaps Jamieson deserves the accolade of most eminent Scottish lexicographer. Be that as it may, what is clear is that, along with the writers and the mass of ordinary folk who continue to speak Scots, the lexicographers have played a central role in building the prestige that the Scots language enjoys today.

14

THE PERIOD DICTIONARIES

Michael Adams

14.1 INTRODUCTION

UPON its completion, the *Oxford English Dictionary* (*OED*) had so far exceeded even the most ambitious expectations for historical lexicography that most could not imagine a subsequent generation of historical dictionaries. 'It might well be supposed,' wrote William A. Craigie, one of the *OED*'s principal editors, 'that with the completion of such a work as this, the task of English lexicography had almost reached a final stage for the present, and that little more would have to be done for some time to come, but that is far from the case. The increased study of English which has grown up since the *Dictionary* was planned and commenced, and new and clearer views on the development of the language which the *Dictionary* itself has been instrumental in creating, call for further work in a closer and more thorough investigation of each of the various periods into which the history of our language naturally falls' (Craigie 1929: 400).

In his lecture to the Philological Society in 1919 on 'new dictionary schemes' (Craigie 1931), Craigie had envisioned several period and regional dictionaries written on historical principles, that is, modelled on the *OED*. He later argued (1937: 54–5) that the 'period dictionaries' could usefully augment the *OED* in several ways: (1) by collecting considerably more material, which would 'present a fuller record of the language during the period covered' and 'constantly carry back the date of words from one period into that preceding it', thus antedating the *OED*; (2) by gathering both 'usual' words, which might otherwise be taken for granted, and words too rare to warrant treatment in the *OED*; (3) by supplying quotations that suggest contextual meanings too subtle for definitions to capture; and (4) by ascertaining the regional affiliations of certain words or forms of words.

Primary among the period dictionaries Craigie conceived were those of Middle and Early Modern English, though scholars eventually realized that Old English deserved similar treatment. The Early Modern dictionary was organized first, but it remains unfinished and is no longer in progress. The *Middle English Dictionary*, adopted by the University of Michigan in 1930, suffered two false starts before 1945, when Hans Kurath reorganized it and finally saw it into print, beginning in 1952. The dictionary text was completely published in 2001, and a revised *Plan and Bibliography* appeared in 2007. The *Dictionary of Old English*, begun much later than the other two, in 1969, is still under way.

While the Early Modern and Middle English dictionaries were intertwined projects in their early years (they were housed in the same building in the 1930s), all three projects are in fact interrelated: they all descend from the *Oxford English Dictionary*, yet, as in most families, offspring only partially resemble the parent, and siblings can look surprisingly dissimilar. The histories of the 'period dictionaries' are partly accounts of their shared characteristics, but also of how, by planning or accident, they became distinctive limbs of the lexicographical family tree.

14.2 THE *EARLY MODERN ENGLISH DICTIONARY* PROJECT

The *Early Modern English Dictionary* (*EMED*) that Craigie had in mind would treat English vocabulary roughly from the beginning of printing in England in 1476 (Craigie suggested the date 1500) to John Dryden's death in 1700. Craigie was 'single-minded' in his lexicography, disciplined, and the most experienced of English lexicographers at the time of his proposal (Bailey 1980: 200). In proposing the *EMED*, however, he may have been overly optimistic: work on it began in 1927 but was discontinued in 1939, and, though the project was renewed in the 1970s, the dictionary remains unpublished.

14.2.1 *Rationale for an Early Modern English Dictionary*

Jürgen Schäfer carefully investigated the *OED*'s treatment of Early Modern English vocabulary, especially its inclusiveness and the accuracy of its dating, and concluded that, given more balanced and thorough excerption of materials, thirty per cent of the *OED*'s first citations could be antedated by at least fifty years, and seven per cent of the main entries 'would change their century of first citation' (Schäfer 1980: 67). For instance, Sir Thomas Wyatt had used *revulse* 127 years before the earliest text quoted in the *OED* (ibid. 171); Thomas Nashe had used *artificiality* 171 years earlier than recorded in the *OED* (ibid. 139); and Sir Thomas Malory's use of *communal* antedates the *OED*'s earliest quotation by 341 years (ibid. 167).

Later, he examined 134 dictionaries and glossaries of Early Modern English and discovered nearly 1,000 words unregistered in the *OED*, such as *obliquilined* (Schäfer 1987: 2.175) and *semidimetient* (ibid. 2.203), and nearly five hundred unregistered senses of words that the *OED* included. On the basis of just those dictionaries, he located quotations for two hundred entries at least twenty-five years later than the most recent provided in the *OED*, and quotations that antedated the first citations provided in the *OED* for approximately 1,500 entries by at least twenty-five years, including one from Richard Sherry's *A Treatise of Schemes and Tropes* (1550) that illustrates the rhetorical sense of *enumeration* 312 years before the *OED*'s earliest citation (ibid. 2.119). While *artificiality* and *communal* are not common English words, they are, in Craigie's sense, 'usual', whereas *obliquilined* and *semidimetient*, both geometrical terms, are rare, technical terms. Schäfer's sustained and systematic research confirms Craigie's predictions about the value of period dictionaries.

Schäfer wrote eloquently of the results of his work: '[N]owhere is the principle of "registering every word found in the literature", originally envisaged but later abandoned in compiling the *OED* documentation, more pressing than for this period. Early Modern English is of supreme importance not only because it harbours the greatest name in English literature, but also because its rapid lexical transmission enabled it to comprehend the totality of the age's knowledge . . . . Vast and structured documentation is necessary in order to reflect the fluid state of the English lexicon in the sixteenth century, a period afloat on uncharted seas of new words' (Schäfer 1987: 70). Hypothetically, an *EMED* would pilot the period into a lexicographical safe haven.

14.2.2 EMED: *The Once and Future Dictionary*

14.2.2 (i) The first attempt

In December 1927, Craigie invited C. C. Fries, a professor of English at the University of Michigan, to edit the *EMED* (Bailey 1980: 200). Between 1928 and 1930, Fries received about two million slips from Oxford (Bailey 1978: viii). He generated 700,000 new slips through an intensive reading programme of his own and, with the help of 460 readers, had amassed 4.5 million slips by 1934, greatly enriching the *OED* collection (Aitken 1987: 96). (All of the slips have since been returned to the *OED* in order to assist in the production of the Third Edition.) Most of those who read texts and excerpted quotations were volunteers, but the project as a whole was nonetheless expensive. The University of Michigan provided much basic financial and administrative support for the *EMED*, but Fries also arranged funds from the General Education Board and the Rockefeller Foundation, and temporary clerical staff through the Works Progress Administration. Between 1928 and 1938, outside sources provided nearly a quarter of a million dollars to the project (Bailey *et al.* 1975: ix).

On the strength of these funds, Fries assembled a small but remarkable staff, including Morris P. Tilley, Albert H. Marckwardt, and H. V. S. Ogden, all professors in the University of Michigan's English Department; Hereward T. Price, one of James Murray's assistants on the *OED* and author of a two-volume German dictionary of economic and commercial vocabulary; and Hope Emily Allen, a prominent American medievalist. Assistants on the *EMED* included Frederic G. Cassidy and Harold B. Allen; both had remarkable careers stimulated, in part, by their early lexicographical work.

The editors and assistants at the *EMED* were highly productive. Cassidy, who was also an assistant on the *Middle English Dictionary*, later co-edited the *Dictionary of Jamaican English*, organized the *Dictionary of American Regional English* (*DARE*), and saw its first two volumes into print. Tilley's *A Dictionary of the Proverbs in England in the Sixteenth and Seventeenth Centuries* (1950) assembled and analysed material in the *EMED* files. Hope Allen edited *The Book of Margery Kempe* (1940) with Sanford B. Meech, one of the *MED*'s assistant editors. Price was interim editor of the *MED*, in the year or so between Thomas A. Knott's retirement and Kurath's arrival in Ann Arbor. Thus while the *EMED* remains in one sense a failed project, it nevertheless directly and indirectly produced significant scholarly by-products and established a culture of historical lexicography in America extending from the *OED* into the twenty-first century. One may object that the *EMED*'s success was not equal to its influence, but we might reconsider the equation and decide that its influence was, in fact, its success.

For some years, alongside the reading programme, Fries developed his plan for editing and producing the *EMED*; we rely primarily on edited specimens for evidence of what that plan was. Originally, Fries and his colleagues expected to write encyclopedic information into their entries. In a specimen for the word *sonnet* circulated for comment in 1932, the opening note runs to eighteen lines of print, and includes editorial intrusions like 'The English use of the word sonnet to indicate a 14-line poem, each line consisting of 5 accents and riming according to certain fixed patterns, begins in the 16th c. after Wyatt's imitations of Italian verse.' This may seem unexceptionable, a commonplace of literary history, but a

2. One who takes two or more academic degrees at once. Cp. ACCUMULATE vb. 2.

1625 in King *PP* II Pref. p. xxxvi: [They took their degrees of B.D. and D.D. as] accumulators and compounders. 1691 Wood *Ath. Oxon.* I. 851: Charles Croke of the same house, an Accumulator & Compounder.

ACCUR, *vb.* [L. *accurrere.*] *intr.* To run together; to meet. Hence, *trans.*, to meet. Perh. in quot. 1677 with admixture of sense of OCCUR.

c1555 Harpsfield *Marryage* P 30: Both these impediments accurre in this marriage. 1651 A.B. tr *Raleigh Ghost* 340: When we vehemently apply our minde to understand, and apprehend any thing, we scarcely observe and note such things, as do accurre our sense. 1677 tr *Amelot de la Houssaye* 5: I have not suppress'd or lessen'd the honour of their Actions where they accur'd in my Discourse.

ACCURACY, *sb.* [ACCURATE. See -ACY.] The state of being accurate; precision; correctness.

[1652] 1712 H. More *Ath.* II. x. 70: Which perfect artifice and accuracy might have been omitted. 1683 Cave *Eccles.* Pref. vii: He falls short of him in judgment and accuracy.

ACCURANCE, *sb.* [L. *accurare*+-NCE.] A taking care; solicitude.

1677 Hale *C* II. 23: Can a woman,..forget a Child, a piece of her self, her sucking Child...when her natural Love is heightned by a pitiful accurance.

ACCURATE, *adj.* [L. *accuratus.*] 1. Executed with care; careful.

[1621] 1632 Burton *A M* II. ii. iv. 276: Those acurate diaries of Portugals, Hollanders. [a1680] 1759 Butler *Rem.* III. 2: A Learn'd Society.. Agreed..To search the Moon by her own light; And make an accurate Survey Of all her lands.

2. In careful or exact conformity to truth or to some standard; precise; correct; exact, esp., but not always, as the result of care;—of things and persons.

1596 Coote *Sch.*: *Accurate*, cunning. 1617 Collins *E* II. x. 461: Perfecter then any Monke, ἀκριβέστερον ζῶν, more accurate of his wayes, more exact in his courses. 1685 Boyle *MW* 68: The accuratest way, I know, is by comparing the differing weights.

ACCURATELY, *adv.* In an accurate manner; also, so as to produce an accurate result; precisely; correctly; exactly.

1611 *Bible* Pref. 7: It got credit with the Iewes, to be called κατὰ ἀκρίβειαν, that is, accuratly done. 1691 E. Taylor *Behmen Life* 425: He grew more and more accurately attentive to his duty to God.

ACCURATENESS, *sb.* The quality of being accurate; careful exactness; precision.

1617 Collins *E* Suppl. 544: He had required passing accuratenesse and strictnesse at their hands. 1695 *Philos. Trans.* 174: The Latitude thereof was observed..with great accurateness.

ACCURATION, *sb.* [L. *accuratio.*] Accurateness; precision.

1653 Whistler *Bapt.* Pref. 2: Accuration of eloquence in variety of languages.

ACCURENT[1], *adj.* [ME.] Flowing or passing in time.

c1500 *Epitaph* in *Archaeol. Cant.* XVIII: Katryn Burlton subterrat ix day with yn June Thowsand iiii c lxxxxviith yer accurrent.

ACCURRENT[2], *sb.* [AC-+CURRENT, or from the adj.] Confluence of events.

[c1630] 1664 Mun *Trade* x. A 47: Thus by a course of traffick (which changeth according to the accurrents of time) the particular members do accommodate each other.

ACCURSE, *vb.* [ME. *acursen.*] To pronounce or imprecated a curse upon (a thing or person); to devote to perdition or misery; to anathematize.

?1520 *Lyfe St. Thomas* A 7: Seynt Thomas gat a bulle for to accurse theym that so dyd ayenst hym. 1582 Whetstone *Heptam.* VI. s 4: Euyll Education wyll accurse their blessyng in hauyng of Chyldren. 1670 Prynne *K. John* Ep. Ded. d 1b: To..accurse, damn them to all eternity, for opposing or denying this their transcendent power.

ACCURSED, ACCURST, *adj.* [ME. *acursed.*] 1. Lying under a curse or anathema; anathematized; doomed to perdition or misery. Also absol.

?1520 *Lyfe St. Thomas* A 7: Saunt Thomas..the auctoryte of ye popes bull openly denounced theim accursed vnto ye tyme they came to amendement. 1597 *RJ* IV. iii. 34. 1694 Hopkins *Poems* Tib. II. iv. 106: O, to all Ages, let him stand accurst, Who e're began this Trade in loving first.

2. Worthy of the curse; accompanied by a curse; damnable; detestable.

1597 Shaks. *RJ* IV. v. 43 (1 1b): Accurst, vnhappy, miserable time. [a1681] 1684 Lacey *Buf.* V. iii. 46: I'll find some other way to destroy thee, thou accursed villain.

ACCURSEDLY, *adv.* [ME. *acursedli.*] In an accursed manner; damnably.

1610 Hall *Brownists* 13: That Euangelium aeternum of the Friers, whose name they accursedly borrowed from Reuel. 14. 6.

FIG. 14.1. Extract from specimen pages of the *Early Modern English Dictionary*, 1936

dictionary is not a book about literary history. Those supervising the dictionary from afar, at the Oxford University Press, were not impressed with the specimen (Bailey 1980: 212). Fries and his colleagues tried a different approach.

In 1936, they submitted entries in the range A–ATR to public scrutiny. The text in Figure 14.1 suggests that the *EMED*'s plan was still underdeveloped. For instance, three entries, those for *accur*, *accurent*, and *accurrent*, misrepresent their headwords. The first, *accur*, is a variant spelling of *occur* and should probably be entered under it; the etymology, then, is also mistaken, since English *occur* is a reflex of Latin *occurere*, not *accurere*. Entries for *accurent* and *accurrent* display further editorial confusion and disorganization. *Accurent* is an *a*-prefixed form of *current* "running in time, in progress" (*OED* s.v. *current* a. 3.a-b); in fact, *accurent* is not a Middle English form, though labelled as such; dated first from 1608, it belongs in the *EMED*, though perhaps not under this headword. *Accurrent* is attested from the mid-fifteenth century (perhaps the label was misplaced under *accurent*), but it cannot be defined as 'confluence of events', which does not substitute for the word in context: 'Thus by a course of traffick (which changeth according to the confluence of events of time' does not really make sense. In 1936, then, Fries and his colleagues still struggled to conceptualize treatment of Early Modern English vocabulary.

While these missteps justify criticism, they represent the intractability of Early Modern English: it is no accident that the *EMED* is the one period dictionary left unfinished, twice attempted and twice abandoned. One can see Fries' attempt to impose order on that lexicon: he entered the prefix *ac-* earlier in the specimen, appropriately, because Early Modern (and not Middle English) writers sometimes reanalyzed words as having taken the Latin prefix *ad-*, which becomes *ac-* when it assimilates to base words beginning with *c-* (like *current*). Thus, *accur* and *accurent* were examples of an Early Modern lexical phenomenon for which the *EMED* had to account, because it belongs particularly to the period.

Fries adhered to the plan that accompanied the 1936 specimen, in which he wrote that, 'Not more than five quotations should amply illustrate all meanings that run through the period.' The entries for *accurse* and *accursed*, illustrated in the figure, clearly conform to this principle, providing only three quotations for each. The amount of quotation would not seem to amplify the evidence for Early Modern English as much as Craigie had hoped, but probably responded to concerns about the eventual length and cost of a too expansive *EMED*.

When the number of quotations per sense is sharply restricted, editors may be tempted to include quotations from famous authors, excluding the mass of writers and text-types from entries. Fries resisted that temptation. '[I]f it is necessary,' Fries wrote in the same document, 'to choose between a good quotation from an unknown writer and an equally good one from an important literary figure we should choose the former because of the light which the obscure writers throw upon the usage of the more important ones.' Early Modern English was not the special province of great writers, and the obscure writers (who far outnumbered the famous ones), were not writing simply to illuminate the illustrious. But consider the quotations that appear under *accurse* and *accursed*: both senses of the latter include quotations from Shakespeare's *Romeo and Juliet*, but the works of Charles Hopkins, William Prynne, and George Whetstone are comparatively obscure. Here Fries seems to have fulfilled his declared intentions, and it is worth noting that none of the *EMED*'s quotations for *accurse* or *accursed* appears in the corresponding *OED* entries.

Bailey (1980: 207–8) identified Fries's two most interesting innovations in historical lexicographical method, though it is far from clear that either was desirable. First, Fries proposed to include a section of ambiguous quotations in some entries, in order, as he put it in one of his 'decisions' (1936), 'to explain a transition in meaning ... demonstrate the existence and range of double or unspecialized meanings ... or to oppose recorded judgments that have given either wrongly specialized or too specialized meanings'. So in the *sonnet* entry he wrote, 'in many quotations it is impossible to determine the precise meaning of the word sonnet, for the same writer sometimes uses the word in all three of its major senses'. Thus Fries follows his own rule: 'In all cases *the points at issue* should be explained in lieu of the usual definitions of meaning'. Nearly all quotations in the *sonnet* entry were ambiguous, but historical lexicographers tend to put such explanations aside in favour of definitions: ambiguity is not an excuse to avoid sense analysis and defining.

Second, Bailey observed that Fries proposed, 'experimentally for the present', as he wrote in his 1936 'decisions', to include a section of 'contemporary comments' in entries where such would 'throw particular light upon meanings, range of use, or attitude toward the word and its various uses'. That is, Fries had invented yet another category of encyclopedic material for his entries: 'These contemporary comments are to be regarded not solely as *evidence* of meaning or use but as the explicit thought of the people of the time concerning their own language'. If the specimens are good evidence, 'the people' are all illustrious, and their comments put forward as evidence for the significance of some cultural phenomenon, but not as evidence of the word in question *per se*—the comments are not about words so much as the 'things' they supposedly represent.

Fries's innovations were certainly adventurous and marked the *EMED*'s method as distinct from that of the *OED*: indeed, most historical lexicographers prefer to include quotations that both explain phenomena underlying the word in question and illustrate use of the word among the other quotations, within the same semantic analysis. Interestingly, Fries's experiment may have influenced Cassidy, who introduced a quasi-encyclopedic technique into *DARE* entries (Adams 2002c: 375–8); he did not include the same sort of encyclopedic material as Fries, but he did depart from practices favoured by the *OED* and the *MED*. In other words, working for Fries may have loosened the constraints on Cassidy's lexicographical imagination.

After assessing the problems with editorial method revealed by the *sonnet* specimen, Fries and Thomas A. Knott, then editor of the *Middle English Dictionary*, decided in 1935 to edit portions of the letter L together, that is, to set *EMED* and *MED* editors to work as teams to prepare entries for their respective dictionaries with each other's help, so that the two dictionaries would 'fit' well together and describe between them a continuous history of English words from the Middle Ages into the Early Modern period. Some of the *MED*'s assistant editors, notably Sanford B. Meech and Harold Whitehall, believed that the approach, while promoting social contact, was a waste of time (Adams 1995: 153–8). They also lacked confidence in the specimens produced as the result of this experiment, L–LEEWARDNESS in the case of *EMED* (1936) and L–LAIK in the case of the *MED* (1937). Both Kenneth Sisam, at the Press, and Craigie sharply criticized the *EMED*'s specimen and further work on L was suspended (Bailey 1980: 216).

The editors turned to work on A thereafter, but in March 1939, the University of Michigan decided to suspend work on the *EMED* in order to concentrate its limited resources on the *MED* (see Lewis 2007: 4). Taking on both projects was, perhaps, too much for one university to fund and administer. But Fries's specimens had not met with approval at OUP, either, and some observers thought that Fries's enthusiasm had waned towards the end of the project (Bailey 1980: 213). It made sense, in any event, to treat Middle English before attempting the later, much larger, and much better attested vocabulary of Early Modern English.

14.2.2 (ii) The second attempt

In 1965, R. C. Alston proposed a *Dictionary of Tudor English 1475–1640*, the announcement of which prompted a new attempt to organize the *EMED* at Michigan (Aitken 1987: 97), led by Richard W. Bailey, James W. Downer, and Jay L. Robinson. With funding from the National Endowment for the Humanities, the American Council of Learned Societies, and the Horace H. Rackham Foundation at the University of Michigan, they assembled and analysed the *EMED*'s 38,500 quotations illustrating twelve auxiliary verbs, producing what they called 'the primary index', and then analysed the 57,000 other words besides those twelve auxiliaries that occurred in those 38,500 quotations, called 'the secondary index'. The results were published on microfiche and described in *Michigan Early Modern English Materials* (Bailey *et al.* 1975), which also compiled the *EMED*'s extensive bibliography of some 14,000 items (Bailey *et al.* 1975: vii), a stage at which the project received considerable support from Xerox University Microfilms.

The most important innovation associated with this stage of the *EMED* was its use of computers to generate the fiche. In this sense, along with the *Dictionary of American Regional English* and the nascent *Dictionary of Old English*, the *EMED* project was forward-looking and explored the technological basis for lexicography at the earliest possible time; while such technology has changed considerably since the 1960s, later dictionaries benefited from the *EMED*'s example. 'Unlike most lexical research,' Bailey wrote, the *EMED* project was 'committed to a corpus publically [sic] available (through computer tape and microfiche), separate presentation of data and interpretation, maximum use of contemporary technology, and, through computer networks, cooperative efforts joining scholars with common interests but differing institutional affiliation' (Bailey 1980: 220). It was a splendid and influential vision of a new historical lexicography, but funding for the revived *EMED* ran out in 1975 and was not renewed, so the project once again ground to a halt, even though Bailey continued to work on the *EMED*'s materials for several years and assembled some 4,000 additions and antedatings to the *OED*, published in 1978.

According to Bailey *et al.* (1975: xix), the *EMED* project consumed some three hundred lexicographer-years. Bailey and his colleagues made some progress towards a product called 'The Early Modern English Dictionary', but it was, as they wrote, 'only the first stage of a work of greater value', the as yet unpublished work of which 'the final shape will depend upon the interest and support of many scholars, at least as many as the two thousand who have already contributed since the first citations were collected for the *OED* more than a century ago' (Bailey *et al.* 1975: xxxii). Such 'interest and support' has not recently been forthcoming, but, after all, the *EMED* was always an optimistic project, a once and future dictionary, and we can look forward to a third attempt.

14.3 THE MIDDLE ENGLISH DICTIONARY

After Craigie's call for a historical dictionary of Middle English, the Modern Language Association and American Council of Learned Societies sought an

American home and an American leader for the project, as opposed, for instance, to a British leader for an American project, as when Craigie became editor of the *Dictionary of American English* at the University of Chicago in 1925. In 1927, they settled on Clark Northup, a professor at Cornell University, who inherited the materials of Ewald Flügel, a Stanford University professor who had begun a Chaucer glossary but had not been able to finish it before he died. Northup arranged for access to the *OED*'s Middle English slips, and A–G were transferred to Cornell at some point late in the 1920s (Lewis and Williams 2007: 3). For reasons not entirely clear (funding was certainly a problem), Northup did not make much progress. Charles C. Fries, already leading the Early Modern English Dictionary project at the University of Michigan, apparently convinced the university to adopt the Middle English dictionary project as well. Fries negotiated with Craigie to transfer the rest of the relevant *OED* slips to Ann Arbor, and the slips under Northup's control were shipped there too, altogether amounting to some 430,000 quotations, both those included and those rejected for publication in the *OED* (Lewis and Williams 2007: 3).

14.3.1 *Two false starts*

Michigan and the Modern Language Association jointly approved Samuel Moore as editor of the *Middle English Dictionary* in 1930. (This section draws freely on Adams 1995 and 2002b, unless otherwise indicated.) Moore was a well-respected scholar of Old and Middle English, and, though he had no lexicographical experience, he grasped immediately the work that would be required before editing could begin. He hired Sanford B. Meech, Harold Whitehall, and James Rettger as assistant editors, and together they launched an ambitious reading programme to supplement the *OED* material (Jost 1985 and 1986). This additional programme involved more than a hundred volunteer readers, closely supervised by Meech. It added nearly 300,000 quotations to those borrowed from the *OED*, Northup, and Flügel, so that the total number of slips available for editing approached 900,000. Middle English had no standard dialect until well into the fourteenth century, and the rise of a standard then by no means led to diminution of the historical regional dialects. Moore realized that any durable dictionary of Middle English would have to account for dialects in some fashion, so he and his colleagues began to assess the dialectal value of the material in their possession and to articulate the positions on dialect that would inform the published dictionary (Moore, Meech, and Whitehall 1935).

Like Fries, and perhaps under his influence, Moore conceived of his *MED* as an Oxford dictionary. For the most part, it relied on printed texts without much concern for textual variation—a problematic decision, since many Middle English texts were unedited in 1930, or edited badly. In 1932, Meech travelled to England to search libraries and collections of public records for unknown manuscripts useful in the dialect survey and editing generally; he located hundreds, but missed hundreds more, and the bibliography he compiled in 1934 was thinner than it should have been, much thinner than the *MED*'s ultimate bibliography. As a result, any *MED* that Moore and his colleagues edited would have constituted a large supplement to the *OED*, and the archival record of Moore's editorship suggests that he intended to follow the *OED*'s entry structure, right down to the typographical distinctions for which the *OED* is justly admired. The grip of the *OED* on the *MED* and *EMED* was strong, not least because the University of Michigan had entered into publishing agreements with the Oxford University Press that helped to subsidize the projects; the Press often turned to Craigie and C. T. Onions, the other surviving principal editor of the *OED*, for advice about the American dictionaries—which rarely met their expectations, partly because the period dictionary editors were Americans. In any event, the *OED*, so recently completed (the 1933 *Supplement* was still in press), exerted a centripetal lexicographical force too strong for novice editors, like Moore, to resist.

Moore died unexpectedly in 1934 and was replaced by Thomas A. Knott. Knott had been the first choice as editor in 1930, but he declined because he was then the executive editor of *Webster's New International Dictionary of the English Language, Second Edition* (1934). By the time Moore died, and with Knott's work for the Merriam-Webster Company all but complete, he accepted the renewed offer of the *MED*. In spite of his experience of leading a major dictionary project, despite the fact that, like Moore, he was a noted scholar of Old and Middle English, Knott proved ill-equipped to manage the *MED*. He never clearly conceived what an *MED* should be, especially given the constraints on length imposed by the Press: he vacillated between a dictionary with a literary bias and a general one and between treating dialect and avoiding it as too complicated. He found encyclopedic explanation irresistible and the disciplines of etymology and sense-analysis challenging. All of these problems were evident in the specimen of entries L–LAIK published by the Press in 1937 and circulated for comment among prominent medievalists. The comments were mixed, but the most prominent and experienced among the respondents were highly critical.

By the time they were editing the specimen, some members of the staff were restive: they lacked confidence in Knott, whose failings Meech exposed to the Modern Language Association Committee responsible for the dictionary. Meech had already had a disruptive argument with Hope Allen over their respective roles in editing *The Book of Margery Kempe*, and his treachery in this case was a final straw for his senior colleagues at Michigan. He and Whitehall were fired in

1938, partly because funds were tight, partly because their dissent made them expendable. Struggling against the Depression, then the onset of war, Knott regrouped and edited a portion of A—once again circulated, once again criticized—and he appears then to have lost his will to continue. Though the *EMED* had been suspended in 1939, in order to concentrate resources and focus attention on the *MED*, Knott made little progress—most of that in collecting and preparing crucial texts—and the project, after fourteen years of continuous operation at Michigan, was in disarray.

In 1944, Hereward T. Price, once an editor on the *EMED*, was appointed interim editor of the *MED*. He harboured ambitions of becoming the *MED*'s permanent editor, but these were dashed when Michigan offered the position to Hans Kurath. The Modern Language Association objected to the appointment because Kurath had no experience in lexicography (neither had Moore, however, and experience failed to support Knott through his difficulties) and was not a scholar of Middle English. He was, however, a proven leader of a complex scholarly project, the Linguistic Atlas of the United States and Canada, the first component of which, the *Linguistic Atlas of New England*, he had published in four volumes between 1939 and 1943. Michigan, after all the primary source of the *MED*'s funding, asserted its right to hire its own personnel. The Modern Language Association felt that the university had violated their agreement about joint management of the project, so retired from its supporting position. The *MED* entered a new era.

14.3.2 *Kurath's* MED

Kurath had a very different idea of the *MED* from Moore and Knott: he viewed it, not as a supplement to the *OED* but as an independent dictionary loosely in the *OED*'s tradition of lexicography on historical principles. Kurath was an arch-empiricist, sceptical about knowledge of semantics and of editorial judgement: he privileged evidence over everything. Kurath's *MED*—the *MED* finally published—eschews encyclopedic information, favours glossarial definitions, and offers terse etymologies; but each entry lists all attested spelling variants, analyses senses thoroughly, and provides as many quotations as possible, given constraints of evidence and space. Like A. J. Aitken—editor, after Craigie, of the *Dictionary of the Older Scottish Tongue*—Kurath believed that 'definitions remain subservient to the citations themselves', because 'their function is simply to identify separate sets of citations; more specifically, they serve as finding-aids or sign-posts to particular sections of a long entry, they specify the criteria which distinguish one division of citations from one another' (1973: 259).

One can see the differences between Knott's editorial design and procedures and Kurath's easily, by comparing Knott's 1937 specimen to the treatment of the same range of entries, L–LAIK, in the published *MED*. Knott devoted eleven double-column, *OED*-style pages to the range; the *MED* treatment, in contrast, fills nearly twenty-four double-column pages, just over twice as many as Knott had produced. Remarkably, even granting the page-space efficiency of Kurath's spare entry format, which minimizes spacing and distinguishing typography, the *MED* includes 1,506 quotations in its treatment, whereas Knott managed to include only 560—Kurath's plan includes roughly three times the evidence in roughly twice the space. The difference in these ratios of evidence and space can be explained only by difference in editorial plan and technique. (Knott entered 121 lemmata, compared to the *MED*'s ninety, but several of Knott's entries were absorbed into the *MED*'s entry for *ladi(e* 'lady'. That is, the same material is distributed differently, as compounds formed on *ladi(e* are treated as derivative in the *MED*.)

If one compares the entries for *lai* in the general senses 'song' and 'short narrative poem', one immediately recognizes profound differences of content, method, and style that distinguish Knott's conception of the *MED* from Kurath's, much to Kurath's credit. Knott's entry is interrupted by a lengthy encyclopedic comment on the Breton lai as a literary form; though the note accompanying sense 2b. is only seventeen lines long, compared to twenty-seven lines of quotations, the note is set in type so large that it fills two column inches of space, whereas all the quotations for all three senses occupy but two and a half column inches. Knott shared encyclopedic tendencies with Fries, then, very likely because they worked out their method side by side. It is not difficult to gauge the difference between Knott's and Kurath's temperaments as lexicographers—there is no similar intrusion in Kurath's entry, though evidence of the phrase *lai of Breton* is noted laconically in the definition (see Fig. 14.2).

Like his predecessor Moore, as well as his colleague Fries, Knott thought of the *MED* as a sort of extended supplement to the *OED*, as the 1937 specimen entry for *lai* illustrates: the ' + ' symbol marks an etymology that supposedly improves the *OED*, the encyclopedic commentary just discussed, and the antedating represented by the quotation from the *Lai le Freine*—a1330 beats c1330. Kurath reconceived the *MED* as a dictionary on its own terms, related to the *OED* in scope and method, but edited from scratch according to principles suited specifically to the Middle English lexicon and justified without reference to the *OED*. Kurath resisted commentary and annotation as speculation: he wanted to say only what could be proved, so that the *MED* would stand the test of time and avoid misinforming users. He restricted etymologies to noting the immediate

influenced by OF. *lei commune*.
1429 *Rolls Parl.* IV. 360: Yan ye partie yat feleth hym greved, shal take ayenst hym an action at *ye commen laye*, of trespas and disceit.

LAI[3], *sb.* OD: Lay, *sb.*[4] [OF. *lai*, +of Celtic origin; cp. Irish *laoi laoidh*, song, poem, OIr. *lōid*, Gaelic *laoidh* poem, verse.] **1.** A lyric poem or song of either religious or secular character.
a1250 Brown *English Lyrics XIII.* 8/167: Ich habbe i-sungen þe [the Virgin] ðesne englissce *lai*. **a1400** Chaucer *E. Mch.* 1881: And in a lettre wroot he al his sorwe, In manere of a compleynte or a *lay*, Unto his faire, fresshe lady May.

2a. A short narrative poem of romantic adventure;—in some cases intended to be sung with or without musical accompaniment.
a1330 *Sir Tristrem* 551: An harpour made *alay*, Þat tristrem, aresound he. **a1400** *Gawain & Green Knight* 30: If ȝe wyl lysten þis *laye* bot on littel quile, I schal telle hit astit, as I in toun herde, with tonge,..In stori stif and stronge. **a1450** *Wars Alex.* 6: Sum has langing of lufe *lays* to herken, How ledis for þaire lemmans has langor endured.

+**b.** *Specif.* A 'Breton lay', a short narrative poem of romantic adventure with a purported Breton original. The six poems in ME. which call themselves lays and claim Breton origin are: *Sir Orfeo*, *Lai le Freine*, Chaucer's *Franklin's Tale*, *Erle Toulouse*, *Sir Gowther*, and *Emare*. *Sir Launfal*, which calls itself a lay but does not claim a Breton original, is generally grouped with the above six; *Degare* (a1330), which neither calls itself a lay nor purports to be of Breton origin, has also been grouped with them by some scholars. These eight poems are all short, unified, and coherent. In only three, *Lai le Freine*, *Franklin's Tale*, and *Degare* is the locale of the story in Brittany. Numerous lays of purported Breton origin were written in OF. in the second half of the twelfth century, in the thirteenth century, and in the first quarter of the fourteenth century, among the most famous of which are those written by Marie de France, c1170.
+**a1330** *Lai le Freine* 14: In Breteyne bi hold time Þis *layes* were wrouȝt, so seiþ þis rime. **c1330** *Sir Orfeo* 13: In Brytayn þis *layes* arne ywryte, Furst yfounde and forþe ygete—Of aventures þat fillen by dayes, Wherof Brytouns made her layes; When þey myght owher heryn Of aventures þat þer weryn, Þey toke her harpys wiþ game, Maden *layes* and ȝaf it name. **a1400** Chaucer *F. Fkl.* 710: Thise olde, gentil Britons, in hir dayes, Of diverse aventures maden *layes*, Rymeyed in hir firste Briton tonge, Whiche layes with hir instrumentz they songe. **a1400** *Launfal*, 4: A *ley* þat was ysette, þat hyȝt Launual. **a1440** *Erle Toulouse* 1220: Yn Rome thys gest cronyculyd ys, A *lay* of Bretayn callyd ywys. **a1450** *Sir Gowther* 28: A *lai* of Breyten long y soȝght And owt þerof a tale have broȝht, þat lufly is to tell. **a1450** *Emare* 1030: Thys ys on of Brytayne *layes*, That was vsed by olde dayes.

3. Song of birds.
a1300 *K. Alis.* 5211: The foules syngeth her *lay*. **a1400** Chaucer *B. Th.* 1959: The thrustelcok made eek hir *lay*. **a1420** Lydg. *Troy Book* I. 1198: Þe larke with a blissed *lay*. **c1430** Lydg. *Churl & Bird* in Hammond Eng. Verse 109/346: The cokkow syngen can but oo *lay* In othir tunys she hath no fantasye.

LAI[4], *sb.* OD: Lay, *adj.* & *sb.* [OF. *lai* a secular person.]

FIG. 14.2. Extract from specimen pages of the *Middle English Dictionary*, 1937

etymon of the precise Middle English reflex: in the case of *lai*, the *MED* records 'OF', that is, Old French, as the etymology; in contrast, Knott took *lai* back to Celtic etyma. No example better demonstrates Kurath's insight: the current *OED*

lai n. (2) Also **lei.** [OF]
(a) A short narrative poem of love, adventure, etc., to be sung and accompanied on instruments, especially the harp; ~ **of Britoun,** a Breton lay; also, a tale; (b) a song, lyric; (c) the song of a bird.

(a) c1330 Orfeo 50/599: Harpours.. made her-of a lay [vr. ley] of gode likeing.. swete is þe note. c1380 Firumb.(1) 1602: What halt hit muche her-of to telle to drecchen ous of our lay [rime: play]? (c1395) Chaucer CT.Fkl. F.710, 712: Thise.. Britons in hir dayes Of diuerse auentures maden layes.. Whiche layes with hir instrumentz they songe Or elles redden hem for hir plesaunce. c1400(?a1300) KAlex. 2840: Tofore þe kyng com on harpoure And made a lay of gret sauoure. c1450(?a1400) Wars Alex. 6: When folk ere festid & fed.. sum has langing of lufe lays to herken. (a1470) Malory Wks. 618/10: I woll make a lay for hym and.. make an harpere to syng hit. a1500(?c1400) EToulouse 1220: Yn Rome thys geste cronyculyd ywys; A lay of Bretayne callyd hyt ys. a1500(?c1400) Gowther 28: A lai of Breyten long y soȝght And owt þerof a tale have broȝht. a1500 Orfeo (Hrl) 2/3: The layes that ben of harpyng.. ben of wele & sum of wo.. of bourdys.. of rybaudy.. of trechery.. of happes þat fallen by whyle. (b) a1250 Cristes milde moder 167: God.. unne me.. alle mine ureondmen þe bet beo nu to-dai Þet ich habbe i-sungen þe ðesne englissce lai. c1300 SLeg.Dunstan (Hrl) 170: Harpe he louede suyþe wel.. A day.. he sat in solaz and a lay þeron drouȝ. (a1393) Gower CA 8.1670: Sche harpeth many a lay And lich an Angel sang withal. (c1395) Chaucer CT.Mch. E.1881: In a lettre wroot he al his sorwe In manere of a compleynt or a lay.

(c) (c1390) Chaucer CT.Th. B.1959: The thrustelcok made eek his lay [rime: nay, spray]. (a1393) Gower CA 7.1046: Every brid upon his lay [rime: Maii] Among the griene leves singeth. c1400(?a1300) KAlex. 5202: Mery tyme it is in Maij! Þe foules syngeþ her lay. c1400(a1376) PPl.A(1) (Trin-C) 9.57: Vndir a lynde.. lenide I me a stounde To lerne þe laies þat louely briddis maden. (a1420) Lydg. TB 1. 1198: Þe larke with a blissed lay [rime: day] Gan to salue the lusty rowes rede Of Phebus char. a1425 By a forest 27: I.. askesd [read: asked].. why sche song in her lay, 'Parce michi domine'. a1450-1509 Rich. (Brunner) 3760: Merye is in þe tyme off May, Whenne foules synge in here lay. a1475 (?a1430) Lydg. Pilgr. 14383: The Cookkoow.. vp-on o lay halt so long. a1500(?a1410) Lydg. CB 346: The cookkow syngen can but o lay [rime: May].

Fig. 14.3. Extract from the *Middle English Dictionary*

explicitly excludes a Celtic origin; ironically, Knott's '+', rather than marking an improvement, warns the user of potential error.

Kurath's editorial plan was syncretic: though he rejected essentially all of Knott's work, he embraced what was useful in that of his other predecessors.

As Norman Blake observes, 'Kurath subsumed Moore's working practices, and many of Flügel's, within his "Editor's Guide", issued in 1947. Particular attention was paid to documents which could be localised and early texts were read with special care. Attention was given to personal and place names' (2002: 57). But the plan was also boldly new. Among many small innovations, three stand out. First, quotation paragraphs were carefully balanced, to whatever extent the evidence would allow. Editors were expected to begin a paragraph with the quotation of earliest date and to supply quotations at roughly twenty-five-year intervals, simultaneously exhibiting all attested spellings. The assemblage of quotations under each sense was expected to provide evidence of subtle semantic development, syntactic patterns of use, regional variation, and also, represented by the array of text types, social variation.

MED entry for *lai* certainly achieves a chronological density beyond that of Knott's earlier choice of quotations, especially revealing in the case of the *MED*'s sense (b), which corresponds to Knott's sense 1: Knott's evidence jumps 150 years, while Kurath's illustrates a more continuous history of the meaning, with the largest jump in the evidence less than a hundred years—of course, one can only illustrate facts insofar as the evidence allows (see Fig. 14.3).

The *MED* evidence also suggests a more complex semantics for *lai* than possible with Knott's selection: in 1300, according to the *MED*, a lay can be sung in 'solas' whereas in the quotation from Chaucer that both treatments share, the song is one of 'sorwe'. The *MED*'s quotation from a1500 *Orfeo* indicates that, by the end of the Middle English period, *lai* meant 'poem about sex, treachery, or things that happen'. Knott quoted the c1330 *Orfeo*, in which *lai* means 'poem of adventure', but the *MED* captures that sense in the quotation from Chaucer's *The Franklin's Tale*. Whereas Knott's *lai* is made, wrought, sung, or heard in the town (depending on the quotation), the *MED*'s, given the quotation from the *Wars of Alexander*, is something to which those with love-longing should 'herken', that is, 'listen' or 'take heed', shades of meaning missing from the specimen, though available in the literature.

In its larger array of quotations, the *MED* suggests, even certifies, facts about the use of *lai* beyond the reach of Knott's specimen entry. For instance, Knott's entry concentrates too much on the use of *lai* in lays, where the *MED* adds several quotations from other types of works, such as the legend of Saint Dunstan and Malory's *Works*, referring to the tradition of lays and their singing. Another way of expressing the same difference is to note that more prose works are quoted in the *MED* entry than in Knott's specimen entry. If one wondered whether *lai* was an item of exclusively poetic diction, one would arrive at different conclusions from the two entries—the one derived from Knott's evidence would be wrong, the one from the *MED* as right as the available evidence could support.

The *MED* better represents use of *lai*, not only in courtly romance, but in common song, historical poems like those by Lydgate, and in works as idiosyncratic and uncourtly as *Piers Plowman*. And while Knott captures a Northwest Midlands example of *lai* by quoting the romance *Gawain and the Green Knight*, the *MED*, while for some reason excluding that, supplies South-western evidence in the quotation from the romance *Sir Firumbras* and Northern evidence in that from *Piers Plowman*, given the manuscript quoted. While one can criticize the range of dialectal use represented in the *MED*, then, its treatment still improves on that in Knott's specimen, primarily because, in the course of editing, more evidence and evidence of more kinds was taken into account.

The *MED*'s second great innovation solved a bibliographic problem. Kurath and Margaret Ogden, who originally designed and compiled both the *MED*'s working bibliography (the densely informative collection of file cards used by editors and staff) and the published version based on it (Kurath, Ogden, Palmer, and McKelvey 1954), had to resolve an intractable textual problem of profound consequence to every entry, indeed, every quotation, as it had to do with assigning accurate dates to Middle English texts: a text may be represented by many manuscripts, and those manuscripts may be of various dates and dialects; but, unless the original manuscript is extant, all of the manuscripts will postdate the text's composition, on occasion by as much as a hundred years. A manuscript may reflect the speech of its underlying text's author, of the scribe of the exemplar manuscript, or the scribe of the manuscript cited in the entry. Kurath and Ogden decided to treat all manuscripts separately (contrary to the *OED*'s practice and that of all other period and regional dictionaries compiled on the *OED*'s pattern), and, for each quotation, to provide both a manuscript date and composition date, a novel system of 'double dating' (Adams 2005: 701–3 and Lewis and Williams 2007: 5).

The third innovation is simply Kurath's extreme reticence. All of the information described above went into entries without editorial commentary: if the quotations demonstrated two hundred years or so of use, from 1225 to 1425, say, in Northern religious texts, but in no other regions or text types, commentary was unnecessary—the scholar using the *MED*, for it was conceived as a scholarly dictionary, would draw his or her own conclusion from the evidence presented. As we learned more about Middle English and language generally, then users would draw better informed conclusions. The evidence, in Kurath's view, would speak for itself; editors, if given the chance, would speak too much and introduce error at the expense of evidence. All of this placed a heavy burden on quotation paragraphs, heavier than that expected of those in the *OED*, or in Moore's or Knott's versions of the *MED*, not to mention a considerable burden on editors responsible for preparing them.

Ogden had joined the *MED* staff in 1933; Richard McKelvey, who served as director of production for over thirty years, joined late in Knott's tenure. In 1948, Kurath hired Sherman M. Kuhn, a young but prematurely distinguished scholar of Old English, as his associate editor, perhaps on Ogden's recommendation (Adams 2005: 706). With these and other editors, like Charles E. Palmer, and several assistants in place, Kurath pushed hard to vindicate the dictionary in the wake of Knott's ineffectiveness, and finally saw the first fascicle, that for the letter E, into print in 1952. Kurath and the Oxford University Press had agreed to part ways in the late 1940s, and the dictionary was published, instead, by the University of Michigan Press. In order to save costs and to make the dictionary available to interested medievalists, Kurath chose to print the dictionary by a lithographic process resulting in entries that were criticized as difficult to read, because they were tightly printed with essentially no typographical distinctions among layers of information. But the *MED* was suddenly a fact rather than a glint in Craigie's eye. The dictionary's original *Plan and Bibliography* were published in 1954; the bibliography was so clearly an important reference tool that it was issued separately in the same year, to universal acclaim (Adams 2005: 703–4). From then on, from two to four 128-page fascicles were published yearly, until the entire dictionary was in print in 2001.

14.3.3 Kuhn and Lewis: Improving Kurath's Dictionary

Kurath retired in 1961 and was succeeded by Kuhn, who remained editor-in-chief until 1983. His successor, Robert E. Lewis, began as co-editor in 1982 and saw the dictionary to completion in 2001 (Lewis and Williams 2007: 32). Though the dictionary at completion was fundamentally as designed by Kurath, Kuhn and Lewis were progressively less reticent and changed many small matters of method and presentation over time. Every page of Kuhn's copy of Kurath's 1947 Editorial Manual, now held in the *Middle English Dictionary* archives at the University of Michigan's Bentley Historical Museum, is covered with revisions, and the revisions continued under Lewis. Where Kurath had rarely labelled a form as belonging to a particular dialect, Kuhn relaxed what was nearly a prohibition on doing so. 'Our guiding principle,' Lewis wrote of his own editorial period, 'has been to try to "capture the generality", as I constantly used to tell editors, that is, to present what Kurath called "types of meanings", but at the same time to give the reader as much help as we can with the difficult quotations and with the subtleties of meaning. It is too difficult for the reader, even the knowledgeable, discriminating reader . . . At times I have wondered if some of our distinctions have not been overly precise or overly subtle or overly contextual, but I then think of our obligation to those who consult the *MED* and conclude that it is better to err in this direction (sometimes with caveats) than to be too general' (2002: 81). Widely admired, the *MED* was nevertheless regularly criticized for not handling (or mishandling) the copious evidence it presented (see Blake 2002); Kurath thought erring in the minimal direction preferable, and he enforced that presumption so effectively that, even as Kuhn and Lewis loosened that restraint, their loosening was restrained.

Kuhn oversaw editing of the *MED* from G through P. Editing with a small staff was slow going, especially as the editors began to encounter large letters, like L, M, P, R, S, and T. In 1974, Kuhn applied to the Andrew W. Mellon Foundation for a grant to expand the editorial staff significantly; the application was successful, and from 1975 through 1996, the staff included from seven to thirteen full-time editors, including John Reidy, who served as review editor from 1983 to 1987; his successor, Mary Jane Williams, who was also the *MED*'s bibliographer from 1983, after McKelvey's retirement; Marilyn S. Miller, who joined Williams as a review editor in 1991 and was also responsible for automated aspects of the dictionary's operations; and Elizabeth Girsch, who joined the team of review editors in 1995. The expense of bringing the project to a conclusion from 1980 forward was generously supported by the Mellon Foundation and the National Endowment for the Humanities, to which Lewis made five successful applications. But the University of Michigan and the University of Michigan Press deserve recognition as the greatest continuous sources of support, their commitment to historical lexicography surpassed only by that of the Oxford University Press.

Lewis oversaw publication of the dictionary from R through Z. He and Williams published additions to the *Plan and Bibliography* in 1984 and then, with Miller's assistance, revised and completed work on the *Plan and Bibliography, Second Edition*, published in 2007. The last is very welcome: Ogden's bibliography (1954) included 4,257 entries, but the process of reading new texts continued throughout the project's history, and the fully revised bibliography includes more than 7,100 items; additionally, Lewis has replaced Kurath's laconic 'plan' with a full history of the project, thorough explanation of the principles that underlie it, and helpful account of editorial practices. Of course, it was easier to write the details after the project was complete and open to retrospection.

Lewis gradually incorporated the findings of the *Linguistic Atlas of Late Mediaeval English* (McIntosh, Samuels, Benskin, *et al.* 1986) into the later alphabetical range, and the effect of that work can be gauged by an appendix on dialect in the 2007 plan (Lewis and Williams 2007: 21–4).

14.3.4 *The* Middle English Compendium

In 1998, the National Endowment for the Humanities began to subsidize creation of the *Middle English Compendium*, under the general editorship of Frances McSparran, who had, at various times, been an *MED* editor, serving as administrative head of the dictionary for a period during Kuhn's editorial tenure. The *Compendium* includes an electronic version of the *MED*, a remarkably flexible 'Hyperbibliography', and many digitally reproduced Middle English texts, all of which are fully searchable and interconnected, thanks to John Price-Wilkin of the University of Michigan's Humanities Text Initiative (McSparran 2002). The electronic format allows for an ever-expanding historical lexical resource: for instance, the Hyperbibliography registers the connections between the *MED* and the *Linguistic Atlas of Late Mediaeval English* initiated by Lewis throughout the bibliography, which can be accessed with a click on any citation through any entry. Given the potential for development inherent in the medium, the *MED*, though finished, is a continuing project under the *Compendium*'s umbrella.

14.4 THE *DICTIONARY OF OLD ENGLISH* (*DOE*)

Last among the period dictionaries to begin, the *DOE* gained considerably from the examples of *EMED* and *MED*, even though, in many respects, it is not a dictionary on historical principles. Nevertheless, especially in terms of automation and the development of related but freestanding resources, the *DOE* in turn sets an example for future historical dictionaries.

14.4.1 *Origins*

In 1919, Craigie suggested that *An Anglo-Saxon Dictionary* (1898), compiled by Joseph Bosworth and T. Northcote Toller, once supplemented by Toller (1921), would adequately represent Old English vocabulary and obviate the need for a period dictionary of Old English parallel to those projected for Middle and Early Modern English. He was wrong, though it took a long time for specialists in Old English to act on their dissatisfaction with Bosworth–Toller, as the earlier dictionary is usually called. In the late 1960s, Angus Cameron, of the University of Toronto, and C. J. E. Ball, of Lincoln College, Oxford, stimulated by Cameron's work towards a B.Litt. thesis on the semantics of Old English colour words, in which the inadequacies of Bosworth–Toller were manifest (Leyerle 1985: 9), began to formulate plans for an ultimate dictionary of Old English.

By 1968, the University of Toronto's Centre for Medieval Studies had decided to sponsor a new dictionary, under the direction of Cameron and Ball. In order to promote international support and chart the project's future, the Centre hosted a series of conferences: the first took place in March 1969 and focused on automation; the second, in September 1970, considered the state of Old English texts, concordances of Old English, and the structure of the proposed dictionary and the form of its entries; in May 1977, the conference included sessions on automation and concordances, non-literary evidence of Old English, and criticism of the editors' work to that date on entries in D.

The *DOE* was particularly well conceived and well planned. While one should not underestimate the genius of its editors, part of that genius was a clear-sighted view of the problems inherent in large-scale historical lexicography, those amply illustrated in the histories of projects like the *OED*, *EMED*, and *MED*. It is significant that Richard W. Bailey and Jay L. Robinson, leaders of the renewed *EMED*, and John Reidy, at various periods an *MED* editor, participated in the 1969 conference (Cameron, Frank, and Leyerle 1970: ix–x). They were joined at the 1970 conference by Frederic G. Cassidy, an assistant on both of those projects in the 1930s and chief editor of *DARE* (Cameron and Frank 1973: 2). Sherman M. Kuhn, then editor-in-chief of the *MED*, attended the third conference, in 1977 (Cameron and Amos 1978: 292). Thus both within the conference structure and in casual conversation, the *DOE* editors were encouraged to think of their project in historical terms; the resulting dictionary suggests that they learned a great deal about dictionary-making from their colleagues, past and present.

One test of the preliminary work was the degree of stability it has provided for the project given some unfortunate personnel changes. Ball withdrew from the project in 1976 (Aitken 1987: 103); Cameron died in 1983 (and was succeeded by Ashley Crandall Amos, the assistant editor, who died shortly thereafter, in 1989 (Amos 1984: 12; Holland 1989: 18)); then Antonette diPaolo Healey, who had been with the project since 1978 (Amos 1979: 15) and had been co-editor with Amos since 1985 (Holland 1986: 21), took the helm. Cameron was able to direct editing of the first published fascicle, but did not see it to completion. Nevertheless, parts of the dictionary have appeared regularly since, more or less within the lines drawn in Cameron and Ball's original plan.

14.4.2 *Character*

In 1977, the editors could describe the *DOE* as including roughly 35,000 entries treating the English lexicon within the period 600–1150 CE. They had an advantage over editors of the other period dictionaries: they could examine every bit of extant evidence, though the dictionary would not comprehend all of that evidence, especially in the case of grammatical words (articles and prepositions, for instance), too numerous in the record to analyse effectively in dictionary form, even in a dictionary designed for a scholarly audience.

After the first two conferences and considerable deliberation, Cameron and Roberta Frank published *A Plan for the Dictionary of Old English* (1973), a work in the tradition of the *MED*'s *Plan and Bibliography* (1954) and *Michigan Early Modern English Materials* (1975). Like them, it includes a bibliography, 'A List of Old English Texts', prepared by Cameron, which, unlike them, organizes the texts broadly according to type (verse, prose, inscriptions, glosses), notes all of the extant manuscripts, facsimiles, and editions of each text, and cross-refers them to standard bibliographical works, especially Neil R. Ker's *Catalogue of Manuscripts Containing Anglo-Saxon* (1957). Each text is identified by a number, conventionally known today as its 'Cameron number'. Altogether, the *DOE* bibliography includes 3,037 items (Healey 2002: 157). Some Old English texts had not been edited reliably, and Helmut Gneuss developed a procedure for editing such texts to maximize their value to the *DOE*, articulated in a chapter of the *Plan*. In attempting to provide a textual foundation for the dictionary, he followed in the footsteps of F. J. Furnivall, who established the Early English Text Society to enhance the quality of early texts used in the *OED* (Benzie 1983: 117), but developments at the dictionary soon made new critical editions of Old English texts unnecessary for lexicographical purposes.

Ball and Cameron contributed a chapter to the *Plan* with sample entries. These established the *DOE* entry structure as it appears in published fascicles to this date. Each entry begins with a headword (usually a late West Saxon form); lists all attested spellings; provides grammatical information (the word's function, gender, stem-class, etc.); states the number of occurrences, distributed over the text types identified in Cameron's 'A List of Old English Texts'. Senses are analysed and citations provided to illustrate them; Latin equivalents are identified, when appropriate, as are related Old English words (synonyms and antonyms, for instance) and Middle and Modern English reflexes. There are no etymologies, and, in contrast to the *MED*, place-names and personal names are not cited as evidence.

Cameron and Amos claimed that 'while technical innovation has not been one of the purposes of the project, the dictionary has made as much use as possible of modern technology' (1978: 290). Later, though, Cameron realized that the *DOE*'s innovative approach to automating lexical resources might guide us to new forms of dictionary and strategies of dictionary use (1983: 18–20). Advances made in the course of developing many historical dictionaries confirmed Cameron's insight; in quite different ways, this set of technologically advanced dictionaries eventually

dryhten

→ ðriht-, ðryht-, drehten, drehtnen, dreyhten, drhiten, drhten, drhtne, drichten, drichtin, dricten, drih, drihcten, drihne, drihny, drihtæn, drihtan, drihten, drihtin, drihtn, drihton, drihtten, drihtyn, driten, drith-, dritnes, driyhten, driyten, dryctin, dryghtne, dryh, dryhnes, dryhtæn, dryhtin, dryhtn-, dryhtnæs, dryhtyn, dryten, drythten, ryht'

Noun, m., cl. 1

Att. sp.: dryhten (2000x), drihten (8000x), drehten (HomU 35.2, PsGlE), driyhten (PsGlE), drhten (PsGlK); drhiten (PsGlK); drichten (BenRW, PsGlE), dricten (PsGlE), drihcten (PsGlE), drihtten (PsGlK); drithen (PsGlE), drythten (PsGlE), drithten (PsGlE); dryten (PsGlA, HomS 2), driten (Solil); ðryhten (PsGlAB), ðrihten (PsGlE, Bede, LS 16) | dryhtæn (Mart 5), drihtæn (PsCaE, PsGlE) | dryhtin (ChronE), drihtin, dryctin (CædN) | dryhtyn (WSGosp MS Cp), drihtyn (PsCaC, PsGlC, WSGosp MS Cp) | drihtan (HomS 5) | drihton (BenRW) | drihter (Li); ðrihter (Li).

dryhtnes, drihtnes (1500x), drehtnes (HomU 35.2); drichtnes (PsGlE); dryhnes (Mart 4), drihnes; drithnes (xii); dritnes (PsGlG); ðrihtnes (PsCaE) | drihtnæs (PsGlE) | drihtnys, drihnys (PsGlC) || dryhtenes, drihtenes; drihttenes (PsGlK); drihtennes | drihtines, drichtines (xii, xiii) | drihtones (LS 14) || ðryhtne (Bede).

dryhtne, drihtne (1500x), drhtne (PsGlF); dryghtne (PsGlE), drihne (PsGlC, BenRGl); drithne (PsCaE); ðryhtne (PsGlB, Bede), ðrihtne (Bede) | drihtny (PsGlC), drihny (PsGlC) | drihtno (Li, DurRit) || drihtnen (Li), drehtnen (HomU 35.2) | drihtnum (BenR) || dryhtene, drihtene, drhtene (PsGlK); drihtenne | drihtine || drihtenum (ProspGl).

dryhtnas, drihtnas.

dryhtna, drihtna | drihtena, drihtenna.

Also in an inscription now lost: dryhtnæs (RuneBewcastle).

Abbrev. forms in glosses: d', dr', dreyht', drht', drih', driht', dry', dryh', dryht', dryt', ryht', ðrih', ðriht', ðryht'; inflected: drih'es, driht'es, drih'e, drih'ne, drihtn', dryhtn'.

Forms without mark of abbrev.: dryht | driht | drihte (nom.sg) || drihtes || drihte (see sense 4).

Late: drichtin (xiii); driyten (xiii)

ca. 15,500 occ.

1. in poetry and laws: lord, ruler, chief (mainly with genitive complement, e.g. *Creca, Geata, Wedera, eorla, gumena;* cf. *dryhtna*

dryhten sense 2.a.i)

1.a. in poetry 22x (in Beo 15x in sense 1, 14x in sense 2)

GenA 2227: **drihten** min, do swa ic þe bidde (Sarah addressing Abraham about taking Hagar as his wife).
Sea 39: forþon nis þæs modwlonc mon ofer eorþan, ne his gifena þæs god, ne in geoguþe to þæs hwæt, ne in his dædum to þæs deor, ne him his **dryhten** to þæs hold, þæt he a his sæfore sorge næbbe, to hwon hine dryhten gedon wille.
Beo 1999: Biowulf maðelode, bearn Ecgðioes: þæt is undyrne, **dryhten** <Higelac>.
Beo 2752: ða ic snude gefrægn sunu Wihstanes æfter wordcwydum wundum **dryhtne** [Beowulf] hyran heaðosiocum.
Beo 2788: he ða mid þam maðmum mærne þioden, **dryhten** sinne [Beowulf], driorigne fand ealdres æt ende.
Met 26.13: for wiges heard Creca **drihten** [Agamemnon] campsted secan.
Met 26.19: diore gecepte **drihten** Creca [Agamemnon] Troia burg tilum gesiðum.
Beo 2482: Hæðcynne wearð, Geata **dryhtne**, guð onsæge.
Beo 1484: mæg þonne on þæm golde ongitan Geata **dryhten** [Hygelac], geseon sunu Hrædles ... þæt ic gumcystum godne funde beaga bryttan.
Beo 2575: hond up abræd Geata **dryhten** [Beowulf], gryrefahne sloh incgelafe.
Beo 2900: nu is wilgeofa Wedra leoda, **dryhten** Geata [Beowulf], deaðbedde fæst.
Beo 2183: hean wæs lange, swa hyne Geata bearn godne ne tealdon, ne hyne on medobence micles wyrðne <**drihten** Wedera> gedon wolde (*drihten* supplied from B, MS wereda).
Jud 19: hie þæt fæge þegon, rofe rondwiggende, þeah ðæs se rica ne wende, egesful eorla **dryhten** [Holofernes].
Beo 2337: heht him þa gewyrcean wigendra hleo eallirenne, eorla **dryhten** [Beowulf], wigbord wrætlic.
Brun 1: her Æþelstan cyning, eorla **dryhten**, beorna beahgifa, and his broþor eac, Eadmund æþeling, ealdorlangne tir geslogon æt sæcce.
Dan 612: ða for ðam gylpe gumena **drihten** [Nabuchodonosor] forfangen wearð and on fleam gewat.
Beo 1822: gif ic þonne on eorþan owihte mæg þinre modlufan maran tilian, gumena **dryhten** [Hrothgar] ... ic beo gearo sona.

FIG. 14.4. Extract from the *Dictionary of Old English*

included the *OED* and *MED*, but *DARE* and *DOE*, and to a lesser extent *EMED*, were well in front.

DOE demonstrates the value of computer-enhanced entries, for instance, as Aitken explains, when providing 'statistics of word-frequency, such as the surprising and previously wholly unnoticed, indeed all but unknowable, fact that of 15,500 occurrences of *dryhten* [="lord, the Lord"] almost all refer to the Christian Lord and only 28, mostly in verse, to secular lords, of which 15 are in *Beowulf*' (1987: 111). Astonishing indeed, and well worth knowing. Yet Aitken's focus on what automation provides the reader overlooks how it improves the editorial process. The *DOE*'s value has been determined partly (and unexpectedly) by its commitment to automation, on the one hand, as a component of the editorial and production apparatus, and, on the other, as an entry into a corpus of lexical data and instrument of data manipulation.

The architect of the *DOE*'s computerized system was Richard L. Venezky, of the University of Wisconsin when the project began, later of the University of Delaware. Venezky constructed an archive that can 'serve as a distributable data base for linguistic and literary research' (Cameron and Frank 1973: 311), a tool not unlike the *MED*'s working bibliography in its data and purpose, but fully searchable, so that editors would not need to shuffle through drawers of file cards to look for a text's date of composition or dialect, etc. In cooperation with the editors, Venezky designed a code with which to mark up texts, so that they were analysed uniformly and were searchable; the marked-up texts were transferred, in the first instance, to magnetic tape by optical scanning. By this means, Venezky built a database of all known Old English text: the editors could generate concordances from the database; they could generate slips for editorial use directly from the concordances, saving the editors (and their assistants) considerable labour.

14.4.3 *Results*

Materials required to edit the *DOE* came in various forms and far exceeded the dictionary itself.

14.4.3 (i) Materials for the Study of Old English

As with Bailey and Robinson, Cameron and his colleagues believed that the raw materials and by-products of their dictionary should be published, in one form or another, so that scholars would have access to them while the dictionary was in progress. The proceedings of the first conference were published as *Computers and*

Old English Concordances (Cameron, Frank, and Leyerle 1970); the *Plan* (Cameron and Frank 1973), including its indispensable list of Old English texts, appeared soon after. Having searched for every article about an Old English word or words, they compiled *Old English Word Studies: A Preliminary Author and Word Index* (Cameron, Kingsmill, and Amos 1983), with articles listed under their authors in the printed book but under the words they treat on five accompanying microfiches.

Most important among these publications, however, are the results of automation. Venezky collaborated with Healey on a lemmatized concordance of Old English (1980) excluding function words; he then collaborated with Sharon Butler on a concordance of 197 'high-frequency words' (1985). In conception, these were editorial tools, but the editors quickly realized that they were useful in their own rights, and that scholars would gratefully accept access to them. Similarly, the fully searchable corpus was published in several iterations, on magnetic tape (Cameron, Amos, Butler, and Healey 1981), diskette (Healey *et al.* 1993), and finally the World Wide Web (Healey *et al.* 1995) under the aegis of the Humanities Text Initiative at the University of Michigan, where John Price-Wilkin designed the Web interface (Healey 2002: 158). The corpus is published by the University of Michigan Press, in the series Sources of Early English and Norse Electronic Texts, with the most recent revision dated 2000.

14.4.3 (ii) The *Dictionary of Old English*

While a print version of the dictionary is expected to appear eventually, fascicles are currently published on microfiche, which (as with *Michigan Early Modern English Materials*) can be computer-generated as well as accessible on the World Wide Web. The first fascicle, with entries under D, was published in 1986; entries under C followed in 1988; B appeared in 1991 and Æ in 1992; A was published in 1994 and E in 1996; F was issued in 1999 with the other six, on CD-ROM; and G was published in 2007, on the Web, CD-ROM, and microfiche. In all, then, eight of twenty-two fascicles have been published to date.

14.5 CONCLUSION

Every vocabulary requires individual treatment: the characteristics of Old, Middle, and Early Modern English diverge in both obvious and subtle ways, and the techniques appropriate to treating one will differ from those best suited to another. The *EMED*, *MED*, and *DOE* are independent dictionaries distinguished by editorial procedures and methods of presentation developed to deal with the idiosyncrasies of their respective lexicons and to achieve visions of what historical lexicography can and should be. But they were not developed in isolation and their histories are partly shared, as the histories of historical dictionaries meant to address deficiencies in the *OED* are likely to be.

REFERENCES

Besides the published resources listed at the end of the book, there are significant archives of material relating to the *Middle English Dictionary* and the Early Modern English Dictionary project in the Bentley Historical Library of the University of Michigan and the Oxford University Press Archives (see especially dropped file 4665). Richard W. Bailey owns an apparently unique copy of the 1936 specimen of the *EMED*, from which figure 14.1 is reproduced with his permission. Materials underlying the present chapter are cited and fully described in Adams 1995 and 2002, Bailey 1980, and Bailey, Downer, and Robinson 1975.

15

DICTIONARIES OF CARIBBEAN ENGLISH

Jeannette Allsopp

15.1 INTRODUCTION

IT is a natural sociolinguistic development that where a recognized language exists there should be a dictionary to ensure that the variety selected by the speech community concerned is codified, and that this dictionary should be generally recognized as the authority in matters of usage. This is no less true of Caribbean English than of any other variety of the English language as we know it today. Caribbean English is historically the oldest variety of English after its progenitor, British English, having first been brought to the region in the sixteenth century by such seafaring knights as Hawkins, Drake, and Raleigh, seeking to gain a foothold in the region so as to establish settlements for the British Crown. The English-based Creoles that then developed through the 'triangular trade' that flourished between the seventeenth and eighteenth centuries, and involved an influx of several million West African slaves, paved the way, first via creolization and later via decreolization, for the rise of the variety that is known today as Caribbean English.

Efforts to chronicle it have been quite regionally polarized in that, unlike Canadian or New Zealand English, which are spoken on one land mass and are therefore largely homogeneous varieties, Caribbean English is a series of sub-varieties of English, distributed over many different territories that are separated from each other by the Caribbean Sea. Two of those, Guyana and Belize, are in geographically distant parts of the South and Central American mainland, but their history is similarly one of British colonization and settlement and so qualifies their varieties of English to be included in any representative study of Caribbean English lexicography.

15.2 EARLY WORKS IN CARIBBEAN ENGLISH LEXICOGRAPHY

Caribbean English lexicography began as early as 1905, in Guyana, with a small book by J. A. Van Sertima called *The Creole Tongue*, followed by J. G. Cruikshank's *Black Talk–Notes on Negro Dialect in British Guiana*. More seminally important in the development of Caribbean English lexicography, however, is Frank Collymore's *Barbadian Dialect*, which appeared in 1955 and is somewhat more comprehensive than either of the two works mentioned above. Indeed, the full title given to Collymore's work is *Notes for a Glossary of Words and Phrases of Barbadian Dialect* because, as the author explains, he was extremely conscious that accuracy of definition and etymology were two formidable challenges, and that meeting them would have required more time and in-depth knowledge of the historical background of the island than he possessed. Furthermore, having had recourse to dictionaries of Standard British English, Collymore realized that there were definitely semantic shifts that had taken place between the standard British variety and the Barbadian variety, and that these, too, needed to be taken into account.

Other early Caribbean English lexicographic work includes *Popular Phrases in Grenada Dialect* by C. W. Francis in 1971; *Creole Talk of Trinidad and Tobago* by C. R. Ottley in 1965 and 1971; *Virgin Islands Dictionary* (St Croix) by G. A. Seaman in 1967; and *Dictionary of Guyanese Folklore* by A. J. Seymour, in 1975. There are also *Random Remarks on Creolese* by C. A. Yansen in 1975, which is a commentary on Guyanese Creole; *What a Pistarckle* (St John and the US Virgin Islands) by L. Valls, in 1981; and *Cote ce Cote la* (Trinidad and Tobago) by John Mendes, in 1985. There is also a small work called *The Belizean Lingo* by George McKesey, published in 1974. These works illustrate the many attempts made to grapple with the varieties of English found at the local level within the much wider regional entity that is Caribbean English. They are useful in that they are pioneering efforts, unsophisticated in terms of the professional standards that would later develop in Caribbean English lexicography, but making definite attempts to chronicle the idiosyncrasies of the individual varieties with which they deal.

15.3 CARIBBEAN TERRITORIAL ENGLISH DICTIONARIES

15.3.1 The Dictionary of Jamaican English *(DJE)*

The first major territorial scholarly dictionary that appeared in the Anglophone Caribbean was the *Dictionary of Jamaican English*, compiled by Frederic Cassidy and Robert Le Page and published in 1967 by Cambridge University Press. A second edition appeared in 1980. Designed on historical principles, the *DJE* was intended to be a complete inventory of Jamaican Creole as well as a record of more educated Jamaican English. The *DJE* is based on transcribed tape-recordings of a variety of informants from all over the island. The recordings were responses to a questionnaire patterned after that of the Linguistic Atlas of the United States and Canada, but adapted to Jamaican conditions by Cassidy. They thus described the activities of small farmers, hog-hunters, boat-builders, cane-planters, cattlemen, fishermen, domestics, schoolteachers, and social workers. They also documented tales, songs, and biographies. The material was classified according to the language status and geographical distribution of the speakers and it formed the basic content of the *Dictionary*. It was combined with a list of dialect words and phrases collected from a competition held by the *Daily Gleaner* of Kingston in 1943. This brought in several hundred entries from all parts of Jamaica. They ranged from a few words on a single sheet of paper to a hundred or more items on several sheets. This collection was passed on to Le Page, who made a file of them and donated the originals to the *Dictionary*. The items cited are entered in the *DJE* as '1943 GL' followed by the name of the parish from which the entry came, when known; they appear in the *Dictionary* as in the following example:

(1) **COCOOCHAWYER** sb and adj dial; prob a form of COCO-TAYA. A mean or insignificant person.
1943 *GL* StAnn, Cocochawyer, mean, low, not countable.

There was also the collection of Mr H. P. Jacobs, who had gathered lexical items in Jamaica for many years. Mr Jacobs donated to the Survey the transcribed version of his collection, which covered about half the letters of the alphabet and was gathered between 1935 and 1948, and also gave freely of his advice. This material was incorporated into the *Dictionary* and, where his citations are used, they carry the date of the observation followed by HPJ and the parish from which they originated. Wherever Mr Astley Clark, who assisted in transcribing the items, added his own notes, they are cited as 'A. Clark in HPJ', as the following example illustrates:

(2) **BARQUADIER** sb arch; 1774 1823
1838 barquadier, 1970 barguadier, 1808 barquedia, 1940 barkadere; <Sp *embarcadero*, a wharf; the form is that of a French word, but no record of such has been found; this word, like some others, was probably Gallicized by Englishmen. Cf *OED embarcadere*.[1]
1. An export wharf. BL ...
2. Attrib: *barquedier road*, a road from a property to the barquadier; *barquedier cattle*, cattle employed in drawing produce to the barquadier; *barquadier (wagon)*, a waggon used to transport produce to the barquadier, etc.

1863 Waddell 134 (year 1838), The 'barquadier road', led from Frankfort wharf [Ocho Rios] up the sides of the mountains. 1935 HPJ Tre, Barquadier road, waggon, cattle. 1940 Astley Clark [in HPJ] 'Now "barkadere".

Another body of material was that collected by the Institute of Education of the then University College of the West Indies, now the University of the West Indies (UWI), in Jamaica. It consisted of the transcribed recordings, made by researchers like Astley Clark, of the spontaneous conversation of children in school playgrounds or in their homes, using any spelling that seemed to reflect the pronunciation. The material was then collated and analysed for the Institute and made available to Le Page, who took citations for the *Dictionary* from it. Those citations are recorded in the *DJE* as '1957 JN', followed by the relevant parish when that is known, as the following example shows:

(3) **DOWN** /doun, dong/ prep dial; for *down at.* (Also in London vulgar speech. LeP.) At, down at. *G*

1957 JN Clar, Mrs Rickman, down Trout Hall, mam; StE, Tree a wee de here wid we father but one down Mountainside live wid Missa Rogers. [*Three of us are here with our father but one at Mountainside lives with Mr R.*]

[1] The citations of the first and second senses of the word have both been left out because only Mr Clark's input is being recognized here.

Other material came from Mrs Jean Brown, secretary to the English Department of the University College, who contributed a number of citations which are usually recorded in the *DJE* as JB preceded by the date. Several other sources were tapped, such as students and staff at the University College and at University College Hospital, individual members of the public, the Botany Department of the UCWI and the West Indian Medical Journal.

Cassidy and Le Page also faced some descriptive challenges, as was to be expected, because of the nature of the material with which they were dealing. The first was the fact that, because of the limited standard of education of many of the informants, the spelling of items could only approximate to what was heard; wherever possible, however, the spelling of the original material has been retained. Such a problem led to the difficulty experienced in relation to the phonetic representation of the items in the *DJE* to represent as accurately as possible the pronunciation of the folk dialect. The *DJE* covers a range of dialects from the Creole to a more educated form of Jamaican English, and uses Received Pronunciation (RP) as a point of reference against which the quality of the sounds of Jamaican English can be measured.

In order to formulate his phonemic notation, Cassidy used the descriptions of educated southern English usage by several seventeenth- and eighteenth-century English pronunciation experts, such as Gil (1619), Cooper (1687), and Douglas (*c*.1740). Also contributing to the notation were the descriptions of those West African languages, Twi by Chistaller (1875) and Ewe by Westermann (1907), seen to have the greatest influence on the formation of Jamaican English. Cassidy felt that since, until comparatively recently, RP was the model for educated speakers of Jamaican English, it was reasonable to show that the vowel and consonant phonemes of Jamaican Creole were reflexes of the appropriate RP phonemes. This has been done in great detail in the section on Historical Phonology in the front matter of the *DJE*. In that section, Cassidy has merged the reflex vowel and consonant phonemes of Jamaican Creole from British RP with the relevant sounds of Twi and Ewe, showing that, whereas tone is an important factor in sound production and meaning in a language like Twi, for example, it cannot be used in the same way to represent syllabic stress in English. In addition, the consonants of Twi and Ewe, as presented by Christaller and Westermann, have been compared with the consonants of English and it has been found that many usages in Jamaican English which seem to be Africanisms also occur in one or more British English dialects. There is extensive treatment of consonant clusters, assimilation, metathesis, aphesis, intrusives, and parasitics.

For example, we may look at the unstressed vowel /i/ in Jamaican as in the word *peeny* /piini/, where the unstressed /i/ is equivalent to the British English sound [ɪ] rather than [i:]. With regard to consonants, initial /k/ and /g/ tend to be palatalized before low-front [a] and [a:], for example, /gyaadn/ for *garden* but not before low-back vowels like [ ]:], for example, /gaadn/ for *Gordon*. Consequently, the phonemic rendering of *garden egg* is /gyàadn ég/.

Another feature of Jamaican Creole is that the diphthong /uo/ is the regular reflex of RP /oɪ/, conservative RP /]χ/ wherever that phoneme derives from a seventeenth-century /uω/, /oɪ/ or /]ω/ before [r] as in *pork* /puok/, *four* /fuo/, *more* /muo/. Some other phonological features are the following. Vowels in final unstressed positions in Jamaican Creole can occur without diphthongization or any loss of quality, unlike RP, where this only occurs with /ɪ/ and then only in some cases. Examples are /neba/ *never*, /sense/ *senseh-fowl* (a fowl with no neck feathers). Initial and final consonant clusters are lost, such as /st/ and we find /tan/ for *stand*, /san/ for *sand*. There are also assimilations, /aaredi/ for *already*, and /sk/ metathesis, /aks/ for *ask*, as well as /r/ and /l/ metathesis, /prakapain/ for *porcupine* and /flim/ for *film*. The normal British English tendency to aphesis in speech, such as *'cos* for *because*, is also common in Jamaican Creole in words like /gens/ for *against*. There is also the occurrence of intrusive consonants such as /b/ which gives /tambran/ for *tamarind*.

As the entries cited above illustrate, etymologies are given wherever possible, but they are not enclosed within or identified by *the* use of square brackets, and in some entries there are brief notes on the usage of the item which come at the end of the citation. Glossing is concise but also fully informative. The use of fully dated citations throughout the text, which reflects the historical nature of the work, is one of its greatest strengths. As has been pointed out in the introduction to the *Dictionary of Caribbean English Usage* (*DCEU*), the *DJE* is a fully documented basic Jamaican Creole lexicon, together with upper-level Jamaican originals in international English (R. Allsopp 1996: xx). It is the first scholarly work in Caribbean English lexicography, but, unfortunately, its design makes it unable to meet the general everyday needs of its intended users whose usage of language it includes. Consequently, it is perhaps naturally seen as only pertaining to Jamaica, although its high level of linguistic scholarship makes it regional in scope and importance. Furthermore, it is not generally used by Caribbean educators at either secondary or tertiary level in their respective territories.

15.3.2 The Dictionary of Bahamian English *(DBE)*

The Dictionary of Bahamian English, by John Holm and Alison Watt Shilling, appeared in 1982, 'the result of four years of fieldwork and research' (1982: iii) and is the second regional scholarly dictionary to be published. It is the first comprehensive study of colloquial Bahamian English, and forms 'a link between the Caribbean Creoles, such as Jamaican English, and the English spoken today by many black people in the United States'. Since the *DBE* is meant to reflect the English spoken in the Bahama Islands, of which there are seven hundred, only thirty being inhabited, the authors had to restrict themselves to the more accessible islands of the chain, while at the same time selecting so judiciously among them that the dictionary manages to remain representative of the whole (Robertson 1982: 109). This was one of the major challenges that the compilers faced.

The introduction to the *DBE* includes the historical aspects considered by Holm and Shilling to be important, but their description of the process of creolization is flawed in that it leans heavily on the theory of simplification. They account for European-based Creoles brought to the Caribbean as simplified languages with the lexicon of the particular European language and a basically African structure which evolved into the Caribbean Creoles. However, further on in the same essay, very pertinent aspects of West African origin are listed without explanation, contradicting the earlier claims of simplification which is, in any case, a rather troublesome and largely unsubstantiated explanation of creolization.[2] There is no denying the European contribution to creolization, but the West African input, in terms of structure, is also crucial.

A claim is also made for a Bahamian–Gullah connection through the citing of a list of nine items by Parsons (1923), including such items as *day clean* for *daybreak*, *meet* for *find*, and *man* as a form of address. However, such items and some of the others listed among the nine are in wide and current use in the southern Caribbean, where there is little historical support for a link with Gullah.

Like its predecessor and counterpart, the *DJE*, the *DBE* is designed on historical principles. Another useful aspect of the *DBE* is that it identifies the entries according to the islands on which they are used. That geographical identification is what helps to weld the dictionary together as being representative of Bahamian English in general, as is seen in the following entry where the territory is identified by name—Andros:

(4) **fowl-crow** [also Gul. ADD] *n.* the crowing of roosters, marking different periods of the pre-dawn hours: 1977 *before daylight next morning, just about second 'fowl-crow'* (Albury 17) <Andros, Long>

[2] Compare the retention of the base verb in Bahamian dialect, with tense and aspect being indicated by preverbal markers, with the verbal system of the Yoruba languages spoken in Nigeria and also with a similar structure in Elizabethan English, such as 'The country cocks do crow, the clocks do toll' where the *do* would not have emphatic use as in standard English today. This indicates the use of such markers could have either an English or a West African source, or both.

Far from emphasizing separation, the names of the different islands in different entries show that each entry is a part of the wider entity of Bahamian English, as the reality is that the Bahamas are a collection of separate islands administered by one government as one entity.

As illustrated by the entry below, etymologies—which are given in most cases—occur immediately after the headword and before the pronunciation. This closely follows Cassidy's phonemic notation as used in the *DJE*, except in cases where the pronunciation needs to be indicated immediately because there are variant spellings, as in the following example:

(5) **gillembo** /gílembow/ <Berry>; **gelabo** /gélabow/ (Nassau) [W Car.; cf. MCC *gilamba* Prov. *Gálembo* (Washbaugh 1974: 161). Belize *gilanbòr* (Dayley), all (blue) parrot fish] *n.* a fish, the mature slippery dick (*Irido bivittatus*). Cf. BLUE RAINBOW, BLUE WIMBO, PORG

Although glossing is largely both detailed and informative, it must also be noted that there are some items which appear to have been just slipped in and which are very cursorily treated, such as:

(6) **gumma bush** [etym?] *n.* a shrub (sp?) up to three feet in height with broad green leaves. <Andros, San Sal.>

Many plants can be so described and there is no attempt to include a scientific name for this item. There are other such entries which may be considered incomplete and which, despite the detailed treatment of the majority of entries, mar the professionalism of the work, which is otherwise of a scholarly standard.

It is also regrettable that, like its predecessor the *DJE*, the *DBE*, despite its regional reach and its importance as a landmark in the production of dictionaries of Caribbean English, and the development of Caribbean English lexicography, is not in regular use by educators at either secondary or tertiary level in the Caribbean territories.

15.3.3 Other Caribbean dictionaries as precursors to the DCEU

So far in this account, the trend established in the Anglophone Caribbean is for territorial dictionaries to be compiled, and a sample follows of the less ambitious attempts to follow this trend. I am referring specifically to three small territorial dictionaries which are of some significance when dealing with the development of Caribbean English lexicography. Chronologically, the first is *The Belizean Lingo* (1974), by George McKesey, which seeks to record Belizean Creole and also adds radio commentary, some Anancy stories and some Belizean proverbs and expressions. The second is *What a Pistarckle* (1981) by Lou Valls, which attempts to inventory the English of the Virgin Islands for popular consumption, and the third is *Cote ce Cote la* (1985), by John Mendes, which does the same for the English of Trinidad and Tobago. This last work includes a special list of items representing Carnival characters, costumes, and a list of popular sayings.

The Belizean Lingo is a basic list of Creole words and expressions which are morphosyntactically classified. The definitions are in many cases one-word equivalents, although there are some that may aim to define the meaning of the particular item in slightly more detail. There is no phonological representation of pronunciation. For example, note the item **kyato'**, which is defined as follows:

(7) **kyato'** (n.): ('kya' is one syllable)
Catfish

Compare the item **jook**:

(8) **jook** (n., v.): a puncture; to stick or puncture,
especially the skin. (Rhymes with 'book')

After the first listing of single items, there is a second listing of compounds or short phrases which are not related to any other words, such as:

(9) **yu coco roas**: you are in good circumstances
Warry-sahma: Machete – a long straight edged tool used for
cutting grass, bush, wood, etc.

Occasionally, there is mention of a parallel in American dialect or something from the West Indian islands, Guyana or Nigeria. No explanation of exactly what is meant by American dialect is given, but one can see the very early beginnings of cross-referencing. The rest of the book is devoted to the reproduction of some radio broadcasts on Belizean dialect and the last section is a short one on Belizean proverbs such as:

(10) Ebry man know whitch part y own house leak. (Every man knows where his own house leaks).
Meaning: Every man knows his weaknesses.

Here, the proverb is given in Creole, followed by a literal English rendering and finally the meaning of the proverb in the form of the equivalent English proverb. This far predates the *Book of Afric Caribbean Proverbs*, by Richard Allsopp (2004), which also gives the Creole proverb, then an English translation, but continues with a much more detailed treatment which includes historical details in some cases. However modest in scale, McKesey's work is an important precursor of the major work to come in the form of the *DCEU.*

The work of Lou Valls is equally worthy of mention, because although it is really a glossary of Virgin Islands English, compiled basically to inform and appeal to the general public and to tourists, it is very useful as an organized record of local speech. Although there is no attempt to provide systematic grammar labelling (e.g. vi, vt, det, adj.) or to reproduce pronunciations, there is some effort to classify certain items and to describe how they are pronounced, although this is done quite unscientifically. There is some recognition of different senses of words and, in that case, the senses are numbered consecutively. Note the following example:

(11) **FA** 1. Modal. 'Me fa done.' I am finished. 'Me fah noh no.' I don't know. 2. For. Pertaining to. Belong to. Employed by. People and property are said to be 'fa.' 'Ivan fa Frederiksen.' Ivan, who is employed by Frederiksen. 'Prosperity, fa Miss Bee Christensen.' Prosperity, the plantation belonging to Miss Bee Christensen. 'De beel fa she.' Her car.

Similarly, when items of flora or fauna are treated, the scientific name is always included, which assists greatly in the identification of the particular item, as can be seen in the following example:

(12) **GINGER THOMAS** Yellow cedar or yellow elder tree (*Tecoma stans*) and Flower. Leaves are used in medicinals to cure jaundice, colds, fevers, diabetes and headaches. In P.R., 'Roble Amarillo' or 'Saúco Amarillo.' In Trinidad, 'Christmas Hope.' Proclaimed the official flower of the Virgin Islands by Gov. Paul M. Pearson, 20 June 1935.

In this entry, too, there is an attempt to cross-reference the item to equivalents in both Spanish and English and some encyclopedic information is also given, as is the case in many entries. Valls's work may be regarded as having a basic lexicographical style, which was to reach its fullest level of refinement in the later *DCEU.*

In Trinidad and Tobago, there was a parallel work in the form of a glossary called *Cote ce Cote la* by John Mendes. It is also very basic in design, being a listing of words and glosses that give the meaning of the items and also include encyclopedic information. The work treats not only Trinbagonian[3] English words and phrases

[3] A typically Caribbean adjective of nationality which is a blend of Trin(idadian) and (To)bagonian and usually refers to a citizen of the twin-island state.

but also French Creole and Indic items that have become absorbed into the lexicon of Trinidadian English. There is no attempt at syntactic classification, but there is sometimes basic phonological representation in the form of spelling pronunciation. There is also very rudimentary cross-referencing in the form of 'See items'. Some items of flora, particularly trees, are usually referred to by their scientific names. On the whole, it is a very useful, informative work that can easily be used by the general public. Unlike *What a Pistarckle*, it does not include any sense numbering but it does put similar items like popular ideophones together in a section called 'Sayings'. An example of this is the item 'buck tong a-bun dong' meaning that your business is going badly, while you are enjoying yourself. *Cote ce Cote la* also includes a list of items which is specially dedicated to Carnival, the all-inclusive national festival of Trinidad and Tobago, as well as a list of well-known proverbs and popular sayings. The fact that it is an illustrated glossary also adds to its appeal. Examples of entries are the following:

(13) **GRU-GRU BOUEF**
Pronounced *Groo-groo-bef*
The fruit from a palm-type tree. Round about 3.6 mm/1.5 ins in diameter, and very difficult to chew, as its fibrous kernel is covered with a thick, gummy substance. The tree and the branches are covered with thorn or picant. See MONKEY KNOW under SAYINGS.

This single item is French Creole. The pronunciation is given according to a respelling system, and the definition follows. There is cross-referencing to 'Monkey Know', a well-known popular saying which is found in the list at the back of the book.

The next item is a saying:

(14) **ONE-ONE DOES FULL BASKET**
One by one may seem slow, but eventually it will fill the basket.
Even though the going may seem tedious, sure success lies ahead.

The final item that will be cited is one describing Carnival-type characters:

(15) **IMPS**
Characters in Devil Band. Servants and messengers of hell. They wear Skin-fits with wings, tails and half-masks with horns. In their hands they carry axes, horns, dice and face cards. Their movement is sprightly.

Cote ce Cote la therefore treats a full cultural range of material in the English of Trinidad and Tobago and provides useful information for the general public.

It must be noted that, chronologically, these three works appeared quite close to each other in the 1970s and the 1980s. This fact indicates that there were people who regarded their local language varieties as important enough to be recorded and their culture quite worthy of being chronicled through those varieties. The works represent a highly significant change in consciousness and show that the cultural insecurity normally associated with post-colonial societies and referred to earlier was very slowly giving way to a more positive cultural self-image.

The combination of both scholarly territorial work in the form of the *DJE* and the *DBE* and the less scholarly editions that appeared in Belize, the Virgin Islands, and Trinidad and Tobago, for example, showed that the time was ripe for the appearance of an all-embracing master work of regional reach, combining pan-Caribbean linguistic scholarship, cultural power and authenticity, and lexicographical professionalism. All these characteristics are fused into one work, namely the *Dictionary of Caribbean English Usage* (*DCEU*), by Richard Allsopp.

15.4 REGIONAL CARIBBEAN ENGLISH LEXICOGRAPHY

15.4.1 The Dictionary of Caribbean English Usage *(DCEU)*

15.4.1 (i) Genesis

The *Dictionary of Caribbean English Usage* originated in the late 1940s as an idea in the mind of its eventual author, Richard Allsopp, prompted by two experiences. The first occurred when he was an undergraduate student of French attending summer school in France and was asked to translate into English the French phrase for *It had stopped raining*. He proudly rendered his translation as 'The rain had held up', only to be reprimanded by his tutor. Quite piqued by the clear signal from his tutor that his English was not all that he thought it was, his pride was further bruised when his English fellow students agreed wholeheartedly with his tutor. That was the first time that Allsopp realized that his 'English', and indeed the English used in the Caribbean as a whole, was not exactly the same as British Standard English. The second experience was when he began to teach French on his return to his native British Guiana in 1948 and found on one occasion that some of his French students translated *une pierre* as 'a brick', rather than 'a stone'. Those two experiences were responsible for the genesis of the all-embracing work on Caribbean English, the *DCEU*.

From this point on, as he recognized that his students would be writing examination papers for the Oxford and Cambridge Examinations Board, Allsopp began collecting in an exercise book the words, phrases, and idioms that he knew would be unacceptable to a British Examining Board. As his collection of exercise books grew, they became filled with material taken not only from the work of his students but also from personal experiences and encounters, surreptitious recordings, and journalistic literature. He then replaced his exercise books with 6×4 cards as, at that time, his intention was to publish a glossary of Guianese words and phrases. The collection was stored in shoeboxes. His first publication in the journal *Kyk-over-al*, in the form of an article called 'The language we speak', was also his first unconscious foray into the field of lexicography. Shortly after this, Allsopp went to University College London to read for an MA in English, and the thesis produced for the award of that degree—entitled 'Pronominal Forms in the Dialect of English Spoken in British Guiana'—was, historically, the first MA thesis in the field of Creole studies. It was followed by his Ph.D. thesis on Guianese verb forms, and he was now well on his way to producing what would eventually turn out to be the *Dictionary of Caribbean English Usage* (J. Allsopp 1998: 38).

The defining moment in Allsopp's lexicographical career came when he began, as a member of staff of the UWI in Barbados, to cross-reference his Caribbean examples to his Guianese items, as one result of a 1967 resolution passed by the Association of Caribbean Headmasters and Headmistresses,[4] and later in response to the Ford Foundation's funding of the Caribbean Language Research Programme,[5] for which he additionally proposed the compilation of a dictionary of West Indies usage. Thus there came into being Richard Allsopp's Caribbean Lexicography Project, housed at the UWI Cave Hill Campus, with him as director/coordinator.

15.4.1 (ii) Data-collection: 1972–82

Allsopp's data-collection workshops, thirty-eight in all, began to operate in 1972, first in the territories of the Eastern Caribbean, and later going as far as Belize and the Bahamas, and including the smaller territories such as the Cayman Islands, Montserrat, Tobago, and Nevis. These workshops were usually set up by teachers and they made the fact even clearer to him that, despite the magnitude of the

[4] The Association referred to passed a resolution that the relevant department in the UWI be asked to compile a list of lexical items in each territory and circulate these to schools for the guidance of teachers. Richard Allsopp took action on it.

[5] A UWI programme funded by the Ford Foundation which provided support for Caribbean linguists in their work on language development in the region.

task, there was an unmistakable need for such a reference work on Caribbean English as a whole.

However, despite the model provided earlier by Cassidy and Le Page in the *DJE*, Allsopp realized, quite early in his lexicographical work, that he could not compile a dictionary on historical principles, like the *DJE* or the *OED*, in view of the geographical scale of the Caribbean region. That aspect was therefore abandoned. The monumental task of data-collection nonetheless continued from Guyana to Belize, covering twenty-two territories, with an invaluable input from research assistants loaned by the University of Guyana, who zealously collected and collated workshop data over a number of years. Also invaluable was the provision by the Barbados Government of a secondary school teacher as a research assistant to the project at UWI Cave Hill Campus in Barbados for eight years, and the secondment of teachers from the Trinidad school system (funded by the Trinidad Government), who also functioned as research assistants and contributed very valuable data to the project.

During this period, Allsopp recognized the vital fact that Caribbean English does not derive from the English language only, or, more specifically, from English Creoles only, or only non-standard English dialects of the United Kingdom. The English of the islands, which at some time in the region's colonial past were under the domination of the French—such as Trinidad, Grenada, St Lucia, and Dominica, includes French Creole items.[6] Additionally, a wide variety of loan-words exists, taken from the indigenous languages of the Caribbean as well as from those languages which came into the Caribbean through colonization and settlement by European powers—the Spanish, the French, the Dutch, and the Portuguese. Furthermore, a vast number of proverbs and phrases, clearly calques of the numerous Niger-Congo languages spoken by the millions of West African slaves, were brought across the Atlantic during the era of the slave trade and have their counterparts right across the language varieties of the Caribbean, including the French, Spanish, and Dutch-based Creoles. Finally, as a result of later developments, such as East Indian immigration, a large number of Indic loanwords also came to form part of Caribbean English. The painstaking research required into the etymologies of this huge number of items, since it is in the etymologies that so much of our cultural history lies, caused the compilation of the *DCEU* to take much longer than the earlier dictionaries cited (J. Allsopp 1998: 40).

[6] See *souse-glo*, the French Creole word for POND-FLY, which is a combination of French Creole *susé* (<Fr *sucer*) 'suck' + *glo* (<Fr *de l'eau*) 'water', i.e. 'suck-water' referring to the insect's posture when it alights on water.

15.4.1 (iii) Content of the *DCEU*

The content of the *DCEU* includes as complete an inventory as practicable of items reflecting the Caribbean environment and lifestyle, as known and spoken in each territory, but not recorded in standard British and American dictionaries. Descriptions of ostensive items include a physical description of the item, followed by encyclopedic information, which is separated from the description by a semicolon. All items are cross-referenced since Caribbean English has many different names for one item, and, conversely, one name for many different items. This was one of the challenges faced by the author. In the *DCEU*, the many names for one item have been called ALLONYMS or 'other names'. However, since a referent is defined only once in the *Dictionary*, one allonym, a 'main' or 'primary allonym', is chosen according to a frequency of occurrence principle (it is usually also the name most widely used). All other names, which are called 'secondary allonyms' and indicated by two forward slashes (//), are referred to the entry for the main allonym for the definition of the item. Territorial labelling of each item is therefore obligatory. For example, the following entries may be noted:

(16) **dunk(s)*** [dʌŋk(s) ~ dʌŋs] *n (pl)* (Bdos, Guyn, StKt, StVn) //***byre*** (Guyn)// ***coco-plum*** (CayI) //***coolie-plum*** 1. (Jmca) //***dum(b)-fruit*** (StKt) //***dumps*** (Antg) //***dungs*** (Guyn) //***governor-plum*** 2. (Belz) //***Jew-plum*** (CayI) //***juju (be)*** (Baha, Jmca) //***koko-kouli, ponm siwèt*** (StLu) //***pomme-surette*** (Angu, Nevs, StKt) A small apple-shaped plum, yellow shading into light-brown when ripe, with a white, brittle, sweetish-sour flesh around a single, stone-hard seed; it is borne on a medium-sized, spreading, and very prickly tree many varieties of wh stink when in blossom; *Ziziphus Mauritania* or *Z. jujuba (Rhamnaceae)*. [Orig *dung-tree* from the distinctly dung-like smell of the young blossoms in the wind. However, the objectionable naming of the fruit ***dung*** by back-formation led to several euphemisms, principally ***dunk***, but also ***dumb, dump***] □Since the word occurs mostly in the pl in ref to the fruit, the form ***dungs*** pronunc [dʌŋs ~ dʌŋz] (also spelt ***dounce*** by E. Mittelholzer) is used in Guyn. Other variant spellings abound: ***donce, dngs, donks, down(e)s, dums, duncks***, etc.

Note that the item **dunk(s)** has twelve allonyms or other names. Each of the other names is entered in its correct alphabetical place in the body of the *DCEU*. The item **byre** would be treated as follows:

(17) **byre** [baωr] *n* (Guyn) [Indic] //DUNKS (Bdos, Guyn, Trin) [Bhoj < Hin *ber* 'plum, jujube'] □This name is restricted to rural Indic people, the tree being of particular religious significance to Muslims.

Here, the primary allonym is indicated by both double slashes (//) and small capitals. There is no definition because the definition will be found under the primary allonym **dunk(s)**, but there is an etymology and a usage note indicated by the small square box preceding it. In other words, entries for secondary allonyms do not carry definitions but may contain other elements of a dictionary entry such as citations, etymologies, and usage notes.

It is also to be noted that the primary allonym **dunk(s)** is followed by an asterisk. This happens with all items that are to be found in the *Multilingual Supplement* to the *DCEU* compiled by this writer, and which will be dealt with as a separate development of Caribbean English lexicography.

Whenever one name can have several referents, there is sense numbering, as in the entry for **pepperpot.** This item carries two consecutively numbered senses as words with different senses are so treated in the *DCEU.* The primary allonym in the second part of the entry also carries one sub-sense indicated by a bold Roman numeral:

(18) **pep.per-pot (pep.per-pot)** [pɛp□pɒt] /1'12/ *n* **1.** (Bdos, Gren, Guyn) A dark-brown stew prepared by boiling together pieces of any kind of wild or regular meat (except fish) with red peppers and other seasoning, sugar and CASAR-EEP for several hours, usu in a large earthenware pot; it is kept on the fire-place, with meat, CASAREEP and seasoning being added from time to time, so that the same pot may actually be served from (in *Guyn*) for weeks, months, or even years. **2.** (Angu, Antg, Jmca) //CALALU **2.** (i) (Dmca, etc) □Note that the two senses apply to meals of very different appearance and taste.

In the same entry, **pepperpot**, the pitch-contour or tone pattern of the headword is rendered by a system of digits between slashes. In entries where the pitch-pattern is included, it comes immediately after the pronunciation. The digits from 1 to 4 represent the range of pitch from low to high, although there can be a much wider range in Caribbean English. Stress is included in the pitch-contour, and it must be noted that the main stress on a word does not always coincide with the highest pitch. Stress is conveyed by a single raised comma, which comes immediately after the tone number, whether this is 1, 2, or 3. The pitch-contour of highest frequency for disyllables in Caribbean English is /1'2/, and for trisyllables /1'12/, and usually these are not indicated.

There are cases in which pitch-contour differentiates meaning and then it is always indicated, usually by superscript numbers, and sometimes with an added usage note. Consider, for example, **one-time** /1'1/ as opposed to /1'2/ or /3'1/.

(19) **one-time**[1] *adv* (CarA) [*IF*] [A compound with distinct senses differentiated by pitch contrasts wh must be noted]. **1.** /1'1/ [with even low stress] Once in

the past. **2.** /2'2/ At one and the same time; in full and at once. **2.** *PHRASES* **2.1 one time and done** *adv phr* [*AF/IF*] At once and have done with it; completely while you are about it; once and for all. **2.2 one time so!** *adv phr* [*AF*] Fully and without hesitation. **3.** /3'1/ [In story telling] Once upon a time. **4.** /3'1/ ~ '3'3/ [with notable stress] [In emotive contexts] There and then; instantly; without a moment's hesitation or a second thought. **5.** /1'2/ [In non-emotive contexts] Right away, so as to avoid delay or risk.

one-time[2] /1'2/ *adj* (CarA) [*IF*] **1.** Of some time in the past. **2.** Rare; exceptional.

Both these headwords, which carry superscript numbers to separate their syntactic functions, also carried citations illustrating the use of each sense. These have been omitted because the chief points to note here would be the pitch-contour and its influence on the meaning of the item, and the corresponding sense numbering to indicate the different meanings.

The other feature to be noted would be the status-labelling, represented by the italicized capitals in square brackets that occur just after the territorial label. Indications of status are an element of the entry that is, so far, unique to the *DCEU*, as compared to the other dictionaries referred to in this chapter, and it is one of its prescriptive aspects.

The lexicographer usually records or describes usage, as we have seen in the *DCEU*, but the lexicographer may also prescribe. Allsopp has similarly prescribed usage in the *DCEU*, both as a Caribbean himself, but also as a linguist reflecting the Caribbean public's perception of the level of formality of its own language, which is reflected largely in citations that reflect the usage of the items in question. This obviates the need to argue about what is 'standard', 'substandard', or 'nonstandard' in Caribbean English (Allsopp 1996: lvi). As Allsopp further explains in the Introduction to the *DCEU*, the hierarchy of formality may be structured using four descending levels—'Formal', 'Informal', 'Anti-Formal', 'Erroneous'. The Anti-Formal level will be further sub-categorized into 'Creole', 'Jocular', 'Derogatory', and 'Vulgar', represented as [*AF-Cr*], [*AF-Joc*], [*AF-Derog*] and [*AF-Vul*]. Formal [*F*] is what is accepted as educated, recognized as Internationally Accepted English (IAE), and is also applied to any regionalism that is not replaceable by any other designation. Informal [*IF*] is what is accepted as familiar, usually well-structured, casual, relaxed speech, sometimes illustrating morphosyntactic reductions of English structure, or some remainders of decreolization. Consider the phrase **come and go (along)**, used Caribbean-wide, which is a relaxed way of saying 'Let's go!' and implying that time should not be wasted on whatever may be preventing those involved from going about their business. Anti-Formal [*AF*] is deliberately familiar and intimate, involving a wide range of speech from close and friendly through jocular to crude and vulgar, or any creolized or Creole form or structure a bit too loosely formulated and used to suit context or situation. Erroneous or Disapproved [*X*] marks an item or sense that is not permissible in IAE but considered to be so by the user. Disapproved may involve such stated grounds as spelling as in **ackee** 3. [*X*] = **akee**, indicating that the former cannot be used as an alternative to the latter, *akee*, since they represent totally different popular fruits.

Another of the most significant challenges was the treatment of the huge body of idiomatic phrases in CE which often incorporate single Standard English verbs, in particular, such as **have**, **give**, **make**, nouns, such as **duppy**, conjunctions such as **before**, prepositions such as **behind**, adjectives such as **long** and adverbs such as **one-time**. The resulting phrases often defy syntactic classification, and, where this is extremely problematic, the syntactic class is given as *id phr*, standing for 'idiomatic phrase'. For example, the treatment of **long** is as follows:

(20) **long**[1] *adj* (CarA) [*AF/IF*] **1.** [Of a person] Notably tall; of ungainly height and bearing. **2.** [In many uses, it denotes size or intensity rather than length; so it is often uncomplimentary or Derog; note foll phrs, and separate entries below] *PHRASES* **2.1 cry long water** *vb phr* (CarA) See CRY Phr 1. ... **2.2 foot is long** *id phr*, (Guyn) [*AF-Joc*] See FOOT Phr. 2.4 **2.3 hand [is] long; hand [is] longer than your foot** *id phrs* (Gren) [*AF*] See HAND[1] Phr 4.11 **2.4 have a long head** *vb phr* (Guyn) [*IF*] To be far-sighted. [Cp IrE *You have a quare long head on you, son* 'You've got brains, can plan for the future'–L.Todd]

The entry, as cited, is not quite complete in that some phrases and their supporting citations have been left out, but it gives an idea of the kinds of phrases that are based on single Standard English words, and of how the West African world view is reflected in the idiomatic phrases of Caribbean English via calquing within the creolization process. The phrases make use of English words but the concepts expressed are certainly not English or European as *PHRASES* **2.1** ... **2.2** suggest. Note that, in the entry, the phrases are given as sub-senses of the second sense. The same goes for other parts of speech that give rise to phrases in Caribbean English.

Perhaps the greatest challenge in the recording and analysis of Caribbean English is in the etymologies. In many cases the sources are African, in many others, English dialect, in some others, French, Spanish, or Portuguese, and for the Indic items, Bhojpuri or Hindi. Also, not to be discounted, is the indigenous Amerindian contribution to Guyanese English. This takes the form of hundreds of nouns from the nine languages of its identified ethnic groups which include two Arawakan—Arawak (Lokono) and Wapishana; six Cariban—Akawaio, Arekuna, Makushi, Patamuna, Carib, Wai-Wai; and one Warrau language.[7] In the

[7] Arawakan loanwords, such as *mora* and *wallaba* (two types of timber), are found in Guyanese English and sometimes in the English of Trinidad.

case of the African, Indic, and Amerindian sources, data had to be sought directly from African, Indian, and Amerindian informants and that took up much time. The African informants, for example, were academics based in universities in Nigeria—Ibadan, for example—as well as in universities in North America, who still retained control of their mother tongues. Similarly, there had to be in-depth research into written sources, such as the *English Dialect Dictionary*, the *OED*, and French, Spanish, Portuguese, and Hindi dictionaries; Arawak and Carib dictionaries; numerous glossaries; and other written sources. Etymologies are enclosed in bold square brackets, since square brackets are used for other purposes in the *DCEU*, such as enclosing status and subject labels, indicating explanatory material in glosses, and marking off words that are optional in phrases.

The final aspect of the *DCEU* that must be noted is its cultural reach as reflected in the cross-referencing of entries pertaining to flora and fauna, folklore, festivals, religion, foods, beliefs, superstitions, and folk wisdom—to name just some of the categories treated. As Allsopp says in his introduction to the *DCEU*:

> Many aspects of Caribbean life—foods, festivals, ceremonies, beliefs, practices related to births, marriages, cures, burials, etc. have a massive vocabulary which is sometimes suggestively African—
>
> **dokunu; jonkunu; queh-queh** ...
>
> sometimes clearly Anglophone
>
> **Carnival; big-drum dance; tie-heads**, etc.
>
> sometimes a mixture of both—
>
> **bake bammy for somebody; to obeah somebody**, etc. (Allsopp 1996: xxxiii)

He goes on to point out that he has tried in a number of ways to sensitize the reader to the 'reality, nature and dimensions of the Caribbean's African background, and to invite investigative intelligence to dislodge the old programmed contempt for Black African culture' (Allsopp 1996: xxxii). This declaration shows that Allsopp was continuing, in greater depth, the work begun by Cassidy and Le Page in the *DJE* and continued on a smaller scale by Holm and Shilling in the *DBE*. However, Allsopp went further in that he also included the East Indian contribution that is so much a part of the English of Guyana and Trinidad, and also led the user to an understanding of the character and culture of the Caribbean East Indian, thereby endorsing a more all-embracing form of Caribbean cultural integration. Note the following item:

(21) **dho.ti** [dhoti ~ doti] *n* (Guyn, Trin) [Indic] //***capra*** 1. (Trin)
An EAST INDIAN man's white loin cloth consisting of a single piece
Of cloth wrapped around the waist, folded over and passed loosely
Between the legs. [Hin *dhoti* 'loin cloth']

The great educational and cultural value of this work is indisputable in that it shows Caribbean people who they are and explains to them both their linguistic and cultural identity. As a guide to teachers of English and other languages, the *DCEU*, together with its *Multilingual Supplement* (J. Allsopp 1996: 669–97), is invaluable in that it informs its readers as to the nature and origins of Caribbean English, going from the formal right through to the disapproved, then extending across the major language divisions of the Caribbean region.

15.5 FURTHER DEVELOPMENTS IN CARIBBEAN LEXICOGRAPHY

15.5.1 The Book of Afric Caribbean Proverbs *(BACP)*

The natural successor of the *DCEU* is the *Book of Afric Caribbean Proverbs* by Richard Allsopp, which appeared in November 2004. Allsopp's intention in this dictionary is to chronicle in one work those collective sayings of the folk that reflect our West African heritage. The term 'Afric', with which he deals in the Introduction to the book, is meant to denote the ethnic descendants of the people of the continent of Africa, but 'who are native to to the continents and islands of the West Atlantic (or emigrants therefrom to Europe)' (Allsopp 2004: xiv). Consequently, in this work, Allsopp is dealing with the folk wisdom as originally culled from the stock of our African forebears, brought with them from Africa and so becoming the heritage of Afric peoples in the Caribbean. The concentration on Afric proverbs in the Caribbean is indicative of the depth of the influence of sub-Saharan Africa on the life and culture of the Caribbean, as opposed to the imprint of other groups such as the East Indians, the Chinese, and the Amerindians, there being very little recorded material for the first two communities and none for the last.

The collection of over 1,300 proverbs in the *BACP* comes almost exclusively out of Afric-Caribbean folklife as expressed in the various Creoles, and lists their numerous sub-Saharan African language correlates. It also illustrates the numerous duplications of Creole proverbs spread over the twenty-two Caribbean territories in which they were collected. It is not meant to be a complete collection but a representative sample of the total stock.

15.5.1 (i) Content of the BACP

The *BACP* gives a listing of proverbs arranged alphabetically by headword, in that the headwords chosen usually convey the most significant part of the message of the proverb. There is, however, an Index of other significant words that are not headwords, preceded by explanatory notes that will help the searcher. The content and structure of the entries are as follows in each case:

(i) P – the original form of the proverb,
(ii) T – its translation into Internationally Accepted English for those who would prefer to receive the message in that form,
(iii) R – the author's rendering in rhyming couplets, intended to be a mnemonic for young people,
(iv) E – an explanation of any feature that needs clarification and a commentary on aspects of Caribbean Social History,
(v) M – the meaning of the proverb expressed in simple English, and
(vi) N – a note of comparative, historical, or other interest (often illustrating the universality of folk thinking in certain aspects of life, worldwide).

Territorial labelling similar to that of the *DCEU* is used in the *BACP*, and there is also a similar system of cross-referencing, features seen in the following example:

(22) **broom** *Baha, Belz, Guyn, Jmca*

P (a) New broom sweep clean, but is de ol(d) one know all de corner –*Belz, Guyn, Jmca*

(b) // Ol(d) broom know where de dirt is –*Baha*

T *The old broom knows where the dirt is.*

R *The old broom's shape gets dirt from under bases;*
The new broom cleans only the open places.

E The old broom, shaped from long use, gets into places where the new broom does not.

M The older person can anticipate the tricks of others from experience, which aggressive younger person lacks.

N Compare (*S.Ghana*) Gã-Adangme proverb *An old broom is better than new one – MEWP* #1560, also BrE *A new broom sweeps clean – ODEP* (1564p.564

However, the *CarA* version extends the message to warn against overlooking the value of age and experience.

This example contains all the elements of a typical entry in the *BACP*. The correlates in both a West African language and British English must be noted, as must also the extension of meaning found in the Caribbean version. Allsopp states in his Introduction to the *BACP* that proverbs are the 'orature' or 'oral literature' of the folk, everywhere, through recorded time. This oral literature is what embodies 'mountains of human experience and wisdom from which literature itself will have gained much, but can hardly challenge in quantum, on the ground of human enlightenment' (Allsopp 2004: xvii). The example given above contains cultural, historical, and linguistic material, presented in a form which is meant to teach the reader about the life-ways of Afric Caribbean people, and also to enlighten non-Caribbean people about Caribbean language, life, and culture.

The *BACP* is a direct descendant of Caribbean Anglophone lexicography in general, but there is another descendant of much greater linguistic and cultural reach, which chronicles not only the English of the Caribbean but also its French, Creole, and Spanish. This is the *Caribbean Multilingual Dictionary of Flora, Fauna and Foods (CMD)* (2004), in English, French, French Creole, and Spanish, produced by this writer. It is the first volume of a large work spanning to date the major official languages of the Caribbean, already named, but with the intention of including the other official language, Dutch, which has not yet been done.

15.5.2 The Caribbean Multilingual Dictionary of Flora, Fauna and Foods *(CMD)*

This work introduces a new dimension into Caribbean lexicography in that it is a thematic dictionary treating its material under such heads as flora, fauna, foods, and, in a second volume currently being prepared, folklore, festivals, music, dance, and religion. The *CMD* originates from the *Multilingual Supplement* to the *DCEU*, and is a listing of primary allonyms of flora and fauna found in the *DCEU* for which equivalents are given in the four Caribbean varieties of French and four Caribbean varieties of Spanish. Consequently, the *Supplement* supplies the equivalents for about eight times the actual entries contained in it, since the French and Spanish equivalents would apply to the secondary allonyms as well, identified by their scientific names. Those names serve as the means of determining that the secondary allonyms refer to the same item of flora or fauna. Apart from the themes mentioned above, other themes will be treated as well. The *CMD* is worthy of mention in a history of English lexicography in that it is a unidirectional dictionary going from Caribbean English into Caribbean French, French Creole, and Spanish.

The fifty pages of front matter in the *CMD* are written largely in English, but with the summaries of the content and purpose of the work in French and Spanish; and it contains three sections on Caribbean flora, fauna, and foods. The headwords are English and territorially labelled, as are the glosses, which take the same form as those in the *DCEU* and consist of description, followed by encyclopedic information. The listing is largely of ostensive items, in that they name fruits, flowers, trees, shrubs, animals, including insects, amphibians, reptiles, birds, etc., but verbs or phrases derived from those items are also treated. There is also cross-referencing to entries in English, but handled differently from the *DCEU*, and, wherever necessary, citations in English. After this, French equivalents are supplied, usually with citations, followed by French Creole equivalents, wherever possible, and finally by Spanish equivalents, usually with citations—all cross-referenced and territorially labelled. The French, French Creole, and Spanish equivalents are taken from the four Francophone Caribbean territories and from five representative Hispanophone territories—Cuba, Puerto Rico, the Dominican Republic, Costa Rica, and Venezuela—the latter two having a coast washed by the Caribbean Sea, thus justifying their inclusion. The ethnic composition of these territories, which is made up of indigenous, Hispanic, and African peoples and is similar to that of the Francophone and Anglophone Caribbean, is also relevant.

Unlike the *Supplement* and like the main body of the *DCEU*, the *CMD* treats French Creole items, since they are an authentic part of Caribbean English. This point needs to be made because the listing of primary allonyms which comprises the *Supplement* did not include any French Creole item as a primary allonym, but listed only the Caribbean English name of the particular item. In the case of items of flora and fauna, the scientific names are given for accuracy of identification. Etymologies, where given, are included in usage notes at the end of entries. A typical *CMD* entry, though with citations excluded, would be the following:

(23) **gar.den-bal.sam** (*Bdos, Jmca, Trin, USVI*) [g(y)ardn-bzlzχm] *n. Justicia pectoralis (Acanthaceae).* **Guyn** ***toyo***; **Jmca** ***fresh-cut***; **Trin** ***carpenter-grass.*** A small, flowering shrub about 0.3 m high, with slender stems and small, pink, white, or pale blue flowers, often cultivated for its aromatic leaves; it is often used as a remedy for colds.
FrCa ***carmentin*** *m.*; **Guad, Hait, Mart** ***herbe à charpentier(s)*** *f.*;
Hait ***z'herbe charpentier*** *f.*; **FrCr Guad, Hait, Mart** ***herbe (zèb à charpentier)***; **Hait** ***charpentier (sepantye)***; **Cuba** ***tila*** *f.*, ***tilo*** *m.*;
PtRi, StDo ***curia*** *f.*; **StDo** ***carpintero*** *m.*, ***yerba carpintera*** *f.* *No relative to the European balsam; it is so called because of its aromatic properties and because it is often cultivated for use.

All French and Spanish items are syntactically classified, but the French Creole items do not carry grammatical gender. The item ***z'herbe charpentier*** is not a French Creole item but an item of what is called 'français créolisé' or 'creolized French', a variety which may have Creole elements but in general their forms are morphologically those of metropolitan French. The *z'* of ***z'herbe charpentier*** is the Creole element, but the rest of the item—***herbe*** and ***charpentier***—is made up of two perfectly ordinary standard French words so that the item can be given grammatical gender based on the first element of the compound which is feminine, as it is a compound word.

This natural development from Caribbean Anglophone into Caribbean multilingual lexicography is the logical offshoot of the *DCEU*, and the *CMD* brings to the reader's attention the fact that the Caribbean is multilingual and multicultural.

15.5.3 Historical Dictionary of Trinidad and Tobago

Another interesting development in Caribbean English lexicography is Michael Anthony's *Historical Dictionary of Trinidad and Tobago*, published in 1997, which includes a variety of entries under place-name, events, and persons. Although this is not a dictionary—in that the treatment of its material is not like that of a regular dictionary but rather more like an encyclopedia—it nevertheless forms part of the collection of Caribbean English dictionaries. Based on well-researched historical content, the *Historical Dictionary of Trinidad and Tobago* gives an in-depth view of the history, culture, and development of Trinidad and Tobago, and as such is worthy of mention in this chapter. An example of an event that is contained in the timeline of Trinidad and Tobago's history is seen in the following entry:

(24) 1748 French expedition from Martinique attempts to settle Tobago in defiance of Treaty of Aix-la-Chapelle.

15.6 CONCLUSION

The major Caribbean English dictionaries that have been examined in this chapter are certainly agents of standardization for spelling, pronunciation, and general usage. The *DCEU* has led the way in this regard, supplying many variant spellings for the items treated, capturing the vagaries of pronunciation through the use of standard IPA, and chronicling general usage, from the formal to the disapproved. The *DJE* and the *DBE* have also contributed to the standardization of the individual varieties they treat—Jamaican English and Bahamian English—the former particularly in relation to capturing the standard pronunciation of Jamaican English Creole words through a system of phonemic representation specially designed for the purpose. This initiative was later followed by the *DBE*, which used a revised form of Cassidy's system. Crucially, however, the three major dictionaries of Caribbean English, the *DCEU*, the *DJE*, and the *DBE*, have sought to bolster the faltering cultural self-assurance normally witnessed in post-colonial societies—referred to earlier in this chapter—by contributing to the building of a positive Caribbean cultural self-image. Central to this has been the recognition of the huge input of sub-Saharan African languages and cultures into the languages and cultures of the Caribbean, both Anglophone and non-Anglophone.

However, with so much already achieved, what is the future for dictionaries of Caribbean English? Cassidy and Le Page of the *DJE* have both passed on, Holm and Shilling have not attempted any further work on Bahamian English; the promised *Dictionary of Trinidadian English* has not yet materialized; and there has been no attempt to encourage—or even consider the production of—a second edition of the *DCEU*. Nevertheless, there has been an attempt on the part of Richard Allsopp to produce a considerably reduced *Supplement* to the *DCEU* in the form of the *New Register of Caribbean English Usage*. This is still unfinished. But besides its completion, we still need to see the compilation of more territorial dictionaries, a revised edition of the *DCEU*, and the production of school dictionaries and specialized glossaries relating to various aspects of Caribbean life and culture.

It is expected that the Centre for Caribbean Lexicography, intended to be the umbrella body for the entire Caribbean Lexicography Programme, Anglophone and Multilingual, housed at the UWI Cave Hill Campus in Barbados, whose work is to be directed by this writer, will undertake some of the tasks mentioned, such as the revision of the *DCEU*, the completion of the *Supplement* already begun, and the production of school dictionaries and specialized glossaries and dictionaries of Caribbean English and other Caribbean languages.

The ground-breaking, pioneering work undertaken by the *DCEU* and its predecessors, which proudly affirms Caribbean linguistic and cultural identity as well as unity, should not be allowed to stand still, especially in view of the positive moves towards regional integration at all levels currently being pursued in the Anglophone Caribbean and without which the region, as a cultural and political entity, cannot survive.

16

THE ELECTRONIC *OED*: THE COMPUTERIZATION OF A HISTORICAL DICTIONARY

Edmund Weiner

16.1 INTRODUCTION

THE purpose of this chapter is to trace the progress from the printed, unrevised, 16-volume *OED* to its database version, published online. Around 1982, when the story began, the *OED* existed in two alphabetical sequences, the first edition of 1884–1928 and its Supplement, begun in 1957; the latter was then approaching completion. In the first decade of the century, the electronic *OED* is in the process of revision and continual updating. This presentation is organized under headings representing the main problems that had to be solved. It is broadly a sequential narrative, but the logic of the arrangement necessitates one or two disjunctures in the chronology.

16.2 STAGE 1—*OED2*, THE OEDIPUS SYSTEM, AND CD-ROM, 1982–1992

16.2.1 Securing the future of the OED

In the early 1980s, the editing of *A Supplement to the Oxford English Dictionary* was nearing completion, and Volume 4 (Se–Z) was on schedule for publication in 1986. The senior management of the Oxford University Press, the publishers of the *OED*, began to be concerned about the future of the dictionary, recognized as both a national monument and an international resource, which they held in trust. The *OED* was the flagship of the OUP range of dictionaries, but how it could be further developed to the advantage of the scholars who used it and the publishers themselves was not readily apparent. In 1983, the 50-year copyright of the 1933 first edition would come to an end. The *OED* might be vulnerable to exploitation by parties other than OUP. (There was a suspected case of piracy of the *OED* at this time.) Moreover, OUP had a skilled team of historical lexicographers, equipped with an invaluable set of resources—its voluminous quotation files, its specialist library, and all the infrastructure developed during the thirty years of work on the *Supplement*. They needed to be productively employed, at the very least in order to underpin the future development of the profitable Oxford trade dictionaries. But, first and foremost, it was recognized by most parties that the *OED* needed revision.

16.2.2 *Integrating the First Edition and the* Supplement

An obvious solution to the immediate question of securing the copyright would be to combine the contents of the *Supplement* with those of the first edition in order to produce an integrated edition of the *OED*. The *OED* had to be kept in print, and an integrated edition would protect the copyright on the first edition while giving the reader the convenience of having the entries from the Supplement inserted in their proper places. In 1982, Robin Denniston, who held the senior post of Publisher at OUP, suggested, doubtless with reservations about the practicalities, the 'biggest scissors-and-paste job in history'. Editors would place the supplementary material in the correct positions in the main *OED*, making appropriate adjustments where needed, and the resultant text would be reset and printed. Richard Charkin, Head of Reference, immediately responded with a more ambitious idea. OUP had just installed its first production system for editing text electronically and was beginning negotiations to publish some of its printed materials in electronic formats. Charkin argued that this technology was likely in due course to enter the mainstream of publishing. Why not use it to transform the *OED*? First, the whole of the two texts could be computerized. Then, using the new technology, the two could be blended together and edited. Moreover, online databases were becoming familiar, accessed in those days via modem and standard telephone connections: the *OED* itself had a subscription to the Nexis/Lexis database. Why not make the *OED* available commercially as an online database? (Indeed, at this very early stage, at least one online database company, Mead Data Central who owned Nexis/Lexis, expressed an interest in hosting the electronic *OED* if it came into existence.)

16.2.3 *Identifying the end product*

Once it had been decided that the *OED* should be converted into an electronic resource which would allow unlimited editing, the long-term aim of updating and revising the *OED* became more realistic. The OUP management asked the Dictionary Department to study the feasibility of such a project in greater detail. Lexicographers working on the *OED Supplement* and on the *New Shorter OED* had from their vantage point a clear picture of what was needed, and could imagine what they would do, using conventional methods, to get there (even though the scale of the task was immense). The main purpose of the *Supplement* had been to add new words and meanings, not to update the first edition, and *Supplement* staff were familiar with those aspects of the parent volume that were now very outdated, including, for example, definitions reflecting old-fashioned social, technological, and scientific situations or expressed in terms that had become obscure or ambiguous. The *New Shorter* staff, meanwhile, had been revising the histories and etymologies of thousands of words on the basis of a great body of new evidence that had been collected since the time of the first edition of the *OED*. Accordingly, in March 1982, Robert Burchfield commissioned one of the two senior editors on the *OED Supplement*, John Simpson, and the Chief Editor of the *New Shorter*, Lesley Brown, to list the activities and estimate the person-years required in order to revise and update the *OED*, assuming that some kind of computing equipment would be available. They concluded that both the conversion of the texts by manual keyboarding and their integration by experienced editors were feasible.

16.2.4 *Organizing a project of unprecedented size and complexity*

16.2.4 (i) Identifying external partners

By contrast with the editorial resources available, OUP had little expertise in any of the computational processes that could be envisaged. It decided early in 1983 to issue a Request for Tender, combined with descriptions of the existing *OED*, the desired end product, and the processes required to get from one to the other. This procedure was put into the hands of the Information Systems Department, under Ewen Fletcher. The computing requirements were compiled by one of his senior staff, Richard Sabido, and the lexicographical information by another senior member of the *OED Supplement* staff, Edmund Weiner. The document, entitled *A Future for the Oxford English Dictionary*, was sent in June to a wide range of computer companies, software houses, government agencies, and academic departments (in all about a hundred copies were sent out, with a deadline of 1 August 1983). There were several promising responses. Charkin and Weiner made a number of visits, both in the UK and in North America. Four companies submitted formal tenders.

Two things became clear. No single agency could carry out everything OUP wanted; it would have to work with a number of partners. And OUP would have to take on the central managing role. Accordingly a department was set up under an experienced OUP project director, Tim Benbow. When the project (at this stage called 'The New OED') was launched officially at the Royal Society on 15 May 1984, OUP's partners were: International Computaprint Corporation (a subsidiary of Reed International), with a straightforward business contract to convert the text to machine-readable form; IBM UK, who under the auspices of their Academic Programme donated computer equipment and staff to form the nucleus of a team of system designers based at OUP; and the University of Waterloo in Canada, who were to have full access to the machine-readable data for the purpose of research into the electronic handling of large texts, in exchange for making available to OUP the software developed in the course of this research. The UK Department of Trade and Industry gave a subvention of £288,750 to support the necessary research.

A number of personal initiatives, some arising fortuitously, had given the project its momentum. An enquiry from IBM UK Ltd on a different topic led OUP through the corporate hierarchy to its director, John Fairclough, who was able to negotiate the donation. After OUP had held inconclusive discussions with Reed, Hans Nickel, the President of its subsidiary, ICC, took the initiative and demonstrated that his company could and should carry out the data conversion. Dr Douglas Wright, President of the University of Waterloo, became aware of OUP's plans via a chain of personal acquaintances and saw at once how the project would mesh with his university's aspirations in the field of computer applications. Sir Fred Dainton, then Chancellor of Sheffield University, smoothed the way for the application to the Department of Trade and Industry. The Chief Executive of OUP, George Richardson, felt that it was vital that the Press should get its feet wet in the new environment of digital publishing, and OUP's governing body of academics, the Delegates, were impressed by the calibre of the parties supporting the project idea—including researchers in the University of Oxford and within IBM (both in the UK and in the US)—and agreed that it was a sensible solution to the copyright problem. Two advisory bodies were established: an

Advisory Council to represent the main partners to the project and handle business questions and an Editorial Board of scholars with relevant language expertise.

16.2.4 (ii) Organizing the project internally

Early thinking had been that the chosen supplier would convert the two texts into electronic form, merge them, and supply the output to OUP, where editorial staff, using OUP's text editing system, would revise and correct the dictionary interactively and pass it on to be typeset and published. It was now realized that this was far too much to manage in one step. The first stage alone, merging the first edition and *Supplement*, was a substantial undertaking, but at least its parameters were easily defined. The second stage, the full revision and updating of the *OED*, could at that stage hardly be envisaged and would need careful research and planning. It was therefore decided to publish the integrated edition on paper and subsequently in electronic form as the second edition of the *OED*. The revision and updating that would create a third edition was deferred to a second phase.

The Project Director compiled an overall plan identifying all the major activities within the project, their interrelationships, the time each would take, and the resources of staff, equipment, and finance each required. The activities were: conversion of the data, initial proof-reading, computer development, automatic processing of the machine-readable text, editing of entries on the screen, composition of galley proofs, final proof-reading, and final page composition. For each of these a detailed plan was made. In July 1985, when the outline design of the computer system had been completed, it became possible to estimate the times required to build and run the system; these times were added in, and a firm 'Plan of Record' with fixed dates for the completion of each activity was established; it was at this point that publication was set for March 1989. Probably for the first time in the history of the Oxford Dictionaries, project planning software was employed to project and monitor time and cost; and the plan was adhered to.

16.2.5 Handling the text by computer

In October 1984, an *Outline statement of user requirements for a computer system* was drawn up by the project team, setting out the aims of the project and the operations which the computer system should perform. In July 1985, the computing team issued an *Outline design for a computer system* and over the ensuing eighteen months built a dictionary system to carry out these functions. The dictionary text, once it had been captured, was held (at OUP) on an IBM 4341 mainframe computer (systems based on a network of servers were still being developed) within an SQL database management system. Each new version of the data resulting from successive stages of the project was retained and nothing overwritten. The hardware and software used were of reasonably generous speed and proportions for their time, though by the standards of even a few years later they were limited and slow. The technical design had to work with very small amounts of storage space and memory. There were no windows in the editing system and, if a checking process was running on a user's workstation, he or she could do nothing else.

16.2.6 Converting the text to electronic form

Tests were undertaken very early on to see whether conversion of the text by optical character recognition (OCR) would be practicable. OCR would require each page to be scanned by an optical device and the images converted into digital text. However, the printed text of the first edition of the *OED* was of relatively poor quality, with many broken characters, so that a very large amount of correction would be required. Moreover, OCR could introduce only typographical mark-up (such as italics, bold, small capitals, different point sizes, and so on). By contrast, ICC had the scale and expertise to keyboard and proof-read the text so as to make it virtually error-free; and they had skilled copy editors who could handle structural mark-up (i.e. markers in the text which conveyed the meaning of the various typographical devices, such as bold type indicating a headword, small capitals a cross-reference, and so on). Therefore, although this might have seemed an unsophisticated approach, keyboarding was adopted. A sample tape of a hundred dictionary pages supplied by ICC in December 1984 proved that they could introduce a level of mark-up sufficient to reproduce the basic format of the dictionary text. From then on, the copy editors at ICC inserted a mixture of structural and typographical mark-up symbols (see 16.2.7, below) on enlarged dictionary pages which were passed to the data-capture personnel for keying. Data validation routines and sample proof-reading were carried out by ICC, the tapes and proofs were shipped to OUP, and the *OED* team, coordinated by an experienced former member of the *Supplement* staff, Yvonne Warburton, conducted a full proof-read. The cycle of data capture, proof-reading, and data correction occupied the eighteen months January 1985–June 1986. A vital aspect of the reading was that textual mark-up was checked as well as literal text. This was greatly assisted by the running of the prototype parser on the data (see 16.2.8, below). The approved text was estimated to have a residual error-rate of only 1 in 235,000 characters.

16.2.7 *Making the text machine-readable*

The OUP project team had appreciated that mark-up which only identified typographical features would not be enough. The aim from the start, then, was to transform the text into an electronic database, in which every part of the text had its own identifying tag; these tags would form the basis both for complex text searching and for versatile text representation. The editors' very first step towards achieving this aim was literally to take a copy of a sample entry and shade each identifiable element with a differently coloured crayon. From this, a sophisticated schema of textual elements was developed. The IBM group recommended that OUP should develop an *OED* version of Generalized Mark-up Language, which had fortuitously just then come into general use and was soon to be refined as SGML. Over time, the mark-up used for the *OED* has varied in its complexity, but the trend has been constantly towards a finer-grained reflection of the structure of the dictionary. Early analysis during 1984 concentrated on discovering exactly what all the structural elements contained in the dictionary were: these were believed to be of the order of forty. ICC staff could not themselves enter a set of structure tags of this complexity, since too often they would face decisions about the status of a particular string of text that only an *OED* lexicographer could make. It was agreed that their keyboarders would enter a mixed system which incorporated about fifteen major structural tags (such as headword, pronunciation, etymology, sense section, quotation, quotation date, author, and so on) together with conventional typographic mark-up at the lower levels (such as italics marking various different kinds of label or cited form). The conversion of the latter was deferred to the parsing stage (see 16.2.8, below).

During Stage 2 of the project, incidentally, further mark-up was introduced and, in Stage 3, this was accompanied by a reconsideration of the structure of an *OED* entry (see 16.4.1). Under Pasadena, introduced at Stage 3, the mark-up would not only allow more powerful text searching but also support more efficient editing and workflow.

16.2.8 *Introducing mark-up into the text*

As stated above, the first stage made use of a mixed set of tags, some marking such major structural elements as entry, headword, part of speech, pronunciation, etymology, sense section, quotation paragraph, and quotation (which the ICC

Man-ha·ndle, *v.* [f. MAN *n.*[1] + HANDLE *v.*; in sense 3 cf. dial. *manangle* (Devon) to mangle, which may belong to MANGLE *v.* (AF. *mahangler*).]

† **1.** *trans.* To handle or wield a tool. *Obs.*

1457 R. FANNANDE *Mon. Christ's Hosp. Abingdon* xiii, The Mattok was man-handeled right wele a whyle.

2. *Naut.*, etc. 'To move by force of men, without levers or tackles' (Adm. Smyth).

1867 SMYTH *Sailor's Word-bk.* **1894** *Times* 27 Jan. 10/2 The larger weapons will be worked by electricity, but are also capable of being man-handled. **1902** *Blackw. Mag.* Mar. 331/2 I'm going to man-handle my gun down the slope. **1903** *Daily Chron.* 19 Feb. 3/3 Stalwart Punjabis..hand out bags of stores,..or manhandle a fractious, restive animal.

3. *slang.* To handle roughly; to pull or hustle about.

1865 *Hotten's Slang Dict.*, *Man-handle*, to use a person roughly, as to take him prisoner, turn him out of a room, give him a beating. **1886** *Century Mag.* Apr. 905/1 Two of our roughs began to haze him: but they mistook their calling, and in two minutes were so mauled and manhandled that it was reported aft. **1888** CLARK RUSSELL *Death Ship* II. 253, I..was for..manhandling him, ghost or no ghost. **1891** KIPLING *Light that failed* iii, I'll catch you and man-handle you, and you'll die. **1894** R. H. DAVIS *Eng. Cousins* 24 The cry of 'Welsher',..which sometimes on an English race-course means death from man-handling.

FIG. 16.1. *OED1*, formatted

+1000 man-ha +11 ndle, +PS v. +ET +OB f. +SC Man +I n. +R +HM,1 +SC Handle +I v. +R; in sense 3 cf. dial. +I manangle +R (Devon) to mangle, which may belong to +SC Mangle +I v. +R (AF. +I mahangler +R). +EB +SS +31 1. +IR trans. +R +63 To handle or wield a tool. +I +63 Obs. +QP 1457 +SC R. Fannande +I Mon. Christ's Hosp. Abingdon +R xiii, +QT The Mattok was man-handeled right wele a whyle. +SS 2. + IR Naut. + R, etc. + 63 + 17 To move by force of men, without levers or tackles + 18 (Adm. Smyth). +QP 1867 +SC Smyth +I Sailor's Word-bk. +QN 1894 +I Times +R 27 Jan. 10/2 +QT The larger weapons will be worked by electricity, but are also capable of being man-handled. +QN 1902 +I Blackw. Mag. +R Mar. 331/2 +QT I'm going to man-handle my gun down the slope. + QN 1903 + I Daily Chron. + R 19 Feb. 3/3 +QT Stalwart Punjabis +10 hand out bags of stores, +10 or manhandle a fractious, restive animal. +SS 3. +IR slang. +R +63 To handle roughly; to pull or hustle about. +QP 1865 + I Hotten's Slang Dict. + R, + QT + I Man-handle, + R to use a person roughly, as to take him prisoner, turn him out of a room, give him a beating. +QN 1886 + I Century Mag. +R Apr. 905/1 +QT Two of our roughs began to haze him: but they mistook their calling, and in two minutes were so mauled and manhandled that it was reported aft. +QN 1888 +SC Clark Russell +I Death Ship +R II. 253, I +10 was for +10 manhandling him, ghost or no ghost. +QN 1891 +SC Kipling +I Light that failed +R iii, +QT I'll catch you and man +H handle you, and you'll die. +QN 1894 +SC R. H. Davis +I Eng. Cousins +R 24 +QT The cry of +17 Welsher +18, +10 which sometimes on an English race-course means death from man-handling.

FIG. 16.2. *OED1*, with ICC tagging

team were trained to recognize), while others indicated only typographical features within these elements. This meant that some elements were not distinguished (because they had no special typographical marker) and others were distinguished only (for example) by italics, which indicated a range of different elements. The ICC tags were more rudimentary than SGML and XML tags are, in that they only marked a transition from one state to another: so, for example, the +I tag marked the beginning of italic text, a + R tag marked a shift back to roman, a +SC tag marked the beginning of small capitals, another +R tag a shift back to roman, and so on; SGML and XML tags, of course, enclose the whole string within a pair of opening and closing tags. (For a sample of ICC's tagged text, see Fig. 16.2.)

Meanwhile the in-house computer team drawn from IBM and OUP staff had been assembled and had begun planning the computer system. The aim was to build a suite of software consisting of a number of components that would be run sequentially, producing at the end a roughly integrated version of the *OED* text. Their most urgent priority was to identify a means of converting the ICC tags to the target schema. At this stage (1985), the research group at the University of Waterloo, led by Gaston Gonnet and Frank Tompa, stepped in with a solution. They had already been working with the first output from ICC and had produced early sketches of a potential database structure. They had come to an important conclusion about the eventual shape of the searchable database. The dictionary text, instead of being slotted into a complex relational database, should be held as a simple string of words and tags, and the intelligence required to execute search requests should reside in the search software, which they undertook to design (see further below, 16.3.2). In order to help the OUP team transform the dictionary into this form, they now came up with parsing software based on the concept of 'finite state transduction'.

This concept was based on the fact that the regularity of the dictionary text made it possible to analyse its constituents as if they were components of a language with a rule-governed syntax. A University of Waterloo master's student, Rick Kazman, developed a parsing program that could be built into the suite of project software (Kazman 1986). The 'grammar' of the text was written at Oxford by running a postulated grammar against the text to establish whether it could be transformed into the desired new structure without rejection of the input or ambiguity in the output. The grammar had to accommodate as much of the pre-existing variation in textual structure as possible so that lexicographical judgement would not be overridden and only minor re-editing would be needed to make the text pass the parser. In September 1986, when automatic processing of the dictionary data began, the first process (after validation routines) was the running of the parser in its final form. In the ensuing three months 5,711 editorial corrections were made as a result. (For a sample of *OED2* tagged text, see Fig. 16.3.)

<entry>
<hwsec>
<hwgp><hwlem>man-ha&sd.ndle</hwlem>, <pos>v.</pos></hwgp>
<etym>f.
<xra><xlem><man </xlem><pos>sb.</pos><hom>1</hom></xra>
+
<xra><xlem>handle </xlem><pos>v.</pos></xra>
; in <rxra>sense <sn>3</sn><rxra> cf. dial. <cf>manangle </cf>
(Devon) to mangle, which may belong to
<xra><xlem>mangle</xlem><pos>v.</pos></xra>(AF.
<cf>mahangler</cf>).
</etym>
</hwsec>
<signif>
<sen para=t status=obs lit='1.'><lab>trans.</lab>&es.To handle or wield a tool.&es.<lab>Obs. </lab>
</sen>
<qbank>
<quot>
<qdat>1457 </qdat><auth>R. Fannande </auth><wk>Mon. Christ's Hosp. Abingdon </wk> xiii,
<qtxt>The Mattok was man-handeled right wele a whyle. </qtxt>
</quot>
</qbank>
<sen para=t lit='2'><lab>Naut.,</lab>etc.&es.&oq.To move by force of men, without levers or tackles&cq. (Adm. Smyth).
</sen>
<qbank>
<quot>
<qdat>1867 </qdat><auth>Smyth </auth><wk>Sailor's Word-bk.</wk>
</quot>
<quot>
<qdat>1894 </qdat><wk>Times </wk> 27 Jan. 10/2
<qtxt>The larger weapons will be worked by electricity, but are also capable of being man-handled. </qtxt>
</quot>
<quot>
<qdat>1902 </qdat><wk>Blackw. Mag. </wk> Mar. 331/2
<qtxt>I'm going to man-handle my gun down the slope. </qtxt>
</quot>
<quot>
<qdat>1903 </qdat><wk>Daily Chron. </wk> 19 Feb. 3/3
<qtxt>Stalwart Punjabis&dd.hand out bags of stores,&dd.or manhandle a fractious, restive animal. </qtxt>
</quot>
</qbank>
<sen para=t lit='3.'> <la>slang.</la>&es.To handle roughly; to pull or hustle about.

(*Continued*)

```
</sen>
<qbank>
<quot>
<qdat>1865 </qdat><wk>Hotten's Slang Dict. </wk>,
<qtxt><i>Man-handle</i>, to use a person roughly, as to take him prisoner, turn him out of a room, give him a beating. </qtxt>
</quot>
<quot>
<qdat>1886 </qdat><wk>Century Mag. </wk>Apr. 905/1
<qtxt>Two of our roughs began to haze him: but they mistook their calling, and in two minutes were so mauled and manhandled that it was reported aft. </qtxt>
</quot>
<quot>
<qdat>1888 </qdat><auth>Clark Russell </auth><wk>Death Ship </wk> II. 253,
<qtxt>I&dd.was for&dd.manhandling him, ghost or no ghost. </qtxt>
</quot>
<quot>
<qdat>1891 </qdat><auth>Kipling </auth><wk>Light that failed </wk>iii,
<qtxt>I'll catch you and man&dubh.handle you, and you'll die. </qtxt>
</quot>
<quot>
<qdat>1894 </qdat><auth>R. H. Davis </auth><wk>Eng. Cousins </wk> 24
<qtxt>The cry of &oq.Welsher&cq.,&dd.which sometimes on an English race-course means death from man-handling. </qtxt>
</quot>
</qbank>
</signif>
</entry>
```

Fig. 16.3. *OED1*, after parsing, with *OED2* tagging

It should be stressed that the *OED* tagging system used the conventions of SGML, but could not be made to conform to SGML proper. This was because it was impossible to create for the *OED1* text a full 'document type definition' (the declaration which prescribes the exact syntax by which the tags are related to each other within the text). Such a DTD would have had to be far more rigid than the looser grammar developed for the parsing program. This is an important qualification that had a bearing on later developments.

16.2.9 *Matching partial* Supplement *entries with their* OED *parents*

The central goal of this stage of the whole project was the integration in their correct places in the main *OED* text of *partial* entries from the *Supplement* (the *complete* entries were easily slotted into place alphabetically). A component of the system was built that, using the mark-up, could match the corresponding pieces of text, first by headword, part of speech, and homonym number, and then by sense number, and insert both definition text and banks of quotations in the right place. Instructions already present in the printed text of the *Supplement* (identified during parsing as 'integration instructions') assisted in this. Typical instructions included 'Add to def.:', followed by supplementary definition text and '(Further/earlier/later examples)', followed by a series of quotations. The program was designed to work out where in the parent *OED1* entry the additional piece of definition text and the additional quotations should be inserted. It became clear that in many cases the placing would not be exact, mainly because of the variability and complexity of the text being merged. Accordingly, after integration, editors had to examine all the resulting text and edit some of it carefully. Nonetheless, the program successfully handled about eighty per cent of the text and saved between fifty and sixty per cent of the work that would otherwise have had to be carried out interactively. Automatic integration began in March 1987, and the automatic processing of the whole text of the *Dictionary* was completed at the end of May.

16.2.10 *Editing the text*

While simple word-processing was well developed by the mid-1980s, programs for managing editorial work at remote workstations on a large textual database held on a mainframe were still undeveloped. A leading IBM scientist, Dr Mike Cowlishaw, was working on a program named LEXX, which he was able to adapt. For *OED* purposes it was named the 'OED Integration, Publishing, and Updating System' (OEDIPUS). It allowed access to the dictionary data for editing, enabled entries to be proofed for immediate checking, and incorporated checks and controls over the integrity of the text. Because this subsystem was designed to work with structured mark-up, editing could operate on textual components such as quotations and senses as well as on running text. The screen display presented the components of the text indented and differentiated by colour, a design that has been followed by the two subsequent editorial systems.

Because of its size, the dictionary text was handled by the computer in forty separate alphabetical ranges or 'tables'. The editors wrote corrections on proofs of the automatically integrated text for each table and these corrections were entered online by keyboard operators, while other textual changes were keyed by lexicographers at the same stage.

16.2.11 *Making systematic text changes: automatic and interactive*

Two large and complex problems of data change throughout the text had to be solved. One concerned the thousands of cross-references, many of which would be invalidated by integration, since the addresses of their targets (headword spellings, parts of speech, homonym numbers, and sense numbers) might be altered by the addition of adjacent text. Each cross-reference was identified by the parser, numbered, and copied. After integration, the stored copies were automatically matched with their targets, and, where integration had caused the target to change, they were adjusted; the copies were then written back into the text. Many cross-references were too imprecise to be dealt with automatically and printed reports of these were produced; those that were definitely inaccurate were changed editorially, but others that were not misleading were left as they were. It was not possible using either this system (or indeed its successor) to link cross-references to their targets so that they would be updated automatically: this refinement came with the Pasadena system (see 16.4).

It was also decided that the pronunciations, given in a transcription system devised by James Murray and peculiar to the *OED*, should be translated into a variety of the International Phonetic Alphabet. The pronunciations were identified by the parser, copied, translated into IPA according to a set of rules, and restored to the text. Here again, reports of items that were problematic were printed out on paper for the editors to correct.

What is perhaps most surprising is that even though the *OED* text was machine-readable, the editorial group had no tool for searching it. In order to identify particular features known to need changing, editors had to request the computer group to run searches and print out the results, and they then worked from these printed reports. This highlighted the fact that, in the longer term, revision of the *OED* would have to be centred on an efficient search system with a high-quality display of entries and immediate access via the editing system to each item found.

16.2.12 *Typesetting a text of 350,000,000 characters*

The system had no component that would handle composition. Instead, the integrated text of each table was sent to an outside typesetting company, Filmtype Services Ltd, of Scarborough, North Yorkshire. This meant that a further set of routines had to be written to convert the structural mark-up to the typographic style of the printed book. (The typographic design itself was made by the OUP design department.) A further full round of editing was performed at the galley proof stage, using OEDIPUS, and page proofs were generated over again from the tape output of the new version. Conversion involved not only a range of fonts and type sizes but upwards of six hundred special characters, many of which were unique, and all of which had had to be recorded and classified by the editorial team from the start of data capture. The divisions between the twenty volumes were inserted at a late stage. Film was sent to Rand McNally & Company, Taunton, Massachusetts, where the book was manufactured. The finished Second Edition was published on paper in March 1989, with 21,730 pages, 291,500 entries, and 59 million words of text.

16.2.13 *Publishing the* OED *electronically*

While the project was in its early stages, CD-ROM technology came to the fore as a more convenient medium than the online database accessed by modem. It was decided that once *OED2* had been published in print form, development of a CD version would begin. In fact, a CD-ROM of the unintegrated text of the first edition was published in 1987 by TriStar, ICC's sister company, which proved the feasibility and utility of the idea. By the early 1990s, Windows (and the similar Mac software) offered a much better platform for this application than the simple DOS environment in which the 1987 CD operated. In 1990, OUP commissioned the Dutch software company AND to develop the first CD-ROM of *OED2* (published in 1993). This offered searching both on full text and on a range of elements including headword, pronunciation, etymologies, senses, and the main elements of the quotation. A notable feature, not repeated in the CD-ROM of 2000, was that full indexes of the words contained in each of these elements could be browsed: one could browse indexes of main and subordinate headwords, of pronunciations, of variant forms, of cited forms, of authors, and of work titles. In order to make searches run properly, a great deal more regularization of the data structure was carried out. In particular, a canonical set of parts of speech permitted to occur with headwords was established and irregular occurrences were standardized. Other inconsistencies in the data were handled by the search software. For instance, the wide variety of names and abbreviations for the same language or language group, such as *Algonquin*, *Algonquian*, and *Algonkin* (a legacy of a century of etymology-writing by many different editors who had had no simple means of cross-checking their terminology) was handled by tables of equivalences built into the search engine. It was a remarkable triumph of data compression that the whole text and the searching software could be accommodated, after an early two-disk version, on a single disk.

The CD-ROM reissue in 2000 was made both to coincide with and to conform in function and appearance to the simultaneously published online version of *OED2* (see 16.3.4, below). This changed its nature but simplified the processes of production, maintenance, and user support.

16.2.14 *Ancillary activities*

At the time of writing, the handling and remote searching of large text databases is a commonplace activity. In 1983, the *OED* project was a pioneering venture. The *OED* project team found themselves in the unaccustomed company of computer scientists and computational linguists, some rather eminent in their fields, exploring similar territory. A series of conferences (1985–1994), held in partnership with the Centre for the New OED which had been set up by the University of Waterloo, enabled much fruitful interchange to take place. Also in conjunction with Waterloo, the *OED* conducted a user survey (Benbow *et al.* 1990) early in 1985 in order to discover the likely ways in which users might wish to interrogate the electronic *OED* database once it became available. The responses mostly confirmed the guesses already made about what users would want.

In order to support the editorial aspects of the project, codification of policies and procedures was undertaken on an unprecedented scale. For each step a manual was written: there were manuals for proof-reading, for integration, for pronunciation checking, and for keyboarding, for example. This approach has continued in later stages of the project so that the manuals for general training, use of the computer system, editing specialized kinds of entry or parts of entries, and, most notably, bibliographical principles, form an intranet to themselves.

To accompany publication of *OED2*, supporting text was compiled, notably an integrated 'Bibliography' (or more accurately, list of major works cited), explanatory prelims, and a history of the project. In keeping with the conservative policy of *OED2*, *OED1*'s 'General explanations' were amplified but not radically rewritten. For the publication of *OED Online* (see 16.3.4, below), new policy outlines were written and placed on the website; unlike the magisterial statements of James Murray, they are likely to be revised and rethought as *OED3* itself changes.

16.3 STAGE 2—*OED3, THE TESS SYSTEM, AND ONLINE PUBLISHING, 1992–2005*

16.3.1 *Making the source data fully interactive*

The *OED* was founded upon the collections of quotations excerpted by readers from texts. In preparation for the Third Edition, this original, and continuing, basis was being further broadened. A more systematic and extensive UK-based

Reading Programme had already been set up to support the work of the *New Shorter OED* and the New Words series (see 16.3.5). A counterpart North American Reading Programme (NARP) was established in 1989. The decision was taken to switch the collection and storage of this evidence from paper to electronic form. A format for the electronic 'slip' was designed, which enabled each quotation to be displayed on the screen much like a physical slip, but with the difference that every word in the corpus was instantly accessible via the in-house search engine (see below). A software-neutral system for keying quotations was pioneered for NARP. It used a simple template which enabled readers to key in the details of a quotation in an ASCII format that could then be parsed for incorporation into the 'Incomings' database. The latter (into which the UK Reading Programme in due course also fed) rapidly grew in size until its content was comparable to the British National Corpus (assembled from a collection of excerpts from texts in a balanced range of subjects and genres), which itself became available to *OED* lexicographers after 1993. Alongside this, a 'Historical Corpus' (a collection of texts from the Middle Ages to the early twentieth century that were publicly available from various textual archives) was assembled. This was searchable via the project workstations and was a valuable resource at a time when historical texts were still scarce on the Web. The 'Incomings' database contains between one and two million quotations and about fifty million words: 200,000 quotations are added each year. Since the beginning of the revision programme, quotations have been collected from pre-twentieth century sources (see 16.3.4), and these also are now added to the electronic database. The backlog of several million paper-based quotations held on file by the *OED* remains as yet undigitized, however.

16.3.2 Searching the whole text

The collaboration with the University of Waterloo bore all the fruit that had been hoped for. The crucial role played by their parsing software in regularizing the tagging of the text has already been described. The main focus of their interests was the development of software for ordinary users to search large textual databases by computer. Using the *OED* data they developed a fast search engine known as PAT. It was based on an established approach to programming known as 'Patricia trees' (hence the name). PAT could either operate on simple ASCII strings or be tailored (during operation) to make use of the tagging structure, so that one could find items within particular textual elements. Linked to PAT was a method of displaying the data (in the *OED*'s case, the text of each entry containing a search hit) on the screen in a variety of formats, including ones similar to a column of printed text; this was called Lector. The University of Waterloo also worked on a text editor to be linked with PAT.

PAT and Lector, which ran under UNIX, were adopted by OUP initially to assist in the editing of the *New Shorter OED*, which was the Dictionary Department's priority until 1993. (The University of Waterloo also, in 1989, built a suite of software which converted the electronic text of the OED to the abridged format of the *New Shorter*, enabling the editing of the latter to become much swifter and more efficient.) They were then made available to the OED team, whose editorial work at this time was focused on the writing of entries for new words.

16.3.3 *Revising the whole standing text*

16.3.3 (i) **Building an electronic environment for revision**

In 1993, when OUP published the *New Shorter OED*, resources used for this project were released for the next phase of the *OED* project. At the same time the *OED* team completed work on the CD-ROM (see 16.2.13, above) and the first two *Additions* volumes (see 16.3.5, below) and were ready to start revising the *OED*. In 1994, a new set of system requirements was drawn up, but this time it was decided that development would be carried out by the in-house computer group. The text encoding scheme remained the same in principle: still SGML-like, but allowing variation and lacking a strict DTD (this ruled out using SGML-intelligent software at this stage); the tag set had, however, been revised, augmented, and streamlined. (For samples of *OED2* and *OED3* text in the revised tagging, see Figures 16.4 and 16.5.) The applications were Open Systems compliant, using for example X-windows, Unix, and (for a short time) Motif. By this date, of course, screen windows were available on the desktop and it was possible to have the whole dictionary available for editing, but updates of the searchable text could only be run weekly, using the time available over a weekend (after a few years, nightly updates became possible).

The new suite of editorial software was built in-house. The principles behind PAT and Lector were used to construct the search engine TESS and the display module SID. These were able to operate not only on the text of the *OED* but also on the constantly growing stock of in-house databases. The latter were created by parsing electronic texts into, or capturing them in, the *OED* mark-up (which, as mentioned above, resembled SGML but did not conform to it exactly). Eventually this collection of texts included 'Incomings' and the Historical Corpus (see 16.3.1, above), the major Oxford dictionaries, and the *OED* style manual. A new text editor, linked to TESS, and named TED, was built. For the user it resembled

<hg>
<hw>man-&sm.handle</hw>, <ps>v.</ps>
</hg>
<etym>f.
<xr><x>man</x> <ps>n.<hm>1</hm></ps></xr>
+
<xr><x>handle</x> <ps>v.</ps></xr>
; in sense
<xr><xs>3</xs></xr>
cf. dial. <cf>manangle</cf> (Devon) to mangle, which may belong to
<xr><x>mangle</x> <ps>v.</ps></xr>
(AF. <cf>mahangler</cf>).
</etym>
<s4 num="1" st="obs"><gr>trans.</gr>&es.To handle or wield a
tool.&es.<la>Obs.</la></s4>
<qp>
<q><d>1457</d> <a>R. Fannande</a> <wk>Mon. Christ's Hosp. Abingdon</w>
xiii,
<qt>The Mattok was man-handeled right wele a whyle.</qt></q>
</qp>
<s4 num="2"><la>Naut.</la>, etc.&es.&oq.To move by force of men, without
levers or tackles&cq. (Adm. Smyth).</s4>
<qp>
<q><d>1867</d> <a>Smyth</a> <w>Sailor's Word-bk.</w></q>
<q><d>1894</d> <w>Times</w> 27 Jan. 10/2
<qt>The larger weapons will be worked by electricity, but are also capable of being
man-handled.</qt></q>
<q><d>1902</d> <w>Blackw. Mag.</w> Mar. 331/2
<qt>I'm going to man-handle my gun down the slope.</qt></q>
<q><d>1903</d> <w>Daily Chron.</w> 19 Feb. 3/3
<qt>Stalwart Punjabis&dd.hand out bags of stores,&dd.or manhandle a fractious, restive animal.</qt></q>
</qp>
<s4 num="3"><la>slang.</la>&es.To handle roughly; to pull or hustle about.</s4>
<qp>
<q><d>1865</d> <w>Hotten's Slang Dict.</w>,
<qt><i>Man-handle</i>, to use a person roughly, as to take him prisoner, turn him out of a room, give him
a beating.</qt></q>
<q><d>1886</d> <w>Century Mag.</w> Apr. 905/1
<qt>Two of our roughs began to haze him: but they mistook their calling, and in two minutes were so mauled
and manhandled that it was reported aft.</qt></q>
<q><d>1888</d> <a>Clark Russell</a> <w>Death Ship</w> II. 253,
<qt>I&dd.was for&dd.manhandling him, ghost or no ghost.</qt></q>
<q><d>1891</d> <a>Kipling</a> <w>Light that failed</w> iii,
<qt>I'll catch you and man&dubh.handle you, and you'll die.</qt></q>
<q><d>1894</d> <a>R. H. Davis</a> <w>Eng. Cousins</w> 24
<qt>The cry of 'Welsher',&dd.which sometimes on an English race-course means
death from man-handling.</qt></q>
</qp>
</e>

Fig. 16.4. *OED2* (1993–), with *OED3* (pre-Pasadena) tagging
There is no change in content, since the Supplement added nothing new.

<hg>
<hw>manhandle</hw>
<pr>
<la>Brit.</la> <ph>"manhandl</ph>, <ph>%man"handl</ph>,
<la>U.S.</la> <ph>"m{n%h{nd@l</ph>
</pr>, <ps>v.</ps>
</hg>
<lhg type="fmly"><lhw>man-handle</lhw><ps>v.</ps></lhg>
<vfl>Forms: see <xr><x>man</x> <ps>n.<hm>1</hm></ps></xr><ann>xch abc 200002</ann> and <xr><x>handle</x> <ps>v.<hm>1</hm></ps></xr>
</vfl>
<etym>Perh. orig. a variant of <xr><x>mangle</x>
<ps>v.<hm>1</hm></ps></xr><ann>xch abc 200002</ann> (cf. modern regional
<cf>manghangle</cf>, <cf>manangle</cf>
to mangle or confuse (<w>Eng. Dial. Dict.</w>)), but in all quots. as if &from;
<xr><x>man</x><ps>n.<hm>1</hm></ps></xr><ann>xch abc 200002</ann>+
<xr><x>handle</x> <ps>v.<hm>1</hm></ps></xr>, and in senses
<xr><xs>2</xs><oxr><xs>1</xs></oxr></xr><ann>xch dff 9906</ann> and
<xr><xs>3</xs><oxr><xs>2</xs></oxr></xr><ann>xch dff 9906</ann> evidently taken to be so.&es;In modern use in sense
<xr><xs>1</xs><oxr><xs>3</xs></oxr></xr><ann>xch dff 9909</ann> perh. a development from sense <xr><xs>3</xs><oxr><xs>2</xs></oxr></xr><ann>xch dff 9906</ann>.
<n><w>N.E.D.</w> (1905) gives only the pronunciation with primary stress on the second syllable.</n>
</etym>
<s4 num="1" onum="3"><gr>trans.</gr>&es;Now somewhat
<la>colloq.</la>&es;
<s6 num="a" st="obs">To attack (an enemy).&es;<la>Obs.</la></s6>
<s6 num="b">More generally: to handle roughly; to assault, maul, or beat up (a person; occas. <la>spec.</la> a woman).</s6>
</s4>
<qp>
<q d="med" fd="yes"><d>(&a;1470)</d> <a>Malory</a> <w>Morte Darthur</w><bib>y</bib> (Winch. Coll.) 428
<qt>Hit were shame&dd.that he sholde go thus away onles that he were manne-handled.</qt></q>
</qp>
<qp>
<q d="sl"><d>1851</d> <a>H. Melville</a> <w>Moby-Dick</w> liv. 280
<qt>The valiant captain danced up and down&dd.calling upon his officers to manhandle that atrocious scoundrel.</qt><ch>99</ch></q>
<q><d>1864</d> <a>J. C. Hotten</a> <w>Slang Dict.</w> (new ed.),
<qt><i>Man-handle</i>, to use a person roughly, as to take him prisoner, turn him out of a room, give him a beating.</qt></q>
<q><d>1886</d> <w>Cent. Mag.</w><bib>y</bib> Apr. 905/1
<qt>Two of our roughs began to haze him: but they mistook their calling, and in two minutes were so mauled and manhandled that it was reported aft.</qt></q>
<q><d>1888</d> <a>W. C. Russell</a> <w>Death Ship</w> II. 253,
<qt>I&dd.was for&dd.manhandling him, ghost or no ghost.</qt></q>
<q><d>1891</d> <a>R. Kipling</a> <w>Light that Failed</w> iii. 51
<qt>I'll catch you and manhandle you, and you'll die.</qt><ch>99</ch></q>
<q d="oed"><d>1902</d> <a>G. Ade</a> <w>Girl Proposition</w> 58
<qt>To worship one who could be pawed over and man-handled by anything that wore a Derby hat.</qt></q>
<q d="sl"><d>1955</d> <w>Times</w> 17 Aug. 8/6

<qt>They smashed doors, threw stones through windows, and manhandled a member of the staff.</qt></q>
<q d="sl"><d>1988</d> <a>M. Chabon</a> <w>Mysteries of Pittsburgh</w> viii. 69,
<qt>I had&dd.been torn from the register stand, manhandled, and driven away.</qt></q>
<q d="inc"><d>1992</d> <w>N.Y. Times</w> 14 June <pt>i.</pt> 1/2
<qt>Elite young officers were mauling and manhandling female colleagues and civilian women.</qt></q>
</qp>
<s4 num="2" onum="1" st="obs"><gr>trans.</gr>&es;To handle or wield (a tool).&es;<la>Obs.</la></s4>
<qp>
<q><d>&q;&a;1500</d> in <ba>J. H. Parker</ba> <w>Some Acct. Domest. Archit. Eng.</w><bib>y</bib> (1859) I. ii. 42
<qt>The Mattok was man handeled right wele a whyle.</qt><ch>y:med, man-handeled; ghj 9905</ch></q>
</qp>
<s4 num="3" onum="2"><gr>trans.</gr>&es;To move (a large object) by hand, or by manpower, without the help of machinery or mechanical power (orig. <la>Naut.</la>); to move, manoeuvre, or transport with great effort.&es;Freq. with <ps>adv.</ps></s4>
<qp>
<q d="sl"><d>1851</d>
<a>H. Melville</a> <w>Moby-Dick</w> xcviii. 475
<qt>The enormous casks are slewed round and headed over&dd.at last man-handled and stayed in their course.</qt><ch>99</ch></q>
<q><d>1867</d> <a>W. H. Smyth</a> <w>Sailor's Word-bk.</w><bib>y</bib> 466
<qt><i>Man-handle, to</i>, to move by force of men, without levers or tackles.</qt><ch>y:</ch></q>
<q><d>1894</d> <w>Times</w> 27 Jan. 10/2
<qt>The larger weapons will be worked by electricity, but are also capable of being man-handled.</qt></q>
<q><d>1902</d> <w>Blackwood's Mag.</w> Mar. 331/2
<qt>I'm going to man-handle my gun down the slope.</qt></q>
<q><d>1903</d> <w>Daily Chron.</w> 19 Feb. 3/3
<qt>Stalwart Punjabis&dd.hand out bags of stores,&dd.or manhandle a fractious, restive animal.</qt></q>
<q d="sl"><d>1908</d> <w>Westm. Gaz.</w> 2 Oct. 9/4
<qt>The 12-pounder guns which are used in the competition are man-handled with an ease and rapidity which is truly marvellous.</qt></q>
<q d="oed"><d>1953</d> <w>Word for Word</w> (Whitbread & Co.) 35/2
<qt>Before the improvement of roads under Telford and MacAdam, he had to 'trounce', i.e., push and manhandle the dray over the innumerable potholes and hazards.</qt></q>
<q d="sl"><d>1988</d> <w>N.Y. Times</w> 13 Apr. <pt>a</pt>26/5
<qt>In the end, my wife and I&em;both 70 years old&em;had to manhandle it there ourselves. There was no elevator.</qt></q>
</qp>
</e>

Fig. 16.5. *OED3* (2000), with *OED3* (pre-Pasadena) tagging
The entry has been revised with new and changed content.

OEDIPUS but, with the advance in computing power, he or she was now of course able to call up and edit any entry in the dictionary. Not all the facilities which the editorial team wanted could in the end be provided; but because the system was Unix-based (operating on powerful SUN workstations) users were able to compile their own macros and scripts which could be run on copies of entries transferred into the powerful software within the Unix system. Editorial consistency was facilitated by a large number of text validation routines written by the lexicographical group, which were also run on the native Unix software rather than inside the *OED*-designed software. Thus much could be carried out automatically, but the processes were not all part of an integrated system.

16.3.3 (ii) Devising editorial plans for revision

In 1994, plans for the revision of the *OED* began to be formulated. No large-scale modification of the text of the dictionary had been made since its completion in 1928, and no one since then had tried to compile entries for polysemous words whose history stretched back to medieval times, drawing the documentation from the full range of available sources; indeed there was no one alive who had done it. Plans therefore had to be evolved gradually, experimentally, and cautiously. Alongside the development of editorial *policy*, which has been modified continuously ever since, in finer and finer detail, editorial *procedures* (and concomitantly, project organization) had to be developed—many of them dependent upon the computer resources available.

In the earliest stages, it was thought possible that revision might be determined purely by existing resources, such as the recently published *New Shorter OED* (together with its valuable file of earlier and later examples of word senses, new etymological information, and revised grammatical model), other scholarly dictionaries (such as the *Middle English Dictionary* and the *Dictionary of the Older Scottish Tongue*), and the huge quotation files that had been amassed since 1957. Experimentation soon showed that this would not go far enough and that a thoroughgoing review of every aspect of every entry would be required to give a balanced picture of the history of the English language. Moreover, a new and extensive reading programme covering Early Modern English (1500–1700) would be needed to complement the wealth of new medieval and Scots documentation coming from the scholarly dictionaries just mentioned. Furthermore, in 1997, the OED Project acquired from the University of Michigan the entire collection of slips that had been gathered (including those donated from *OED1* materials) for the *Early Modern English Dictionary* planned by Charles C. Fries in the 1930s but never compiled, and began to draw upon them systematically. This enhancement of policy meant that *OED3* would move to the forefront of research in lexical history rather than merely mirroring the patchwork of research done by others.

An important role was played by a new Advisory Committee set up by the Delegates of OUP in 1993. A series of meetings were held (1993–95) between them and the senior staff of the *OED*. The then Co-editors presented a number of policies in papers to the Committee, which were generally endorsed; the Committee also made recommendations regarding questions put to them by the Co-editors. These proceedings covered the following areas. On historical coverage, it was agreed to retain the *OED*'s starting date of 1150 (rather than change it to 1485 or 1500), not to attempt an exhaustive account of Old and Middle English but rather to direct the main burden of revision to the Early Modern and subsequent periods; accordingly, the Early Modern English reading programme was endorsed. As regards bibliography, it was decided to give priority to the date of book publication when dating plays and poetry, and to use manuscript dating for works that appeared before printing. British and American pronunciations were to be included for all non-obsolete entries. A system of grammatical terminology was agreed, and details such as the marking of transitivity and the passive voice were decided. In the etymologies, the regular use of reconstructed proto-forms and references to standard etymological authorities were to be abandoned. Numerous other topics were touched on, such as inclusion policy, the upgrading of important nested compounds (e.g. *Alzheimer's disease*) to entry status, and the organization of function word entries and phrasal verbs.

The editors took the view that the *OED*, in the early part of the alphabet, reflects the problems which their predecessors had faced in beginning to compile the First Edition, and in particular the unsettled state of their policy—leading to inconsistency of treatment—and their shortage of evidence—leading to gaps in the documentation and to unhistorical entry structure. Since the present team of editors themselves would also at the beginning be grappling with policy decisions, it was decided to begin revision at M, a point in the *OED2* text where it was a reasonable assumption that the lexicography of both *OED1* and the *Supplement* had become mature and consistent and the supply of evidence had become more plentiful.

The revision programme came to cover all the following areas: selection of the current headword form; presentation of British and US pronunciation (and other regional pronunciation when the word is chiefly used in that region); citation of all historical spellings in full form (not truncated as in *OED1*) with centuries or century ranges; ascertainment of all pertinent etymological facts, covering not only etymons and cognates in other languages but also relevant related forms when cultural diffusion is significant; treatment for words originating from non-European languages as full, in principle, as had been customary for those from major European languages; explanation of morphological development and pronunciation history within English; consistent grammatical and syntactic description; chronologically based sense structure; full research and presentation of the documentation of every sense of a word; comprehensive review of definitions, with attention to currency of language and expert advice on technicalities; consistent and up-to-date usage, currency, and subject labelling; standardization of all elements of citation style; checking of quotation text in all cases of doubt; and clear presentation of phrases, compounds, derivatives, phrasal verbs, and affixes with their own supporting quotation evidence. (A fuller description is given in the online Introduction to the Third Edition.)

Supporting this programme the *OED* department identified within its staff, or appointed, specialists to deal with (among other areas): new words and senses; scientific words; North American words; general European etymologies; Latin and Greek etymologies; words of non-European origin; historical syntax; variant forms; Old English documentation; Middle English and Older Scots bibliography; general bibliography; library research; database evidence searching; online database subscriptions; reading programme management; and workflow monitoring. The interplay between these areas has varied constantly and will continue to do so as different challenges and resources come and go.

16.3.4 *Publishing the revised text* (OED3)

How *OED3* would be published was a question frequently asked throughout the 1990s. The standard answer was that at the end of the revision process it would be made available both in printed and electronic form, but it was recognized that electronic publication was increasingly favoured as a means of using large reference resources. Around 1994, the World Wide Web came into being, bringing the new resource of online texts immediately available to everyone's computer. The *OED* on CD-ROM had established the indispensability of the electronic *OED*. In September 1994, the then director of NARP (see 16.3.1, above), Dr Jeffery Triggs, proposed a Web-based 'Oxford Online Electronic Text Center' (offered on a subscription basis) containing the *OED* as the 'flagship resource', along with smaller Oxford dictionaries, encyclopedic resources such as the *Dictionary of National Biography*, and the *OED Historical Corpus*, with hypertext links between some or all of these texts and an interactive form allowing scholars to make suggestions to *OED* and submit documentation online.

Building on his experimental prototype of such a website, OUP set up a project to pursue the publication of *OED* online. It was decided both to make the complete second edition available, and to begin the serial publication of the revised edition (mirroring the serial paper publication of the first edition). From March 2000, a section of *OED3* was published on the Web every quarter. The *OED* department was reorganized so as to facilitate online publication. The entries prepared from M to R were reviewed, with two new emphases: (i) text was to go through all stages as far as 'passing for press' so that regular portions could be published, and (ii) many newly available online resources were to be used as fully as possible to help update the text. Resources already in use, such as the *Middle English Dictionary* on paper, were now to be searched online, and other online textual databases were to be routinely drawn on. Over the succeeding period more of these were used as the Web expanded.

A number of adjustments to the publishing pattern have occurred since 2000, each essential to the concept: the amount revised each quarter has increased; every quarterly issue now incorporates updates to the whole published *OED3* text, in addition to the new alphabetical range; entries for new words and senses are published throughout the alphabet, not just in the revised range (see 16.3.5, below); and, instead of being presented as separate texts, *OED3* and *OED2* are dovetailed into a single resource.

16.3.5 *Publishing new words and meanings*

As has been described in previous chapters, the Editors of the first edition coped with new words and meanings arising or coming to their notice after a given part of the alphabet had been passed by collecting the data during the main project and publishing it all in a one-volume *Supplement* five years after its completion (1933). OUP then suspended all further data collection until 1957 when a revision and expansion of the 1933 *Supplement* came to form the four-volume series of 1972–86. At the end of this, learning from past experience, an editorial group immediately began compiling new entries for words and senses throughout the alphabet (known as the New English Words Series or NEWS). Under the editorship of John Simpson, 5,000 of these were incorporated into the Second Edition (since their position was not specially marked in the text a full list can now only be reconstructed by comparison of the second edition with its parent volumes). The work, of course, was ongoing, and after the publication of *OED2* three new volumes of 'Additions' were published, two in 1993 and one in 1997.

When *OED* went online the contents of the *Additions* volumes were included with *OED2*. From then on other new items falling within each quarterly revision range were routinely edited and published with their range. Finally (as mentioned above, 16.3.4) in 2001 it was decided to publish online new words and meanings from any part of the alphabet, so as not to delay the appearance of important vocabulary items in the *OED* until alphabetical revision reached them. As a result, the goal of keeping coverage of the whole vocabulary up to date had finally come in sight.

16.4 STAGE 3—*OED3 AND THE PASADENA SYSTEM, AFTER 2005*

16.4.1 *Towards a fully integrated editorial, publishing, and workflow system*

In the 1990s, the TESS/TED system was a pioneer. But by 2000, the complexity of the project and the need to maximize efficiency, together with the sheer age of the system in software terms, required the building of a new and more comprehensive system. The lexicographical team had for a long time had very clear ideas about the facilities they needed to cut down drudgery and improve efficiency. Some of these were imagined (in a slightly fanciful form) in Weiner (1994a).

A French software company, IDM, with a record of building web-based dictionary editing systems, was chosen to develop the new system, which was named Pasadena and commissioned in 2005. As regards hardware and software, it is notable for employing desktop PCs running Microsoft Windows and servers using Linux. With the growth in storage space and memory, it is quite possible now to hold many copies of the *OED* on one computer, but it can still be a problem that the *OED* contains millions of items needing to be checked, and the proprietary Oracle database software can be strained by the fact that some entries are as long as an entire minidictionary. With the proliferation of apparently instantaneous look-up through search engines on the World Wide Web, users' expectations are much higher, and this gave system designers the problem of balancing complexity (enabling much drudgery to be carried out by the computer) with speed of delivery (enabling lexicographers to move rapidly through their work).

As regards user requirements, the ideal followed this time round was as far as possible to integrate all editorial functions. In addition to the database, Search Interface, and Entry Editor, the system contains a Dictionary Browser, allowing display of entries both in-house and to authorized remote users; an External Research Manager, which channels library research and consultancy requests out of an entry and back in when completed; and a Schedule Manager, by which work is allocated to editors and progress is automatically monitored. Very importantly, the citations of the quotations, both in the dictionary and in the database of additional examples (the 'Incomings') are held in a Bibliographical System which allows bibliographers to control and regularize citation style so that inconsistencies are ironed out. There is full compatibility between all the texts held on the system, so that quotations can be loaded into dictionary entries without recopying. Within entries, the editing software facilitates the moving of textual components by reordering and/or renumbering elements that occur as items in lists, such as senses and subordinate lemmas. Cross-references are now actual links which remain in place whenever changes are made to the target, so that their surface manifestation is automatically reset.

With the introduction of XML mark-up in place of the SGML-like tagging used previously, a proper document-type definition was adopted, so that a consistent text structure became mandatory. After many years of re-editing *OED* entries, a much more consistent picture of entry structure had emerged, and it was no longer necessary to allow for 'loose' structures, except as an interim measure while the whole dictionary was loaded into Pasadena. In order to structure the dictionary more consistently and make it susceptible of a greater number of automatic operations, the tag set employed in Pasadena has about 144 members (compared with about forty-six used for *OED2*).

Concomitant with the new system, it was decided to remodel the structure of the *OED* entry for almost the first time. The main effect has been to remove items that are not part of a chronological sequence from the main sense-numbering schema, and to place nested lexical items in distinct sections. An entry now potentially has the following components: headword section, pronunciation section, inflections section, variants section, etymology section, sense section, lemma section (which may be of a number of types: affix, phrase, phrasal verb, compound, adjectival special use, or derivative section). All these elements existed in the text before, but they were not embodied in such an equal, regular, and consistent way. The essential ideas had been advocated by the lexicographical team as early as October 1993, but it had not been possible to implement them during Stage 2. (For a sample of *OED3* text in Pasadena tagging, see Fig. 16.6.)

16.5 SUMMARY

The *OED* has been re-imagined: it is a register of information about the English language that can respond to new data and discoveries, thereby remaining

<Entry ch_pre 1700="1" cn="00301117" linkID="00139889" pbldate="20000914" wotd="1">
<hwSect>
<hw>manhandle</hw>
</hwSect>
<prSect>
<pr>
<prBrit> <ph>"manhandl</ph><ph>%man"handl</ph></prBrit>
<prUS> <ph>"m{n%h{nd@l</ph></prUS>
</pr>
</prSect>
<vfSect ch_variants="1">
<header>see
<xr refentry="113198" refid="38341619" rel="S" style="S"> <xmain>
<xhw>man</xhw><ps hm="1" type="n."></ps></xmain></xr>
and
<xr refentry="83880" refid="2002548" rel="S" style="S"> <xmain>
<xhw>handle</xhw><ps hm="1" type="v."></ps></xmain></xr>
</header>
</vfSect>
<etymSect>
<etym>Perh. orig. a variant of <etymon> <xr refentry="113421" refid="38409160"
rel="S" style="S"> <xmain> <xhw>mangle</xhw><ps hm="1"
type="v."></ps></xmain></xr></etymon>
(cf. modern regional <cf>manghangle</cf>, <cf>mangle</cf> to mangle or
confuse (<w>Eng. Dial. Dict.</w>)), but in all quots. as if <from></from>
<xr refentry="113198" refid="38341619" rel="S" style="S">
<xmain><xhw>man</xhw><ps hm="1" type="n."></ps></xmain></xr> +
<xr refentry="83880" refid="2002548" rel="S" style="S">
<xmain><xhw>handle</xhw><ps hm="1" type="v."></ps></xmain></xr>
and in senses
<xr refentry="113449" refid="38415498" rel="S" style="S"> <xmain>
<xs>2</xs></xmain></xr>
and
<xr refentry="113449" refid="38415514" rel="S" style="S"> <xmain>
<xs>3</xs></xmain></xr>
evidently taken to be so. In modern use in sense
<xr refentry="113449" refid="38415402" rel="S" style="S"> <xmain>
<xs>1</xs></xmain></xr>
perh. a development from sense
<xr refentry="113449" refid="38415514" rel="S" style="S"> <xmain>
<xs>3</xs></xmain></xr>
.
<etymNote>
<w>N.E.D.</w> <dat>1905</dat>) gives only the pronunciation with primary stress
on the second syllable.</etymNote>
</etym>
</etymSect>
<senseSect>
<s1> <ps type="v."></ps>
<s4 num="1" onum="3"> <def> <gr>trans.</gr> Now somewhat <la>colloq.</la>
<subDef num="1" onum="a" st="obs">To attack (an enemy).
<la>Obs.</la></subDef>
<subDef num="2" onum="b">More generally: to handle roughly; to assault, maul,
or beat up (a person; occas. <la>spec.</la>a woman).</subDef></def>
<qp>
<q d="med" qid="2893944"> <cit citid="2532"> <d dorder="147006"
type="a">1470</d><bibMain> <a>Malory</a><w>Morte

Darthur</w><ms>Winch. Coll.</ms><loc
lid="136396">428</loc></bibMain></cit>
<qt>Hit were shame.. that he sholde go thus away onles that he were manne-
handled.</qt></q>
</qp>
<qp>
<q d="sl" qid="2893945" status="u"> <cit citid="1"> <d
dorder="185118">1851</d><bibMain> <a>H. Melville</a><w>Moby-
Dick</w><loc lid="27100">liv. 280</loc></bibMain></cit>
<qt>The valiant captain danced up and down.. calling upon his officers to manhandle that atrocious scoundrel.</qt></q>
<q qid="2893946"> <cit citid="903310"> <d
dorder="186418">1864</d><bibMain> <a>J. C. Hotten</a><w>Slang
Dict.</w><edn>new ed.</edn></bibMain></cit>
<qt>
<i>Man-handle</i>, to use a person roughly, as to take him prisoner, turn him out of a
room, give him a beating.</qt></q>
<q qid="2893947" status="u"> <cit citid="319678"> <d
dorder="188618">1886</d><bibMain> <w>Cent. Mag.</w><di>Apr.</di><loc
lid="216696">905/1</loc></bibMain></cit>
<qt>Two of our roughs began to haze him: but they mistook their calling, and in two
minutes were so mauled and manhandled that it was reported aft.</qt></q>
<q qid="2893948" status="u"> <cit citid="124453"> <d dorder="188818">1888</d>
<bibMain> <a>W. C. Russell</a><w>Death Ship</w><vmr>II.</vmr><loc
lid="173028">253,</loc></bibMain></cit>
<qt>I.. was for.. manhandling him, ghost or no ghost.</qt></q>
<q qid="2893949"> <cit citid="7404"> <d dorder="189118">1891</d><bibMain>
<a>R. Kipling</a><w>Light that Failed</w><loc lid="53739">iii.
51</loc></bibMain></cit>
<qt>I'll catch you and manhandle you, and you'll die.</qt></q>
<q d="oed" qid="2893950" status="u"> <cit citid="174760"> <d
dorder="190218">1902</d><bibMain> <a>G. Ade</a><w>Girl
Proposition</w><loc lid="139297">58</loc></bibMain></cit>
<qt>To worship one who could be pawed over and man-handled by anything that
wore a Derby hat.</qt></q>
<q d="sl" qid="2893951" status="u"> <cit citid="32090"> <d
dorder="195518">1955</d><bibMain> <w>Times</w><di>17 Aug.</di><loc
lid="200581">8/6</loc></bibMain></cit>
<qt>They smashed doors, threw stones through windows, and manhandled a member
of the staff.</qt></q>
<q d="sl" qid="2893952" status="u"> <cit citid="62864"> <d
dorder="198818">1988</d><bibMain> <a>M. Chabon</a><w>Mysteries of
Pittsburgh</w><loc lid="245293">viii. 69,</loc></bibMain></cit>
<qt>I had.. been torn from the register stand, manhandled, and driven
away.</qt></q>
<q d="inc" qid="2893953" status="u"> <cit citid="35540"> <d
dorder="199218">1992</d><bibMain> <w>N.Y. Times</w><di>14 June</di><loc
lid="261078"> <pt>i</pt>. 1/2</loc></bibMain></cit>
<qt>Elite young officers were mauling and manhandling female colleagues and
civilian women.</qt></q>
</qp>
</s4>
<s4 num="2" onum="1" st="obs"> <def> <gr>trans.</gr> To handle or wield (a
tool). <la>Obs.</la></def>
<qp>
<q qid="2893954" status="checked"> <cit citid="737071"> <d dorder="150012"
type="qa">1500</d><bibSub></bibSub><bibMain> <a>J. H.
Parker</a><w>Some Acct. Domest. Archit.

(*Continued*)

Eng.</w><dp>1859</dp><vmr>I.</vmr><loc lid="734044">ii.
42</loc></bibMain></cit>
<qt>The Mattok was man handeled right wele a whyle.</qt></q>
</qp>
</s4>
<s4 num="3" onum="2"> <def> <gr>trans.</gr> To move (a large object) by hand,
or by manpower, without the help of machinery or mechanical power (orig.
<la>Naut.</la>); to move, manoeuvre, or transport with great effort. Freq. with <ps
type="adv."></ps></def>
<qp>
<q d="sl" qid="2893955" status="u"> <cit citid="1"> <d
dorder="185118">1851</d><bibMain> <a>H. Melville</a><w>Moby-
Dick</w><loc lid="27100">xcviii. 475</loc></bibMain></cit>
<qt>The enormous casks are slewed round and headed over.. at last man-handled and
stayed in their course.</qt></q>
<q qid="2893956"> <cit citid="914069"> <d
dorder="186718">1867</d><bibMain> <a>W. H. Smyth</a><w>Sailor's Word-bk.</w><loc
lid="876457">466</loc></bibMain></cit>
<qt> <i>Man-handle, to</i>, to move by force of men, without levers or
tackles.</qt></q>
<q qid="2893957" status="u"> <cit citid="554553"> <d
dorder="189418">1894</d><bibMain> <w>Times</w><di>27 Jan.</di><loc
lid="510785">10/2</loc></bibMain></cit>
<qt>The larger weapons will be worked by electricity, but are also capable of being
man-handled.</qt></q>
<q qid="2893958" status="u"> <cit citid="657244"> <d dorder="190218">1902</d>
<bibMain> <w>Blackwood's Mag.</w><di>Mar.</di><loc
lid="468742">331/2</loc></bibMain></cit>
<qt>I'm going to man-handle my gun down the slope.</qt></q>
<q qid="2893959" status="u"> <cit citid="688752"> <d
dorder="190318">1903</d><bibMain> <w>Daily Chron.</w><di>19
Feb.</di><loc lid="111286">3/3</loc></bibMain></cit>
<qt>Stalwart Punjabis.. hand out bags of stores,.. or manhandle a fractious, restive
animal.</qt></q><q d="sl" qid="2893960" status="u"> <cit citid="691208"> <d
dorder="190818">1908</d><bibMain> <w>Westm. Gaz.</w><di>2 Oct.</di><loc
lid="187757">9/4</loc></bibMain></cit>
<qt>The 12-pounder guns which are used in the competition are man-handled with an
ease and rapidity which is truly marvellous.</qt>
</q>
<q d="oed" qid="2893961" status="u"> <cit citid="43828"> <d
dorder="195318">1953</d><bibMain> <w>Word for Word</w><ob>Whitbread &
Co.</ob><loc lid="24597">35/2</loc></bibMain></cit>
<qt>Before the improvement of roads under Telford and MacAdam, he had to
'trounce', i.e., push and manhandle the dray over the innumerable potholes and
hazards.</qt></q>
<q d="sl" qid="2893962" status="u"> <cit citid="737072"> <d
dorder="198818">1988</d><bibMain> <w>N.Y. Times</w><di>13 Apr.</di><loc
lid="734045"> <pt>a</pt>26/5</loc></bibMain></cit>
<qt>In the end, my wife and I—both 70 years old—had to manhandle it there
ourselves. There was no elevator.</qt></q>
</qp>
</s4>
</s1>
</senseSect>
</Entry>

FIG. 16.6. *OED3* (2006), with Pasadena tagging

manhandle, *v. Brit.* /ˈmanhandl/, /ˌmanˈhandl/, *U.S.* /ˈmænˈhændəl/

Forms: see MAN *n.*[1] and HANDLE *v.*[1]

[Perh. orig. a variant of MANGLE *v.*[1] (cf. modern regional *manghangle, manangle* to mangle or confuse (*Eng. Dial. Dict.*)), but in all quots. as if < MAN *n.*[1] + HANDLE *v.*[1], and in senses 2 and 3 evidently taken to be so. In modern use in sense 1 perh. a development from sense 3.

N.E.D. (1905) gives only the pronunciation with primary stress on the second syllable.]

1. *trans.* Now somewhat *colloq.* †(*a*) To attack (an enemy). *Obs.* (*b*) More generally: to handle roughly; to assault, maul, or beat up (a person; occas. *spec.* a woman).

*a***1470** MALORY *Morte Darthur* (Winch. Coll.) 428 Hit were shame..that he sholde go thus away onles that he were manne-handled.
1851 H. MELVILLE *Moby-Dick* liv. 280 The valiant captain danced up and down..calling upon his officers to manhandle that atrocious scoundrel. **1864** J. C. HOTTEN *Slang Dict.* (new ed.), *Man-handle*, to use a person roughly, as to take him prisoner, turn him out of a room, give him a beating. **1886** *Cent. Mag.* Apr. 905/1 Two of our roughs began to haze him: but they mistook their calling, and in two minutes were so mauled and manhandled that it was reported aft. **1888** W. C. RUSSELL *Death Ship* II. 253, I..was for..manhandling him, ghost or no ghost. **1891** R. KIPLING *Light that Failed* iii. 51 I'll catch you and manhandle you, and you'll die. **1902** G. ADE *Girl Proposition* 58 To worship one who could be pawed over and man-handled by anything that wore a Derby hat. **1955** *Times* 17 Aug. 8/6 They smashed doors, threw stones through windows, and manhandled a member of the staff. **1988** M. CHABON *Mysteries of Pittsburgh* viii. 69, I had..been torn from the register stand, manhandled, and driven away. **1992** *N.Y. Times* 14 June I. 1/2 Elite young officers were mauling and manhandling female colleagues and civilian women.

†**2.** *trans.* To handle or wield (a tool). *Obs.*

? *a* **1500** in J. H. Parker *Some Acct. Domest. Archit. Eng.* (1859) I. ii. 42 The Mattok was man handeled right wele a whyle.

3. *trans.* To move (a large object) by hand, or by manpower, without the help of machinery or mechanical power (orig. *Naut.*); to move, manoeuvre, or transport with great effort. Freq. with *adv.*

1851 H. MELVILLE *Moby-Dick* xcviii. 475 The enormous casks are slewed round and headed over..at last man-handled and stayed in their course. **1867** W. H. SMYTH *Sailor's Word-bk.* 466 *Man-handle, to*, to move by force of men, without levers or tackles. **1894** *Times* 27 Jan. 10/2 The larger weapons will be worked by electricity, but are also capable of being man-handled. **1902** *Blackwood's Mag.* Mar. 331/2 I'm going to man-handle my gun down the slope. **1903** *Daily Chron.* 19 Feb. 3/3 Stalwart Punjabis..hand out bags of stores,..or manhandle a fractious, restive animal. **1908** *Westm. Gaz.* 2 Oct. 9/4 The 12-pounder guns which are used in the competition are man-handled with an ease and rapidity which is truly marvellous. **1953** *Word for Word* (Whitbread & Co.) 35/2 Before the improvement of roads under Telford and MacAdam, he had to 'trounce', i.e., push and manhandle the dray over the innumerable potholes and hazards. **1988** *N.Y. Times* 13 Apr. A 26/5 In the end, my wife and I–both 70 years old–had to manhandle it there ourselves. There was no elevator.

FIG. 16.7. *OED3* (2006), formatted

continuously up to date, and with the development of technology it can offer its users more and increasingly varied ways of accessing, collecting, and collating this information. Equipped with a more powerful editorial system, and with the experience of six years of online publishing to draw on, the project team is now (2006) considering two main areas for future development. As regards the inner working of the project, policy and procedures are being carefully reviewed in order to increase efficiency and enable publication to proceed as rapidly as is consistent with the maintenance of the scholarly standards of the dictionary. As regards the text published online, a number of possibilities are being explored: releasing the working version of the whole dictionary, in which there are thousands of corrected quotations not currently available; publishing revised entries from parts of the alphabet outside the main block of text that is being expanded entry by entry; linking the *OED* to other online dictionaries; the incorporation of a thesaurus element to enable searching by semantic fields and synonyms; the improvement of functionality and navigation; and the reorganization and expansion of the access pages so as to make it easier for unfamiliar users to learn to use and explore the OED.

UNPUBLISHED SOURCES

OED archives at Oxford University Press

Note: numerous other materials relating to sections 16.1, 16.2, and 16.3 of this chapter are stored in the *OED* archives but few have yet been assigned archival references. Those listed below are numbered in order of their internal dates.

1. *A Future for the Oxford English Dictionary* (request for tender, June 1983)
2. *The New Oxford English Dictionary* (project description for launch, May 1984)
3. *New Oxford English Dictionary Workbook* (a collection of working papers, 1984)
4. OUP. New Oxford English Dictionary Project Phase 1. *Outline statement of user requirements for a computer system.* October 1984.
5. OUP. New Oxford English Dictionary Project Phase 1. *Evaluation criteria for the computer system design.* October 1984.
6. OUP. New Oxford English Dictionary Project Phase 1. *Outline design for a computer system.* July 1985.

7. New Oxford English Dictionary Project. *Computer System Standard. Change Management Procedures.* November 1985.

8. New Oxford English Dictionary Project. *Computer System Standard. Problem Management Procedures.* November 1985.

9. New Oxford English Dictionary. *Composition Requirements.* April 1986.

10. Julia Swannell. *A user's guide to LEXX* (i.e. OEDIPUS). 2 June 1986.

11. *OEDIPUS user trials: report.* 6 March 1987.

12. OUP. New Oxford English Dictionary computer system series. No. 1. *New Oxford English Dictionary Project Phase 1. Development of the New OED computer system.* June 1987.
    Contents:
    A Future for the Oxford English Dictionary (=item 1)
    Outline statement of user requirements for a computer system (=item 4)
    Evaluation criteria for the computer system design (=item 5)
    New OED Phase Reviews Nos.1 (5 August 1985) –5 (22 July 1987)

13. OUP. New Oxford English Dictionary computer system series. No. 2. *System Design* (=item 6)

14. OUP. New Oxford English Dictionary computer system series. No. 4. *New Oxford English Dictionary Project Phase 1. Description of the computer system of the New OED.* July 1987.

15. OUP. New Oxford English Dictionary computer system series. No. 5. *New Oxford English Dictionary Project Phase 1. Description of the processed text of the New OED.* July 1987.

16. OUP. New Oxford English Dictionary computer system series. No. 6. *New Oxford English Dictionary Project Phase 1. Management of the computer system.* June 1987.

ONLINE REFERENCES

Elliott, L. (2000). 'How the Oxford English Dictionary Went Online', *Ariadne* Issue 24 (21 June), http://www.ariadne.ac.uk/issue24/oed-tech/intro.html.

Simpson, J. A. (2000–). *Oxford English Dictionary.* (Third Edition Online: in progress.) http://oed.com. Oxford: Oxford University Press. (Quarterly updates of new and revised material from March 2000.)

References

DICTIONARIES AND RELATED REFERENCE WORKS

In both volumes of the *History*, dictionaries and related reference works are arranged with the author's or editor's name first, e.g., Robinson, M., and the date and title second and third: e.g. (1985). *The Concise Scots Dictionary.* Occasionally, the name of the author will not be given, in which case the title of the book will be given first and the date second: e.g., *Collins Scots* Dictionary (2000).

Académie française. (1694). *Le Dictionnaire de l'Académie françoise, dedié au Roy.* Paris: J. B. Coignard.

Accademia della Crusca. (1612). *Vocabolario degli Accademici della Crusca.* Venice.

—— (1691). *Vocabolario degli Accademici della Crusca.* (Fourth edition, 1729–38.) Firenze: Stamperia dell'Accademia della Crusca.

Accarigi, A. (1543). *Vocabolario, grammatica, et orthographia de la lingua volgare.* Cento: the author.

Adelung, J. C. (1783–96). *Neues grammatisch-kritisches Wörterbuch der englischen Sprache für die Deutschen.* Leipzig: Schwickertsch.

Adler, G. J. (1848, 1857, 1902). A *Dictionary of the German and English Languages.* (Revised by F. P. Foster and E. Althaus.) New York: D. Appleton & Co.

Ainsworth, R. (1736). *Thesaurus Linguae Latinae compendiarius.* (Second edition, 1746.) London: Printed for J. and P. Knapton.

Aleksandrov, A. (1879). *Polnyi anglo-russkii slovar'/Complete English–Russian Dictionary* (Two parts.) Saint Petersburg: Tipografiia Morskogo Ministerstva.

—— (1883, 1885). *Polnyi russko-angliiskii slovar'/Complete Russian–English Dictionary* (Two parts.) Saint Petersburg: Tipografiia Morskogo Ministerstva.

—— (1897). *Polnyi russko-angliiskii slovar'/Complete Russian–English Dictionary* (Second edition.) Saint Petersburg: Voennaiia tipografiia.

Allsopp, J. (2003). *Caribbean Multilingual Dictionary of Flora, Fauna and Foods* (*CMD*). Jamaica: Arawak Publications.

Allsopp, S. R. R. (1996). *Dictionary of Caribbean English Usage* (*DCEU*). Oxford: Oxford University Press.

—— (2004). *Book of Afric Caribbean Proverbs* (*BACP*). Jamaica: Arawak Publications.

Altieri, F. (1726–27). *Dizionario Italiano ed Inglese.* (Second edition 1749; also 1750, 1751.) London: William and John Innys.

Alunno, F. (1543). *Le Ricchezze della lingua volgare.* Venice: Figliuoli di Aldo.

ANDREWS, E. A. (1852). *A Copious and Critical Latin–English Lexicon.* (Founded on the Larger Lexicon of Dr Wilhelm Freund . . .) New York.

ANON. (1618). *Le Grand Dictionaire François–Flamen.* Rotterdam: J. Waesbergue.

ANON. (1716). *Teutsch–Englisches Lexicon.* (Second edition, 1745, third edition, 1765, fourth edition, 1789.) Leipzig: T. Fritsch.

ANTHONY, M. (1977). *Historical Dictionary of Trinidad and Tobago.* Lanham, MD: Scarecrow Press.

APRESIAN, IU. D., and MEDNIKOVA, È. M. (1993). *Novyi bol'shoi anglo-russkii slovar'* (Three volumes.) Moscow: 'Russkii iazyk'.

—— *et al.* (1979). *Anglo-russkii sinonimicheskii slovar'.* Moscow: 'Russkii iazyk'.

ARNOLD, T. (1739). *Neues Deutsch–Englisches Wörterbuch.* Leipzig.

ASOMUGHA, C. N. C. (1981). *Nigerian Slangs: Dictionary of Slangs and Unconventional English in Nigeria.* Onitsha: Abic Publishers.

ATKINS, B. T., DUVAL, A., MILNE, R. C. *et al.* (1978, 1987, 2007). *Robert Collins Dictionnaire français–anglais anglais–français.* London, Glasgow, Toronto, & Paris: Robert Collins.

AUSSIE TALK: The Macquarie Dictionary of Australian Colloquialisms. (1984). McMahons Point: Macquarie Library.

AVIS, W. S. (1967). *A Dictionary of Canadianisms on Historical Principles.* Toronto: W. J. Gage.

BAEDEKER, K. (1889). *Baedeker's Conversation Dictionary. In Four Languages, English, French, German, Italian.* Leipsic: Baedeker.

BAILEY, N. (1721). *An Universal Etymological English Dictionary.* London: E. Bell.

—— (1721). *An Universal Etymological English Dictionary.* (Fourth edition, 1728.) London: E. Bell.

—— (1727). *The Universal Etymological English Dictionary,* Vol. II. London: Printed for T. Cox.

—— (1730). *Dictionarium Britannicum.* London: Printed for T. Cox.

—— (1736a). *Dictionarium Britannicum.* (Second Edition.) London: Printed for T. Cox.

—— (1755). *A New Universal Etymological English Dictionary.* (Revised by Joseph Nicol Scott.) London: T. Osborne, J. Shipton *et al.*

BANKS, IA. (1840). *Russko-angliiskii slovar'.* (Two volumes.) Moscow: Tipografiia Avgust Semen.

BANKS, J./IA. (1838). *A Dictionary of the English and Russian Languages/Angliisko-russkii slovar'.* (Two volumes.) Moscow: Tipografiia Avgust Semen.

BARBER, K. (1998). *The Canadian Oxford Dictionary.* (Second edition 2004.) Don Mills: Oxford University Press.

BARCLAY, J. (1792). *A Complete and Universal English Dictionary on a New Plan.* (First edition, 1774.) London: J. F. and C. Rivington.

BARET, J. (1574). *An Aluearie or Triple Dictionarie, in Englishe, Latin, and French.* London: H. Denham.

—— (1580). *An Aluearie or Quadruple Dictionarie.* London: H. Denham.

Baretti, J. (1760). *A Dictionary of the English and Italian Languages.* (also 1771, 1778, 1787, 1790.) London: C. Hitch.

Baretti, J. (1778). *A Dictionary, Spanish and English, and English and Spanish.* (Second edition.) London: Printed for J. Nourse.

Barnhart, C. L. (1947). *American College Dictionary.* New York: Random House.

—— and Barnhart, R. (1963). *World Book Dictionary.* (Two volumes.) Chicago: World Book.

Bartlett, J. R. (ed.) (1848). *Dictionary of Americanisms: A Glossary of Words and Phrases Usually Regarded as Peculiar to the United States.* New York: Bartlett and Welford. (Reprint, New York: Crescent Books 1989.)

Bauer, W. (1949–52, 1958) *Griechisch–Deutsches Wörterbuch zu den Schriften des Neuen Testaments und der übrigen urchristlichen Literatur.* (Fourth edition; fifth edition De Gruyter.) Berlin: Töpelmann.

Beattie, J. (1779). *A List of Two Hundred Scoticisms.* Aberdeen.

—— (1787). *Scoticisms, arranged in alphabetical order, designed to correct improprieties of speech and writing.* Edinburgh: William Creech.

Becmanus, C. (1619). *Manuductio ad Latinam Linguam.* Hanover: Impensis D. & D. Aubriorum & C. Schleichii.

Beeton, D. R. and Dorner, H. (1975). *A Dictionary of Usage in Southern Africa.* Cape Town: Oxford University Press.

Binnart, M. (1744). *Dictionarium teutonico-latinum novum.* Revised by Johannis de Wilde. Amsterdam.

Bischoff, B. *et al.* (1988). *The Épinal, Erfurt, Werden and Corpus Glossaries.* (EEMF 22.) Copenhagen: Rosenkilde and Bagger.

Bischoff, B. and Lapidge, M. (1994). *Biblical Commentaries from the Canterbury School of Theodore and Hadrian.* (CSASE 10.) Cambridge: Cambridge University Press.

Blount, T. (1656). *Glossographia.* London: T. Newcomb.

Bomhoff, D.(1822). *New Dictionary of the English and Dutch Language. Nieuw Woordenboek der Nederduitsche en Engelsche Taal.* Nijmegen & Arnhem: Thieme

Boom, D. J. (1888). *Dutch, French, English & German Dictionary.* 's-Gravenhage: van Cleef.

Bosman, D. B. *et al.* (eds.) (1931, 1936). *Tweetalige Woordeboek Bilingual Dictionary.* Cape Town: Tafelberg.

Bosworth, J. and Toller, T. N. (eds.) (1882–98). *Anglo-Saxon Dictionary.* Oxford: Oxford University Press.

Boyer, A. (1699). *The Royal Dictionary. In Two Parts. First, French and English. Secondly, English and French.* London: Printed for R. Clavel.

—— (1700). *The Royal Dictionary Abridged. In Two Parts. I. French and English. II. English and French.* London: Printed for R. Clavel.

—— (1764). *Le Dictionnaire royal françois–anglois et anglois–françois.* London: T. Osborne.

Bradley, H. (1900). *Dialogues in French and English by William Caxton.* (EETS ES 79.) London: Kegan Paul, Trench, Trübner.

Branford, J. (1978). *A Dictionary of South African English.* (Third edition 1987.) Cape Town: Oxford University Press.

Branford, W. (1987). *The South African Pocket Oxford Dictionary.* (Second edition 1994.) Cape Town: Oxford University Press.

Breitsprecher, R. et al. (1983). *Collins English–German Dictionary.* London: Collins.

Brown, T. (1845). *A Dictionary of the Scottish Language.* London: Simpkin & Marshall, and J. Gilbert.

Bullokar, J. (1616). *An English Expositor.* London: J. Legatt.

Burchfield, R. W. (1972–86). *A Supplement to the Oxford English Dictionary.* (Four volumes.) Oxford: Clarendon Press.

Burckhardt, G. F. (1839). *Complete English–German and German–English Pocket Dictionary.* (Two volumes.) Berlin: Amelang.

Butuzov, V. (1867). *Slovar' osobennykh slov, fraz i oborotov angliiskogo narodnogo iazyka i upotrebitel'neishikh amerikanizmov, ne vvedennykh v obyknovennye slovari. Nastol'naia kniga dlia izuchaiushchikh angliiskii iazyk, dlia perevodchikov i chitatelei angliiskikh literaturnykh proizvedenii.* Saint Petersburg.

Calepinus, A. (Calepino). (1502). *Dictionarium.* Reggio: D. Berthocus.

—— (1586). *Dictionarium Decem Linguarum.* Lyon.

Cambridge Signorelli. (1985). *Dizionario italiano–inglese inglese–italiano dal Cambridge Italian Dictionary.* Milano: Signorelli.

Cameron, A., Amos, A. C., Healey, A., *et al.* (eds.) (1986–). *Dictionary of Old English.* (Eight parts to date.) Toronto: University of Toronto Press.

Casas, C. de las (1570). *Vocabulario de las dos Lenguas Toscana y Castellana.* Seville: A. Escrivano.

Casselman, B. (2006). *Canadian Words and Sayings.* Toronto: McArthur and Company.

Cassidy, F. and Le Page, R. (1967). *Dictionary of Jamaican English* (*DJE*). (Second edition, 1980.) Cambridge: Cambridge University Press.

Cassidy, F. G., Hall, J. H., *et al.* (eds.) (1985–). *Dictionary of American Regional English* (*DARE*). (Four volumes to date.) Cambridge, MA: Belknap Press.

Cawdrey, R. (1604). *A Table Alphabeticall.* London: I. R. for E. Weaver.

Chambaud, L. (1805). *Nouveau dictionnaire François–Anglois, & Anglois–François.* (Nouvelle édition par. J. Th. H. des Carrières; deux volumes.) London: Cadell and Davies.

Chambers, E. (1728). *Cyclopaedia; Or, An Universal Dictionary of Arts and Sciences.* London: J. and J. Knapton.

Cleishbotham the younger (1858). *A Handbook of the Scottish Language.* Edinburgh: J. L. Smith.

Clifton, C. E. and Grimaux, A. (1876). *Dictionnaire anglais–français et français–anglais composé sur un plan nouveau.* Paris: Garnier.

Cockeram, H. (1623). *The English Dictionarie.* London: E. Weaver.

COLERIDGE, S. T. *et al.* (1818–45). *General Introduction to the Encyclopaedia Metropolitana.* London.

COLES, E. (1676). *An English Dictionary.* London: S. Crouch.

—— (1677). *A Dictionary, English–Latin, and Latin–English.* (Second edition, 1679, thirteenth edition, 1736.) London: Printed by John Richardson.

Collins Scots Dictionary (2003). Glasgow: Collins.

COLLYMORE, F. A. (1955). *Notes for a Glossary of Barbadian Dialect.* Bridgetown, Barbados: Barbados National Trust.

CONNELLY, TH. and HIGGINS, TH. (1797–98). *A New Dictionary of the Spanish and English Languages.* Madrid: Pedro Julian Pereyra.

COOPER, T. (1565). *Thesaurus Linguae Romanae & Britannicae.* London: For H. Wykes.

COOTE, E. (1596). *The English Schoole-maister.* London: Widow Orwin for H. Jackson.

CORRÉARD, M. H. and GRUNDY, V. (1994). *The Oxford-Hachette French Dictionary French–English English–French.* Oxford, New York, and Toronto: Oxford University Press.

CORRO, A. del (1586). *Reglas gramaticales para aprender la lengua Española y Francesa.* Oxford: J. Barnes.

—— and THORIE, J. (1590). *The Spanish Grammer* [sic] *With a Dictionarie adioyned vnto it... by Iohn Thorius.* London: J. Wolfe.

COTGRAVE, R. (1611). *A Dictionarie of the French and English Tongues.* London: Adam Islip.

—— and SHERWOOD, R. (1632). *A Dictionarie of the French and English Tongues compiled by Randle Cotgrave. Whereunto is also annexed a Most Copious Dictionarie, of the English set before the French, by R. S. L.* [Robert Sherwood, Londoner.] London: A. Islip.

COVARRUBIAS HOROZCO, S. de (1611).*Tesoro de la Lengua Castellana, ó española.* Madrid: Luis Sánchez.

CRAIGIE, W. A., AITKEN, A. J., *et al.* (eds.) (1931–2001). *A Dictionary of the Older Scottish Tongue.* Oxford: Oxford University Press.

—— and HULBERT, J. R. (eds.) (1936–44). *A Dictionary of American English on Historical Principles.* (Four volumes.) Chicago: University of Chicago Press.

—— and ONIONS C. T. (eds.) (1933). *A New English Dictionary on Historical Principles. Founded on the Materials Collected by the Philological Society.* (Edited by J. A. H. Murray, H. Bradley, W. A. Craigie, C. T. Onions.) 'Introduction', 'Supplement', and 'Bibliography'. Oxford: Clarendon Press.

CRUIKSHANK, J. G. (1916). *Black Talk–Notes on Negro Dialect in Br. Guiana.* Georgetown, Guyana: The Argosy Co.

CUYÁS, A. (1903). *Appleton's New Spanish–English and English–Spanish Dictionary.* New York: Appleton.

D'ALBERTI DI VILLANUOVA, F. (1797–1805). *Dizionario Universale critico-enciclopedico della lingua italiana.* Lucca: Presso Domenico Marescandoli.

DE BERMINGHAM, A. (1877). *New Dictionary of the English and Italian Languages.* Paris: Garnier.

DE MAURO, T. (2000). *Il dizionario della lingua italiana.* Torino: Paravia.

DELBRIDGE, A. (1981). *The Macquarie Dictionary.* (Second edition 1982.) McMahons Point: The Macquarie Library.

DEVERSON, T. and KENNEDY, G. (2005). *The New Zealand Oxford Dictionary.* Melbourne: Oxford University Press.

DOLAN, T. P. (1998). *A Dictionary of Hiberno-English: The Irish Use of English.* Dublin: Gill & Macmillan.

DUBOIS-CHARLIER, F. *et al.* (1980). *Dictionnaire de l'anglais contemporain.* Paris: Larousse.

DUNCAN, A. (1595). *Appendix Etymologiae ad copiam exemplorum, una cum indice interprete.* Edinburgh: Robert Waldegrave.

DYCHE, T. and PARDON, W. (1735). *A New General English Dictionary.* London: R. Ware.

EBERS, J. (1796–99). *The New and Complete Dictionary of the German and English Languages.* Leipzig: Printed for Breitkopf and Haertel.

EDGREN, A. H. (1902). *An Italian and English Dictionary. With pronunciation and brief etymologies.* (Edited by H. Edgren, assisted by G. Bico and J. L. Gerig.) London: William Heinemann.

ELFFERS, H. and VILJOEN, W. J. (1908). *English–Dutch and Dutch–English Dictionary.* Capetown: J. C. Juta & Co.

ELWELL, W. O. (1850). *A New and Complete American Dictionary of the English and German Languages.* New York: G. & B. Westermann Brothers.

ELYOT, T. (1538). *The Dictionary of Syr Thomas Elyot knyght.* London: T. Berthelet.

—— (1542). *Bibliotheca Eliotae Eliotis librarie.* London: T. Berthelet.

—— revised Cooper, T. (1548). *Bibliotheca Eliotae Eliotis librarie.* London: T. Berthelet.

—— revised Cooper, T. (1552). *Bibliotheca Eliotae Eliotes Dictionarie.* (Another edition, 1559.) London: T. Berthelet.

EMERY, H. G. and BREWSTER, K. G. (1927). *The New Century Dictionary of the English Language.* (Three volumes, later two volumes.) New York: The Century Company.

ENDE, C. VAN DEN (1681). *Le Gazophylace de la langue françoise et flamende.* (Third edition.) Rotterdam: Izaac Naeran.

ENTICK, J. (1796). *Entick's New Spelling Dictionary. By William Crakelt.* London: C. Dilly.

Èntsiklopedicheskii Slovar' (1890). (Volume I.) Saint Petersburg: F. A. Brokgauz and I. A. Èfron. 384.

BROKGAUZ, F. A. and ÈFRON, I. A. (1890). *Èntsiklopedicheskii slovar'* (Volume I). Saint Petersburg, 384.

[ESTIENNE, R.] (1538). *Dictionarium Latino–Gallicum.* Paris: R. Stephanus.

—— (1542). *Dictionariolum puerorum* Paris: R. Stephanus.

—— (1544). *Les Mots Francois selon lOrdre des Lettres tournez en Latin pour les Enfants.* Paris: R. Estienne.

ESTIENNE–Veron. See below, under Stephanus.

EVANS, B. and EVANS, C. (1957). *A Dictionary of Contemporary American Usage.* New York: Random House.

FALLA, P. S. (1984). *The Oxford English–Russian Dictionary.* Oxford: Clarendon Press.

FARMER, J. S. (1889). *Americanisms, Old and New.* London: T. Poulter.

Fee, M. and McAlpine, J. (1997). *Guide to Canadian English Usage.* Toronto: Oxford University Press.

Fenwick De Porquet, L. Ph. R. (1832). *New French–English and English–French Dictionary.* London: Fenwick De Porquet.

Fick, J. Ch. (1802). *Vollstandiges englisch–deutsches und deutsch–englisches Lexicon.* Erlangen: Palm.

Fleming, Ch., Tibbins, J. (1839–43). *The Royal Dictionary, English and French and French and English.* Vol. I English and French, Tome II Français–Anglais. Paris: Didot.

Flexner, S. B. (1987). *The Random House Dictionary of the English Language, Second Edition.* New York: Random House.

Florio, J. (1598). *A Worlde of Wordes.* London: A. Hatfield.

—— (1611). *Qveen Anna's New World of Words.* London: M. Bradwood.

Florio, J. and Torriano, G. (1659). *Vocabolario Italiano & Inglese . . . Formerly compiled by John Florio . . . Whereunto is added a dictionary English & Italian . . . by Gio: Torriano . . .* London: T. Warren.

Flügel, J. G. (1830). *Complete Dictionary of the English and German Language.* Braunschweig.

Follett World-Wide Latin Dictionary. Latin–English/English–Latin (1967). (Edited by E. B. Levine, G. B. Beach, V. E. Bocchetta.) Chicago and New York: Follett.

Follett, W. (1966). *Modern American Usage.* New York: Hill & Wang.

Fowler, H. W. (1926). A *Dictionary of Modern English Usage.* London: H. Milford.

Francis, C. W. (*c.*1971). *Popular Phrases in Grenada Dialect.* St George's, Grenada.

Frisch, J. L. (1741). *Teutsch-Lateinisches Wörter-Buchs.* Berlin.

Frisius, J. (1556). *Dictionarium Latino–Germanicum Editio Noua.* Zurich: C. Froschoverus.

Fungerus, J. (1605). *Etymologicum Latinum.* Frankfurt: I. Rhodius.

Funk, I. K. (1893–94; 1895). *Funk & Wagnalls Standard Dictionary of the English Language.* New York: Funk & Wagnalls.

—— (1913). *Funk & Wagnalls New Standard Dictionary of the English Language.* New York: Funk & Wagnalls.

Furetière, A. (1690). *Dictionaire universel.* The Hague/Rotterdam: Arnout and Reinier Leers.

Gal'perin, I. R. (1977). *New Russian–English Dictionary/Bol'shoi anglo-russkii slovar'* (Second edition, two volumes; first edition 1972). Moscow: 'Russkii iazyk'.

—— (1980). *A Supplement to the New Russian–English Dictionary/Dopolnenie k Bol'shomu anglo-russkomu slovariu.* Moscow: 'Russkii iazyk'.

Gámez, T. de, Forbath, G. N., Page C. D., *et al.* (1973). *Simon and Schuster's International Dictionary.* New York: Simon and Schuster.

Gasc, F. E. A. (1873). *Gasc's Dictionary of the French and English Languages.* London: Bell & Daldy.

Giral Delpino, J. (1763). *A Dictionary Spanish and English, and English and Spanish.* London: A. Millar.

Girard, D. (1982). *Dictionnaire de l'anglais d'aujourd'hui. Anglais–français/français–anglais.* Paris: Julliard.

Glare, P. G. W. (1982). *Oxford Latin Dictionary.* Oxford: Clarendon Press.

Glogger, P. (1901–08). *Das Leidener Glossar.* (Three parts.) Augsburg: P. Pfeiffer.

Glossographia Anglicana Nova. (1707). London: D. Brown.

Gneuss, H. (1968). *Hymnar und Hymnen im englischen Mittelalter.* Tübingen: Niemeyer.

Goetz, G. (1888–1923). *Corpus glossariorum latinorum (CGL).* (Seven volumes.) Leipzig and Berlin: Teubner.

Goosens, L. (1974). *The Old English Glosses of MS. Brussels, Royal Library, 1650 (Aldhelm's De Laudibus Virginitatis).* Brussels: Koninklijke Academie van Belgie.

Gouldman, F. (1664). *A Copious Dictionary In Three Parts.* (Second edition, 1669, third edition, 1674, fourth edition 1678.) London: Printed for John Field.

Gove, P. B. (ed.) (1961). *Webster's Third New International Dictionary.* Springfield, MA: G. & C. Merriam.

Grab, F. (1897). *The Grimm-Webster German–English and English–German Dictionary.* Chicago: Laird & Lee.

Graham, W. (1977). *The Scots Word Book (Scots–English/English–Scots).* Edinburgh: Ramsay Head Press.

Grammatin, N. (1808). *A New Dictionary English and Russian, Composed upon the Great Dictionary English and French of M. Robinet/Novoi angliisko-rossiiskoi slovar' sostavlennoi po bol'shomu Angliisko-Frantsuzskomu Slovariu G. Robineta* (Volume I, A–I). Moscow: Tipografiia Dubrovina i Merzliakova.

Grant, W. and Murison, D. D. (1931–76). *The Scottish National Dictionary.* Edinburgh: Scottish National Dictionary Association Ltd.

Gregor, W. (1866). *The Dialect of Banffshire: with a Glossary of Words not in Jamieson's Scottish Dictionary.* London: Philological Society.

Grieb, Ch. F. (1842–47). *Englisch–Deutsch, Deutsch–Englisch Wörterbuch.* Stuttgart: Paul Neff.

Gwara, S. and Porter, D. W. (ed. and transl.) (1997). *Anglo-Saxon Conversations: The Colloquies of Ælfric Bata.* Woodbridge: Brewer.

H[arrison], L. (1571). *A dictionarie French and English.* London: H. Bynneman.

Halma, F. (1717). *Le Grand Dictionaire François & Flamend.* Amsterdam: R. and G. Wetstein.

Hankin, N. (1992). *Hanklyn-Janklin: Guide to some Words, Customs and Quiddities Indian and Indo-British.* New Delhi: Banyan Books. (Second and much enlarged edition. New Delhi: India Research Press, 2003.)

Hanks, P. and Potter, S. (1971). *Encyclopedic World Dictionary.* London: Hamlyn.

Harris, J. (1704). *Lexicon Technicum.* London: D. Brown *et al.*

Harris, W. T. (1909). *Webster's New International Dictionary of the English Language.* Springfield, MA: G. & C. Merriam.

Hazon, M. (1961). *Grande dizionario inglese–italiano italiano–inglese.* Milano: Garzanti.

Head, R. (1673). *The Canting Academy.* London: F. Leach for M. Drew.

Herrtage, S. J. H. and Wheatley, H. B. (1881). *Catholicon Anglicum.* (EETS OS 75.) London: Trübner.

Hessels, J. H. (1890). *An Eighth-Century Latin–Anglo-Saxon Glossary Preserved in the Library of Corpus Christi College, Cambridge.* Cambridge: Cambridge University Press.

—— (1906). *A Late Eighth-Century Latin–Anglo-Saxon Glossary Preserved in the Library of the Leiden University.* Cambridge: Cambridge University Press.

Hexham, H. (1647–48). *A Copious English and Netherduytch Dictionarie.* Rotterdam: A. Leers.

—— (1648). *Het Groot Woorden-boeck, gestelt in't Neder-duytsch ende in't Engelsch.* Rotterdam: A. Leers.

Hilpert, J. H. (1828–45). *A Dictionary of the English and German Languages.* (Four volumes.) Karlsruhe.

Hince, B. (2000). *The Antarctic Dictionary: A Complete Guild to Antarctic English.* Collingwood: CSIRO Publishing and the Museum of Victoria.

Hoare, A. (1915). *An Italian Dictionary.* (Second edition 1925.) Cambridge: Cambridge University Press.

Hollyband, C. (Desainliens, C.) (1580). *The Treasurie of the French Tong.* London: H. Bynneman.

—— (1593). *A Dictionarie French and English.* London: T[homas] O[rwin].

Holm, J. and Shilling, A. W. (1982). *Dictionary of Bahamian English (DBE).* New York: Lexik House.

Holtrop, J. (1789). *A New English and Dutch Dictionary.* Dordrecht/Amsterdam: A. Blussé.

Holyoke, F. See below under Rider, J. and Holyoke, F.

Holyoke, T. (1677). *A Large Dictionary In Three Parts: I. The English before the Latin... II. The Latin before the English... III. The Proper Names of Persons, Places,....* London: Printed by W. Rawlins.

Hornby, A. S., Gatenby, E. V., and Wakefield, H. (1942). *Idiomatic and Syntactic English Dictionary.* Tokyo: Kaitakusha.

Howell, J. (1660). *Lexicon Tetraglotton, an English–French–Italian–Spanish Dictionary.* London: T. Leach.

Huloet, R. (1552). *Abcedarium Anglico–Latinum pro tyrunculis.* London: W. Riddel.

—— (1572). *Huloets Dictionarie, newelye corrected,... and enlarged... by lohn Higgins.* London: T. Marsh.

Jakobsen, J. (1928–32). *An Etymological Dictionary of the Norn Language in Shetland.* London: David Nutt.

James, W. (1846). *A Complete Dictionary of the English and German languages for General Use.* (Two volumes.) Leipzig: Tauchnitz.

—— and Grassi, G. (1854). *Dizionario italiano–inglese e inglese–italiano.* Leipzig: Tauchnitz.

—— (1808). *An Etymological Dictionary of the Scottish Language.* (Two volumes.) Edinburgh: Creech, Constable and Blackwood.

—— (1818). *An Etymological Dictionary of the Scottish Language... abridged by the author.* Edinburgh.

—— (1825). *Supplement To the Etymological Dictionary of the Scottish Language.* (Two volumes.) Edinburgh: W. and C. Tait.

—— (1879–87). *An Etymological Dictionary of the Scottish Language... A new edition, carefully revised and collated, with the entire supplement incorporated by J. Longmuir,... and D. Donaldson...* (Four volumes and Supplement.) Paisley: Alexander Gardner.

Jauncey, D. (2004). *Bardi Grubs and Frog Cakes: South Australian Words.* South Melbourne: Oxford University Press.

Johnson, S. (1755). *A Dictionary of the English Language: in which the Words are Deduced from their Originals, and Illustrated in their Different Significations by Examples from the Best Writers.* (Two volumes.) London: W. Strahan.

—— (1756). *A Dictionary of the English Language... Abstracted from the Folio edition.* London: J. Knapton *et al.*

—— (1773). *A Dictionary of the English Language.* (Fourth edition.) London: W. Strahan.

—— (1786). *A Dictionary of the English Language.* (Seventh edition.) London: W. Strahan.

—— (1799). *A Dictionary of the English Language.* (Eighth quarto edition, two volumes.) London.

—— (1818). *A Dictionary of the English Language.* (Revised and enlarged by H. J. Todd; enlarged further by R. G. Latham (1866–70)). London: Printed for Longman, Rees, *et al.*

—— and Todd, H. J., abridged by A. Chalmers (1820). *A Dictionary of the English Language.* London.

—— and ——, ed. by J. E. Worcester (1827). *Johnson's English Dictionary: as Improved by Todd and Abridged by Chalmers; with Walker's Pronouncing Dictionary.* Boston: Ewer and Carter.

Junius, A. [= H] (1585). *The Nomenclator or Remembrancer.* (Translated by J. Higgins.) London: R. Newberie and H. Denham.

Junius, H. (1555). *Nomenclator Omnium Rerum Propria Nomina.* Augsburg. (Edition of 1567, Antwerp: C. Plantinus.).

K., J. (1702). *A New English Dictionary.* London: H. Bonwicke.

Kalbhen, U. (2003). *Kentische Glossen und kentischer Dialekt im Altenglischen.* (TUEPh 28.) Frankfurt am Main: Lang.

Katzner, K. (1984). *English–Russian, Russian–English Dictionary.* New York: John Wiley and Sons.

Kersey, J. (1706). *The New World of Words... Compiled by Edward Phillips, Gent. The Sixth Edition, Revised, Corrected, and Improved by J. K.* London: Printed for J. Phillips.

—— (1708). *Dictionarium Anglo-Britannicum.* London: J. Wilde.

Korhammer, M. (1976). *Die monastischen Cantica im englischen Mittelalter und ihre altenglischen Interlinearversionen.* (TUEPh 6.) Munich: W. Fink.

Kornexl, L. (1993). *Die 'Regularis Concordia' und ihre altenglische Interlinearversion.* (TUEPh 17.) Munich: W. Fink.

Kramer, M. (1700–2). *Das herrlich-Grosse Teutsch-Italiänische Dictionarium.* Nuremberg: J. A. Endter.

Kritzinger, M. S. B. (1926). *Woordeboek: Afrikaans–Engels Engels–Afrikaans Dictionary.* Pretoria: J. L. van Schalk.

Kroll, A. (1800). *A Commercial Dictionary, in the English and Russian Languages with a Full Explanation of the Russia Trade.* London: Printed for S. Chappel by T. Plummer.

Kunin, A. V. (1967). *Anglo-russkii frazeologicheskii slovar'.* (Third edition, two volumes.) Moscow: 'Sovetskaia Èntsiklopediia'.

Kunst, P. J. (1840). *Ein Amerikanisches Wörterbuch der Englischen und Deutschen Sprache.* Harrisburg, PA: G. S. Peters.

Kurath, H., Kuhn, S. M., Lewis, R. E., *et al.* (eds.) (1952–2001). *Middle English Dictionary.* Ann Arbor, MI: University of Michigan Press.

Lampe, G. W. H. (1961–68). *A Patristic Greek Lexicon.* Oxford: Clarendon Press.

Ledésert, R. P. L. and Ledésert, M. (1972, 1980). *Harrap's New Standard French and English Dictionary.* London: Harrap.

Levins, P. (Levens). (1570). *Manipulus Vocabulorum.* London: H. Bynneman. (1617). *Ηγεμων εις τά γλωσσας, id est Ductor in Linguas.* London: J. Browne.

Lewanski, R. (1963). *A Bibliography of Slavic Dictionaries, Volume III: Russian.* New York: The New York Public Library.

Lewis, C. T. (1879). *A Latin Dictionary Founded on Andrews' Edition of Freund's Latin Dictionary.* (Revised, Enlarged and in Great Part Rewritten by C. T. Lewis and Charles Short.) Oxford: Clarendon Press.

—— (1891), *An Elementary Latin Dictionary.* Oxford: Clarendon Press.

Liddell, H. G. and Scott, R. (1843). *A Greek–English Lexicon.* (Based on the German Work of Francis Passow.) Oxford: Clarendon Press.

—— and —— (1968). *A Greek–English Lexicon.* (A Supplement, Edited by E. A. Barber.) Oxford: Clarendon Press.

Lighter, J. E. (1994–). *Random House Historical Dictionary of American Slang.* (Vol. I, A–G.) New York: Random House.

Lindheim, B. von (1941). *Das Durhamer Pflanzenglossar.* Bochum-Langendreer: Pöppinghaus.

Lindsay, W. M. (1921). *The Corpus Glossary.* Cambridge: Cambridge University Press.

—— *et al.* (1926–31). *Glossaria Latina.* (*GL*) (Five volumes.) Paris: Les Belles Lettres.

Littleton, A. (1678). *A Latine Dictionary, In Four Parts.* (Second edition, 1684, third edition, 1693.) London: Printed for T. Basset.

—— (1678). *Linguae Latinae Liber Dictionarius Quadripartitus.* London: printed for T. Basset.

Louw, J. P. and Nida, E. A. (1988). *Lexical Semantics of the Greek New Testament: a Supplement to the Greek–English Lexicon Based on Semantic Domains.* Atlanta, GA: Scholars Press. [c.1992]

Ludolf, H. W. (1696). *Grammatica Russica.* Oxford: Sheldonian Theatre.

Ludwig, C. (1706). *A Dictionary English, German and French.* (Second edition, 1736, third edition, 1763, fourth edition, 1791.) Leipzig: T. Fritsch.

Lysle, A. de R. (1913, 1915). *Nuovo dizionario moderno-razionale-pratico inglese–italiano.* (Two volumes.) Torino: Sella & Guala.

Mackay, C. (1888). *A Dictionary of Lowland Scotch.* Edinburgh: privately printed.

Macleod, I. and Cairns, P. (eds.) (1996). *Essential Scots Dictionary.* Edinburgh: Edinburgh University Press.

MacTaggart, J. (1824). *The Scottish Gallovidian Encyclopedia.* London: printed for the author.

Mansion, J. E. (1934–39). *Harrap's Standard French and English Dictionary.* London: Harrap.

Marin, P. (1701). *Nouveau dictionnaire hollandois & françois.* (Eighth edition, 1773, ninth edition, 1787.) Amsterdam: de Weduwe Gysbert de Groot.

Martin, B. (1749). *Lingua Britannica Reformata.* London: J. Hodges.

Martin, W. and Tops, G. A. J. (eds.) (1984). *Van Dale Groot Woordenboek Engels–Nederlands.* Utrecht & Antwerpen: Van Dale.

Marwick, H (1929). *The Orkney Norn.* London: Oxford University Press.

Mathews, M. M. (1951). *A Dictionary of Americanisms on Historical Principles.* Chicago: The University of Chicago Press.

Mayhew, A. L. (1908). *The Promptorium Parvulorum.* (EETS ES 102.) London: Oxford University Press.

McKean, E. (2005). *The New Oxford American Dictionary.* Oxford: Oxford University Press. (Second edition; first edition of 2001 edited by E. J. Jewell and F. Abate, 2001.) (Based on *The New Oxford Dictionary of English*, edited by Judy Pearsall, 1998.)

McKesey, G. (1974). *The Belizean Lingo.* Belize: National Printers.

Meadows, F. C. (1834). *New Italian and English Dictionary.* London: printed for Thomas Tegg.

Meijer, L. (1745). *L. Meijers Woordenschat.* (Tenth edition.) Amsterdam: Jeronimus Ratelband.

Melzi, G. B. (1892). *Nuovo dizionario inglese–italiano italiano–inglese.* Milano: Fratelli Treves.

Mendes, J. (1985). *Cote Ce Cote La.* Trinidad and Tobago: Syncreators Ltd.

Meritt, H. D. (1945). *Old English Glosses, a Collection.* New York and London: Oxford University Press.

Michaelis, H. (1906). *A New Dictionary of the Portuguese and English Languages . . . based on a manuscript of J. Cornet.* (Second edition.) London: Pitman & Sons.

Miège, G. (1677). *A New Dictionary French and English, With Another English and French* (also 1679.) London: Printed by Tho. Dawks for Thomas Basset.

—— (1679). *A Dictionary of Barbarous French.* London: Printed by J. C. for Thomas Basset.

—— (1684). *A Short Dictionary English and French, with another French and English.* London: Printed for Thomas Basset.

—— (1688). *The Great French Dictionary in Two Parts. The First, French and English; the Second English and French.* London: Printed by J. Redmayne for Thomas Basset.

Milfull, I. B. (1996). *The Hymns of the Anglo-Saxon Church: A Study and Edition of the 'Durham Hymnal'.* (CSASE 17.) Cambridge: Cambridge University Press.

Miller, A. D. and Mirskii, D. P. (1936). *Anglo-russkii slovar'.* Moscow: 'Sovetskaia Èntsiklopediia'.

—— and Ozerskaia, T. A. (1937). *Anglo-russkii slovar'.* Moscow: 'Sovetskaia Èntsiklopediia'.

Millhouse, J. (1849, 1853). *New English and Italian Pronouncing and Explanatory Dictionary.* (Two volumes.) Milan: Printed for the heirs of J. Millhouse.

Minsheu, J. (1599). *A Dictionarie in Spanish and English.* (Second edition, 1623.) London: E. Bollifant.

Minsheu, J. (1617). *Ηγεμων εις τά γλωσσας, id est Ductor in Linguas. The Guide into Tongues.* London: J. Browne for the author.

Mitchell, H. (1782). *Scotticisms, Vulgar Anglicisms and Grammatical Improprieties Corrected,....* Glasgow: printed by Falconer & Willison.

Montgomery, M. B. and Hall, J. S. (2004). *Dictionary of Smoky Mountain English.* Knoxville: The University of Tennessee Press.

Moore, B. (2004). *The Australian Oxford Dictionary.* (Second edition.) South Melbourne: Oxford University Press.

Morelius, G. (1558). *Verborum Latinorum cum Graecis Gallicisque conjunctorum Commentarij.* Paris: Morelius.

—— [and ?Fleming, A.] (1583). *Verborum Latinorum cum Graecis Anglicisque coniunctorum, locupletissimi Commentarij.* London: H. Bynneman.

Morris, E. E. (1898). *Austral English: A Dictionary of Australasian Words, Phrases and Usages.* London: Macmillan. (Facsimile, Menston: Scholar Press 1971.)

Morwood, J. (1994). *The Pocket Oxford Latin Dictionary.* Oxford: Oxford University Press.

—— (1995). *Oxford Latin Minidictionary.* Oxford: Oxford University Press.

—— and Taylor, J. (2002). *Pocket Oxford Classical Greek Dictionary.* Oxford: Oxford University Press.

Mulcaster, R. (1582). *The First Part of the Elementarie.* London: T. Vautroullier.

Müller, V. K. (1946). *English–Russian Dictionary/Anglo-russkii slovar'* (Second edition; first edition 1943). Moscow: Gosudarstvennoe izdatel'stvo inostrannykh i natsional'nykh slovarei.

—— (1960). *English–Russian Dictionary/Anglo-russkii slovar'* (Seventh edition). New York: E. P. Dutton and Co.

—— (1978). *English–Russian Dictionary/Anglo-russkii slovar'* (Seventeenth edition). Moscow: 'Russkii iazyk'.

—— (1994). *Modern English–Russian Dictionary/Novyi Anglo-russkii slovar'.* Moscow: 'Russkii iazyk'.

—— (2004). *Complete English–Russian Dictionary/Bol'shoi Anglo-russkii slovar'.* Moscow: Ripol klassik; Tsitadel-treid.

—— and Boyanus, S. K. (1928). *Anglo-russkii slovar' s ukazaniiem proiznosheniia i internatsional'noi foneticheskoi transkriptsii.* Moscow: 'Sovetskaia èntsiklopediia'.

—— and —— (1935). *Russian English Dictionary/Russko-angliiskii slovar'* (Third edition; second edition 1932; first edition 1930.) Moscow: 'Sovetskaia èntsiklopediia'.

Muret, E. and Sanders D. (1891–1901). *Enzyklopädisches Wörterbuch der englischen und deutschen Sprache.* (Four volumes.) Berlin: Langenscheidt.

Murray, J. A. H., Bradley, H., Craigie, W. A., and Onions, C. T. (eds.) (1884–1928). *A New English Dictionary on Historical Principles.* (Twelve volumes.) Oxford: Clarendon Press.

—— —— —— and —— (1933). *The Oxford English Dictionary, being a corrected reissue, with Supplement.* (Thirteen volumes.) Oxford: Clarendon Press. (*OED1*)

—— —— —— and —— (1971). *The Oxford English Dictionary.* (Compact edition.) Oxford: Oxford University Press.

Napier, A. S. (1900). *Old English Glosses Chiefly Unpublished.* Oxford: Clarendon Press.

Nebrija, E. A. de (1492). *Diccionario Latino–espanol.* Salamanca.

Neilson, W. A. (ed.) (1934). *Webster's New International Dictionary of the English Language.* (Second edition.) Springfield, MA: G. & C. Merriam.

Nicot, J. (1606). *Thresor de la Langue Françoyse.* Paris: D. Douceur.

Niermeyer, J. F. (1976). *Mediae Latinitatis Lexicon Minus.* Leiden and Boston: Brill.

Nihalani, P., Tongue, R. K., and Hosali, P. (1979). *Indian and British English: A Handbook of Usage and Pronunciation.* Delhi: Oxford University Press.

—— —— and —— (2004). *Indian and British English: A Handbook of Usage and Pronunciation.* (Second edition.) New Delhi: Oxford University Press.

Ó Muirithe, D. (2002). *Irish Words and Phrases.* Dublin: Gill and Macmillan.

—— (2004). *A Glossary of Irish Slang and Unconventional Language.* Dublin: Gill and Macmillan.

Ogilvie, J. (1876). *The Imperial Dictionary.* London: Blackie and Son.

Oldecop, A. (1841). *Nouveau dictionnaire de poche français—russe et russe—français, précédé d'une Grammaire abrégée de chacune de ces deux langues, et suivi d'une Table de Noms de Baptème les plus usités et des noms historiques et mythologiques les plus connus; d'un Index géographique, et d'un Tableau comparatif des poids, mesures et monnaies des deux nations.* (Third edition, two volumes.) Saint Petersburg: Chez Fd. Bellizard et C°, libraires-éditeurs.

Oliphant, R. T. (1966). *The Harley Latin-Old English Glossary.* The Hague: Mouton.

Orsman, E. and Orsman, H. W. (1994). *The New Zealand Dictionary.* Auckland: New House.

Orsman, H. W. (1979). *Heinemann New Zealand Dictionary.* Auckland: Heinemann.

—— (ed.) (1997). *The Dictionary of New Zealand English: A Dictionary of New Zealandisms on Historical Principles.* Auckland: Oxford University Press.

Osselton, N. and Hempelman, R. (eds.) (2003). *The New Routledge Dutch Dictionary: Dutch–English/English–Dutch.* London: Routledge.

Ottley, C. R. (1965, 1971). *Creole Talk of Trinidad and Tobago.* Port-of-Spain, Trinidad and Tobago.

Oudin, C. (1607). *Tesoro de las dos Lenguas Francesa y Española.* Paris: M. Orry.

Oxford Russian Dictionary (1995). (English–Russian: P. Falla (ed.); Russian–English: M. Wheeler and B. Unbegaun (eds.); revised by C. Howlett.) Oxford: Oxford University Press.

Ozhegov, S. I. (1960). *Slovar' russkogo iazyka* (Fourth edition). Moscow: Gosudarstvennoe izdatel'stvo inostrannykh i natsional'nykh slovarei.

—— and Shvedova, N. Iu. (1993). *Tolkovyi slovar' russkogo iazyka.* Moscow: 'Az'.

Page, R. I. (1973). 'Anglo-Saxon Scratched Glosses in a Corpus Christi College, Cambridge, Manuscript', in Folke Sandren (ed.), *Otium et Negotium.* (Festschrift for Olof von Feilitzen.) Stockholm: Norstedt, 209–15.

—— (1979). 'More Old English Scratched Glosses', *Anglia* 97: 27–45.

Paikeday, T. M. (1990). *The Penguin Canadian Dictionary.* Markham: Penguin Books Canada.

Palsgrave, J. (1530). *Esclarcissement de la Langue Francoyse.* London: R. Pynson.

Parenogo, M. (1811). *A New Dictionary English and Russian, Composed Upon the English Dictionaries of Mrs. Johnson, Ebers and Robinet/Novoi angliisko-rossiiskoi slovar', sostavlennyi po Angliiskim Slovariam GG. Dzhonsona, Ebers i Robineta* (Volume II, I–R). Moscow.

Passerini Tosi, C. (1989). *Dizionario italiano–inglese Italian–English.* Torino: Paravia.

Passow, F. (1813). *Handwörterbuch der griechischen Sprache.* Leipzig: F. G. W. Vogel.

Pelegromius, S. (1580). *Synonymorum sylua.* (Translated by H. F.) London: T. Vautrollerius.

Percyvall, R. (1591). *Bibliotheca Hispanica.* London: J. Jackson.

—— and Minsheu, J. (1599). *A dictionarie in Spanish and English... enlarged and amplified... by Iohn Minsheu.* London: E. Bollifant.

Petronj S. E. and Davenport, J. (1824). *A New Dictionary, English and Italian, Italian and English, with the Equivalents in French.* London: Treuttel and Wurtz, 1828.

Pettman, C. (1913). *Africanderisms: A Glossary of South African Colloquial Words and Phrases and of Place and other Names.* London: Longmans, Green. (Reprint, Detroit: Gale Research 1968.)

Pheifer, J. D. (1974). *Old English Glosses in the Épinal-Erfurt Glossary.* (Reprinted, 1998.) Oxford: Oxford University Press.

Phillips, E. (1658). *The New World of English Words.* London: E. Tyler.

—— (1706). *The New World of Words. Or a General English Dictionary. ... The Sixth Edition, Revised, Corrected, and Improved... by J. K.* London: Printed for J. Phillips.

Picchi, F. (1999). *Grande Dizionario Inglese–Italiano Italiano–Inglese.* Milano: Hoepli.

Picken, E. (1818). *A Dictionary of the Scots Language.* Edinburgh: Printed for James Sawers.

Pickering, J. (1816). *A Vocabulary; or Collection of Words and Phrases which have been supposed to be peculiar to the United States.* Boston: Cummings and Hilliard.

Pickering, J. (1848). *Catalogue of the Philological, Classical, and Law Library, of the Late Hon. John Pickering.* Boston: A. Mudge.

Pickett, J. (2000). *The American Heritage Dictionary of the English Language, Fourth Edition.* Boston: Houghton Mifflin.

Pineda, P. (1740). *Nuevo dicionario, Español e Inglés e Inglés y Español.* London: F. Gyles.

Pollux, J. (1541). *Onomasticon.* (Translated by R. Gualtherus.) Basle: Winter.

Pomey, F. (1664). *Le Dictionnaire Royal des langues françoise et latine.* Lyon: A. Molin.

—— (1671). *Le Dictionnaire Royal augmenté.* (Second edition.) Lyon: A. Molin.

PORTER, N. (1890). *Webster's International Dictionary.* Springfield, MA: G. & C. Merriam.

PRATT, T. K. (1988). *Dictionary of Prince Edward Island English.* Toronto: University of Toronto Press.

PULSIANO, P. (2001). *Old English Glossed Psalters: Psalms 1–50.* Toronto: University of Toronto Press.

—— and DOANE, A. N. (1997). *Anglo-Saxon Manuscripts in Microfiche Facsimile. 5. Latin Manuscripts with Anglo-Saxon Glosses.* (MRTS 175.) Tempe, AZ: Medieval and Renaissance Texts and Studies.

RAGAZZINI, G. (1967). *Dizionario inglese–italiano italiano–inglese.* Bologna: Zanichelli.

RAMSON, W. S. (ed.) (1988). *The Australian National Dictionary: A Dictionary of Australianisms on Historical Principles.* (Second edition 1997.) Melbourne: Oxford University Press.

RAY, J. (1674). *A Collection of English Words not Generally Used.* London: H. Bruges.

REAL ACADEMIA ESPAÑOLA (1726). *Diccionario de la lengua castellana. en que se explica el verdadero sentido de las voces, su naturaleza y calidad, con las phrases o modos de hablar, los proverbios o refranes, y otras cosas convenientes al uso de la lengua . . . Compuesto por la Real Academia Española.* (Tomo primero. Que contiene las letras A. B.) Madrid: Imprenta de Francisco del Hierro. (Facsimile of the 1726 edition. Madrid: Editorial Gredos, *c.*1976.)

REIFF, C. P. and REIF, F. (1835–36). *Dictionnaire russe–français dans lequel les mots russes sont classés par familles, ou dictionnaire étymologique de la langue russe/Russko-frantsuzskii slovar', v kotorom russkie slova raspolozheny po proiskhozhdeniiu.* (Two volumes.) Saint Petersburg: Tipografiia N. Grecha.

RENIER, F. G. (1949). *Dutch–English and English–Dutch Dictionary.* London: Routledge & Kegan Paul.

REYNOLDS, B. (1962, 1981). *Cambridge Italian Dictionary. Vol. I Italian–English Vol. II English–Italian.* Cambridge: Cambridge University Press.

RICHARDSON, C. (1815). *Illustrations of English Philology.* London: Gale and Fenner.

—— (serial publ. 1817–; 1836–37). *A New Dictionary of the English Language.* London: W. Pickering.

RICHELET, C.-P. (1680). *Dictionnaire françois.* Geneva: Jean Herman Wiederhold.

RIDER, J. (1589). *Bibliotheca Scholastica.* Oxford: J. Barnes.

—— and HOLYOKE, F. (1606). *Riders Dictionarie . . . wherein Riders index is transformed into a dictionarie etymologicall . . . by Francis Holyoke.* (Edition of 1626 revised by N. Gray.) London: A. Islip.

RIDLEY, M. (1996). *A Dictionarie of the Vulgar Russe Tongue.* (Bausteine zur slavischen Philologie und Kulturgeschichte.) Köln: Bohlau Verlag.

ROBERTSON, W. (1681). *Phraseologia Generalis.* Cambridge: John Hayes.

ROBINSON, M. (1985). *The Concise Scots Dictionary.* Aberdeen: Aberdeen University Press.

ROONEY, K. (and SOUKHANOV, A., US ed.). (2004). *Encarta Webster's Dictionary of the English Language, Second Edition.* New York: Bloomsbury. (Originally pub. under the title *Encarta World English Dictionary,* 1999.)

Ross, T. W. and Brooks, E. (1984). *English Glosses from British Library Additional Manuscript 37075*. Norman, OK: Pilgrim Books.

Ruddiman, T. (1710). *Virgil's Æneid, translated into Scottish verse, by... Gawin Douglas... A new edition. ... To which is added a large glossary, Which may serve for a Dictionary to the Old Scottish Language....* Edinburgh: Andrew Symson and Robert Freebairn.

Salesbury, W. (1547). *Dictionary in Englyshe and Welshe*. London: J. Waley.

Sani, L. (1974). *Vocabolario inglese–italiano italiano–inglese*. Roma: Società editrice Dante Alighieri.

Sansoni Harrap (1970, 1976). *Dizionario delle lingue italiana e inglese*. Ed. Vl. Macchi Firenze: Sansoni; London: Harrap.

Scholze-Stubenrecht, W., Sykes, J. B. *et al.* (eds.) (1999). *The Oxford–Duden German Dictionary*. Oxford: Oxford University Press.

Schlutter, O. B. (1912). *Das Epinaler und Erfurter Glossar*. Hamburg: Grand. (Facsimile of *Erfurt*.)

Seaman, G.A. (1967). *Virgin Islands Dictionary*. St Croix, US Virgin Islands.

Seaton, A. (1995). *Times-Chambers Essential English Dictionary*. (Second edition 2002.) Singapore: Chambers Harrap and Times Media.

Sewel, W. (1691). *A New Dictionary English and Dutch*. Amsterdam: By de Weduwe van Steven Swart.

—— (1708). *A Large Dictionary English and Dutch*. Amsterdam: By de Weduwe van Steven Swart. (Second edition; third edition, 1727, also 1735; fourth edition, 1749, fifth edition, 1754.)

—— (1766). *A Compleat Dictionary English and Dutch*. (Reviewed, augmented and improved by Egbert Buys.) Amsterdam: Kornelis de Veer.

Seymour, A. J. (1975). *Dictionary of Guyanese Folklore*. Georgetown, Guyana.

Sheridan, T. (1797). *A Complete Dictionary of the English Language*. (Fourth edition.) London: Printed for Charles Dilly.

Shishukov, I. (1808–11). *Slovar' rossiisko-angliiski*. Saint Petersburg.

Silva, P. (ed.) (1996). *A Dictionary of South African English on Historical Principles*. Oxford: Oxford University Press.

Simpson, J. A. (2000) *The Third Edition of the Oxford English Dictionary*. Online at **www.oed.com** (*OED3*)

—— and Proffitt, M. J. (1997). *Oxford English Dictionary Additions Series*, Volume 3. Oxford: Clarendon Press.

—— and Weiner, E. S. C. (1989). *The Oxford English Dictionary*. (Second edition; twenty volumes.) Oxford: Clarendon Press. (*OED2*)

—— and —— (1992). *Oxford English Dictionary*. (Second Edition on Compact Disc.) Oxford: Oxford University Press.

—— and —— (1993a). *Oxford English Dictionary Additions Series*, Volume 1. Oxford: Clarendon Press.

—— and —— (1993b). *Oxford English Dictionary Additions Series*, Volume 2. Oxford: Clarendon Press.

—— and —— (1999). *Oxford English Dictionary* (Second Edition: CD-ROM Version 2.0). Oxford: Oxford University Press.

Sinclair, J. (1782). *Observations on the Scottish Dialect.* Edinburgh: William Creech.

Skeat, W. W. (1871–87). *The Gospels According to Saint Matthew... in Anglo-Saxon, Northumbrian, and Old Mercian Versions.* Cambridge: Cambridge University Press. (Reprint in two volumes, Darmstadt: Wissenchaftliche Buchgesellschaft, 1970.)

Skene, J. (1597). *De Verborum Significatione. The Exposition of the Termes and Difficill Wordes, conteined in the Foure Buikes of Regiam Majestatem....* Edinburgh.

Skey, M. (1978). *Dizionario inglese–italiano italiano–inglese.* Torino: Società editrice internazionale.

Slovar' na shesti iazykakh: Rossiiskom, Grecheskom, Latinskom, Frantsuzkom, Nemetskom i Angliskom. (1763). Saint Petersburg: Imperatorskaia Akademiia Nauk.

Slovar' sovremennogo russkogo literaturnogo iazyka. (1950–65). (Seventeen volumes). Moscow, Leningrad: Izdatel'stvo Akademii Nauk SSSR.

Smirnitskii, A. I. and Akhmanova, O. S. (1975). *Russian English Dictionary/Russko-angliiskii slovar'* (Tenth edition; first edition 1948). Moscow: 'Russkii iazyk'.

Smith, C., Bermejo Marcos, M., and Chang-Rodriguez, E. (1971). *Collins Spanish–English English–Spanish Dictionary.* London and Glasgow: Collins.

Smith, W. (1814). *A French Dictionary on a plan entirely new.* London.

Somner, W. (1659). *Dictionarium Saxonico-Latino–Anglicum.* Oxford: W. Hall.

South African Pocket-Dictionary. Dutch–English and English–Dutch. (1912). (In simplified spelling and containing many Cape Dutch words.) Cape Town: Dusseau; Johannesburg: Bussy.

Spiers A. (1846–49). *General English and French Dictionary.* (Two volumes.) Paris and London: Baudry's European Library.

Spinelli, N. (1929, 1930). *Dizionario italiano–inglese inglese–italiano.* Torino: Società editrice internazionale.

Springer, O. (ed.) (1962–75). *Langenscheid Enzyklopädisches Wörterbuch Englisch.* Berlin & München: Langenscheidt.

Stein, J. (1966). *The Random House Dictionary of the English Language.* New York: Random House.

Steinmetz, S. (1997). *Random House Webster's College Dictionary.* (Second edition.) New York: Random House.

Steinmeyer, E. and Sievers, E. (1879–22). *Die althochdeutschen Glossen.* (Five volumes.) Berlin: Weidman.

Stephanus (Estienne), C. (1553). *Dictionarium historicum, geographicum, poeticum.* Paris: C. Stephanus.

Stephanus (Estienne), R. and Veron, J. (1552). *Dictionariolum puerorum tribus linguis... cui Anglicam interpretationem Ioannes Veron nunc primum adiecit.* London: R. Wolfe.

Stevens, Captain J. (1705–06). *A New Spanish and English Dictionary. Part I A Dictionary Spanish and English. Part II A Dictionary English and Spanish.* (Second edition, 1726.) London: George Sawbridge.

Stevenson, W. H. and Lindsay, W. M. (1929). *Early Scholastic Colloquies.* Oxford: Clarendon Press.

Story, G. M., Kirwin, W. J., and Widdowson, J. D. A. (1982). *Dictionary of Newfoundland English.* (Second edition with supplement, 1990.) Toronto: University of Toronto Press.

Stracke, J. R. (1972). *The Laud Herbal Glossary.* Amsterdam: Rodopi.

Tabbert, R. (1991). *Dictionary of Alaskan English.* Juneau: Denali Press.

Tachard, G. (1689). *Dictionnaire nouveau françois–latin.* Paris: A. Pralard.

Tardy, Abbé. (1811). *An Explanatory Pronouncing Dictionary of the French Language.* (First edition 1799.) London: Longman, Hurst, Rees, Orme & Brown.

Tarver, J. Ch. (1847, 1858). *Tardy's Explanatory Pronuncing Dictionary.* (A New Edition Corrected and much Enlarged by J. Ch. Tarver.) London: Longman, Hurst, Rees, Orme & Brown.

Thieberger, N. and McGregor, W. (1994). *Macquarie Aboriginal Words.* McMahons Point: Macquarie Library.

[Thomas, T.] (1587). *Dictionarium linguae Latinae et Anglicanae.* Cambridge: T. Thomas.

—— (1589). *Thomae Thomasii Dictionarium.* Cambridge: J. Legate. (Tenth edition 1615, with supplement by Philemon Holland.)

Thomas, W. (1550). *Principal Rules of the Italian Grammar, with a Dictionarie.* London: T. Berthelet.

Tilley, M. P. (ed.) (1950). *Dictionary of the Proverbs in England in the Sixteenth and Seventeenth Centuries.* Ann Arbor: University of Michigan Press.

Tooke, J. H. (1786). *Epea ptepoenta, or, The diversions of Purley.* London: J. Johnson.

Torriano, G. See under Florio, J. and Torriano, G.

Triebel, L. A (1923). *English–German and German–English Dictionary. The Glotta English–German and German–English Dictionary.* London: Richard Jaschke.

Ushakov, D. N. (ed.) (1935–40). *Tolkovyi slovar' russkogo iazyka.* (Four volumes.) Moscow: 'Sovetskaia Èntsiklopediia'.

Valls, L. (1981). *What a Pistarckle: A Glossary of Virgin Islands English Creole.* St John.

Van Sertima, J. A. (1905). *The Creole Tongue.* Georgetown, Guyana.

Verheul, J. (1908, 1913). *Hill's Dutch–English and English–Dutch Vest-Pocket Dictionary and Self-Instructor, with conversations and idioms.* Hill's Vest-Pocket Dictionaries.

Veron, J. and Waddington, R. (1575). *A Dictionary in Latine and English... corrected and enlarged... by R. Waddington.* London: H. Middelton: for John Harison.

—— and —— revised by Fleming, A. (1584). *A Dictionarie in Latine and English.* London: R. Newberie and H. Denham.

Walker, J. (1791). *Critical Pronouncing Dictionary and Expositor of the English Language.* London: J. Richardson.

Wall, R. (1987). An *Anglo-Irish Glossary for Joyce's Works.* Syracuse, NY: Syracuse University Press.

—— (1995). A *Dictionary and Glossary for the Irish Literary Revival.* Gerrards Cross, Bucks.: Colin Smyth.

Warrack, A. (1911). *Chambers Scots Dictionary.* Edinburgh: Chambers.

WASE, C. (1662). *Dictionarium minus: A Compendious Dictionary English–Latin & Latin–English.* (Second edition, 1675.) London: D. Maxwell.

WATSON, G. (1923). *Roxburghshire Word Book.* Edinburgh: Scottish Dialects Committee.

WEBSTER, N. (1806). *A Compendious Dictionary of the English Language.* Hartford and New Haven: Sidney's Press.

—— (1828). *An American Dictionary of the English Language.* (Two volumes.) New York: S. Converse.

—— ed. by J. Worcester (1829). *Primary School Dictionary.* New York: S. Converse.

—— (1841). *An American Dictionary of the English Language.* (First edition in octavo; two volumes.) New Haven: Noah Webster.

—— rev. by C. A. Goodrich (1847). *An American Dictionary of the English Language: New Revised Edition.* Springfield, MA: George and Charles Merriam.

—— rev. by C. A. Goodrich (1859). *An American Dictionary of the English Language: Pictorial Edition.* Springfield, MA: George and Charles Merriam.

—— (1864). *Webster's Dictionary of the English Language.* (Revised by C. A. Goodrich and N. Porter.) London: Bell and Daldy.

—— rev. by C. A. Goodrich and N. Porter. (1864). *An American Dictionary of the English Language: Royal Quarto Edition, Unabridged.* Springfield, MA: G. & C. Merriam (called the 'Webster-Mahn' or 'the unabridged').

WEIR, E. (1889). *Cassell's New German Dictionary in Two Parts: German–English English–German.* London: Cassell.

WELY, F. P. H. P. van (1952) *Cassell's English–Dutch Dutch–English Dictionary.* London: Cassell.

WESSELY, E. (1883). *Thieme–Preusser: A New and Complete Critical Dictionary of the English and German Languages.* Part 1, *English–German.* Hamburg: Haendcke and Lehmkuhl.

WHEELER, M. and UNBEGAUN, B. O. (1972). *The Oxford Russian–English Dictionary.* Oxford: Clarendon Press.

WHITNEY, W. D. (1889–91). *The Century Dictionary.* (Six volumes.) New York: The Century Company.

—— (1895). *The Century Dictionary and Cyclopedia.* (Ten volumes.) New York: The Century Company.

WHITWORTH, G. C. (1885). *An Anglo-Indian Dictionary.* London: Kegan Paul, Trench and Co.

WIELAND, G. R. (1983). *The Latin Glosses on Arator and Prudentius in Cambridge University Library, MS Gg. 5.35.* Toronto: Pontifical Institute of Medieval Studies.

WILCOCKE, S. H. (1798). *A New and Complete Dictionary of the English and Dutch Languages.* London: Printed for C. Dilly.

WILDHAGEN, K. (1938). *Englisch-deutsches deutsch-englisches Wörterbuch.* (Based on the dictionary by William James.) Leipzig: Tauchnitz.

WILKINS, J. (1668). An Essay towards a Real Character and a Philosophical Language. London: printed for Sa. Gellibrand and for J. Martyn.

WILLIAM, J. (1846, 1929). *A Complete Dictionary of the English and German Languages for General Use.* (Second and fifty-second editions.) Leipzig: Tauchnitz.

WILLIAMS, E. B. (1955). *Holt Spanish and English Dictionary.* New York: Holt.

—— (1968). *Bantam New College Spanish & English Dictionary.* New York: Bantam.

WILSON, E. A. M. (1982). *The Modern Russian Dictionary for English Speakers.* Oxford: Pergamon Press.

WINSCHOOTEN, W. (1681). *Wigardus à Winschootens Seeman.* Leiden: Johannes de Vivie.

WITHALS, J. (1553). *A Shorte Dictionarie for Yonge Begynners.* London: T. Berthelet.

WORCESTER, J. E. (1830). *A Comprehensive Pronouncing and Explanatory Dictionary of the English Language.* Boston: Jenks and Palmer.

—— (1846). *A Universal and Critical Dictionary of the English Language.* Boston: Wilkins, Carter.

—— (1851). *A Universal Critical and Pronouncing Dictionary of the English Language, including Scientific Terms.* London: Henry G. Bohn

—— (1855). *A Pronouncing, Explanatory, and Synonymous Dictionary of the English Language.* Boston: Hickling, Swan, and Brewer.

—— (1860). *A Dictionary of the English Language.* Boston: Hickling, Swan, and Brewer.

WRIGHT, A. (1891). *Baboo English as 'tis Writ; being Curiosities of Indian Journalism.* London: T. F. Unwin.

WRIGHT, J. (1898–1905). *English Dialect Dictionary.* London: H Froude.

WRIGHT, T. and WÜLCKER, R. P. (1884). *Anglo-Saxon and Old English Vocabularies.* (Second edition; two volumes.) London. (Reprint Darmstadt.) (*WW*)

YANSEN, C. A. (1975). *Random Remarks on Creoles.* Margate, England.

YULE, H. and BURNELL, A. C. (eds.) (1886). *Hobson–Jobson: A Glossary of Colloquial Anglo-Indian Words and Phrases.* London: John Murray. (Reprint NewYork: Humanities Press, 1968).

ZHDANOV, P. (1784). *A New Dictionary English and Russian/Novoi slovar' angliskoi i rossiiskoi.* Saint Petersburg: Tipografiia Morskogo Shliakhetnogo Kadetskogo Korpusa.

—— (1801). *Angliskaia Grammatika.* Saint Petersburg: Tipografiia Morskogo Shliakhetnogo Kadetskogo Korpusa.

ZUPITZA, J. (1880). *Ælfrics Grammatik und Glossar.* (Third edition, with a preface by Helmut Gneuss, 2001.) Berlin.

OTHER REFERENCES

AARSLEFF, H. (1967). *The Study of Language in England, 1780–1860.* Princeton: Princeton University Press.

ADAMS, M. (1995). 'Sanford Brown Meech at the Middle English Dictionary', *Dictionaries: Journal of the Dictionary Society of North America* 16: 151–85.

—— (ed.) (2002). '*The* Middle English Dictionary *and Historical Lexicography*', special issue of *Dictionaries: Journal of the Dictionary Society of North America.*

—— (2002a). 'Phantom Dictionaries: the Middle English Dictionary before Kurath', in M. Adams (ed.), 85–114.

—— (2002b). '*DARE*, History, and the Texture of the Entry', *American Speech* 77: 370–82.

—— (2005). 'Articulating the Middle English Lexicon: Margaret Ogden, Medieval Medical Texts, and the *Middle English Dictionary*', in J. Chance, (ed.), *Women Medievalists and the Academy.* Madison, WI: University of Wisconsin, 697–710.

Adamska-Sałaciak A. (2006). *Meaning and the Bilingual Dictionary.* Frankfurt am Main: Lang.

Aitken, A. J. (1964). 'Completing the Record of Scots', *Scottish Studies* 8: 129–40.

—— (1971). 'Historical Dictionaries and the Computer', in R. A. Wisbey (ed.), 3–17.

—— (1973). 'Definition and Citations in a Period Dictionary', in R. I. McDavid and A. Duckert (eds.), *Lexicography in English.* New York: New York Academy of Sciences, 259–65.

—— (1980). 'On some Deficiencies in our Scottish Dictionaries', in W. Pijnenburg and F. de Tollenaere (eds.), 33–56.

—— (1981). 'DOST: How we Make it and What's in it', in R. J. Lyall and F. Riddy (eds.), *Proceedings of the Third International Conference on Scottish Language and Literature. (Medieval and Renaissance.)* Stirling/Glasgow, 33–51.

—— (1987a). 'The Extinction of Scotland in Popular Dictionaries of English', in R. W. Bailey (ed.), 99–135.

—— (1987b). 'The Period Dictionaries,' in R. Burchfield (ed.), *Studies in Lexicography.* Oxford: Clarendon Press, 94–116.

—— (1988). 'The Lexicography of Scots: the Current Position', in K. Hyldegaard-Jensen (ed.), 323–33.

—— (1989). 'The Lexicography of Scots: Two Hundred Years Since: Ruddiman and his Successors', in J. L. Mackenzie and R. Todd (eds.), *In Other Words: Transcultural Studies in Philology, Translation, and Lexicology.* Dordrecht: Foris, 235–45.

—— (1990). 'The Lexicography of Scots', in F. J. Hausmann, O. Reichmann, H. E. Wiegand, and L. Zgusta (eds.), 2: 1983–7 *Wörterbücher/Dictionaries/Dictionnaires*, Vol. 2. Berlin: de Gruyter, 1983–7.

—— (1992). 'Scottish dictionaries', in T. McArthur (ed.), *The Oxford Companion to the English Language.* Oxford: Oxford University Press, 901–3.

—— (1993). 'Lexicography', in D. Daiches (ed.), *The New Companion to Scottish Culture.* Edinburgh: Polygon, 182–3.

—— and Bratley, P. (1967). 'An Archive of Older Scots Texts for Scanning by Computer', *English Studies* 48: 60–1.

Alekseev, M. P. (1944). 'Angliiski iazyk v Rossii i russkii iazyk v Anglii', *Uchenye zapiski Leningradskogo Gosudarstvennogo Universiteta, seriia filologicheskikh nauk*, Vypusk 9: 77–137.

Alekseev, M. P. (1968). *Slovari inostrannykh iazykov v russkom azbukovnike XVII veka.* Leningrad: 'Nauka'.

—— (1982). *Russko-angliiskie literaturnye sviazi (XVIII vek—pervaia polovina XIX veka).* (Literaturnoe nasledstvo, Vol. 91.) Moscow: 'Nauka'.

—— and Levin, Iu. D. (1994). *Vil'iam Rol'ston—propagandist russkoi literatury i fol'klora* Saint Petersburg: 'Nauka'.

Alford, H. (1864). *A Plea for the Queen's English. Stray Notes on Speaking and Spelling.* London: W. Strahan.

Allsopp, J. (1996). 'French and Spanish Supplement', in S. R. R. Allsopp (ed.), *Dictionary of Caribbean English Usage.* Oxford: Oxford University Press, 669–97.

—— (1998). 'Richard Allsopp and the Dictionary of Caribbean English Usage—An Appreciation', in I. McDonald and V. Radzik (eds.), I. Robertson (guest ed.), *Kyk-Over-Al* 48: 37–44.

Allsopp, S. R. R. (1949). 'The Language We Speak (I)', *Kyk-Over-Al* 29: 13–14.

—— (1971). 'Some Problems in the Lexicography of Caribbean English', *Caribbean Quarterly* [Jamaica] 17: 10–24.

—— (1982). 'The Need for Sociolinguistic Determinants for Status-Labeling in a Regional Lexicography', in D. Hobar (ed.), *Papers of the Dictionary Society of North America, 1977.* Terre Haute, IND: Indiana State University for the Dictionary Society of North America, 64–77.

—— (1983). 'A Good Belly-Feed for All You So', *English World Wide. A Journal of Varieties of English* 4: 92–6.

—— (1987). '"Like If I Say You See a Jumbie or a Duppy": Problems of Definitional Differentiae in a Complex of Anglophone Cultures', in R. W. Bailey (ed.), *Dictionaries of English. Prospects for the Record of our Language.* Ann Arbor: University of Michigan Press, 75–98.

Alston, R. C. (1965–). *A Bibliography of the English Language from the Invention of Printing to the Year 1800.* Printed for the author by a variety of printers.

—— (1985). *A Bibliography of the English Language from the Invention of Printing to the Year 1800. Volume Twelve, Part One: The French Language, Grammars, Miscellaneous Treatises, Dictionaries.* Otley: Smith Settle.

Alston, R. C. (1999). *A Bibliography of the English Language from the Invention of Printing to the Year 1800. Volume Thirteen: The Germanic Languages.* Otley: Smith Settle.

—— (2002). *A Bibliography of the English Language from the Invention of Printing to the Year 1800. Volume Sixteen, Part One: Latin 1651–1800.* Otley: Smith Settle.

Alvar Ezquerra, M. (2003). 'Dictionaries of Spanish in their Historical Context', in R. R. K. Hartmann (ed.), 2: 343–74.

Amos, A. C. (1979). 'Dictionary of Old English: 1978 Progress Report', *Old English Newsletter* 12: 13–15.

Anon (1857) 'Proposal for a Complete Dictionary of the English Language'. *Notes and Queries* IV: 81–4.

—— (1984). 'Dictionary of Old English: 1983 Progress Report', *Old English Newsletter* 17: 12–13.

ATKINS, B. T. S. (2002). 'Bilingual Dictionaries: Past, Present and Future', in Corréard, M.-H. (ed.), *Lexicography and Natural Language Processing. A Festschrift in Honour of B. T. S. Atkins.* Euralex, 2002: 1–29.

AUTY, R. *et al.* (eds.) (1977–99). *LexMA: Lexikon des Mittelalters.* (Ten volumes.) Munich and Zurich: Artemis; Later LexMA; Later Stuttgart: Kröner (CD-ROM version).

BAIGENT, E., BREWER, C., and LARMINIE, V. (2005). 'Women and the Archive: The Representation of Gender in the *DNB* and the *OED*', *Archives* 30: 13–35.

BAILEY, R. W. (1978). *Early Modern English: Additions and Antedatings to the Record of English Vocabulary 1475–1700.* Hildesheim: Georg Olms Verlag.

—— (1980). 'Progress toward a Dictionary of Early Modern English', in W. Pijnenburg and F. de Tollenaere (eds.), 199–221.

—— (ed.) (1987). *Dictionaries of English. Prospects for the Record of our Language.* Ann Arbor: University of Michigan Press.

—— (1991). *Images of English: A Cultural History of the Language.* Ann Arbor: University of Michigan Press.

—— (1996). 'Origins [of *The Century Dictionary*]', *Dictionaries: Journal of the Dictionary Society of North America* 17: 1–16.

—— DOWNER, J. W., ROBINSON, J. L., and LEHMAN, P. V. (1975). *Early Modern English Materials.* Ann Arbor: Xerox University Microfilms and University of Michigan Press.

BAKER, P. S. (1988). '*A Supplement to OED: Sc–Z*', *Notes and Queries* 233: 148–53.

BAKER, S. J. (1945). *The Australian Language.* London: Angus & Robertson. (Second edition Sydney: Currawong, 1966.)

BARNES, J. (1982). 'The Social Democratic Phase', *New Statesman*, 16 July, 20–21.

BARNHART, C. L. (1978). 'American Lexicography, 1947–1973', *American Speech* 53: 83–140.

BARNHART, R. K. (1996). 'Aftermath [of the publication of *The Century Dictionary*],' *Dictionaries: Journal of the Dictionary Society of North America* 17: 116–25.

BATELY, J. (1983). 'Miège and the Development of the English Dictionary', in E. G. Stanley and D. Gray (eds.), *Five Hundred Years of Words and Sounds. A Festschrift for Eric Dobson.* Cambridge: D. S. Brewer, 1–10.

BATELY, J. M. (2001). 'Wase, Torriano and Sherwood: some Unacknowledged Lexical Debts', in C. J. Kay and L. M. Sylvester (ed.), *Lexis and Texts in Early English.* Amsterdam: Rodopi, 13–30.

BÉJOINT, H. and THOIRON, PH. (eds.) (1996). *Les dictionnaires bilingues.* Louvain-la-Neuve: Duculot.

BENBOW, T. J., CARRINGTON, P., JOHANNESON, G., TOMPA, F., and WEINER, E. S. C. (1990). 'Report on the New Oxford English Dictionary User Survey', *International Journal of Lexicography* 3.3: 155–203.

BENZIE, W. (1983). *Dr. F. J. Furnivall. A Victorian Scholar Adventurer.* Norman, OK: Pilgrim Books.

BERG, D. L. (1992). *A Guide to the Oxford English Dictionary.* Oxford: Oxford University Press.

BERGMANN, R. (ed.) (2003). *Volkssprachig-lateinische Mischtexte und Textensembles in der althochdeutschen, altsächsischen und altenglischen Überlieferung.* Heidelberg: Winter.

BIVENS, L. (1982). 'Noah Webster's Etymological Principles', *Dictionaries: Journal of the Dictionary Society of North America* 4: 1–13.

BLAKE, N. F. (2002). 'On the Completion of the *Middle English Dictionary*', in M. Adams (ed.), 48–75.

BOULTON, J. (1971). *Johnson: The Critical Heritage.* London: Routledge and Kegan Paul.

BRADLEY, H. (1917). 'Sir James Murray, 1837–1915'. *Proceedings of the British Academy* 8: 545–51.

BRENGELMAN, F. H. (1981). 'Dialectology in Seventeenth-Century Dictionaries', *Papers of the Dictionary Society of North America*: 1–8.

BREWER, C. (1993). 'The Second Edition of the *OED*', *Review of English Studies* (New Series.) 44: 313–42.

—— (2004). 'The Electronification of the *OED*', *Dictionaries* 25: 1–43.

—— (2005). 'Authority and Personality: Usage Labels in the *OED*', *Transactions of the Philological Society* 103: 261–301.

—— (2005–). 'Examining the *OED*'. **http://oed.hertford.ox.ac.uk/main/.**

—— (2007). *Treasure-house of the Language: the Living OED.* New Haven and London: Yale University Press.

BRODRIBB, C. W. (1928). 'Our Dictionary', *Times Literary Supplement*: 277–8.

BRONSTEIN, A. J. (1986). 'The History of Pronunciation in English-Language Dictionaries', in R. R. K. Hartmann (ed.), *The History of Lexicography.* Amsterdam: Benjamins, 23–33.

BROOKS, N. (ed.) (1982). *Latin and the Vernacular Languages in Early Medieval Britain.* Leicester: Leicester University Press.

BURCHFIELD, R. W. (1958). '*O.E.D.* A New Supplement', *The Periodical* XXXII. 261: 229–31.

—— (1961). '*O.E.D.*: A New Supplement', *Essays & Studies* 14: 35–51.

—— (1974). 'The Treatment of Controversial Vocabulary in the *OED*', *Transactions of the Philological Society*: 1–28.

—— (1975). 'The Art of the Lexicographer', *Journal of the Royal Society of Arts* 123: 349–61.

BURCHFIELD, R. W. (1980). 'Aspects of Short-Term Historical Lexicography', in W. Pijnenburg and F. de Tollenaere (eds.), 271–9.

—— (1984). 'The End of an Innings but not the End of the Game', *Incorporated Linguist* 23: 114–19.

—— (1989). *Unlocking the Language.* London: Faber & Faber.

—— and AARSLEFF, H. (1988). *The OED and the State of the Language.* Washington: Library of Congress.

BURKETT, E. M. (1979). *American Dictionaries of the English Language before 1861.* Metuchen, NJ and London: Scarecrow Press.

CAMERON, A. (1973). 'A List of Old English Texts', in R. Frank and A. Cameron (eds.), *A Plan for the Dictionary of Old English.* Toronto: Toronto University Press, 25–306.

—— (1983). 'On the Making of the *Dictionary of Old English*', *Poetica* 15–16: 13–22.

—— and Amos, A. (1978). 'The Dictionary of Old English: A Turning Point', *English Studies* 59: 289–94.

—— —— Butler, S., and Healey, A. (1981). *The Dictionary of Old English Corpus in Electronic Form* [magnetic tape]. Toronto: University of Toronto Press.

—— Frank, R., and Leyerle, J. (eds.) (1970). *Computers and Old English Concordances.* Toronto: University of Toronto Press.

—— and Healey, A. (1979). 'The Dictionary of Old English', *Dictionaries: Journal of the Dictionary Society of North America* 1: 87–96.

—— Kingsmill, A., and Amos, A. C. (1983). *Old English Word Studies: A Preliminary Author and Word Index.* Toronto: University of Toronto Press.

Chapman, R. L. (1967). 'A Working Lexicographer Appraises *Webster's Third New International Dictionary*', *American Speech* 42: 202–10.

Chapman, R. W. (1946). 'The World of Worlds', *Times Literary Supplement*, 12 October: 492.

Claes, F. (1980). *A Bibliography of Nederlandic (Dutch, Flemish) Dictionaries.* München: Kraus.

Cleminson, R. M. (1995). 'The History of Russian Language Learning in England', in R. M. Cleminson (ed.), *Russian Language Learning: Past, Present and Future.* (Papers from a Conference held at the University of Portsmouth, 11–13 April 1994.) Portsmouth: University of Portsmouth, 1–12.

Coleman, J. (2004). *A History of Cant and Slang Dictionaries. Volume I: 1567–1785.* Oxford: Oxford University Press.

Coleridge, H. (1859). *A Glossarial Index to the Printed English Literature of the Thirteenth Century.* London: Trubner & Co.

—— (1860). 'A Letter to the Very Rev. The Dean of Westminster'. Appended to Trench (1860): 71–8.

Coles, E. (1674). *The Compleat English Schoolmaster.* London: Peter Parker.

Collison, R. L. (1982). *A History of Foreign-Language Dictionaries.* London: André Deutsch.

Cormier, M. (2006). 'De l'influence de la lexicographie française sur la lexicographie bilingue français–anglais: le *Royal Dictionary* (1699) d'Abel Boyer', *Cahiers de lexicologie* 88.2: 163–82.

—— and Fernandez, H. (2004). 'Influence in Lexicography: A Case Study. Abel Boyer's *Royal Dictionary* (1699) and Captain John Stevens' *Dictionary English and Spanish* (1705)', *International Journal of Lexicography* 17.3: 291–308.

—— and —— (2005).'From the *Great French Dictionary* (1688) of Guy Miège to the *Royal Dictionary* (1699) of Abel Boyer: Tracing Inspiration', *International Journal of Lexicography* 18.4: 479–507.

—— and Francœur, A. (2004a). 'Claudius Holyband: Pioneer Huguenot Lexicographer in England', *Proceedings of the Huguenot Society* 28: 160–75.

—— and —— (2004b). 'French–English Bilingual Dictionaries in the 16th and 17th Centuries: Achievements and Innovations by French-Speaking Protestants', *Dictionaries* 25: 77–106.

Cormier, M. and Francœur, A. (2006). 'La réduction dictionnairique: l'exemple du *Short Dictionary* (1684) de Guy Miège et du *Royal Dictionary Abridged* (1700) d'Abel Boyer', *Cahiers de lexicologie* 88.1: 27–51.

Cowie, A. P. (1999). *English Dictionaries for Foreign Learners: A History.* Oxford: Clarendon Press.

Cowlishaw, M. F. (1987). 'LEXX–a Programmable Structured Editor', *IBM Journal of Research and Development* 31: 73–80.

Craigie, W. A. (1931). 'New Dictionary Schemes Presented to the Philological Society, 4th April, 1919', *Transactions of the Philological Society* (1925–30): 6–13.

—— (1929). 'The Oxford English Dictionary and Afterward', *The English Journal* 18: 396–403.

—— (1937). 'The Value of the Period Dictionaries', *Transactions of the Philological Society*: 53–62.

Cram, D. (1991). 'Birds, Beasts and Fishes versus Bats, Mongrels and Hybrids: The Publication History of John Ray's *Dictionariolum* (1675)', *Paradigm* 6 (October). [**http:w4.ed.uiuc.edu/faculty/Paradigm/cram.html, accessed 10 February 2006**]

Cross, A. (1993). *Anglo–Russica: Aspects of Cultural Relations between Great Britain and Russia in the Eighteenth and Early Nineteenth Centuries.* Oxford: Berg Publishers Limited.

—— (1997). *By the Banks of the Neva: Chapters from the Lives and Careers of the British in Eighteenth-Century Russia.* Cambridge: Cambridge University Press.

De Maria, R. (1986). *Johnson's Dictionary and the Language of Learning.* Chapel Hill: University of North Carolina Press.

Delbridge, A. (1981). 'Delbridge on Dictionaries', *The Macquarie Dictionary Society* [newsletter] 1.1: 1–2.

Derolez, R. (ed.) (1992). *Anglo-Saxon Glossography: Papers Read at the International Conference* held in the Koninklijke Academie voor Wetenschappen. Brussels: WLSK.

Dixon, R. W. (1857). 'Fore-elders', *Notes and Queries* (Second series.) IV: 208–9.

Dolezal, F. (2000). 'Charles Richardson's *New Dictionary* and Literary Lexicography, being a Rodomontade upon Illustrative Examples', *Lexicographica* 16: 104–51.

Dolezal, F. (1985). *Forgotten but Important Lexicographers: John Wilkins and William Lloyd. A Modern Approach to Lexicography before Johnson.* Tübingen: Niemeyer.

Edwards, A. S. G. (ed.) *The Index of Middle English Prose* (*IMEP*). *Handlist I*: 1984–*Handlist XVIII*: 2006 (still in progress). Cambridge: Brewer.

'Eirionnach' (1859). 'Bishop Wetenhall's Books', *Notes and Queries* (Second series.) VII: 271–3.

Elliott, L. (2000). 'How the Oxford English Dictionary Went Online', *Ariadne* Issue 24 (21 June) [**http://www.ariadne.ac.uk/issue24/oed-tech/intro.html**].

—— and Williams, S. R. (2006). 'Pasadena: a New Editing System for the Oxford English Dictionary', in E. Corino, C. Marello, and C. Onesti (eds.), *Proceedings XII Euralex International Congress.* Alessandria: Edizioni dell'Orso, 257–64.

Ellis, A. J. (1873). 'Second Annual Address of the President to the Philological Society', *Transactions of the Philological Society* (1873–74) 200–52.

—— (1874). 'Third Annual Address of the President to the Philological Society', *Transactions of the Philological Society* (1873–74) 354–460.

Farina, D. M. T. Cr. (1992). 'The Meaning of Definition in Soviet Lexicography: The Leningrad Academic Dictionaries', *Lexicographica* 8: 69–99.

—— (1996). 'The Bilingual Lexicographer's Best Friends', in *The Translational Equivalent in Bilingual Lexicography*, thematic section of *Lexicographica* 12: 1–15.

—— (2001a). 'Dictionaries of the Soviet Period', in D. Jones (ed.), *Censorship: An International Encyclopedia.* London: Fitzroy Dearborn Publishers, 3. 2103–5.

—— (2001b). 'Dal's Dictionary', in D. Jones (ed.), *Censorship: An International Encyclopedia.* London: Fitzroy Dearborn Publishers, 3. 2101–3.

Fawcett, H. (1991). *PAT 3.3 User's Guide.* Waterloo, Ontario, Canada: University of Waterloo Centre for the New OED.

Fowler, R. (2004). 'Text and Meaning in Richardson's Dictionary', in J. Coleman and A. McDermott (eds.), *Historical Dictionaries and Historical Dictionary Research.* Tübingen: Niemeyer: 53–62.

Frank, R. and Cameron, A. (eds.) (1973). *A Plan for the Dictionary of Old English.* Toronto: University of Toronto Press.

Franzen, C. (1991). *The Tremulous Hand of Worcester: A Study of Old English in the Thirteenth Century.* Oxford: Oxford University Press.

Friend, J. H. (1967). *The Development of American Lexicography 1798–1864.* The Hague: Mouton.

Fries, C. C. (1932). 'The Early Modern English Dictionary', *Publications of the Modern Language Association* 47: 893–7.

Furnivall, F. J. (1861). *List of Books Already Read, or Now (July 12, 1861) Being Read for the Philological Society's New English Dictionary.* London: The Philological Society.

—— (1862). 'On the Next Step in the Dictionary Plan', *Proceedings of the.Philological Society* 328.

—— (1864). *Circular to the Members of the Philological Society, 18 October 1864.* London: The Philological Society.

—— (1865). *Circular to the Members of the Philological Society, 26 October 1865.* London: The Philological Society.

Garmonsway, G. N. (1939). *Ælfric's Colloquy.* (Several reprints.) Methuen and Manchester University Press.

Gee, W. (1863). *The Philological Society's New English Dictionary. Vocabulary of Words Beginning with the Letter B.* Hertford: Stephen Austin.

Geikie, A. C. (1857). 'Canadian English', *Canadian Journal of Industry, Science, and Art* 2: 344–55.

Gilman, E. W. (1996). 'Definitions and Usage [in *The Century Dictionary*]', *Dictionaries: Journal of the Dictionary Society of North America* 17: 55–67.

Gneuss, H. (1996). *English Language Scholarship: a survey and Bibliography from the Beginnings to the End of the 19th Century.* (Medieval and Renaissance Texts and Studies 125.) Binghampton, NY.

—— (2001). *Handlist of Anglo-Saxon Manuscripts.* Tempe, AZ: Arizona Center for Renaissance Studies.

Gonnet, G. (1987). *Pat 3.1: An Efficient Text Searching System.* Waterloo, Ontario, Canada: University of Waterloo Centre for the New OED.

Gouws R.H. (2007). 'On the Development of Bilingual Dictionaries in South Africa: Aspects of Dictionary Culture and Government Policy', *International Journal of Lexicography* 20.3: 313–27.

Gove, P. (1940). 'Notes on Serialization and Competitive Publishing', *Proceedings of the Oxford Bibliographical Society* 5: 305–22.

Grant, W. and Dixon, J. M. (1921). *Manual of Modern Scots.* Cambridge: Cambridge University Press.

Greenfield, S. B. and Robinson, F. C. (1980). *A Bibliography of Publications on Old English Literature to the End of 1972.* Toronto: University of Toronto Press.

Gretsch, M. (1999). *The Intellectual Foundations of the English Benedictine Reform.* (CSASE 25.) Cambridge: Cambridge University Press.

H. W. (1851). 'Meaning of Sinage; Distord; Slander', *Notes and Queries* (First series.) IV: 6.

Hall, D. J. (2004). 'Sewel, Willem (1653–1720)', in *Oxford Dictionary of National Biography.* Oxford: Oxford University Press. [**http://www.oxforddnb.com/view/article/25139, accessed 20 June 2006**]

Hamilton-Smith, N. (1971). 'A Versatile Concordance Program for a Textual Archive', in R. A. Wisbey (ed.), 235–44.

Hancher, M. (1996). 'Illustrations [in *The Century Dictionary*]', *Dictionaries: Journal of the Dictionary Society of North America* 17: 79–115.

Hartmann, R. R. K. (ed.) (1986). *The History of Lexicography.* Amsterdam: Benjamins.

—— (ed.) (2003). *Lexicography. Critical Concepts.* (Three volumes.) London: Routledge.

Hausmann, F. J. (1991). 'La lexicographie bilingue anglais–français, français–anglais', in F. J. Hausmann, O. Reichmann, H. E. Wiegand, and L. Zgusta (eds.), 3: 2956–60.

—— and Cop, M. (1985). 'Short History of English–German Lexicography', in K. Hyldgaard-Jensen and A. Zettersten (eds.), *Symposium on Lexicography II.* Tübingen: Max Niemeyer, 183–97.

Hausmann, F. J., Reichmann, O., Wiegand, H. E., and Zgusta, L. (eds.) (1989–91). *Wörterbücher. Ein internationales Handbuch zur Lexicographie/Dictionaries. An International Encyclopedia of Lexicography/Dictionnaires. Encyclopédie internationale de lexicographie.* Berlin/New York: Walter de Gruyter.

—— and Werner, R. O. (1991). 'Spezifische Bauteile und Strukturen zweisprachiger Wörterbücher: eine Übersicht', in F. J. Hausmann, O. Reichmann, H. E. Wiegand, and L. Zgusta (eds.), 3: 2729–69.

HEALEY, A. (1995). *The Dictionary of Old English Corpus in Electronic Form* [Web version]. Ann Arbor: University of Michigan Press.

—— (1997). 'The Dictionary of Old English', in K. H. van Dalen-Oskam, K. A. C. Depuydt, W. J. J. Pijneburg, and T. H. Schoonheim (eds.), *Dictionaries of Medieval Germanic Languages: A Survey of Current Lexicographical Projects.* Turnhout: Brepols, 55–61.

—— (2002). 'The Dictionary of Old English: From Manuscripts to Megabytes', in M. Adams, 156–79.

HEALEY, A., HOLLAND, J. *et al.* (1993). *The Dictionary of Old English Corpus in Electronic Form* [diskette]. Toronto: University of Toronto Press.

[Hickes, G.] (1678). *Ravillac Redivivus being a Narrative of the Late Tryal of Mr. James Mitchel, a Conventicle-Preacher.* London: Henry Hills.

HILL, G. (1989). 'Common Weal, Common Woe', *Times Literary Supplement*, 21–27 April: 411–14.

HOLLAND, J. (1986). 'Dictionary of Old English: 1985 Progress Report', *Old English Newsletter* 19: 21–2.

—— (1989). 'Dictionary of Old English: 1989 Progress Report', *Old English Newsletter* 23: 18–20.

HOUSEHOLDER, F. W. and SAPORTA, S. (eds.) (1962). *Problems in Lexicography. Proceedings of the Conference on Lexicography, Indiana University 11–12 1960* (IJAL 28 no. 2 Part IV). Bloomington IN: Indiana University Press.

HULL, W. I. (1933). *Willem Sewel of Amsterdam 1653–1720. The first Quaker historian of Quakerism.* Swarthmore: Swarthmore College.

HÜLLEN, W. (1999). *English Dictionaries, 800–1700.* Oxford: Clarendon Press.

HUME, D. (1752). *Political Discourses.* Edinburgh.

HUNT, T. (1989). *Plant Names of Medieval England.* Cambridge: Brewer.

—— (1991). *Teaching and Learning Latin in 13th Century England.* (Three volumes.) (I: Texts; II: Glosses; III Indexes.) Cambridge: Brewer.

HYLDEGAARD-JENSEN, K. (ed.) (1988). *Symposium on Lexicography III: Proceedings of the Third International Symposium on Lexicography.* Tübingen: Niemeyer.

IANNUCCI, J. E. (1962). 'Meaning Discrimination in Bilingual Dictionaries', in F. W. Householder, and S. Saporta (eds.), 201–16.

ISPOLATOV, N. M. (1971). 'Pervye anglo-russkie slovari v Rossii', *Vestnik LGU, seriia istoriia–iazyk–literatura* 4: 131–41.

JAMES, G. C. A. (2000). 'Bilingualisation as a Genre', in *Colporul. A History of Tamil Dictionaries.* Chennai: Cre-A, 450–8; reprinted in R. R. K. Hartmann (ed.), (2003), 3:135–46.

JOHNSON, S. (1747). *The Plan of a Dictionary of the English Language.* London: J. and P. Knapton.

JOST, D. (1984). 'The Reading Program of the *Middle English Dictionary*: Evaluation and Instructions', *Dictionaries: Journal of the Dictionary Society of North America* 6: 113–27.

JOST, D. (1985). 'Survey of the Reading Program of the *Middle English Dictionary*', *Dictionaries: Journal of the Dictionary Society of North America* 7: 201–13.

KAZMAN, R. (1986). *Structuring the Text of the Oxford English Dictionary through Finite State Transduction.* Waterloo, Ontario, Canada: University of Waterloo.

KER, N. R. (1957). *Catalogue of Manuscripts Containing Anglo-Saxon.* Oxford: Oxford University Press.

KERLING, J. (1979). *Chaucer in Early English Dictionaries.* Leiden: University Press.

KERNERMAN, A. (2006). 'Summing Up Two Decades of Pedagogic Lexicography', in E. Corino, C. Marello, C. Onesti (eds.). *Atti del XII Congresso Internazionale di Lessicografia, Proceedings XII Euralex International Congress.* Alessandria: Edizioni dell'Orso, 1263–9.

KEY, N. E. (2004). 'Littleton, Adam (1627–1694)', in *Oxford Dictionary of National Biography.* Oxford: Oxford University Press. [**http://www.oxforddnb.com/view/article/16780, accessed 2 Aug 2006**]

'The King's Congratulations on the Completion of the Dictionary'. (1928). *The Periodical* XIII: 73.

KITTLICK, W. (1998). *Die Glossen der Hs. British Library, Cotton Cleopatra A.III.* Frankfurt am Main: Lang.

KNAPPE, G. (2004). *Idioms and Fixed Expressions in English Language Study before 1800.* Frankfurt am Main: Lang.

KORHAMMER, M. (1980). 'Mittelalterliche Konstruktionshilfen und altenglische Wortstellung', *Scriptorium* 34: 18–58.

KRAPP, G. P. (1925). *The English Language in America.* (Two volumes.) (Reprint New York: Frederick Ungar, 1966.)

KURATH, H, OGDEN, M. S., PALMER, C., and MCKELVEY, R. (1954). *Middle English Dictionary: Plan and Bibliography.* Ann Arbor: University of Michigan Press.

L., I. (2003). 'Slovo o sostavitele slovaria', *Novoe russkoe slovo*, 2–3 August.

L. L. L. (1867). 'The Philological Society's "English Dictionary"', *Notes and Queries* (Third series.) X: 169.

LANCE, D. M. (1996). 'Pronunciation [in *The Century Dictionary*]', *Dictionaries: Journal of the Dictionary Society of North America* 17: 68–78.

LANDAU, S. I. (1974). 'Of Matters Lexicographical: Scientific and Technical Entries in American Dictionaries', *American Speech* 49: 241–4.

—— (2001). *Dictionaries: the Art and Craft of Lexicography.* (Second edition.) New York: Cambridge University Press.

—— (2005). 'Johnson's Influence on Webster and Worcester in Early American Lexicography', *International Journal of Lexicography* 18: 217–29.

LAPIDGE, M. *et al.* (eds.) (1999). *The Blackwell Encyclopedia of Anglo-Saxon England (BEASE).* Oxford: Blackwell.

LARIN, B. A. (1959). *Russko-angliiskii slovar'–dnevnik Richarda Dzhemsa (1618–1619 gg.).* Leningrad: Izdatel'stvo Leningradskogo universiteta.

LAUGHLIN, R. M. (1967). 'The Predecessors of *That* Dictionary,' *American Speech* 42: 105–13.

LAW, V. (1997). *Grammar and Grammarians in the Early Middle Ages.* London: Longman.

LEAVITT, R. K. (1947). *Noah's Ark, New England Yankees, and the Endless Quest: A Short History of the Original Webster Dictionaries, with Particular Reference to their First Hundred Years as Publications of the G. & C. Merriam Company.* Springfield, MA.: G. & C. Merriam.

LENDINARA, P. (1999). *Anglo-Saxon Glosses and Glossaries.* (Variorum Collected Studies Series.) Aldershot: Ashgate.

LEWIS, R. E. (2002). 'The *Middle English Dictionary* at 71', in M. Adams (ed.), 76–94.

—— WILLIAMS, M. J., and MILLER, M. S. (2007). *Middle English Dictionary: Plan and Bibliography: Second Edition.* Ann Arbor: University of Michigan Press.

LEYERLE, J. (1985). 'In Memoriam: Angus Cameron (1941–1983)', in A. Bammesberger (ed.), *Problems of Old English Lexicography.* Regensburg: Verlag Friedrich Pustet.

LIBERMAN, A. (1996). 'Etymology [in *The Century Dictionary*]', *Dictionaries: Journal of the Dictionary Society of North America* 17: 29–54.

LIFE, P. (2004). 'Coles, Elisha (*c*.1640–1680)', in *Oxford Dictionary of National Biography.* Oxford: Oxford University Press. **[http://www.oxforddnb.com/view/article/5892, accessed 2 Aug 2006]**

LINDSAY, W. M. (1921). *The Corpus, Épinal, Erfurt and Leiden Glossaries.* London: Oxford University Press.

—— (1996). *Studies on Mediaeval Latin Glossaries*, ed. M. Lapidge (Variorum Collected Studies Series.) Aldershot: Ashgate.

LUNA, P. (2000). 'Clearly Defined. Continuity and Innovation in the Typography of English Dictionaries', *Typography Papers* 4: 5–56.

—— (2005). 'The Typographic Design of Johnson's *Dictionary*', in J. Lynch and A. McDermott (eds.), 175–97.

LYNCH, J. (2005). 'Johnson's encyclopedia', in J. Lynch and A. McDermott (eds.), 129–46.

—— and MCDERMOTT, A. (eds.) (2005), *Anniversary Essays on Johnson's Dictionary.* Cambridge: Cambridge University Press.

MACAFEE, C. and MACLEOD, I. (eds.) (1987). *The Nuttis Schell: Essays on the Scots Language.* Aberdeen: Aberdeen University Press.

MALKIEL, Y. (1962). 'A Typological Classification of Dictionaries on the Basis of Distinctive Features', in F. W. Householder and S. Saporta (eds.), 3–24.

MARELLO, C. (1989). *Dizionari Bilingui.* Bologna: Zanichelli.

—— (1998). 'Hornby's Bilingualized Dictionaries', *International Journal of Lexicography* 11.4: 292–314.

MARSH, G. P. (1860). *Lectures on the English Language.* New York: Scribner.

MATHEWS, M. M. (1985). 'George Watson and the Dictionary of American English', *Dictionaries: Journal of the Dictionary Society of North America* 7: 214–24.

MCARTHUR, T. (ed.) (1992). *The Oxford Companion to the English Language.* Oxford: Oxford University Press.

McClure, J. D. (ed.) (1983). *Scotland and the Lowland Tongue.* Aberdeen: Aberdeen University Press.

McDermott, A. (2005). 'The Compilation Methods of Johnson's *Dictionary*', *The Age of Johnson* 16: 1–20.

—— (2005a). 'Johnson the prescriptivist? The case for the defense', in J. Lynch and A. McDermott (eds.), 113–28.

McSparran, F. (2002). 'The Middle English Compendium: Past, Present, and Future', in M. Adams (ed.), 126–41.

Meier, H. H. (1962). 'Review of *A Dictionary of the Older Scottish Tongue*', *English Studies* 43: 444–5.

Mencken, H. L. (1936). The *American Language.* (Fourth edition.) New York: Alfred A. Knopf.

Meritt, H. D. (1954). *Fact and Lore about Old English Words.* Stanford: Stanford University Press.

—— (1968). *Some of the Hardest Glosses in Old English.* Stanford: Stanford University Press.

Metcalf, A. (1996). 'Typography [of *The Century Dictionary*]', *Dictionaries: Journal of the Dictionary Society of North America* 17: 17–28.

Micklethwait, D. (2000). *Noah Webster and the American Dictionary.* Jefferson, North Carolina and London: McFarland.

Milton, C. (1995). '*Shibboleths o the Scots*: Hugh MacDiarmid and Jamieson's Etymological Dictionary of the Scottish Language', *Scottish Language* 14–15: 1–14.

Moore, B. (ed.) (2001). *Who's Centric Now? The Present State of Post-Colonial Englishes.* South Melbourne: Oxford University Press.

Moore, S., Meech, S. B., and Whitehall, H. (1935). 'Middle English Dialect Characteristics and Boundaries', in *Essays and Studies in English and Comparative Literature.* Ann Arbor: University of Michigan Press, 1–60.

Morton, H. C. (1994). *The Story of Webster's Third: Philip Gove's Controversial Dictionary and its Critics.* New York: Cambridge University Press.

Mugglestone, L. C. (2000). 'Labels Revisited: The Problems of Objectivity and the *OED*', *Dictionaries* 21: 27–36.

—— (2002a). '"An Historian and not a Critic": The Standard of Usage in the *OED*', in L. C. Mugglestone (ed.), 189–206.

Mugglestone, L. C. (2002b). '"Pioneers in the Untrodden Forest": The *New* English Dictionary', in L. C. Mugglestone (ed.), 1–21.

Mugglestone, L. C. (ed.) (2002c). *Lexicography and the OED: Pioneers in the Untrodden Forest.* Oxford: Oxford University Press.

—— (2005). *Lost for Words. The Hidden History of the Oxford English Dictionary.* London and New York: Yale University Press.

—— (2007). '"The Indefinable Something". Taboo and the English Dictionary', in M. Gorji (ed.), *Rude Britannia.* London: Routledge: 22–32.

Müller, F. M. (1878). *Observations by Professor Max Müller on the Lists of Readers and Books Read for the Proposed English Dictionary.* Oxford: Clarendon Press.

Murison, D. (1987). 'Scottish Lexicography', in C. Macafee and I. Macleod (eds.), *The Nuttis Schell: Essays on the Scots Language*, 17–24.

Murray, J. A. H. (1873). *The Dialect of the Southern Counties of Scotland: its Pronunciation, Grammar and Historical Relations.* London: The Philological Society.

—— (1879a). *An Appeal to the English-Speaking and English-Reading Public to Read Books and Make Extracts for the Philological Society's New Dictionary.* Oxford: Clarendon Press.

—— (1879b). 'Eighth Annual Address of the President to the Philological Society', *Transactions of the Philological Society* (1877–79): 561–621.

—— (1880). 'Ninth Annual Address of the President to the Philological Society', *Transactions of the Philological Society* (1880–81): 117–74.

—— (1881). 'Report on the Dictionary of the Philological Society', *Transactions of the Philological Society* (1880–81): 260–9.

—— (1884). 'Thirteenth Annual Address of the President to the Philological Society', *Transactions of the Philological Society* (1882–84): 501–31.

—— (1888). *Preface to Volume I. A New English Dictionary on Historical Principles, Founded Mainly on the Materials Collected by the Philological Society.* Vol. I, *A and B.* Oxford: Clarendon Press, v–xiv.

—— (1900). *The Evolution of English Lexicography.* Oxford: Clarendon Press.

—— (1993). 'The Evolution of English Lexicography', *International Journal of Lexicography* 6: 100–22. (Reprint of The Romanes Lecture, 1900.)

Murray, K. M. E. (1977). *Caught in the Web of Words. James A. H. Murray and the Oxford English Dictionary.* London and New Haven: Yale University Press.

'A New Dictionary', *The Times*, 22 March 1788: 3.

N[orman]., J. M. (1859). 'Diablerie Illustrated by Harsnet', *Notes and Queries* (Second series.) VII: 144–5.

'Notes on Books, etc'. (1857). *Notes and Queries* (Second series.) IV: 139–40.

O'Connor, D. (1990). *A History of Italian and English Bilingual Lexicography.* Firenze: Leo S. Olschki Editore.

—— (1991). 'Bilingual Lexicography: English–Italian, Italian–English', in F. J. Hausmann, O. Reichmann, H. E. Wiegand, and L. Zgusta (eds.), 3: 2970–6.

—— (2004). 'Baretti, Giuseppe Marc'Antonio (1719–1789)', in *Oxford Dictionary of National Biography.* Oxford: Oxford University Press. [**http://www.oxforddnb.com/view/article/1367, accessed 7 Dec 2005**]

O'Connor, D. (1978). 'Ancora sui primi dizionari italiano–inglesi', *Lingua Nostra* 38: 94–8.

Ogilvie, S. (2004). 'From "Outlandish Words" to "World English": The Legitimization of Global Varieties of English in the *OED*', G. Williams and S. Vessier in *Proceedings of the Eleventh Euralex International Congress* (eds.), Lorient, Université de Bretagne-Sud: 651–8.

Onions, C. T. (1928). 'The Great Oxford Dictionary. Completion Today', *The Times* 19 April: 10.

Osselton, N. E. (1958). *Branded Words in English Dictionaries before Johnson.* Groningen: Wolters.

—— (1964). 'Early Bi-lingual Dictionaries as Evidence for the Status of Words in English', in *English Studies Presented to R. W. Zandvoort on the Occasion of His Seventieth Birthday.* Amsterdam: Swets & Zeitlinger, 14–20.

—— (1969). 'The Sources of the First Dutch and English Dictionary', *Modern Language Review* 64: 355–62.

—— (1973). *The Dumb Linguists. A Study of the Earliest English and Dutch Dictionaries.* London: Oxford University Press.

—— (1991). 'Bilingual Lexicography with Dutch', in F. J. Hausmann, O. Reichmann, H. E. Wiegand, and L. Zgusta (eds.), 3: 3034–9.

—— (1995) 'Phrasal Verbs: Dr Johnson's Use of Bilingual Sources', in *Chosen Words: Past and Present Problems for Dictionary Makers.* Exeter: University of Exeter Press: 93–103.

—— (1996). 'Authenticating the Vocabulary. A Study in Seventeenth-Century Practice', *Lexikos* 6: 215–32.

—— (1999) 'English Specialized Lexicography in the late Middle Ages and in the Renaissance', in L. Hoffmann *et al.* (eds.), *Fachsprachen. Languages for Special Purposes.* Berlin: De Gruyter, 2458–65.

—— (2000). 'Murray and his European Counterparts', in L. Mugglestone (ed.), 59–76.

—— (2006). 'Usage Guidance in Early Dictionaries of English', *International Journal of Lexicography* 19: 99–105.

Oxford University Press (1993). *The Oxford English Dictionary Second Edition on Compact Disk.* User's manual. Oxford: Oxford University Press.

'The Oxford English Dictionary. Completion of a Great Work. A Retrospect'. (1928). *The Times*, 16 April: 11.

Parsons, E. C. (1923). 'Folklore of the Sea Islands, South Carolina', *Memoirs of the American Folklore Society* 13.

Patrick, S. (1746). 'The Preface', in R. Ainsworth, *Thesaurus Linguae Latinae compendiarius.* (Second edition.) London: W. Mount, xxvi–xxvii.

Pätzold, K.-M. (1991). 'Bilingual Lexicography: English–German, German–English', in F. J. Hausmann, O. Reichmann, H. E. Wiegand, and L. Zgusta (eds.), 3: 2961–9.

Periodical, The. (1934). Journal of Oxford University Press. Vol. XIX, no. 173.

[Philological Society]. (1859). *Proposal for the Publication of a New English Dictionary.* London: Trübner & Co.

Pijnenburg, W. and de Tollenaere, F. (eds.) (1980). *Proceedings of the Second International Round Table Conference on Historical Lexicography.* Dordrecht: Foris.

Piotrowski, T. (1988). 'English and Russian: Two Bilingual Dictionaries', *Dictionaries* 10: 127–41.

Quemada, B. (1967). *Les dictionnaires du français moderne (1539–1863). Etude sur leur histoire, leurs types et leurs méthodes.* Paris, Brussels, and Montreal: Didier.

Quirk, R. (ed.) (1982). *Style and Communication in the English Language.* London: Edward Arnold.

Ramsay. A. (1945–74). *The Works of Allan Ramsay.* (Six volumes.) Edinburgh: Scottish Text Society.

Read, A. W. (1934). 'The Philological Society of New York', *American Speech* 9: 131–6.

—— (1938). 'Plans for "A Historical Dictionary of Briticisms"', *American Oxonian* 25: 186–90.

—— (1966). 'The Spread of German Linguistic Learning in New England During the Lifetime of Noah Webster', *American Speech* 41: 163–81.

—— (1987). 'A Dictionary of the English of England: Problems and Findings', *Dictionaries* 9: 149–63.

—— (2002). *Milestones in the History of English in America.* (Publication of the American Dialect Society, 86.) Durham: Duke University Press.

Reddick, A. (1996). *The Making of Johnson's Dictionary, 1746–1773.* (Revised edition.) Cambridge: Cambridge University Press.

—— (1997). 'Johnson beyond Jacobitism: Signs of Polemic in the *Dictionary* and the *Life of Milton*', in *English Literary History* 64: 983–1005.

—— (1998). 'Johnson's *Dictionary of the English Language* and its Texts: Quotation, Context, Anti-Thematics', *Yearbook of English Studies* 28: 66–76.

—— (2005). *Johnson's Unpublished Revisions to the Dictionary of the English Language: A Facsimile Edition.* Cambridge: Cambridge University Press.

Reed, J. W., Jr. (1962). 'Noah Webster's Debt to Samuel Johnson', *American Speech* 37: 95–105.

Reiser, G. R. (1998). 'XXV. Works of Science and Information', in A. E. Hartung (ed.), *A Manual of the Writings in Middle English 1050–1500*, Vol. 10. New Haven, CT: The Connecticut Academy of Arts and Sciences.

Relton, F. B. (1851). 'Meaning of "Stickle" and "Dray"', *Notes and Queries* (First series.) IV: 209.

Riola, H. (1878). *Key to the Exercises of the Manual for Students of Russian (Based on the Ollendorffian System of Teaching Languages and Adapted for Self-Instruction).* London: Trübner & Co.

—— (1880). *A Graduated Russian Reader, with a Vocabulary of all the Russian Words Contained in It.* Boston: Houghton, Osgood and Company.

—— (1915). *How to Learn Russian: A Manual for Students of Russian (With a Preface by W. R. S. Ralston).* (New edition; first edition 1878.) London: Kegan Paul, Trench, Trübner & Co. Ltd.

Roberts, J., Kay, C., and Grundy, L. (1995). *A Thesaurus of Old English.* (Two volumes; King's College London Medieval Studies 11.) London: King's College London. Second impression, 2000.) Amsterdam-Atlanta, GA: Rodopi.

Robertson, I. (1983). 'Review of J. A. Holm and A. W. Shilling, *Dictionary of Bahamian English*', *Nieuwe West Indies Gid*, 108–12.

Roe, K. (1977). 'A Survey of the Encyclopedic Tradition in English Dictionaries', *Papers of the Dictionary Society of North America*: 16–23.

Rosier, J. L. (1961). 'The Sources and Methods of Minsheu's *Guide into the Tongues*', *Philological Quarterly* 40: 68–76.

—— (1963). 'Lexical Strata in Florio's *New World of Words*', *English Studies* 44: 415–23.

Ross, A. S. C. (1934). [review of *OED Supplement* of 1933] *Neuphilogische Mitteilungen* 35: 128–32.

Sauer, H. (1997). 'Knowledge of Old English in the Middle English Period?', in R. Hickey and S. Puppel (eds.), *Language History and Linguistic Modelling: A Festschrift for Jacek Fisiak on his 60th Birthday*. Berlin: Mouton de Gruyter, 791–814.

—— (1999). 'Angelsächsische Glossen und Glossare und ihr Fachwortschatz', in L. Hoffmann *et al.* (eds.) *Fachsprachen/Languages for Special Purposes*. Berlin: De Gruyter, 2452–58.

—— (2007). 'Old English Words for People in the *Épinal-Erfurt Glossary*', in H. Sauer and R. Bauer (eds.), *Beowulf and Beyond*. Frankfurt am Main, 119–81.

Ščerba, L. V. (1940 [1982], [1995]). 'Opyt obščej teorii leksikografii', Izvestija Akademii Nauk SSSR, Otdelenije literatury i jazika 3:89–117; German translation by W. Wolski 'Versuch einer allgemeinen Theorie der Lexikographie', in W. Wolski (ed.) (1982). *Aspekter der sowjetrussischen Lexikographie: Übersetzungen, Abstracts, bibliographische Angaben*. Tübingen: Narr; English translation by D. M. T. Cr. Farina 'Towards a General Theory of Lexicography', *International Journal of Lexicography* 8.4: 314–50.

Schabram, H. (1965). *Superbia: Studien zum altenglischen Wortschatz*. Munich: Fink.

Schäfer, J. (1980). *Documentation in the OED: Shakespeare and Nashe as Test Cases*. Oxford: Clarendon Press.

—— (1987). 'Early Modern English: *OED*, *New OED*, *EMED*', in R. W. Bailey (ed.), 66–74.

—— (1989). *Early Modern English Lexicography. Volume 1: A Survey of Monolingual Printed Glossaries and Dictionaries 1475–1640*; *Volume 2: Additions and Corrections to the OED*. Oxford: Clarendon Press.

Scheurweghs, G. (1960). 'English Grammars in Dutch and Dutch Grammars in English in the Netherlands Before 1800', *English Studies* 41: 129–67.

Silva, P. (2000). 'Sense and Definition in the *OED*', in L. Mugglestone (ed.), 77–80.

Simmons, E. J. (1964). *English Literature and Culture in Russia (1553–1840)*. (Harvard Studies in Comparative Literature, Vol. 12.) New York: Octagon Books.

Simpson, J. A. (1986a). 'The New Oxford English Dictionary Project: a New Dimension in Lexicography', *Proceedings of the Association for Literary and Linguistic Computing*, 47–57.

Simpson, J. A. (1986b). 'The New OED Project', in G. Johannesen (ed.), *Information in Data: the First Conference of the UW Centre for the New Oxford English Dictionary: Proceedings of the Conference* (6–7 November, 1985). Waterloo, Ontario, Canada: University of Waterloo, 1–6.

—— (1987). 'The New OED project: a Year's Work in Lexicography', *University Computing* 9: 2–7.

—— (1988a). 'The New Vocabulary of English', in E. G. Stanley and T. F. Hoad (eds.), *Words: for Robert Burchfield's Sixty-fifth Birthday.* Woodbridge: D. S. Brewer, 143–52.

—— (1988b). 'Computers and the New OED's New Words', in M. Snell-Hornby (ed.), *ZüriLEX '86* Proceedings. (Papers read at the EURALEX International Conference, University of Zürich, 9–14 September 1986.) Tübingen: Francke Verlag, 437–44.

—— (1999). 'Editing the OED: beyond Completion', in A. Moerdijk and R. Tempelaars (eds.), *Van A tot Z en verder?: Lezingen bij de Voltooiing van het WNT.* Den Haag: Sdu Uitgevers; Antwerp: Standaard, 53–72.

—— (2000–). *Oxford English Dictionary.* (Third Edition Online: in progress.) http://oed.com. Oxford: Oxford University Press. (Quarterly updates of new and revised material from March 2000.)

—— (2001). 'The Oxford English Dictionary on the Web', *Bollettino dell'Opera del Vocabolario Italiano,* Supplemento I: La Lessicografia Storica e I Grandi Dizionari delle Lingue Europee, 19–26.

—— (2003). 'The Revolution in English Lexicography', *Dictionaries* 23: 1–23 and in (2003) R. R. K. Hartmann (ed.), *Critical Perspectives in Lexicography.*

—— (2004). 'The *OED* and Collaborative Research into the History of English', *Anglia* 122.2: 185–208.

—— Weiner, E. S. C., and Durkin, P. N. R. D. (2004). 'The Oxford English Dictionary Today', *Transactions of the Philological Society* 102: 335–74.

Skeat, W. W. (1867). 'The Philological Society's Dictionary', *Notes and Queries* (Third series.) X: 256.

—— (1886). 'Report upon "Ghost-words", or Words which have no Real Existence', *Transactions of the Philological Society* (1885–87) ii: 350–74.

Sledd, J. and Ebbitt, W. R. (1962). *Dictionaries and THAT Dictionary.* Chicago: Scott, Foresman.

—— and Kolb, G. J. (1955). *Dr. Johnson's Dictionary: Essays in the Biography of a Book.* Chicago: University of Chicago Press.

Smalley, V. E. (1948). *The Sources of* A Dictionarie of the French and English Tongues *by Randle Cotgrave.* Baltimore: Johns Hopkins Press.

Smith, D. S. (ed.) (1989). *D. S. Mirsky: Uncollected Writings on Russian Literature.* Berkeley: Berkeley Slavic Specialties.

Smith, R. D. (2004). 'Ainsworth, Robert (1660–1743)', in *Oxford Dictionary of National Biography.* Oxford: Oxford University Press. [**http://www.oxforddnb.com/view/article/241, accessed 24 July 2006**]

Stanley, E. (1990). 'The *OED* and *Supplement*: The Integrated Edition of 1989', *Review of English Studies (New Series).* 41: 76–88.

Starnes, D. T. (1937). 'Bilingual Dictionaries of Shakespeare's Day', *Publications of the Modem Language Association of America* 52: 1005–18.

Starnes, D. T. (1954). *Renaissance Dictionaries, English–Latin and Latin–English.* Austin: University of Texas Press.

—— (1965). 'John Florio Reconsidered', *Texas Studies in Literature and Language* 6: 407–22.

—— and Noyes, G. E. (1946). *The English Dictionary from Cawdrey to Johnson, 1604–1755.* Chapel Hill: University of North Carolina Press. (New edition with an introduction and select bibliography by Gabriele Stein. Amsterdam: Benjamins, 1991.)

Steger, S. A. (1913). *American Dictionaries: A Dissertation.* Baltimore: J. H. Furst.

Stein, G. (1983). 'Review of *A Supplement to the OED*, Vol. 3', *Anglia* 101: 468–75.

—— (1985a). 'English–German/German–English Lexicography: Its Early Beginnings', *Lexicographica* 1: 134–64.

—— (1985b). *The English Dictionary before Cawdrey.* Tübingen: Niemeyer.

—— (1997). *John Palsgrave as Renaissance Linguist.* Oxford: Clarendon Press.

Steiner, R. J. (1970). *Two Centuries of Spanish and English Lexicography (1590–1800).* The Hague and Paris: Mouton.

—— (1984). 'Guidelines for Reviewers of Bilingual Dictionaries', *Dictionaries*, 1984.6: 166–81.

—— (1986). 'The Three-Century Recension in Spanish and English Lexicography', in R. R. K. Hartmann (ed.), *The History of Lexicography*, Amsterdam: Benjamins 229–39; reprinted in R. R. K. Hartmann (ed.) (2003), 2: 85–95.

—— (1991). 'Bilingual Lexicography: English–Spanish and Spanish–English', in F. J. Hausmann, O. Reichmann, H. E. Wiegand, and L. Zgusta (eds.), 3: 2949–56.

Stephen, L. and Lee, S. (eds.) (1949–50). *The Dictionary of National Biography.* London: Oxford University Press, Vol. 16. [A second edition has been published and is available via the Internet: www.oxforddnb]

Stone, J. (2005). 'The Law, the Alphabet, and Samuel Johnson', in J. Lynch and A. McDermott (eds.), 147–59.

Strang, B. (1974). 'Review of Second Supplement, Vol. 1', *Notes and Queries* 219: 2–13.

—— (1977). 'Review of Second Supplement, Vol. 2', *Notes and Queries* 22: 388–99.

Sweet, H. (1885). *The Oldest English Texts.* (EETS OS 83.) London. Trübner.

Swift, J. (1712). *Proposal for Correcting, Improving, and Ascertaining the English Tongue.* London: printed for Benj. Tooke at the Middle Temple Gate.

Terras, V. (1991). *A History of Russian Literature.* New Haven: Yale University Press.

Thomson, D. (1979). *A Descriptive Catalogue of Middle English Grammatical Texts.* New York: Garland.

Trench, R. C. (1851). *On the Study of Words.* London: John W. Parker & Son.

—— (1855). *English Past and Present. Five Lectures.* London: John W. Parker & Son.

—— (1860). *On Some Deficiencies in our English Dictionaries, being the Substance of Two Papers Read Before the Philological Society, Nov. 5th and Nov. 19th, 1857.* (Second edition.) London: John W. Parker & Son.

Trench, R. C. *et al.* (1860). *Canones Lexicographici; or Rules to be Observed in Editing the New English Dictionary of the Philological Society.* London: The Philological Society.

TRITHEN, F. H. (1843). 'On the Structure of the Russian Verb', *Proceedings of the Philological Society* I: 96–101.

VENEZKY, R. and BUTLER, S. (1985). *A Microfiche Concordance to Old English: The High-Frequency Words.* Toronto: Pontifical Institute.

—— and HEALEY, A. (1980). *A Microfiche Concordance to Old English.* Toronto: Pontifical Institute.

Vestnik Evropy (1878). 'Zametka: Russkaia grammatika v Anglii', Book 7 (July): 398–9.

VIZETELLY, F. H. (1923). *The Development of the Dictionary of the English Language.* New York: Funk & Wagnalls.

WARBURTON, Y. L. (1989). 'From Dictionary to Database', *The Stag* 4 (Summer).

—— and RAYMOND, D. R. (1987). *Computerization of Lexicographical Activity on the OED.* (Technical Report OED 87–03.) Waterloo, Ontario, Canada: University of Waterloo Centre for the New OED.

WARFEL, H. R. (1936). *Noah Webster: Schoolmaster to America.* New York: Macmillan.

—— (ed.) (1953). *Letters of Noah Webster.* New York: Library Publishers.

WATSON, G. (1916). 'The Story of Scottish Dictionary-Making', *Transactions of the Hawick Archaeological Society*, 7–12.

WEBSTER, N. (1800). Letter, *Windham Herald* [Connecticut] June 4, 3.

—— (1817). A Letter to the Honorable [sic] John Pickering on the Subject of his Vocabulary. Boston: West and Richardson.

WEDGWOOD, H. (1844). 'Notices of English Etymology', *Proceedings of the Philological Society* II: 1–6.

WEINER, E. S. C. (1985a). 'The *New OED*: Problems in the Computerization of a Dictionary', *University Computing* 7: 66–71.

—— (1985b). 'Computerizing the Oxford English Dictionary', *Scholarly Publishing* 16.3: 239–53.

—— (1985c). 'The New Oxford English Dictionary', *Journal of English Linguistics* 18.1: 1–13.

—— (1986a). 'New Uses for the New OED', *The Bookseller*, 25 January, 332–6.

—— (1986b). 'The New Oxford English Dictionary and World English', *English World-Wide* 7.2: 259–66 (reprinted in *English Today* (1987) 11: 31–4).

—— (1986c). 'A Conversation with a Dictionary', in S. Nash (ed.), *Science and Intelligence.* Northwood: Science Reviews Ltd., 117–32.

—— (1987). 'The *New Oxford English Dictionary*: Progress and Prospects', in R. W. Bailey (ed.), 30–48.

—— (1988a). 'The Electronic English Dictionary', *Oxford Magazine* 18: 6–9 (reprinted in *The Cambridge Review* (1988) 109 (October): 122–6).

—— (1988b). 'Standardization and the New Oxford English Dictionary', in V. Liedloff (ed.), *Standardization in Computerized Lexicography.* (Proceedings of the IV Forum Information Science and Practice, 15–17 October 1986.) Saarbrücken: IAI, 53–67.

—— (1989a). 'Editing the OED in the Electronic Age', in L. M. Jones (ed.), *Dictionaries in the Electronic Age.* (Proceedings of the 5th Annual Conference of the University of

Waterloo Centre for the New OED.) Waterloo, Ontario, Canada: University of Waterloo, 23–31.

—— (1989b). Translated article on the Second Edition of the OED, in *Gakuto* (Maruzen Co. Ltd., Tokyo), November, 26–8.

—— (1990). 'The Federation of English', in C. Ricks and L. Michaels (eds.), *The State of the Language.* London and Boston: Faber & Faber, 492–502.

—— (1994a). 'The Lexicographical Workstation and the Scholarly Dictionary', in B. T. S. Atkins and A. Zampolli (eds.), *Computational Approaches to the Lexicon.* Oxford: Oxford University Press, 413–38.

—— (1994b). 'Local History and Lexicography', *The Local Historian* 24: 164–73.

—— (2000a). 'Medieval Multilingualism and the Revision of the OED', in D. A. Trotter (ed.), *Multilingualism in Later Medieval Britain.* Woodbridge: D. S. Brewer, 169–74.

—— (2000b). 'A New Web of Words', *Oxford Today* 12.3: 24.

—— Silva, P. M., *et al.* (2000). 'Brook Symposium on the Revised OED and English Historical Lexicography: A Report', in J. Coleman and C. J. Kay (eds.), *Lexicology, Semantics and Lexicography: Current Issues in Linguistic Theory.* (Selected Papers from the Fourth G. L. Brook Symposium.) Amsterdam: John Benjamins, 230–9.

Wells, J. C. (1985). 'English Pronunciation and its Dictionary Representation', in R. Ilson (ed.) *Dictionaries, Lexicography and Language Learning.* Oxford–New York: Pergamon Press 45–51.

Wells, R. (1973). *Dictionaries and the Authoritarian Tradition.* The Hague: Mouton.

Wilson, H. H. (1843). 'Opening Address to the meeting of the Philological Society held on 27 January 1843', *Proceedings of the Philological Society* I: 13.

—— (1844). 'Opening Address to the meeting of the Philological Society held on 26 January 1844', *Proceedings of the Philological Society* I: 169.

Wisbey, R. A. (ed.) (1971). *The Computer in Literary and Linguistic Research.* Cambridge: Cambridge University Press.

Worcester, J. E. (1854). *A Gross Literary Fraud Exposed; relating to the publication of Worcester's Dictionary in London.* Boston: Jenks, Hickling, and Swan.

'Word Lists'. (1882). *Notes and Queries* (Sixth series.) v: 86, 107, 146, 167.

Zgusta, L. (1971). *Manual of Lexicography.* Prague: Academia.

Zgusta, L. (1987). 'Translational Equivalence in a Bilingual Dictionary: Bāhukośyam', *Dictionaries* 9: 1–47.

—— (1991). 'Jacob Grimm's *Deutsches Wörterbuch* and other Historical Dictionaries of the 19th Century', in A. Kirkness, P. Kühn, and H. E. Wiegand (eds.), *Studien zum Deutschen Wörterbuch von Jacob Grimm und Wilhelm Grimm.* Tübingen: Niemeyer: 595–626.

—— (2006). 'Chapter One: History and Dictionaries', in F. Dolezal and T. Creamer (eds.), *Lexicography Then and Now: Selected Essays.* Tübingen: Niemeyer: 1–86.

Zöfgen, E. (1991). 'Bilingual Learner's Dictionaries', in F. J. Hausmann, O. Reichmann, H. E. Wiegand, and L. Zgusta (eds.), 3: 2888–2903.

INDEX